MACROECONOMICS
Theories and Policies

Fourth Edition

MACROECONOMICS
Theories and Policies

RICHARD T. FROYEN
University of North Carolina at Chapel Hill

Macmillan Publishing Company
New York

Maxwell Macmillan Canada
Toronto

Maxwell Macmillan International
New York • Oxford • Singapore • Sydney

Editor: Jill Lectka
Production Supervisor: Margaret Comaskey
Production Manager: Paul Smolenski
Text Designer: Susan Frankenberry
Cover Designer: Cathleen Norz
Marketing Manager: David Borkowsky

This book was set in New Baskerville by Publication Services, Inc. and printed and bound by R. R. Donnelley and Sons. The cover was printed by Lehigh Press.

Macmillan Publishing Company is part
of the Maxwell Communication Group of Companies.

Macmillan Publishing Company
866 Third Avenue, New York, New York 10022

Maxwell Macmillan Canada, Inc.
1200 Eglinton Avenue East
Suite 200
Don Mills, Ontario M3C 3N1

LIBRARY OF CONGRESS CATALOGING IN PUBLICATION DATA
Froyen, Richard T.
    Macroeconomics, theories and policies / Richard T. Froyen. —4th ed.
        p.   cm.
    Includes index.
    ISBN 0-02-339591-5
    1. Macroeconomics.   I. Title.
HB172.5.F76   1993
339–dc20   92-10762
                                                           CIP

Printing: 1 2 3 4 5 6 7 8   Year: 3 4 5 6 7 8 9 0 1 2

To Linda
Katherine, Sara, and Andrea

Preface

The years since 1970 have been challenging ones for macroeconomists. Key variables in macroeconomics—the levels of output, inflation, unemployment; interest rates; foreign exchange rates—have proved difficult to explain and predict. This period has also been an active one in macroeconomic theory. It has been a period of controversy but also of progress. The 1970s saw a broadening of the issues in the *monetarist–Keynesian* controversy. Additionally, a new challenge to the Keynesian position, the *new classical* economics, emerged. During the 1980s, Keynesian policy prescriptions came under attack from a group called the supply-side economists. The 1980s also witnessed the development of two contrasting lines of research on the business cycle: the *new Keynesian economics* and the *real business cycle theory*. There has, however, been progress as well as controversy. During the past twenty years there have been significant improvements in the handling of expectations, in our understanding of labor market institutions, in accounting for the macroeconomic implications of various market structures, in modeling of open economies, and in other areas as well.

In this book I have tried to explain macroeconomics, inclusive of recent developments, in a coherent way, but without glossing over the fundamental disagreements among macroeconomists on issues of both theory and policy. The major modern macroeconomic theories are presented and compared. Important areas of agreement as well as differences are discussed. An attempt is made to demonstrate that the controversies among macroeconomists center on well-defined issues that are based on theoretical differences in the underlying models.

Features

Distinguishing features of the approach taken here are the following:

- An up-to-date summary of the Keynesian position, including recent research that has come to be called the new Keynesian economics.
- A detailed analysis of the modern challenges to the Keynesian position by the monetarists, new classical economists, and real business cycle theorists.
- An extensive treatment of monetary policy which considers the optimal strategy for monetary policy, including intermediate targeting on monetary aggregates versus targeting on interest rates.
- An analysis of the post-1970 slowdown in U.S. output growth, capital formation, and growth in labor productivity. It is within this context of intermediate-run growth that the views of the supply-side economists are considered.
- Thorough coverage of money demand, including recent difficulties in predicting money demand and the effects of ongoing innovations in the financial sector.
- An analysis of the question of rules versus discretion in macroeconomic policymaking. Rules for monetary policy as well as a constitutional amendment for balancing the federal budget are considered. The *public-choice* view of macroeconomic policymaking is examined.
- Consideration of foreign exchange rate determination including discussion of recent proposals for policy coordination and target zones for exchange rates.

Organization

The organization of the book is as follows. Part I (Chapters 1–2) discusses the subject matter of macroeconomics, the recent behavior of the U.S. economy, and questions of measurement. Part II presents the major macroeconomic models, beginning with the classical system (Chapters 3–4). Consideration of the classical system at the start is useful because the Keynesian model can then be viewed as an attack on the classical orthodoxy. The recent challenges to the Keynesian position can then be rooted in the parts of the classical model that provide starting points for their analysis: the quantity theory of money for the monetarists, and the classical labor market clearing assumptions and choice-theoretic-based behavioral functions for the new classical economists. The classical analysis is also useful for a later examination of the policy prescriptions of the supply-side economists.

The Keynesian model is analyzed in detail in Chapters 5–8, beginning from a very simple model; more complex models are built up to incorporate monetary influences, wage and price flexibility, changing price expectations, and shocks to aggregate supply. Chapters 9 and 10 examine monetarism and the issues in the monetarist–Keynesian controversy. Chapter 9 focuses on the monetarist view of the importance of money. Chapter 10 examines the monetarist view of the unemployment–inflation trade-off, the *natural rate* theory, as well as the Keynesian view on the same issue. Chapter 11 considers the *new classical* theory with its central concepts of *rational expectations* and market clearing. The Keynesian response to the new classical economics is then considered. Chapter 12 examines two very recent directions in macroeconomic research. One, very strongly rooted in the classical tradition, is the *real business cycle theory*. The second, the *new Keynesian economics*, is, as its name suggests, firmly in the Keynesian tradition. Chapter 13 summarizes and compares the different models.

Part III presents extensions of the models and considers parts of the models in greater detail. The chapters here and in Part IV are designed to be self-contained so that the instructor can choose topics as time and interest allow. Chapter 14 is a more detailed examination of the components of private sector demand: consumption and investment spending. Chapter 15 considers money demand and Chapter 16 the money supply process. Chapter 17 returns to the supply side of macroeconomic models to discuss long-run equilibrium growth and the determinants of growth over intermediate-run periods, periods too long to fit the short-run framework of the models in Part II, but not necessarily situations of long-run equilibrium.

Part IV deals with macroeconomic policy—fiscal policy in Chapter 18 and monetary policy in Chapter 19. A historical appendix to Part IV describes major macroeconomic policy actions over the period since the Great Depression of the 1930s.

Part V considers *open-economy* macroeconomics. Chapter 20 focuses on exchange rate determination and the choice of an international monetary system. An appendix to Part V considers monetary and fiscal policy in the open economy.

In the section on macroeconomic models, the conceptual approach taken here is to develop each model within the aggregate demand–aggregate supply framework in order to facilitate comparisons among the models. Throughout the book the aim is to provide a clear and rigorous, primarily graphical and verbal, analysis. Other pedagogical features are the explanatory captions provided for the graphs in the text, end-of-chapter questions, and a list of selected readings following each chapter.

Most chapters also contain one or more *Perspectives* sections, which relate the material in the text to events in the real economy.

New Features in the Fourth Edition

- A new chapter (Chapter 12) has been added on recent lines of macroeconomic research. The first half of the chapter analyzes the real business cycle model. The relationship of the real business cycle model to the original classical model and to the new classical model is considered.

- The new chapter also provides an expanded coverage of the new Keynesian economics. General features of this approach are described. Several variants of the new Keynesian economics are then considered. These include sticky wage (menu cost) models, efficiency wage models, and insider–outsider models of the labor market.
- The discussion of long-term economic growth has been expanded to take account of interesting recent research on models exhibiting endogenous technological change. These models are shown to have important policy implications.
- As with the third edition, *Perspectives* have been added and deleted. The goal has been to make perspectives provide more international and historical comparisons.
- The discussion of policy issues has been thoroughly updated to include developments through mid-1992.
- The section on national income accounting has been revised to reflect the shift of emphasis in the United States from gross national product (GNP) to gross domestic product (GDP).

Teaching Aids and Supplements

A complete set of supplements to the new edition includes the following:

1. An Instructor's Manual has chapter summaries, answers to all end-of-chapter questions, and test materials that include a greatly increased number of problems, essay questions, and multiple-choice questions.
2. A Study Guide by Lawrence Davidson contains a review outline, problems, multiple-choice questions, and exercises on concepts and techniques for each chapter.
3. In addition, a package of computer software, POLICYMAKER: A Macroeconomic Simulation, allows students to simulate models in the text under various assumptions.

Acknowledgments

Many people have been helpful in preparing the various editions of this book. In preparing this edition, I have benefited from comments on earlier editions by Roger Waud, Art Benavie, Alfred Field, Pat Conway, and Alfred Guender, all from the University of North Carolina, as well as by Lawrence Davidson and Williard Witte, Indiana University; Allin Cottrell, Wake Forest University; David Van Hoose, University of Alabama; Michael Bradley, George Washington University; Rexford Santerre and Michael Tucci, Bentley

College; Art Goldsmith, Washington and Lee University; Thomas Havrilesky, Duke University; Sang Sub Lee, University of South Florida; David Bowles, Clemson University; Michael Loy and Lawrence Ellis, Appalachian State University; and Richard Selden, University of Virginia.

Reviewers recruited by Macmillan provided many useful suggestions for this and previous editions. These reviewers include Ed Day, University of Louisville; Edward M. Gamber, Oberlin College; Gary Gigliotti, Rutgers University; William Goffe, Southern Methodist University; James Keeler, Kenyon College; John Lapp, North Carolina State University; Thomas McCaleb, Florida State University; John Trapani, University of Texas–Arlington; Doug Waldo, University of Florida; Jack Adams, University of Arkansas; Lawrence DeBoer, Ball State University; Mario Pastore, Ithaca College; John Vahaley, University of Louisville; H.W. Whitmore, University of Cincinnati; John A. Orr, California State College–Chico; Jeurgen von Hagen, Federal Reserve Bank of St. Louis; and Subarna Samanta, Trenton State College.

Editors at Macmillan have been helpful at all stages in this project. I am grateful to Jill Lectka for many useful suggestions in preparing the current revision. Again with this edition, I look forward to working with the outstanding Macmillan sales force and our new Marketing Manager, David Borkowsky.

Contents

xiii

MACROECONOMICS
Theories and Policies

Introduction and Measurement

The two chapters in this opening part of the book discuss the subject matter of macroeconomics, the recent behavior of the U.S. economy, and the measurement of macroeconomic variables. The first two of these tasks are undertaken in Chapter 1, the Introduction. In this chapter we also develop some of the central questions in macroeconomics, to which we return in later chapters. Chapter 2 deals with questions of measurement. The main macroeconomic aggregates, the behavior of which later chapters try to explain, are defined there. Central to this task is an examination of the U.S. national income accounts.

1 Introduction

1.1 • WHAT IS MACROECONOMICS?

This book examines theories and policy questions in the branch of economics called **macroeconomics**. The British economist Alfred Marshall defined economics as the "study of mankind in the ordinary business of life; it examines that part of individual and social action which is most closely connected with the attainment and with the use of the material requisites of well being."[1] In macroeconomics we study this "ordinary business of life" in the aggregate; that is, we look at the behavior of the economy as a whole. The key variables we study include total output in the economy, the aggregate price level, employment and unemployment, interest rates, wage rates, and foreign exchange rates. The subject matter of macroeconomics includes factors that determine both the levels of these variables and how the variables change over time: the rate of growth of output, the inflation rate, changing unemployment in periods of boom and recession, appreciation or depreciation in foreign exchange rates.

Macroeconomics is a policy-oriented part of economics. Much of our analysis focuses on how macroeconomic variables are affected by government policies. To what degree can government policies affect the level of output and employment in the economy? To what degree is inflation the result of unfortunate government policies? What government policies are *optimal* in the sense of achieving the most desirable behavior of aggregate variables such as the level of unemployment or the inflation rate? Should government policy attempt to achieve a *target* level for foreign exchange rates?

Looking at concrete examples, we ask to what degree were government policies to blame for the massive unemployment during the world depression of the 1930s or for the simultaneously high unemployment and inflation of the 1970s? What role did "Reaganomics" have in the sharp decline in

---

[1] Alfred Marshall, *Principles of Economics*, 8th ed. (New York: Macmillan, 1920), p. 1.

inflation and rise in unemployment in the early 1980s? Were government policies responsible for the extreme variability of foreign exchange rates throughout the 1980s?

On these policy questions we find considerable disagreement among economists. In large part the controversy over policy questions stems from differing views of the factors that determine the aggregate variables listed previously. Questions of theory and policy are interrelated. In our analysis we examine different macroeconomic theories and the policy conclusions that follow from these theories. It would be more satisfying to present *the* macroeconomic theory and policy prescription. Satisfying, but such a presentation would be misleading because there *are* fundamental differences among what can be termed schools of macroeconomists. In comparing different theories, however, we see that there are substantial areas of agreement as well as disagreement. Controversy does not mean chaos. The approach taken here will be to isolate the key issues that divide macroeconomists and to explain the theoretical basis for each position.

Over the past two decades the public has become much more interested in macroeconomic issues. The 1970s were a decade of unstable growth, high inflation, *and* high unemployment. During the early 1980s, inflation declined but unemployment rose to record post–World War II levels. Later in the 1980s, record federal budget and foreign trade deficits created uncertainty about the economy's future. The 1990s began with a protracted recession. In stable times we take for granted the behavior of the economy as a whole and concentrate on our individual economic decisions. When the macroeconomy misbehaves, when individuals cannot find jobs although they have the required skills, when the value of the earnings of the employed are eroded by high inflation rates, then we become more interested in the behavior of aggregates.

With the increased interest in macroeconomics has also come a dissatisfaction with the explanation of economic events and the policy prescriptions provided by the established macroeconomic theory. The years since 1970 have been, as economist James Tobin calls them, "troubled times" for macroeconomics. We analyze the macroeconomic orthodoxy as it existed when the 1970s began, what is termed **Keynesian economics**. The roots of Keynesian theory as an attack on an earlier orthodoxy, the **classical economics**, is explained. We then examine the challenges to the Keynesian position, theories that have come to be called **monetarism** and the **new classical economics.** We examine the theory of the **supply-side economists** who have also attacked the Keynesian position. *Supply-side* views were an important element in the redirection of macroeconomic policy that took place when the Reagan administration came into office in 1981. Finally, we consider two recent directions in macroeconomic research. One, strongly rooted in the classic tradition, is the **real business cycle theory.** The other, the **new Keynesian theory,** is, as its name suggests, in the Keynesian tradition. How each theory explains the events of the 1970s and 1980s, as well as the policies each group of economists propose to provide for better future performance of the economy, is a central concern of our analysis.

To start, it is useful to examine the performance of some important macroeconomic variables in the United States over the past three decades.

1.2 • POST–WORLD WAR II U.S. ECONOMIC PERFORMANCE

Our tasks here and in the next section are to sketch the broad outline of U.S. macroeconomic performance over the post–World War II period and to suggest some of the central questions addressed in our later analysis. Tables 1.1 to 1.3 provide data for selected postwar years for several important macroeconomic variables.

TABLE 1.1   Real Output in the United States 1953–91

Year	Real GNP (billions)	Percentage Change in GNP	Year	Real GNP (billions)	Percentage Change in GNP
1953	1435.3	4.0	1970	2416.2	−0.3
1954	1416.2	−1.3	1971	2484.8	2.8
1955	1494.9	5.6	1972	2608.5	5.0
1956	1525.6	2.1	1973	2744.1	5.2
1957	1551.1	1.7	1974	2729.3	−0.5
1958	1539.2	−0.8	1975	2695.0	−1.3
1959	1629.1	5.8	1976	2826.7	4.9
1960	1665.3	2.2	1977	2958.6	4.7
			1978	3115.2	5.3
1961	1708.7	2.6	1979	3192.4	2.5
1962	1799.4	5.3	1980	3187.1	−0.2
1963	1873.3	4.1	1981	3248.8	1.9
1964	1973.3	5.3			
1965	2087.6	5.8	1982	3166.0	−2.5
1966	2208.3	5.8	1983	3279.1	3.6
1967	2271.4	2.9	1984	3501.4	6.8
1968	2365.6	4.1	1985	3618.7	3.4
1969	2423.3	2.4	1986	3717.9	2.7
Average (1953–69)		3.4	1987	3845.3	3.4
			1988	4016.9	4.5
			1989	4117.7	2.5
			1990	4155.8	0.9
			1991	4120.3	−0.8
			Average (1970–91)		2.4

Sources: Economic Report of the President, 1991; Survey of Current Business, various issues.

Output

Table 1.1 shows the level of output for the United States for the years 1953–91. The table also shows the growth rate in output for each year. The output measure in the table is *real* **gross national product** (GNP).[2] Gross national product measures current production of goods and services; real means that the measures in Table 1.1 have been corrected for price change. The figures measure growth in the actual quantity of goods and services produced.

As Table 1.1 indicates, output has increased substantially over the 1953–91 period, rising from $1435.3 billion in 1953 to $4120.3 billion in 1991. Looking at the data in more detail, it can be seen that GNP growth in the period since 1970 has been more irregular than was the case for the 1961–69 period. In fact, real GNP has declined in six of the last twenty-two years. The 1961–69 period was one of steady expansion. In this respect the period since 1970 has been more like the decade of the 1950s, when, as can be seen from Table 1.1, there were two years when GNP fell. The instability of GNP growth in the period since 1970 can also be seen from Figure 1.1,

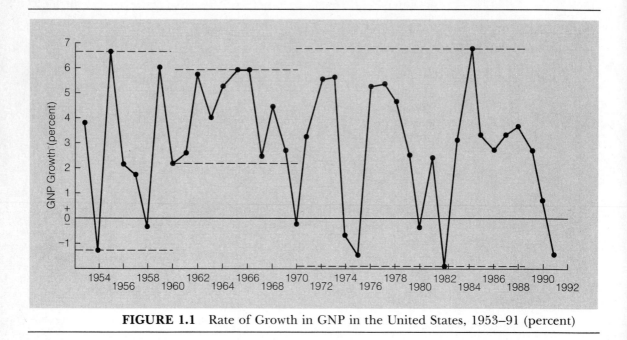

FIGURE 1.1   Rate of Growth in GNP in the United States, 1953–91 (percent)

[2]Gross national product is one of two widely reported measures of aggregate output. The other, gross domestic product, is introduced in Chapter 2, where the difference between the two is explained.

TABLE 1.2 U.S. Unemployment Rate, 1953–91

Year	Unemployment Rate (percent)	Year	Unemployment Rate (percent)
1953	2.9	1970	4.9
1954	5.5	1971	5.9
1955	4.4	1972	5.6
1956	4.1	1973	4.9
1957	4.3	1974	5.6
1958	6.8	1975	8.5
1959	5.5	1976	7.7
1960	5.5	1977	7.0
Average (1953–60)	4.9	1978	6.0
		1979	5.8
1961	6.7	1980	7.1
1962	5.5	1981	7.6
1963	5.7	Average (1970–81)	6.4
1964	5.2		
1965	4.5	1982	9.7
1966	3.8	1983	9.6
1967	3.8	1984	7.5
1968	3.6	1985	7.2
1969	3.5	1986	7.0
Average (1961–69)	4.7	1987	6.2
		1988	5.5
		1989	5.3
		1990	5.5
		1991	6.7
		Average (1982–91)	7.0

Sources: Economic Report of the President, 1989, 1992.

which plots the GNP growth rate for the period 1953–91. Fluctuations in GNP since 1970 have been substantially greater than for the 1960s and more similar to the pattern of the 1950s.

Table 1.1 also shows that not only has GNP growth been more unstable since 1970, but the growth rate has been lower on average, 2.4 percent for the 1970–91 period, compared to 3.4 percent for the 1953–69 period.

Unemployment

Table 1.2 shows the **unemployment rate** for each year since 1953. The unemployment rate is the percent of the labor force that is not employed. For example, in 1991 125.3 million people were in the labor force and 8.4 million or 6.7 percent of these were unemployed. The instability of output growth in the 1970s is mirrored in the fluctuations in the unemployment

TABLE 1.3 U.S. Inflation Rate, 1953–91

Year	Inflation Rate (percent)	Year	Inflation Rate (percent)
1953	0.6	1970	5.5
1954	−0.5	1971	3.4
1955	0.4	1972	3.4
1956	2.9	1973	8.8
1957	3.0	1974	12.2
1958	1.8	1975	7.0
1959	1.5	1976	4.8
1960	1.5	1977	6.8
Average (1953–60)	1.4	1978	9.0
		1979	13.3
1961	0.7	1980	12.4
1962	1.2	1981	8.9
1963	1.6	Average (1970–81)	8.0
1964	1.2		
1965	1.9	1982	3.9
1966	3.4	1983	3.8
1967	3.0	1984	4.0
1968	4.7	1985	3.8
1969	6.1	1986	1.1
Average (1961–69)	2.6	1987	4.4
		1988	4.4
		1989	4.6
		1990	6.1
		1991	3.1
		Average (1982–91)	3.9

Sources: Economic Report of the President, 1989, 1992.

rate over this period. Similarly, the strong, steady expansion of the 1960s is reflected in a steady decline in the unemployment rate. Also, relative to the 1960s or the 1950s, the average unemployment rate has been quite high in the period since 1970. The average unemployment rate was 6.4 percent for 1970–81 and 7.0 percent for 1982–91, compared to average unemployment rates of 4.9 percent for 1953–60 and 4.7 percent for 1961–69.

Inflation

Table 1.3 shows the rate of **inflation** for 1953–91. To calculate the rate of inflation, we use a *price index* that measures the aggregate (or general) price level relative to a base year. The inflation rate is then computed as the percentage rate of change in the price index over a given period. In Table 1.3 the inflation rate is measured by the **consumer price index** (CPI), with other price indexes considered in the next chapter. The CPI measures the retail prices of a fixed "market basket" of several thousand goods and services purchased by households.

It can be seen from the table that the inflation rate was low and relatively stable in the 1950s and early 1960s. In the late 1960s an upward trend in inflation is apparent. This upward trend continued and intensified in the 1970s. The early 1980s were a period of *disinflation,* meaning a decline in the inflation rate. The inflation rate remained fairly low throughout the 1980s. There was an upward blip in the inflation rate in 1990, partly due to a sharp rise in energy prices following Iraq's invasion of oil-rich Kuwait. This was reversed in 1991 as energy prices fell with the allied victory in Kuwait.

It can also be seen from Table 1.3 that variability in the inflation rate has been much greater over the period since 1970. This variability, as well as the upward trend in inflation through 1981 and subsequent disinflation, show up clearly in the plot of inflation in Figure 1.2.

Inflation and Unemployment

Figure 1.2 also shows a plot of the annual unemployment rate for 1953–91. It is interesting to note that in the early portion of this period, through the late 1960s, a negative relationship between the inflation rate and unemployment rate is obvious; years of relatively high rates of inflation are years of relatively low unemployment. In the period since 1970 no such simple relation-

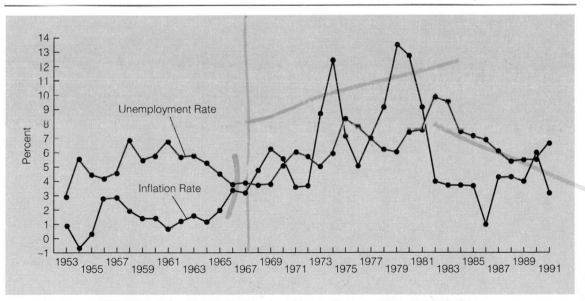

FIGURE 1.2   U.S. Inflation and Unemployment Rates, 1953–91

ship is evident. During parts of the 1970s, for example 1973–75, the unemployment and inflation rates both rose sharply. In the early 1980s the negative relationship seemed to return, with unemployment rising sharply as inflation declined. Later in the 1980s, the inflation rate remained low while the unemployment rate steadily declined. Between 1990 and 1991, the unemployment rate rose and the inflation rate fell, but the behavior of the inflation rate appears to have been due to factors connected with the Iraq–Kuwait war, rather than any underlying unemployment–inflation relationship.

These changes in the relationship between the inflation rate and unemployment rate can be seen in Figure 1.3. In parts *a* and *b* of the figure the

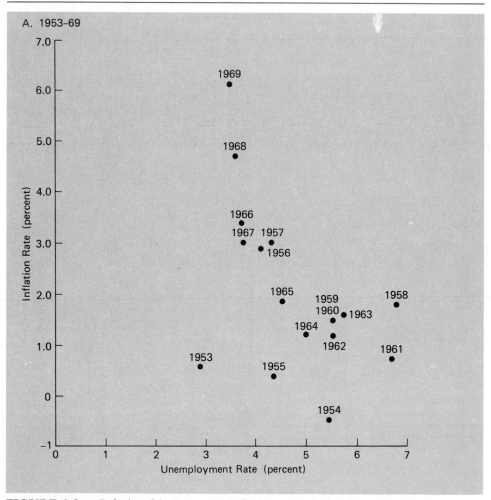

FIGURE 1.3a   Relationship Between Inflation and Unemployment, 1953–69

inflation rate is measured on the vertical axis, and the unemployment rate is on the horizontal axis. Part *a* is for the years 1953–69, and the negative relationship between the two variables is evident. Part *b* is for 1970–91, and for these years there is no apparent relationship between inflation and unemployment.

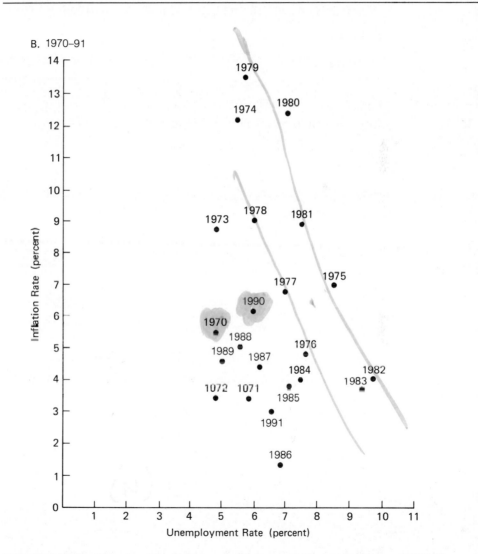

FIGURE 1.3b Relationship Between Inflation and Unemployment, 1970–91

The Twin Deficits

We have seen that during the post–1970 period, the economy was less stable than in the earlier post–World War II years. Looking at the previous tables and graphs, however, it can be seen that each of the variables we considered—output growth, inflation, and unemployment—showed signs of settling down as we moved into the late 1980s. By 1989, output growth had been positive for six straight years, the inflation rate had remained low for a similar period, and the unemployment rate had fallen below 6 percent. Still, polls taken in the later 1980s revealed that respondents were very uncertain about continued stability, a majority forecasting worse economic conditions. Important sources of this uncertainty were the large U.S. federal government deficits and U.S. international trade deficits that emerged in the 1980s.

Figure 1.4 plots U.S. federal government expenditures and receipts since 1950. Over the 1950s and 1960s, growth in revenues roughly kept pace with growth in expenditures. There were some government deficits (excesses

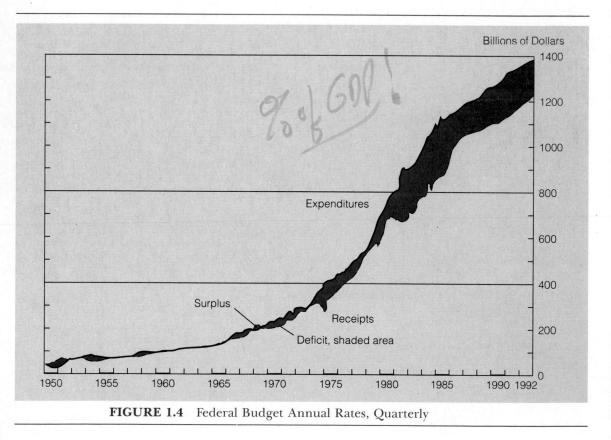

FIGURE 1.4   Federal Budget Annual Rates, Quarterly

of expenditures over receipts), but they were generally small. There were sizable deficits in the mid-1970s during a severe recession, but it was only in the 1980s that we had persistent very large deficits. In 1986 the deficit was $200 billion. The deficit declined later in the 1980s, falling to $124 billion by 1989, but then reversed course and rose to $201 billion by 1991. Projected deficits for 1992 and 1993 are in excess of $300 billion.

Figure 1.5 shows the U.S. merchandise trade deficit for the years since 1950. The trade deficit is the excess of U.S. imports over exports. Persistent trade deficits emerged in the late 1970s, but, as with the federal budget deficit, it was in the 1980s that the trade deficit ballooned, rising to $160 billion by 1988. Thereafter, the trade balance improved steadily, with the deficit falling to $108 billion by 1990 and $66 billion in 1991—still, however, high by historic standards.

The other side of the coin for these two excesses of spending above earnings was the emergence of large debts. In the 1980s, the outstanding amount of federal government debt more than doubled (a reflection of the huge

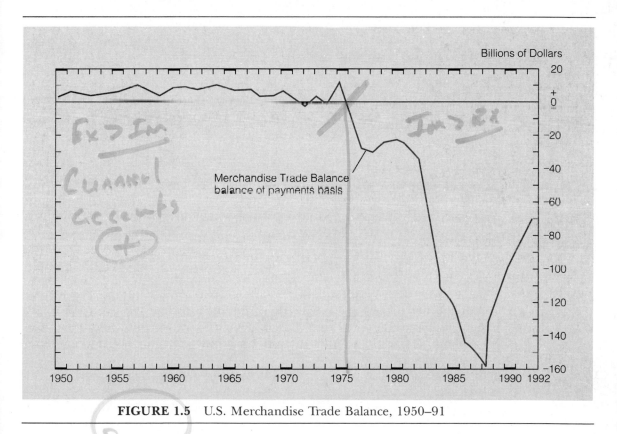

FIGURE 1.5   U.S. Merchandise Trade Balance, 1950–91

federal government deficits), and internationally the United States went from being the world's largest creditor nation to the world's largest debtor (a reflection of our excess of spending abroad [imports] over our earnings on sales abroad [exports]).

1.3 • CENTRAL QUESTIONS IN MACROECONOMICS

The data for output growth, unemployment, and inflation in the foregoing tables and figures suggest some important macroeconomic questions.

Increased Economic Instability

Why did the behavior of output, employment, and inflation become more unstable in the period after 1970? In contrast, what factors explain the steady expansion of output in the 1960s or the price stability of the 1950s? To answer these questions requires a general explanation of the determinants of output, employment, and the price level over periods of several years—that which is termed the *cyclical* behavior of the economy. The macroeconomic theories in Part II attempt to do just this.

The Output–Inflation Relationship

What relationship exists between unemployment and inflation? Why were both the unemployment rate *and* the inflation rate so high during much of the 1970s? What became of the negative relationship that existed between these two variables in the 1950s and 1960s (Figure 1.3a)?

The presence of both high inflation rates and high unemployment rates during the 1970s was especially puzzling to macroeconomists. The experience of the 1950s and the 1960s had led economists to explain substantial inflation as a symptom of too high a level of total demand for output. Substantial unemployment was considered the result of inadequate demand. Such an explanation is consistent with the negative relationship between inflation and unemployment during the 1953–69 period, as shown in Figure 1.3a. When demand was high, the inflation rate was high and unemployment was low; when demand was low, the inflation rate was low but unemployment was high. But this line of reasoning cannot explain simultaneously high unemployment and high inflation. Total demand for output cannot be both too high and too low.

The events of the 1970s caused economists to reconsider and modify earlier theories of inflation and unemployment, as we see in the analysis that follows. An important part of this reconsideration of existing theory concerns the role of total demand for output, what is termed **aggregate demand,** in determining output, employment, and inflation.

All in all, the relationship between unemployment and inflation has been much more complex in the post–1970 period than in earlier years. The macroeconomic theories we consider try to explain why.

A Growth Slowdown with Rising Unemployment

What explains the decline in the growth rate in output, as measured by real GNP, in the period since 1970? As we saw previously, output grew at an average annual rate of 3.4 percent in the 1953–69 period, compared to 2.4 percent for 1970–91. Are we witnessing a *secular* decline in the growth rate of the U.S. economy? Mired in recession, the 1990s did not get off to a good start as a high-growth decade.

Together with slower growth in the post–1970 period, the unemployment rate was higher than in the 1950s or 1960s. In the late 1980s, there was considerable improvement in unemployment. The recession that began in 1990, however, pushed the unemployment rate back up above 7 percent, the average for the 1982–91 period. What explains this apparent trend toward higher unemployment, a trend also seen in many European countries?

Implications of the Twin Deficits

What will be the future economic effects of the U.S. federal budget and trade deficits? Is the U.S. economy heading for what an editorial in the *Financial Times* called a "rendezvous with disaster"? Or do these deficits pose problems of a more subtle, long-term kind, as some have said, more akin to termites in the basement than the wolf at the door?

1.4 · CONCLUSION

There is no shortage of questions. Let us look ahead at how we will pursue the answers.

We begin in Chapter 2 with a consideration of the measurement of macroeconomic variables. In that chapter we tie the variables considered in later chapters to their counterparts in the U.S. economy. Chapters 3 to 13 (Part II) present and compare four major schools of macroeconomic theory: the classical theory (Chapters 3 and 4), Keynesian economics (Chapters 5 to 8), monetarism (Chapters 9 and 10), and the new classical economics (Chapter 11). We then (Chapter 12) discuss two recent directions in macroeconomic research: real business cycle theory and the new Keynesian economics. These chapters examine the models that each of these groups of economists have constructed to analyze the cyclical or short-run behavior of macroeconomic variables. We also examine the policy conclusions that follow from each of these models. In Chapter 13 we summarize the major issues on which macroeconomists are divided.

Chapters 14 to 17 (Part III) consider elements of the models in Part II in more detail and extend the models in several ways. Chapter 17, for example, expands the time frame of our models beyond the short run, enabling us to examine questions such as the potential causes of a slowdown in U.S. economic growth over a period of more than a decade.

In Chapters 18 and 19 (Part IV) we consider macroeconomic policy. How best might government policy be conducted to achieve macroeconomic goals such as low unemployment and inflation rates and stable economic growth?

Chapter 20 (Part V), which concludes the volume, considers U.S. international economic relations.

Review Questions and Problems

1. What are some of the important variables that comprise the subject matter of macroeconomics? How does macroeconomics differ from microeconomics, the other major branch of economic theory?

2. Summarize the behavior of the inflation rate and unemployment rate since 1980. Did the movements of the inflation and unemployment rates over this period more closely resemble those of the 1970s or of the 1950s and 1960s?

3. Compare the behavior of inflation, output growth, and the unemployment rate of the U.S. economy in the post–1970 period with the behavior of the same variables for the 1960s; for the 1950s. In which period was the performance of the macroeconomy, as measured by these variables, the most "desirable"? the least desirable?

4. There appear to have been several shifts in the output–inflation relationship over the 1953–91 period. Explain the nature of these shifts.

5. Using the *Economic Report of the President* or other sources for the most recent years, update the data in Tables 1.1 to 1.3.

6. Consider the behavior of output growth, unemployment, and inflation for the years 1983–91. Which earlier decade does this period most resemble— the 1950s, 1960s, or 1970s?

Measurement of Macroeconomic Variables

2

In subsequent chapters we examine a number of *macroeconomic models.* These models are simplified representations of the economy, which attempt to capture important factors determining aggregate variables such as output, employment, and the price level. The elements of such models are hypothesized theoretical relationships among aggregative economic variables, including macroeconomic policy variables. To understand such theoretical relationships, it is best to begin by carefully defining the real-world counterparts of the variables that appear in our models. It will also prove useful to consider some of the accounting relationships that exist among these variables, since we make use of these relationships to construct our theoretical models. We begin by describing the key variables measured in the **national income accounts.**

2.1 • THE NATIONAL INCOME ACCOUNTS

One reads with dismay of Presidents Hoover and then Roosevelt designing policies to combat the Great Depression of the 1930s on the basis of such sketchy data as stock price indices, freight car loadings, and incomplete indices of industrial production. The fact is that comprehensive measures of national income and output did not exist at the time. The Depression, and with it the growing role of government in the economy, emphasized the need for such measures and led to the development of a comprehensive set of national income accounts.[1]

---

[1] Nobel Prize winning economists Simon Kuznets and Richard Stone played pioneering roles in the development of national income accounting. See Simon Kuznets, *National Income and Its Composition, 1919–38* (New York: National Bureau of Economic Research, 1941). During World War II the Commerce Department took over the maintenance of the national income accounts. National income accounts data are published in the *Survey of Current Business.* Historical data series can be found in *Business Statistics,* a biennial supplement to the *Survey.*

Like the accounts of a business firm, the national income accounts have two sides: a product side and an income side. On the product side, production and sales are measured. The income side measures the distribution of the proceeds from sales.

On the product side there are two widely reported measures of overall production: gross national product (GNP), which we looked at in Chapter 1, and gross domestic product (GDP). They differ in their treatment of international transactions. GNP includes earnings of U.S. corporations overseas and U.S. residents working overseas: GDP does not. Conversely, GDP includes earnings from current production in the United States that accrue to foreign residents or foreign-owned firms, while GNP excludes these items. To give an example, profits earned in the United States by a foreign-owned firm would be included in GDP but not in GNP.

For the United States, there is little difference between these two product measures. This is because few U.S. residents work abroad, and the overseas earnings of U.S. firms are about the same as the U.S. earnings of foreign firms. The difference between GNP and GDP is large for a country like Pakistan, with a large number of residents working overseas, or Canada, in which there is much more foreign investment than there is Canadian investment abroad. In 1991 the U.S. national income accountants shifted emphasis from GNP to GDP. Our explanation of the product side of the national accounts therefore concentrates on this measure of output. The GNP concept enters into the discussion at a later point.

On the income side of the national accounts, the central measure is national income, although we also discuss some related income concepts.

2.2 · GROSS DOMESTIC PRODUCT

Gross domestic product (**GDP**) is a measure of all currently produced final goods and services evaluated at market prices. A number of aspects of this definition require clarification.

Currently Produced.   GDP includes only currently produced goods and services. It is a flow measure of output per time period—for example, per quarter or per year—and includes only goods and services produced during this interval. Such market transactions as exchanges of previously produced houses, cars, or factories would not enter into GDP. Exchanges of assets, such as stocks and bonds, are examples of other market transactions that do not directly involve current production of goods and services and are therefore not in GDP.

Final Goods and Services.   Only the production of *final* goods and services enters gross domestic product. Goods that are used in the production of other goods rather than being sold to final purchasers, what are termed intermediate goods, are not counted separately in GDP. Such goods show up in GDP because they contribute to the value of the final goods in whose production they are used. Counting them separately is double counting. To give an example, we would not want to count the value of flour used in making bread separately, then again when the bread is sold.

However, two types of goods used in the production process are counted in GDP. The first of these is currently produced *capital goods*—business plant and equipment purchases. Such capital goods are ultimately used up in the production process, but within the current period only a portion of value of the capital good is used up in production. This portion, termed *depreciation*, can be thought to be embodied in the value of the final goods that are sold. If capital goods were not included separately in GDP, it would be equivalent to assuming that they depreciated fully in the current time period. In gross national product, the whole value of the capital good is included as a separate item. In a sense this is double counting since, as just noted, the value of depreciation is embodied in the value of final goods. At a later point we will subtract out depreciation to construct a *net* output measure.

The other category, containing essentially intermediate goods, that is part of GDP is *inventory investment*—the net change in inventories of final goods awaiting sale or of materials used in the production process. Additions to inventory stocks of final goods belong in GDP because they are currently produced output. To get the timing of national product correct, they should be counted in the current period as they are added to stocks; they should not be counted later when they are sold to final purchasers. Inventory investment in materials similarly belongs in GDP because it also represents currently produced output whose value is not embodied in *current* sales of final output. Notice that inventory investment can be negative as well as positive. If final sales exceed production, for example, due to a rundown of inventories (negative inventory investment), GDP will fall short of final sales.

Evaluated at Market Prices.   GDP is the *value* of goods and services determined by the common measuring rod of market prices. This is the trick to being able to measure apples plus oranges plus railroad cars plus.... But this does exclude from GDP goods that are not sold in markets, such as the services of homemakers or output of home gardens, as well as nonreported output from illegal activities such as the sale of narcotics, gambling, and prostitution.[2] Also, since it is a measure of the value of output in terms of market prices, GDP, which is essentially a *quantity* measure, will be sensitive to

---

[2] For some services that are not actually sold on the market, the Commerce Department does try to *impute* the market value of the service and include it in GDP. An example is the services of owner-occupied houses, which the Commerce Department estimates based on rental value.

TABLE 2.1   Nominal GDP and Its Components, Selected Years[a] (billions of dollars)

Year	GDP	Consumption	Investment	Government Purchases of Goods and Services	Net Exports
1929	103.9	77.3	16.7	8.9	1.1
1933	56.0	45.8	1.6	8.3	0.4
1939	91.3	67.0	9.5	13.6	1.2
1945	213.4	119.6	11.3	83.0	−0.5
1950	288.3	192.1	55.1	38.8	2.2
1960	513.4	332.4	78.7	99.8	2.4
1970	1010.7	646.5	150.3	212.7	1.2
1980	2708.0	1748.1	467.6	507.1	−14.7
1991	5672.6	3889.1	726.7	1087.5	−30.7

[a] Components may not sum to total due to rounding error.

Source: Economic Report of the President, 1989; 1992 *Federal Reserve Bulletin,* May 1989.

changes in the average price level. The same physical output will correspond to a different GDP level as the average level of market prices varies. To correct for this, in addition to computing gross domestic product in terms of current market prices, a concept termed *nominal* GDP, the national income accountants also calculate *real* GDP, which is the value of domestic product in terms of constant prices from a base year. The way in which the latter calculation is made is discussed later in the chapter.

GDP can be broken down into the components shown in Table 2.1.[3] The values of each component for selected years are also given in the table. The data in the table suggest a number of trends and patterns which will be of interest to us later.

The **consumption** component of GDP consists of the household sector's purchases of currently produced goods and services. Consumption can be further broken down into consumer durable goods (e.g., automobiles, televisions), nondurable consumption goods (e.g., foods, beverages, clothing), and consumer services (e.g., medical services, haircuts). Consumption is the largest component of GDP, between 60 and 69 percent of GDP in recent years.

The **investment** component of GDP in Table 2.1 consists of three subcomponents. The largest of these is business fixed investment, which amounted

---

[3] The GDP series goes back only to 1959; for earlier years, GNP is used to measure total output.

to $550.4 billion, 76 percent of the total investment in 1991. Business fixed investment consists of purchases of newly produced plant and equipment— the capital goods discussed previously. The second subcomponent of investment is residential construction investment, the building of single- and multifamily housing units, which in 1991 totaled $196.5 billion. The final subcomponent of investment is inventory investment, which is the change in business inventories. As noted, inventory investment may be positive or negative. In 1991, inventory investment was $−20.2 billion, meaning that there was a decrease of $20.2 billion in inventories during that year.

Over the years covered by the table, investment was a volatile component of GDP, ranging from 2.9 percent of GDP in 1933 to 19.1 percent of GDP in 1950. This volatility of investment behavior has implications for the construction of the macroeconomic models considered later.

The figures in Table 2.1 are *gross* rather than net, meaning that no adjustment for depreciation has been made. The investment total in the table is gross investment, not net investment (net investment equals gross investment minus depreciation). In 1991, for example, depreciation, which is also called the capital consumption allowance, was $623.5 billion. Therefore, net investment was $103.2 billion (726.7 − 623.5).[4]

The next component of gross domestic product in the table is **government purchases** of goods and services. This is the share of the current output of goods and services bought by the government sector, which includes the federal government as well as state and local governments. It is important to note that not all government expenditures are part of gross domestic product because not all government expenditures represent a demand for currently produced goods and services. Government transfer payments to individuals (e.g., social security payments) and government interest payments are examples of expenditures that are not included in GDP. From the table it can be seen that government's share in gross domestic product has increased in the post–World War II period relative to the prewar period. In 1929, government purchases of goods and services were 8.6 percent of total output. Not surprisingly, in 1945, during World War II, the government component of output, swollen by the military budget, had risen to 39 percent. But in the postwar period the government sector did not return to its prewar size. Government purchases of goods and services were approximately 20 percent or one-fifth of GDP in both 1960 and 1991. Trends in the size of the government budget—both purchases of goods and services and other

---

[4] In 1933, depreciation was $7.6 billion. Since gross investment was only $1.6 billion, *net* investment was negative. This means that the capital stock declined in that year since gross investment was insufficient to replace the portion of the capital stock that wore out.

components not included in the national income accounts—are analyzed in some detail in a later chapter, when we consider *fiscal* or government budget policy.

The final component of GDP given in Table 2.1 is **net exports.** Net exports equals total (gross) exports minus imports. These items represent the direct contribution of the foreign sector to GDP. Gross exports are currently produced goods and services sold to foreign buyers. They are a part of gross domestic product. Imports are purchases by domestic buyers of goods and services produced abroad and should not be counted in gross domestic product. Imported goods and services are, however, included in the consumption, investment, and government spending totals in GDP. Therefore, we need to subtract the value of imports to arrive at the total of domestically produced goods and services. Net exports remain as the (net) direct effect of foreign-sector transactions on GDP. As can be seen from the table, net exports were negative in 1991, reflecting the excess of imports relative to exports.

Before turning from the product to the income side of the national income accounts, it should be noted that the breakdown of GDP into consumption, investment, government purchases, and net exports (exports minus imports) results from the attempt to group purchases by type of buyer—rather than, for example, by type of product. This is done with an eye toward explaining the levels of such components by isolating the factors that motivate each group of purchasers. Consumers in general would be expected to be influenced by household incomes, businesses by profit opportunities, the government by macroeconomic policy considerations, and so on. Not all the macroeconomic theories discussed use a sectoral approach to modeling GDP determination, but one, the Keynesian theory, does.

Read Perspectives 2.1.

2.3 • NATIONAL INCOME

We turn now to the income side of the national accounts. In computing national income, our starting point is the GNP total, not GDP. This is because, as explained earlier, it is GNP that includes income earned abroad by U.S. residents and firms but excludes earnings of foreign residents and firms from production in the United States. This is the proper starting point because we want a measure of the income of U.S. residents and firms.

To go from GDP to GNP, we add foreign earnings of U.S. residents and firms, which totaled $148.9 billion in 1991. We then subtract earnings in the United States by foreign residents and firms—a total of $135.7 billion in 1991. This results in a GNP of $5685.8 billion compared to a GDP of $5672.6 billion. As noted previously, there is little difference between these two production measures for the United States.

PERSPECTIVES

2.1

What GDP Is Not

GDP is the most comprehensive measure of a nation's economic activity. Policymakers use GDP figures to monitor short-run fluctuations in economic activity as well as long-run growth trends. It is worthwhile, however, to recognize some important limitations of the GDP concept.

NONMARKET PRODUCTIVE ACTIVITIES ARE LEFT OUT

Because goods and services are evaluated at market prices in GDP, nonmarket production is left out. (As noted earlier, for instance, homemaker services are left out.) Cross-country comparisons of GDP overstate the gap in production between highly industrialized countries and less developed nations where largely agrarian nonmarket production is of greater importance.

THE UNDERGROUND ECONOMY IS LEFT OUT

Also left out of GDP are illegal forms of economic activity and legal activities that are not reported to avoid paying taxes, the *underground economy*. Gambling and the drug trade are examples of the former. Activities not reported for purposes of tax avoidance take many forms; for example, repairmen who are paid in cash for services may underreport or fail to report the income. It is hard to estimate the size of the underground economy for obvious reasons. Rough estimates for the United States range from 5 to 15 percent of GDP. For countries where tax evasion is more widespread—Italy is often cited as an example—estimates of the underground economy are 25 percent of GDP or more.

GDP IS NOT A WELFARE MEASURE

GDP measures production of goods and services; it is not a measure of welfare or even of material wellbeing. For one thing, GDP gives no weight to leisure. If we all began to work 60-hour weeks, GDP would increase, yet would we be better off?

GDP also fails to subtract for some welfare costs to production. If, for example, production of electricity causes acid rain, and consequently water pollution and dying forests, we count the production of electricity in GDP but do not subtract the economic loss from the pollution. In fact, if the government spends money to try to clean up the pollution, we count that too!

GDP is a useful measure of the overall level of economic activity, not of welfare.

National income is the sum of all factor earnings from current production of goods and services. Factor earnings are incomes of factors of production: land, labor, and capital. Each dollar of GNP is one dollar of final sales, and if there were no charges against GNP other than factor incomes, GNP and national income would be equal. There are, in fact, some other charges against GNP that cause national income and GNP to diverge, but the two concepts are still closely related. The adjustments required to go from GNP to national income, with figures for the year 1991, are shown in Table 2.2.

Externalities
Environmental

TABLE 2.2   Relationship of Gross National Product
and National Income, 1991 (billions of dollars)

Gross national product	5685.8
Minus: Depreciation	623.5
Net national product	5062.3
Minus: Indirect taxes and Other	519.8
National income	4542.5

Sources: Federal Reserve Bulletin, May 1992; *Economic Report of the President,* 1992; Economic Indicators, March 1992.

The first charge against GNP that is not included in national income is depreciation. The portion of the capital stock used up must be subtracted from final sales before national income is computed; depreciation represents a cost of production, not factor income. Making this subtraction gives us **net national product,** the net production measures referred to earlier. From this total, both indirect taxes—sales and excise taxes—and the net amount of some additional items labeled "Other" in the table are subtracted to yield national income. An indirect tax such as a sales tax represents a discrepancy between the market price of a product, which includes the tax (the amount entered in GNP), and the proceeds of the seller, from which factor incomes are paid. The "Other" category in Table 2.2 includes relatively minor adjustments for some additional discrepancies between factor earnings and the market prices of items included in GNP.[5]

Table 2.3 shows the components of national income and the level of each component in 1991. Compensation of employees, which includes wages and

TABLE 2.3   Components of National Income, 1991
(billions of dollars)

Compensation of employees	3388.2
Corporate profits	307.2
Proprietors' income	379.6
Rental income of persons	−12.7
Net interest	480.2
	4542.5

Sources: Federal Reserve Bulletin, May 1992; *Economic Report of the President,* 1992; *Economic Indicators,* March 1992.

[5]An example of the type of item included in the "Other" category is bad debts to the business sector, which is termed a business transfer payment. Since such debts are uncollected, they are not factor earnings, yet they represent sales included in GNP.

salary payments as well as supplementary benefits, is the largest element in national income, 74.6 percent in 1991. Corporate profits were 6.8 percent of national income in that year. The next item in the table, proprietors' income, is the income of unincorporated business. In 1991 this amounted to 8.4 percent of national income. The final two items are (net) rental income of persons and net interest income, which together totaled 10.3 percent of national income.[6]

Later we return to the discussion of national income and derive some useful relationships between national income and national product. First we consider two other income concepts.

2.4 • PERSONAL AND PERSONAL DISPOSABLE INCOME

National income is a measure of income earned from current production of goods and services. For some purposes, however, it is useful to have a measure of income received by *persons* and regardless of source. For example, we noted that consumption expenditures by households would be influenced by income. The relevant income concept would be one of all income received by persons. Also, we would want a measure of income after deducting personal tax payments, since income needed to make tax payments could not be used to finance consumption. **Personal income** is the national income accounts measure of the income received by persons from all sources. When we subtract personal tax payments from personal income, we get a measure of **disposable (after-tax) personal income.**

To go from national income to personal income, we have to subtract elements of national income that are not received by persons and add income of persons from sources other than current production of goods and services. The necessary adjustments are shown in Table 2.4. The first items subtracted from national income are the portions of the corporate profits item in the national income accounts that are not paid out as dividends to persons. The portion of corporate profits not paid out in dividends includes corporate profits tax payments, undistributed profits (retained earnings), and a valuation adjustment made by the Commerce Department to correct for a distortion of reported profits figures because of inflation. The first two of these should require no explanation. The details of the valuation adjustment need not concern us here except to recognize that since this adjustment was made to the corporate profits entry in the national income, but did not actually affect profits that can be paid out to persons, it must

---

[6]The net rental income item equals gross rental income minus depreciation of rental property. It was negative in 1991 because depreciation exceeded gross rental income.

TABLE 2.4　Relationship of National Income, Personal Income, and Disposable Income, 1991 (billions of dollars)

National income	4,542.5
Less	
Corporate profits tax payments, undistributed profits, and valuation adjustment	175.3
Contributions to Social Security	527.3
Plus	
Transfer payments to persons	757.2
Personal interest income	238.2
Personal income	4,835.3
Less	
Personal taxes	616.1
Personal disposable income	4,219.2

Source: Survey of Current Business, March 1992; *Economic Indicators,* March 1992.

be subtracted in computing personal income. Also subtracted from national income in computing personal income are contributions to Social Security by the employer and employee. Such payroll taxes are included in the employee compensation term in national income but go to the government, not directly to persons.

The items added in going from national income to personal income are payments to persons that are not in return for current production of goods and services. The first of these are *transfer payments* to persons. These are predominantly government transfer payments such as Social Security payments, veterans' pensions, and payments to retired federal government workers. There is also a relatively small amount of business transfers to persons that, in the national income accounts, includes gifts to charities. The other item to be added in going from national income to personal income is personal interest income—mostly interest payments by the government to persons. Government interest payments are made on bonds previously issued by federal, state, and local governments. Personal interest payments here do *not* include interest payments by corporations. These are considered to be payments for factor services and, as we noted, were included in national income. With these adjustments we can calculate personal income, which in 1991 equaled $4835.3 billion. We then subtract personal taxes to get personal disposable income, which was $4219.2 billion in 1991.

Table 2.5 shows how we used our disposable income in 1991. Most of it, $3889.1 billion, was spent for consumption, the household sector's purchases of goods and services. There were two other expenditures. The first was interest paid to business (installment credit and credit card interest). The second, a very small component of personal expenditures, was transfers

TABLE 2.5 Disposition of Personal Disposable Income, 1991 (billions of dollars)

Personal disposable income	4,219.2
Less	
Personal consumption expenditures	3889.1
Interest paid to business	106.8
Personal transfer payments to foreigners	
(net)	3.0
Personal saving	220.3

Sources: *Economic Report of the President, Survey of Current Business,* March, 1992.

to foreigners (e.g., gifts to foreign relatives). Personal saving is the part of personal disposable income that is not spent. In 1991 personal saving was $220.3 billion, or 5.2 percent of personal disposable income.

2.5 • SOME NATIONAL INCOME ACCOUNTING IDENTITIES

The interrelationships among gross national (or domestic) product, national income, and personal income form the basis for some accounting definitions or *identities* that are used to construct the macroeconomic models considered. In deriving these identities in this section, we simplify the national income accounting structure by ignoring a number of items discussed previously. This simplified accounting structure is carried over into several of the models in the next part.

The simplifications we impose are as follows:

1. The foreign sector will be omitted. This means that we drop the *net exports* term from GDP (Table 2.1) and the *net foreign transfers* item from personal outlays in breaking down the disposition of personal income (Table 2.5). The foreign sector is reintroduced into our models later in the book, when we consider questions of international macroeconomics. In excluding the foreign sector, we also exclude foreign earnings of U.S. residents and firms, as well as U.S. earnings of foreign residents and foreign-owned firms. GNP and GDP are thus equal. *These two terms are used interchangeably except where we reintroduce the foreign sector.*

2. Indirect taxes and the other discrepancies between GNP and national income will be ignored (Table 2.2). We assume that national income and national product or output are the same. *The terms national* income *and* output *are used interchangeably throughout this book.*

3. Depreciation will also be ignored (except where explicitly noted). Therefore, gross and net national product will be identical.

4. Several simplifications are made in the relationship between national income and personal disposable income (Table 2.4). We assume that all corporate profits are paid out as dividends; there are no retained earnings or corporate tax payments, and there is no valuation adjustment (see Table 2.4). We assume that all taxes, including social security contributions, are assessed directly on households. Also, business transfer payments will be ignored. Consequently, we can specify personal disposable income as national income (or output) minus tax payments (Tx) plus government transfers (Tr), which include government interest payments.[7] Letting *net* taxes (*T*) equal tax payments minus transfers,

$$T \equiv \text{Tx} - \text{Tr} \tag{2.1}$$

we have (personal) disposable income Y_D equal to national income (Y) minus net taxes:

$$Y_D \equiv Y - \text{Tx} + \text{Tr} \equiv Y - T$$

With these simplifications, we have the following accounting identities. Gross domestic (or national) product (Y) is defined as

$$Y \equiv C + I_r + G \tag{2.2}$$

that is, as consumption (C) plus *realized* investment (I_r) plus government purchases of goods and services (G).[8] The subscript (r) on the investment term is included since we will want to distinguish between this *realized* investment total that appears in the national income accounts and the *desired* level of investment spending.

From the income side of the national income accounts, again making use of simplifications 1 to 4 *and ignoring interest paid to business* (in Table 2.5), we have the identity

$$Y_D \equiv Y - T \equiv C + S \tag{2.3}$$

which states that, with the simplifying assumptions we have made, all disposable income, which equals national income (Y) minus *net* tax payments (T = tax payments minus transfers), goes for consumption expenditures or personal saving (S). We can write (2.3) as

$$Y \equiv C + S + T$$

---

[7] This excludes that part of personal interest income in Table 2.4 that is not paid to households by the government.

[8] It is important to distinguish identities such as (2.1) and (2.2), which are indicated by the three-bar symbol ($\equiv$), and equations, which are indicated with the usual equal sign ($=$). Identities are relationships that follow from accounting or other definitions and therefore hold for any and all values of the variables.

and since Y is both national income and output, we can combine (2.2) and (2.3) to write

$$C + I_r + G \equiv Y \equiv C + S + T \tag{2.4}$$

This identity states that expenditures on GDP ($C + I_r + G$) must by definition be equal to the dispositions of national income ($C + S + T$) and will be useful in the construction of the Keynesian macroeconomic model. By canceling the consumption term (C) on both the left and right in (2.4), we can rewrite this fundamental identity as

$$I_r + G \equiv S + T \tag{2.5}$$

This form of the expenditures–income identity will also be employed.

2.6 • MEASURING PRICE CHANGES: REAL VERSUS NOMINAL GDP

So far the figures we have been discussing are for *nominal* GDP, which is the output of currently produced goods and services evaluated at current market prices or in current dollar terms. Since gross domestic product is the value of currently produced goods and services measured in market prices, it will change when the overall price level changes as well as when the actual volume of production changes. For many purposes we want a measure of output that varies only with the quantity of goods produced. Such a measure would, for example, be most closely related to the level of employment; more workers are not needed to produce a given volume of output simply because it is sold at a higher price. To construct a measure of output that changes only when quantities and not prices change, what is termed *real* GDP, we measure output in terms of constant prices or constant-valued dollars from a base year. Using 1987 as a base year, for example, we can compute the value of GDP in 1959, 1980, or 1991 *in terms of the price level or value of the dollar in 1987*. Changes in GDP in 1987-valued dollars then measure quantity changes between these years.

Column 1 of Table 2.6 shows the nominal GDP for selected years. Column 2 shows the value of real GDP as measured in 1987 prices for each of these years. In 1987 real and nominal income are the same since base-year prices are current prices. In prior years, when current prices were lower than 1987 prices, real GDP is higher than nominal GDP. Conversely, in the years after 1987, when prices were higher, nominal GDP exceeds real GDP.

Table 2.6 shows that real GDP often behaves quite differently from nominal GDP. Nominal GDP changes whenever the quantity of goods produced changes *or* when the market price of those goods changes; real GDP changes only when production changes. It is therefore when prices are changing

TABLE 2.6   Nominal GDP, Real GDP, and Implicit Price Deflator, Selected Years

Year	(1) Nominal GDP (Billions of current dollars)	(2) Real GDP (Billions of 1987 dollars)	(3) Implicit GDP Deflator $\left(\dfrac{\text{Column 1}}{\text{Column 2}} \times 100\right)$
1959	494.2	1,931.3	25.6
1960	513.4	1,973.2	26.0
1970	1,010.7	2,875.8	35.1
1973	1,349.6	3,268.6	41.3
1974	1,458.6	3,248.1	44.9
1975	1,585.9	3,221.7	49.2
1978	2,232.7	3,703.5	60.3
1979	2,488.6	3,796.8	65.5
1980	2,708.0	3,776.3	71.7
1987	4,539.9	4,539.9	100.0
1990	5,513.8	4,884.9	112.9
1991	5,672.6	4,848.4	117.0

Source: Economic Report of the President, 1992.

dramatically that the movements of the two measures diverge sharply. It can be seen from the table, for example, that while nominal GDP rose by over $200 billion from 1973 to 1975, real GDP actually declined between those two years. Again, between 1979 and 1980 there was a rapid increase in nominal GDP but a fall in real GDP. In both periods, real GDP declined because the actual production level of goods and services declined. Prices, however, rose rapidly enough in these inflationary years to make nominal GDP rise. At such times, the distinction between real and nominal figures is especially important.

Now consider the numbers in column 3 of Table 2.6, which gives the ratio of nominal GDP to real GDP (nominal GDP ÷ real GDP), where the ratio is multiplied by 100 (following the procedure in the national income accounts). The ratio of nominal GDP to real GDP is a measure of the value of current production in current prices (e.g., in 1991) relative to the value of the *same* goods and services in prices for the base year (1987). Since the same goods and services appear at the top and bottom, the ratio of nominal GDP to real GDP is just the ratio of the current price level of goods and services relative to the price level in the base year. It is a measure of the aggregate (or overall) price level, which in the previous chapter we called a *price index*. This index of the prices of goods and services in GDP is called the *implicit GDP deflator*.

We measure changes in the aggregate price level by comparing values of the implicit GDP deflator in different years. First, consider a comparison of the implicit price deflator between the base year, 1987, and 1991. In the base year, real and nominal GDP are the same and the implicit price deflator has a value of 100. From Table 2.6 we see that in 1991 the value of the implicit GDP deflator was 117.0. This means that GDP at current prices in 1991 (nominal GDP) was 17 percent higher than the same goods and services valued at 1987 prices. The aggregate price level, as measured by the GDP deflator, rose 17 percent between 1987 and 1991.

We can also use the implicit GDP deflator to measure price changes between two years, neither of which is the base year. Between 1990 and 1991, for example, the implicit GDP deflator rose from 112.9 to 117.0. As measured by this index, the percentage rise in the aggregate price level (or rate of inflation) between 1990 and 1991 was

$$[(117.0 - 112.9) \div 112.9] \times 100 = 3.6\%$$

Before going on, consider how the GDP deflator got its name. The ratio of nominal to real GDP is termed a *deflator* because we can divide nominal GDP by this ratio to correct for the effect of inflation on GDP—to deflate GDP. This follows because

$$\text{GDP deflator} = \frac{\text{nominal GDP}}{\text{real GDP}}$$

$$\text{real GDP} = \frac{\text{nominal GDP}}{\text{GDP deflator}}$$

confusing!

Less obvious is why the adjective *implicit* is attached to the name of this price index. The GDP deflator is an implicit price index in that we first construct a quantity measure, real GDP, and then compare the movement in GDP in current and constant dollars to gauge the changes in prices. We do not try, directly or explicitly, to measure the average movement in prices. Two examples of explicit price indices are considered in the next section.

2.7 • THE CONSUMER PRICE INDEX AND THE PRODUCER PRICE INDEX

Since the GDP deflator measures changes in the prices of all currently produced goods and services, it is the most comprehensive and in that sense the preferable measure of the rate of price change. Two other price indices are *CPI* widely reported, however, and have their particular uses and advantages.

The **consumer price index** (CPI) measures the retail prices of a fixed "market basket" of several thousand goods and services purchased by households. The CPI is an explicit price index in the sense that it directly measures movements in the weighted average of the prices of the goods and services

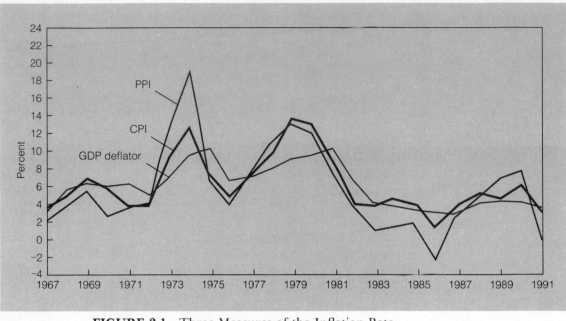

FIGURE 2.1 Three Measures of the Inflation Rate

in the market basket through time. The CPI is the price index most relevant to consumers because it measures the prices of only goods and services directly purchased by them. Many government pensions, including the level of Social Security benefits and many wage rates, are indexed to the CPI, meaning they have provisions for automatic increases geared to increases in the CPI.

Another widely reported explicit price index is the **producer price index** (PPI), which measures the wholesale prices of approximately 3000 items. Since these items sold at the wholesale level include many raw materials and semifinished goods, movements in the producer price index signal future movements in retail prices, such as those measured in the CPI. Both the consumer price index and the producer price index have the advantage that they are available monthly, whereas the implicit GDP deflator is available only quarterly.

Figure 2.1 shows the annual inflation rates for the years 1967–91 as measured by the three price indices we have discussed. In terms of broad movement in the inflation rate, the three indices show similar patterns. The acceleration of inflation in the 1973–75 and 1979–80 periods is evident in each series, as is the disinflation in the 1980s. There are, however, some differences in the three series that reflect their different composition. The producer price index, for example, gives a larger weight to raw materials than either of the others and therefore rose substantially more than the CPI or GDP deflator in 1973 and 1974, when agricultural and crude oil prices skyrocketed. Conversely, when these raw material prices declined during the 1982–86 period, the decline in the inflation rate registered by the producer price index was the largest among the three inflation measures.

2.8 • MEASURES OF CYCLICAL VARIATION IN OUTPUT

Most of the analysis in this book focuses on short-run or cyclical movements in output and employment—fluctuations over periods of perhaps one to four years. In these short-run periods, fluctuations in output and employment come primarily from variations in actual output around **potential output,** where potential output is defined as the level of real output that the economy could produce at high rates of resource utilization. Such short-run movements in output consist of changes in the utilization rates of labor and capital. It is in the longer run that growth of potential output, which implies growth in the available quantity of factors of production (capital and labor), becomes an important determinant of the growth of output. We have already discussed the measurement of actual real output (real GNP or GDP); what remains for this section is to explain the measurement of potential real output and thus of deviations of actual GNP from potential GNP[9]

The first step in estimating potential output is to choose benchmark measures of high resource utilization. Potential output is then estimated as the level of real output that would be forthcoming at those high utilization rates. In the 1960s the Council of Economic Advisors, which then compiled the official estimates of potential output, simply estimated the output level that corresponded to a 4 percent unemployment rate; that is, a 4 percent unemployment rate was taken as the benchmark level of high employment. This reflected an assumption that at an unemployment rate of 4 percent of the labor force, existing unemployment was of a frictional or seasonal nature— workers between jobs, just entering, or reentering the labor force, or workers whose employment has a seasonal pattern. During the 1970s this procedure was modified to take account of the utilization rate of capital.

In the 1970s economists and policymakers became less certain about the appropriate benchmark for high employment. It was generally agreed that the unemployment rate that would correspond to output being at its

---

[9]Our discussion of potential output focuses on the GNP measure of output. This is because the constructed potential output series are for GNP. Since GNP and GDP differ only slightly, which output measure we use does not have a substantive effect.

potential level had risen above 4 percent. Among the reasons for this increase in the benchmark unemployment rate were changes in the age–sex composition of the labor force, which seem likely to have raised the levels of unemployment that would exist even in a high-employment situation. Specifically, young workers and female workers had increased relative to older male workers as a proportion of the labor force. Since the former groups include a greater number of new entrants or reentrants to the labor force, and tend to change jobs more frequently as well as to combine spells of employment with periods of alternative activity (school or work in the home), they would be expected to have more frequent episodes of unemployment. In the 1970s and 1980s, beyond these demographic factors, there may have been additional forces raising the unemployment rate that would have existed even if the economy were running at its potential level. These forces are considered in Chapter 17.

For our purpose here, which is to provide a broad description of the cyclical movements in output over recent decades, the precise benchmark unemployment rate used to construct a potential output series is not important. For later policy questions concerning how low we might expect the unemployment rate to be reduced, the question of the proper benchmark unemployment rate is important.

Figure 2.2 shows annual values of actual real output and two measures of potential output. The first is shown by the line marked "Trend GNP." This measure does not use any benchmark unemployment rate to represent high employment, but simply assumes that potential output grew throughout the period at the trend (or average) rate of growth of real output. The second measure, the dashed line marked "High-employment GNP," uses 6 percent as the high-employment benchmark unemployment rate. Shaded areas in the graph represent recessions, when the level of economic activity was declining.

Looking at the figure, one can trace the cyclical course of output. In the late 1960s the economy was overheated, with actual output above potential output. This was the period of high Vietnam war expenditures imposed on an economy already operating at high resource utilization rates. The result was employment pushed above a sustainable rate for the long run.[10] Another result was an accelerating inflation rate as demand exceeded capacity.

In the wake of restrictive policies, the boom conditions of the late 1960s gave way to a mild recession in 1970, followed by a strong expansion that again pushed actual output above potential output by 1973. Then came the

---

[10]During this period, the unemployment rate was not only below the 6 percent benchmark used for the figure, but also below the 4 percent benchmark used at that time.

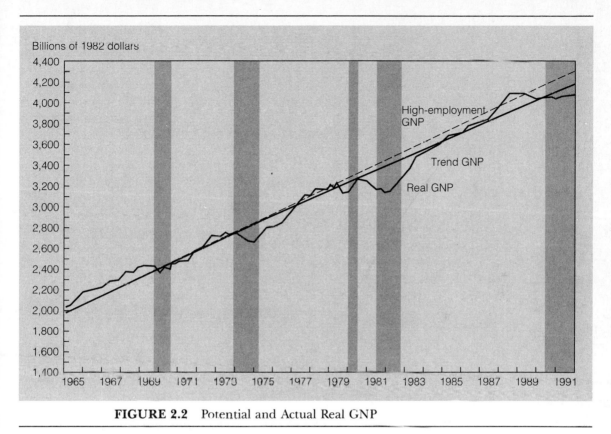

FIGURE 2.2   Potential and Actual Real GNP

severe recession of 1974–75 when actual output fell more than 5 percent below potential output.

After a recovery in the late 1970s, output again fell below potential output in the recession of 1980. Before a sustained recovery occurred, another recession began in 1981. This was the most severe recession of the post–World War II period, with output falling 9 percent below potential output. A long economic expansion then began in late 1982. By 1988 the unemployment rate was below the 6 percent benchmark. Output, however, again fell below potential output during the most recent recession, which began in mid–1990.

The fluctuations in actual output around the level of potential output, as illustrated in Figure 2.2, together with the associated variations in other important macroeconomic aggregates, form the subject matter for much of the analysis to come.

2.9 • CONCLUSION

We have now discussed the real-world counterparts to the central variables that appear in the models of the next section—with one exception. The exception is money. The quantity of money is a key variable in all the models we consider later. Control of the quantity of money through **monetary policy** is one important type of stabilization policy. The question of the definition of money turns out to be somewhat more complicated than it seems at first glance and is best put off until later, when questions of money supply and demand are examined in detail. For now it is adequate to take the term *money* in our models to refer to the stock of currency plus "checkable" deposits (deposits on which checks may be written).

We return to questions of measurement at several later points. In addition to further discussion of the empirical definition of money (Chapter 15), we also need to consider foreign exchange rates and measures of our international transactions (Chapter 20) and go into more detail concerning the federal government budget (Chapter 18). Some other variables (e.g., the wage rate and the interest rate) are defined as they are encountered in our analysis. At this point it is time to turn to the task of explaining rather than just measuring the behavior of macroeconomic variables.

Review Questions and Problems

1. Define the term *gross domestic product* (GDP). Explain carefully which transactions in the economy are included in GDP.

2. What is the difference between gross national product and gross domestic product?

3. Define the term *national income* (NI). Why is national income not equal to gross national product?

4. Define the terms *personal income* and personal *disposable income*. Conceptually, how do these income measures differ from national income? Of what usefulness are these measures?

5. Three price indices were considered in this chapter: the GDP deflator, the consumer price index, and the producer price index. Explain the differences among these different measures of *the* price level.

6. Using the data in Table 2.6, compute the percentage change in the price level between 1959 and 1960; between 1959 and 1970, between 1959 and 1991.

7. Explain the concept of *potential output*. How would you interpret a situation such as that in the late 1960s when the economy was above *potential output*?

Selected Readings

Abraham, W. I., *National Income and Economic Accounting.* Englewood Cliffs, N.J.: Prentice-Hall, 1969.

Nordhaus, William, and Tobin, James, "Is Growth Obsolete?" in *Economic Growth,* 50th Anniversary Colloquium, Vol. 5. New York: National Bureau of Economic Research–Columbia University Press, 1972.

Okun, Arthur, "Potential GDP, Its Measurement and Significance," *1962 Proceedings of the Business and Economic Statistics Sections of the American Statistical Association,* pp. 98–104. Also reprinted as an appendix to Arthur Okun, *The Political Economy of Prosperity.* Washington, D.C.: Brookings Institution, 1970.

Ruggles, Nancy, and Ruggles, Richard, *The Design of National Income Accounts.* New York: National Bureau of Economic Research–Columbia University Press, 1970.

Sommers, Albert T. *The U.S. Economy Demystified.* Lexington, Mass.: Lexington Books, 1985.

II Macroeconomic Models

CHAPTER OUTLINE

The chapters of this part trace the development of several competing macroeconomic theories. This approach, rather than the discussion of a unified macroeconomic theory, is made necessary by the existence of different explanations of the economic phenomena described in Chapter 1 and correspondingly different positions on central macroeconomic policy questions. We begin with an analysis of the *classical* macroeconomic model (Chapters 3 and 4). Succeeding chapters discuss the *Keynesian* model (Chapters 5 to 8), the *monetarist* model (Chapters 9 and 10), and the *new classical* model (Chapter 11). We then discuss two recent directions in macroeconomic research: *real business cycle theory* and the *new Keynesian economics* (Chapter 12). The final chapter in this part summarizes the positions of these different "schools" of macroeconomic theory.

3 Classical Macroeconomics (I): Equilibrium Output and Employment

[handwritten: Renc]

[handwritten: Who was the economists were the economists responsible for this mess?]

3.1 • THE STARTING POINT

The term *macroeconomics* originated in the 1930s. That decade witnessed substantial progress in the study of aggregative economic questions. The forces that determine income, employment, and prices had been receiving greater attention since the turn of the century, after a long period in which microeconomic questions dominated the field of economics. The world depression that began in 1929 added urgency to the study of macroeconomic questions. The products of this research were a number of theories of the "business cycle" and accompanying sets of policy prescriptions for stabilizing economic activity. One such theory and set of policy conclusions swept the field and was to become a new orthodoxy in macroeconomic thought. The book containing this theory was *The General Theory of Employment, Interest and Money* by John Maynard Keynes, and the process of change in economic thinking that resulted from this work has been called the Keynesian Revolution. But revolution against what? What was the old orthodoxy? Keynes termed it "classical economics," and it is this body of macroeconomic thought that we study in this chapter and the next.

The ideas that formed the Keynesian revolution, as well as the evolution of these ideas in the post-Keynesian period, are central to our analysis. A prerequisite for this analysis is a knowledge of the classical system that Keynes attacked. Classical theory also plays a more positive role in the later development of macroeconomics. Although many early Keynesian writers viewed the classical theory as ready for the scrap heap of outmoded ideas, with time such overreaction subsided, and modern Keynesian economics contains many ideas that originated with the classical economists. The classical model also provides the starting point for the two main challenges that have been mounted against the Keynesian theory, those of the *monetarists* and of the *new classical economists.*

Keynes used the term *classical* to refer to virtually all economists who had written on macroeconomic questions prior to 1936. More conventional modern terminology distinguishes between two periods in the development of economic theory before 1930. The first, termed *classical,* is the period dominated by the work of Adam Smith (*Wealth of Nations,* 1776), David Ricardo (*Principles of Political Economy,* 1st ed., 1817), and John Stuart Mill (*Principles of Political Economy,* 1st ed., 1848). The second, termed the *neoclassical* period, had as its most prominent English representatives Alfred Marshall (*Principles of Economics,* 8th ed., 1920) and A. C. Pigou (*The Theory of Unemployment,* 1933). The theoretical advances distinguishing the classical and neoclassical periods related primarily to microeconomic theory. Keynes felt that the macroeconomic theory of the two periods was homogeneous enough to be dealt with as a whole. Our treatment here follows Keynes in that respect.

To the classical economists the normal or equilibrium level of income at any time was a point of *full employment,* or in terms of the variables described in Chapter 2, a point when actual output was equal to potential output. Equilibrium for a variable refers to a state in which all the forces acting on that variable are in balance and, consequently, there is no tendency for the given variable to move from that point. It was an important tenet of classical economists that only such full-employment points could be positions of even short-run equilibrium. Away from full employment the classical economists assumed that there were forces not in balance acting to bring output to the full-employment level. The classical equilibrium economics examined the factors that determined the level of full-employment output along with the associated levels of other important aggregates, such as employment, prices, wages, and interest rates.

3.2 · THE CLASSICAL REVOLUTION

Classical economics also emerged as a revolution against an earlier orthodoxy. The classical economists attacked a body of economic doctrines known as *mercantilism.* Mercantilist thought was associated with the rise of the nation-state in Europe during the sixteenth and seventeenth centuries. Two tenets of mercantilism that classical writers attacked were *bullionism,* a belief that the wealth and power of a nation were determined by its stock of precious metals, and the belief in the need for state action to direct the development of the capitalist system.

An adherence to bullionism led countries to attempt to secure an excess of exports over imports and, hence, to earn gold and silver through foreign trade. Methods used to secure this favorable balance of trade included export subsidies, import duties, and development of colonies to provide export markets. State action was assumed to be necessary to cause the developing capitalist system to act in line with the interests of the state. Foreign trade was carefully regulated and the export of bullion was prohibited in many places to serve the ends of bullionism. The use of state action was also advocated on a broader front to develop home industry, reduce consumption of imported goods, and develop both human and natural resources.

In contrast to the mercantilists, classical economists emphasized the importance of *real* factors in determining the *Wealth of Nations* and stressed the optimizing tendencies of the free market in the absence of state control. Classical analysis was primarily *real* analysis; the growth of an economy was the result of increased stocks of the factors of production and advances in techniques of production. Money played a role only in facilitating transactions as a *means of exchange*. Most *real* questions in economics could be answered without an analysis of the role of money. Classical economists mistrusted government and stressed the harmony of individual and national interest when the market was left unfettered by government regulations, except for those necessary to see that the market remained competitive. Both of these aspects of classical economics—the stress on real factors and the belief in the efficacy of the free-market mechanism—developed in the course of controversies over long-run questions, concerns about the determinants of long-run economic development. These classical positions on long-run issues were, however, important in shaping classical economists' views on short-run questions.

The attack on bullionism led classical economists to stress that money had no intrinsic value. Money was held only for the sake of the goods it could purchase. It was on the role of money as a means of exchange that classical economists focused. Another role money had played in the mercantilist view was as a spur to economic activity. In the short run, many mercantilists argued, an increase in the quantity of money would lead to an increase in demand for commodities and would stimulate production and employment. For classical economists to ascribe this role to money in determining real variables, even in the short run, was dangerous in light of their deemphasis of the importance of money.

The classical attack on the mercantilist view of the need for state action to regulate the capitalist system also had implications for short-run macroeconomic analysis. One role for state action in the mercantilist view was to ensure that markets existed for all goods produced. Consumption, both domestic and foreign, must be encouraged to the extent that production advanced. The classical response is stated by John Stuart Mill:

> In opposition to these palpable absurdities it was triumphantly established by political economists that consumption never needs encouragement.[1]

As in other areas, classical economists felt that the free-market mechanism would work to provide markets for any goods that were produced: "The legislator, therefore, need not give himself any concern about consumption."[2] The classical doctrine was that, in the aggregate, production of a given quantity of output will generate sufficient demand for that output; there could never be a "want of buyers for all commodities."[3] Consequently, classical economists gave little explicit attention to factors that determine the overall demand for commodities, which in Chapter 1 we termed *aggregate demand,* or to policies to regulate aggregate demand.

Two general features of the classical analysis, then, arose as part of their attack on mercantilism:

1. Classical economics stressed the role of real as opposed to monetary factors in determining real variables such as output and employment. Money had a role in the economy only as a means of exchange.
2. Classical economics stressed the self-adjusting tendencies of the economy if left free of government intervention. Government policies to ensure an adequate demand for output were among those state actions considered by the classical economists to be unnecessary and generally harmful.

We turn now to the model constructed by classical economists to support these positions.

3.3 · PRODUCTION

A central relationship in the classical model is the **aggregate production function.** The production function, which is based on the technology of individual firms, provides a relationship between the level of output and

---

[1] J. S. Mill, "On the Influence of Consumption on Production," in *Essays on Economics and Society,* Vol. IV of *Collected Works* (Toronto: University of Toronto Press, 1967), p. 263.

[2] Ibid., p. 263.

[3] Ibid., p. 276.

the level of factor inputs. For each level of inputs, the production function shows the resulting level of output and can be written as

$$y = F(\overline{K}, N) \tag{3.1}$$

where y is real output, K the stock of capital (plant and equipment), and N the quantity of the homogeneous labor input.[4] For the short run the stock of capital is assumed to be fixed, as indicated by the bar over the symbol for capital. The state of technology and the population are also assumed to be constant over the period considered. For this short-run period output varies solely with variations in the labor input (N) drawn from the fixed population. In Figure 3.1a we plot the output that will be produced by the efficient utilization of each level of labor input. As drawn, the production function has several characteristics of interest. At low levels of labor input (below N'), the function is assumed to be a straight line. Since the slope of the line gives the increment in output that is forthcoming for a given increment in labor input, this straight-line (constant-slope) portion of the curve exhibits constant returns to increases in labor input. For very low levels of labor utilization it might be presumed that additional workers could be applied to a given amount of plant and equipment without a fall in the productivity of the last worker added. For the most part, however, we consider situations to the right of N', between N' and N'', where adding additional labor input will result in an increment to output, but where the size of the increments to output declines as more labor is employed. Past N'', increments to labor produce no increment to output.

In Figure 3.1b we plot the increment to output per increment to the labor input, termed the **marginal product of labor** (MPN). The marginal product of labor curve is the slope of the production function ($\Delta y / \Delta N$) in Figure 3.1a.[5] As N increases below N', the line is flat, representing the constant marginal product of labor. Past N', the marginal product of labor is positive but declining and the curve hits the horizontal axis at N''.

The short-run production function plotted in Figure 3.1a is a technological relationship that determines the level of output given the level of labor input (employment). Classical economists assumed that the quantity of labor employed would be determined by the forces of demand and supply in the labor market.

---

[4] Functional notation such as that used in (3.1) will be used at numerous points in our analysis. In each case such equations have the interpretation that the function involved (in this case F) is a relationship that determines a unique value of the left-hand variable (in this case y) for each combination of the levels of the *arguments* of the function (in this case K and N).

[5] The differencing symbol Δ (delta) indicates the change in the variable it precedes (e.g., Δy is the change in y.)

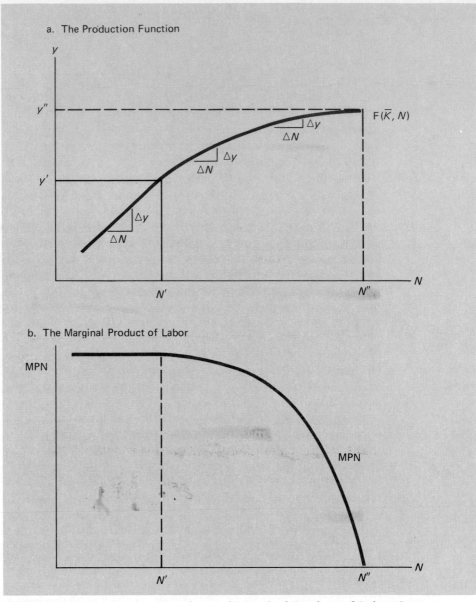

a. The Production Function

b. The Marginal Product of Labor

FIGURE 3.1 Production Function and Marginal Product of Labor Curves
Part *a* is the graph of the production function showing the level of output (*y*) for each level of employment (*N*). As employment rises, output rises, but at a diminishing rate. The slope of the production function ($\Delta y/\Delta N$) is positive, but diminishes as we move along the curve. The marginal product of labor (MPN), plotted in Part *b*, is the increment to output as a result of the addition of one further unit of labor input. The marginal product of labor is measured by the slope of the production function ($\Delta y/\Delta N$) and is a downward-sloping curve when plotted against the level of employment.

3.4 • EMPLOYMENT

The hallmark of classical labor market analysis is the assumption that the market works well. Firms and individual workers optimize. They all have perfect information about relevant prices. There are no barriers to the adjustment of money wages; the market *clears*.

Labor Demand

On the demand side of the market, purchasers of labor services are firms that produce commodities. To see how the aggregate demand for labor is determined, we begin by considering the demand for labor on the part of an individual firm, denoted the ith firm. In the classical model firms are considered to be perfect competitors who choose their output level so as to maximize profits. In the short run, output is varied solely by changing the labor input, so that choice of the level of output and quantity of the labor input are essentially one decision. The perfectly competitive firm will increase output until the marginal cost of producing a unit of output is equal to the marginal revenue received from its sale. For the perfectly competitive firm, marginal revenue is equal to product price.[6] Since labor is the only variable factor of production, the marginal cost of each additional unit of output is the marginal labor cost. Marginal labor cost equals the money wage divided by the number of units of output produced by the additional unit of the labor input. We defined the units of output produced by the incremental unit of labor employed as the marginal product of labor (MPN). Thus marginal cost for the ith firm (MC_i) is equal to the money wage (W) divided by the marginal product of labor for that firm (MPN_i).[7]

$$MC_i = \frac{W}{MPN_i} \qquad (3.2)$$

---

[6]A perfectly competitive firm faces a horizontal product demand curve. By assumption, the firm is so small a portion of the market that its own increase in output can be sold without depressing product price. The analysis could be reformulated for the firm facing a downward-sloping demand curve without substantially changing the conclusions that we reach in this chapter. The question of whether or not firms are perfect competitors does, however, have important implications at future points in our analysis.

[7]The i subscript does not appear on the price or wage variables since these are uniform across firms. The marginal product of labor for each firm (MPN_i) is derived from the production function for each firm, assumed to be identical over all firms; that is,

$$y_i = F\left(\overline{K}_i; N_i\right)$$

for each firm.

If, for example, the wage is \$6 per hour and the additional unit of labor input will produce 3 units of output, the marginal cost of a unit of output would be \$2.

The condition for short-run profit maximization is

$$P = \text{MC}_i = \frac{W}{\text{MPN}_i} \qquad \qquad (3.3)$$

$$MC = \frac{6}{3} = 2$$

Alternatively, (3.3) can be written as

$$\frac{W}{P} = \text{MPN}_i \qquad \qquad (3.4)$$

$\$/hr$

$\$/unit$

$unit/hr$

In this form the condition for profit maximization is that the real (W/P) paid by the firm must equal the marginal product of labor (which is measured in units of the commodity, i.e., in real terms).

From this condition for profit maximization we can see that, plotted against the real wage, the demand for labor schedule for the firm is the marginal product of labor schedule, as illustrated in Figure 3.2. At a real wage such as 3.0 (e.g., a money wage of \$6 and a product price of \$2), the firm will hire 500 units of labor. At a quantity of labor below 500, say 400, the marginal product of labor (4.0 at 400) exceeds the real wage (3.0). The payment to the worker in real terms is less than the real product he produces. Profits would be increased by hiring additional units of labor. Alternatively, at quantities of labor input above 500, if the real wage is 3.0, the real wage will be above the marginal product of labor. The payment to labor will exceed the real product of the marginal worker, and marginal cost will exceed product price. The firm will reduce labor input to increase profit.

Thus, the profit-maximizing quantity of labor demanded by a firm at each level of the real wage is given by the quantity of labor input that equates the real wage and marginal product of labor. The marginal product curve is the firm's demand curve for labor. This implies that labor demand depends inversely on the level of the real wage. The higher the real wage, for example, the lower the level of labor input that will equate the real wage to the marginal product of labor. In Figure 3.2, if the wage were 4.0 instead of 3.0, labor demand would be 400 instead of 500. The aggregate demand curve for labor is the horizontal summation of the individual firms' demand curves. For each real wage this curve will give the sum of the quantities of labor input demanded by the firms in the economy. We write this aggregate labor demand function (N^d) as

$$N^d = f\left(\frac{W}{P}\right) \qquad \qquad (3.5)$$

where in the aggregate, as with individual firms, an increase in the real wage lowers labor demand.

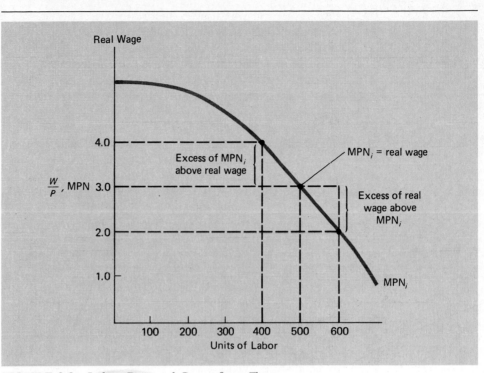

Real Wage

4.0

Excess of MPN$_i$ above real wage

MPN$_i$ = real wage

$\frac{W}{P}$, MPN 3.0

Excess of real wage above MPN$_i$

2.0

1.0

MPN$_i$

100 200 300 400 500 600

Units of Labor

FIGURE 3.2 Labor Demand Curve for a Firm

The condition for profit maximization is met at the point where the real wage (W/P) is equated with the marginal product of labor (MPN). If the real wage is 3.0, then the firm will maximize profits by hiring 500 units of the labor input. At a lower labor input, 400 units, the marginal product of labor (4.0) exceeds the real wage of 3.0 and the firm can increase profits by hiring additional labor. At a higher labor input, 600 units, the marginal product of labor (2.0) falls short of the real wage of 3.0 and the firm will increase profits by reducing the number of labor units employed.

Labor Supply

The last relationship necessary for determining employment, and hence output, in the classical system is the labor supply curve. Labor services are supplied by individual workers in the economy. As was the case with labor demand, the labor supply curve can best be explained by first considering an individual's labor supply decision. Classical economists assumed that the individual attempts to maximize *utility* (or satisfaction). The level of utility depended positively on both real income, which gave the individual a command over goods and services, and leisure. There is, however, a trade-off between the two goals since income is increased by work that reduces available leisure time.

Consider, for example, how individual j allocates one 24-hour period between leisure hours and hours worked: N_j^s, his supply of labor. Figure 3.3a illustrates the choice facing the individual. On the horizontal axis we measure hours of work per day. Starting from the zero point at the right, work hours are measured from right to left to a maximum of 24. Leisure is equal to 24 minus hours worked. Real income is measured on the vertical axis and is equal to the real wage W/P multiplied by the number of hours the individual works (N_j^s). The curved lines in the graph (labeled U_1, U_2, U_3) are *indifference curves*. Points along one of these lines are combinations of income and leisure that give equal satisfaction to the individual; hence he is indifferent as to which point along a given curve he achieves. The slope of the indifference curve gives the rate at which the individual is willing to trade off leisure for income, that is, the increase in income he would have to receive to be just as well off after giving up a unit of leisure, increasing N_j^s by a unit. Notice that, as drawn, the curves become steeper as we go from right to left. For the eighteenth hour of work one would require greater compensation to maintain a given utility level than for the fifth hour of work. The hour of leisure the individual gives up (sleep, no doubt) in the former case would have more subjective value than the hour given up in the latter case. Curves higher and to the right represent progressively greater levels of utility. All points along U_2, for example, yield greater satisfaction than any point on U_1. The individual attempts to achieve the highest possible indifference curve.

The straight-line rays originating at the zero point on the horizontal axis give the budget lines facing the individual. Starting from the zero point (no work, all leisure) the individual can trade off leisure for income at a rate equal to the hourly real wage W/P; the slope of the budget line is the real wage. The higher the real wage, the steeper the budget line, reflecting the fact that at a higher real wage if we increase hours of work by 1 unit (move 1 unit to the left along the horizontal axis) we will receive a larger increment to income (move farther up the vertical axis along the budget line) than we would at the lower real wage. Three budget lines, corresponding to real wage rates of 2.0, 3.0, and 4.0, are shown in Figure 3.3a.

To maximize utility for any given real wage rate, the individual will choose the point where the budget line corresponding to that wage rate is tangent to one of his indifference curves. This point has the property that the rate at which he is able to trade off leisure for income (the slope of the budget line) is just equal to the rate at which he is willing to make that trade-off (the slope of his indifference curve). In Figure 3.3a, at a real wage of 2.0 the worker will choose point A, where he supplies 6 hours of labor services, has 18 hours of leisure, and has a real income of 12. At real wage rates of 3.0 and 4.0, respectively, points B and C are chosen. As the figure is constructed, more labor services are supplied at the higher real wage rates.

In Figure 3.3b, we construct the labor supply curve for the jth individual. This supply curve consists of points such as A, B, and C from Figure 3.3a,

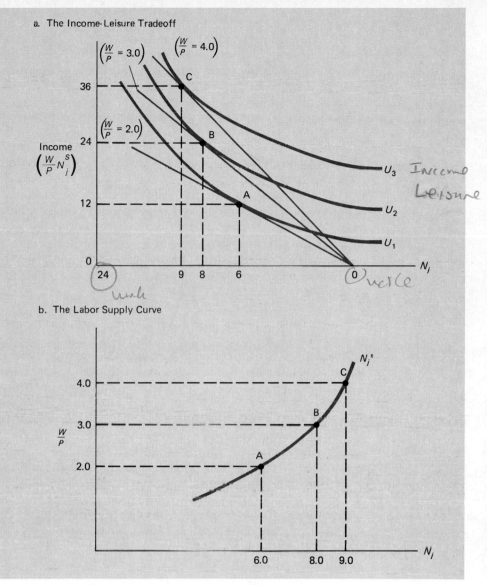

a. The Income-Leisure Tradeoff

b. The Labor Supply Curve

FIGURE 3.3 Individual Labor Supply Decision

Part a depicts the individual's labor–leisure choice. The individual will supply labor (N_j^s) up to the point where the rate at which labor may be traded for income in the marketplace, which is given by the real wage (W/P), is equated with the rate at which the individual is willing to trade labor (give up leisure) in return for income, which is measured by the slope of the individual's indifference curves (U_1, U_2, U_3). At a real wage of 2.0, 6 hours of labor will be supplied (point A); at a real wage of 3.0, 8 hours of labor will be supplied (point B); at a real wage of 4.0, 9 hours of labor will be supplied (point C). In Part b these amounts of labor supplied for given values of the real wage are plotted to give the individual's labor supply curve (N_j^s).

giving the amount of labor the individual will supply at each real wage rate. The aggregate labor supply curve is obtained by horizontally summing all the individual labor supply curves and gives the total labor supplied at each level of the real wage. This aggregate labor supply curve can be written as

$$N^s = g\left(\frac{W}{P}\right) \tag{3.6}$$

Two features of the classical labor supply theory require further comment. First, note that the wage variable is the *real wage*. The worker receives utility ultimately from consumption, and in making the labor–leisure decision his concern is with the command over goods and services he receives for a unit of his labor. If, for example, his money wage rose from $2 per hour to $4 per hour while all product prices doubled, he would supply the same amount of labor after the change as before.

Second, by the construction of Figure 3.3, the labor supply curve is positively sloped; more labor is assumed to be supplied at higher real wage rates. This reflects the fact that a higher real wage rate means a higher price for leisure in terms of forgone income. At this higher price we assume that the worker will choose less leisure. This effect is analogous to the "substitution effect" in the theory of consumer demand. There is another effect, the equivalent of the "income effect" in consumer demand theory. As the real wage increases, the worker is able to achieve a higher level of real income. At higher levels of real income, leisure may become more desirable relative to further increments in income. With successive increases in the real wage, a point may be reached when the worker chooses to supply less labor as the real wage increases and consumes more leisure. At this point the income effect outweighs the substitution effect; the labor supply curve assumes a negative slope and bends back toward the vertical axis. Almost certainly, at extremely high wage rates we would reach a backward-bending portion of the labor supply curve, and perhaps wage rates need not be so "extremely" high. Although the empirical evidence on this question is inconclusive, we will assume that for wage rates that have been observed in industrialized nations, the aggregate labor supply curve does have a positive slope; the substitution effect outweighs the income effect.

3.5 • EQUILIBRIUM OUTPUT AND EMPLOYMENT

To this point the following relationships have been derived:

$$y = F(\overline{K}, N) \quad \text{(aggregate production function)} \tag{3.1}$$

$$N^d = f\left(\frac{W}{P}\right) \quad \text{(labor demand schedule)} \tag{3.5}$$

$$N^s = g\left(\frac{W}{P}\right) \quad \text{(labor supply schedule)} \tag{3.6}$$

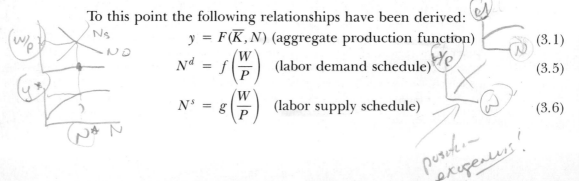

These relationships, together with the equilibrium condition for the labor market,

$$N^s = N^d \tag{3.7}$$

determine output, employment, and the real wage in the classical system. In terminology we use frequently, output, employment, and the real wage are designated as the *endogenous* variables in the classical model to this point, where endogenous variable means one that is determined within or by the model.

Equilibrium within the classical model is illustrated in Figure 3.4. Part *a* of the graph shows the determination of the equilibrium levels of employment (N_0) and the real wage ($W/P)_0$ at the point of intersection between the aggregate labor demand and labor supply curves. This equilibrium level of labor input (N_0) results in an equilibrium level of output (y_0) given by the production function, as shown in Figure 3.4*b*.

The Determinants of Output and Employment

We now consider which factors in the economy are the ultimate determinants of output and employment in the classical theory. What are the *exogenous* factors that, when changed, in turn cause changes in output and employment, where exogenous factors or variables are those determined outside the model? In the classical model the factors that determine output and employment are the factors that determine the positions of the labor supply and demand curves and the position of the aggregate production function.

The production function is shifted by technical change that alters the amount of output forthcoming for given input levels. As graphed in Figure 3.4*b*, the production function also shifts as the capital stock changes over time. The labor demand curve is the marginal product of labor curve, the slope of the production function. Consequently, the position of the labor demand curve will shift if the productivity of labor changes due to technical change or capital formation. From the derivation of the labor supply curve, one can see that this relationship would change as the size of the labor force changes. Population growth would, for example, shift the labor supply curve out to the right. The labor supply curve would also shift with changes in individuals' preference functions expressing their labor–leisure trade-offs (i.e., U_1, U_2, U_3 in Figure 3.3*a*).

A common feature of the factors determining output in the classical model is that they are all variables that affect the supply side of the market for output—the amount that firms choose to produce. *In the classical model, the levels of output and employment are determined solely by such supply factors.*

Since the supply-determined nature of output and employment is a crucial feature of the classical system, it is worthwhile to demonstrate this property of the model more formally. To do so, it is necessary to further consider the properties of the labor supply and demand functions just discussed. Figure

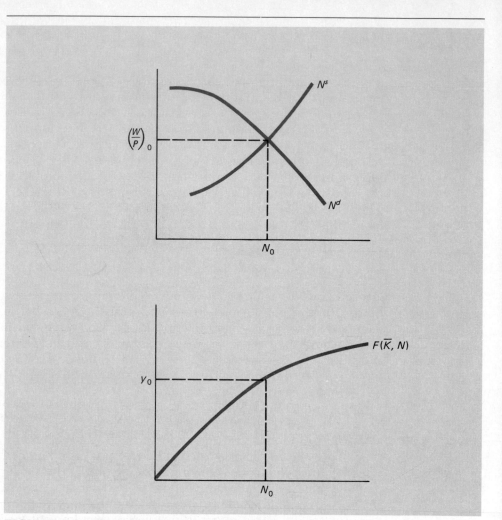

FIGURE 3.4 Classical Output and Employment Theory
Part *a* depicts the determination of labor market equilibrium at the level of the real
wage $(W/P)_0$ which just equates labor supply and demand. The resulting equilibrium
level of employment is N_0. Once the equilibrium level of employment is determined,
we find the equilibrium level of output, y_0, along the production function curve in
Part *b*.

3.5*a* reproduces the aggregate supply and demand curves for labor. Figure 3.5*b* plots labor supply and labor demand as functions of the money
wage (W). We first consider the form of each of the latter relationships.
For labor supply, we can draw a positively sloped curve such as $N^s(P_1)$,
which gives the amount of labor supplied for each value of the money wage,
given that the price level is P_1. The curve is upward sloping because at the given

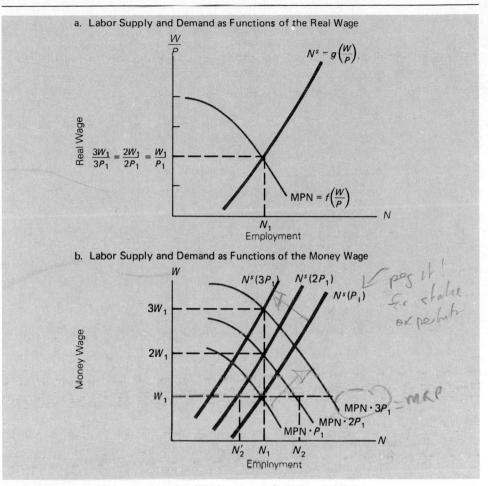

FIGURE 3.5   Labor Market Equilibrium and the Money Wage

Part *a* shows the determination of equilibrium employment (at N_1) where labor supply equals labor demand. In Part *b* labor supply and demand are plotted as functions of the money wage. Increases in the price level (from P_1 to $2P_1$, then to $3P_1$) shift the labor supply and demand schedules upward proportionately. The money wage rises proportionately with the price level (from W_1 to $2W_1$, then to $3W_1$). The real wage and level of employment are unchanged.

price level a higher money wage means a higher real wage. Since workers are interested in the real wage, each price level will have a different curve. For a given money wage each price level will mean a different real wage and, hence, a different amount of labor supplied. At a price level of $2P_1$, or twice that of P_1, the labor supply curve in Figure 3.5*b* shifts to $N^s(2P_1)$.

It will be noticed that less labor is supplied for any money wage because at the higher price level a given money wage corresponds to a lower real wage. A rise in the price level shifts the labor supply curve (plotted against the money wage) upward to the left. That the individual worker is interested *only* in the real wage can be seen from the fact that the same level of labor (N_1) is supplied at a money wage of W_1 and a price level of P_1 (real wage W_1/P_1), as at money wage and price combinations of $2W_1, 2P_1$ or $3W_1, 3P_1$ (real wage $= W_1/P_1$ at both points). *Equiproportional increases (or decreases) in both money wages and the price level leave the quantity of labor supplied unchanged.*

Now consider the labor demand curve plotted against the money wage, where in Figure 3.5 we use the fact that the labor demand $[f(W/P)]$ and marginal product of labor (MPN) schedules are equivalent. Recall that the condition met at all points along the labor demand curve is

$$\frac{W}{P} = \text{MPN} \tag{3.8}$$

If we want to know the quantity of labor that will be demanded at any money wage, as was the case for the quantity supplied, the answer depends on the price level. Given the money wage, the firm will choose the level of employment at which

$$W = \text{MPN} \cdot P \tag{3.9}$$

At successively higher price levels ($P_1, 2P_1, 3P_1$) the labor demand curve plotted against the money wage shifts to the right (from $\text{MPN} \cdot P_1$ to $\text{MPN} \cdot 2P_1$ to $\text{MPN} \cdot 3P_1$). For a given money wage, more labor is demanded at higher price levels since that money wage corresponds to a lower real wage rate.[8] *The demand for labor depends only on the real wage.* Equiproportional increases in the money wage and the price level from (W_1, P_1) to $(2W_1, 2P_1)$ and $(3W_1, 3P_1)$ leave labor demand unchanged at level N_1. They leave the real wage unchanged at W_1/P_1, which corresponds to the demand N_1 in Figure 3.5a.

The information in Figure 3.5 is useful in constructing the classical **aggregate supply function**—a relationship that makes clear the supply-determined nature of output in the classical model. The aggregate supply curve is the macroeconomic analog to the microeconomic concept of the firm's supply curve. For the firm, the supply curve gives the output forthcoming at each level of the product price. For the perfectly competitive firm, profits are maximized, as we have seen, where marginal cost (W/MPN_i for the ith firm) equals product price (P), or equivalently where

---

[8]Condition (3.9) has a simple economic interpretation. For profit maximization, the money wage paid to the incremental worker (W) must just equal his contribution to the firm's revenue. The worker's contribution to money revenues equals his marginal product multiplied by product price (MPN · P), which is termed his marginal revenue product.

$$\text{MPN}_i = \frac{W}{P} \tag{3.10}$$

the marginal product equals the real wage. The individual firm will take the money wage as fixed in deciding on the optimal output to supply and therefore the quantity of labor to hire. One firm would not expect its effort to hire more labor to cause the money wage to change because the firm is a small part of the overall market. Since the money wage is assumed to be fixed, the output supply curve for the firm is positively sloped as a function of price. Higher prices mean lower real wages, and consequently the firm demands more labor and produces more output. In constructing the aggregate supply curve for the economy, we cannot assume that the money wage remains fixed as output and labor input are varied. The money wage must adjust to maintain equilibrium in the labor market. With this important difference, the aggregate supply curve addresses the same question as its microeconomic analog: How will the level of output supplied vary when we change the product price?

In Figure 3.6 we construct the classical aggregate supply function. Consider the output supplied at the three successively higher price levels, P_1, $2P_1$, and $3P_1$ which were plotted in Figure 3.5. At price level P_1 and money wage W_1, employment was N_1 and we assume that the resulting output is y_1, as shown in Figure 3.6.[9] How will output supplied vary as we go to a price level of $2P_1$? At a price level of $2P_1$, *if* the money wage remained at W_1, we can see from Figure 3.5*b* that labor demand would increase to N_2. The higher price would mean a lower real wage, and firms would try to expand both employment and output. The money wage will not, however, remain at W_1. At a price level of $2P_1$ the labor supply curve in Figure 3.5*b* will have shifted to $N^s(2P_1)$, and at a money wage of W_1, labor supply will be only N_2' units. There will be an excess demand for labor equal to $(N_2 - N_2')$ units and the money wage will rise.

The process at work here is one of some firms responding to higher prices by attempting to expand employment and production. To expand employment, they raise money wages in an effort to bid workers away from other firms. Firms that lag in the process of raising money wages suffer higher quit rates and lose workers. This process of rising money wages will stop only when the money wage has increased sufficiently to reequilibrate supply and demand in the labor market. As can be seen in Figure 3.5*b*, this happens at a money wage of $2W_1$, where the money wage has increased proportionately with the price level. At this point the initial real wage is restored and employment is back at its original level. Consequently, output supplied at price level $2P_1$ is equal to y_1, the output level for price level P_1. At a still

---

[9]This output level is read from the production function curve given in Figure 3.4.

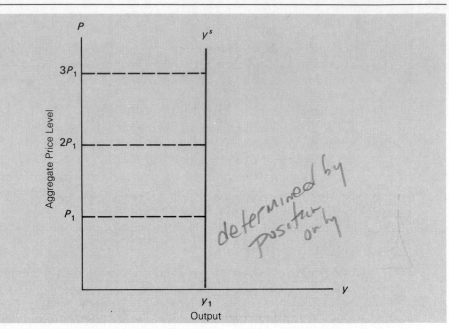

FIGURE 3.6   Classical Aggregate Supply Curve
The vertical classical aggregate supply curve reflects the fact that higher values of
the price level require proportionately higher levels of the money wage for labor
market equilibrium. The real wage, employment, and therefore level of output are
the same at P_1, $2P_1$, and $3P_1$. The vertical aggregate supply curve implies that output
is completely supply-determined in the classical system.

higher price level of $3P_1$, the money wage rises to $3W_1$, but again output is
unchanged at y_1. The aggregate supply curve is vertical. Higher prices provide a spur to output only if they are not matched by proportionately higher
money wages—only if they lower the real wage. Given the assumptions we
have made, however, equilibrium in the labor market requires that money
wages rise proportionately with prices to maintain the unique equilibrium
real wage in that market.

The vertical aggregate supply curve in the classical model illustrates the
supply-determined nature of output. An aggregate demand curve could be
constructed and added to Figure 3.6, but whatever the shape and position
of such a curve, it would clearly not affect equilibrium output. For output
to be in equilibrium, we must be on the supply curve; output must be at y_1.

Factors That Do Not Affect Output

It is also of interest to consider the factors that will *not* affect output and employment in the classical model. Because output and therefore employment

are supply-determined in the classical system, the level of aggregate demand will have *no* effect on output. As John Stuart Mill advised the legislator, "He need not give himself concern over the demand for output." Factors such as the quantity of money, level of government spending, and level of demand for investment goods by the business sector are all demand-side factors that have no role in determining output and employment. The case of government tax policy is more complex. Changes in taxes, to the degree that they affect the demand side, will not affect output or employment. But changes in tax rates also have incentive or supply-side effects that do matter for output and employment, as we see in Chapter 4.

Read Perspectives 3.1.

PERSPECTIVES

Real Business Cycles

It was argued in Section 3.5 that the determinants of output in the classical model are all supply-side variables. The traditional view has been that these supply-side variables change only slowly over time. But if output is determined by variables that change only slowly over time, how can the classical model explain sharp cyclical movements in output? Real GDP, for example, fell by 2.5 percent in 1982, rose by 6.8 percent in 1984, and fell by 30 percent between 1929 and 1933. It was the apparent failure of the classical equilibrium model to explain such cyclical movements in output that led to the Keynesian revolution.

In the 1980s, however, some economists have argued that the business cycle *is* caused by changes in *real* supply-side variables, much along classical lines. These economists do not accept the view that supply-side factors change only slowly over time. They believe that changes in technology, shocks that affect capital formation and labor productivity, as well as disturbances that influence the availability and prices of natural resources can explain the short-run fluctuations in output as well as its long-run growth path. The models

these economists have constructed are called *real business cycle* models.

In the model in this chapter, the real business cycle theorists see fluctuations in real output and employment as resulting from shifts in the production function and labor demand schedules in Figure 3.4. If preferences of workers change, the labor supply schedule could also shift.

Events such as the OPEC (Organization of Petroleum Exporting Countries) oil-price shock in 1974 led all economists to recognize that at times supply-side shocks can affect the cyclical behavior of output. Still, most economists are skeptical that real supply-side influences can fully explain the business cycle. We will consider real business cycle models in more detail in Chapter 12.[1]

---

[1] For a survey of real business cycle models, see Mark Rush, *Real Business Cycles,* Federal Reserve Bank of Kansas City *Review,* 72 (February 1987), pp. 20–32. For a critique of these models, see Bennett T. McCallum, "On 'Real' and 'Sticky Price' Theories of the Business Cycle," *Journal of Money, Credit and Banking,* 18 (November 1986), pp. 397–414.

3.6 · CONCLUSION

The striking feature of the classical model is the supply-determined nature of real output and employment. This property of the model follows from the vertical classical aggregate supply curve. The classical aggregate supply curve is vertical, as we have just seen, because of the assumptions that we have made about the labor market. It is worthwhile to recognize explicitly the nature of these assumptions. Generally, the foregoing portrayal of the labor and product markets can be characterized by the term *auction market*. Labor and output are assumed to be traded in markets that are continually in equilibrium and in which all participants make decisions based on announced real wage rates and product prices. A contemporary market that has characteristics similar to these would be a stock exchange. Two assumptions implicit in this classical representation of the labor market are as follows:

1. Perfectly flexible prices and wages.
2. Perfect information on the part of all market participants about market prices.

For whatever time period we assume that the equilibrium model determines employment and output, equilibrium must be achieved. If such a model is to explain employment and output in the short run, prices and wages must be perfectly flexible in that time period.

The auction market characterization of the labor market also requires that market participants have perfect information about market prices. Both suppliers and purchasers of labor must know the relevant trading prices. This requires that when selling and buying labor at a given money wage W, both workers and employers know the command over commodities that will result from such a wage (W/P).

These two assumptions, essential for the nature of the classical equilibrium theory of employment and output, are elements of the classical theory that Keynes attacked. Prior to considering the nature of that attack, we discuss the other major elements of the classical equilibrium theory and the classical economists' own analysis of the results of weakening these assumptions.

Review Questions and Problems

1. In what respects was the classical attack on mercantilism important in shaping the classical economists' views on macroeconomic questions?

2. Explain the concept of an aggregate production function. How would you expect the production function in Figure 3.1 to be affected by an increase in the average and marginal productivity of labor for a given output level, owing, for example, to increased education of the labor force? How would such a shift in the production function affect the levels of output and employment in the classical model?

3. Explain the classical theories of labor supply and demand. Why is the labor demand schedule downward-sloping when plotted against the real wage, whereas the labor supply schedule is upward-sloping on the same graph?

4. Suppose that the public's taste changes in such a way that leisure comes to be more desirable relative to commodities. How would you expect such a change to affect output, employment, and the real wage in the classical model?

5. We termed the classical view of the labor market an *auction market* characterization. What assumptions underlie this characterization?

6. In microeconomics we would expect the supply curve for the firm to slope upward to the right when drawn against price. The classical aggregate supply curve is based on this microeconomic theory of the firm but is vertical. Why?

7. What factors are the major determinants of output and employment in the classical system? What role does aggregate demand have in determining output and employment?

Selected Readings

Ackley, Gardner, *Macroeconomic Theory.* New York: Macmillan, 1961, Chaps. 5–8.

Eagly, Robert V., *The Structure of Classical Economic Theory.* London: Oxford University Press, 1974.

Makinen, Gail, *Money, the Price Level, and Interest Rates.* Englewood Cliffs, N.J.: Prentice-Hall, 1977, Chaps. 1–4.

Rush, Mark, *Real Business Cycles.* Federal Reserve Bank of Kansas City *Review,* 72 (February 1987), pp. 20–32.

Stockman, Alan C., "Real Business Cycle Theory: A Guide, an Evaluation and New Directions," Federal Reserve Bank of Cleveland *Economic Review,* 24 (1988, Quarter 4), pp. 24–47.

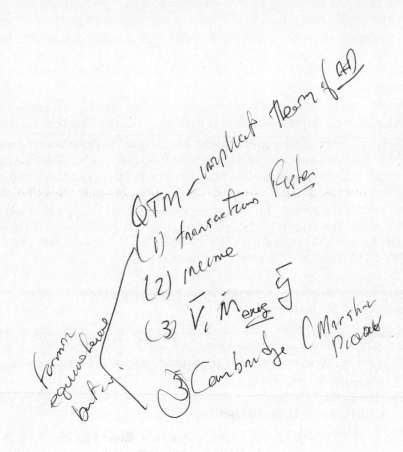

QTM — implicit theory of (A)

(1) transactions Peter

(2) income

(3) $\bar{V}, M_{exg} \xi$

③ Cambridge CMarshar Pigou

Formn
equivalence
but -

4 The Classical System (II): Money, Prices, and Interest

Money Feng

In this chapter we complete our discussion of the classical model. We analyze the classical theory of aggregate price level determination, which brings in the demand side of the model. Determination of the interest rate is also discussed. Next, we consider the policy conclusions that emerge from the classical equilibrium model—the classical views on monetary and fiscal policy. We then analyze the role of rigid money wages in the classical system, where it will be seen that money wage rigidity can explain the existence of unemployment in the classical system.

4.1 • THE QUANTITY THEORY OF MONEY

To understand the determination of the price level in the classical system, it is necessary to analyze the role of money. In the classical theory, the quantity of money determines the level of aggregate demand, which, in turn, determines the price level.

The Equation of Exchange

The starting point for the classical **quantity theory of money** is the equation of exchange, which is an identity relating the volume of transactions at current prices to the stock of money times the turnover rate of each dollar. This *turnover rate* for money, which measures the number of times each dollar is used in transactions during the period, is called the **velocity of money**. In the form used by the most prominent American quantity theorist, Irving Fisher, this identity is expressed as

$$MV_T \equiv P_T T \tag{4.1}$$

where M is the quantity of money, V_T the transaction velocity of money, P_T the price index for the items traded, and T the volume of such transactions.

63

This relationship is an identity because of the *ex post* definition of velocity. If, for example, over a given period the value of transactions in current dollars ($P_T T$) were \$3600 billion and the money stock (M) were \$300 billion, we could *define* the transactions velocity (or turnover rate) of money as the number of times the average dollar was used in transactions:

$$V_T \equiv \frac{P_T T}{M} = \frac{3600}{300} = 12 \tag{4.2}$$

The transaction variable (T) includes not only sales and purchases of newly produced goods but also exchanges of previously produced goods and financial assets. Another expression of the equation of exchange focuses only on income transactions:

$$MV \equiv Py \tag{4.3}$$

M is again the quantity of money, and V is now the *income velocity* of money, the number of times the average dollar is used in a transaction involving current output (income). The price index for currently produced output is given by P and the level of current output by y. Again this relationship would be an identity as long as income velocity was defined residually, as the level necessary to make the equality hold:

$$V \equiv \frac{Py}{M} \tag{4.4}$$

In the form (4.3), the variables in the equation of exchange are easier to measure and are more central to our concerns in analyzing the classical theory, so it is on this form of the equation of exchange that our interest is focused.

The equation of exchange is a "truism" and by itself does not explain the variables it contains. Fisher and other quantity theorists, however, postulated that all the *equilibrium* values of the elements in the equation of exchange, with the exception of the price level, were determined by other forces. Thus the equation of exchange served to determine the price level. As Fisher put it:

> We find that, under the conditions assumed, the price level varies (1) directly as the quantity of money in circulation (M), (2) directly as the velocity of its circulation (V), (3) inversely as the volume of trade done by it (T). The first of these three relations is worth emphasis. It constitutes the "quantity theory of money."[1]

The level of real output (or transactions) was a measure of real economic activity. As we have seen in Chapter 3, the classical economists regarded this variable as supply-determined. Most simply, money was assumed to be a metallic money such as gold, but considering paper money and bank deposits

---

[1] Irving Fisher, *The Purchasing Power of Money* (New York: Macmillan, 1922).

does not seriously complicate the analysis as long as we confine ourselves to equilibrium situations. The important assumption was that the quantity of money was exogenously controlled by the monetary policy authority.

In equilibrium, Fisher argued that the velocity of money was determined by the payments habits and payments technology of society. To give some examples, factors such as the average length of the pay period, the practice of using charge accounts or bank charge cards, and the prevalence of trade credit among businesses all affect the velocity of circulation. Shorter pay periods lead to smaller average money holdings over the pay period for any given income level, hence an increase in velocity. Frequent use of charge accounts by consumers or trade credit by businesses also increases velocity, the number of transactions per unit of money. According to Fisher and other quantity theorists, the equilibrium level of *velocity was determined by such institutional factors and could be regarded as fixed for the short run.*

If velocity is a predetermined constant and not simply defined residually to equate MV and Py, the equation of exchange is no longer merely a definition. With the volume of output fixed from the supply side, the equation of exchange now expresses a relationship of proportionality between the exogenously given money stock and the price level:

$$M\overline{V} = P\overline{y} \tag{4.5}$$

or

$$P - \frac{\overline{V}}{\overline{y}}M \tag{4.6}$$

The bar over the V and y indicates that these terms can be taken as given. Equation (4.6) indicates the dependence of the price level on the stock of money. A doubling of M doubles P, or a 10 percent increase in M leads to a 10 percent increase in P. This is the basic result of the quantity theory of money; *the quantity of money determines the price level.*

The Cambridge Approach to the Quantity Theory

The mathematics of the quantity theory may be clear from (4.5) and (4.6), but what about the economics? How do changes in the money stock affect the price level? This question can be answered more easily after considering another variant of the quantity theory, the Cambridge or cash balances approach.

The **Cambridge approach**, named after Cambridge University, the academic home of its originators Alfred Marshall and A. C. Pigou,[2] again

---

[2] John Maynard Keynes, who was also at Cambridge University, participated in the development of this approach to the quantity theory in the earlier "pre-Keynesian" phase of his career.

demonstrated a proportional relationship between the exogenous quantity of money and the aggregate price level. The foundation of this relationship was, however, less mechanistic than the transactions or Fisherian (after Irving Fisher) version of the quantity theory considered previously. Marshall began by focusing on the individual's decision on the optimal amount of money to hold. Some money will be held because of the convenience that money provides in transactions compared to other stores of value. Money also provides security by lessening the possibility of inconvenience or bankruptcy from failing to be able to meet unexpected obligations. But as Pigou notes, "currency held in the hand yields no income," so money will be held only insofar as its yield in terms of convenience and security outweighs the income lost from not investing in productive activity or satisfaction lost by not simply using the money to purchase goods for consumption. On these criteria, how much money will it be optimal to hold?

Marshall and the other Cambridge economists assumed that the demand for money would be a proportion of income and wealth. In most formulations the distinction between income and wealth has been neglected, and the Cambridge equation has been written as

$$M^d = kPy \tag{4.7}$$

Money demand (M^d) is assumed to be a proportion (k) of nominal income, the price level (P) times the level of real income (y). Since the primary desirable property of money is its usefulness for transactions, it follows that the demand for money depends on the level of transactions, which may be supposed to vary closely with the level of income. The proportion of income that would be optimal to hold in the form of money (k) is assumed to be relatively stable in the short run, depending, as in the Fisherian formulation, on the payments habits of the society.

In equilibrium, the exogenous stock of money must equal the quantity of money demanded.

$$M = M^d = kP\overline{y} \tag{4.8}$$

With k treated as fixed in the short run and real output $(\overline{y})$ determined, as before, by supply conditions, the Cambridge equation also reduces to a proportional relationship between the price level and money stock. As in the Fisherian approach, the quantity of money determines the price level.

The formal equivalence of the Cambridge equation and Fisher's version of the equation of exchange can be seen by rewriting (4.8) as

$$M\frac{1}{k} = P\overline{y} \tag{4.9}$$

One can see by comparing this with Fisher's equation (4.5) that the two formulations are equivalent with V equal to $1/k$. If, for example, individuals wish to hold an amount equal to one fifth of the nominal income in the form of money, the number of times the average dollar is used in income transactions will be five.

While the two formulations of the quantity theory are formally equivalent, the Cambridge version represents a step toward more modern monetary theories. The Cambridge focus was on the quantity theory as a theory of the demand for money. The proportional relationship between the quantity of money and the price level resulted from the fact that the proportion of nominal income people wished to hold in the form of money (k) was constant and the level of real output was fixed by supply conditions. Following up on Pigou's analysis of the alternatives to holding wealth in the form of money, Keynes attacked the quantity theory by providing a new theory of money demand. The monetarists, as we will see, also take the Cambridge form of the quantity theory as the starting point for their theory of money demand.

Additionally, the Cambridge focus on the quantity theory as a theory of money demand leads naturally to an answer to the question raised about the mechanism by which money affects the general price level. Let us suppose that we begin at equilibrium and then consider the effects of doubling the quantity of money. Initially, there will be an excess of money supply over the amount demanded. Individuals try to reduce their money holdings to the optimal proportion of their income by putting this excess into alternative uses of consumption and investment in production activities. They increase their demand for goods for both consumption and investment. This increased demand for commodities puts upward pressure on prices. In the language of the classical economists, there is too much money chasing too few goods. If output is unchanged, as it would be in the classical model, and k is constant, a new equilibrium will be reached only after the general price level is doubled. At that point nominal income and hence money demand will have doubled. This was the direct link in the classical system between money and prices; an excess supply of money led to increased demand for commodities and upward pressure on the general price level.

The Classical Aggregate Demand Curve

The quantity theory was thus the *implicit* theory of the aggregate demand for output within the classical system. We can use the quantity theory to construct a classical aggregate demand curve.

The construction of the aggregate demand curve is illustrated in Figure 4.1. For concreteness we assign some numerical values to the variables with which we are concerned. Let the value of k be one fourth so that velocity is 4. Initially, let the stock of money be 300 units. For either equation (4.8) or (4.5) to hold, $P \times y$ (nominal income) must be equal to 1200 (4 × 300). In Figure 4.1, with price on the vertical axis and real output on the horizontal axis, the line labeled $y^d (M = 300)$ connects all the points where $P \times y$ equals

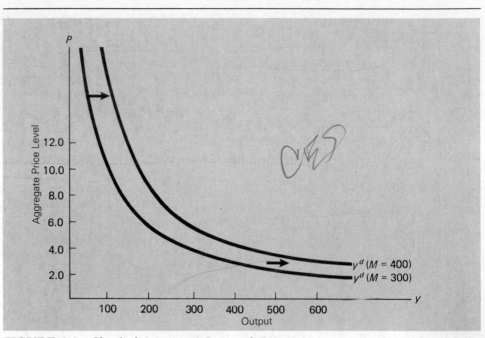

FIGURE 4.1 Classical Aggregate Demand Curve
The classical aggregate demand curve plots the combinations of the price level (P) and real output (y) consistent with the quantity theory equation $Py = M\overline{V}$, for a given money stock (M) and fixed velocity ($\overline{V}$). With $M = 300$ and velocity assumed to be 4, points such as $P = 12.0$ and $y = 100$ or $P = 6.0$ and $y = 200$ ($Py = 1200 = MV$ in each case) lie along the aggregate demand schedule. An increase in the money stock to $M = 400$ shifts the aggregate demand schedule to the right.

1200 units.[3] Points lying on the schedule, for example, are real income levels of 300 and 600 with accompanying price levels of 4.0 and 2.0, respectively.

Now consider a higher value of the money stock of, for example, 400 units. To satisfy either equation (4.8) or (4.5) with k still equal to one fourth ($V = 4$), $P \times y$ must now equal 1600. The schedule $y^d(M = 400)$ corresponding to a value of M equal to 400 lies above and to the right of the $y^d(M = 300)$ schedule and shows all $P \times y$ combinations of 1600. *An increase in the money stock shifts the aggregate demand curve to the right.*

[3]The schedule $y^d(M = 300)$ and the other such aggregate demand curves are constructed to have the property that the product of the value of the variable on the vertical axis times the value of the variable on the horizontal axis, ($P \times y$) in this case, is equal at all points along the schedule. Such a curve is a rectangular hyperbola.

For a given stock of money, we trace out a downward-sloping aggregate demand curve that can be put together with the vertical aggregate supply curve constructed in Figure 3.6 to illustrate the determination of price and output in the classical model. This is done in Figure 4.2.

Figure 4.2 reproduces the vertical aggregate supply curve (y_1^s) from Figure 3.6 and also contains several aggregate demand schedules [$y^d(M_1)$, $y^d(M_2)$, $y^d(M_3)$] drawn for successively higher values of the money stock (M_1, M_2, M_3). As just explained, increasing the money stock shifts the aggregate demand curve upward to the right. Because the supply curve is vertical, increases in demand do not affect output. Only the price level increases. Also note that for a given value of k (or V), *a change in the quantity of money is the only factor that shifts the aggregate demand curve.* Since the equilibrium value of k (or V) was considered to be stable in the short run, aggregate demand varied only with the stock of money.

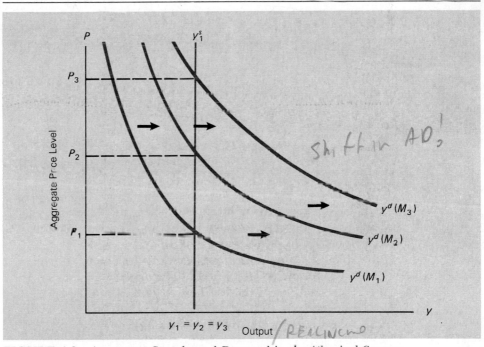

FIGURE 4.2 Aggregate Supply and Demand in the Classical System
Successive increases in the money stock, from M_1 to M_2 and then to M_3, shift the aggregate demand curve to the right, from $y^d(M_1)$ to $y^d(M_2)$ to $y^d(M_3)$. The price level rises from P_1 to P_2, then to P_3. Output, which is completely supply-determined, is unchanged ($y_1 = y_2 = y_3$).

The classical theory of aggregate demand has been termed an *implicit* theory, and it is worthwhile to consider its nature more carefully. The theory is not explicit in the sense of a theory that focuses on the components of aggregate demand and explains the factors that determine their level. Instead, in the classical theory a given value of MV [or $M(1/k)$] implies a level of $P \times y$ that *must* pertain for equilibrium in the money market—for money demand to equal the existing money supply. If money demand exceeds (falls short of) money supply, there will be a spillover to the commodity market as individuals try to reduce (increase) their expenditures on commodities. Points along the y^d schedule are points at which firms and households are in equilibrium with regard to their money holdings and, hence, are also at equilibrium rates of expenditures on commodities. It is in this sense that the classical theory

PERSPECTIVES

4.1

Money in Hyperinflations

The relationship between money and the price level that is postulated by the quantity theory can be seen clearly during hyperinflations. A hyperinflation is a period when the price level simply explodes. The inflation rate reaches astronomical levels. When this happens, the money supply *always* explodes as well. This can be seen from Table 4.1, which shows the *monthly* inflation rates and growth rates in the money supply from four hyperinflations. In each case the extremely high inflation rate (19,800 percent

per month for Hungary!) is matched by an extremely high rate of growth in the money supply (e.g., 12,200 percent for Hungary).

As we will see in later chapters, many economists do not accept the quantity theory of money as applied to economies in normal circumstances. The data for hyperinflation do, however, illustrate an implication of the quantity theory on which there is general agreement—sustained very high inflation rates require accommodating high money growth rates.

TABLE 4.1 Inflation and Money Growth in Four Hyperinflations

	Time Period	Inflation Rate (monthly, percent)	Money Growth Rate (monthly, percent)
Germany	August 1922 to November 1923	322	314
Greece	November 1943 to November 1944	365	220
Hungary	August 1945 to July 1946	19,800	12,200
Poland	January 1923 to January 1924	81.4	72.2

Source: Philip Cagan: "The Monetary Dynamics of Hyperinflation," in Milton Friedman, ed., *Studies in the Quantity Theory of Money* (Chicago: University of Chicago Press, 1956), p. 26.

of aggregate demand is implicit. Equilibrium levels of commodity demand are those price–output combinations that provide equilibrium in the money market and, implicitly, equilibrium levels of commodity demand.

Read Perspectives 4.1.

4.2 • THE CLASSICAL THEORY OF THE INTEREST RATE

In the classical system the components of aggregate commodity demand—consumption, investment, and government spending—play their explicit role in the determination of the equilibrium interest rate. It is, in fact, the interest rate that guarantees that exogenous changes in the particular components of demand do not affect the aggregate level of commodity demand.

The equilibrium interest rate in the classical theory was the rate at which the amount of funds that individuals desired to lend was just equal to the amount others desired to borrow. For simplicity, we assume that borrowing consists of selling a standard bond, a promise to pay certain amounts in the future. Lending consists of buying such bonds. Later we consider the properties of bonds in more detail, but for now the simplest assumption is that the standard bond is a "perpetuity," a bond that pays a perpetual stream of interest payments with no return of principal.[4] The rate of interest measures the return to holding such bonds and equivalently the cost of borrowing. The interest rate depends on the factors that determine the levels of bond supply (borrowing) and bond demand (lending).

In the classical system the suppliers of bonds were the firms, which financed all investment expenditures by the sale of bonds, and the government, which might sell bonds to finance spending in excess of tax revenues.[5] The level of the government deficit (excess of spending over revenues) as well as the portion of the deficit the government might choose to finance by selling bonds to the public are exogenous policy variables. In the classical model the level of business investment was a function of the expected profitability of investment projects and the rate of interest. The expected profitability of investment projects was assumed to vary with expectations of product demand over the life of these projects, and the state of these expectations was subject to exogenous shifts.

---

[4] Also for simplicity, no resale market for such bonds is allowed. This and the other simplifying assumptions may be dropped without substantive change in the analysis.

[5] The word *might* is used concerning the government's sale of bonds to finance a deficit because, as discussed in section 4.3, the alternative of financing the deficit by printing money is available to the government. Also note that *investment* refers to expenditure by firms on plant, durable equipment, and inventories—investment in the national income accounts sense. The term *investment* does *not* refer to the purchase of financial assets such as bonds.

For a given expected profitability, investment expenditures varied inversely with the interest rate. The classical economists explained this relationship as follows. A firm would have a number of possible investment projects offering various expected returns. It could rank these projects in order of the level of expected profits. The rate of interest represents the cost of borrowing funds to finance these investment projects. At a high interest rate fewer of these projects will be profitable net of interest costs. At successively lower rates of interest (lower borrowing costs) more and more projects will become profitable, net of interest costs, and investment will increase. We look at investment in more detail later but obtain the same general result. Investment depends inversely on the rate of interest. Thus, on the supply (borrowing) side of the bond market, government bond supply is exogenous, and the business supply of bonds equals the level of investment expenditure. Investment varies inversely with the interest rate and is also influenced by exogenous shifts in the expected profitability of investment projects.

On the demand (lending) side of the bond market are the individual savers who purchase the bonds.[6] In the classical model, saving was taken to be a positive function of the rate of interest. The act of saving is the act of foregoing current consumption to have a command over consumption goods in a future period, a trade-off of current consumption for future consumption. As the interest rate increases, the terms of the trade-off become more favorable. A dollar saved today will earn a higher interest return for the saver, a greater command over consumption goods in future periods. The classical economists assumed that individuals would take advantage of this more favorable trade-off of consumption in the future for consumption today; they would save more at higher rates of interest.

But saving need not go into bonds; money is also a potential store of wealth. Since money paid no interest, the classical economists assumed that bonds would always be preferred as a store of wealth. As discussed previously, some money would be held for the convenience and security it offered. Wealth accumulated through new saving, however, would be held in the form of bonds. Classical economists believed that people might shift their wealth into the form of money in times of severe general economic distress. At such times, with bank panics and bankruptcies being prevalent, people might worry about bond default and "hoard" money, but for normal times the classical assumption was that saving was a demand for bonds.

Determination of the interest rate in the classical system is illustrated in Figure 4.3. Saving (s) is plotted as an upward-sloping function of the rate of

---

[6]Households may lend to each other, but this is not formally considered in the simple classical system; saving can be considered net saving of households.

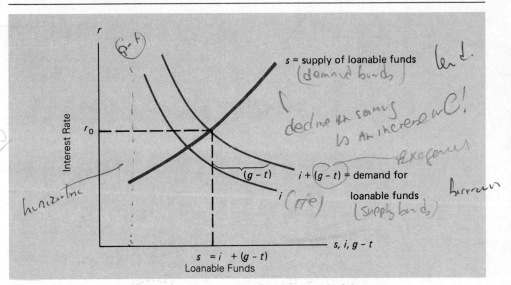

FIGURE 4.3 Interest Rate Determination in the Classical System
The equilibrium interest rate r_0 is the rate that equates the supply of loanable funds,
which consists of new saving (s), with the demand for loanable funds, which consists
of investment (i) plus the bond-financed government deficit $(g - t)$.

interest. Saving provides the demand for bonds, or as the classical economists
called it, the *supply of loanable funds*. Investment (i) is a negatively sloped
schedule plotted against the interest rate. Investment plus the exogenously
determined government deficit $(g - t)$, all of which we assume to be financed
by selling bonds, equals bond supply. In the classical terminology, this is the
demand for loanable funds. In the diagram, r_0 is the equilibrium interest rate,
the rate of interest that equates the demand and supply for bonds or loanable
funds.

The interest rate plays a stabilizing role in the classical system, as can be
seen by examining the effects of a change in the expected profitability of
investment. Recall that in the short run, investment depends on the interest rate and the expected future profitability of investment projects. Let us
suppose that as a result of an exogenous event (e.g., fear of a future war),
business managers in general revise downward their expectation about such
future profits from investment. This would have the effect of reducing
investment and, hence, reducing the demand for loanable funds *at each
interest rate*.

Figure 4.4 illustrates the effect of this autonomous decline in investment
demand. For simplicity, we assume that the government budget is balanced
$(g = t)$, so there is no government borrowing. Investment is the only source

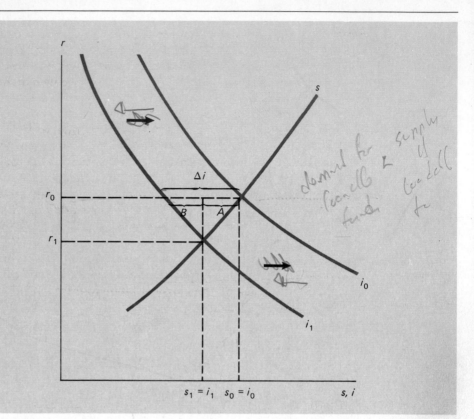

FIGURE 4.4   Autonomous Decline in Investment Demand
An autonomous decline in investment shifts the investment schedule to the left from
i_0 to i_1—the distance Δi. The equilibrium interest rate declines from r_0 to r_1. As the
interest rate falls, there is an interest-rate–induced increase in investment—distance
B. There is also an interest-rate–induced decline in saving, which is an equal increase
in consumption—distance A. The interest-rate–induced increases in consumption
and investment just balance the autonomous decline in investment ($A + B = \Delta i$).

of the demand for loanable funds. The fall in expected profitability of investment projects is shown as a shift in the investment schedule downward from
i_0 to i_1. At a given rate of interest, the amount of the decline in investment
is measured by Δi in Figure 4.4.

At the initial equilibrium interest rate of r_0, after the fall in investment
demand the supply of loanable funds exceeds demand, putting downward
pressure on the rate of interest. As the rate of interest declines, two adjustments occur. First, saving declines, which means that current consumption
increases. The amount of this decline in saving and the equal increase in

current consumption demand is given by the distance marked A in Figure 4.4.[7] Second, investment is somewhat revived by the decline in the interest rate. This interest-rate–induced increase in investment is measured by the distance B in Figure 4.4. Equilibrium is restored at interest rate r_1 with saving (the supply of loanable funds) again equal to investment (the demand for loanable funds). At the new equilibrium, the increase in consumption (fall in saving) plus the increase in investment caused by the drop in the interest rate, the distance $A+B$ in Figure 4.4, is just equal to the original autonomous decline in investment demand, the distance Δi in Figure 4.4. Because of the adjustment of the interest rate, the sum of private-sector demands $(c + i)$ is unaffected by the autonomous decline in investment demand.

This stabilizing role of the interest rate is important to the classical system. The interest-rate adjustment is the first line of defense for full employment. Shocks that affect consumption demand, investment demand, or government demand will *not* affect the demand for output as a whole. These shocks will not shift the aggregate demand curve in Figure 4.2. Even if they did, there would be no effect on output or employment. This is because of the self-adjusting properties of the classical labor market as reflected in the vertical aggregate supply curve—the second line of defense for full employment.

4.3 • POLICY IMPLICATIONS OF THE CLASSICAL EQUILIBRIUM MODEL

In this section we analyze the effects of monetary and fiscal policy actions within the classical model. We consider the effects that various policy shifts will have on output, employment, the price level, and the interest rate.

Fiscal Policy

Fiscal policy is the setting of the federal budget and is thus comprised of decisions on government spending and taxation. In considering the classical view of fiscal policy, it is convenient to begin with government spending.

Government Spending

Consider the effects of an increase in government spending in the classical model. The question of how the increased spending is financed arises first. Like a business or household, the government has a **budget constraint,** a condition that states that all expenditures must be financed from some source. The government has three sources of funds: taxation, selling bonds

---

[7]It is important to note that as saving declines there is a dollar-for-dollar increase in current consumption. Real income is fixed, as are taxes, so *all* changes in saving are mirrored in changes in current consumption.

to the public (borrowing funds from the public), or financing by the creating of new money. The creation of new money can take several forms, but in our discussion of the classical system, it will do no harm to assume that the government simply prints new currency to finance its spending.

To increase spending, then, the government must increase taxation, sell additional bonds to the public, or increase the money supply. For now, to avoid bringing in a monetary policy change, we assume the money supply to be fixed, We also assume that tax collections are fixed. The increased government expenditures are therefore assumed to be financed by selling bonds to the public.

It follows from our analysis to this point that a bond-financed increase in government spending will not affect the equilibrium values of output or the price level. This must be the case since we constructed both the aggregate demand and aggregate supply curves, which together determine output and the price level, without reference to the level of government spending. Since output is not affected by changes in government spending, employment must also be unaffected. To understand these results, it is necessary to examine the effect on the interest rate of a change in government spending.

The effect in the loanable funds market of an increase in government spending financed by a sale of bonds to the public is shown in Figure 4.5. We assume that prior to the increase in government spending the government budget was in balance ($g - t = 0$). The government deficit is then equal to the increase in spending ($\Delta g = g - t$). Initially, with no government deficit, the demand for loanable funds comes only to finance investment and is given by schedule i in Figure 4.5. The increase in government spending shifts the demand for loanable funds to the $i + \Delta g$ schedule in the figure. Note that the distance of the horizontal shift in the curve, the increase in the demand for loanable funds at a given interest rate, measures the amount of the increase in government spending. This amount is measured by the distance Δg in Figure 4.5.

The increase in government spending creates an increased demand for loanable funds as the government sells bonds to the public to finance the new spending. This creates an excess of borrowers over lenders at the initial interest rate r_0, and the interest rate is pushed up to r_1. The increase in the interest rate has two effects. Saving increases from s_0 to s_1; this is the distance A in Figure 4.5. As was explained in the preceding section, an increase in saving is mirrored by an equal decline in consumption demand. Second, investment declines with the higher interest rate. At r_1 we can read the new level of investment as i_1, along the i schedule. The investment decline is the distance B in Figure 4.5.

It can be seen from the figure that the amount of the decline in consumption demand, which equals the amount of increased saving (distance A), plus the decline in investment (distance B) just equals the amount of the increase in government spending (Δg). The increase in government spending

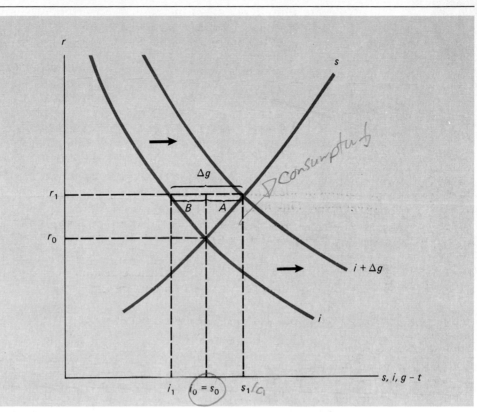

FIGURE 4.5 Effect of Increase in Government Spending in the Classical Model
An increase in government spending shifts the demand for loanable funds schedule
to the right from i to $i + \Delta g$, a distance Δg. The equilibrium interest rate rises from
r_0 to r_1. The rise in the interest rate causes a decline in investment from i_0 to i_1,
a distance B, and an increase in saving, which is an equal decline in consumption,
from s_0 to s_1, a distance A. The decline in investment and consumption just balances
the increase in government spending $(A + B - \Delta g)$.

financed by selling bonds to the public pushes the interest rate up by enough
to "crowd out" an equal amount of private expenditure (consumption
plus investment). Private expenditures are discouraged because the higher
interest rate causes households to substitute future consumption for current
consumption—to save more. Investment declines because fewer projects appear profitable with higher borrowing costs. It is this crowding out that keeps
aggregate demand from increasing when the government component of
demand rises. Since aggregate demand is not changed, increases in government expenditures financed by bonds do not affect the price level.

What are the effects of an increase in government spending if, alternatively, the government prints money to finance the new spending? Here, since the quantity of money is changed, the price level will be changed proportionately. We have previously analyzed the way in which an increase in the money stock shifts the aggregate demand curve up along the vertical aggregate supply curve, raising the price level (see Figure 4.2). In the classical system the source of the increase in the money stock does not matter. A given change in the money stock has the same effect whether it enters the economy to finance an increase in government spending or in another manner. Put differently, and this is the crucial point, *the increase in government spending has no independent effect on aggregate demand.*

Tax Policy

Demand-Side Effects.   As long as we consider only the possible effects on aggregate demand, analysis of a change in taxes produces results that are analogous to those for government spending. For example, by increasing the disposable income of households, a tax cut might stimulate consumption demand. If, however, the government sold bonds to the public to replace the revenues lost by the tax cut, the same crowding-out process would follow, as in the case of a bond-financed increase in government spending. The equilibrium interest rate would rise, investment demand would fall, and there would also be an interest-rate–induced rise in saving, meaning that consumption would fall back toward the pre–tax-cut level. In the case of a tax cut, as with an increase in spending, aggregate demand would not be affected.

If revenues lost because of the tax cut are replaced by printing new money, then, as with an increase in government spending, the money creation *will* increase aggregate demand, and the tax cut will cause the price level to rise. Again, though, it would simply be the increase in the money supply that affected the price level. The tax cut would have no *independent* effect on aggregate demand.

Supply-Side Effects.   If the tax cut were simply a *lump-sum* cut, meaning, for example, that every household received a tax cut of $100, then the demand-side effects would be all that we would need to consider.[8] But suppose the tax cut was in the form of a reduction in income tax rates. Suppose the *marginal* income tax rate were cut from an initial rate of 40 percent to a

---

[8] Since the tax cut would affect wealth, which in turn might influence the labor–leisure choice, even a lump-sum tax cut would affect the supply side. We are neglecting wealth effects here as being of secondary importance.

new rate of 20 percent. Instead of having 40 cents of every additional dollar taken as a tax payment, only 20 cents would now be taken. In the classical model, such a change would have an incentive effect on labor supply. The change would affect the supply side of the model and *would* affect output and employment.

Figure 4.6 illustrates the effect of a cut in the marginal income tax rate within the classical model. Part *a* shows the effects in the labor market. A cut in the tax rate would increase labor supply at any value of the (pretax) real wage and shift the labor supply schedule out to the right. This follows

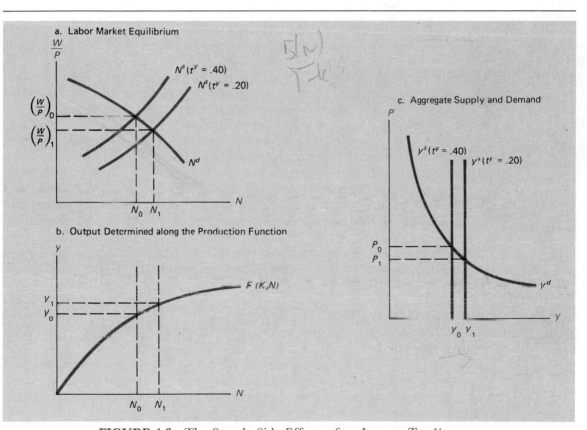

FIGURE 4.6 The Supply-Side Effects of an Income Tax Cut
In Part *a*, a reduction in the marginal income tax rate (from 0.40 to 0.20) increases the after-tax real wage for a given value of the pretax real wage. The labor supply curve therefore shifts out to the right. Employment and output increase, as shown in Part *b* of the graph. This increase in output is represented by the shift to the right in the aggregate supply curve in Part *c*.

because the worker is concerned about the *after-tax* real wage, which in this case is $(1 - t^y)W/P$, where t^y is the marginal income tax rate. If we had included an income tax in our model of the classical labor market in Chapter 3, the labor supply function would have been

$$N^s = g\left((1 - t^y)\frac{W}{P}\right) \tag{3.6'}$$

For a given value of the pretax real wage (W/P), a cut in the income tax represents an increase in the after-tax real wage and therefore increases labor supply.

In Figure 4.6a, as the marginal income tax rate falls from 0.40 to 0.20, the labor supply schedule shifts from $N^s(t^y = .40)$ to $N^s(t^y = .20)$. The equilibrium level of employment increases from N_0 to N_1. Part b of Figure 4.6 shows the aggregate production function. The increase in employment from N_0 to N_1 as a result of the increase in labor supply leads to an increase in output from y_0 to y_1.

In part c of the figure, this increase in the supply-determined level of output (from y_0 to y_1) is shown as a shift to the right in the classical aggregate supply curve from $y^s(t^y = .40)$ to $y^s(t^y = .20)$. Because the level of aggregate demand is unchanged (determined by the level of the money stock), this increase in aggregate supply results in a fall in the price level.[9]

To summarize, changes in government spending or taxes have no independent effects on aggregate demand because of the interest rate adjustment and resulting crowding-out effects on the components of private-sector demand. Changes in marginal income tax rates would have additional supply-side effects. A reduction in the marginal income tax rate, for example, stimulates labor supply and leads to an increase in employment and output.

Read Perspectives 4.2.

Monetary Policy

The role of money in the classical system has been dealt with already, and here we simply summarize our findings. The quantity of money determines the price level and, for a given real income, the level of *nominal* income. In this sense monetary policy was quite important to classical economists. Stable money was a requirement for stable prices.

---

[9]The aggregate demand curve is fixed as long as revenues that were lost because of the cut in the income tax rate are replaced by increased bond sales to the public. If instead lost revenue were replaced by printing money, then the aggregate demand curve would shift to the right and the price level might not fall.

PERSPECTIVES

Supply-Side Economics—A Modern Classical View

Classical economists in the nineteenth and early twentieth centuries did not give much attention to the supply-side effects of changes in income tax rates. The reason for this neglect is simple; at the time the classical economists wrote, the marginal income tax rate was very low and pertained only to the relatively wealthy. As can be seen from Table 4.2, in the United States, the average marginal income tax rate (averaged across each tax bracket) in 1920 was only 4.6 percent and by 1929 had declined to 3.5 percent. Moreover, in the late 1920s fewer than 15 percent of U.S. households had incomes that were high enough to require filing an income tax return.

As can also be seen from Table 4.2, the situation was quite different in the post–World War II period. By 1980 the average marginal income tax rate was above 30 percent, and a large majority of U.S. households had incomes that were high enough to be subject to the income tax. In the 1970s a group that became known as the *supply-side economists* argued, much along the lines of the analysis in this subsection, that such taxes formed a "wedge" between the real wage paid by employers and that received by the worker. Reducing the size of that wedge, they argued, would increase the incentives to supply labor and result in higher output and employment, as illustrated in Figure 4.6.

By the late 1970s, economists such as Robert Mundell of Columbia University and Arthur B. Laffer, then at the University of Southern California, had popularized the idea that tax cuts would have strong favorable "supply-side" effects. Representative Jack Kemp and Senator William Roth accepted the supply-siders' argument, and in 1977 they introduced a bill calling for across-the-board cuts of 10 percent in personal income tax rates in each of three successive years. In 1980 Ronald Reagan endorsed the Kemp–Roth proposal, and in 1981, in what then Senator Howard Baker called "a riverboat gamble," the Reagan–Kemp–Roth tax bill, calling for a 23 percent across-the-board income tax cut over three years, was passed. Later, the Tax Reform bill of 1986 further reduced marginal income tax rates.

The effects of these tax cuts, as well as other elements of supply-side economics and "Reaganomics," are considered in Chapter 17, where we examine the classical roots of supply-side economics in more detail.

TABLE 4.2 Average Marginal Tax Rate, Selected Years (percent)

1916	1.2	1950	19.6
1920	4.6	1970	24.3
1929	3.5	1980	30.4

Source: Robert J. Barro and Chaipat Sahasakul, "Measuring the Average Marginal Tax Rate from the Individual Income Tax," *Journal of Business,* 56 (October 1983), pp. 434–35, Table 2.

In another sense money was not important. The quantity of money did not affect the equilibrium values of the real variables in the system: output, employment, *and the interest rate*. The supply-determined nature of output and employment was the subject of Chapter 3. The theory of the equilibrium interest rate we have constructed here is a real theory that did not mention the quantity of money. Factors determining the interest rate were real investment demand, real saving, and the real value of the government deficit—what the classical economists called the forces of "productivity and thrift."

To classical economists, money was a "veil" that determined the nominal values in which we measure such variables as the level of economic activity, but had no effect on real quantities.

4.4   THE CLASSICAL SYSTEM WITH RIGID MONEY WAGES— ONE EXPLANATION OF UNEMPLOYMENT

So far we have assumed that the money wage is perfectly flexible. It is the instantaneous adjustment of the money wage that guarantees that the labor market will be in equilibrium. Thus, in the classical system perfect money-wage flexibility is a requirement for full employment.

Classical economists recognized that wages might be somewhat rigid, especially in the downward direction. There were several reasons for downward rigidity in wages. Consider the response of the money wage to a change that produced a fall in the demand for labor. Clearly, workers might try to prevent the fall in the money wage required to reequate supply and demand. Individual workers in the type of "auction" market setting by which the classical economists characterized the labor market would have little power to keep their wages from falling in response to market conditions. Classical economists, however, witnessed the growth of organized labor unions and congresses of unions. They recognized that labor organizations might effectively resist wage cuts that would be required to maintain equilibrium in the labor market during periods when the demand for labor was declining. Disruptions, work slowdowns, strikes, and even a general strike were weapons that could be (and were) used by organized labor for this purpose.

Additionally, government policies might make the money wage inflexible in a downward direction. The most obvious example of government policies that keep wages from falling are minimum-wage laws. In addition, during periods when the level of economic activity was falling, government often tried to keep wages and prices from falling, believing that this would minimize economic distress. An example is Franklin Roosevelt's attempt in 1933–34 to get employers to agree to codes limiting wage cuts.

The effect of downward rigidity in the money wage in the classical system can be analyzed within the graphical framework of Chapter 3 (see Figure 3.5). In Figure 4.7 we plot both labor supply and demand as functions of the *money* wage. As explained in Chapter 3, each schedule must be drawn for a given price level; the curves will shift as shown in Figure 3.5 when the price level changes.

In Figure 4.7 we assume that labor supply and demand are given initially by $N^s(P_1)$ and $N^d(P_1)$, respectively, where P_1 is the initial price level. Equilibrium in the labor market would be at N_1 with money wage W_1 and the real wage W_1/P_1. Assume instead, however, that the money wage is fixed at $\overline{W}$, a level too high for equilibrium, and does not fall despite the fact that at $\overline{W}$ labor supply $\overline{N}_1^s$ exceeds labor demand $\overline{N}_1^d$. The wage is assumed to be rigid at this level, as a result, for example, of organized labor's resistance to a

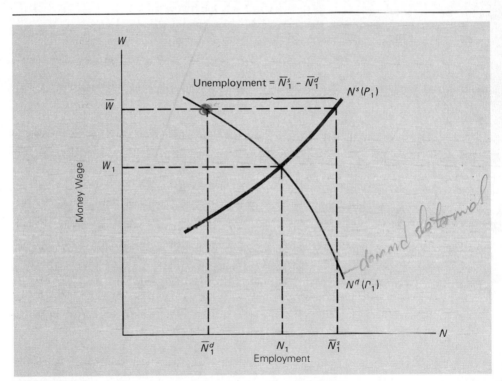

FIGURE 4.7 A Rigid Money Wage in the Classical System
The equilibrium point for the labor market with price level P_1 is at a money wage W_1 and level of employment N_1. If the money wage is fixed at $\overline{W}$ above W_1, employment will be determined by labor demand, $\overline{N}_1^d$, and unemployment will be equal to $(\overline{N}_1^s - \overline{N}_1^d)$.

wage cut following a decline in labor demand. In this situation, firms will hire labor only up to the point at which the marginal product of labor equals the real wage. This results in employment of $\overline{N}_1^d$, the point on the labor demand curve corresponding to $\overline{W}$. Labor supply is $\overline{N}_1^s$ at $\overline{W}$ so unemployment is equal to $\overline{N}_1^s - \overline{N}_1^d$. Thus a possible explanation for unemployment that is consistent with the classical system is that wages are rigid in the downward direction.

If wages are rigid downward, it is no longer the case that the levels of employment and output are completely supply-determined; the aggregate supply curve is no longer vertical. To see this, consider the effect on employment of an increase in the price level from P_1 to a higher value P_2, as illustrated in Figure 4.8. The increase in the price level with the money wage

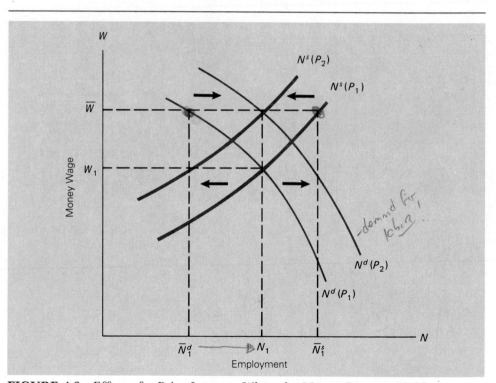

FIGURE 4.8 Effect of a Price Increase When the Money Wage Is Rigid
With the money wage fixed at $\overline{W}$, an increase in the price level from P_1 to P_2 will shift the labor demand schedule from $N^d(P_1)$ to $N^d(P_2)$. Employment will rise from $\overline{N}_1^d$ to N_1. The increase in price will also shift the labor supply schedule leftward from $N^s(P_1)$ to $N^s(P_2)$, but given the initial excess supply of labor, this will not prevent the expansion in employment.

held at $\overline{W}$ will reduce the real wage and shift the demand-for-labor curve to the right to $N^d(P_2)$. The fall in the real wage does cause labor supply to decline. The labor supply schedule shifts to the left to $N^s(P_2)$. As long as there is unemployment, however, and supply exceeds demand, this fall in supply has no effect. In other words, as long as the real wage is too high for equilibrium, demand—not supply—is the factor constraining employment. A fall in the real wage increases employment. In Figure 4.8 the increase in the price level to P_2 is just sufficient to achieve equilibrium employment N_1. The rise in the price level is sufficient to generate a real wage $\overline{W}/P_2$ equal to W_1/P_1.

The implications of a rigid money wage for the slope of the aggregate supply curve and for the output effects of changes in aggregate demand can be seen from Figure 4.9. At price level P_1 and the fixed money wage

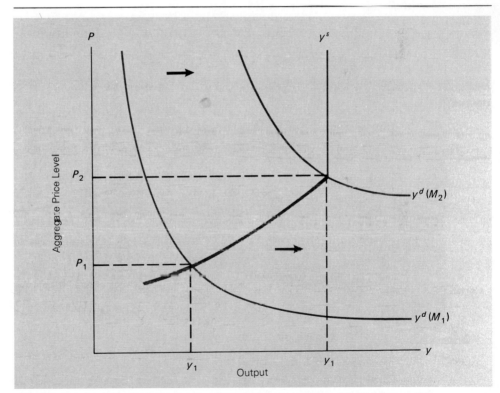

FIGURE 4.9 Classical Aggregate Supply Curve with a Rigid Money Wage
At price level P_1 output is at $\overline{y}_1$. An increase in the money stock from M_1 to M_2 will shift the aggregate demand schedule from $y^d(M_1)$ to $y^d(M_2)$; the price level will rise to P_2 and, in the case of a rigid money wage, output will rise to y_1.

($\overline{W}$), output would be at $\overline{y}_1$, the level produced with employment $\overline{N}_1^d$ in Figure 4.7. In the figure this price level (P_1) is shown to be consistent with the money stock being at M_1, giving the aggregate demand curve $y^d(M_1)$. At a price level of P_2, as we have seen in Figure 4.8, employment would increase to N_1. Output would then increase to y_1. The price level could be pushed up to P_2 if the money stock were increased to M_2, shifting the aggregate demand curve to $y^d(M_2)$.

The aggregate supply curve would be upward sloping at price levels below P_2 since over that range $\overline{W}/P$ is above the equilibrium value in Figure 4.7. Movements of the price level above P_2 would *not* increase output supplied. At P_2 with wage $\overline{W}$, labor supply equals labor demand. Further increases in the price level would simply lead to proportionate increases in the money wage. The money wage is not assumed to be rigid in the upward direction, so at price levels above P_2 the derivation of the aggregate supply curve remains as discussed in Chapter 3.

To summarize, downward money wage rigidity was one explanation of unemployment in the classical system. If unemployment was caused by such downward rigidity—if the real wage was too high for full employment—then an increase in the money stock would increase employment. A higher money stock would increase aggregate demand. The price level would rise and the real wage would fall toward its equilibrium value.

Monetary policy could affect the level of output with a rigid money wage, but that does not mean that such policy actions were viewed as desirable by classical economists. If there was unemployment because the money wage was too high, then classical economists believed that a fall in the money wage was the preferable way to lower the real wage and restore full employment. To use monetary policy to raise the price level would encourage organized labor to attempt to push wages above equilibrium levels and to depend on the government to validate this wage inflation with an expansionary monetary policy. Classical economists also recommended changes that would increase wage flexibility by restricting the power of organized labor to fix money wages.

4.5 · CONCLUSION

Our analysis of the classical system has been detailed since the properties of the system are crucial to the theories we consider later. The Keynesian theory is an attack on the classical system. The monetarist and new classical economic frameworks are reformulations of the classical system.

The classical economists stressed the *self-adjusting tendencies of the economy.* Free from destabilizing government actions, the private sector would be stable, and full employment would be achieved. The first of these self-stabilizing mechanisms is the interest rate, which adjusts to keep shocks to sectoral demands from affecting aggregate demand. The second set of stabilizers in the classical system is freely flexible prices and money wages, which keep changes in aggregate demand from affecting output. As we saw when we considered the effects of a rigid money wage, such price and wage flexibility is crucial to the full-employment properties of the classical system. The inherent stability of the private sector led the classical economists to what can be termed *noninterventionist* policy conclusions. To be sure, many of the interventionist mercantilist policies that the classical economists opposed (tariffs, trading monopolies, etc.) were a far cry from the macroeconomic stabilization policies of today, but the model itself argues for nonintervention in a very general sense.

A second central feature of the classical system is the *dichotomy between the factors determining real and nominal variables.* In the classical theory real (supply-side) factors determine real variables. Output and employment depend primarily on population, technology, and capital formation. The interest rate depends on productivity and thrift. Money is a veil determining the nominal values in which quantities are measured, but monetary factors do not play a role in determining these real quantities (assuming wage flexibility).

In the next theoretical system that we consider—the Keynesian theory— we will see that the policy conclusions that emerge are much more interventionist. We will also see that monetary and real variables are much more interrelated in the Keynesian system.

Review Questions and Problems

1. Explain the role that money plays in the classical system. Specifically, in the classical model, what role does money have in determining real output, employment, the price level, and the interest rate? Explain how money affects these variables; or, if money has no effect on some of them, explain why this is the case. (Here assume the money wage is flexible.)

2. What are the differences between the Fisherian and Cambridge versions of the quantity theory of money?

3. Define the term *velocity of money.* What factors determine the velocity of money in the classical system? What is the relationship between the velocity of money and the Cambridge k?

4. Explain how aggregate demand is determined within the classical model. What would be the effects on output and the price level of an increase in aggregate demand?

5. The classical economists assumed that velocity was stable in the short run. But suppose that, because of a change in the payments mechanism— for example, greater use of credit cards—there was an exogenous rise in

the velocity of money. What effect would such a change have on output, employment, and the price level within the classical model?

6. Explain how the interest rate is determined in the classical theory.

7. Explain how the interest rate works in the classical system to stabilize aggregate demand in the face of autonomous changes in components of aggregate demand such as investment or government spending.

8. Within the classical model, analyze the effects of an increase in the marginal income tax rate. Explain how output, employment, and the price level are affected. Consider both the case in which the increased revenue produced by the tax increase results in a decline in bond sales to the public and when it results in lower money creation.

9. We saw in section 4.4 that when the money wage was fixed, an increase in the money stock *would* lead to an increase in output. Would an increase in government spending also increase output in this case? Explain.

10. What are the major policy conclusions of classical economics? Explain how these policy conclusions follow from the key assumptions of the classical theoretical system.

11. How are the classical policy conclusions modified if we assume that the money wage is rigid rather than perfectly flexible?

12. Suppose that we are in the situation depicted in Figure 4.7 in which the money wage is fixed (at $\overline{W}$) above the equilibrium level. Using a graphical analysis combining Figures 4.7 and 4.9, show the effects on output and employment of a policy action, such as some type of antiunion legislation, that resulted in an exogenous fall in the money wage to a level $\overline{W}'$, below $\overline{W}$ but still above the equilibrium money wage (W_1).

Selected Readings

Ackley, Gardner, *Macroeconomic Theory*. New York: Macmillan, 1961, Chaps. 5–8.

Fisher, Irving, *The Purchasing Power of Money*. New York: Macmillan, 1922, especially Chap. 4.

Makinen, Gail, *Money, the Price Level and Interest Rates*. Englewood Cliffs, N.J.: Prentice-Hall, 1977, Chaps. 1–4.

Patinkin, Don, "On the Short-Run Non-neutrality of Money in the Quantity Theory," *Banca Nazionali del Lavoro Quarterly Review*, 25 (March 1972), pp. 3–22.

Pigou, A. C., "The Value of Money," *Quarterly Journal of Economics*, 32 (1917–18), pp. 38–65. Reprinted in Friedrich Lutz and Lloyd Mints, eds., *Readings in Monetary Theory*. Homewood, Ill.; Irwin, 1951.

5 The Keynesian System (I): The Role of Aggregate Demand

5.1 • THE PROBLEM OF UNEMPLOYMENT

Keynesian economics developed against the background of the world Depression of the 1930s. The length and severity of the decline in economic activity that occurred at that time were unprecedented. The effect of the Depression on the U.S. economy can be seen in Figure 5.1, which shows the annual unemployment rates for the years 1929–41. The unemployment rate rose from 3.2 percent of the labor force in 1929 to 25.2 percent of the labor force in 1933, the low point for economic activity during the Depression. Unemployment remained over 10 percent throughout the decade. Real GNP fell by 30 percent between 1929 and 1933 and did not reach the 1929 level again until 1939.

The British economist John Maynard Keynes, whose book *The General Theory of Employment, Interest and Money* is the foundation of the Keynesian system, was more heavily influenced by events in his own country than those in the United States. In Great Britain high unemployment began in the early 1920s and persisted into and throughout the 1930s.[1] The high unemployment in Great Britain led to a debate among economists and policymakers over the causes of unemployment and the proper policy response to increased unemployment. Keynes was a prominent participant in this debate, during the course of which he developed his revolutionary theory of macroeconomics.

---

[1] The unemployment rate in Great Britain was above 10 percent as early as 1923 and remained above 10 percent, except for one brief fall to 9.8 percent, until 1936, the year in which *The General Theory* was published.

89

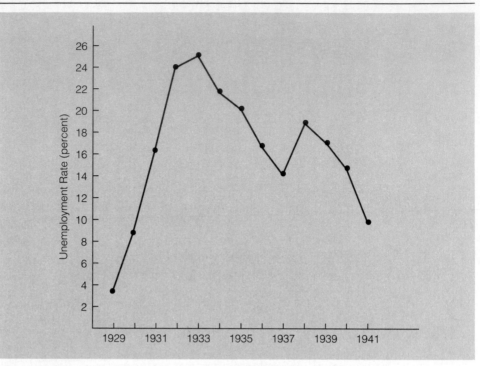

FIGURE 5.1   U.S. Unemployment Rate, 1929–41 (percent)

According to Keynes's theory, the high unemployment in Great Britain and the United States (as well as in other industrialized countries) was the result of a deficiency in *aggregate demand*. Aggregate demand was too low because of inadequate investment demand. Keynes's theory provided the basis for economic policies to combat unemployment. Policies should be aimed at stimulating aggregate demand. At the time of the Depression Keynes favored fiscal policy measures, primarily government spending on public works projects, to stimulate demand. More generally, the Keynesian theory argues for the use of monetary and fiscal policies to regulate the level of aggregate demand. To understand the revolutionary nature of this theory, it is useful to consider the state of macroeconomic thinking about unemployment as an economic policy question at the time Keynes's thought was developing.

Classical economists clearly recognized the human cost of unemployment, as stated with great feeling, for example, by Alfred Marshall:

> Forced interruption to labour is a grievous evil. Those, whose livelihood is secure, gain physical and mental health from happy and well-spent holidays. But want of work, with long continued anxiety, consumes a man's best strength without any

return. His wife becomes thin; and his children get, as it were, a nasty notch in their lives, which is perhaps never outgrown.[2]

But Marshall had little to say about the causes of unemployment. He noted that unemployment existed in early times and argued that knowledge was the cure, in that knowledge would increase the skills of labor and also keep laborers and firms from making poor economic decisions that result in business failures and unemployment. When Marshall suggested ways in which to diminish fluctuations in employment, the following was the first given.

> Those causes of discontinuity which lie within our scope, and are remediable, are chiefly connected in some way or other with the want of knowledge; but there is one which is willful: it is fashion. Until a little while ago only the rich could change their clothing at the capricious order of their dressmakers: but now all classes do it. The histories of the alpaca trade, the lace trade, the straw hat trade, the ribbon trade, and a multitude of others, tell of bursts of feverish activity alternating with deadening idleness.[3]

To the modern reader this analysis must appear quaint; it was hardly a basis for meaningful solutions to the unemployment problem of Britain in the 1920s. Marshall and the other economists relying on the classical equilibrium theory had little else to offer. In the classical system unemployment could result from downward rigidity of the money wage. Money wage cuts could be, and were, suggested as a possible remedy for unemployment. The money wage, however, fell in the United States by one third between 1929 and 1933 without stopping the rise in unemployment. Just as wage cuts did not appear to provide an adequate remedy to the Depression, rigid money wages did not provide a satisfactory explanation of the massive unemployment. The failure of the money wage to fall in response to a decline in the demand for labor would result in unemployment, but why was the demand for labor falling so disastrously? Was not the decline in labor demand the ultimate source of the unemployment? Recently, economists have tried to explain the Depression in ways not inconsistent with the classical model, but economists at the time were dissatisfied and were casting about for alternatives to the orthodox classical analysis.

Much of the debate over economic policy in Great Britain at that time focused on the question of the desirability of government spending on public works as a cure for unemployment, what we would now term an expansionary fiscal policy action. The argument advanced by Keynes and others was that such actions would increase output and employment. Such expenditures would stimulate output and employment both directly and

---

[2]Alfred Marshall, *Money, Credit and Commerce* (London: Macmillan, 1922), p. 260.

[3]Ibid.

Public works

Classical response

indirectly because they would increase the income and hence consumer expenditure of those employed by the public works projects, thus generating secondary employment.

Those arguing against his view drew primarily on the classical equilibrium analysis that we have presented. Increases in government expenditure, unless financed by money creation and thus changes in monetary policy, would not affect either employment or the price level. If public works projects were financed by creating money, the price level but not the levels of output or unemployment would be affected. This classical theory was the basis for the official position of the Conservative Party in Great Britain, which was in power for the bulk of the 1920s and early 1930s. As Winston Churchill explained this position: "It is the orthodox Treasury dogma, steadfastly held, that whatever might be the political or social advantages, very little employment can, in fact, as a general rule, be created by state borrowing and state expenditure."

In the United States, policy prescriptions consistent with the classical position were also influential. Far from trying to raise demand and stimulate output and employment, during the height of the Depression, in 1932, the administration of Herbert Hoover engineered a large tax *increase*. Hoover's reason for increasing tax rates was to balance the federal budget. Higher tax rates were needed to balance the federal budget in the wake of falling tax revenues as income declined. Since, in the classical system, fiscal policy had no effect on income, prudent budget management had come to mean simply balancing spending with tax revenues.[4] When Franklin Roosevelt ran against Hoover for the presidency in 1932, he attacked Hoover for failing to balance the budget and argued for *cuts* in government spending. Would not the income tax increase or cut in government spending lower aggregate demand, output, and employment? Not in the classical system, since output and employment were supply-determined. In any case, in the classical model fiscal policy did not affect aggregate demand. As we will see, such a tax increase or spending cut is just the opposite of the "correct" policy action indicated by the Keynesian model.

To sum up, the situation in the early 1930s was one of massive unemployment that was not well explained by the classical system and for which classical economics provided no remedy. Many economists and political figures argued in favor of various policy actions, including public works projects, to try to increase aggregate demand. The classical economists pointed out that such policies would not work in the classical system, where output and employment were not demand-determined. As Keynes pointed out: "The strength

---

[4]This ignores the supply-side effects of a change in the tax rate, discussed in section 4.3. As explained there, the classical economists gave little consideration to those effects, though they have become an important policy consideration in recent years.

of the self-adjusting school depends on its having behind it almost the whole body of organized economic thinking and doctrine of the last hundred years."[5] Keynes ranged himself among the "heretics" to the classical view of the self-adjusting properties of the economy. Of the heretics, he wrote: "They are deeply dissatisfied. They believe that common observation is enough to show that facts do not conform to the orthodox reasoning. They propose remedies prompted by instinct, by flair, by practical good sense, by experience of the world—half right, most of them, half wrong."[6] Keynes felt that the heretics would never prevail until the flaw in the orthodox classical theory had been found. He believed that flaw to be the lack of an explicit theory of the aggregate demand for output and, hence, of the role of aggregate demand in determining output and employment. We discuss next the theory provided by Keynes and his followers to fill this gap in the classical system.

Our analysis of the Keynesian system proceeds as follows. In the remainder of this chapter we analyze a very simple version of the Keynesian model. This model will be useful in developing the basic elements of Keynes's theory of aggregate demand. Our simple model neglects complications that come from allowing for the effects of money and interest rates in the model. It also neglects the effect of changes in the price level and the money wage. Money and interest rates are introduced into the model in Chapter 6. Chapter 7 analyzes policy effects in the resulting version of the Keynesian model. In Chapter 8, which takes account of the effects of price and wage changes in the Keynesian system, we explain the Keynesian theory of aggregate supply.

5.2 • THE SIMPLE KEYNESIAN MODEL: CONDITIONS FOR EQUILIBRIUM OUTPUT

A central notion in the Keynesian model is that for a level of output to be an equilibrium level requires that *output be equal to aggregate demand.* In our simple model, this condition for equilibrium can be expressed as

$$Y = E \tag{5.1}$$

where Y is equal to total output (GNP) and E equals aggregate demand or desired expenditures on output. Aggregate demand (E) consists of three components: household consumption (C), desired business investment demand (I), and the government sector's demand for goods and services (G). Thus in equilibrium we have

$$Y = E = C + I + G \tag{5.2}$$

---

[5] John M. Keynes, *Collected Works,* Vol. 13 (London: Macmillan, 1973), p. 489.

[6] Ibid., pp. 488–89.

The simple form of (5.2) and of the identities discussed later results from neglecting a number of complexities in the definitions of gross national product and national income. These simplifications, discussed in Chapter 2, are noted here briefly again. Exports and imports do not appear in equation (5.2). Here we are dealing with a "closed" economy, neglecting foreign trade.[7] Depreciation is also neglected, so we do not need to distinguish between gross national product and net national product. We also assume that gross national product and national income are equivalent. This means we do not include items in the model that cause a discrepancy between the two totals (primarily indirect business taxes). A final assumption has to do with the units in which each of the variables is measured. For this chapter we assume that *the aggregate price level is fixed.* All variables are *real* variables, and all changes are changes in real terms.

With national product Y also measuring national income, we can write

$$Y \equiv C + S + T \tag{5.3}$$

Equation (5.3) is an accounting definition or identity stating that national income, all of which is assumed to be paid to households in return for factor services, is either consumed (C), paid out in taxes (T), or saved (S).[8] Additionally, from the fact that Y is a national product, we can write

$$Y \equiv C + I_r + G \tag{5.4}$$

Equation (5.4) *defines* national product as equal to consumption, plus *realized* investment (I_r), plus government spending.

Using the definitions given in equations (5.3) and (5.4), we can rewrite the condition for an equilibrium level of income given in equation (5.2) in two alternative ways, which will help us to understand the nature of equilibrium in the model. Since, by (5.2), in equilibrium Y must equal ($C + I + G$), and from (5.3), Y is defined as ($C + S + T$) *in equilibrium,*

$$C + S + T \equiv Y = C + I + G$$

or, equivalently,

$$S + T = I + G \tag{5.5}$$

---

[7] The roles of imports and exports in the simple Keynesian model are considered in the appendix to this chapter. Notice also that for a closed economy we need not distinguish between gross national product (GNP) and gross domestic product (GDP), the other output measure defined in Chapter 2.

[8] The model does not allow for retained earnings. All profits are assumed to be paid out as dividends. Also, firms are assumed to make no tax payments; all taxes are paid by households.

In similar fashion, from equations (5.2) and (5.4) we can see that in equilibrium

$$C + I_r + G \equiv Y = C + I + G$$

or, by canceling terms,

$$I_r = I \tag{5.6}$$

There are then three equivalent ways to state the condition for equilibrium in the model:

$$Y = C + I + G \tag{5.2}$$

$$S + T = I + G \tag{5.5}$$

$$I_r = I \tag{5.6}$$

To help interpret the meaning of these conditions, we turn to the flow chart given in Figure 5.2. Each of the magnitudes in the chart (each of the variables in our model) is a *flow* variable. The magnitudes are measured in dollars per period. In the national income accounts they are measured as billions of dollars per quarter or year. The flow marked with the uppermost arrow in the diagram is the flow of national income from the business sector to the household sector. This flow consists of payments for factor services (wages, interest, rents, dividends). Such payments are assumed to sum to national income, which is equal to national product. There is a corresponding flow from the household sector to the business sector, consisting of the factor services supplied by the household sector. This flow and similar flows are not shown in the diagram because they are not money flows.

National income is distributed by households into three flows. There is a flow of consumption expenditures that goes back to the business sector as

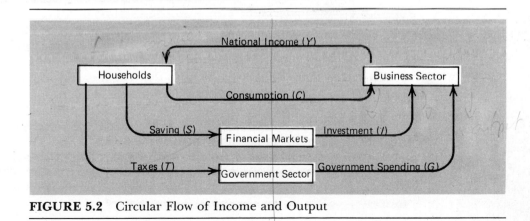

FIGURE 5.2   Circular Flow of Income and Output

a demand for the output produced. Thus the inner loop of our diagram depicts a process whereby firms produce output (Y), which generates an equal amount of income to the household sector, which in turn generates a demand for the output produced (C).

Not all national income returns directly to the firms as a demand for the output produced. There are two flows out of the household sector in addition to consumption expenditure—the saving flow and the flow of tax payments. If we regard the inner loop of our diagram, linking the households (as suppliers of factor services and demanders of output) and the business sector (as suppliers of output and demanders of factor services) as the central income- and output-generating mechanism, the saving and tax flows are *leakages* from this central loop.

The saving leakage flows into the financial markets. By this we mean that the part of income that is saved is held in the form of some financial asset (currency, bank deposits, bonds, equities, etc.). The tax flow is paid to the government sector. The tax flow in the diagram is *net* taxes, that is, gross tax payments minus transfer payments from the government to the household sector (Social Security benefits, welfare payments, unemployment compensation, etc.). Consequently, when we talk later about a tax increase or tax cut, this can be interpreted equivalently as a change in the opposite direction in the level of transfer payments.

Although each dollar of output and, hence, national income does not directly generate one dollar of demand for output on the part of the household sector, this does not mean that total demand must fall short of output. There are additional demands for output on the part of the business sector itself for investment, and from the government sector. In terms of the circular flow, these are *injections* into the central loop of our diagram. The investment injection is shown as a flow from financial markets to the business sector. The purchasers of the investment goods are actually the firms in the business sector themselves. These purchases must, however, be financed by borrowing in financial markets. Thus the dollar amount of investment represents an equivalent flow of funds lent to the business sector. Government spending is a demand for the output of the business sector and is shown as a money flow from the government to the business sector.

We are now in a position to examine the three equivalent expressions for equilibrium given by equations (5.2), (5.5), and (5.6). Production of a level of output Y generates an equivalent amount of income to households. A portion of this income, equal to consumption demand (C), returns directly to the firms as a demand for that output. The level of output will be an equilibrium level if this directly generated demand (C), when added to desired investment expenditures of firms (I) and government spending (G), produces a total demand equal to Y, that is, if

$$Y = C + I + G \tag{5.2}$$

From the second version of the condition for equilibrium income

$$S + T = I + G \tag{5.5}$$

we see that a flow rate of output will be an equilibrium rate if the leakages $(S + T)$ from the central loop of our flow diagram are just balanced by injections $(I + G)$ into this central income and output circular flow. This ensures that the amount of income households do not spend on output $(S + T)$, and therefore the amount of output that is produced but not sold to households $(Y - C \equiv S + T)$, is just equal to the amount the other two sectors wish to buy $(I + G)$. This is equivalent to saying that total output equals aggregate demand and is thus equivalent to the first way of stating the condition for equilibrium.

The third way of expressing the condition for equilibrium, equation (5.6) $(I = I_r)$, states that in equilibrium desired investment must equal actual or realized investment. What does it mean for desired investment to differ from realized investment? The GNP accountant computes investment as the total volume of business spending on plant and equipment, plus inventory investment, the increase (or decline) in inventories.[9] We can assume that desired spending on plant and equipment equals actual spending as recorded by the GNP accountant. It is in the last category, inventory investment, that desired and realized totals may differ. The GNP accountant will record all goods that are produced by a firm and not sold as inventory investment—*whether such investment was intended or not.*

To see how realized and intended inventory investment can differ, consider what happens when a level of output $(Y = C + I_r + G)$ is produced that exceeds aggregate demand $(E = C + I + G)$. In this case

$$Y > E$$
$$C + I_r + G > C + I + G \tag{5.7}$$
$$I_r > I$$

where $I_r - I$ is the *unintended inventory accumulation.* The amount by which output exceeds aggregate demand $(I_r - I)$ will be unsold output over and above the amount of inventory investment that the firm desired. This excess is unintended inventory accumulation.

In the reverse situation, in which aggregate demand exceeds output, we have

$$E > Y$$
$$C + I + G > C + I_r + G \tag{5.8}$$
$$I > I_r$$

---

[9] Here, to keep the discussion simple, we are ignoring residential construction investment. In Chapter 6 the investment concept will be broadened.

where $I - I_r$ is the *unintended inventory shortfall*. Demand is greater than output, and firms sell more than was planned. Inventories end up at less than the desired level. The equilibrium point ($I = I_r$) is a level of production that, after all sales are made, leaves inventory investment at just the level desired by firms. As can be seen from equation (5.7) or (5.8), this is the level at which output equals aggregate demand and hence is equivalent to the other two ways of expressing the condition for equilibrium in the model.

Looked at from this third way of expressing the condition for equilibrium in the model, it is easy to see the reason why there cannot be an equilibrium at any other point. If, at a given level of output, firms are accumulating undesired inventories or are seeing their inventories depleted, there is a tendency for output to change. If production exceeds demand ($Y > E$), firms are accumulating unwanted inventories ($I_r > I$) and there is a tendency for output to fall as firms cut production to reduce the level of inventories. If, alternatively, demand is outstripping production ($E > Y$), there is an inventory shortfall ($I_r < I$) and a tendency for output to rise as firms try to prevent further falls in inventories. Only when aggregate demand equals output will firms be satisfied with their current level of output. There is neither an unintended inventory buildup nor a shortfall and, therefore, no tendency for output to change. This is what is meant by equilibrium.

5.3 • THE COMPONENTS OF AGGREGATE DEMAND

We have expressed the condition for equilibrium in the simple Keynesian model in terms of the components of aggregate demand. To see the factors that determine the level of income, we need to consider the factors that affect the components of aggregate demand: the determinants of consumption, investment, and government spending. We look at each of these in turn. The determinants of saving and the role of taxes also enter into our discussion.

Consumption   New Concepts

Consumer expenditure is the largest component of aggregate demand, amounting to between 60 and 69 percent of GNP in recent years. Consumption plays a central role in the Keynesian theory of income determination.

Keynes believed that the level of consumer expenditure was a stable function of disposable income, where disposable income (Y_D) in our simple model is national income minus net tax payments ($Y_D = Y - T$).[10] Keynes did not deny that variables other than income affect consumption, but believed that

---

[10]Recall here that T is net taxes; i.e., gross tax payments minus transfer payments. Disposable income ($Y_D = Y - T$) is therefore national income minus gross taxes plus transfer payments.

income was the dominant factor determining consumption. As a first approximation, other influences could be neglected.

The specific form of the consumption–income relationship, termed the **consumption function**, proposed by Keynes was as follows:

$$C = a + bY_D, \quad a > 0, \quad 0 < b < 1 \tag{5.9}$$

Figure 5.3 graphs this relationship. The intercept term a, which is assumed to be positive, is the value of consumption when disposable income equals zero. As such, a can be thought of as a measure of the effect on consumption of variables other than income, variables not explicitly included in this simple model. The parameter b, the slope of the function, gives the increment to consumer expenditure per unit increase in disposable income. In notation we frequently use

$$MPC = b = \frac{\Delta C}{\Delta Y_D} \tag{5.10}$$

where, as in Chapter 3, the differencing symbol, Δ, indicates the change in the variable it precedes. The value of the increment to consumer expenditure per unit increment to income (b) is termed the **marginal propensity to consume** (MPC). The Keynesian assumption is that consumption will

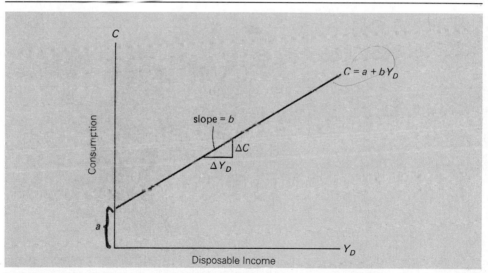

FIGURE 5.3 Keynesian Consumption Function
The consumption function shows the level of consumption (C) corresponding to each level of disposable income (Y_D). The slope of the consumption function ($\Delta C / \Delta Y_D$) is the marginal propensity to consume (b), the increase in consumption per unit increase in disposable income. The intercept for the consumption function (a) is the (positive) level of consumption at a zero level of disposable income.

increase with an increase in disposable income ($b > 0$), but that the increase in consumption will be less than the increase in disposable income ($b < 1$).

From the definition of national income previously discussed,

$$Y \equiv C + S + T \tag{5.3}$$

we can write

$$Y_D \equiv Y - T \equiv C + S \tag{5.11}$$

which shows that disposable income is, by definition, consumption plus saving. Thus a theory of the consumption–income relationship also implicitly determines the saving–income relationship. In the case of the Keynesian theory, we have

$$S = -a + (1 - b)Y_D \tag{5.12}$$

If consumption is a units with Y_D equal to zero, then *at that point*

$$S \equiv Y_D - C = 0 - a$$
$$= -a$$

If a one-unit increase in disposable income leads to an increase of b units in consumption, the remainder of the one-unit increase $(1 - b)$ is the increase in saving:

$$\frac{\Delta S}{\Delta Y_D} = 1 - b \tag{5.13}$$

This increment to saving per unit increase in disposable income $(1 - b)$ is called the **marginal propensity to save** (MPS). The graph of the saving function is shown in Figure 5.4.

Investment

Investment was also a key variable in the Keynesian system. Changes in desired business investment expenditure were one of the major factors that Keynes thought were responsible for changes in income.

As noted previously, Keynes believed that consumption was a stable function of disposable income. This did not imply that the level of consumption expenditures would not vary over time. It did imply that in the absence of other factors that caused income to change, consumption expenditures would not be an important independent source of variability in income. Consumption was primarily *induced* expenditure, by which we mean expenditure that depends directly on the level of income.

To explain the underlying causes of movements in aggregate demand and, hence, income, Keynes looked to the *autonomous* components of aggregate demand. These were the components that were determined, in large part, independently of current income. When these expenditure compo-

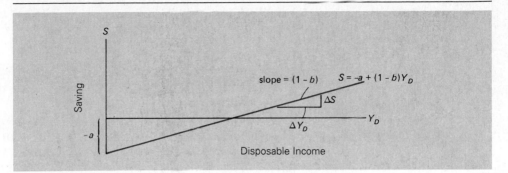

FIGURE 5.4 Keynesian Saving Function
The saving function shows the level of saving (S) corresponding to each level of disposable income (Y_D). The slope of the saving function is the marginal propensity to save ($1 - b$), the increase in saving per unit increase in disposable income. The intercept for the saving function ($-a$) is the (negative) level of saving at a zero level of disposable income.

nents varied, they caused income to vary. Keynes believed that investment was the most highly variable of the autonomous components of aggregate demand. He believed that it was the variability of such investment spending that was primarily responsible for the instability in income.

Table 5.1 contains figures for investment and consumption as percentages of gross national product in selected years. The years shown in the table contrast investment and consumption spending in prosperous years (1929, 1955, 1973, 1979, 1989) with corresponding spending in subsequent

TABLE 5.1 Consumption and Investment as a Percentage of Gross National Product, Selected Years

Year	Investment	Consumption
1929	15.7	74.8
1933	2.5	82.1
1955	17.1	63.5
1958	13.8	64.5
1973	16.1	62.6
1975	12.5	64.0
1979	16.0	62.7
1982	13.1	65.3
1989	11.0	67.1
1991	9.6	68.5

$$GNP = C + I + G.$$

depression or recession years (1933, 1958, 1975, 1982, 1991). Investment spending does appear to be more volatile and is a logical choice as a factor explaining income variability. The question remains: What determines investment?

Keynes suggested two variables as the primary determinants of investment expenditures in the short run: the interest rate and the state of business expectations.

In explaining the relationship between investment and the rate of interest, Keynes's analysis did not differ from the classical view. Again the level of investment is assumed to be inversely related to the level of the interest rate. At higher interest rates there are fewer investment projects that have a prospective return high enough to justify borrowing to finance them. This link will be important in Chapter 6. For now, since we have not explained how the interest rate is determined in the Keynesian model, we neglect this effect of the interest rate on investment. We focus instead on the second factor determining investment, the expected yield on investment projects.

Business managers' expectations about the future profitability of investment projects are a central element in Keynes's analysis of the sources of economic instability. Keynes emphasizes the "uncertain knowledge" upon which expectations of the future must be based. In planning a project that will produce output over 20 or 30 years, to know how profitable the project will be, a manager needs a great deal of knowledge about the future. He needs to know the future demand for the product, which requires knowledge about future consumer tastes and the state of aggregate demand. He needs knowledge about future costs, including money wages, interest rates, and tax rates; a well-grounded forecast of such variables cannot be made for 20 or 30 years into the future.

Nevertheless, investment decisions are made. Keynes felt that rational managers faced with the need to make decisions under such extreme uncertainty formed expectations using the following techniques:

1. They tended to extrapolate past trends into the future, ignoring possible future changes, unless there was specific information about a prospective change.
2. "Knowing that our own individual judgment is worthless, we endeavor to fall back on the judgment of the rest of the world which is perhaps better informed. That is, we endeavor to conform with the behavior of the majority or the average. The psychology of a society of individuals each of whom is endeavoring to copy the others leads to what we may strictly term a *conventional* judgment."[11]

---

[11]John M. Keynes, "The General Theory of Employment," *Quarterly Journal of Economics* (February 1937), p. 214.

Keynes believed that an expectation formed in this manner would have the following property.

> In particular, being based on so flimsy a foundation, it is subject to sudden and violent changes. The practice of calmness and immobility, of certainty and security, suddenly breaks down. New fears and hopes will, without warning, take charge of human conduct. The forces of disillusion may suddenly impose a new conventional basis of valuation. All these pretty, polite techniques, made for a well-panelled board room, are liable to collapse. At all times the vague panic fears and equally vague and unreasoned hopes are not really lulled, and lie but a little way below the surface.[12]

To summarize, expectations of the future profitability of investment projects rested on a very precarious base of knowledge, and Keynes felt that such expectations could shift frequently, at times drastically, in response to new information and events. Consequently, investment demand was unstable. Investment expenditure is the component of autonomous expenditures that Keynes believed to be responsible for instability in the behavior of income.

Government Spending and Taxes

The level of government spending (G) is a second element of autonomous expenditures. Government spending is assumed to be controlled by the policymaker and therefore does not depend directly on the level of income.

We assume that the level of tax receipts (T) is also controlled by the policymaker and is a policy variable. A more realistic assumption is that the policymaker sets the tax rate and tax receipts vary with income. This would complicate our calculations somewhat but would not change the essential conclusions (more complex tax structures are discussed in Chapter 18, where we consider fiscal policy in more detail).

5.4 • DETERMINING EQUILIBRIUM INCOME

We now have all the elements needed to determine the level of equilibrium income (output).[13] The first form of the condition for an equilibrium level of income was

$$Y = C + I + G \tag{5.2}$$

---

[12] Ibid., 214–15.

[13] Recall that national output and income are identical under the assumptions we have made. These terms are used interchangeably in our discussion.

The level of equilibrium income (Y) is the *endogenous* variable to be determined. The *autonomous* expenditure terms I and G are given, as is the level of T; these are the *exogenous* variables determined by factors outside the model. Consumption is, for the most part, *induced* expenditure determined *endogenously* by the consumption function

$$C = a + bY_D = a + bY - bT \tag{5.9}$$

where the second equality uses the definition of disposable income ($Y_D \equiv Y - T$).

Substituting the equation for consumption given by (5.9) into the equilibrium condition (5.2), we can solve for $\overline{Y}$, the equilibrium level of income, as follows:

$$Y = C + I + G$$
$$Y = a + bY - bT + I + G$$
$$Y - bY = a - bT + I + G$$
$$Y(1 - b) = a - bT + I + G$$
$$\overline{Y} = \frac{1}{1 - b}(a - bT + I + G) \tag{5.14}$$

In Figure 5.5 the determination of equilibrium income is depicted graphically. The level of income is measured along the horizontal axis, and the components of aggregate demand are measured along the vertical axis. The 45° line is drawn to split the positive quadrant of the graph. All points along this line have the property that the value of the variable measured on the vertical axis is equal to that of the variable measured on the horizontal axis. The consumption function ($C = a + bY_D$) is shown on the graph, and we have also plotted the ($C + I + G$) or aggregate demand (E) schedule, which is obtained by adding the autonomous expenditure components, investment and government spending, to consumption spending at each level of income. Since the autonomous expenditure components (I, G) do not depend directly on income, the ($C + I + G$) schedule lies above the consumption function by a constant amount. Similarly, the line plotting these autonomous expenditure components alone, the $I + G$ line, is horizontal, reflecting the fact that their level does not depend on Y. The final line, marked $S + T$ in the graph, plots the value of saving plus taxes. This schedule slopes upward because saving varies positively with income.

The equilibrium level of income is shown at the point where the ($C + I + G$) schedule crosses the 45° line, and aggregate demand is therefore equal to income (Y). At this point it must also be true that the ($S + T$) schedule crosses the ($I + G$) schedule. This reflects the equivalence of our various expressions of the equilibrium condition, as discussed in section 5.2. That this must be the case in the graph can be seen as follows. The distance between

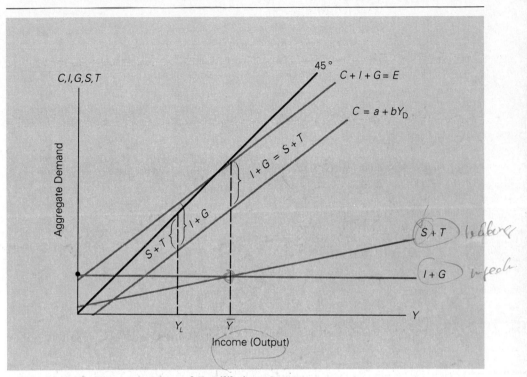

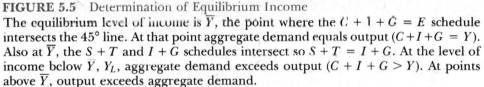

FIGURE 5.5 Determination of Equilibrium Income
The equilibrium level of income is $\overline{Y}$, the point where the $C + I + G = E$ schedule intersects the 45° line. At that point aggregate demand equals output ($C+I+G = Y$). Also at $\overline{Y}$, the $S + T$ and $I + G$ schedules intersect so $S + T = I + G$. At the level of income below Y, Y_L, aggregate demand exceeds output ($C + I + G > Y$). At points above $\overline{Y}$, output exceeds aggregate demand.

the consumption schedule and the 45° line is always ($S + T$), by definition ($Y \equiv C + S + T$) The distance between the consumption schedule and the ($C + I + G$) line is always equal to ($I + G$). Where the ($C + I + G$) schedule hits the 45° line, these two distances, ($S + T$) and ($I + G$), are equated. Also note that at $\overline{Y}$, actual investment is just equal to desired investment ($C + I + G = Y \equiv C + I_r + G$; therefore, $I = I_r$).

The understanding of the properties of an equilibrium level of income is aided by considering why other points on the graph are not points of equilibrium. Consider a level of income below $\overline{Y}$, for example, the point marked Y_L in Figure 5.5. A level of income equal to Y_L will generate consumption as shown along the consumption function. When this level of consumption is added to the autonomous expenditures ($I + G$), the total aggregate demand exceeds income; the $(C + I + G)$ schedule is above the 45° line. Equivalently, at this point $I + G$ is greater than $S + T$, as can be seen from the graph. It also follows that with demand outstripping production, desired investment will exceed actual investment at points such as $Y_L (C + I + G > Y \equiv C + I_r + G$; therefore, $I > I_r$). There will be an unintended inventory shortfall at such points below $\overline{Y}$ and therefore a tendency for output to rise.

Analogously, at levels of income above $\overline{Y}$ in Figure 5.5, output will exceed demand (the 45° line is above the $C + I + G$ schedule), unintended inventory investment will be taking place ($Y \equiv C + I_r + G > C + I + G$; therefore, $I_r > I$), and there will be a tendency for output to fall. It is only at $\overline{Y}$ that output is equal to aggregate demand; there is no unintended inventory shortfall or accumulation and, consequently, no tendency for output to change.

Returning to our expression for equilibrium income, equation (5.14), we can rewrite this equation in a form that gives the essence of Keynes's view of the income determination process. Our expression for equilibrium consists of two parts:

$$\overline{Y} = \frac{1}{1 - b}(a - bT + I + G)$$

(5.15)

$$\overline{Y} = \left(\begin{array}{c} \text{autonomous expenditure} \\ \text{multiplier} \end{array} \right) \times \left(\begin{array}{c} \text{autonomous} \\ \text{expenditures} \end{array} \right)$$

The first term, $1/(1 - b)$, is what we will refer to as the **autonomous expenditure multiplier.** Note that b is the fraction of any increment to disposable income that will go to consumption, what we termed the marginal propensity to consume (MPC). The term $1/(1 - b)$ or $1/(1 - \text{MPC})$ is then 1 divided by a fraction and, hence, some number greater than 1. Some examples are as follows:

$$b = 0.5: \quad \frac{1}{1 - b} = \frac{1}{1 - 0.5} = \frac{1}{0.5} = 2$$

$$b = 0.8: \quad \frac{1}{1 - b} = \frac{1}{1 - 0.8} = \frac{1}{0.2} = 5$$

$$b = 0.9: \quad \frac{1}{1 - b} = \frac{1}{1 - 0.9} = \frac{1}{0.1} = 10$$

We call this term the autonomous expenditure multiplier because every dollar of autonomous expenditure is multiplied by this factor to get its contribution to the level of equilibrium income.

The second term in the expression is the level of autonomous expenditures. We have already discussed two elements of autonomous expenditures, investment (I) and government spending (G). The first two terms (a and $-bT$) require a few words of explanation. These terms measure the autonomous component of consumption expenditures (a) and the autonomous effect of tax collections on aggregate demand $(-bT)$, which also works through consumption. Consumption is, for the most part, induced expenditures, as explained previously. The two terms (a and $-bT$), however, affect the amount of consumption *for a given level of income* (Y). In terms of Figure 5.5, they determine the height of the consumption function. Like G and I, they affect the amount of aggregate demand for a given level of income rather than being themselves directly determined by income. They are thus appropriately included as autonomous factors affecting aggregate demand.

Keynes's theory in its simplest form can be stated as follows. Since consumption is a stable function of income, the marginal propensity to consume is stable. Changes in income come primarily from changes in the autonomous components of aggregate demand, especially from changes in the unstable investment component. A given change in an autonomous component of aggregate demand causes a larger change in equilibrium income due to the multiplier, for reasons we explain later. Equation (5.15) makes clear that in the absence of government policies to stabilize the economy, income will be unstable because of the instability of investment. From equation (5.15) one can also see that by appropriate changes in government spending (G) and taxes (T), the government could counteract the effects of shifts in investment. Appropriate changes in G and T could keep the sum of the terms in parentheses (autonomous expenditures) constant even in the face of undesirable changes in the I term. This is the basis for the interventionist policy conclusions that Keynes reached.

Before giving examples of such stabilization policies, we consider the working of the autonomous expenditure multiplier in more detail.

5.5 • CHANGES IN EQUILIBRIUM INCOME

Consider the effect on equilibrium income of a change in autonomous investment demand. We assume that the other determinants of autonomous expenditures, the other items in parentheses in equation (5.15), are fixed. We solve for the change in equilibrium income from equation (5.15) as follows:

$$\Delta \overline{Y} = \frac{1}{1-b}\Delta I \qquad (5.16)$$

or

$$\frac{\Delta \overline{Y}}{\Delta I} = \frac{1}{1-b} \qquad (5.17)$$

multiplier

A one-unit change in investment causes a change in income of $1/(1-b)$ units. If b is 0.8, for example, Y changes by five units for each one-unit change in investment. Why does income change by a multiple of the change in investment, and why by the precise amount $1/(1-b)$?

One means of explaining the process behind the multiplier is the analogy of the "ripple effect" of a stone dropped in a pond. There is the initial effect as the stone disturbs the water. Added to this is the effect on the rest of the water surface as the disturbance by the water displaced by the stone spreads out to the adjoining water, with intensity that diminishes with the distance from the initial point of impact. The investment change is the initial disturbance; let us assume this equals 100 units. As some firms experience increased demand as a result of this increased investment, their output increases. In consequence, their payments to factors of production (wages, rents, interest, dividends) increase. To the households this is an increase in income and, since taxes are fixed, an equal increase in disposable income. Consumption will then increase, although by less than the increase in income. This is the beginning of the indirect effects of the shock. With ΔI equal to 100 as assumed, if the MPC were 0.8, for example, there would now be an additional 80 units of consumer demand.

The process does not stop here, since this 80 units of new consumer expenditure, with the resulting increase in production, generates a second-round increase in income for some households of 80 units. There will be a further increase in consumer demand (64 units if the MPC is 0.8). The reason then for income rising by more than the autonomous rise in investment is that the rise in investment leads to induced increases in consumer demand as income increases.

Why is the increase in income per dollar increase in investment just equal to $1/(1 - b)$? With the other elements of autonomous expenditures fixed, we can write the change in equilibrium income as investment varies as

$$\Delta Y = \Delta I + \Delta C \tag{5.18}$$

To restore the equality of income and aggregate demand, equilibrium income must rise by an amount equal to the increase in investment (ΔI) plus the income-induced increase in consumer demand. Rearranging terms in equation (5.18), we have

$$\Delta Y - \Delta C = \Delta I$$

or[14]

$$\Delta S = \Delta I \tag{5.19}$$

Condition (5.19) can also be seen to follow from our second way of expressing the condition for equilibrium income:

$$S + T = I + G \tag{5.5}$$

---

[14]Note that tax collections are fixed, so $\Delta Y = \Delta Y_D$. Thus $\Delta Y = \Delta Y_D \equiv \Delta C + \Delta S$ and, therefore, $\Delta Y - \Delta C = \Delta S$.

With T and G fixed, for equilibrium S must rise by the amount of the increase in I, as required by equation (5.19). To restore equilibrium, income must rise by enough to generate new saving equal to the new investment. Put differently, the increase in income must be such that after the induced consumption demand is satisfied, sufficient new output will be left to satisfy the increased investment demand.

Since ΔS is equal to $(1 - b)\,\Delta Y$, we have, from equation (5.19),

$$(1 - b)\Delta Y = \Delta I$$

$$\frac{\Delta \overline{Y}}{\Delta I} = \frac{1}{1 - b} = \frac{1}{1 - \text{MPC}} = \frac{1}{\text{MPS}} \tag{5.20}$$

If, for example, b equals 0.8, the marginal propensity to save (MPS = $1 - b$) is equal to 0.2. Each dollar increase in income will generate 20 cents worth of new saving and a five-dollar increase in income will be required to generate the one dollar of new saving to balance a one-dollar increase in investment. The value of the multiplier in this case is 5.

The effect of an increase in autonomous investment is illustrated in Figure 5.6. Initially, with investment at I_0 and government spending and taxes at G_0 and T_0, equilibrium income is at $\overline{Y}_0$. Now let investment increase to the higher level I_1. The aggregate demand (E) schedule shifts up by the amount ($\Delta I = I_1 - I_0$), from $E_0(= C + I_0 + G_0)$ to $E_1(= C + I_1 + G_0)$. The $(I + G)$ schedule shifts up by the same amount. Equilibrium is restored at $\overline{Y}_1$, where income is now equal to the higher value of aggregate demand. Note that the increase in income is equal to the initial increase in investment plus an induced increase in consumption (ΔC), as shown in the graph. Note also that at the new equilibrium, saving has increased by the same amount as investment ($\Delta S = \Delta I$).

The multiplier concept is central to Keynes's theory because it explains how shifts in investment caused by changes in business expectations set off a process that causes not only investment but consumption to vary. The multiplier shows how shocks to one sector are transmitted throughout the economy. Keynes's theory also implies that other components of autonomous expenditure affect the overall level of equilibrium income. The effect on equilibrium income of a change in each of the two policy-controlled elements of autonomous expenditures, government spending and taxes, can be calculated from equation (5.15).

We proceed just as we did in considering the effects of a change in investment and let one component of autonomous expenditures change while each of the others is held constant. For a change in government spending (G), we have

$$\Delta \overline{Y} = \frac{1}{1 - b}\Delta G$$

$$\frac{\Delta \overline{Y}}{\Delta G} = \frac{1}{1 - b} \tag{5.21}$$

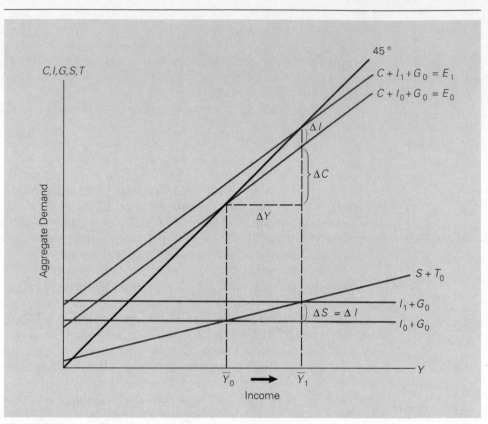

FIGURE 5.6 Effect on Equilibrium Income of an Increase in Autonomous Investment

An increase in autonomous investment from I_0 to I_1 shifts the aggregate demand schedule upward from $C + I_0 + G_0 = E_0$ to $C + I_1 + G_0 = E_1$. The $I + G$ schedule shifts up from $I_0 + G_0$ to $I_1 + G_0$. Equilibrium income rises from $\overline{Y}_0$ to $\overline{Y}_1$. The increase in income is equal to the initial increase in investment (ΔI) plus an income-induced increase in consumption (ΔC) as we move along the consumption function from $\overline{Y}_0$ to $\overline{Y}_1$. Note also that at $\overline{Y}_1$ saving has increased by the same amount as investment ($\Delta S = \Delta I$).

For a change in taxes, we have

$$\Delta \overline{Y} = \frac{1}{1-b}(-b)\Delta T$$

$$\frac{\Delta \overline{Y}}{\Delta T} = \frac{-b}{1-b}$$

(5.22)

For government spending we see that a one-dollar increase has just the same effect as a one-dollar increase in investment. Both are one-dollar increases in autonomous expenditures. The multiplier process, whereby the initial increase in income generates induced increases in consumption, is the same for an increase in government spending as for investment. In terms of Figure 5.6, an increase in government spending of ΔG units would shift up the $(C + I + G)$ schedule by the same amount as an equal increase in investment.

From the expression given in equation (5.22), we see that the effect of an increase in taxes is in the opposite direction to those of increased government spending or investment. A tax increase lowers the level of disposable income $(Y - T)$ for any level of national income (Y). This shifts the aggregate demand schedule down since it reduces consumption spending *for any level of national income*. The effect on equilibrium income from a tax increase is illustrated in Figure 5.7. We assume that taxes rise by ΔT from T_0 to T_1. The aggregate demand schedule shifts from $(C + I + G)_0$ down to $(C + I + G)_1$. This is the consequence of the downward shift in the consumption function shown to result from the rise in taxes from T_0 to T_1. Equilibrium income falls from $\overline{Y}_0$ to $\overline{Y}_1$.

Notice that the aggregate demand schedule shifts down by $(-b\,\Delta T)$, that is, by only a fraction (b) of the increase in taxes. This is because at a given level of income, a one-dollar increase in taxes reduces disposable income by one dollar but lowers the consumption component of aggregate demand by only b dollars. The rest of the one-dollar decline in disposable income is absorbed by a fall of $(1 - b)$ dollars in saving. Unlike changes in government expenditures and investment, which have a dollar-for-dollar effect on autonomous aggregate demand, a one-dollar change in taxes shifts the aggregate demand schedule by only a fraction $(-b)$ of one dollar. It is this fraction $(-b)$ times the autonomous expenditure multiplier, $1/(1 - b)$, that gives the effect on equilibrium income of a one-dollar change in taxes, $b/(1 \quad b)$.

There is a relationship between the absolute values of tax and government expenditure multipliers, which can be seen in the following examples.

$$b = 0.5: \quad \frac{1}{1 - b} = \frac{1}{1 - 0.5} = 2; \quad \frac{-b}{1 - b} = \frac{-0.5}{1 - 0.5} = -1$$

$$b = 0.8: \quad \frac{1}{1 - b} = \frac{1}{1 - 0.8} = 5; \quad \frac{-b}{1 - b} = \frac{-0.8}{1 - 0.8} = -4$$

$$b = 0.9: \quad \frac{1}{1 - b} = \frac{1}{1 - 0.9} = 10; \quad \frac{-b}{1 - b} = \frac{-0.9}{1 - 0.9} = -9$$

The tax multiplier is always one less in absolute value than the government expenditure multiplier. This fact has an interesting implication for the effects of an increase in government spending accompanied by an equal increase in taxes, a balanced budget increase. To find the effects of such a combination of policy changes, we add the two policy multipliers to get the following

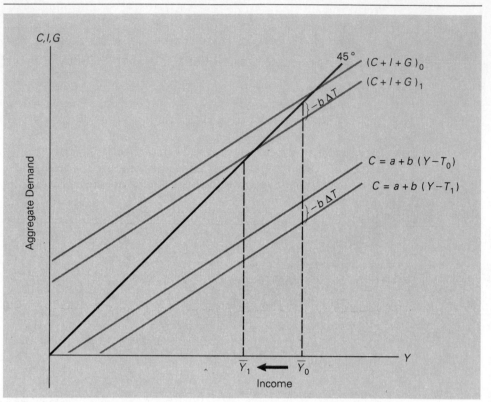

FIGURE 5.7   Effect on Equilibrium Income of an Increase in Taxes
An increase in taxes from T_0 to T_1 shifts the consumption schedule downward from $C = a + b(Y - T_0)$ to $C = a + b(Y - T_1)$. The aggregate demand schedule also shifts downward, from $(C + I + G)_0$ to $(C + I + G)_1$. Equilibrium income falls from $\overline{Y}_0$ to $\overline{Y}_1$.

expression:

$$\frac{\Delta \overline{Y}}{\Delta G} + \frac{\Delta \overline{Y}}{\Delta T} = \frac{1}{1 - b} + \frac{-b}{1 - b} = \frac{1 - b}{1 - b} = 1$$

A one-dollar increase in government spending financed by a one-dollar increase in taxes increases equilibrium income by just one dollar. This result, termed the *balanced-budget multiplier*, reflects the fact that tax changes have a smaller per-dollar impact on equilibrium income than do spending changes. The value of 1 for the multiplier results because the tax multiplier is one less in absolute value than the spending multiplier. The latter result does not carry through in many more complex models, but the result that tax changes affect aggregate demand by less per dollar than changes in government spending is quite general.

5.6 · FISCAL STABILIZATION POLICY

Since the level of equilibrium income is affected by changes in government spending and taxes, these fiscal policy instruments can be varied to offset the effects of undesirable shifts in private investment demand. In other words, the government can use these fiscal policy instruments to stabilize the total of autonomous expenditures and, therefore, equilibrium income, even if the investment component of autonomous expenditures is unstable.

An example of fiscal stabilization policy is illustrated in Figure 5.8. The economy is assumed to be in equilibrium at a full-employment (potential) level $\overline{Y}_F$, with aggregate demand at E_F equal to $(C + I_0 + G_0)$. We assume that from this point autonomous investment declines from I_0 to I_1, as a result of

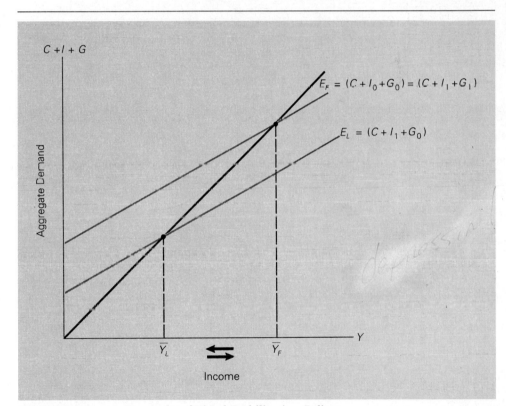

FIGURE 5.8 An Example of Fiscal Stabilization Policy

A decline in autonomous investment expenditure from I_0 to I_1 shifts the aggregate demand schedule downward from $E_F = (C + I_0 + G_0)$ to $E_L = (C + I_1 + G_0)$. A compensating increase in government spending from G_0 to G_1 shifts the aggregate demand schedule back to $C + I_1 + G_1 = E_F = C + I_0 + G_0$. Equilibrium income is again at $\overline{Y}_F$.

an unfavorable change in business expectations. In the absence of a policy action, aggregate demand declines to E_L, equal to $(C + I_1 + G_0)$. The new level of equilibrium income is below full employment at $\overline{Y}_L$.

Within the model, an appropriate fiscal policy response would be to increase government spending by an amount sufficient to restore equilibrium at $\overline{Y}_F$. In the graph, a rise in government spending from G_0 to G_1 shifts the aggregate demand curve back up to E_F, now equal to $(C + I_1 + G_1)$. Alternatively, a tax cut could be used to restore the initial level of aggregate

PERSPECTIVES

5.1

Fiscal Policy in Practice

An example of fiscal stabilization policy within the Keynesian framework is the Kennedy–Johnson tax cut of 1964. There had been a serious recession in 1958, during which the unemployment rate rose to 6.8 percent. Recovery from this recession was short-lived. The economy sank back into a recession in 1960, which many believe cost Richard Nixon the presidency that year in his first try for the office. The Kennedy administration came into office in 1961 with a program to "get the economy moving again"—a program called "the new economics"—which meant the application of Keynesian theory to macroeconomic policy. The Kennedy administration proposed a large cut in both personal and business taxes.

Kennedy's economic advisers believed that aggregate demand was too low for the economy to operate at the full-employment or potential level. The unemployment rate in 1961, for example, was 6.7 percent, compared to the 4.0 percent then considered to be "full" employment. In terms of Figure 5.8, the economy in the early 1960s was at such a point at $\overline{Y}_L$. The tax cut was intended to shift the aggregate demand schedule upward

to move the economy to potential output ($\overline{Y}_F$ in Figure 5.8).

The Kennedy administration could not move the tax cut through Congress, mainly because congressional leaders worried over the budget deficit it would create. After Kennedy's assassination, President Lyndon Johnson persuaded Congress to enact the tax cut of 20 percent for persons and 10 percent for businesses early in 1964. Output and employment then grew rapidly, with the unemployment rate falling to 4.8 percent by the first half of 1965, and to 3.8 percent in 1966. This was the high point of influence for the Keynesian theory of fiscal policy.

As U.S. involvement in the Vietnam war grew in the 1966–68 period, government spending on defense increased rapidly. This increase in aggregate demand, with the economy already at potential output, generated inflationary pressures. In terms of Figure 5.8, the aggregate demand schedule was being pushed above the level consistent with potential output (Y_F). The 1960s demonstrated that, in practice, fiscal policy could destabilize as well as stabilize the economy.

demand. Since the tax multiplier is smaller, the appropriate tax cut would be somewhat larger than the required spending increase, but in theory this poses no particular problem.

Read Perspectives 5.1.

5.7 • CONCLUSION

The model in this chapter is incomplete. We need to consider money and interest rates and to explain the behavior of prices and wages before we complete our analysis of the Keynesian system. Several features of the Keynesian system are highlighted by considering this simple model, and these will carry over to more complex models.

The simple model clearly illustrates the role of aggregate demand in determining income in the Keynesian system. As we will see later, it *overstates* the role of aggregate demand. Still a key feature of all the Keynesian models we consider is that demand plays a crucial role in income determination. In the Keynesian view, changes in the autonomous elements of aggregate demand, especially investment demand, are key factors causing changes in the equilibrium level of income. By means of the multiplier process, such changes in autonomous expenditures also induce changes in consumption spending. Inadequate investment, and as a consequence a low level of aggregate demand, was the Keynesian explanation for massive unemployment in the Depression of the 1930s.

The model also illustrates the role of fiscal stabilization policy in managing aggregate demand to cushion equilibrium output from shifts in the unstable investment demand. Although the simple expressions we derive for the government expenditure and tax multipliers require modification, the principles behind them remain intact.

Review Questions and Problems

1. Explain how the origins of the Keynesian revolution can be found in the problem of unemployment.

2. Interpret each of the three ways of writing the condition for equilibrium income in the simple Keynesian model [equations (5.2), (5.5), (5.6)]. Explain why the three ways of writing the equilibrium condition are equivalent.

3. Carefully explain the difference between realized and desired investment. In which component of investment does the discrepancy between the two totals occur?

4. Explain Keynes's theory of how expectations affect investment demand. How is this theory related to Keynes's view that aggregate demand would be unstable in the absence of government stabilization policies?

5. Consider the numbers in Table 5.1 giving consumption as a percentage of income in prosperous years (1929, 1955, 1973, 1979, 1989) compared to recession years (1933, 1958, 1975, 1982, 1991). Notice that in each case consumption is higher as a percentage of income in the recession years. Is this what you would predict on the basis of Keynes's consumption function given by equation (5.9)? Explain.

6. In the simple Keynesian model, an increase of one dollar in autonomous expenditure will cause equilibrium income to increase by a multiple of this one-dollar increase. Explain the process by which this happens.

7. Explain carefully why the tax multiplier $[\Delta Y/\Delta T = -b/(1 - b)]$ is negative and why it is smaller in absolute value than the government expenditure multiplier $[\Delta Y/\Delta G = 1/(1 - b)]$.

✱ 8. Suppose that for a particular economy, for some time period, investment was equal to 100, government expenditure was equal to 75, net taxes were fixed at 100, and consumption (C) was given by the consumption function

$$C = 25 + 0.8Y_D$$

where Y_D is disposable income and Y is GNP.

    a. What is the level of equilibrium income (Y)?

    b. What is the value of the government expenditure multiplier $(\Delta Y/\Delta G)$? the tax multiplier $(\Delta Y/\Delta T)$?

    c. Suppose that investment declined by 40 units to a level of 60. What will be the new level of equilibrium income?

✱9. Suppose that initially equilibrium income was 200 units and that this was also the full-employment level of income. Assume that the consumption function is

$$C = 25 + 0.8Y_D$$

and that, from this initial equilibrium level, we now have a decline in investment of 8 units. What will be the new equilibrium level of income? What increase in government spending would be required to restore income to the initial level of 200? Alternatively, what reduction in tax collections would be sufficient to restore an income level of 200?

✱ 10. Suppose that government spending was increased by 10 units and that this increase was financed by a 10-unit increase in taxes. Would equilibrium income change or remain the same as a result of these two policy actions? If equilibrium income changed, in which direction would it move, and by how much?

11. Suppose that, instead of a fixed level of taxes, we had an income tax so that

$$T = t_1 Y$$

where t_1 was the income tax rate. Following the procedure of section 5.4, derive an expression for equilibrium income ($\bar{Y}$) analogous to (5.14) for this case where the level of tax collections depends on income. What is the expression equivalent to the autonomous expenditure multiplier $[1/(1 - b)]$ for this case of an income tax?

12. In question 8, assume that, beginning from the initial equilibrium position (investment equal to 100, government expenditure equal to 75, and net taxes fixed at 100), there was an autonomous fall in consumption and increase in saving such that the consumption function shifted from

$$C = 25 + 0.8Y_D$$

to

$$C = 5 + 0.8Y_D$$

a. Find the change in equilibrium income resulting from this autonomous increase in saving.

b. Calculate the actual level of saving and before and after the shift in the consumption and, therefore, saving function. How do you explain this result?

Selected Readings

Ackley, Gardner, *Macroeconomics: Theory and Policy.* New York: Macmillan, 1978, Chaps. 6 and 7.

Branson, William, *Macroeconomic Theory and Policy,* 3rd ed. New York: Harper & Row, 1989, Chap. 3.

Hutchison, T. W., *A Review of Economic Doctrines.* London: Oxford University Press, 1953, Chap. 24.

Keynes, John M., "The General Theory of Employment," *Quarterly Journal of Economics* (February 1937), pp. 209–23.

Klein, Lawrence, *The Keynesian Revolution,* 2nd ed. New York: Macmillan, 1966.

Surrey, M. V. C., *Macroeconomic Themes.* London: Oxford University Press, 1976, Chap. 1: readings pertaining to the material in the present chapter and the following three chapters on the Keynesian system.

Tobin, James, *The New Economics, One Decade Older.* Princeton, N.J.: Princeton University Press, 1974.

Appendix
Exports and Imports in the Simple Keynesian Model

Here we consider the effects of introducing exports and imports into the simple Keynesian model. The focus is on the roles of imports and exports in determining equilibrium income. We will also see that the expression for the autonomous expenditure multiplier changes when we allow for the fact that consumption includes purchases of imports as well as domestic products.

Recall from Chapter 2 that GNP or GDP (Y) consists of consumption, investment, and government spending *plus* net exports. Net exports are exports minus imports. The condition for equilibrium output in the *open* economy (including exports and imports) is then

$$Y = E = C + I + G + X - Z \qquad (A.5.1)$$

Compared to (5.2), the condition for equilibrium in the *closed* economy, we have added exports (X) to aggregate demand and subtracted imports (Z). Exports are the foreign demand for domestic output and therefore belong in aggregate demand. Also, since imports are included in C, I, and G but are *not* demands for domestic goods, we must subtract them out of aggregate demand.

To find an expression for equilibrium GNP in the open economy model, we follow the same procedure as we did for the closed economy case; we take investment and government spending as exogenous—as autonomous expenditure components. Consumption is given by the consumption function

$$C = a + bY \qquad (A.5.2)$$

where since they play no essential role in our discussion here, we have left out taxes and therefore do not need to distinguish between GNP(Y) and disposable income ($Y_D = Y - T$). To compute equilibrium output for the open economy case, we need to specify the determinants of imports and exports.

To simplify our analysis, we assume that imports consist solely of consumption goods. The demand for imports is assumed to depend on income and to have an autonomous component.

$$Z = u + vY \qquad u > 0, \quad 0 < v < 1 \qquad (A.5.3)$$

The parameter u represents the autonomous component of imports. The parameter v is the marginal propensity to import, the increase in import demand per unit increase in GNP, a concept analogous to the marginal propensity to consume (b) in (A.5.2).[1]

---

[1] Note that because consumption includes imports, b is the marginal propensity to consume *both* domestic and imported goods. Since v is the marginal propensity to import (consumption goods), $b - v$ is the marginal propensity to consume domestic goods.

The demand for U.S. exports will be a part of the *foreign* demand for imports. The foreign demand for imports will depend on the level of *foreign* income, being determined by an import demand function analogous to equation (A.5.3). From the point of view of this country, foreign income and, hence, the demand for our exports are considered exogenous.

Additional variables that one would surely expect to influence both U.S. demand for imports and foreign demand of U.S. exports are the relative price levels in the two countries and the level of the exchange rate. These variables will determine the relative costs of the two countries' products to citizens of either country. Note that for now we are assuming that price levels and the exchange rate are fixed. The effects on imports and exports of changes in the domestic price level or exchange rate are examined later.

With imports given by equation (A.5.3) and exports assumed to be exogenous, we can compute equilibrium income from equation (A.5.1), as follows:

$$Y = C + I + G + X - Z \tag{A.5.1}$$

$$= \overbrace{a + bY}^{C} + I + G + X \overbrace{-u - vY}^{-Z}$$

$$Y - bY + vY = a + I + G + X - u$$

$$(1 - b + v)Y = a + I + G + X - u$$

$$\overline{Y} = \frac{1}{1 - b + v}(a + I + G + X - u) \tag{A.5.4}$$

One way to examine the effects of allowing for foreign trade in the model is to compare equation (A.5.4) with the equivalent expression for equilibrium income from the closed economy model (5.14). This expression, omitting the tax variable (T), can be written as

$$\overline{Y} = \frac{1}{1 - b}(a + I + G) \tag{A.5.5}$$

In both equations (A.5.4) and (A.5.5) equilibrium income is expressed as the product of two terms (as explained in the chapter), the autonomous expenditure multiplier and the level of autonomous expenditures. Consider how each of these is changed by adding imports and exports to the model.

Take first the autonomous expenditure multiplier, $1/(1-b+v)$ in equation (A.5.4) as opposed to $1/(1-b)$ in equation (A.5.5) for the closed economy model. Since v, the marginal propensity to import, is greater than zero, the multiplier in (A.5.4), $1/(1 - b + v)$, will be *smaller* than the multiplier in (A.5.5), $1/(1 - b)$. To give an example, if $b = 0.8$ and $v = 0.3$, we would then have

$$\frac{1}{1 - b} = \frac{1}{1 - 0.8} = \frac{1}{0.2} = 5$$

and

$$\frac{1}{1 - b + v} = \frac{1}{1 - 0.8 + 0.3} = \frac{1}{0.5} = 2$$

From these expressions it can be seen that the more open an economy is to foreign trade (the higher is v), the lower will be the autonomous expenditure multiplier.

The autonomous expenditure multiplier gives the change in equilibrium income per unit change in autonomous expenditures. It follows, therefore, that the more open an economy is (the higher v), the smaller will be the response of income to aggregate demand shocks such as changes in government spending or autonomous changes in investment demand. The decline in the value of the autonomous expenditure multiplier with a rise in v can be explained with reference to our previous discussion of the multiplier process. A change in autonomous expenditures—a change in government spending, for example—will have a direct effect on income and an induced effect on consumption with a further effect on income. The higher the value of v, the larger the proportion of this induced effect on consumption that will be a change in demand for *foreign*, not domestic, consumer goods. Consequently, the induced effect on demand for domestic goods and hence, on domestic income will be smaller.[2] The increase in imports per unit of income constitutes an additional *leakage* from the circular flow of (domestic) income at each round of the multiplier process and reduces the value of the autonomous expenditure multiplier.

Now consider the second term in the expression for equilibrium income in the open economy case [equation (A.5.4)], the level of autonomous expenditures. In addition to the elements for a closed economy ($a + I + G$), autonomous expenditures for the open economy include the level of exports and the autonomous component of imports. Recall that autonomous components of aggregate demand are those that are not directly determined by income. Rather, shifts in the components of autonomous expenditures affect the level of aggregate demand *for a given level of income* and result in changes in equilibrium income. Thus changes in the level of exports and autonomous changes in import demand are additional shocks that will change equilibrium income.

From equation (A.5.4) we can compute the multiplier effects of changes in X and u.

---

[2]Recall from footnote 1 that $b - v$ is the marginal propensity to consume domestic goods. A higher v (given b) therefore means a lower MPC for domestic goods and a lower value for the multiplier.

$$\frac{\Delta \overline{Y}}{\Delta X} = \frac{1}{1 - b + v} \tag{A.5.6}$$

$$\frac{\Delta \overline{Y}}{\Delta u} = \frac{-1}{1 - b + v} \tag{A.5.7}$$

An increase in the demand for our exports is an increase in aggregate demand for domestically produced output and will increase equilibrium income just as would an increase in government spending or an autonomous increase in investment.[3]

In contrast, an autonomous increase in import demand, an increase in u, is seen to cause a decline in equilibrium income. An autonomous increase in import demand represents a shift from demand for domestic goods to demand for foreign goods. For example, because of the large rise in gasoline prices, U.S. consumers shifted demand from domestic to (smaller) foreign automobiles. As such, the autonomous increase in import demand is a *decline* in demand for domestic output and causes equilibrium income to decline.

To summarize, an increase in the demand for our exports has an expansionary effect on equilibrium income, whereas an autonomous increase in imports has a contractionary effect on equilibrium income. Clearly, this should not be interpreted to mean exports are good and imports harmful in their economic effects. Countries import goods that can be more efficiently produced abroad, and trade increases the overall efficiency of the worldwide allocation of resources. The expansionary effect of increases in exports and contractionary effect of increases in imports do, however, explain why at times nations have tried to stimulate the domestic economy by subsidizing exports and restricting the flow of imports.

As in the closed economy case, the open-economy simple Keynesian model is incomplete. We return to international economic relations in Chapter 20.

Review Problem

1. Suppose that we now include taxes in the open-economy model and disposable income ($Y_D = Y - T$) therefore replaces GNP(Y) in the consumption function (A.5.2). Compute the expression for equilibrium income for this version of the open-economy model. Compute an expression for the tax multiplier ($\Delta Y / \Delta T$) in the model.

---

[3] Note that from equation (A.5.4) we can also compute
$$\frac{\Delta \overline{Y}}{\Delta G} = \frac{\Delta \overline{Y}}{\Delta I} = \frac{1}{1 - b + v}$$

6 The Keynesian System (II): Money, Interest, and Income

In Chapter 5 we were able to ignore the interest rate and monetary policy only because we neglected the effect of the interest rate on investment or other components of aggregate demand. Here we explain the role of the interest rate and money in the Keynesian system and construct a model that shows how both the equilibrium interest rate and the equilibrium level of income are jointly determined. In Chapter 7 we use this model to provide a more realistic view of how income depends on aggregate demand and make clear how monetary policy can affect income by means of an effect on aggregate demand. We also see how the results in Chapter 5 concerning fiscal policy are modified by the inclusion of a money market in the model.

6.1 • MONEY IN THE KEYNESIAN SYSTEM $M_d \to r \to Y$

Fundamental to Keynes's theory of money was his view that money affects income by means of an effect on the interest rate. An increase in the money stock, for example, would lower the interest rate, which, in turn, would increase aggregate demand and income. We need to examine two links in the chain of events connecting changes in the money stock and changes in income. The first is the relationship between money and the interest rate. The second is the effect of the interest rate on aggregate demand. In the next two subsections we look at these relationships, beginning with the latter one.

Interest Rates and Aggregate Demand

We have already considered the reasons why business investment demand depends on the interest rate. Briefly, an investment project will be pursued only if its expected profitability exceeds the cost of borrowing to finance the

123

project by an amount sufficient to justify the risks of the project. At a high interest rate (borrowing cost), fewer projects satisfy this criterion.

When considering the possible influences of the interest rate, we also need to consider components of aggregate demand other than business investment. The first of these is residential construction investment. Residential construction is a component of investment in the national income accounts, but the reason such investment will be affected by the level of the interest rate requires further explanation. The value of newly constructed houses enters the GNP accounts as the houses are built. One element of building cost is the cost of short-term borrowing to finance construction of the house. Higher interest rates mean higher costs to the builder and, other things equal, this discourages housing starts. Moreover, an important factor determining the rate of new housing construction is the overall state of demand for houses, existing and newly constructed. Most purchases of houses are financed by long-term borrowing in the mortgage market, and high interest rates include high rates of mortgage interest. High mortgage rates increase the cost of buying a house and reduce the demand for new and existing homes. This reduced demand in the housing market will lower the volume of new residential construction.

Additional components of aggregate demand are not counted as investment by the national income accounts, but would be included in a broader definition of investment and may be affected by interest rate changes. The first of these is consumer expenditures on durable goods. Such expenditures are counted as current-quarter consumption in the national income accounts, but to the consumer the purchase of a car or an appliance such as a refrigerator or television set is a form of investment. Such purchases are often financed by borrowing, especially in the case of new-car purchases. Higher interest rates will raise the cost of such purchases when one includes the financing cost and should lower this component of aggregate demand. Several early studies did not reveal much evidence of an effect of interest rates on consumer durable purchases, but later studies do seem to find such evidence.

A final component of aggregate demand that may be affected by interest rates is a subcomponent of government spending. Government spending in the national income accounts includes state and local government spending for services, consumption goods, and investment goods. In the models constructed here, we take government spending to be exogenously fixed by the policymaker. The actual policymaker would be the federal government, and the appropriate policy variable is federal government expenditures. State and local government spending can more properly be considered to be included with private consumption and investment spending. Much of state and local government investment spending is financed by borrowing through bond issues. High interest rates should, in theory, increase such borrowing costs and discourage this part of state and local government expenditures.

There are, however, many determinants of the level and timing of such state
and local government spending projects, and how important the effect of
interest rates is in practice remains uncertain.

Within the simple model of Chapter 5, the effects on aggregate demand
and equilibrium income as a result of a change in the level of the interest
rate are illustrated in Figure 6.1. Initially, we assume that the economy is in
equilibrium at $\overline{Y}_0$ with aggregate demand at E_0 equal to $(C + I + G)_0$, corresponding to an interest rate of r_0. A decline in the interest rate to r_1 shifts
the aggregate demand curve up to E_1, equal to $(C + I + G)_1$. This shift represents the combined effects of the interest rate on business investment, residential construction investment, consumer expenditures on durable goods,
and state and local government investment spending. Equilibrium income
rises to $\overline{Y}_1$.

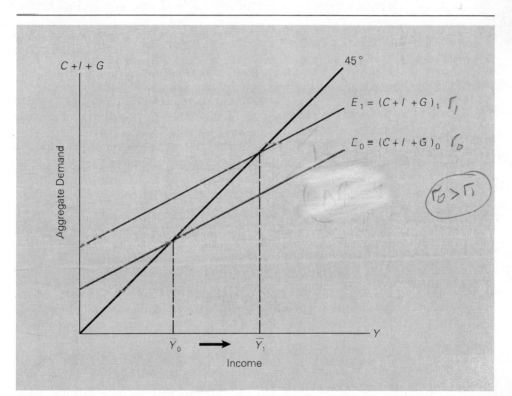

FIGURE 6.1   Effect on Equilibrium Income from a Decline in the Rate of Interest
The initial level of equilibrium income is $\overline{Y}_0$, corresponding to a level of aggregate
demand $E_0 = (C + I + G)_0$ at the initial interest rate r_0. A decline in the interest rate
to r_1 increases aggregate demand to $E_1 = (C + I + G)_1$; equilibrium income rises
to $\overline{Y}_1$.

Clearly, one important factor determining the extent of the change in equilibrium income $(\overline{Y}_1 - \overline{Y}_0)$ that will occur for a given change in the interest rate is the size of the shift in aggregate demand caused by the change in the interest rate. The more sensitive the various components of aggregate demand discussed previously are to interest-rate changes, the larger will be the shift in the aggregate demand function in Figure 6.1 and the greater the effect on equilibrium income. The interest sensitivity of aggregate demand will therefore be important in determining how effective monetary policy, which works through interest rates in the Keynesian system, will be in affecting equilibrium income. In the models we consider we represent the effect of interest rates on aggregate demand as simply an effect on I, the investment component of aggregate demand. The discussion of this section should, however, be kept in mind. To account fully for the effects of interest rates on aggregate demand, we must consider investment as broadly defined to include the other components of aggregate demand discussed here.

Read Perspectives 6.1.

The Keynesian Theory of the Interest Rate

The next relationship we consider is that between the quantity of money and the rate of interest. Keynes believed that the quantity of money played a key role in determining the rate of interest and structured his theory of interest-rate determination in such a way as to highlight that role.

The Keynesian analysis begins with some simplifying assumptions. First, Keynes assumed that all financial assets can be divided into two groups: (1) money and (2) all nonmoney assets, which we term *bonds*.

Money can be thought of as the narrowly defined money stock that in the official U.S. monetary statistics is called M1. M1 consists of currency plus bank accounts on which one can write checks. The "bond" category includes actual bonds plus other long-term financial assets, primarily corporate equities (stock). The *long-term* (bonds) versus *short-term* (money) distinction between the two assets is the crucial one. Additionally, for a long time bonds were the interest-earning asset, and money paid no interest. It is still true that part of the money stock, currency and some checkable accounts, pay no interest, but interest is paid on some components of M1. We first explain the Keynesian theory of interest-rate determination *under the assumption that all money pays no interest.* We then explore the implications for the theory of having interest paid on some parts of the money stock.

Also, to keep things simple, we consider the "bonds" in the model to be homogeneous in all respects. As we did in our discussion of the classical system, we assume that bonds are perpetuities, promises to pay fixed amounts

PERSPECTIVES

6.1

Residential Construction and the Interest Rate

The negative relationship between residential construction investment and the level of interest rates is illustrated in Figure 6.2. Housing starts (new residential construction) in thousands of units at an annual rate (e.g., 1200 = 1.2 million per year) are measured along the left axis and the interest rate (long-term bond rate) is measured, in percentages on the right axis. That housing starts decline markedly when the interest rate rises is evident from the graph. Especially notable is the collapse in the housing market as interest rates rose to record levels in the early 1980s.

Some additional aspects of the relationship between the interest rate and the housing market are discussed in Section 14.2.

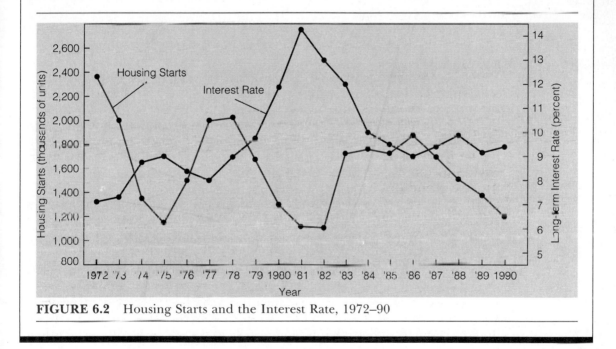

FIGURE 6.2   Housing Starts and the Interest Rate, 1972–90

at fixed intervals throughout the future (e.g., one dollar per year), with no repayment of principal.

Within this simplified framework, Keynes considers the way in which individuals decide how to allocate their financial wealth between the two assets, money (M) and bonds (B). At a point in time, wealth (Wh) is fixed at some level, and since bonds and money are the only stores of wealth, we have

$$\text{Wh} \equiv B + M \tag{6.1}$$

The equilibrium interest rate on bonds is that rate at which the demand for bonds is just equal to the existing stock of bonds. It might seem most natural to develop a theory of the equilibrium interest rate by studying the factors that directly determine the supply of and demand for bonds. Keynes did not proceed in this manner. Note that given equation (6.1), there is only one independent portfolio decision, the split between money and bonds. If for an individual wealth is equal to $1000, the decision to hold $300 in the form of money implicitly determines that bond holdings will be the remainder, $700. In terms of equilibrium positions, this means that if a person is satisfied with the level of his money holdings relative to total wealth, he is by definition [equation (6.1)] satisfied with his bond holdings; he is at the optimal split of his fixed wealth between the two stores of value. To say, for example, that the demand for money exceeds the supply is to say, in the aggregate, that the public is trying to increase the proportion of wealth held in the form of money. This is definitionally the same as to say that the supply of bonds exceeds the demand; the public is trying to reduce the proportion of wealth held as bonds.

Consequently, there are two equally correct ways to describe the equilibrium interest rate—as the rate that equates the supply of and demand for bonds or alternatively, the rate that equates the supply of money with the demand for money. Equilibrium in one market implies equilibrium in the other. Keynes chose the latter of these perspectives because he wished to emphasize the relationship between monetary factors and the interest rate.

This Keynesian view of interest rate determination is illustrated in Figure 6.3. The money supply is assumed to be fixed exogenously by the central bank at M_0^s. The equilibrium interest rate is r_0, the rate at which money demand, given by the money demand schedule M^d in the graph, is just equal to the fixed money supply.

In a more fundamental sense, the equilibrium rate of interest is determined by factors affecting the supply of money and money demand. In the case of supply, the major factor will be the policies of the central bank. We turn now to the factors Keynes believed determined money demand, the factors determining the position and slope of the M^d schedule in Figure 6.3.

The Keynesian Theory of Money Demand

Keynes considered three motives for holding money. The analysis proceeds as if there were separate money demands for each of the motives. It is not presumed that any individual can say which dollars are kept for each of

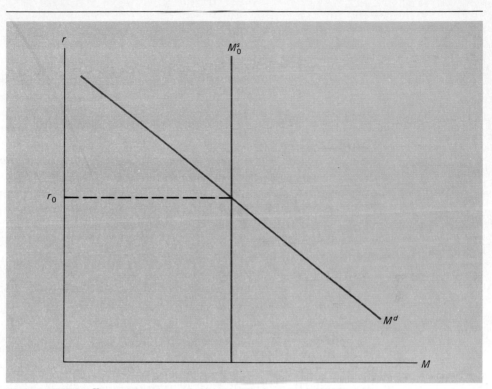

FIGURE 6.3 Determination of the Equilibrium Interest Rate
In the Keynesian system, the equilibrium interest rate (r_0) is the interest rate that
equates money supply and money demand.

the three motives, but Keynes believed it was useful to look at the separate
motives behind the overall level of money holdings.

Transactions Demand

The first motive Keynes considered was the **transactions motive**. Money is
a medium of exchange, and individuals hold money for use in transactions.
Money bridges the gap between the receipt of income and eventual expenditures. The amount of money held for the transactions purpose would vary
positively with the volume of transactions in which the individual engaged.
Income was assumed to be a good measure of this volume of transactions,
and thus the transactions demand for money was assumed to depend positively on the level of income.

When money is received in one transaction, it could be used to buy
bonds, which would then be sold to get money again when the time came
for an expenditure. The gain from doing so is that interest would be earned

for the time the bonds were held. Brokerage fees involved in buying bonds and the inconveniences of a great number of such transactions would clearly make purchases of bonds for small amounts to be held for short periods unprofitable. Some money will be held for transactions. Still, there is room to *economize* on transaction balances by such bond purchases. Since the return to be gained is interest earnings on bonds, we would expect the incentive to economize on transaction balances to be greater the higher the interest rate is. Consequently, in addition to depending positively on income, the transactions demand for money would be expected to be negatively related to the rate of interest.

Keynes did not place much emphasis on the interest rate when discussing the transactions motive for holding money, but it has proven to be of importance, especially for the business sector's transactions demand. Firms with a high volume of transactions can by cash management practices reduce considerably their average holdings of money. The incentive to make the expenditures required for such careful cash management depends on the level of the rate of interest.

Precautionary Demand

Keynes believed that, beyond the money held for planned transactions, additional money balances were held in case unexpected expenditures became necessary. Money would be held for use in possible emergencies, to pay unexpected bills such as medical bills or repair bills of various types. Money held for this motive Keynes termed the **precautionary demand for money.** He believed that the amount held for this purpose depends positively on income. Again, the interest rate might be a factor if people tended to economize on the amount of money held for the precautionary motive as interest rates rose. Since the motives for holding precautionary balances are similar to those for transactions demand, we simplify our discussion here by subsuming the precautionary demand under the transactions demand category, transactions being expected or unexpected ones. The precautionary demand for money receives separate treatment when we return to the subject of money demand in Chapter 15.

Speculative Demand

The final motive for holding money that Keynes considered was the **speculative motive**. This is the most novel part of Keynes's analysis of money demand. Keynes began with the question of why an individual would hold any money above that needed for the transactions and precautionary motives when bonds pay interest and money does not. Such an additional demand for money did exist, Keynes believed, because of the uncertainty about future interest rates and the relationship between changes in the interest rate and the market price of bonds. If interest rates were expected to move in such a way as to cause capital losses on bonds, it was possible that these expected losses would outweigh the interest earnings on the bonds and cause an investor to hold money instead. Such money would be held by those "speculating" on future changes in the interest rate. To see the way in which such speculation works, we begin by analyzing the relationship between the interest rate and the level of bond prices. After that the details of Keynes's theory are considered.

Consider the case of a perpetuity, which is what we have been assuming the bonds in our model to be. Suppose that at some point in the past you paid the then prevailing market price of $1000 to buy a government bond that entitles you to payment of $50 per year, termed the *coupon payment*. You bought a perpetual bond at a price of $1000, at a market interest rate of 5 percent (50/1000 = 0.05 or 5 percent). How much would this bond be worth if you tried to sell it today? The value of a financial asset that entitles the owner to a coupon payment of $50 per year depends on the *current* market rate of interest. First, suppose the current market rate of interest is 5 percent, the same as the interest rate that prevailed when you bought the bond. In this case, the bond would still sell for $1000; at that price it would yield the current interest rate of 5 percent.

Next consider the case in which the market interest rate has risen to 10 percent over the time since you purchased the bond. The going price today for a bond with a coupon payment of $50 per year is $500 (50/500 = 0.10 or 10 percent). Your bond has no feature that will enable you to sell it for more. Even though you paid $1000, given the rise in interest rates, you will be able to sell it only at a *capital loss* for $500, the price that makes it competitive at *current* market rates. *A rise in the market interest rate results in a capital loss on previously existing bonds.*

If, instead, from the time you purchased the bond the market interest rate had fallen, then the value of your bond would have increased. If the interest rate had declined from 5 to 2 percent, the bond price would have increased from the $1000 you paid to $2500. At that price your bond, which has a coupon of $50 per year, will pay 2 percent (50/2500 = 0.02 or 2 percent). Thus *a decline in interest rates results in a capital gain on previously existing bonds.* With this relationship between bond prices and interest rate changes in mind, we return to the question of the relative desirability of money and bonds.

The expected returns on the two assets can be expressed as follows:

$$\text{return on money} = 0$$

$$\text{expected return on bonds} = \begin{array}{l}\text{interest} \\ \text{earnings} \\ (= r)\end{array} \left\{\begin{array}{l}(+)\ \text{expected capital gain} \\ \text{or} \\ (-)\ \text{expected capital loss}\end{array}\right.$$

The return on money is zero, since it earns no interest (our assumption so far) and because its value is not subject to capital gains or losses as interest rates change.[1] Money clearly has a fixed price. The bond will pay an interest rate of r. The *expected* return on bonds will equal this interest return plus or minus any expected capital gain or loss. For reasons just discussed, an investor would expect a capital gain if he expected interest rates to fall and a capital loss if he expected interest rates to rise. It is this uncertainty about the future course of interest rates that is crucial to Keynes's analysis.

Suppose that an investor believes interest rates will fall. Bonds then clearly have the higher expected return. They pay interest and are expected to yield a capital gain. If interest rates are expected to rise, however, it is possible that the expected capital loss on bonds will outweigh the interest earnings. The expected return on bonds would be negative in such a case, and money would be the preferred asset. Money held in anticipation of a fall in bond prices (a rise in interest rates) is Keynes's speculative demand for money.

To this point, we have a relationship between the level of money demanded and expected future *changes* in interest rates. Keynes converts this to a relationship between money demanded and the *level* of the interest rate by an assumption about how people form expectations about future interest rate changes. He assumes that investors have a relatively fixed conception of the "normal" level of the interest rate. When the actual interest rate is above the normal level, investors expect the interest rate to fall. When the interest rate is below the normal rate, a rise in the interest rate is expected. Given this assumption about the way expectations about future movements in interest rates are formed, we can develop a relationship between the level of the speculative demand for money and the interest rate. We do so first for an individual investor and then consider the corresponding aggregate relationship.

For the individual investor the demand curve for speculative balances is shown in Figure 6.4a. Here M_i^2 represents the speculative demand for money by the ith individual and M_i^1 is his transactions demand. We have then

$$MP_i^1 + MP_i^2 \equiv M_i$$

and

$$M_i + B_i \equiv \text{Wh}_i \tag{6.2}$$

where M_i, B_i, and Wh_i are the individual's total money holdings, bond holdings, and wealth, respectively.

Following Keynes's theory, the individual is assumed to have a preconceived view of the normal level of the interest rate. This is shown as r_i^n in

---

[1] Notice that so far we are not allowing for the effect of commodity price changes. The *real* value of money declines proportionately with increases in the aggregate price level. So, however, does the real value of bonds; therefore, the relative returns are not directly affected by allowing for commodity price changes.

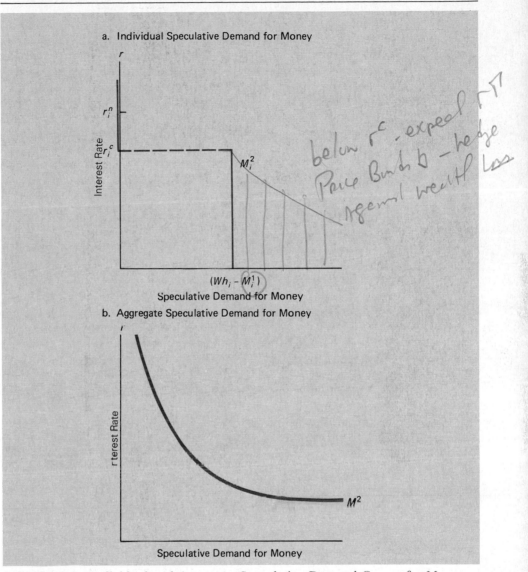

FIGURE 6.4 Individual and Aggregate Speculative Demand Curves for Money The individual's speculative demand for money is shown in part a. At any interest rate above the critical rate (r_i^c), the speculative demand for money is zero. Below the critical interest rate, the individual shifts into money. Part b shows the aggregate speculative demand for money schedule (M^2). As the interest rate becomes lower, it falls below the critical rate for more individuals, and the speculative demand for money rises.

Figure 6.4a. Since at all rates of interest above r_i^n, interest rates are expected to fall, at those rates bonds will be preferred to money as an asset. The speculative demand for money will be zero, and bond holdings will equal $(\mathrm{Wh}_i - M_i^1)$. The speculative demand for money will also be zero for interest rates over a certain range below r_i^n. If the interest rate is not too far below r_i^n, the interest earnings on the bond will be greater than the small expected capital loss. The expected capital loss will be small because only a small rise in r will be expected as r returns to r_i^n.

There is a level of the interest rate below r_i^n, however, at which the expected capital loss on bonds, which increases as the interest rate declines below r_i^n, will come to just equal the interest earnings on the bond. We term this value of the interest rate the individual's *critical* interest rate (r_i^c). Below this rate, money will be preferred. The individual will sell bonds and hold speculative balances of $(\mathrm{Wh}_i - M_i^1)$, which means that he will be holding all his wealth in the form of money.

Different individuals were assumed by Keynes to have different views as to what was a "normal" interest rate. Thus there is no specific critical rate of interest that, if approached, would trigger a massive shift of funds between money and bonds. Instead, as the interest rate fell, beginning, for example, at a very high rate where there was very little speculative demand, declines in the interest rate would move the rate successively below the critical rates of different investors. The lower the interest rate, the more investors would find that, given their view of the normal rate, money was the preferred asset. At very low values of the interest rate, almost all investors would come to expect the interest rate to rise substantially in the future ($r < r_i^c$), and money would be almost universally preferred as an asset. Proceeding in this manner, we can construct the aggregate demand for speculative balances shown in Figure 6.4b.

The curve is smooth, reflecting the gradual increase in the speculative demand for money at successively lower interest rates. The curve flattens out at a very low rate of interest, reflecting the fact that at this low rate, there is a general expectation of capital losses on bonds that outweigh interest earnings. At this rate, increments to wealth would be held in the form of money, with no further drop in the interest rate. Keynes termed this situation the "liquidity trap." For the most part, however, we assume that we are on the downward-sloping portion of the speculative demand for money curve.

The Total Demand for Money

We have looked at the three motives for holding money in the Keynesian system and can now put these together to construct the total money demand function. The transactions demand and the precautionary demand were seen to vary positively with income and negatively with respect to the interest rate.

The speculative demand for money was negatively related to the interest rate. Taken together, then, we can write total money demand as

$$M^d = L(Y, r) \tag{6.3}$$

where Y is income and r is the interest rate. A rise in income increases money demand; a rise in the interest rate leads to a fall in money demand. In the following, we at times make the simplifying assumption that the money demand function is of a linear form:

$$M^d = c_0 + c_1 Y - c_2 r \qquad c_1 > 0, \quad c_2 > 0 \tag{6.4}$$

Equation (6.4) expresses the same information as (6.3) but assumes that we can plot the money demand function as a straight line on our graphs. The parameter c_1 is the increase in money demand per unit increase in income, and c_2 gives the amount by which money demand declines per unit increase in the interest rate.

The Effects of an Increase in the Money Stock

In Figure 6.5, we plot this linear Keynesian money demand schedule [equation (6.4)] as a function of the interest rate and illustrate the effect that an increase in the money supply will have in the money market.

The money demand function M^d is downward-sloping; a decline in the interest rate, for example, increases the demand for money. To fix the position of the money demand function, we must fix the level of income. The curve in Figure 6.5 is drawn for a level of income Y_0. An increase in the level of income would shift the curve to the right, reflecting the fact that, for a given interest rate, money demand increases with income. The money supply is assumed to be an exogenously controlled policy variable set initially at M_0^s.

Now consider the effects of an increase in the money stock to the level shown by the M_1^s schedule in Figure 6.5. At the initial equilibrium level of the interest rate r_0, after the money stock increases, there will be an excess supply of money. At r_0 people will not be content to hold the new money. They will attempt to decrease their money holdings by buying bonds. The increase in the demand for bonds will decrease the rate of interest suppliers of bonds (borrowers) offer to sell their bonds. The fall in the interest rate will cause the demand for money to rise, and a new equilibrium is reached at interest rate r_1.

Some Implications of Interest on Money

As noted previously, in recent years some components of the money supply have begun to pay interest. This is contrary to the assumption we have made that bonds are the only interest-bearing asset. What implications does interest-bearing money have for the Keynesian theory?

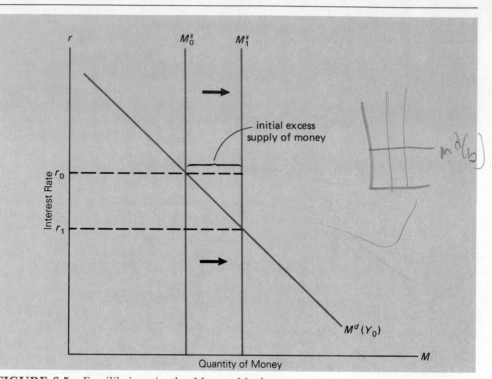

FIGURE 6.5　Equilibrium in the Money Market

An increase in the money stock from M_0^s to M_1^s causes an initial excess supply of money. The equilibrium interest rate falls from r_0 to r_1 to restore equilibrium in the money market.

In Chapter 15 the different definitions of money are discussed. Here we consider only one of these, M1. In the official U.S. monetary statistics, M1 consists of currency, travelers checks (a relatively minor item), demand deposits (regular checking accounts), and a category called "other checkable deposits." Currency, travelers checks, and demand deposits, which together accounted for a little less than two thirds of M1 in 1990, do not pay interest; the "other checkable deposits" do. Moreover, following a period of deregulation of deposit interest rates in the 1980s, banks and other depository institutions can pay whatever interest rate they wish on these deposits.[2]

The place in which this question of interest-bearing money comes into our analysis is in considering the Keynesian theory of money demand and,

---

[2]The types of "other checkable deposits" have varied over time. In the late 1980s, most of these deposits were Super NOW (negotiated order of withdrawal) accounts. Deregulation of the deposit market is discussed in more detail in Chapter 15.

specifically, the relationship of money demand to the interest rate. Suppose the interest rate on bonds rises. From equation (6.4) or from Figure 6.5 we see that the Keynesian theory predicts a decline in money demand as individuals shift into bonds. But this analysis was based on the assumption that money earned no interest.

From the previous discussion, we see that for the majority of the assets in M1, this assumption is valid. For "other checkable deposits" accounts, we might expect the rate paid on deposits to rise as the rate of interest on bonds rises. But we would not expect the rate paid on these deposits to increase by as much as the rise in the interest rate paid on bonds. Banks have costs associated with providing checkable deposits; an important cost results from the fact that banks are required to set aside a certain percentage of such deposits (currently 10 percent) as reserves, on which the bank itself will not be able to earn any interest. Therefore, if the interest rate on bonds rises by 1 percent, the interest rate on "other checkable deposits" will rise by *less* than 1 percent.[3] The *relative* interest rate on bonds will be higher, and there will still be an incentive for individuals to shift from money to bonds.

Because some components of M1 pay no interest, and even for those that pay interest, the rate paid adjusts only partially to changes in the interest rate on bonds, we can continue to assume that the Keynesian money demand function will be downward-sloping, as drawn in Figure 6.5. Money demand depends negatively on the rate of interest, which in our discussion always means the interest rate on bonds. None of this means that the emergence of interest-paying money, one of several financial-sector innovations in recent years, does not have important implications, especially for monetary policy. These implications are discussed in Chapter 19.

Summary

It may seem that we are now ready to analyze the effects of monetary policy in the Keynesian system. We have seen how changes in the money supply affect the interest rate. We have also seen how a change in interest rates affects aggregate demand. Can we not simply combine Figure 6.5 with Figure 6.1 to examine sequentially the effect on income of a change in the money supply? Unfortunately, we cannot.

In Figure 6.5 we analyzed the effects of a change in the money supply in the money market not allowing any effects in other markets. Specifically,

---

[3] Furthermore, several studies have shown that interest rates on checkable deposits are quite "sticky," meaning that depository institutions are slow to adjust deposit rates when market interest rates change. See, for example, Paul O'Brien, "Deregulated Deposit Rate Behavior," Board of Governors of the Federal Reserve, April 1986.

we held income constant (at Y_0) to fix the position of the money demand function. Now as the interest rate drops from r_0 to r_1, we can see from Figure 6.1 (assuming the subscripts have the same meaning in both diagrams) that income increases from Y_0 to Y_1. This rise in income will shift the money demand schedule in Figure 6.5 to the right. There will be a further change in the interest rate back toward r_0 and consequently a further change in income. What we need to find is the effect of changes in the money stock on the equilibrium values of the interest rate and income level, equilibrium values for *both* the money and commodity markets. We have all the relationships required for this, but we need a new framework in which to fit them together. This new framework is the *IS–LM* model, to which we now turn.

6.2 • THE *IS–LM* CURVE MODEL

Our task in this section is to find the values of the interest rate and level of income that simultaneously equilibrate both the commodity market and the money market. Note that since equilibrium in the money market implies equilibrium in the bond market, such a combination will equilibrate all three of these markets (commodities, money, and bonds). First, we identify combinations of income and the interest rate that will equilibrate the money market, neglecting the commodity market. Next, we identify combinations of income and the interest rate that are equilibrium values for the commodity market. These two sets of equilibrium combinations of interest rate and income levels are then shown to contain one combination that equilibrates both markets. To find a unique point of equilibrium, we have to assume that policy variables, including the money stock, government spending, and taxes, are held fixed at some levels. Other autonomous influences on income and interest rates (e.g., the state of business expectations that affects investment) must also be assumed to be fixed. We see that these policy variables and other exogenous influences determine the positions of the equilibrium schedules for the money and product markets, termed below the *LM* and *IS* schedules. In Chapter 7 we see how changes in these policy variables and other exogenous influences affect the equilibrium values of income and the interest rate.

Money Market Equilibrium: The *LM* Curve

Construction of the *LM* Curve

We explained previously that money demand in the Keynesian model was assumed to depend positively on the level of income because of the transactions demand. Money demand also varied inversely with the rate of interest, owing to the speculative demand for money and because the amount of transactions balances held at any income level would decline as the interest rate (the opportunity cost of holding such balances) increased. We expressed this relationship as

$$M^d = L(Y, r) \qquad (6.3)$$

or in linear form

$$M^d = c_0 + c_1 Y - c_2 r \qquad c_1 > 0, \quad c_2 > 0 \qquad (6.4)$$

Now we wish to find all the combinations of r and Y that will equilibrate money demand with a fixed money stock, denoted M_0^s. The schedule of such points is termed the *LM schedule* since along this schedule money demand, for which we use the symbol L [equation (6.3)], is equal to the money stock (M). For simplicity, we discuss the case in which money demand is given by the linear form (6.4). For this case, the condition that must be satisfied for money market equilibrium, the *LM* curve equation, can be written as

$$M_0^s = M^d = c_0 + c_1 Y - c_2 r \qquad (6.5)$$

We have already considered the nature of equilibrium in the money market. In Figure 6.6, for example, three separate demand for money schedules

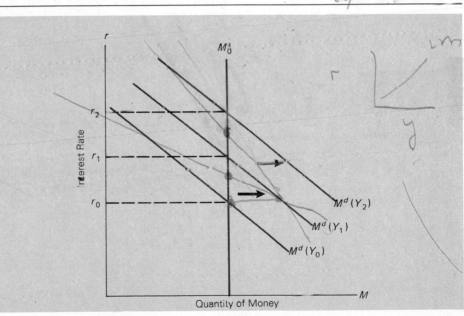

FIGURE 6.6 Equilibrium Positions in the Money Market
Increases in income from Y_0 to Y_1 to Y_2 shift the money demand function from $M^d(Y_0)$ to $M^d(Y_1)$, then to $M^d(Y_2)$. Equilibrium in the money market requires successively higher interest rates r_0, r_1, r_2 at higher levels of income Y_0, Y_1, Y_2.

are drawn, corresponding to three successively higher levels of income, Y_0, Y_1, and Y_2. As income increases from Y_0 to Y_1, then from Y_1 to Y_2, the money demand curve shifts to the right when plotted against the interest rate. The points where these money demand schedules intersect the vertical line, giving the value of the fixed money stock, are points of equilibrium for the money market. The income–interest-rate combinations at which equilibrium occurs, $(Y_0, r_0), (Y_1, r_1)$, and (Y_2, r_2), are points along the *LM* or money market equilibrium curve. These points are plotted in Figure 6.7. Proceeding in this manner, we can find the equilibrium value of the interest rate for each level of income and construct the complete *LM* schedule shown in Figure 6.7.

Notice that the *LM* curve slopes upward to the right. At higher levels of income, equilibrium in the money market occurs at higher interest rates. The reason for the positive slope for the *LM* curve is the following. An increase in income (e.g., from Y_0 to Y_1 in Figures 6.6 and 6.7) will increase money

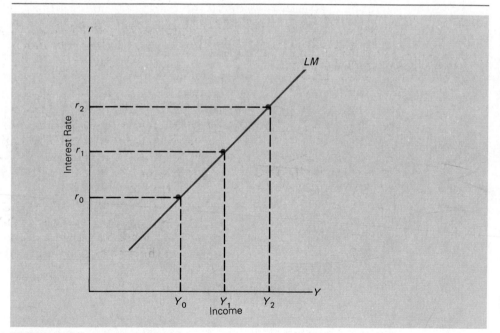

FIGURE 6.7   The *LM* Curve
The *LM* schedule shows the combinations of income (Y) and the interest rate (r) which equilibrate the money market. Equilibrium combinations such as (r_0, Y_0), (r_1, Y_1), and (r_2, Y_2) from Figure 6.6 are points along the *LM* schedule. As we saw in Figure 6.6, at higher levels of income, higher interest rates are required for money market equilibrium; the *LM* schedule slopes upward to the right.

demand at a given interest rate, since the transactions demand for money varies positively with income. To restore demand to a level equal to the fixed money stock, the interest rate must be higher (r_1 instead of r_0 in Figures 6.6 and 6.7). The higher interest rate will result in a lower speculative demand for money and lower the transactions component *corresponding to any level of income*. The interest rate must rise until this decline in money demand is just equal to the initial income-induced increase in transactions demand.

To complete our discussion of the *LM* curve, two questions need to be considered. First, we want to know what determines the value of the slope of the *LM* curve. We know that the curve is upward-sloping, but is it steep or relatively flat? The slope of the *LM* curve is important for our discussion of policy effects later. The second question concerns the position of the *LM* curve in our graph—what factors shift the schedule?

Factors Determining the Slope of the *LM* Schedule

To see which factors determine the slope of the *LM* schedule, we begin by considering the effect on money market equilibrium of an increase in income, ΔY, for example, from Y_0 to Y_1 in Figures 6.6 and 6.7. The income-induced increase in money demand as a result of this change will equal $c_1\Delta Y$, where c_1 is the parameter giving the increase in money demand (for transaction purposes) per unit increase in income from equation (6.4) on page 139. The interest rate will have to rise by enough to offset this income-induced increase in money demand. The higher the value of c_1, the larger the increase in money demand per unit increase in income, and, hence, the larger upward adjustment in the interest rate required to restore total money demand to the level of the fixed money stock. The higher the value of c_1 is, the steeper will be the *LM* curve. The value of c_1 is, however, not a subject of much debate. Controversy on this subject centers on the second factor that determines the slope of the *LM* curve.

For a given income-induced increase in money demand (a given c_1), the amount by which the interest rate has to rise to restore total money demand to the value of the fixed money stock depends on how *elastic* (sensitive) money demand is with respect to changes in the rate of interest.[4] In equation (6.4) the interest elasticity of money demand depends on the value of c_2, which determines the amount of the change in money demand for a given change

---

[4]The concept of elasticity refers to the percentage change in one variable that results from a 1 percent change in another variable. In the case of the interest elasticity of money demand, the elasticity is negative. A 1 percent increase in the interest rate will cause money demand to decline. In the text, the term *high elasticity* refers to the absolute value of the elasticity. If money demand is very responsive to changes in the interest rate, we say that money demand is highly elastic. If money demand is not very responsive to interest rate changes, we term this a low interest elasticity or low interest sensitivity of money demand.

in the interest rate ($-c_2 = \Delta M^d / \Delta r$). This relationship between the interest elasticity of money demand and the slope of the LM curve is illustrated in Figure 6.8.

Part a of the figure illustrates the case of a low interest elasticity of money demand. The money demand curve is steep, reflecting the fact that large changes in the interest rate will not change the level of money demand by very much. To see how the slope of the LM schedule is related to the interest elasticity of money demand, consider how money market equilibrium changes as we consider progressively higher income levels. Increases in income from Y_0 to Y_1 and then to Y_2 will shift the money demand schedule to the right in Figure 6.8a, from $M^d(Y_0)$ to $M^d(Y_1)$, then to $M^d(Y_2)$. These increases in income cause increases in the transactions demand for money equal to $c_1(Y_1 - Y_0)$ and $c_1(Y_2 - Y_1)$, respectively. Since a given increase in the interest rate will not reduce money demand by much (c_2 is small), the interest rate will have to rise by a large amount to reduce money demand back to the fixed M_0^s level. This fact is reflected in the LM curve in Figure 6.8a, which is quite steep.

The case in which money demand is highly interest-elastic is shown in Figure 6.8b. Here the money demand curve is quite flat. A small drop in the interest rate, for example, increases money demand significantly. Here again the money demand curve shifts to the right as income increases from Y_0 to Y_1, then to Y_2. The graph is constructed such that the increase in income and the value of c_1 from equation (6.4) are the same as in Figure 6.8a. Thus, the income-induced increases in money demand are the same in Figure 6.8a and b. Notice that in Figure 6.8b the interest rate must rise by a relatively small amount to restore equilibrium in the money market. As a consequence, the LM curve in Figure 6.8b is relatively flat. If money demand is highly responsive to changes in the interest rate (c_2 is large), a relatively small rise in the interest rate will offset the income-induced increases in transaction balances as income rises from Y_0 to Y_1, then to Y_2.

Two special cases for the slope of the LM curve result from the interest elasticity of money demand taking on the value of zero or, alternatively, becoming extremely high.

First consider the case in which money demand is completely interest-insensitive[c_2 equals zero in equation (6.4)]. Beginning at some initial equilibrium, consider the rise in the interest rate required to reequilibrate the money market if income were to be increased. To have income at a higher level would mean increased transactions demand for money. With money demand completely unresponsive to changes in the interest rate, there is no possible rise in the interest rate that would reduce money demand back to the level of the fixed money supply. In this special case, a rise in the interest rate is assumed not to cause people either to reduce the speculative demand for money or to economize on transactions balances. Consequently, only one

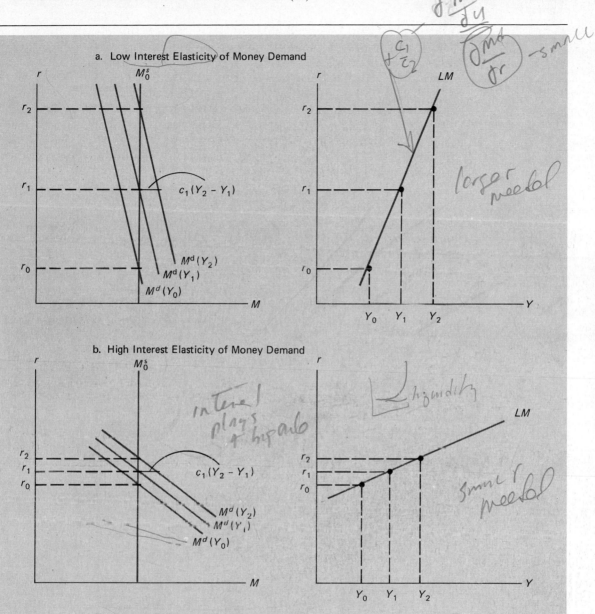

FIGURE 6.8 Interest Elasticity of Money Demand and the Slope of the *LM* Curve
The relatively steep money demand schedule in part *a* reflects the assumption that
the interest elasticity of money demand is low (in absolute value). With a low interest
elasticity of money demand, the *LM* schedule is relatively steep. In part *b*, money
demand is assumed to be highly interest-elastic and, as a result, the money demand
schedule is relatively flat. The *LM* schedule in this case is also relatively flat.

level of income can be an equilibrium level. To see this clearly, notice that with c_2 equal to zero, equation (6.4) becomes

$$M^d = c_0 + c_1 Y$$

and the *LM* curve equation (6.5) is given by

$$M_0^s = c_0 + c_1 Y$$

Consequently, with M fixed at M_0^s for equilibrium we must have

$$Y = \frac{M_0^s - c_0}{c_1} \tag{6.6}$$

Only this one level of income can be an equilibrium level for the money market.

The *LM* curve for this case is shown in Figure 6.9, and we refer to this case as the *classical* case because the Keynesian money demand function *when c_2 equals zero* does not differ substantively from the classical money demand function. As in the classical theory (Section 4.1), money demand depends only on income. The distinguishing feature of the Keynesian theory of

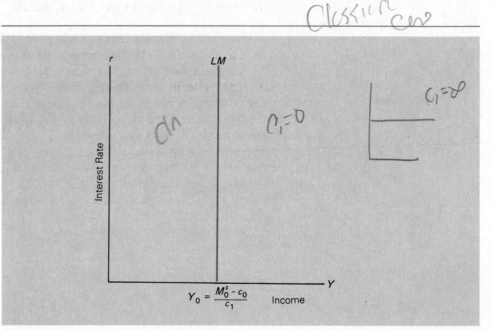

FIGURE 6.9 *LM* Curve, the Classical Case
The *LM* schedule will be vertical if money demand is completely interest-insensitive.

money demand is the negative relationship between money demand and the interest rate.

The alternative extreme case is where the interest elasticity of money demand becomes extremely large, approaching infinity. What causes this to happen? We saw from our discussion of Keynes's theory of the speculative demand for money that as the interest rate becomes very low relative to what is considered a normal value, a consensus develops viewing future interest rate increases as likely. In this situation, with expected future capital losses outweighing the small interest earnings on bonds, the public would hold any increase in money balances with only a negligible fall in the interest rate. It is in this range of the money demand schedule that the interest elasticity of money demand has become extremely high. This case, which Keynes termed the *liquidity trap*, is illustrated in Figure 6.10. Notice that here we have to abandon the linear form of the Keynesian money demand function that we have been discussing. In the liquidity trap case, we are considering a change in the slope of the money demand function. The function becomes very flat at low interest rates.

In Figure 6.10a, consider first the money demand schedules $M^d(Y_0)$ and $M^d(Y_1)$ corresponding to the income levels Y_0 and Y_1 shown in Figure 6.10b. Relative to income levels Y_2 and Y_3, these are low levels of income. Consequently, $M^d(Y_0)$ and $M^d(Y_1)$ are to the left of $M^d(Y_2)$ and $M^d(Y_3)$ in Figure 6.10a.

At such low income levels, with the money stock at M_0^s, the equilibrium interest rate is so low that we are on the flat portion of the money demand schedule. Within this range, a rise in income, from Y_0 to Y_1, for example, requires only a very slight rise in the interest rate to restore equilibrium in the money market; money demand is highly responsive to changes in interest rate. In this range, the *LM* curve in Figure 6.10 is nearly horizontal.

Notice that at higher levels of income, between Y_2 and Y_3, for example, an increase in income would require a larger increase in the interest rate to restore equilibrium in the money market. Here the equilibrium interest rates are such that we are not in the liquidity trap. The interest elasticity of money demand is lower over this portion of the money demand schedule.

We return to this liquidity trap case and to the classical case of the vertical *LM* curve in later discussions of policy effects.

Factors That Shift the *LM* Schedule

Two factors that shift the *LM* curve are changes in the exogenously fixed money stock and shifts in the money demand function. These are the two factors that we have set at given levels in order to determine the position of the *LM* curve. The money stock is assumed to be a policy variable, and when we consider an increase in the money stock, for example, we mean an

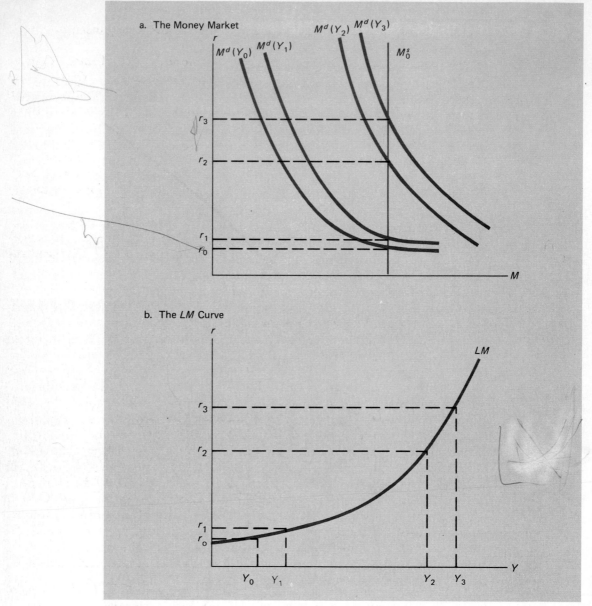

FIGURE 6.10 Keynesian Liquidity Trap

At very low levels of income, Y_0 and Y_1, equilibrium in the money market in part *a* occurs at points along the flat portion of the money demand schedule where the elasticity of money demand is extremely high. Consequently, the *LM* schedule is nearly horizontal over this range of low income levels. At higher income levels, such as Y_2 and Y_3, money market equilibrium is at steeper points along the money demand curves $M^d(Y_2), M^d(Y_3)$, and the *LM* curve becomes steeper.

exogenous policy action changing the setting of this policy instrument to a new fixed level.

We have already considered shifts in the money demand *schedule* drawn against the interest rate *as the level of income changes*. This is *not* what is meant here by a shift in the money demand *function*. A shift in the money demand function means a change in the amount of money demanded for given levels of the *interest rate and income*, what Keynes called a shift in *liquidity preference*. To give an example, if very unsettled economic conditions increase the probability of firms going bankrupt and, hence, the default risk on bonds, the demand for money might increase. This would be a shift in individuals' portfolios away from bonds and toward holding an increased amount of money for given levels of the interest rate and income.

Changes in the Money Stock. Consider first the effect on the *LM* schedule of an exogenous change in the money stock. Figure 6.11 illustrates the

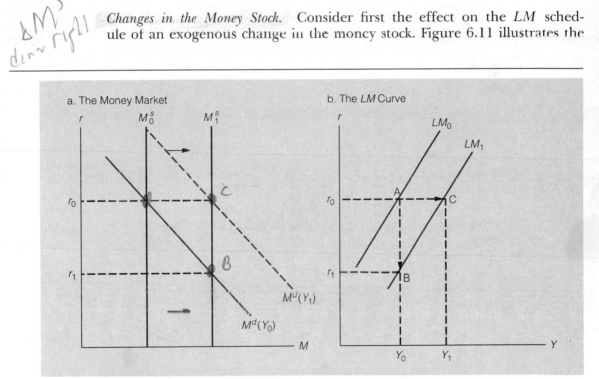

FIGURE 6.11 Shift in the *LM* Curve with an Increase in the Quantity of Money
Initially, with money stock M_0^s, the interest rate r_0 will be an equilibrium rate when income is at Y_0 in part a. This r_0, Y_0 combination is one point (A) on the *LM* schedule, LM_0. If the money stock is increased to M_1^s, r_0 will be an equilibrium interest rate in the money market only with a higher income level Y_1. This r_0, Y_1 combination is one point (C) on the new *LM* schedule, LM_1. The increase in the money stock shifts the *LM* schedule to the right.

effects of an increase in the money stock from M_0^s to M_1^s. With the initial money stock M_0^s, the LM curve is given by LM_0 in Figure 6.11b. Along this initial LM curve, an income level of Y_0, for example, would be a point of money market equilibrium for an interest rate value of r_0, as shown at point A on the graph. Equilibrium in the money market for income level Y_0 is also shown in Figure 6.11a at the intersection of the M_0^s and $M^d(Y_0)$ schedules.

An increase in the money stock from M_0^s to M_1^s can be seen in Figure 6.11a to reduce the equilibrium interest rate to r_1 for a given level of income Y_0. With income fixed, for the new higher money stock to be equal to money demand, the interest rate must be lower, to increase the speculative demand for money and transactions demand for a given income level. In terms of the LM curve in Figure 6.11b, the point on the new LM schedule (for money stock M_1^s) that gives the equilibrium interest rate for income level Y_0 will be at interest rate r_1. This income–interest-rate combination (Y_0, r_1) is a point on the new LM curve, LM_1, as shown at point B on the graph.

In general, with a higher money stock for a given level of income, the interest rate that equilibrates the money market will be lower. The new LM curve, LM_1, will lie below the initial curve LM_0, as shown in Figure 6.11b.

Alternatively, consider the point on the new LM curve that gives the equilibrium level of income corresponding to interest rate r_0. At M_0^s the income level Y_0 was an equilibrium level for interest rate r_0 (point A). With the money stock M_1^s, for r_0 to be an equilibrium value in the money market, income would have to be higher at Y_1, higher by an amount that would shift the money demand schedule in Figure 6.11a out to the dashed schedule shown in the graph. With a higher money stock and a given interest rate, for there to be equilibrium in the money market, income must be at a higher level. The point on the new LM schedule LM_1, corresponding to r_0, must lie to the right of point A. This point is shown as point C in Figure 6.11b. Thus the new LM curve, LM_1, with the higher money stock M_1^s will lie to the right of the original LM schedule in Figure 6.11b.

In sum, *an increase in the money stock shifts the LM schedule downward and to the right*. Clearly, as can be verified by reversing the foregoing analysis, a decline in the money stock shifts the LM schedule upward and to the left.

Shifts in the Money Demand Function. Consider next the effect on the position of the LM curve of a shift in the money demand function. Assume that there is an increase in money demand for a given level of income and the interest rate. A possible reason for such a shift, as suggested previously, is a loss of confidence in bonds. The effects of such an increase in money demand are illustrated in Figure 6.12.

Figure 6.12a shows an initial equilibrium in the money market corresponding to income level Y_0. Initially, money demand is given by $M_0^d(Y_0)$. The equilibrium interest rate is r_0, as shown at point A on the initial LM

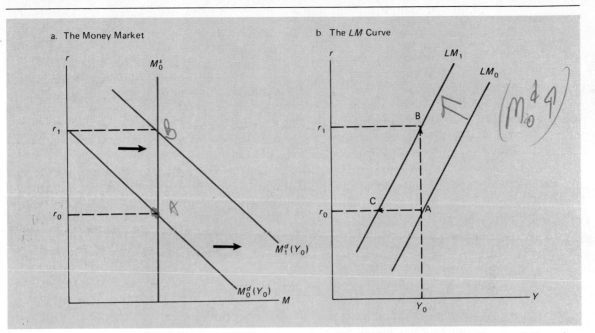

FIGURE 6.12 Shift in the LM Curve with a Shift in the Money Demand Function
A shift in the money demand function that shifts the money demand schedule upward from $M_0^d(Y_0)$ to $M_1^d(Y_0)$ in part a raises the equilibrium interest rate for a given income level. The LM schedule in part b shifts upward to the left from LM_0 to LM_1.

curve LM_0 in Figure 6.12b. Now we assume that the money demand function shifts to $M_1^d(Y_0)$, an increase in money demand for a given level of income. Note here that it is the *function* that shifts, from $M_0^d(Y_0)$ to $M_1^d(Y_0)$. At the unchanged level of income, Y_0, equilibrium in the money market requires an interest rate of r_1. The point on the new LM curve, LM_1 in Figure 6.12b, for a given level of income Y_0 will be above the old LM schedule. This point is shown as point B in Figure 6.12b.

Similarly, maintaining equilibrium in the money market at r_0 after the shift in the money demand curve would require a fall in income to a level below Y_0, which would shift the schedule in Figure 6.12a back down to the level of the original $M_0^d(Y_0)$ line. Thus the point on LM_1 at r_0 is to the left of LM_0. This point is shown as point C in Figure 6.12b.

A shift in the money demand function that increases the demand for money at a given level of both the interest rate and income shifts the LM schedule upward and to the left. A reverse shift in money demand lowering the amount of money demanded at given levels of income and the interest rate shifts the LM curve downward to the right.

The *LM* Schedule: Summary

We now know the essentials about the *LM* curve:

1. It is the schedule giving all the combinations of values of income and the interest rate that produce equilibrium in the money market.
2. It slopes upward to the right.
3. It will be relatively flat (steep) if the interest elasticity of money demand is relatively high (low).
4. It will shift downward (upward) to the right (left) with an increase (decrease) in the quantity of money.
5. It will shift upward (downward) to the left (right) with a shift in the money demand function which increases (decreases) the amount of money demanded at given levels of income and the interest rate.

Product Market Equilibrium: The *IS* Curve

Construction of the *IS* Schedule

The condition for equilibrium in the product market is

$$Y = C + I + G \qquad (6.7)$$

An equivalent statement of this equilibrium condition was seen to be

$$I + G = S + T \qquad (6.8)$$

The product market equilibrium schedule, which is termed the *IS curve*, is most often constructed from this second form of the equilibrium condition, although the same results could be derived using equation (6.7).

We will proceed, as we did with the money market, by finding the set of interest-rate and income-level combinations that produces equilibrium, in this case equilibrium for the product market. Next we examine the factors that determine the slope and position of this product market equilibrium schedule.

To begin, we consider a simplified case in which we neglect the government sector (i.e., G and T equal zero). The more general case is considered subsequently. For this simple case, we can rewrite (6.8) as[5]

$$I(r) = S(Y) \qquad (6.9)$$

Here we indicate the dependence of investment on the interest rate and of saving on the level of income. Our task in constructing the *IS* schedule is

---

[5]The label IS comes from this simple version of the product market equilibrium curve, an equality between investment (I) and savings (S).

to find combinations of the interest rate and level of income that equate investment with saving.

Figure 6.13 illustrates the construction of the IS curve for this simple case. In Figure 6.13a investment is plotted as a negatively sloped function of the interest rate; a decline in the interest rate will increase investment expenditures. Saving is depicted as a positively sloped function of income, the slope being the positive marginal propensity to save.

Consider an interest rate of r_0. For this level of the interest rate, investment spending will be the amount I_0, as shown along the investment schedule. An amount of saving just equal to I_0 is shown as S_0 along the saving function. This level of saving results if income is at Y_0. Thus, for the interest rate r_0, a point of product market equilibrium will be at Y_0. This interest rate–income combination (r_0, Y_0) is one point on the IS curve, shown as point A in Figure 6.13b.

Now consider a higher value of the interest rate, such as r_1. At interest rate r_1, investment will be I_1, a smaller amount than at r_0. For equilibrium, saving must be at S_1, lower than S_0. This saving level is generated by income level Y_1, which is lower than Y_0. Thus a second point on the IS curve will be at r_1 and Y_1, point B on Figure 6.13b. Notice that for the higher interest rate, the corresponding equilibrium income level is lower. *The IS curve has a negative slope.* By choosing additional interest rate values such as r_2 in Figure 6.13a and finding the corresponding income level for equilibrium Y_2, where $I_2 = S_2$, we can find additional points on the IS curve in Figure 6.13b, such as point C. In this way we trace the complete set of combinations of income and interest rate levels that equilibrate the product market.

Factors That Determine the Slope of the IS Schedule

Next consider the factors that determine the degree of the slope of the IS curve. We know that the curve will be negatively sloped, but will it be steep or flat? As with the LM curve, the question is of interest because we will see that the steepness of the IS curve is a factor determining the relative effectiveness of monetary and fiscal stabilization policies.

In constructing the IS curve, we have looked at how investment changes as we vary the interest rate and then at the required change in income to move saving to equal the new investment level. In considering the steepness of the IS curve, we are asking whether, as we look at progressively lower interest rates, for example, equilibrium in the product market requires *much* higher income levels (the curve is relatively flat) or only *slightly* increased income levels (the curve is steep). This will depend on the slopes of the investment and saving functions. Figure 6.14 illustrates how the slope of the IS curve is related to the slope of the investment function. Two investment schedules are depicted. The schedule I is drawn to be very steep, indicating

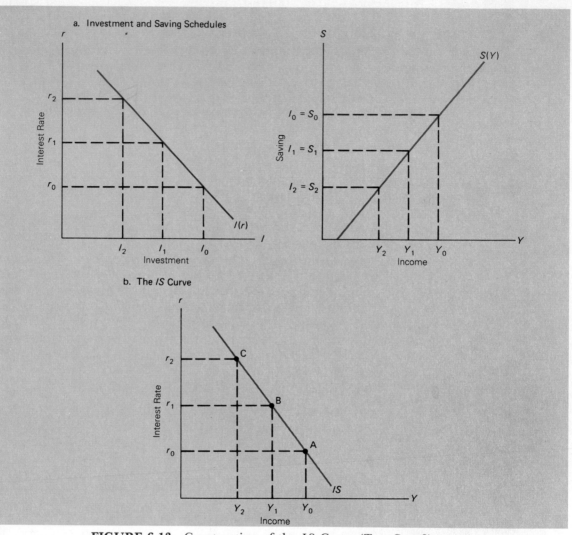

a. Investment and Saving Schedules

b. The *IS* Curve

FIGURE 6.13 Construction of the *IS* Curve ($T = G = 0$)

At interest rates r_0, r_1, r_2, investment levels will be I_0, I_1, and I_2 in part *a*. To generate levels of saving S_0, S_1, S_2 equal to these levels of investment, income must be at Y_0, Y_1, and Y_2, respectively. Therefore, interest-rate income combinations $(r_0, Y_0), (r_1, Y_1)$, and (r_2, Y_2) are points (A, B, C) along the *IS* schedule in part *b*.

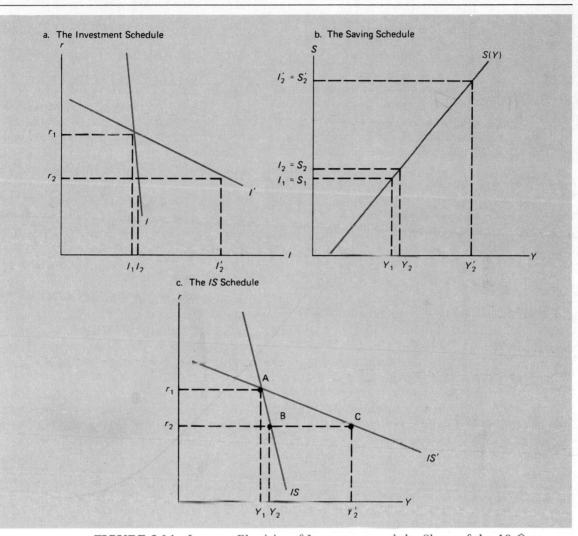

FIGURE 6.14 Interest Elasticity of Investment and the Slope of the IS Curve
Where the investment schedule is steep (I) in part a, a fall in the interest rate will increase investment by only a small amount. Only a small increase in saving and, hence, income is required to restore product market equilibrium. Therefore, the IS schedule in part c (IS in this case) will be steep. Where the investment schedule is relatively flat (I'), investment will increase by more with a fall in the interest rate. Saving, and therefore income, must then increase by more; the IS schedule for this case (IS') will be relatively flat.

that investment is not especially sensitive to changes in the interest rate; the interest elasticity of investment demand is low.[6] The schedule I' is drawn for the case where investment is more sensitive to movements in the interest rate. For either investment schedule, the graph is constructed so that an interest rate of r_1 corresponds to an investment level of I_1 (the curves have different intercepts on the interest rate axis). Equilibrium in the product market for this interest rate will be at Y_1, as can be seen from Figure 6.14b (at that point, $I_1 = S_1$). This will be one point along the product market equilibrium schedules that we construct corresponding to each of these investment schedules. These product market equilibrium schedules, IS for investment schedule I and IS' for investment schedule I', are shown in Figure 6.14c. They have a common point at (Y_1, r_1), point A.

Now consider the point along each of these equilibrium schedules corresponding to a lower interest rate r_2. If investment is given by schedule I in Figure 6.14a, at the lower interest rate r_2 investment will increase to I_2. Equilibrium in the product market requires an equal increase in saving to S_2, which requires that income be at Y_2 in Figure 6.14b. Along the IS schedule we move to point B in Figure 6.14c. Notice that since investment was assumed to be relatively insensitive to changes in the interest rate, the increase in the level of investment when the interest rate falls to r_2 is small. Consequently, the required increase in saving, and therefore income, in Figure 6.14b was small. The IS curve is steep in this case; lower levels of the interest rate correspond to only slightly higher levels of income along the product market equilibrium curve.

Now consider the case in which investment is given by the flatter schedule I' in 6.14a. At the lower interest rate r_2, investment will be at I_2'. The level of income corresponding to r_2 along the investment-equals-saving curve for this case, IS' in Figure 6.14c, would be Y_2' at point C. Saving must increase to S_2', and this requires income level Y_2'. In this case investment is more highly interest-elastic and increases by a greater amount as the interest rate falls to r_2. Consequently, saving must be increased by a greater amount than in the case where investment was interest-inelastic, and for this income must increase by more. The product market equilibrium schedule (IS') is flatter when investment is more sensitive to the interest rate.

This, then, is the first of the factors determining the slope of the IS curve. The curve will be relatively steep if the interest elasticity of investment is low. The curve will be flatter for higher (absolute) values of investment interest elasticity.

---

[6]The concept of elasticity is defined in footnote 4. Here, as in the case of money demand, the interest elasticity is negative; an increase in the interest rate lowers investment demand. By saying that elasticity is low, we again refer to the absolute value of the elasticity.

One extreme case for the slope of the IS curve is when the interest elasticity of investment demand is zero; investment is completely insensitive to the interest rate. In this case the investment schedule in Figure 6.14a will be vertical and, as the reader can verify with a graphical analysis analogous to that given previously, the IS curve will also be vertical. For this case a fall in the interest rate from r_1 to r_2 would not increase investment at all. Consequently, equilibrium in the product market requires the same level of saving, and hence income, at r_2 as at r_1. This means that the IS curve would be vertical. The implications of a vertical IS curve for the effectiveness of monetary and fiscal policies are considered later.

The second factor affecting the slope of the IS curve is the slope of the saving function. Until we consider more elaborate theories of consumption, we do not encounter controversy over the slope of the saving function in Figure 6.14b, which is equal to the marginal propensity to save. Consequently, in this section the value of the MPS does not play much of a role in our discussion of the factors determining the slope of the IS curve or, as we see later, the relative effectiveness of monetary and fiscal policy. It can be shown, however, that the IS curve will be relatively steeper, the higher the MPS.

To see this, first note that the higher the value of the MPS, the steeper the saving function in Figure 6.14b (saving increases by more per unit of income) is. Once we have determined the slope of the investment schedule, we fix the increase in investment for a given change in the interest rate. A given decline of the interest rate, for example, then leads to a given increase in investment, and for product market equilibrium along the IS curve, saving must be higher by the same amount. If the MPS is relatively high, then a smaller increase in income will generate this new saving than if the MPS were low. Thus, for a given fall in the interest rate, the amount by which income would have to be increased for a new point of equilibrium in the product market is smaller (larger) the higher (lower) the value of the MPS. This means that the IS curve is relatively steeper, other factors being as given, the higher the MPS.

Factors That Shift the IS Schedule

Next consider the factors that determine the position of the IS curve and changes that will shift the schedule. Here we drop the assumption that government expenditures and taxes are zero; we bring the government sector back into the model. With the government sector in the model, the condition for product market equilibrium is given by (6.8), which we rewrite as

$$I(r) + G = S(Y - T) + T \tag{6.10}$$

Notice that saving must now be written as a function of *disposable* income ($Y_D = Y - T$), which differs from income by the amount of tax collections.

Construction of the IS curve for this more general case is illustrated in Figure 6.15. In part a we plot both the investment function and the level of investment plus government spending. Note that the $I + G$ schedule is downward-sloping only because investment depends on the rate of interest. The $I + G$ schedule lies to the right of the I schedule by the fixed amount of government spending. In Figure 6.15b the saving schedule is plotted against the level of income. Saving plus taxes $[S(Y - T) + T]$ is also plotted. Since we are assuming that tax collections are fixed exogenously, the saving-plus-taxes schedule lies above the saving schedule by a fixed distance (equal to T).

Consider an interest rate such as r_0 in Figure 6.15. At this interest rate, the level of investment [which can be read from the $I(r)$ curve] plus the fixed level of government spending equals $I_0 + G$. For equilibrium, this must be balanced by an equal total of saving plus tax collections, given by $S_0 + T$ in Figure 6.15b. The level of income that generates this level of saving plus tax collections is given by Y_0. Thus, one point along the IS curve is point A in Figure 6.15c, corresponding to interest rate r_0 and income level Y_0. If we consider a higher interest rate, such as r_1, investment would be less; hence, with government spending unchanged, investment plus government spending would be at the lower level $I_1 + G$. For equilibrium, a lower level of saving plus taxes is required. This level is shown as $S_1 + T$ in Figure 6.15b, where it should be noted that the change is only in the saving component, since taxes are fixed. For this lower level of saving, income must be at Y_1, below Y_0 in Figure 6.15b. The corresponding point on the IS curve is point B in Figure 6.15c.

By similar reasoning, the reader can establish that an interest rate of r_2 will require an income level of Y_2 for equilibrium in the product market (point C in Figure 6.15c). Proceeding in this manner, the complete IS schedule is constructed.

We can now look at factors that would cause a shift in the IS curve. From the equilibrium condition given by (6.10), it can be seen that a change in either the level of government spending (G) or the level of taxes (T) will disturb an initial product market equilibrium position—this will be a shift in the IS curve. Additionally, an autonomous investment change that shifts the investment function will shift the IS curve. The precise nature of this autonomous change in investment is explained later. Generally, note that the factors that shift the IS curve are those that determine autonomous expenditures in the simple Keynesian model of the preceding chapter. The reason for this should become clear as we proceed.

Changes in Government Spending.   Consider first the effects of a change in government spending. The shift in the IS curve when government spending increases from an initial level G_0 to a higher level G_1 is illustrated in

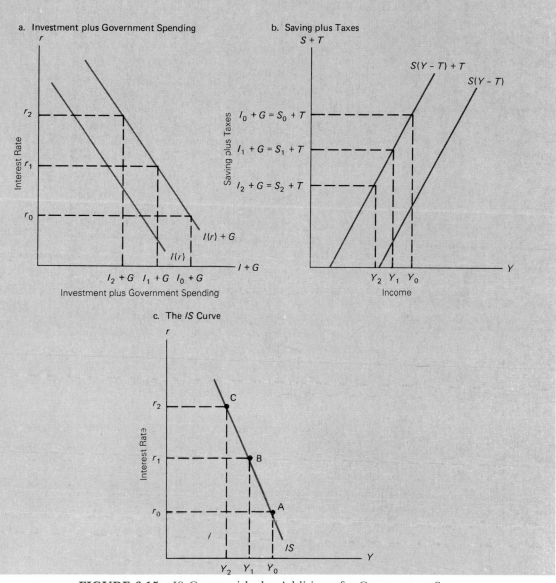

FIGURE 6.15 *IS* Curve with the Addition of a Government Sector

With the inclusion of the government sector, the condition for equilibrium in the goods market becomes $I + G = S + T$. At an interest rate of r_1 in part a, investment plus government spending will be equal to $I_1 + G$. Therefore, equilibrium in the goods market requires that saving plus taxes, as shown in part b, equal to $S_1 + T (= I_1 + G)$, which will be the case at an income level Y_1. Thus, the combination r_1, Y_1 is one point (B) along the (IS) schedule in part c.

Figure 6.16. For the initial level of government spending, the IS schedule is given by IS_0 in Figure 6.16c. An interest rate of r_0, for example, will be an equilibrium level for the product market if income is at Y_0, as shown at point A on IS_0. At interest rate r_0, investment plus government spending will be $I_0 + G_0$, as shown in Figure 6.16a. As shown in Figure 6.16b, an income level of Y_0 generates saving plus taxes just equal to this amount of government spending plus investment ($S_0 + T_0 = I_0 + G_0$).

Now let government spending increase to G_1. In Figure 6.16a it can be seen that this shifts the investment plus government spending schedule out to the right. At a given interest rate, investment will be unchanged, and the sum of investment plus government spending will be higher by the increase in government spending ($\Delta G = G_1 - G_0$).

Equilibrium in the product market requires an equally higher level of saving plus taxes, shown as $S_1 + T_0$ in Figure 6.16b. This level of saving plus taxes will be forthcoming at income level Y_1 above Y_0. Thus, a given interest rate r_0, for equilibrium in the product market, requires a higher level of income when government spending is increased. The increase in government spending will shift the IS curve to the right to IS_1 in Figure 6.16c, where at r_0 the point of equilibrium is at point B, corresponding to the higher income level Y_1.

It will be useful to establish the amount by which the IS curve shifts to the right, the horizontal distance from A to B in Figure 6.16c. For each one-unit increase in government spending with taxes assumed unchanged to restore equilibrium *at a given interest rate* in the product market, saving must be higher by one unit. This can be readily seen by looking at equation (6.10). So the question of the distance of the horizontal shift in the IS curve (e.g., distance A − B) is that of the amount of the increase in income required to generate new saving equal to the increase in government spending. Since the increase in saving per unit increase in income is given by the MPS equal to $(1 - b)$, the required increase in income (the horizontal shift in the IS curve) will be $\Delta G (1/(1 - b))$,

$$\Delta G = \Delta S = (1 - b)\Delta Y|_{r_0}$$
$$\Delta G \frac{1}{1 - b} = \Delta Y|_{r_0} \tag{6.11}$$

where the subscript r_0 on the ΔY term indicates that we are computing the increase in the value of Y that will be required to maintain equilibrium in the product market *at interest rate* r_0. This is the amount of the horizontal shift in the IS schedule.

Notice that the amount of the horizontal shift in the IS curve per unit increase in G is $1/(1 - b)$, the autonomous expenditure multiplier from Chapter 5. In looking at the horizontal distance that the curve shifts, we are

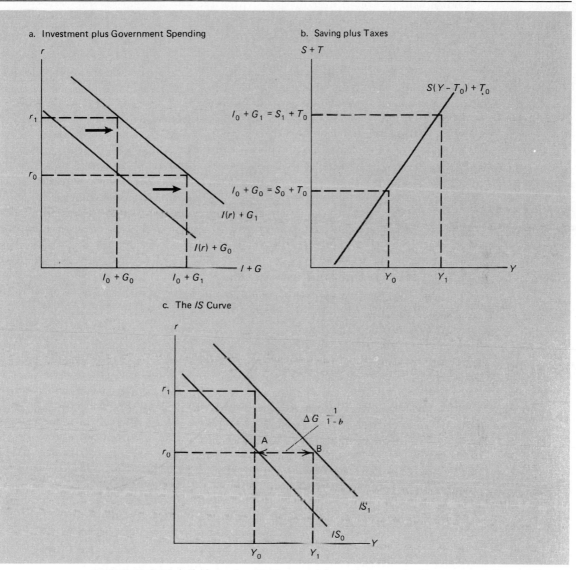

FIGURE 6.16 Shift in the IS Curve with an Increase in Government Expenditures
At interest rate r_0, an increase in government spending increases the total of investment plus government spending from $I_0 + G_0$ to $I_0 + G_1$. To maintain the condition $I + G = S + T$, with a fixed level of taxes, saving must rise from S_0 to S_1, which requires income to be Y_1 instead of Y_0. At interest rate r_0, the equilibrium point in the product market is point B instead of point A. An increase in government spending shifts the IS schedule to the right from IS_0 to IS_1.

holding the interest rate constant, which fixes investment. Once investment is assumed given, our model is identical to that in Chapter 5. We are looking for the increase in income that will come with investment fixed, government spending rising, and with a consequent induced increase in consumption. This is the same question analyzed in Chapter 5, and reassuringly, we get the same answer.

Changes in Taxes.   Next consider the shift in the IS curve with a change in taxes. The effect on the position of the IS curve of a tax increase from T_0 to T_1 is depicted in Figure 6.17. For each one-dollar increase in taxes *at a given income level*, taxes are higher by one dollar and saving is less by $(1 - b)$ dollars. The latter effect follows since an increase of one dollar in taxes lowers disposable income by one dollar and reduces saving by the MPS $(1 - b)$. Since for a given income level the decline in saving is less than the increase in taxes, an increase in taxes will shift the $S + T$ schedule upward. In Figure 6.17b, an increase in taxes from T_0 to T_1 shifts the schedule from $[S(Y - T_0) + T_0]$ to $[S(Y - T_1) + T_1]$.

At an interest rate such as r_0 in Figure 6.17a, we can find the level of government expenditures plus investment along the $I(r) + G$ schedule at $I_0 + G_0$. Equilibrium in the product market requires an equal amount of saving plus taxes. Initially, with taxes at T_0, the equilibrium level of the saving plus taxes is $S_0 + T_0$, and this requires income to be at Y_0. This combination of (r_0, Y_0) is a point on the initial IS curve IS_0, point A in Figure 6.17c.

After the tax increase, for equilibrium in the product market at r_0, we must still have the same total of saving plus taxes. This is the case because there has been no change in investment plus government spending. With the higher level of taxes, for saving plus taxes to be unchanged, saving and therefore income must be lower. The new level of income required for product market equilibrium is given by Y_1 in Figure 6.17b. The corresponding point on the new IS curve is point B in Figure 6.17c. The increase in taxes shifts the IS curve to the left.

As with the change in government spending, we can calculate the magnitude of the horizontal shift in the IS curve as a result of an increase in taxes. *For a given rate of interest* a tax change does not affect the left-hand side of the equilibrium condition for the product market [equation (6.10)]; investment and government spending are unchanged. So for equilibrium at the same interest rate, the right-hand side must also be unchanged; saving plus taxes must be unchanged. This requires that the increase in taxes be exactly balanced by a decline in saving,

$$0 = \Delta S + \Delta T$$

We can express the change in saving as

$$\Delta S = (1 - b)\Delta(Y - T) = (1 - b)\Delta Y - (1 - b)\Delta T$$

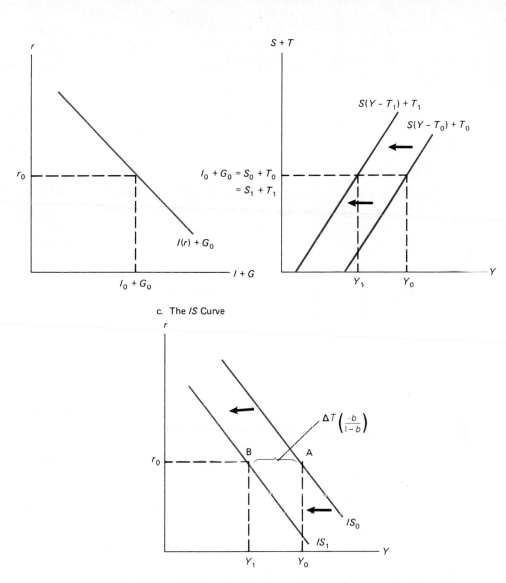

c. The *IS* Curve

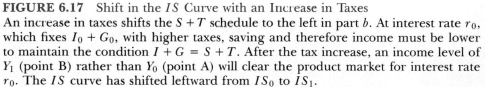

FIGURE 6.17   Shift in the *IS* Curve with an Increase in Taxes

An increase in taxes shifts the $S + T$ schedule to the left in part *b*. At interest rate r_0, which fixes $I_0 + G_0$, with higher taxes, saving and therefore income must be lower to maintain the condition $I + G = S + T$. After the tax increase, an income level of Y_1 (point B) rather than Y_0 (point A) will clear the product market for interest rate r_0. The *IS* curve has shifted leftward from IS_0 to IS_1.

So for (6.10) to hold requires that

$$\Delta S + \Delta T = 0$$

$$(1 - b)\Delta Y - (1 - b)\Delta T + \Delta T = 0$$

$$(1 - b)\Delta Y - \Delta T + b\Delta T + \Delta T = 0$$

$$(1 - b)\Delta Y + b\Delta T = 0$$

$$(1 - b)\Delta Y = -b\Delta T$$

$$\Delta Y|_{r_0} = \frac{-b}{1 - b}\Delta T \qquad (6.12)$$

where again in equation (6.12) the subscript r_0 is used on the ΔY term to indicate that this is the change in income that at interest rate r_0 will be an equilibrium value for the product market. From (6.12) it can be seen that, as demonstrated previously, income must be lower for product market equilibrium at r_0 with a higher level of taxes. Also, it can be seen that the amount by which the IS curve shifts to the left for a one-unit increase in taxes, $-b/(1 - b)$, is just equal to the tax multiplier from the simple Keynesian model of Chapter 5. When we consider the horizontal shift in the IS curve per unit change in taxes, we are fixing the interest rate, which fixes investment. Thus we are calculating the change in equilibrium income per unit change in taxes for a given level of investment. This is what was given in Chapter 5 by the tax multiplier $-b/(1 - b)$.

Autonomous Changes in Investment.   The last factor we consider that shifts the IS curve is an autonomous change in investment. By this is meant a shift in the investment schedule as drawn against the interest rate. For example, an increase in expectations about the future profitability of investment projects increases the level of investment demand *corresponding to each interest rate,* shifting the $I(r)$ schedule and hence the investment plus government spending schedule to the right in Figure 6.16a. This rightward shift in the $I(r)$ schedule, by the amount of the autonomous increase in investment, has exactly the same effect on the IS curve as an equal increase in government spending, analyzed in Figure 6.16. Both changes shift the investment plus government spending schedule and, as was seen in the previous discussion, this shifts the IS curve to the right by $1/(1 - b)$ units per unit increase in government spending, or in this case, autonomous investment expenditures.

In this section we have considered the various factors that shift the IS schedule. We have also generalized the analysis to allow for a government sector and hence enable us to see how fiscal policy variables affect the position of the IS schedule. Because the new variables considered, government spending and taxes, were exogenous, the slopes of the investment plus government spending schedule and of the saving plus taxes schedule were the same as those for the investment and saving schedules considered in the preceding section. Since it is the slopes of these functions that were shown to determine the slope of the IS curve and since they are unchanged, the addition of the government sector to the model in this section requires no revision of the previous discussion of the slope of the IS curve.

The IS Schedule: Summary

In the last two subsections, we derived the following results concerning the IS curve, the equilibrium schedule for the product market:

1. The IS curve slopes downward to the right.
2. The IS curve will be relatively flat (steep) if the interest elasticity of investment is relatively high (low).
3. The IS curve will shift to the right (left) when there is an increase (decrease) in government expenditures.
4. The IS curve will shift to the left (right) when taxes increase (decline).
5. An autonomous increase (decrease) in investment expenditures will shift the IS curve to the right (left).

The IS and LM Curves Combined

In Figure 6.18 we combine the LM and IS schedules. The upward-sloping LM schedule shows all the points of equilibrium for the money market. The downward-sloping IS schedule shows all the points of equilibrium for the product market. The point of intersection between the two curves, point E in the figure, is the (only) point of general equilibrium for both markets. As pointed out at the beginning of our discussion, if the money market is in equilibrium, the bond market must also be in equilibrium. Thus, the interest rate and income level at the intersection of the IS and LM schedules in Figure 6.18, denoted r_0 and Y_0, are values that produce a simultaneous equilibrium for the money market, product market, and bond market.

As was the case with the simpler Keynesian model in Chapter 5, the nature of equilibrium in the IS–LM curve model can be better understood by considering why points other than the point of intersection of the two curves are not points of equilibrium. Figure 6.19 shows a number of points off the IS and LM curves (A, B, C, D).

First consider points above the LM schedule such as points A and B. At all points above the LM schedule, there will be an excess supply of money (XS_M). At the level of income for either point A or B, the corresponding interest rate is too high for money market equilibrium. With an excess supply of money, there is downward pressure on the interest rate, as indicated by the downward-direction arrow. There is a tendency to move toward the LM schedule. Similarly, at points below the LM schedule, such as points C and D, there will be an excess *demand* for money (XD_M), and consequently upward pressure on the interest rate.

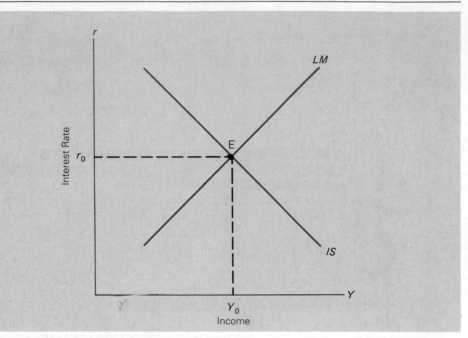

FIGURE 6.18 IS and LM Curves Combined
The point of intersection of the IS and LM curves gives the combination of the interest rate and income (r_0, Y_0), which produces equilibrium for both the money and product markets.

Now consider the same points in relation to the IS curve. At points such as B and C, to the right of the IS schedule, output will exceed aggregate demand or, analogously, saving plus taxes will exceed investment plus government spending. At the levels of the interest rate for either point B or C, the corresponding output level that will equate investment plus government spending to saving plus taxes, an output level given by the point along the IS curve, is below the actual output level. There is an excess supply of output (XS_0), and therefore a downward pressure on output, as indicated by the arrows pointing to the left. Correspondingly, at points to the left of this IS schedule, such as points A and D, actual output is below the level that will just clear the product market. There is an excess demand for output (XD_0) and there will be upward pressure on output, as indicated by the rightward-directed arrows at these points.

Finally, note that points on one schedule but not on the other are also *disequilibrium* points relative to one of the two markets. A point such as F, for example, is a point of equilibrium for the money market but a point of excess supply for the product market. Similarly, any point along the IS curve other

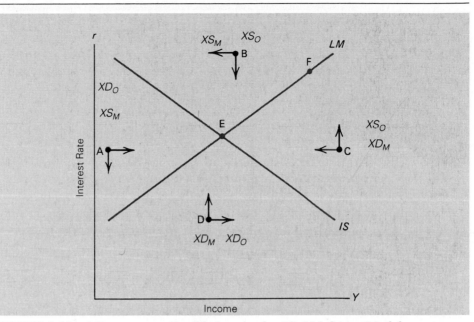

FIGURE 6.19   Adjustment to Equilibrium in the $IS–LM$ Curve Model
At points such as A, B, C and D, there are either excess supplies or demands in the money and product markets, and therefore pressures for the interest rate and output to change. At point F, the product market is out of equilibrium and there is pressure for output to change. Only at point E are both the money and product markets in equilibrium with no pressure for change in either the interest rate or output.

than point E would result in disequilibrium in the money market. It is only at point E that both the money and product market are in equilibrium. There is no excess demand or supply in either the money or product market, and therefore there are no pressures for the interest rate or output to change. This is the condition for equilibrium in the $IS–LM$ curve model.

6.3 • CONCLUSION

In this chapter we have brought the money market into our Keynesian model. The role of money and monetary policy in the Keynesian system was considered. We then analyzed how the equilibrium level of income and the interest rate are simultaneously determined in the $IS–LM$ curve model. The next task is to see how these equilibrium values are affected by monetary and fiscal policy variables as well as by other shocks to the model.

Review Questions and Problems

1. Explain the Keynesian theory of interest-rate determination. What differences do you see between this theory and the classical theory of the interest rate?

2. How would the level of aggregate demand be affected by a rise in the interest rate in the Keynesian theory? Which components would be affected most strongly?

3. What are the three motives for holding money according to Keynes's theory of money demand? Explain each motive.

4. What property is shared by all points along the *LM* schedule? Along the *IS* schedule?

5. Explain why in the *IS–LM* curve model the *IS* curve is negatively sloped and the *LM* curve is positively sloped.

6. What factors determine the magnitude of the slope of the *IS* schedule; that is, what factors determine whether the curve is steep or flat?

7. What variables will shift the position of the *IS* schedule? Explain the way a change in each variable will shift the schedule (to the left or to the right).

8. What factors determine the magnitude of the slope of the *LM* schedule; that is, what factors determine whether the curve is steep or flat?

9. Trace through the procedure for deriving the *IS* schedule, as was done in Figure 6.15, for the case where, rather than a fixed level of taxes (T), we have taxes depending on income

$$T = t_1 Y$$

where t_1 is the marginal income tax rate. Will the *IS* curve for this case be steeper or flatter than when the level of taxes is fixed?

10. What variables will shift the position of the *LM* schedule? Explain the way in which a change in each variable will shift the schedule (to the left or to the right).

11. What condition is required for the *LM* schedule to be vertical? What condition is required for the alternative extreme case, where over a range the *LM* schedule became nearly horizontal?

12. Why are we assured that when the money and product markets are in equilibrium, the bond market will also be in equilibrium?

13. Explain why at a point such as B in Figure 6.19, there is downward pressure on both the level of output and the interest rate.

Selected Readings

Branson, William, *Macroeconomic Theory and Policy.* New York: Harper & Row, 1989, Chaps. 4–5.

Hicks, John, "Mr. Keynes and the Classics: A Suggested Interpretation," *Econometrica*, 5 (April 1937), pp. 147–59. Reprinted in John Hicks, *Critical Essays in Monetary Theory.* London: Oxford University Press, 1967. See also Chap. 8 in that volume, "The 'Classics' Again," and Chap. 9, "Monetary Theory and History—An Attempt at Perspective."

Laidler, David, *The Demand for Money.* New York: Dun-Donnelly, 1977, Chap. 1.

Makinen, Gail, *Money, the Price Level and Interest Rates.* Englewood Cliffs, N.J.: Prentice-Hall, 1977, Chaps. 5–8.

Robertson, D. H., "Mr. Keynes and the Rate of Interest," in D. H. Robertson, *Essays in Monetary Theory.* London: Staples Press, 1940.

Appendix
The Algebra of the *IS–LM* Model

In this appendix, the $IS–LM$ curve model is presented in algebraic form; no new material is covered. This algebraic presentation is simply a supplement to the verbal and graphical explanation given in the chapter.

For simplicity, we deal with a linear form of the IS and LM equations. We have already written out a linear form of the LM equation

$$M^s = M^d = c_0 + c_1 Y - c_2 r \qquad c_1; c_2 > 0 \qquad (6.5)$$

Equation (6.5) states that the fixed money supply (M^s) is equal to the demand for money (M^d), which depends positively on the level of income (Y) and negatively on the interest rate (r).

The condition met for each point on the IS curve is

$$I + G = S + T \qquad (6.8)$$

The level of investment (I) plus government spending (G) is equal to the level of saving (S) plus taxes (T). Let us derive a linear form of this condition.

In Chapter 5 we saw that saving could be represented by the saving function

$$S = -a + (1 - b)Y_D = -a + (1 - b)(Y - T) \qquad (5.12)$$

The level of investment is assumed to have an autonomous component and to depend negatively on the interest rate. In linear form we can write an *investment function* in the following way:

$$I = \bar{I} - i_1 r \qquad i_1 > 0 \tag{A.1}$$

where $\bar{I}$ is the autonomous component of investment and i_1 is a parameter that measures the interest sensitivity of investment (i.e., $-i_1 = \Delta I / \Delta r$).[1] The levels of government spending (G) and taxes (T) are assumed to be fixed exogenously by policymakers.

Substituting equation (5.12) for S and equation (A.1) for I into the IS curve equation (6.8), we can write a linear IS curve equation

$$\bar{I} - i_1 r + G = -a + (1 - b)(Y - T) + T \tag{A.2}$$

If we rearrange terms so that the level of income appears alone on the left-hand side, we have

$$Y = \frac{1}{1 - b}[a + \bar{I} + G - bT] - \frac{i_1 r}{1 - b} \tag{A.3}$$

We can also rearrange the terms in our LM equation (6.5) so that the interest rate (r) is alone on the left-hand side, as follows:

$$r = \frac{c_0}{c_2} - \frac{M^s}{c_2} + \frac{c_1 Y}{c_2} \tag{A.4}$$

Equations (A.3) and (A.4) are linear IS and LM curves. These two equations determine the two endogenous variables in the model, the levels of income (Y) and the interest rate (r). From here we proceed to consider the properties of the LM and then the IS curve, deriving in algebraic form the graphical results in Section 6.2. We then examine the solution of these two equations for the equilibrium levels of income and the interest rate, the analog to the graphical representation of equilibrium in Figure 6.18.

A.1 The *LM* Curve

The Slope of the *LM* Curve

The slope of the LM curve will be the change in r (movement up the vertical axis in the IS–LM curve graph) per unit change in Y (the movement along the horizontal axis), holding constant the factors that fix the position of the

---

[1] A parameter is a given or known value. An example of a parameter in our previous analysis is the marginal propensity to save $(1 - b)$ in (5.12).

curve. From equation (A.4) we compute this slope as $\Delta r/\Delta Y$ for fixed values of (c_0/c_2) and $(-M^s/c_2)$, which gives

$$\Delta r = \frac{c_1}{c_2}\Delta Y$$

$$\text{Slope of } LM = \left.\frac{\Delta r}{\Delta Y}\right|_{LM} = \frac{c_1}{c_2} \qquad \text{(A.5)}$$

From equation (A.5) we see that the LM curve has a positive slope. If the expression for the slope of the curve is large (small), then the curve will be steep (flat). From equation (A.5) it can be seen that the curve will be steeper the higher the value of c_1 and the lower the value of c_2. This means that the more money demand increases per unit increase in income (the higher c_1), and the *less* sensitive money demand is to the interest rate (the lower c_2), the steeper will be the LM schedule.[2]

Factors That Shift the LM Curve

Now let us consider factors that shift the LM curve. One way to look at such shifts mathematically is the change in r for a change in one right-hand-side variable in the LM curve equation (A.4) *holding income and the other right-hand-side variables constant*. This is the vertical displacement of the curve. For example, if the money supply changes, all other variables remaining the same, then

$$\Delta r = \frac{-1}{c_2}\Delta M^s$$

$$\left.\frac{\Delta r}{\Delta M^s}\right|_{LM} = \frac{-1}{c_2} < 0 \qquad \text{(A.6)}$$

An increase in the money supply (M^s) causes a downward shift in the LM schedule; $\Delta r / \Delta M^s$ is negative. This is what we found in Figure 6.11; the curve shifts downward and therefore out to the right.

The other factor we considered that would shift the LM curve was a shift in the money demand *function*, a change in the level of money demand for given levels of income and the interest rate. In our linear version of the IS–LM curve model, such a shift in the money demand function is

---

[2]Notice also from equation (A.5) that, as c_2 approaches zero, the expression becomes extremely large, indicating that the LM curve becomes vertical. This is the so-called classical case illustrated in Figure 6.9. Alternatively, as c_2 becomes extremely large, the expression for the slope of the LM curve approaches zero, indicating that the LM curve becomes flat. This is the liquidity-trap case illustrated in Figure 6.10.

represented as a change in the c_0 term in equation (6.5) and therefore in (c_0/c_2) in equation (A.4). For example, an increase in c_0 would mean that more money was demanded for given levels of income and the interest rate. From equation (A.4) we can see that if c_0 rises, then holding constant the other terms on the right-hand side of equation (A.4), the interest rate will rise. This means that, as illustrated in Figure 6.12, an upward shift in the money demand function will shift the LM schedule upward to the left.

A.2 The IS Curve

The Slope of the IS Curve

To compute an expression for the slope of the IS curve, we again consider the relationship between r and Y given the values of the terms that fix the position of the curve [the terms in brackets in equation (A.3)]. From equation (A.3), holding these terms constant, we can write

$$\Delta Y = \frac{-i_1}{1-b}\Delta r$$

or, after rearranging terms

$$\text{Slope of } IS = \left. \frac{\Delta r}{\Delta Y}\right|_{IS} = -\frac{(1-b)}{i_1} < 0 \tag{A.7}$$

As discussed in Section 6.2, the IS slope is negative. The larger the absolute value of the slope of the IS schedule, the steeper the curve will be. From equation (A.7), it follows that the IS curve will be steeper the larger is $(1-b)$, the higher the marginal propensity to save, and the smaller the value i_1, the parameter measuring the interest sensitivity of investment.[3]

Factors That Shift the IS Schedule

Using equation (A.3), it is most convenient to examine the horizontal shift in the IS schedule as the result of changes in the factors that determine the position of the curve. To do this, we examine how Y changes in equation (A.3) as one of the right-hand-side variables changes, *holding constant the interest rate and the other right-hand-side variables*. If, these other things being equal, an increase in a variable raises (lowers) Y, this represents a shift to the right (left) in the IS curve.

---

[3]A special case for the IS curve is where i_1 approaches zero; investment is almost completely interest-insensitive. Here the slope of the IS curve, given by equation (A.7), becomes extremely large; the curve becomes nearly vertical.

For example, if the level of government expenditure changes, from equation (A.3) we compute

$$\Delta Y = \frac{1}{1-b}\Delta G$$

$$\left.\frac{\Delta Y}{\Delta G}\right|_{IS} = \frac{1}{1-b} > 0$$

(A.8)

This is the same result we found in equation 6.11; an increase in government spending shifts the IS curve to the right. From equation (A.3) we can see that the analogous expression for the horizontal shift in the IS schedule as the result of a change in autonomous expenditure ($\bar{I}$) or in the intercept of the consumption function (a) would be identical to equation (A.8). An increase of one unit in each of these would be an increase in autonomous expenditure of one unit, and each would have identical effects in the IS–LM curve model.

Finally, consider the effect on the IS curve of a change in taxes (T). From equation (A.3) we compute

$$\Delta Y = \frac{1}{1-b}(-b\Delta T)$$

or

$$\left.\frac{\Delta Y}{\Delta T}\right|_{IS} = \frac{-b}{1-b} < 0$$

(A.9)

As in the text (see equation 6.12), we see that an increase in taxes would lower income (other things being equal), shifting the IS curve to the left.

A.3 Equilibrium in the IS–LM Curve Model

An equilibrium point in the IS–LM curve model is a combination of income and the interest rate that satisfies both the IS and LM curve conditions. In terms of our linear IS and LM curves, the equilibrium values of Y and r are the values that satisfy both equations (A.3) and (A.4).

To find these values, we solve the two equations. First, we substitute the value of r from equation (A.4) into equation (A.3). Solving the resulting equation for Y yields the equilibrium value for income (Y_0):

$$Y_0 = \left(\frac{1}{(1-b)+i_1 c_1/c_2}\right)\left[a + \bar{I} + G - bT + \frac{i_1}{c_2}(M^s - c_0)\right]$$

(A.10)

We can then find the equilibrium value of the interest rate (r_0) by substituting equation (A.10) or alternatively equation (A.3) into the LM curve equation (A.4). The resulting expression is

$$r_0 = \left(\frac{1}{(1 - b) + i_1 c_1 / c_2}\right)\left[\frac{(1 - b)}{c_2}(c_0 - M^s) + \frac{c_1}{c_2}(a + \overline{I} + G - bT)\right] \quad (A.11)$$

Notice the difference between the IS and LM curve equations (A.3 and A.4) and the solutions for the equilibrium values of Y and r (equations A.10 and A.11). The former equations are relationships that must hold between the two variables, with both Y and r appearing in each equation. The solution for equilibrium Y and r expresses these endogenous variables as depending on the exogenous variables of the model. In Chapter 7 we examine how these equilibrium values of Y and r change with changes in the exogenous variables. The appendix to Chapter 7 extends this analysis to the linear model considered here.

Review Problem

1. Suppose that

$$C = 60 + 0.8Y_D$$
$$I = 150 - 10r$$
$$G = 250$$
$$T = 200$$
$$M^s = 100$$
$$M^d = 40 + .1Y - 10r$$

   a. Write the equations for the IS and LM schedules.
   b. Find the equilibrium values for income (Y_0) and the interest rate (r_0) in the model.

7 The Keynesian System (III): Policy Effects in the *IS–LM* Model

In this chapter we use the *IS–LM* curve model to analyze the effects of various policy actions on the equilibrium levels of income and the interest rate. Other factors that affect income and the interest rate are also considered. The groundwork for this analysis was established in Chapter 6. Equilibrium levels of income and the interest rate are those given by the intersection of the *IS* and *LM* curves. The factors that change these equilibrium levels are those that shift either the *IS* or the *LM* curve, considered in Chapter 6. Here we see how such shifts affect income and the interest rate when we consider the two schedules jointly in Section 7.1. In Section 7.2 we see how the magnitude of the effects of different policies depends on the slopes of the *IS* and *LM* curves. The slopes of the *IS–LM* curves were shown in Chapter 6 to depend on various features of the economic system, the most important being the interest sensitivity of investment and of money demand. In Section 7.2 we see how policy effectiveness depends on these factors.

7.1 • FACTORS AFFECTING EQUILIBRIUM INCOME AND THE INTEREST RATE

Monetary Influences: Shifts in the *LM* Schedule

Consider the effects on income and the interest rate of changes in the quantity of money. Figure 7.1 illustrates the effects of an increase in the quantity of money from M_0 to M_1. Initially, assume that the *IS* and *LM* schedules are IS_0 and LM_0. Income and the interest rate are at Y_0 and r_0, respectively. As we saw in Chapter 6, an increase in the quantity of money shifts the *LM* schedule to the right to a position such as LM_1 in Figure 7.1. Consequently, the interest rate falls from r_0 to r_1 and income rises from Y_0 to Y_1.

The economic process producing these results is straightforward. The increase in the money stock creates an excess supply of money, which causes

173

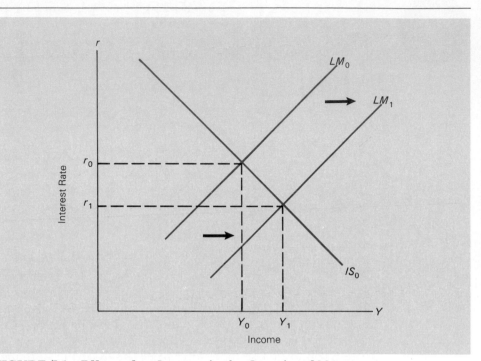

FIGURE 7.1 Effects of an Increase in the Quantity of Money
The initial equilibrium point is at interest rate r_0 and income level Y_0. An increase
in the money stock from M_0 to M_1 shifts the *LM* schedule to the right from LM_0 to
LM_1. The interest rate falls from r_0 to r_1, and income rises from Y_0 to Y_1.

the interest rate to fall. As the interest rate falls, investment demand is
increased, and this causes income to rise, with a further income-induced
increase in consumption demand. A new equilibrium is achieved when the
fall in the interest rate and rise in income jointly increase money demand
by an amount equal to the increase in the money supply. This occurs at the
point where the new *LM* curve intersects the *IS* curve.

A decline in the money stock has just the opposite effects. The *LM* curve
shifts to the left; the equilibrium level of income falls; and the equilibrium
interest rate rises.

The other factor that shifts the *LM* schedule is a shift in the money
demand function. Consider, for example, an increase in money demand *for
given levels of income and the interest rate*. Such a portfolio shift away from
bonds into money will shift the *LM* schedule to the left. As people try to
reduce their bond holdings in order to increase their money holdings, the
interest rate will rise. The higher interest rate will cause income to decline.
An increase in money demand, in the sense of a shift in the function such

that more money is demanded at a given level of income and interest rate, has the same effect as a decline in the money stock. Equilibrium income falls and the interest rate rises. A reverse portfolio shift toward holding more bonds and less money has the opposite effects.

Real Influences: Shifts in the *IS* Schedule

Fiscal policy variables are one set of factors that shift the *IS* schedule and hence affect equilibrium income and the interest rate. Figure 7.2 illustrates the effects of one fiscal policy shift, an increase in government spending from G_0 to G_1. The initial positions of the *IS* and *LM* schedules are given by IS_0 and LM_0. The initial equilibrium values of income and the interest rate are Y_0 and r_0, respectively. The increase in government spending to G_1, as shown in Chapter 6, shifts the *IS* schedule out to the right to a position such as IS_1 in Figure 7.2. The equilibrium level of income rises, as does the equilibrium level of the interest rate.

The force pushing up the level of income is the increase in aggregate demand both directly as government demand rises and then indirectly as a

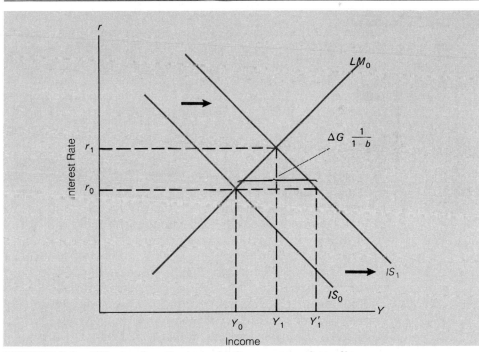

FIGURE 7.2   Effects of an Increase in Government Spending
An increase in government spending shifts the *IS* schedule to the right from IS_0 to IS_1. Income rises from Y_0 to Y_1; the interest rate rises from r_0 to r_1.

result of an income-induced increase in consumer expenditures. The forces pushing up the interest rate require some explanation. Notice that the *LM* schedule does not shift. At a given level of income, equilibrium in the money market, and therefore in the bond market, is undisturbed by the government spending change. It is the rise in income in response to the fiscal policy shift that necessitates the interest rate adjustment. As income increases, the transactions demand for money rises. The money stock is not changed, so the attempt to increase transactions balances requires a decline in the demand for bonds. It is this income-induced increase in money demand and decline in bond demand that causes the interest rate to rise.

In the aggregate, the public cannot increase money holdings; the money stock is fixed. The attempt to do so, however, will push up the interest rate, reducing the speculative demand for money and causing individuals to economize on the amount of transactions balances held for any level of income. At the new equilibrium the interest rate must rise sufficiently that net money demand is unchanged even though income is higher.

It was shown in Chapter 6 that the horizontal distance by which the *IS* curve shifts when government spending increases is equal to $\Delta G(1/(1 - b))$ where ΔG equals $(G_1 - G_0)$. The distance of the shift in the *IS* curve is the increase in government spending times the autonomous expenditure multiplier from the simple (no money market) Keynesian model. This horizontal distance equals the amount by which income would have increased in that simple model. In Figure 7.2 this increase in equilibrium income would have been to Y_1'. When we take into account the required adjustment in the money market, it can be seen that income rises by less than this amount, to Y_1 in Figure 7.2. Why?

The difference between the simple Keynesian model and the *IS–LM* curve model is that the latter includes a money market. When government spending increases, as we have just seen, the rate of interest must rise to maintain equilibrium in the money market. The increase in the interest rate will cause a decline in investment spending. The decline in investment spending will partially offset the increase in aggregate demand resulting from the increase in government spending. Consequently, the increase in income will be less than that in the simple Keynesian model, where investment was taken as completely autonomous. By neglecting the necessary increase in the interest rate and consequent decline in investment that accompany an increase in government spending, the simple Keynesian model *overstated* the effect of an increase in government spending.

Next, consider the effects in the model of an increase in the level of tax collections *(T)* as illustrated in Figure 7.3. An increase in tax collections from T_0 to T_1 will, as shown in Chapter 6, shift the *IS* curve to the left. In the figure this is shown as a shift in the *IS* curve from its initial position IS_0 to IS_1. As can be seen, income declines from Y_0 to Y_1. The interest rate also declines, from r_0 to r_1.

Income falls as taxes rise because the tax increase lowers disposable income $(Y - T)$ and causes consumption to decline. The reason for the drop in the interest rate parallels that for the income-induced interest rate increase when government spending was increased. As income declines as a result of the tax increase, money demand declines and bond demand increases. This causes the interest rate to fall.

As was the case with a change in government spending, Figure 7.3 indicates that income falls by less than the horizontal distance of the shift in the IS curve. The horizontal distance by which the IS curve shifts with a change in taxes is, as explained in Chapter 6, equal to $\Delta T(-b/(1 - b))$, the tax multiplier from the simple Keynesian model times the change in taxes. Thus it is again true that in the IS–LM curve model, fiscal policy multipliers are reduced relative to our results for the simple Keynesian model. For a tax increase, the reason for this is that the decline in the interest rate discussed previously will cause investment to rise, partially offsetting the decline in consumption caused by the tax increase. The simple Keynesian model

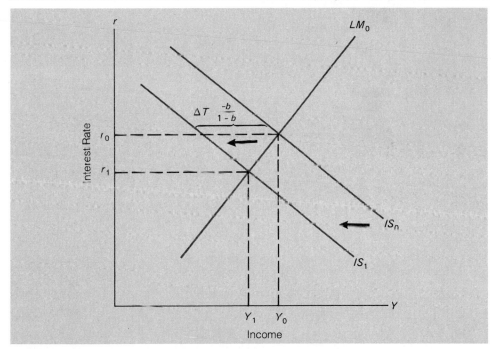

FIGURE 7.3 Effects of and Increase in Taxes
An increase in taxes shifts the IS schedule to the left from IS_0 to IS_1. Income falls from Y_0 to Y_1, and the interest rate falls from r_0 to r_1.

assumed investment to be fixed, neglected this offset, and hence overstated the effects of the tax increase.

A decrease in taxes has just the opposite effects of the tax increase. The *IS* curve shifts to the right, and both income and the interest rate rise. Similarly, a decline in government spending has effects just opposite to those for the increase in government spending.

Within the *IS–LM* curve model, we can derive a result similar to the balanced budget multiplier in Chapter 5, that is, a multiplier giving the effect on income of a change in government spending financed by an equal change in tax collections ($\Delta Y/\Delta G + \Delta Y/\Delta T$). Figure 7.4 illustrates the effects of an increase in government spending financed by an increase in taxes *of an equal amount*. The increase in government spending shifts the *IS* curve to the right, from IS_0 to IS_1' in Figure 7.4. The horizontal distance by which the curve shifts is $\Delta G(1/(1-b))$, as shown in the graph. The increase in taxes shifts the

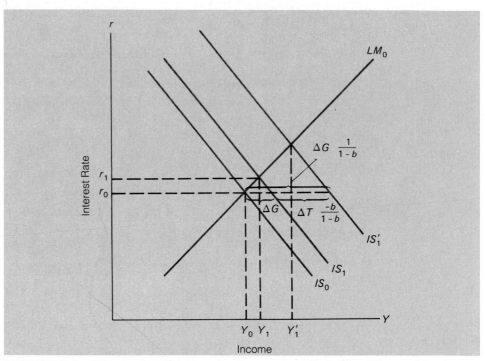

FIGURE 7.4 Effects of an Increase in Government Spending Financed by an Equal Increase in Tax Collections

An increase in government spending shifts the *IS* schedule from IS_0 to IS_1'. An increase of an equal amount in taxes shifts the *IS* schedule to the left from IS_1' to IS_1'. The *IS* curve does not, however, shift all the way back to IS_0. Income rises from Y_0 to Y_1, and the interest rate rises from r_0 to r_1.

IS curve back to the left by an amount equal to $\Delta T(-b/(1-b))$, or equivalently since ΔT equals ΔG by $\Delta G(-b/(1-b))$. In Figure 7.4 this is shown as a shift from IS_1' to IS_1. The crucial point to note here is that the initial shift to the right caused by the increase in government spending is only partially offset by the increase in taxes,

$$\Delta G\left(\frac{1}{1-b}\right) + \Delta G\left(\frac{-b}{1-b}\right) = \frac{\Delta G - b\Delta G}{1-b}$$

$$= \Delta G\left(\frac{1-b}{1-b}\right) = \Delta G \qquad (7.1)$$

There is a net shift to the right in the IS curve by the distance ΔG, the amount of the balanced increase in the size of the government budget. This is the result that parallels the balanced budget multiplier of Chapter 5.

As with the fiscal policy actions considered previously, however, the actual change in income is less than the horizontal shift in the IS curve and therefore less than the multiplier from the simple model, which for this case was unity. As can be seen from Figure 7.4, the net shift in the IS curve from IS_0 to IS_1 increases income to Y_1, an increase of less than ΔG, and causes the interest rate to rise to r_1. As was the case with expansionary fiscal policy actions considered previously, the interest rate must rise to clear the money market as income increases. This causes investment demand to decline and explains why income rises by less than in the simple Keynesian model.

To summarize, as in the simple Keynesian model, government spending changes have a greater per-dollar effect on income than do tax changes. As a consequence, a change in the size of the budget holding the deficit constant (an equal change in spending and taxes) causes income to change in the same direction as the change in the size of the government budget.

Fiscal policy variables are not the only factors that can shift the IS schedule. Any autonomous change in the aggregate demand for output will have this effect. One such change is an autonomous change in investment demand, by which is meant a shift in the function giving the level of investment for each level of the interest rate. Such a change would occur, for example, if, as a result of some exogenous event, the expected profitability of investment projects changed.

Figure 7.5 illustrates the effects of an autonomous decline in investment demand. In Figure 7.5a the investment schedule is plotted. The initial schedule is $I_0(r)$. The autonomous decline in investment of $\Delta \overline{I}$ shifts the schedule to the left to $I_1(r)$ reducing the level of investment at each rate of interest. In Figure 7.5b this autonomous decline in investment demand shifts the IS schedule to the left, from IS_0 to IS_1. Income falls from Y_0 to Y_1. The interest rate declines from r_0 to r_1. Income declines because investment demand at the initial interest rate has fallen (from I_0 to I_1' in Figure 7.5a). As income falls, an income-induced decline in consumption spending also occurs. The

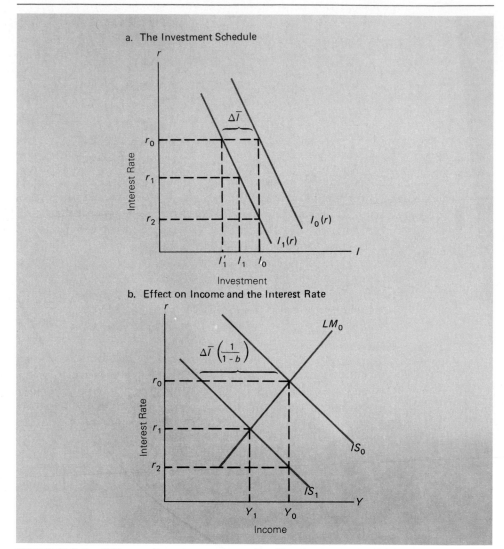

a. The Investment Schedule

b. Effect on Income and the Interest Rate

FIGURE 7.5 Effects of an Autonomous Decline in Investment Demand
An autonomous decline in investment shifts the investment schedule to the left in part a. At the initial interest rate r_0 this shift causes investment to fall from I_0 to I_1'. The shift in the investment function causes the IS schedule in part b to shift to the left from IS_0 to IS_1. Equilibrium income falls from Y_0 to Y_1, and the equilibrium interest rate falls from r_0 to r_1. As a result of the fall in the interest rate, investment is revived somewhat to I_1 in part a.

interest-rate decline is also income-induced, as was the case when we considered the interest-rate effects of fiscal policy changes. The decline in income causes money demand to fall and bond demand to rise; consequently, the interest rate falls.

Notice that the decline in the interest rate causes investment to return somewhat toward its initial level. At the new equilibrium, investment demand is at I_1, in Figure 7.5a, having increased from I_1' to I_1, as a result of the decline in the interest rate.

It is of interest to compare the effects of an autonomous decline in investment in the $IS–LM$ curve version of the Keynesian model, with the effect of the same shift within the classical model analyzed previously (Section 4.2). There the interest rate played a stabilizing role such that a change in investment demand did not affect aggregate demand. The interest rate fell sufficiently to restore aggregate demand to its initial level. In the $IS–LM$ model the interest-rate adjustment is stabilizing but incomplete. For income to be unchanged with an autonomous decline in investment, the interest rate would have to fall to the level r_2 in Figure 7.5b. At that level of the interest rate, income would be at the original level Y_0 along the new IS schedule IS_1. In Figure 7.5a it can be seen that at level r_2, the interest rate has fallen sufficiently to return investment to its initial level I_0. The interest rate falls only to r_1, however; the offset to the initial autonomous drop in investment demand is incomplete.

In one case the offset is complete, that is, where the interest rate would fall to r_2. This is where the LM schedule is vertical. In that case, when the IS schedule shifted from IS_0 to IS_1, we simply moved down the vertical LM schedule to a new equilibrium at the initial income level Y_0 and with the interest rate having declined to r_2. The vertical LM schedule was termed a classical case, so it should not be surprising that classical conclusions result from that assumption. An explanation of these classical results for the vertical LM curve case is provided in the next section.

7.2 • THE RELATIVE EFFECTIVENESS OF MONETARY AND FISCAL POLICY

In Section 7.1 we examined the qualitative effects of monetary and fiscal policy actions within the $IS–LM$ curve model, as summarized in Table 7.1. As can be seen from the table, both monetary and fiscal policy instruments can be used to affect the level of income. In this section we examine the relative effectiveness of the two types of policy actions. By "effectiveness" is meant the size of the effect on income of a given change in the policy variable. The effectiveness of each type of policy (monetary and fiscal) will be shown to depend on the slopes of the IS and LM curves, which in turn are determined by certain behavioral parameters of our model.

Policy Effectiveness and the Slope of the *IS* Schedule

First we examine how the slope of the *IS* curve influences the effectiveness of monetary and fiscal policy. As we saw earlier, the crucial parameter determining the slope of the *IS* schedule is the (absolute value of the) interest elasticity of investment. If investment demand is highly interest-elastic, meaning that a given rise in the interest rate will reduce investment by a large amount, the *IS* curve will be relatively flat. The lower the value of the interest elasticity of investment demand, the steeper will be the *IS* curve.

Here, and when we consider the influence on policy effectiveness of the slope of the *LM* curve later, we proceed as follows. First, we compare the effects of monetary and fiscal policy on income when the schedule, here the *IS* curve, is steep and when it is flat. The monetary policy action considered is an increase in the money stock. The fiscal policy action considered is an increase in government spending. Since both tax changes and spending changes work by shifting the *IS* schedule, tax changes and government spending changes are effective or ineffective in the same circumstances. No separate evaluation of tax policy effectiveness is required.

As a measure of whether fiscal policy actions are effective or not, we compare the effect of the policy action on income with the effect predicted by the simple Keynesian model. In moving to the *IS–LM* curve model, we add a money market to the Keynesian system. By comparing the effect of fiscal policy in the *IS–LM* model with the effect in the simple Keynesian system, where fiscal policy variables are major determinants of income, we see how the addition of the money market modifies our previous results. The distance of the horizontal shift in the *IS* curve for a given fiscal policy action equals the effect on income in the simple Keynesian model (e.g., $\Delta Y = \Delta G(1/(1-b))$, for a government spending change). Consequently, to evaluate the effectiveness of fiscal policy on the following graphs, we compare the change in income with the horizontal shift in the *IS* curve.

To evaluate the effectiveness of monetary policy, we compare the effect on income of the change in the money stock with the horizontal distance of

TABLE 7.1   Effects of Monetary and Fiscal Policy Variables[a]

Effect of		M	G	T
on	Y	+	+	−
	r	−	+	−

[a]M, money stock; G, level of government spending; T, taxes. A + sign indicates that a change in the policy instrument causes the variable in that row (Y or r) to move in the same direction. A − sign indicates the reverse.

the shift in the *LM* schedule. The horizontal shift in the *LM* schedule when the money stock changes is equal to $\Delta M(1/c_1)$ where c_1 is the coefficient on income in the money demand function [equation (6.4)]. The coefficient c_1 gives the amount of the increase in money demand per unit of income; therefore, ΔM $(1/c_1)$ gives the increase in income that could occur for an increase in the money stock if *all* new money balances went to support increased transactions demand for money due to increased income. This is the amount of the increase in income for a given level of the interest rate, and thus the amount of the horizontal shift in the *LM* schedule. This distance measures the maximum possible increase in income for a given increase in the money stock.

Monetary Policy Effectiveness and the Slope of the *IS* Schedule

Figures 7.6*a* and *b* show the effects of an increase in the quantity of money for two differently sloped *IS* schedules. In each case the increase in the money stock shifts the *LM* schedule from LM_0 to LM_1. In Figure 7.6*a* the *IS* schedule is steep, reflecting a low interest elasticity of investment demand. As can be seen from the graph, monetary policy is relatively ineffective in this case. Income rises very little as a result of the increase in the money stock.

In Figure 7.6*b* the slope of the *LM* schedule has been kept the same as in Figure 7.6*a*. The size of the horizontal shift in the *LM* schedule, $\Delta M(1/c_1)$ which fixes the size of the policy action, has also been kept the same. The only difference is in the slope of the *IS* schedule. In Figure 7.6*b* that schedule is drawn much flatter, reflecting a higher interest elasticity of investment demand. As can be seen, monetary policy becomes more effective when the *IS* schedule is flatter.

Within the *IS–LM* curve model, monetary policy affects income by lowering the interest rate and stimulating investment demand. If investment demand is little affected by interest rate changes, which is the assumption in Figure 7.6*a*, monetary policy will be ineffective. In Figure 7.6*b*, where the interest sensitivity of investment is assumed to be substantially greater, monetary policy has correspondingly greater effects. Our first result in this section is, then, that monetary policy is ineffective when the *IS* schedule is steep, that is, when investment is interest-inelastic. Monetary policy is more effective the higher the interest elasticity of investment, and thus the flatter the *IS* schedule.

Here and subsequently, we consider several extreme cases for the slopes of the *IS* or *LM* schedule. Consideration of such extreme cases is helpful in understanding our results in the "normal" cases.

The first extreme case is that of the vertical *IS* schedule. The *IS* curve will be vertical if investment is completely insensitive to changes in the interest rate (interest elasticity equals zero). The effects of an increase in the money

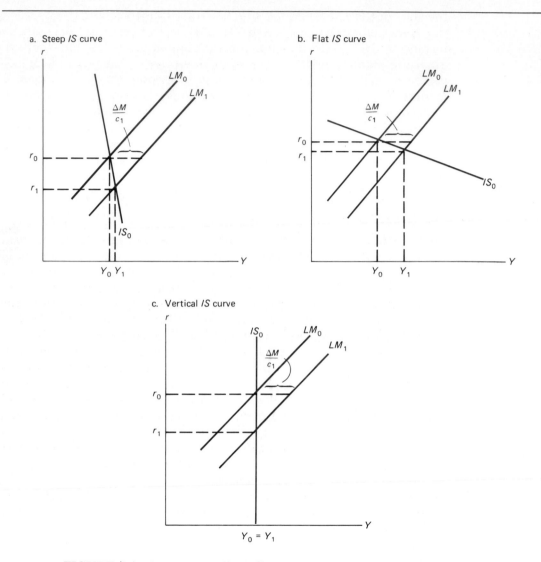

FIGURE 7.6 Monetary Policy Effects and the Slope of the *IS* Schedule
An increase in the money stock shifts the *LM* schedule to the right from LM_0 to LM_1. This expansionary monetary policy action has only a small effect on output in part *a*, where the *IS* curve is steep, but a much larger effect in part *b*, where the *IS* curve is relatively flat. In part *c*, where the *IS* curve is vertical, the increase in the money stock has no effect on equilibrium income.

stock for this case are shown in Figure 7.6c. If the *IS* curve is vertical, as shown in the graph, increasing the money stock simply shifts the *LM* schedule down along the *IS* schedule. The interest rate falls until money demand increases by enough to restore equilibrium in the money market, but income is unchanged. To increase income, the increase in the money stock and resulting fall in the interest rate must stimulate investment demand. When the *IS* curve is vertical, investment is not affected by monetary policy because, by assumption, investment demand does not depend on the interest rate. The steeper the *IS* curve, the closer we come to this extreme case and the less effective is monetary policy.

Fiscal Policy Effectiveness and the Slope of the *IS* Schedule

Figure 7.7a and b show the effects of an increase in government spending in the case of a steep *IS* schedule (7.7a) and a relatively flat *IS* schedule (7.7b). In both cases the increase in government spending shifts the *IS* schedule from IS_0 to IS_1. The horizontal distance of the shift in the curve $\Delta G(1/(1-b))$ is the same in both cases, meaning that the size of the policy action as well as the autonomous expenditure multiplier from the simple Keynesian model are equal in both cases. As can be seen from these graphs, fiscal policy is much more effective where the *IS* schedule is steep (Figure 7.7a).

The steep *IS* curve occurs when investment is relatively interest-inelastic. What we have found is that the less sensitive investment is to the interest rate, the greater the effect of a given fiscal policy action is. To see why, consider the role of the interest-rate change in the adjustment to a new equilibrium after an increase in government spending. As income increases following the rise in government spending, the interest rate must rise to keep the money market in equilibrium. This rise in the interest rate causes investment to decline, partially offsetting the expansionary effect of the government spending increase. It is this interest-rate–induced decline in investment that causes the income response in the *IS–LM* curve model to fall short of the response given by the multiplier from the simple Keynesian system; that is, income rises by less than the horizontal shift in the *IS* schedule.

How important is this effect on investment, which is often referred to as "crowding out"? One factor determining the importance of such crowding out of private investment is the slope of the *IS* curve. If investment is not very sensitive to changes in the interest rate, the assumption in Figure 7.7a, then the interest-rate increase will cause only a slight drop in investment, and income will rise by almost the full amount of the horizontal shift in the *IS* curve. Alternatively, if investment is highly interest-sensitive, the assumption in Figure 7.7b, then the rise in the interest rate will reduce investment substantially, and the increase in income will be reduced significantly relative to the prediction of the simple Keynesian model.

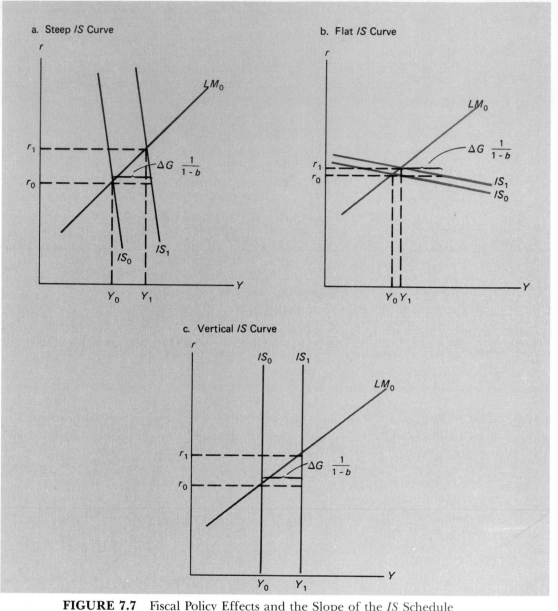

FIGURE 7.7 Fiscal Policy Effects and the Slope of the *IS* Schedule

In each part of the figure an increase in government spending shifts the *IS* curve to the right from IS_0 to IS_1. In part *a*, where the *IS* curve is steep, this expansionary fiscal policy action results in a relatively large increase in income. This fiscal policy action is much less effective (the increase in income is much smaller) in part *b*, where the *IS* curve is relatively flat. Fiscal policy is most effective in part *c*, where the *IS* curve is vertical.

The case of the vertical *IS* curve is shown in Figure 7.7*c*. Here investment is completely interest-insensitive. The increase in government spending causes the interest rate to rise, but this does not result in a decline in investment. Income increases by the full amount of the distance of the horizontal shift in the *IS* curve. In this case, the simple Keynesian model does not overstate the effects of fiscal policy because there is no crowding out of private investment expenditures.

A comparison of the results in this subsection with those in the preceding subsection shows that fiscal policy is most effective when the *IS* curve is steep (low interest elasticity of investment), while monetary policy is most effective when the *IS* curve is flat (high interest elasticity of investment). This is a result of the different role that the interest rate plays in transmitting the effects of these policy actions. Monetary policy affects income by means of an effect on interest rates. Consequently, the greater the effect of interest rates on aggregate demand, *ceteris paribus*, the greater will be the effects of a given monetary policy action. In the case of fiscal policy, the interest-rate change offsets the fiscal policy effects. A larger interest elasticity of investment will mean that more of the expansionary effect of an increase in government spending will be offset by an interest-rate–induced decline in investment, and thus the greater will be the "crowding-out" effect. Fiscal policy will be more effective, again *ceteris paribus*, the lower the interest elasticity of investment.

Policy Effectiveness and the Slope of the *LM* Schedule

The slope of the *LM* schedule has been shown to depend most crucially on the interest elasticity of money demand. A high interest elasticity of money demand causes the *LM* schedule to be relatively flat. At progressively lower values of the interest elasticity of money demand, the *LM* curve will become steeper. If money demand is completely insensitive to the interest rate (interest elasticity is zero), the *LM* schedule will be vertical. In this section we see how monetary and fiscal policy effectiveness depend on the slope of the *LM* schedule and, hence, on the interest elasticity of money demand.

Fiscal Policy Effectiveness and the Slope of the *LM* Schedule

Figure 7.8 illustrates the effects of an increase in government spending for three separate assumptions concerning the slope of the *LM* schedule. In Figure 7.8*a* the *LM* schedule is rather flat, in 7.8*b* the schedule is steep, and in 7.8*c* the *LM* schedule is vertical. In each case the increase in government spending is assumed to shift the *IS* curve from IS_0 to IS_1. The slope of the *IS* curve is the same in each graph. The size of the increase in government expenditure is also the same. As can be seen from the graph, the effect

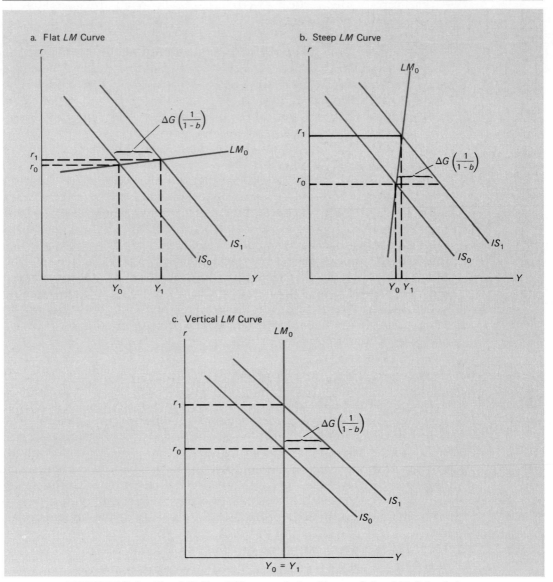

FIGURE 7.8 Fiscal Policy Effects and the Slope of the *LM* Schedule
In each part of the figure an increase in government spending shifts the *IS* schedule
to the right from IS_0 to IS_1. Fiscal policy is most effective in part *a*, where the *LM*
schedule is relatively flat; less effective in part *b*, where the *LM* curve is steeper; and
completely ineffective in part *c*, where the *LM* curve is vertical.

on income of this expansionary fiscal policy action is largest when the *LM* schedule is relatively flat (Figure 7.8*a*) and less when the curve is relatively steep (Figure 7.8*b*). In the extreme case in which the *LM* schedule is vertical, the increase in government spending has no effect on equilibrium income.

Fiscal policy is seen to be most effective when the interest elasticity of money demand is high, making the *LM* schedule relatively flat. The reason for this result again concerns the effect of the interest-rate adjustment on investment following the fiscal policy shift. The increase in government spending causes income to rise. As income rises, the demand for transactions balances increases, and to reequilibrate the money market with an unchanged stock of money requires a rise in the interest rate. The rise in the interest rate must lower the speculative demand for money and cause individuals and corporations to economize on the use of transactions balances. If money demand is highly sensitive to changes in the interest rate, only a small rise in the interest rate is required to restore equilibrium in the money market. This is the case in Figure 7.8*a*, where the interest rate rises by only a small amount, from r_0 to r_1.

Since in this case there is only a small increase in the interest rate, other things being equal, the decline in investment because of the interest rate increase will be small.[1] With little crowding out of private investment, income rises by nearly the full amount of the horizontal shift in the *IS* curve.

When money demand is relatively interest-inelastic (Figure 7.8*b*), a greater increase in the interest rate (from r_0 to r_1 in Figure 7.8*b*) is required to reequilibrate the money market as income rises. The larger increase in the interest rate leads to a larger decline in investment spending, offsetting more of the expansionary effect of the increase in government spending. Consequently, the increase in income for the steeper *LM* curve (Figure 7.8*b*) is a smaller proportion of the horizontal shift in the *IS* curve.

If money demand is completely insensitive to changes in the interest rate (Figure 7.8*c*) only one level of income can be an equilibrium level—the level that generates transactions demand just equal to the fixed money stock. An increase in aggregate demand, caused by an increase in government spending, creates an upward pressure on income at a given interest rate. There is an excess demand for goods (*G* is higher, *C* and *I* are unchanged). However, the attempt to increase income (or a temporary rise in income) leads to an increased demand for transactions balances and causes the interest rate to rise. *Equilibrium* income cannot, in fact, be higher than Y_0, since no possible increase in the interest rate will reequilibrate the money market at a higher level of income. A new equilibrium will be achieved when, in the attempt to acquire transaction balances to support a higher income level, an

---

[1] The primary "other thing" being held equal in this case is the amount by which a given increase in the interest rate will cause investment to decline—the interest elasticity of investment.

attempt that must fail in the aggregate, individuals bid the interest rate up by enough to return aggregate demand to its initial level. In Figure 7.8c this occurs at interest rate r_1. At that point private investment has declined by an amount just equal to the increase in government spending. Crowding out is complete in this case.

The vertical LM case was referred to previously as a "classical" case because the classical economists failed to take account systematically of the dependence of money demand on the interest rate. Implicitly, they assumed that money demand was completely interest-inelastic. Notice that in this classical case our fiscal policy results are classical in nature, even though in other respects (the relationships underlying the IS curve) the model we are using is Keynesian.[2] An increase in government expenditures affects the interest rate but not the level of income. Crowding out is complete.

At the end of Section 7.1 we saw that for this case of a vertical LM curve, an autonomous change in investment demand would also leave income unchanged. The interest-rate adjustment would have completely offset the initial drop in investment demand in the case considered there. Again, for changes in the government component of autonomous expenditures, the interest rate adjusts fully, so that total aggregate demand ($C + I + G$) is not affected by the shift.

A necessary element, then, in the Keynesian view that changes in autonomous expenditure resulting from fiscal policy actions do affect income is the belief that money demand does depend on the rate of interest. This belief follows from considering the role that money plays as an asset, as an alternative store of wealth to bonds. The classical view of money focused simply on its role in transactions, and thus the classical economists were led to neglect the role of the interest rate in determining money demand. Keynes's theory of the relationship between money demand and the interest rate was a crucial part of his theory.

Monetary Policy Effectiveness and the Slope of the LM Schedule

Figure 7.9 shows the effects of an increase in the quantity of money for the same three assumptions about the LM schedule as those considered previously. In part a, the LM schedule is relatively flat. In part b, the LM curve is steeper; and in part c, the schedule is vertical. In each case the increase in the money stock shifts the LM schedule by an equal amount from LM_0 to LM_1.

As can be seen from the figure, monetary policy is least effective in Figure 7.9a, where the LM schedule is relatively flat (the interest elasticity of money demand is high). The effect on income of the increase in the money stock is successively greater as we consider Figure 7.9b, where the interest elasticity

---

[2] The classical analysis of fiscal policy effects is discussed in Section 4.3.

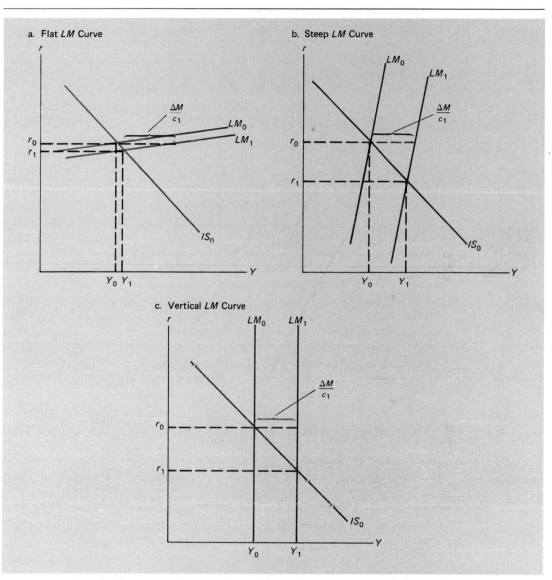

FIGURE 7.9 Monetary Policy Effects and the Slope of the LM Schedule
In each part of the figure an increase in the money stock shifts the LM schedule to
the right from LM_0 to LM_1. Monetary policy is least effective in part a, where the
LM curve is relatively flat; more effective in part b where the LM curve is steeper;
and most effective in part c, where the LM curve is vertical.

of money demand is lower, and then Figure 7.9c, where the interest elasticity of money demand is zero and the *LM* curve is vertical.

The reason for this can be seen by comparing the fall in the interest rate that results from the money stock increase in each case. At the initial level of income and the interest rate the increase in the money stock will create an excess supply of money, causing the interest rate to fall. This fall in the interest rate will stimulate investment and, hence, income. The interest rate must decline to a point where the lower interest rate and higher income level have increased money demand by an amount equal to the increase in the money supply. In Figure 7.9a, where money demand is very interest-sensitive, a small drop in the interest rate is all that is required for this purpose. Consequently, the increase in investment, and hence income, will be small in this case. With a highly interest-elastic demand for money, as the interest rate falls, individuals substantially increase their speculative balances and economize less on transactions balances. Most of the newly created money is used for these purposes, and relatively little ends up as transactions balances required by a higher level of income.

In Figure 7.9b the interest elasticity of money demand is lower, and a larger fall in the interest rate is required to reequilibrate the money market following the increase in the money stock. As a consequence, investment, and therefore income, increase by a greater amount. In Figure 7.9c, where money demand is completely interest-inelastic, there is again a fall in the interest rate following an increase in the money supply. Here the fall in the interest rate itself does nothing to increase the demand for money and restore equilibrium in the money market, since in this case money demand does not depend on the interest rate. The fall in the interest rate, however, causes investment and income to rise. The rise in income will continue until all the new money is absorbed into additional transaction balances. Clearly, this is the maximum possible increase in income for a given increase in the money stock, since all of the new money balances end up as transaction balances required by the higher income level. None of the new money is siphoned off as an increase in speculative demand as the interest rate falls. There is also no tendency for the amount of transactions balances held for a given income level to rise as the interest rate falls.

To summarize, the effect on the level of income of a given increase in the money stock is greater the lower the interest elasticity of money demand.

As in our discussion of the *IS* schedule, we find here that the condition that makes monetary policy most effective makes fiscal policy least effective. Monetary policy effectiveness increases as the interest elasticity of money demand is reduced. Fiscal policy is more effective the higher the interest elasticity of money demand. The reason for this difference is again the differing role of the interest-rate adjustment in transmitting monetary and fiscal policy effects. For the case of monetary policy, which affects income by means of an effect on the interest rate, the *greater* the interest rate response, the more effective the policy action will be. As we have just seen, the interest-rate response is greatest when the interest elasticity of money demand is low (i.e., the *LM* schedule is steep).

For the case of fiscal policy where the interest-rate response, with the resulting crowding out of investment, offsets part of the effect of the policy action, the income response is greater the *smaller* the interest rate response. A high interest elasticity of money demand reduces the effects of a fiscal policy action on the interest rate (compare parts *a* and *b* of Figure 7.8). Therefore, fiscal policy is most effective when the interest elasticity of money demand is high (i.e., the *LM* schedule is flat).

Read Perspectives 7.1.

7.3 • CONCLUSION

In Section 7.1 we examined the effects of monetary and fiscal policy actions on income and the interest rate assuming that the *IS–LM* curves had normal slopes, that is, the slopes of both the *IS* and *LM* schedules were in an intermediate range—neither so steep nor so flat as to make either monetary or fiscal policy impotent. In Section 7.2 the relationships between the slopes of the *IS* and *LM* schedules and the relative effectiveness of monetary and fiscal policies were examined in some detail. The results of that analysis are summarized in Table 7.2.

A relevant question to consider at this point is which of the cases in the table actually characterizes the economy. What are the actual slopes of the relationships in our economy that correspond to the model's *IS* and *LM* curves? We see in our later analysis that this question is still subject to dispute.

TABLE 7.2   Relative Monetary and Fiscal Policy Effectiveness and the Slopes of the *IS* and *LM* Curves

| | **Monetary Policy** | |
	IS Curve	*LM* Curve
Steep	ineffective	effective
Flat	effective	ineffective

| | **Fiscal Policy** | |
	IS Curve	*LM* Curve
Steep	effective	ineffective
Flat	ineffective	effective

PERSPECTIVES

THE MONETARY–FISCAL POLICY MIX: SOME HISTORICAL EXAMPLES

We have seen that either monetary or fiscal policy can, in general, affect income in the Keynesian view. But the effects of each policy on the interest rate, and therefore on investment, are quite different. In the case of expansionary monetary policy, the interest rate declines and investment increases. With an expansionary fiscal policy action—an income tax cut, for example—the interest rate rises and investment declines. This is a significant difference because the level of investment determines the rate of capital formation and is important to longer-term growth of the economy.

Our analysis, then, suggests that within a Keynesian framework there is a preference for a policy *mix* of relatively "tight" fiscal policy and "easy" monetary policy in order to keep the interest rate low and encourage investment. Moreover, whenever fiscal policy actions such as income tax cuts are used to expand the economy, the Keynesians would like to see *an accommodating* monetary policy—an accompanying increase in the money supply that will prevent the interest rate from rising and thus prevent the crowding out of investment. Such a monetary–fiscal policy combination is illustrated in Figure 7.10. At the same time the *IS* curve is shifted to the right by a tax cut, the money stock is increased sufficiently so that the *LM* curve shifts far enough to the right to prevent a rise in the interest rate.

As an example of such a coordinated expansion, the Keynesians point to the tax cut of 1964 and the accompanying increase in money supply growth. As explained in Perspectives 5.1, the tax cut was 20 percent

for individuals and 10 percent for businesses. Growth in the money supply increased to 4.7 percent over the 1964–65 period, compared to 3.7 percent in 1963. The result was a GNP growth of 5.4 percent in 1964 and 5.5 percent in 1965 (rates well above growth in potential output). As a result of the accommodating monetary policy, the interest rate (corporate bond rate) rose only slightly, from 4.0 percent in 1963 to 4.3 percent in 1965. The business tax reductions included in the 1964 tax cut were also aimed at preventing any decline in investment. In fact, fixed business investment increased from 9.0 to 10.5 percent of GNP between 1963 and 1965.

Later, Keynesian economists were critical of the monetary–fiscal policy mix in the first Reagan administration. They interpreted this mix as one of tight monetary policy, as growth in the money stock slowed, and easy fiscal policy, primarily the large cuts in personal and business taxes. The Keynesians saw the two policy moves as canceling each other out in terms of their effects on GNP. Keynesian economist James Tobin compared the Reagan policy to putting a train in New Haven, Connecticut, with an engine on the front headed for Boston and one in the back headed for New York. In graphical terms, the Keynesians saw the Reagan administration's monetary policy shifting the *LM* curve to the left to lower income while fiscal policy shifted the *IS* curve to the right to increase income. They believed that both policies would increase the interest rate (both curves shift upward) with unfavorable effects on investment.

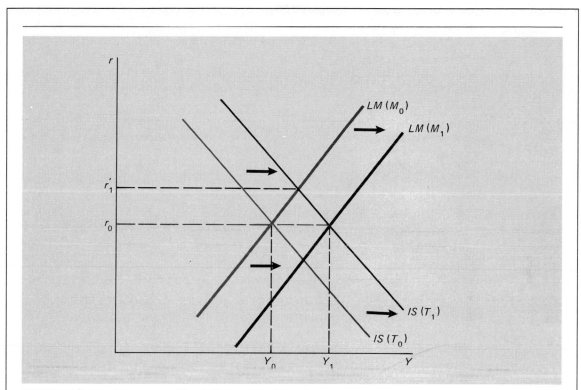

FIGURE 7.10   Monetary–Fiscal Policy Combination

A tax cut from T_0 to T_1 shifts the *IS* schedule from $IS(T_0)$ to $IS(T_1)$. Of itself, this fiscal policy shift would push the interest rate upward to r_1'. If the tax cut were accompanied by an increase in the money stock from M_0 to M_1, the *LM* schedule would shift to the right from $LM(M_0)$ to $LM(M_1)$. Together, the two policy actions would increase output to Y_1, with the interest rate remaining at r_0.

The Reagan administration's macroeconomic policies were, however, much more influenced by the supply-side views of tax cuts (Perspective 4.2) than by Keynesian analysis.

We return to an analysis of the Reagan administration's monetary and fiscal policies in Section 17.3.

Issues concerning the slopes of the *IS* and *LM* schedules form a part of the controversy between the Keynesians and the next group of macroeconomists whose theoretical system we analyze, the monetarists. There is also some divergence between the positions of some of the earlier Keynesians and current-day Keynesians on the issue of the slopes of these schedules. These differences are analyzed later. Here we confine ourselves to the position of the modern-day Keynesians. The modern Keynesian view is that both the *IS* and *LM* curve slopes are in the intermediate or normal range, where both monetary and fiscal policies are effective in controlling income. Our results in Section 7.1—summarized in Table 7.1—characterize this modern Keynesian position.

Review Questions and Problems

1. Within the *IS–LM* curve model, show how income and the interest rate are affected by each of the following changes.

    a. An increase in government spending.
    b. An autonomous decline in investment spending.
    c. An increase in taxes.
    d. An increase in the money stock.
    e. An increase in government spending financed by an equal increase in taxes.

In each case explain briefly why the changes in income and the interest rate occur.

2. What would be the effect within the *IS–LM* curve model of an autonomous increase in saving that was matched by a drop in consumption, that is, a fall in *a* in the consumption function?

$$C = a + b(Y - T)$$

Which curve would shift? How would income and the interest rate be affected?

3. Explain the relationship between the effectiveness of monetary policy and the interest elasticity of investment. Will monetary policy be more or less effective the higher the interest elasticity of investment demand? Explain. Now explain the relationship between the effectiveness of fiscal policy and the interest elasticity of investment demand. Why do the two relationships differ?

4. Explain the relationship between the effectiveness of monetary policy and the interest elasticity of money demand. Will monetary policy be more or less effective the higher the interest elasticity of money demand? Explain. Now explain the relationship between fiscal policy and the interest elasticity of money demand. Why do the two relationships differ?

5. Suppose we had a case in which the interest elasticity of *both* money demand and investment was quite low. Would either monetary or fiscal policy be very effective? How would you interpret such a situation?

6. We saw that the interest rate played a stabilizing role in the classical system, adjusting so that a shock to one component of demand, a decline in autonomous investment, for example, would not affect aggregate demand. Does the interest rate perform a similar stabilizing function in the Keynesian model?

7. How do the fiscal policy multipliers in the *IS–LM* model compare to those from the simple Keynesian model of Chapter 5? Are they larger or smaller? Why?

8. In what sense is the situation in which the *LM* schedule is vertical a "classical case"?

Selected Readings

Branson, William, *Macroeconomic Theory and Policy.* New York: Harper & Row, 3rd ed., 1989, Chaps. 4 and 5.

McCallum, Bennett, *Monetary Economics.* New York: Macmillan, 1989, Chap. 5.

Appendix
Monetary and Fiscal Policy Multipliers in the *IS–LM* Curve Model

Here we extend the algebraic treatment of the *IS–LM* model given in the appendix to Chapter 6. We examine how the equilibrium value of income, which was derived there, changes as monetary and fiscal policy variables are changed. In doing so, we establish algebraically the graphical results in Section 7.1. We then consider the same question taken up in Section 7.2, the relative effectiveness of monetary and fiscal policy, within the linear version of the *IS–LM* model.

A.1   The Effects of Monetary and Fiscal Policy on Income

In the appendix to Chapter 6, we derived the following expressions[1] for the equilibrium values of income (Y_0) and the interest rate (r_0) in the *IS–LM*

---

[1]Since we return to equations in the appendix Chapter 6, to avoid confusion, equations here are numbered consecutively to those equations.

curve model:

$$Y_0 = \left(\frac{1}{(1 - b) + i_1 c_1 / c_2} \right) \left[a + \overline{I} + G - bT + \frac{i_1}{c_2} (M^s - c_0) \right] \quad \text{(A.10)}$$

$$r_0 = \left(\frac{1}{(1 - b) + i_1 c_1 / c_2} \right) \left[\frac{(1 - b)}{c_2} (c_0 - M^s) + \frac{c_1}{c_2} (a + \overline{I} + G - bT) \right] \quad \text{(A.11)}$$

We can use these two equations to see how the interest rate and income change when any of the exogenous variables in the model change. This is the mathematical equivalent to seeing how these equilibrium values changed on the graphs in Section 7.1 with a shift in the *IS* or *LM* curves. In this section we compute expressions that show how income changes with changes in policy variables using equation (A.10). Finding the effects on the interest rate of changes in these variables is left as an exercise (see Review Problem 1).

Fiscal Policy

Consider first how equilibrium income changes with a change in government spending. From equation (A.10), letting G vary but holding constant all other exogenous variables, and for given value of the parameters, we compute

$$\Delta Y = \frac{1}{(1 - b) + i_1 c_1 / c_2} \Delta G$$

$$\frac{\Delta Y}{\Delta G} = \frac{1}{(1 - b) + i_1 c_1 / c_2} > 0 \quad \text{(A.12)}$$

Equation (A.12) indicates that, as we saw graphically (Figure 7.2), an increase in government spending will lead to an increase in equilibrium income within the *IS–LM* curve model. Moreover, it can be seen that the increase in equilibrium income per unit increase in government spending, as given by equation (A.12), is *smaller* than in the simple Keynesian model. Within the simple Keynesian model analyzed in Chapter 5, the increase in equilibrium income per unit increase in government spending was given by the autonomous expenditure multiplier $1/(1 - b)$. The *multiplier* in equation (A.12) contains an additional positive term in the denominator ($i_1 c_1 / c_2$) and is therefore smaller.

Notice also, looking back at equation (A.10), that the change in equilibrium income per unit change in autonomous investment ($\Delta Y / \Delta \overline{I}$) would be exactly the same as with a change in government spending.

The effect on income from a change in taxes is

$$\Delta Y = \frac{1}{(1 - b) + i_1 c_1 / c_2} (-b \Delta T)$$

$$\frac{\Delta Y}{\Delta T} = \frac{-b}{(1 - b) + i_1 c_1 / c_2} < 0 \quad \text{(A.13)}$$

This *tax multiplier* is opposite in sign to the government spending multiplier and smaller in absolute value, since $-b$ rather than 1 appears in the numerator.

Monetary Policy

From equation (A.10) we compute the effects on income from a change in the money supply as

$$\Delta Y = \left(\frac{1}{(1 - b) + i_1 c_1/c_2} \right) \frac{i_1}{c_2} \Delta M^s$$

or

$$\frac{\Delta Y}{\Delta M^s} = \left(\frac{1}{(1 - b) + i_1 c_1/c_2} \right) \frac{i_1}{c_2} > 0$$

which simplifies to

$$\frac{\Delta Y}{\Delta M^s} = \frac{i_1}{(1 - b)c_2 + i_1 c_1} \qquad (A.14)$$

An increase in the money supply causes equilibrium income to rise, as was illustrated in Figure 7.1.

A.2   Policy Effectiveness and the Slopes of the *IS* and *LM* Curves

The expressions given by equations (A.12) and (A.14) are, respectively, fiscal and monetary policy *multipliers*. They give the change in equilibrium income per unit change in the policy variables G and M^s. In this section we examine the relationship between the magnitude of these multipliers and the slopes of the *IS* and *LM* curves. Our results parallel those of Section 7.2.[2]

The *IS* Curve and Policy Effectiveness

In the appendix to Chapter 6 we found that the slope of the *IS* schedule was given by

$$\left. \frac{\Delta r}{\Delta Y} \right|_{IS} = -\frac{(1 - b)}{i_1} \qquad (A.7)$$

---

[2]As in the text, we do not need to consider separately the effectiveness of tax policy. The same factors that influence the effectiveness of changes in G determine the effectiveness of changes in T.

The crucial parameter, over which there is some dispute, is i_1, which measures the interest sensitivity of investment demand. If i_1 is large (small), investment demand is interest-sensitive (insensitive), and the IS curve is flat (steep).

Now examine the role i_1 plays in the two multiplier expressions. We see from equation (A.12) that as i_1 becomes smaller, $\Delta Y / \Delta G$ becomes larger. That is, as investment becomes less sensitive to the interest rate and the IS curve becomes steeper, fiscal policy becomes more effective (see Figure 7.7). If i_1 goes to zero, equation (A.12) reduces to $1/(1 - b)$, the multiplier from the simple Keynesian model in Chapter 5.

We next consider equation (A.14), the monetary policy multiplier. As i_1 gets smaller (the IS curve becomes steeper), the numerator in equation (A.14) becomes proportionately smaller, whereas only one term in the denominator falls. Therefore, the value of the expression declines.[3] The lower the interest elasticity of investment, the steeper the IS curve, and the less effective is monetary policy (see Figure 7.6). In the extreme case, where i_1 is zero (vertical IS schedule), the value of equation (A.14) goes to zero; monetary policy becomes completely ineffective.

The LM Curve and Policy Effectiveness

The expression in the appendix to Chapter 6 for the slope of the LM curve was

$$\frac{\Delta r}{\Delta Y}\bigg|_{LM} = \frac{c_1}{c_2} \tag{A.5}$$

The crucial parameter (again the one subject to some dispute) determining whether the curve is steep or flat is c_2, which measures the interest sensitivity of money demand. If, c_2 is large (small), meaning that money demand is interest-sensitive (insensitive), the LM curve will be relatively flat (steep). This follows since it can be seen that the expression in equation (A.5) decreases in value as c_2 becomes larger.

Now examine the way in which c_2 affects the fiscal policy multiplier given by equation (A.12). As c_2 becomes smaller, the second term in the denominator of equation (A.12) becomes larger. No other terms are affected so the whole expression becomes smaller. The lower the interest sensitivity of money demand, the steeper is the LM schedule and the less effective is fiscal policy (see Figure 7.8). In the extreme case in which c_2 approaches zero, the denominator of equation A.12 becomes extremely large and the whole expression goes toward zero. As the LM becomes vertical, fiscal policy becomes completely ineffective.

---

[3]To see this clearly, rewrite the right-hand side of equation (A.14) as $1/[(1 - b)c_2/i_1 + c_1]$. As i_1 falls, the denominator increases in value and the size of the multiplier declines.

Finally, consider the relationship between c_2 and the effectiveness of monetary policy as measured by equation (A.14). As c_2 becomes smaller, the denominator of equation (A.14) becomes smaller and the expression becomes larger. The less sensitive money demand is to the interest rate, the steeper is the LM curve and the more effective is monetary policy (see Figure 7.9). If c_2 is zero, equation (A.14) reduces to $1/c_1$. The LM schedule is vertical, and equilibrium income will increase by the full amount of the horizontal shift in the LM schedule as the money supply increases (Figure 7.9c).

Review Problems

1. Using equation (A.11), show how the equilibrium value of the interest rate (r) will be affected by

    a. an increase in the money supply (M^s).
    b. an increase in government spending (G).
    c. an increase in taxes (T).

2. Start with the solution for the equilibrium values of Y and r from question 1 in the appendix to Chapter 6. Show how these values would change if government spending rose from 250 to 310.

8 The Keynesian System (IV): Aggregate Supply

The preceding three chapters analyzed the determination of income assuming that the price level and the money wage were fixed. With these assumptions in the Keynesian model, output is determined solely by aggregate demand. We have gone this far assuming wages and prices to be constant, not because of the plausibility of that assumption but because the fixed price–fixed wage version of the Keynesian system highlights the role of aggregate demand. This theory of aggregate demand was Keynes's central contribution. The demand-determined nature of output in this fixed price–fixed wage Keynesian model stands in sharp contrast to the supply determined nature of output in the classical system. In this chapter we examine the Keynesian system when prices and wages are not held constant and see that supply factors as well as demand factors play a role in determining output. In this sense the models considered in this chapter are a synthesis of the classical and Keynesian systems. We see, however, that the key feature in the Keynesian system continues to be the fact that aggregate demand is a factor (here not the only factor) determining aggregate output.

We proceed as follows. In Section 8.1 we illustrate the demand-determined nature of output (income) in the Keynesian system. Here we construct a Keynesian aggregate demand curve. In Section 8.2 this Keynesian aggregate demand curve is put together with the classical supply side to form a model of price and output determination. It will be seen that as long as we retain the classical assumptions of perfect information in the labor market and perfect price and wage flexibility,[1] the substitution of the Keynesian aggregate demand curve does not change the classical nature of the model. As long as the supply curve remains vertical, as it does if the foregoing labor market

---

[1] See Section 3.5.

assumptions are made, aggregate output will be determined independently of the assumptions made about the demand side of the model. For aggregate demand to play a role in output determination, which is necessary for the model to be a Keynesian model, the classical labor market assumptions of perfect information and perfect wage and price flexibility must be modified.

The alternative Keynesian assumptions about the supply side of the economy are analyzed in Sections 8.3 and 8.4. In these sections we develop the Keynesian aggregate supply function. In Section 8.5 we see how shifts in this aggregate supply function play a role in determining price and output in the Keynesian model. Section 8.6 considers the policy implications of such supply shocks. The final section of the chapter compares the classical and Keynesian systems.

8.1 • THE KEYNESIAN AGGREGATE DEMAND CURVE

The simple model of Chapter 5 presented Keynes's theory of the aggregate demand for output. The essential notion embodied in the simple Keynesian model was that for a level of output to be an equilibrium level, aggregate demand must equal output. In Chapters 6 and 7 the effect of the interest rate on investment, and hence on aggregate demand, was considered. It was shown that for an output (Y) and interest-rate (r) combination to be an equilibrium point, output must equal aggregate demand, and money demand must also equal money supply.

What guarantees that this level of output will also be equal to aggregate supply—equal to the amount the business sector will choose to produce? No supply considerations were included in these versions of the Keynesian model. We were able to ignore the supply side because of the assumption that the price level and the level of the money wage were fixed. The assumption we were implicitly making about the aggregate supply curve of output is depicted in Figure 8.1. We assumed that any level of output demanded would be forthcoming at the given price level. Supply was assumed to be no constraint on the level of output.

Such an assumption could be a plausible approximation of conditions when the levels of output being considered are far below the capacity of the economy. In these conditions, for example, during the Depression of the 1930s, increases in output might not put upward pressure on the level of the money wage, given the high level of unemployment. Also, the marginal productivity of labor (MPN) might not fall as more labor is employed when we begin at a low level of employment (see Figure 3.1). As a consequence, the cost of producing additional units of output W/MPN might be expected to remain constant even with increases in output. In more normal conditions, an increase in output would put upward pressure on both the wage and price levels. We would expect the supply curve to be upward-sloping.

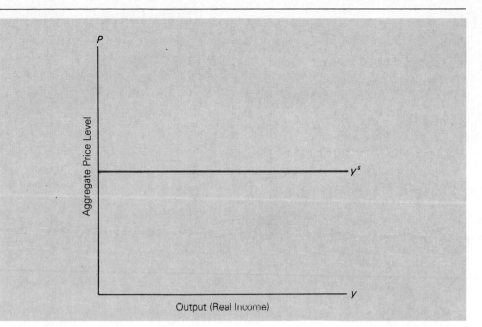

FIGURE 8.1   Aggregate Supply Curve in the Fixed-Price Keynesian Model
In previous chapters on the Keynesian model, where we assumed the price level was fixed and output was determined by aggregate demand, we were implicitly assuming that the aggregate supply curve was horizontal. Supply was no constraint on the level of output.

In this more general case of the upward-sloping aggregate supply curve, we cannot assume that price is given (supply is no constraint) and simply determine output by determining aggregate demand. Output and price will be jointly determined by supply and demand factors. The Keynesian aggregate supply curve is discussed in Sections 8.3 and 8.4. First, we construct the Keynesian aggregate demand curve, the relationship between aggregate demand and the price level implied by the Keynesian model. This aggregate demand curve will later be put together with the Keynesian aggregate supply curve to jointly determine price and output.

The factors that determine aggregate demand in the Keynesian system have been analyzed in detail. These are the factors that determine the positions of the *IS* and *LM* curves and, therefore, the income–interest-rate combination that equilibrates the money market and causes output to equal aggregate demand. In constructing an aggregate demand schedule, we want to find the level of output demanded for each price level. To do this, we examine how the position of the *IS* and *LM* schedules, and consequently the levels of the interest rate and output at which the curves intersect, are affected by price changes. The level of output at which the IS and LM schedules intersect for a given price level is a point on the Keynesian aggregate demand curve. Consider, first, how a change in the price level affects the position of the IS curve. The condition for equilibrium along the IS schedule is

$$i(r) + g = s(y) + t \tag{8.1}$$

where i = investment
g = government spending
s = saving
t = taxes
y = output

Here we return to the notation used in Chapters 3 and 4, where *lower-case letters were used to denote real (constant-dollar) magnitudes, with capital letters used for the corresponding nominal (current-dollar) magnitudes*. To see how the price level influences the position of the IS schedule, consider how each of the variables in (8.1) is affected by price changes.

Two of the variables, government spending (g) and the level of taxes (t), are assumed to be fixed by the government in *real terms*; that is, we have and will continue to assume that their real levels are unaffected by price changes. The level of investment is also assumed to be determined in real terms—a given interest rate determines a level of real investment. Changes in the price level do not directly affect investment. Changes in the price level may affect investment indirectly if they affect the interest rate, but for a given interest rate there is no effect on real investment.

Similarly, *real* saving is assumed to depend on real income and is not directly affected by changes in the price level. Since none of the four terms in (8.1), the IS curve equilibrium condition, depends directly on the price level, a change in the price level does not shift the IS curve.

What about the LM schedule? The equilibrium condition for the money market, the LM schedule equation, is

$$m = \frac{M}{P} = L(y, r) \tag{8.2}$$

The condition equates the real stock of money ($m = M/P$) with the demand for money in real terms (demand for real money balances). The real money stock is equal to the exogenously fixed *nominal* money stock divided by the price level.

The Keynesian theory of the demand for money considered in Chapter 6 related the demand for money in *real* terms to the level of *real* income and to the interest rate, although as long as prices were held constant, there was no need to distinguish between changes in real and nominal values. People wish to hold a certain amount of real money balances for a given volume of transactions measured in real (constant-dollar) terms, where the level of real income is a proxy for the real volume of transactions. Consequently, equilibrium in the money market occurs when the demand for real money balances is just equal to the real money stock. It is the nominal money stock, however—not the real money stock—which can be exogenously fixed by the monetary authority. Any change in the price level will affect the real money stock and consequently shift the LM schedule.

Figure 8.2a illustrates this effect of the price level on the position of the LM schedule. Three price levels are considered, where $P_2 > P_1 > P_0$. Notice that as we consider the effect of a price increase from P_0 to P_1, then from P_1 to P_2, at the higher price level the LM schedule is shifted to the left. The effect of a higher price level is the same as that of a fall in the nominal stock of money; both reduce the real money stock ($M/P = m$). The LM schedule shifts to the left, raising the interest rate and lowering investment and aggregate demand.

In Figure 8.2b we plot the level of the aggregate demand for output corresponding to each of the three price levels considered. This schedule, labeled y^d, is the aggregate demand schedule. It gives the level of output demanded at each price level. As can be seen from the construction of the aggregate demand curve, this level of output demanded is the equilibrium output level from the $IS-LM$ curve model, the output level which for a given price level just equates output and aggregate demand while simultaneously clearing the money market.

The aggregate demand curve reflects monetary influences (factors that affect the LM schedule) as well as direct influences on aggregate demand (factors affecting the IS schedule). Factors that increase the level of equilibrium income in the $IS-LM$ curve model (increase the level of output demanded at a given price level) will shift the aggregate demand curve to the right. Factors that cause equilibrium income to decline in the $IS-LM$ curve framework will shift the aggregate demand schedule to the left.

Consider, for example, the effect of an increase in the money stock, as shown in Figure 8.3. From an initial position $LM_0(P_0)$, the increase in the money stock shifts the LM schedule to $LM_1(P_0)$, as shown in Figure 8.3a. Equilibrium income for a given price level P_0 in the figure increases from y_0 to y_1. The aggregate demand curve shown in Figure 8.3b shifts to the right, from y_0^d to y_1^d.[2] Notice that the distance of horizontal shift in the aggregate demand curve is (y_1-y_0), the amount of the increase in equilibrium income in the $IS-LM$ curve model. This is the increase in income and aggregate demand that results *at a given price level.* Similarly, changes in government

---

[2] For simplicity, the Keynesian aggregate demand curve here and in later graphs is drawn as a straight line rather than the actual nonlinear curve in Figure 8.2. The exact curvature of the aggregate demand curve is not important for our analysis.

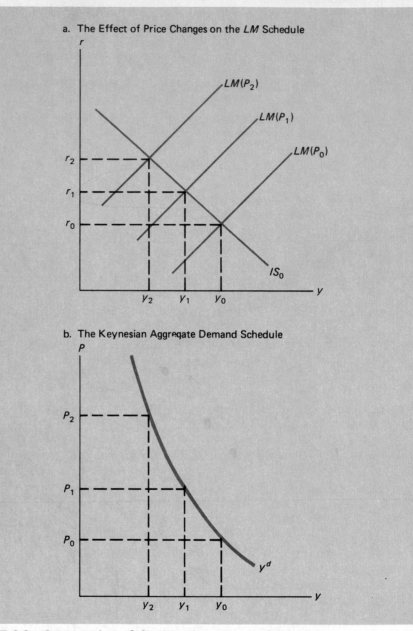

FIGURE 8.2 Construction of the Aggregate Demand Schedule

At successively higher price levels P_0, P_1, P_2, the LM schedule in part a is shifted further to the left. This results in successively lower levels of aggregate demand y_0, y_1, y_2. These combinations of price and aggregate demand are plotted to give the negatively sloped aggregate demand schedule in part b.

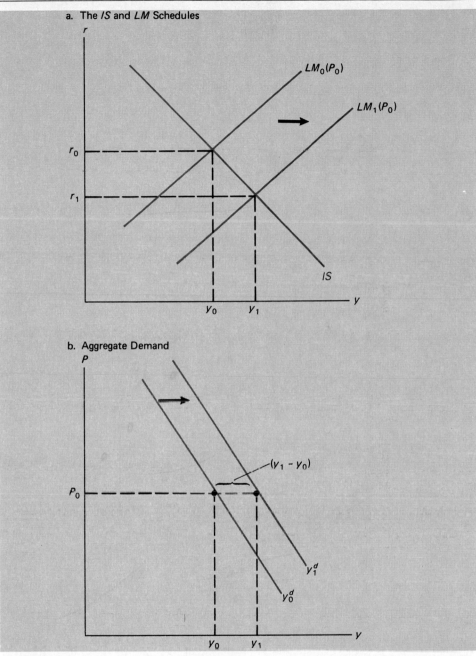

FIGURE 8.3 Effect on Aggregate Demand of an Increase in the Money Stock
An increase in the money stock shifts the *LM* schedule in part *a* to the right from $LM_0(P_0)$ to $LM_1(P_0)$ and shifts the aggregate demand schedule to the right from y_0^d to y_1^d in part *b*.

expenditures or taxes that shift the IS schedule shift the aggregate demand schedule such that the distance of the horizontal shift in the curve equals the amount of the change in equilibrium income from the $IS–LM$ curve model—the amount of the change in aggregate demand for a given price level.

8.2 • THE KEYNESIAN AGGREGATE DEMAND CURVE COMBINED WITH THE CLASSICAL THEORY OF AGGREGATE SUPPLY

When prices and wages are not assumed constant, knowing the effects of policy actions on demand is not enough to determine their effects on income. The effect on income will depend on the assumptions we make about aggregate supply. This is illustrated in Figure 8.4, where the effect of an in-

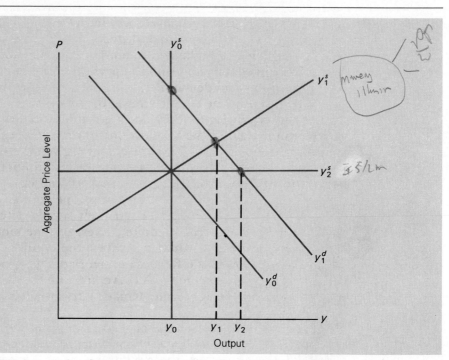

FIGURE 8.4 Role of Aggregate Supply in Determining the Output Response to a Policy Shock

An increase in government spending shifts the aggregate demand curve from y_0^d to y_1^d. If the aggregate supply curve is horizontal (y_2^s), output increases from y_0 to y_2. If the aggregate supply curve slopes upward to the right (y_1^s), output increases only to y_1. If the supply curve is vertical (y_0^s), output is unchanged at y_0.

crease in government spending is compared for three different assumptions about the shape of the aggregate supply curve.

In each case the increase in government expenditures shifts the aggregate demand schedule to the right, from to y_0^d to y_1^d in Figure 8.4. If the supply curve is given by y_2^s, a horizontal schedule, then output increases by the full amount of the horizontal shift in the aggregate demand schedule. Recall from Section 8.1 that this is the increase in equilibrium income from the IS–LM curve model, which implicitly assumed that the supply curve was horizontal. If the supply curve is upward-sloping (y_1^s), prices will rise and the increase in income will be less, $y_1 - y_0$ compared with $y_2 - y_0$ in Figure 8.4. If the supply curve were vertical (y_0^s in Figure 8.4), there would be no increase in income even though aggregate demand increased. Clearly, then, the effects of policy changes on income will depend on the assumption made concerning aggregate supply. In this section we consider the implications of making the "classical" assumptions about supply while maintaining the Keynesian apparatus behind the aggregate demand schedule.

The classical analysis of aggregate supply was explained in Chapter 3. The central elements of this analysis are illustrated in Figure 8.5. In the labor market both supply and demand depend solely on the real wage (W/P), which is assumed to be known to all. Further, the labor market is assumed always to be in equilibrium with the perfectly flexible money wage, adjusting to equate supply and demand. The labor market has the characteristics of an "auction" market. The equilibrium in the labor market is graphed in Figure 8.5a. As shown in Figure 8.5b, for a given level of employment output will be determined along the production function, the relationship giving the output produced by each amount of labor, given the fixed capital stock.

As explained in Chapter 3, the classical assumptions result in a vertical aggregate supply curve (Section 3.5). With the classical assumptions concerning the supply side, the aggregate supply curve would be given by y_0^s in Figure 8.4; output would be completely supply-determined. Factors such as changes in government spending, taxes, and the money stock, which shift the demand schedule, would not affect the equilibrium income.[3] This is the case even though the Keynesian theory of aggregate demand is used to construct the aggregate demand curve, for with the classical supply assumptions the form of the aggregate demand curve is irrelevant for income determination.

The effect of a shift in the aggregate demand curve resulting from an increase in the level of government expenditures is illustrated in Figure 8.6 for this case in which the classical labor market assumptions are made. The increase in government spending shifts the IS schedule from IS_0 to IS_1

---

[3]Some fiscal policy changes, such as a change in the marginal tax rate, have supply-side effects in the classical system, as explained in Section 4.3. These are being ignored here.

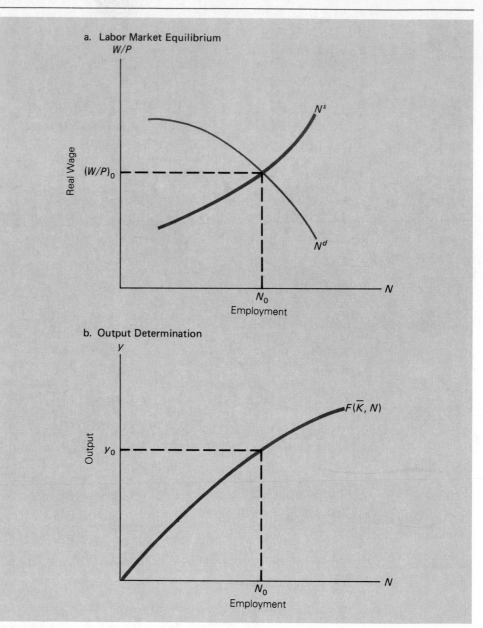

FIGURE 8.5 Classical Supply Assumptions

In the classical model, employment (N_0) is determined at the point where labor supply and demand, both as functions of the real wage, are equated (part *a*). Equilibrium output (y_0) can then be determined using the production function relationship (part *b*).

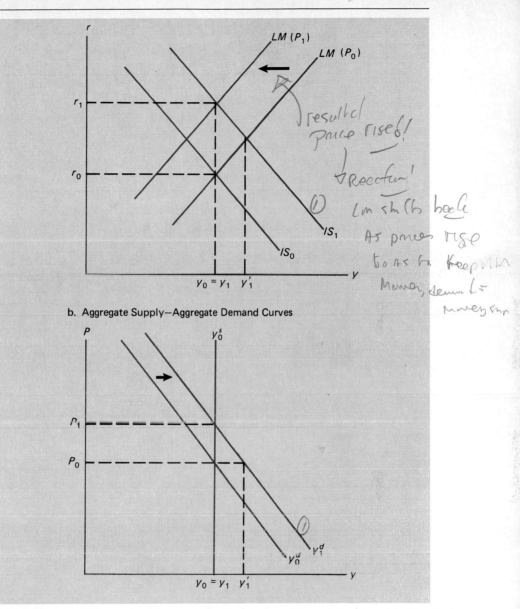

The handwritten annotations on the figure read:

resultd price rises!

↓Recofun!

① Lm shifts back
As prices rise
So as to keep the
Money demand (=
money sup

b. Aggregate Supply–Aggregate Demand Curves

FIGURE 8.6 Effect of an Increase in Government Expenditures with Classical Labor Market Assumptions

An increase in government expenditures shifts the IS schedule to the right from IS_0 to IS_1 (part a) and shifts the aggregate demand schedule to the right from y_0^d to y_1^d (part b). In the classical case the aggregate supply curve (y_0^s) is vertical. The increase in aggregate demand causes the price level to rise from P_0 to P_1, but the level of output is unchanged at y_0. The increase in the price level shifts the LM schedule in part a from $LM(P_0)$ to $LM(P_1)$.

in Figure 8.6a and shifts the aggregate demand curve from y_0^d to y_1^d in Figure 8.6b. If the price level were fixed, output would increase to the level given by y_1' in both figures. The price level will not, however, remain constant. As can be seen in Figure 8.6b, at the initial price level of P_0, aggregate demand exceeds supply. The price level will rise to the level P_1, where demand is reduced just back to the initial level y_0. The increase in the price level will lower the real money stock (from M/P_0 to M/P_1). This will shift the LM schedule from LM (P_0) to LM (P_1) in Figure 8.6a.

It is worth stopping here to consider why the price level must rise by an amount just sufficient to shift the LM schedule in Figure 8.6a to a point where it intersects the IS_1 schedule at the initial income level (y_0). The price level must increase until demand returns to the initial level y_0. As we saw in constructing the aggregate demand schedule, increases in the price level lower the real money stock (M/P), which in turn pushes up the interest rate and lowers investment. With the classical vertical supply curve, the price level must rise until the interest rate has been pushed up and investment has declined by just enough to restore equilibrium at y_0. This occurs when the LM schedule has shifted to the left by enough to intersect the new IS schedule IS_1 at the original income level.

From the analysis of this section it can be seen that *the classical theory of aggregate supply based on the classical auction market characterization of the labor market is fundamentally incompatible with the Keynesian system.* The central feature of Keynesian analysis is the theory of aggregate demand and the influence of aggregate demand on output and employment. With the classical assumptions about aggregate supply, leading to the vertical supply curve, there is *no* role for aggregate demand in determining output and employment. It was therefore necessary for Keynes and his followers, in addition to developing a theory of aggregate demand, to attack the classical supply assumptions and develop a Keynesian theory of the supply side. This theory is the subject of the next two sections.

8.3 · THE KEYNESIAN CONTRACTUAL VIEW OF THE LABOR MARKET

Keynes believed that the money wage would not adjust sufficiently in the short run to keep the economy at full employment. In the classical system both labor supply and demand are functions of the real wage and, as we saw (Figure 8.5), the intersection of the labor supply and demand curves determines an equilibrium real wage and level of employment. Wage bargains are, however, set in terms of money wages, and one assumption crucial to the classical model is that the money wage is perfectly flexible. Adjustments in the money wage are required to equate labor supply and labor demand—to keep the economy at full employment.

Sources of Wage Rigidity

The Keynesian theory offers a number of reasons why the money wage will *not* quickly adjust, especially in the downward direction, to maintain equilibrium in the labor market. The most important of these Keynesian explanations for the *rigidity* of money wages are as follows.

1. The first explanation comes from Keynes. He argued that workers are interested in their relative as well as their absolute wage. There exists in any labor market a set of wage differentials between workers with different trades and skills. Much of the work of wage bargaining is to arrive at a relative wage structure that is acceptable to both labor and management. Wage differentials can be measured by relative money wages, since price-level changes affect all wages symmetrically.

Keynes believed that one reason workers would resist money wage cuts even as the demand for labor fell was that they would see the wage cuts as "unfair" changes in the structure of relative wages. Workers in one firm or industry would see changes in money wages as changes in relative wages because they would have no assurance that if they accepted a cut in money wages, workers in other sectors of the labor market would do the same. A decline in the real wage as a result of a rise in prices would not be seen by labor as affecting the structure of relative wages. Because of this, Keynes believed that declines in real wages caused by price-level increases would meet much less resistance from labor than an equivalent fall in the real wage from a money wage cut.

2. The next factor leading to stickiness in the money wage level is an institutional one. In the unionized sector of the labor market, wages are set by labor contracts, most often of two or three years' duration. Such contracts typically fix the money wage levels for the life of the contract. The money wage will not respond to events, such as a decline in labor demand, over the life of the contract. Indexation of the money wage set in the contract (i.e., provisions that tie changes in the money wage to changes in the price level) provides some flexibility in the money wage over the length of the contract. In the United States, however, when any indexation of labor contracts exists, it is generally incomplete. Thus fixed-money-wage contracts impart stickiness to the money wage.

Once such a labor contract is signed, the decision of how much labor to hire is left to the employer. A labor supply curve such as the classical labor supply function in Figure 8.5 no longer plays any role in determining employment. The firm hires the profit-maximizing amount of labor at the fixed money wage.

3. Even in segments of the labor market when no explicit contract fixes the money wage, there is often an implicit agreement between employer and employee that fixes the money wage over some time period. In particular, such implicit contracts keep employers from cutting money wages in the face of a fall in the demand for their products and consequent decline in labor demand. The incentive for employers to refrain from attempting to achieve such wage cuts, or alternatively from hiring workers from among the pool of the unemployed who might be willing to work for a lower wage, is their desire to maintain a reputation as a "good employer." Firms might achieve a temporary gain by reducing labor costs by forcing a money wage cut, but this could be more than counterbalanced by the effect of poor labor relations with existing employees and difficulties in recruiting new employees. Keynesians believe that the "conventions" of labor markets are such that firms find it in their interest to cut the length of the work week or have temporary layoffs in response to falls in demand rather than to seek money wage cuts.

Keynesians believe that contractual arrangements are central to an understanding of how modern labor markets function. The *contractual* view of the labor market stands in sharp contrast to the frictionless *auction* market view of the classical economists. In the Keynesian view, as expressed by Arthur Okun,

> wages are not set to clear markets in the short run, but rather are strongly conditioned by longer-term considerations involving . . . employer worker relations. These factors insulate wages . . . to a significant degree from the impact of shifts in demand so that the adjustment must be made in employment and output.[4]

We consider the basis for this Keynesian contractual view further in Chapter 11. Here we turn to its implications.

Read Perspectives 8.1.

A Flexible-Price, Fixed-Money-Wage Model

To model this contractual view of the labor market, we assume that, although prices are free to vary, the money wage is *fixed*.[5] A fixed money wage is an extreme version of a sticky wage, and Keynesian economists certainly do not believe that the money wage is completely rigid even in the short run. Still, if the response of the money wage to labor market conditions is slow to materialize, as the contractual approach to the labor market suggests, results based on the assumption of a fixed money wage will be approximately correct for the short run. They will certainly be closer to reality than results based on the classical assumption that the money wage moves instantaneously to clear the labor market.

---

[4] Arthur Okun, *Prices and Quantities* (Washington, D.C.: The Brookings Institution, 1981), p. 233.

[5] The models in this chapter focus on the traditional Keynesian view that wage rigidity is the key explanation of why output and employment must respond to changes in aggregate demand. In Section 12.2 we consider some *new Keynesian* models in which the key rigidity is, instead, product prices.

PERSPECTIVES

PRICE AND QUANTITY ADJUSTMENT IN GREAT BRITAIN, 1929–36

Keynes's view that the money wage would not adjust quickly to clear the labor market was no doubt in part a result of his observation of events in Great Britain. Table 8.1 provides data for the money wage, price level, real wage, and unemployment rate in Britain for the years 1929–36.

The money wage fell over the first part of the period, but only by 5 percent by 1933. After 1933 the money wage rose slowly despite the exceptionally high unemployment rate. Data for the price level, real wage, and unemployment rate clearly indicate that no downward adjustment in the real wage to clear the labor market—the classical labor market adjustment—occurred.

TABLE 8.1   Wages, Prices, and Unemployment in Great Britain, 1929–36

Year	Money Wage (W) (index 1914 = 100)	Price Level (P) (index 1914 = 100)	Real Wage (W/P × 100)	Unemployment Rate (Percent)
1929	193	164	118	11.0
1930	191	157	122	14.6
1931	189	147	129	21.5
1932	185	143	129	22.5
1933	183	140	129	21.3
1934	183	141	130	17.7
1935	185	143	130	16.4
1936	190	147	129	14.3

Source: B. P. Mitchell and P. Deane, *Abstract of British Historical Statistics.* Cambridge: Cambridge University Press, 1962, p. 67, p. 345.

Finally, before we analyze this flexible price-fixed money wage model, it should be pointed out that Keynes's concern was with the downward rigidity of the money wage—the failure of the money wage to fall sufficiently to restore full employment when the demand for labor was less than supply. The main situations to which we would want to apply the fixed-wage model are those in which there is unemployment, an excess supply of labor.

With the money wage fixed and labor supply greater than labor demand, actual employment will be determined by demand. Firms will be able to hire the amount of labor they demand at the going wage and not be forced to hire more. Keynes did not object to the classical theory of labor demand. According to this theory, as explained in Chapter 3, the profit-maximizing firm demands labor up to the point at which the real wage (W/P) is equal to the marginal productivity of labor (MPN) or equivalently to the point at which

$$W = \text{MPN} \cdot P \qquad\qquad (8.3)$$

the money wage paid to labor is just equal to the money value of the marginal product (the marginal revenue product) of labor. Since, with an excess supply of labor and a fixed money wage, employment depends only on labor demand, the determination of employment is as depicted in Figure 8.7. At a fixed money wage $\overline{W}$, labor demand, and therefore employment, will be N_0.

The labor supply schedule is also shown in Figure 8.7, as a dashed line. Notice that at the fixed money wage ($\overline{W}$), the labor supply curve is to the right of N_0, indicating an excess supply of labor. Demand, not supply, is the factor constraining employment. The labor supply curve plays *no* role and is not shown in the subsequent figures in this section. The properties of the Keynesian labor supply function are explained in the next section, where we analyze a Keynesian model in which the money wage is allowed to vary.

The position of the labor demand schedule, the schedule giving the money value of the marginal product of labor corresponding to each level of em-

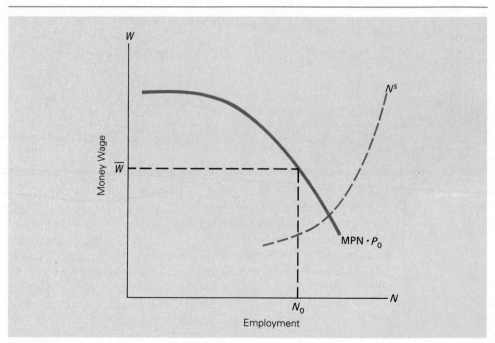

FIGURE 8.7 Employment with a Fixed Money Wage
With the money wage fixed at $\overline{W}$, employment will be at N_0, the amount of labor demanded.

ployment (the $MPN \cdot P_0$ schedule in Figure 8.7), depends on the price level. The number of workers firms will hire, and as a consequence the amount of output they will supply, depends on the price level. This relationship between output supplied and the price level is developed in Figure 8.8.

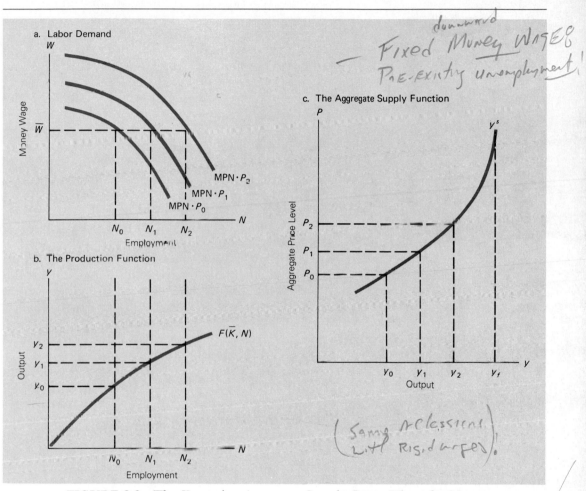

downward
— Fixed Money WAGES
PRE-existing unemployment!

(Same Aclessical)
(with Rigid wages)

FIGURE 8.8 The Keynesian Aggregate Supply Curve When the Money Wage Is Fixed

Part *a* shows the levels of employment N_0, N_1, N_2 for three successively higher price levels P_0, P_1, P_2. Part *b* shows the levels of output y_0, y_1, y_2 that will be produced at these three levels of employment . In part *c* we put together the information in parts *a* and *b* to show the level of output supplied at each of the three price levels. Notice that at higher price levels, employment, and hence, output supplied increases—*the aggregate supply curve (y^s) is upward-sloping.*

Figure 8.8a shows the level of employment that will result at three successively higher price levels, P_0, P_1, and P_2, with the money wage fixed at $\overline{W}$. An
increase in the price level (from P_0 to P_1, then from P_1 to P_2) will increase
the money value of the marginal product of labor corresponding to any level
of employment and therefore will increase labor demand for a given money
wage. The labor demand (MPN · P) schedule shifts to the right and employment increases. As employment increases, output is shown to rise in Figure
8.8b, where we have plotted the aggregate production function giving the
level of output for each level of employment.

Figure 8.8c combines the information from Figures 8.8a and 8.8b to show
the resulting level of output supplied for each price level. Higher price levels
result in higher levels of supply; the aggregate supply function is upward-
sloping. This is the same relationship as for the classical model with *rigid*
wages (Section 4.4). As in the classical model, one would expect that at some
level of income (y_f in Figure 8.8c), full employment would be reached and
further increases in price would have no effect on output. The aggregate
supply curve becomes vertical at this full-employment level.

Below full employment the supply curve will not be vertical; shifts in the
aggregate demand curve will change the level of output. The effects of an
increase in the money stock and the effects of an increase in government
spending are illustrated in Figures 8.9 and 8.10, respectively.

In Figure 8.9a an increase in the money stock is shown to shift the LM
schedule from LM_0 (P_0) to the schedule marked LM_1 (P_0). This is the shift
in the LM curve as a direct result of the change in the money stock. The
increase in the money stock shifts the aggregate demand schedule to the
right in Figure 8.9b, from y_0^d to y_1^d. At the initial price level P_0, output
would be increased to y_1' as shown in Figure 8.9. But for output supplied to
increase, prices must rise and the new equilibrium is reached not at y_1' but
at y_1, where the price level has risen to P_1. The rise in price shifts the LM
schedule in Figure 8.9a to LM_1 (P_1).

Thus we find the same type of Keynesian results from an increase in the
money stock as we did for the fixed-price $IS–LM$ curve model in Chapter
7. Output and employment will rise and the interest rate will fall, from r_0
to r_1 in Figure 8.9a. When the price level is allowed to vary, the increase
in output will be less than when the price level is fixed. Output rises to y_1
instead of y_1'. This is because the increase in the price level reduces the real
money stock (M/P), which *partially* offsets the effects of the increase in the
nominal quantity of money. The interest rate falls only to r_1, not to r_1'. As a
consequence, this expansionary monetary policy action has a smaller effect
on investment and, hence, on output.

The situation is much the same with fiscal policy effects. Again the results are Keynesian in that fiscal policy does affect output, but again the
effect of a given policy action is smaller in magnitude when the price level is

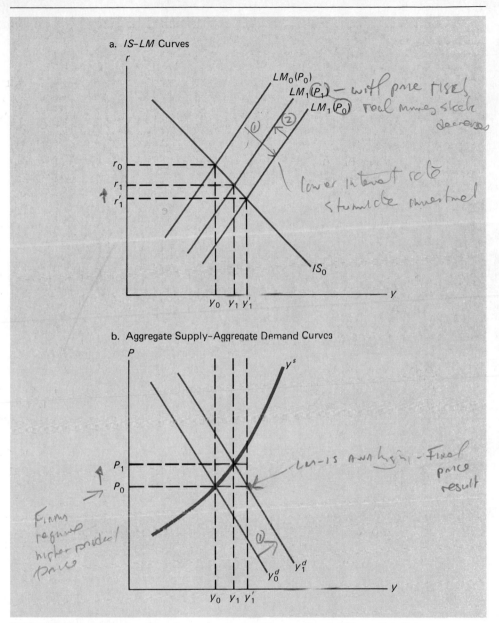

a. *IS-LM* Curves

[handwritten annotations: LM₁(P₁) — with price rises; real money stock decreases; lower interest rate stimulate investment]

[handwritten annotations: Len-IS analysis — Fixed price result; Firms require higher product price]

b. Aggregate Supply-Aggregate Demand Curves

FIGURE 8.9 Effects of an Increase in the Money Stock When the Price Level Is Flexible

An increase in the money stock shifts the *LM* schedule to the right from $LM_0(P_0)$ to $LM_1(P_0)$ (part *a*) and shifts the aggregate demand curve to the right from y_0^d to y_1^d (part *b*). The increase in aggregate demand causes output to rise from y_0 to y_1 and the price level to rise from P_0 to P_1. The increase in the price level shifts the *LM* schedule from $LM_1(P_0)$ to $LM_1(P_1)$.

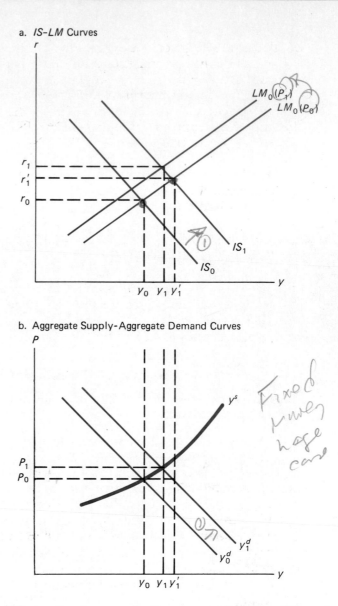

a. *IS-LM* Curves

b. Aggregate Supply-Aggregate Demand Curves

FIGURE 8.10 Effects of an Increase in Government Spending When the Price Level Is Flexible

An increase in government spending shifts the *IS* curve from IS_0 to IS_1 (part *a*) and shifts the aggregate demand curve from y_0^d to y_1^d (part *b*). The increase in aggregate demand causes output to rise from y_0 to y_1 and the price level to rise from P_0 to P_1. The increase in the price level shifts the *LM* schedule from $LM_0(P_0)$ to $LM_0(P_1)$.

variable than when we assumed that the price level was fixed. The effects of an increase in government spending are illustrated in Figure 8.10.

An increase in government spending shifts the IS curve from IS_0 to IS_1 in Figure 8.10a. The increase in government spending has no direct effect on the LM schedule, which is initially given by $LM_0(P_0)$. The increase in aggregate demand as the IS curve shifts right is reflected in Figure 8.10b in the shift of the aggregate demand curve from y_0^d to y_1^d. Output increases to y_1 and the price level rises to P_1. The increase in the price level decreases the real money stock (M/P), causing the LM schedule to shift from $LM_0(P_0)$ to $LM_0(P_1)$ in Figure 8.10a. Output rises only to y_1, not to y_1', the increase in output that would have occurred had the price level remained fixed.

8.4 • LABOR SUPPLY AND VARIABILITY IN THE MONEY WAGE

Free up money wage!

In this section we bring the supply side of the labor market into the picture. We examine the differences in the Keynesian and classical views of labor supply and then examine a version of the Keynesian model in which both the aggregate price level and the money wage are allowed to vary.

The Classical and Keynesian Theories of Labor Supply

The classical economists believed that the supply of labor depended positively on the real wage,

$$N^s = g\left(\frac{W}{P}\right) \tag{8.4}$$

The reasoning behind this formulation was that individuals maximized utility, which depended positively on real income and leisure. A rise in the real wage increased the income that could be gained from an hour's labor or, looked at in reverse, increased the opportunity cost of taking one hour of leisure. Consequently, an increase in the real wage was assumed to increase labor supply.[6] Suppliers of labor were assumed to know the real wage, and a perfectly flexible money wage was assumed to adjust to bring the supply of labor and demand for labor into equality.

The Keynesian theory of labor supply begins with the observation that the wage bargain is struck in terms of the *money* wage, not the real wage.

---

[6] As explained in Section 3.4, the increase in the real wage will increase labor supply only if the "substitution effect" (leisure is now more expensive in terms of income forgone) outweighs the "income effect" (with a higher income level leisure may be more desirable and workers may choose to supply less labor). We continue to assume that the substitution effect dominates.

The classical theory assumes that suppliers of labor (workers) know the price level (P) and money wage (W), and therefore know the real wage (W/P). The Keynesians argue that since the labor bargain is in terms of the money wage, we can assume that workers know the money wage but not the price level. As explained previously, through implicit or explicit contracts, workers agree to provide labor services over some period, let us say for a year. They have no way of knowing the value that the aggregate price level will take on over the coming year. It is this aggregate price level that will determine the purchasing power of any money wage they agree to in a current wage bargain. As a consequence, the Keynesians believe that decisions about labor supply depend on the current money wage and the *expectation* of the aggregate price level. Further, the Keynesian view has been that workers' expectations about the price level depend for the most part on the past behavior of prices.

To see the implications of the Keynesian view of workers bargaining for a known money wage with only imperfect information about prices, we construct a Keynesian labor supply curve, which we compare with the classical labor supply curve [equation (8.4)]. We then consider a model in which the money wage is perfectly flexible, but labor supply is given by the Keynesian version of the labor supply function. In this analysis we neglect the factors enumerated previously, which the Keynesians believe cause the money wage to be sticky. One purpose of this analysis is to show that *even if the money wage were perfectly flexible*, with the Keynesian version of the labor supply curve, the aggregate supply curve would not be vertical. Output and employment would not be completely supply-determined; aggregate demand would also play a role. In reality the Keynesians believe that the money wage *is* sticky in the downward direction and much of the unemployment we observe is the result of the failure of the money wage to clear the labor market. Imperfect information about prices is, however, an important additional factor that the Keynesians believe explains fluctuations in output and employment. A second purpose of this analysis is to explain the factors that influence the money wage in the Keynesian system. What factors, for example, explain the terms of wage settlements in contracts when they are signed?

The Keynesian labor supply function can be written as follows:

$$N^s = t(W/P^e) \tag{8.5}$$

where W is the money wage, an increase in which would be expected to result in an increase in the quantity of labor supplied. An increase in the money wage for a given value of the expected price level (P^e) would increase labor supply, since it would be viewed by workers as an increase in the real wage. An increase in the expected price level will cause labor supply to decline. Fundamentally, workers are assumed to be interested in the real wage, not the money wage, and they reduce their supply of labor when they perceive that the real wage has declined. The difference between the Keynesian and classical labor supply functions is that in the Keynesian version workers must form an expectation of the price level. Labor supply therefore depends on the *expected* real wage. In the classical system workers know the real wage. Labor supply depends on the *actual* real wage.

The Keynesian theory of labor supply is incomplete without an assumption about the way in which workers form an expectation of the price level (P^e). The Keynesian assumption is that such price expectations are based primarily on the past behavior of the price level. Thus

$$P^e = a_1 P_{-1} + a_2 P_{-2} + a_3 P_{-3} + \cdots + a_n P_{-n} \tag{8.6}$$

where $P_{-i}(i = 1, 2, 3, \ldots)$ is the price level from i periods back and the $a_1, a_2, \ldots, a_n$ are the weights given to a number of past observations on the price level in forming the expectation of the current value of the price level. Clearly, there is additional information that might prove useful in accurately predicting the behavior of prices. The Keynesian assumption is that the cost of gathering and processing such additional information is high enough that the price expectations of labor suppliers are reasonably accurately represented by a simple formulation such as equation (8.6). As we will see in later chapters, this assumption has not gone unchallenged.

According to equation (8.6), price expectations are essentially *backward-looking*, simply adjusting to the past behavior of the price level. Moreover, in the Keynesian view there is considerable inertia in this adjustment process; price expectations adjust only *slowly* to the past behavior of the price level. If this is the case, then price expectations do not change as a result of current economic conditions. In analyzing the effects of various policy changes, for example, we can take P^e as constant. In the longer run (after many short periods have passed) we need to take account of how stabilization policies affect P^e, because such policies will have affected price levels from past periods.

The Keynesian Aggregate Supply Curve with a Variable Money Wage

Figure 8.11 illustrates the construction of the aggregate supply curve, where labor supply is given by equation (8.5) and the money wage is assumed to adjust to equate labor supply and labor demand. In Figure 8.11a labor supply (N^s) and labor demand are plotted as functions of the money wage. As in the previous analysis, labor demand is assumed to depend on the real wage, and firms are assumed to know the price level at which they will be able to sell their individual products. The labor demand curve will shift to the right with an increase in the price level. In Figure 8.11a we show labor demand curves for three successively higher price levels, P_0, P_1, and P_2, respectively.

The labor supply curve is drawn for a given value of the *expected* aggregate price level. As explained previously, this expected price level is assumed

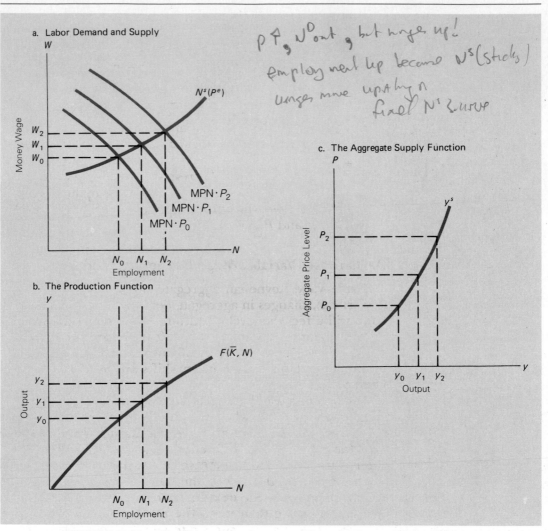

P↑, N^D out, but wages up! employment up because N^s (sticks) wages move up with n final N^s curve

FIGURE 8.11 The Keynesian Aggregate Supply Curve When the Money Wage Is Variable

Part *a* shows the equilibrium levels of employment N_0, N_1, N_2, corresponding to successively higher values of the price level P_0, P_1, P_2. Part *b* gives the level of output y_0, y_1, y_2 that will be produced at each of these employment levels. Part *c* combines the information in parts *a* and *b* to show the relationship between the price level and output supplied. At higher values of the price level, output supplied increases; as in the fixed wage case, *the aggregate supply curve (y^s) is upward-sloping.*

to be fixed in the short run. With the fixed labor supply curve, increases in the price level shift the labor demand curve along the supply curve, with the result that for a higher price level the equilibrium levels of employment and the money wage are increased. The process at work here is as follows. The increase in price (from P_0 to P_1, for example) causes an excess demand for labor at the old money wage (W_0). The money wage is bid up, and for a given value of P^e, an increase in the money wage causes more workers to accept jobs (or increase hours worked in existing jobs); employment rises.

At the higher levels of employment N_1 and N_2, corresponding to the higher price levels P_1 and P_2, output is higher at the levels shown by y_1 and y_2 in Figure 8.11b. Thus, a higher price level corresponds to a higher level of output supplied. This information is reflected in the upward-sloping aggregate supply curve in Figure 8.11c, plotting output supplied for each price level (points such as P_0, y_0; P_1, y_1; and P_2, y_2).

Policy Effects in the Variable-Wage Keynesian Model

Since the variable-wage Keynesian aggregate supply curve is still upward-sloping (nonvertical), changes in aggregate demand that shift the aggregate demand curve will affect the level of output. Increases in the money stock or level of government expenditures will shift the aggregate demand curve to the right, increasing both the level of output and the aggregate price level. Graphical illustrations of such policy shifts are *qualitatively* the same as Figure 8.9 and 8.10.

Suppose that we compare the effects on price and output from a given change in aggregate demand when the money wage is variable with the effects for the case in which we assumed the money wage was fixed. Is there a predictable *quantitative* difference? The answer is yes. When the money wage is variable, a given increase in aggregate demand will cause output to increase by less than when the money wage is fixed. When the money wage is variable, an increase in aggregate demand will cause the price level to rise by more than when the money wage is fixed. The reason for these results is that the aggregate supply curve when the money wage varies is steeper than when the money wage is fixed. As the aggregate demand curve is shifted to the right along the steeper aggregate supply curve, the increased demand results less in increased output and more in increased price.

The reason the aggregate supply curve is steeper in the variable-money-wage case is illustrated in Figure 8.12. In Figure 8.12a the labor market response to an increase in the price level is illustrated for the fixed- and variable-money-wage cases. If the money wage is fixed at $\overline{W} = W_0$, an increase in the price level from P_0 to P_1 shifts the labor demand curve from $MPN \cdot P_0$ to $MPN \cdot P_1$, and employment rises from N_0 to N_1. Recall from the discussion in the previous section that in the fixed-money-wage case, we

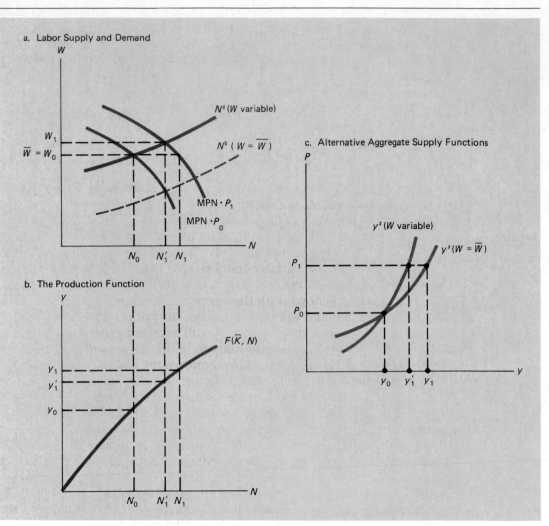

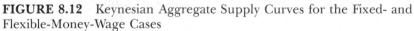

FIGURE 8.12   Keynesian Aggregate Supply Curves for the Fixed- and Flexible-Money-Wage Cases

The aggregate supply schedule in part c for the case when the money wage is variable $[y^s(W$ variable$)]$ is steeper than when the money wage is fixed $[y^s(W = \overline{W})]$. This is because the increase in employment (part a) with a rise in price and therefore the increase in output (part b) are smaller when the money wage is variable than when it is fixed. In essence, this follows because the rise in the money wage in the variable wage case dampens the effect on employment and output from an increase in the price level.

assume that there is an excess supply of labor. The labor supply curve in this case, given by $N^s(W = \overline{W})$, is to the right of N_0 at $\overline{W}$ (as in Figure 8.7). Labor supply is no constraint on employment, which is determined solely by labor demand. For this case of $W = \overline{W}$, output supplied can be seen from Figure 8.12b to rise from y_0 to y_1. The aggregate supply curve is given by $y^s(W = \overline{W})$ in Figure 8.12c.

With a variable money wage, when the labor demand curve shifts from $\text{MPN} \cdot P_0$ to $\text{MPN} \cdot P_1$, as a result of the increase in price, employment rises only to N_1'. Here we are assuming that there is no initial excess supply of labor. At W_0, labor demand just equals supply along the labor supply curve $N^s(W$ variable$)$. The money wage must rise from W_0 to W_1 to get workers to increase labor supply. This increase in the money wage dampens the effect of the original increase in labor demand. Since employment increases by less than in the fixed-wage case, output supplied also increases by less, rising only to y_1', as shown in Figure 8.12b. The increase in the price level leads to a smaller rise in output supplied, and this is reflected in the steeper aggregate supply curve for the variable-money-wage case, as shown in Figure 8.12c, the $y^s(W$ variable$)$ curve.

As Figure 8.13 shows, with the steeper aggregate supply curve an increase in aggregate demand will have a smaller output effect. A shift in the aggregate demand curve from y_0^d to y_1^d will increase output from y_0 to y_1 in the fixed-money-wage case but only to y_1' in the variable-money-wage case. Price rises by more in the variable-money-wage case, to P_1', as opposed to P_1 when the money wage is fixed. Policy multipliers giving output effects for changes in the money stock or for changes in government spending, factors that affect output by means of aggregate demand, will be smaller for the variable-money-wage case than for the fixed-money-wage case.

At this point it is useful to draw some conclusions from the preceding two sections concerning the way in which allowing price and wage flexibility affects the policy implications of the Keynesian system.

In Section 8.3 we saw that when the price level was assumed to vary (the money wage still fixed), policy multipliers were reduced relative to their values in the simple *IS–LM* curve model of Chapter 7, where both the price level and the money wage had been fixed. In that simple *IS–LM* curve model the implicit assumption was that the aggregate supply curve was horizontal. Supply was no barrier to an increase in output. In the model in Section 8.3 we were taking account of the fact that in normal circumstances, as output increases the marginal product of labor declines. Since the unit cost of producing additional units of output is the money wage divided by the marginal product of labor, firms will supply a greater output only at a higher price—even if the money wage is fixed. The aggregate supply curve was seen to be upward-sloping, and increases in aggregate demand consequently had smaller output effects than with the horizontal aggregate supply curve.

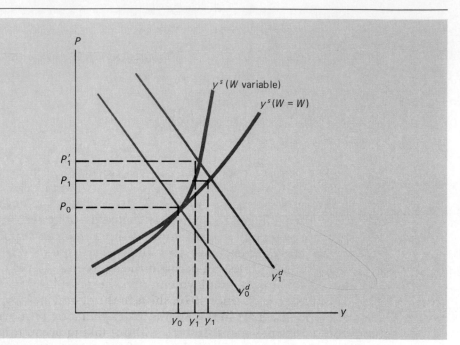

FIGURE 8.13 Effect of an Increase in Aggregate Demand in the Fixed- and Variable-Money-Wage Cases
Since the aggregate supply curve in the variable-money-wage case [$y^s(W$ variable)] is steeper than for the fixed-wage case [$y^s(W = \overline{W})$], a shift to the right in the aggregate demand curve will increase output by a smaller amount (from y_0 to y_1') in the variable-wage case in the fixed-wage case (from y_0 to y_1).

When the money wage is also assumed to be variable, the implied aggregate supply curve becomes steeper. Now as output is increased, not only does the marginal product of labor decline, causing an increase in unit costs (W/MPN), but the rise in the money wage required to induce workers to supply more labor will also push up unit cost. As a result, any increase in output supplied requires a larger increase in price; the aggregate supply curve is steeper. Aggregate demand changes have still smaller output effects.

In the classical system the aggregate supply curve was vertical; output was completely supply-determined. The price and wage were assumed to be perfectly flexible. In the simple $IS–LM$ curve model, output was completely demand-determined. Prices and wages were completely rigid. The models in the preceding two sections, by introducing price and wage flexibility in the Keynesian system, have brought the Keynesian results closer to those of the classical model. Still the models in these sections remain "Keynesian" in the important sense that aggregate demand still plays a role in determining the level of output. The aggregate supply curve is not vertical in the short run.

8.5 • THE EFFECTS OF SHIFTS IN THE AGGREGATE SUPPLY FUNCTION

So far in our development of the Keynesian theory of aggregate supply we have focused on how taking account of supply factors changes the role of aggregate demand in determining output. The output and employment effects of changes in aggregate demand—shifts in the aggregate demand function—depend on the slope of the aggregate supply function. In addition, supply factors have an independent role in determining output and employment. Shifts can occur in the aggregate supply curve, and such shifts will affect output, employment, and the price level.

Over the years since 1970, shifts in the aggregate supply curve have played an important part in the Keynesian explanation of movements in price, output and employment. In fact, without taking account of shifts in the aggregate supply curve, the behavior of price, output, and unemployment over the decade of the 1970s cannot be explained within a Keynesian framework. In this section we consider the causes and effects of shifts in the aggregate supply curve. We begin with an analysis of the behavior of price and output during the 1970s. The role of shifts in the aggregate supply curve during the 1980s and the early 1990s are then discussed.

The Behavior of Price and Output over the 1970s

Figure 8.14 plots the levels of real income and the aggregate price level (GNP deflator) for the years 1973–81. Notice that whereas the price level increased substantially in each year, there were several declines in the level of real output. The relationship between changes in real output and changes in the aggregate price level can be seen in Table 8.2, giving the annual rates of change for real GNP and the GNP deflator for the years 1973–81. From Table 8.2 it is also clear that during this period the years with the greatest growth in real output were not those with the largest rates of price increase. In fact, the three years in which output declined (1974, 1975, and 1980) were three of the four most inflationary years of the period.

This pattern of price and output changes is inconsistent with the Keynesian model unless shifts in the aggregate supply curve are taken into

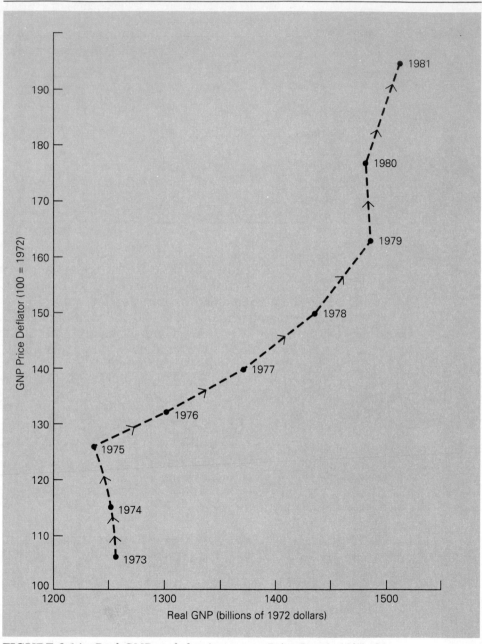

FIGURE 8.14   Real GNP and the Aggregate Price Level, 1973–81

TABLE 8.2 Percentage Growth Rates in Real GNP and the GNP Price Deflator, 1973–81

Year	Growth in Real GNP	Increase in GNP Deflator
1973	5.8	5.8
1974	−0.6	8.8
1975	−1.2	9.3
1976	5.4	5.2
1977	5.5	5.8
1978	5.0	7.4
1979	2.8	8.6
1980	−0.3	9.2
1981	2.5	9.6

account. To see this, consider Figure 8.15. In Figure 8.15a, movements in output and price are caused by shifts in the aggregate demand curve (from y_0^d to y_1^d, then to y_2^d). In this case increases in price (from P_0 to P_1, then to P_2) would *always* be accompanied by increases in output (from y_0 to y_1, then to y_2). The demand schedule shifts to the right along the fixed upward-sloping supply curve, increasing both price and output. Shifts to the left in the aggregate demand curve cause *both* output and price to fall. Therefore, shifts in the aggregate demand schedule do not provide an explanation for the behavior of price and output in years such as 1974, 1975, and 1980, when output fell but price rose, and in fact the rate of price increase accelerated.

In Figure 8.15b, it can be seen that shifts to the left in the aggregate supply curve (from y_0^s to y_1^s and to y_2^s) would result in price increases (from P_0 to P_1, then to P_2) associated with declines in output (from y_0 to y_1, then to y_2). Such "supply shocks" could explain the U.S. economy's experience over the 1970s with inflationary recessions—periods when output declines and prices increase.

Factors That Shift the Aggregate Supply Schedule

The question remains of the causes of shifts in the aggregate supply schedule—the nature of "supply shocks." Recall that points on the aggregate supply schedule give the desired output of the firms in the economy for each value of the aggregate price level. Each firm, and therefore firms in the aggregate, will choose the level of output that maximizes profits. This implies, as discussed in Chapter 3, that firms produce up to the point where P is equal to marginal cost:

$$P = \text{MC} \tag{8.7}$$

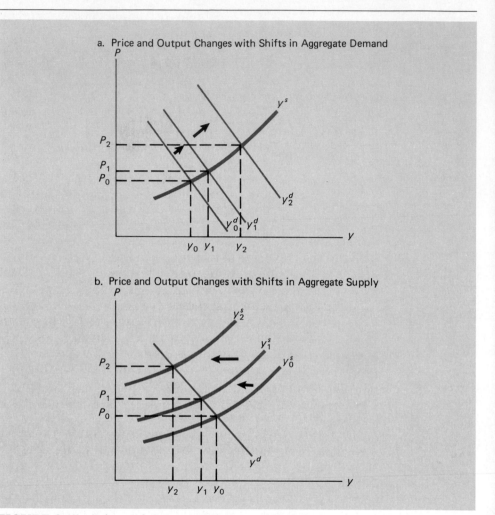

FIGURE 8.15   Price and Output Variations with Shifts in Aggregate Demand and Supply

If changes in output were the result of shifts in the aggregate demand schedule along a fixed supply schedule, as in part *a*, we would expect a positive relationship between price and output changes. If, on the other hand, output changes resulted from shifts in the aggregate supply schedule along a fixed demand schedule, as in part *b*, we would expect a negative association between price and output changes. Shifts to the left in the aggregate supply curve can provide an explanation for the behavior of the U.S. economy in years such as 1974, 1975, and 1980 (see Table 8.2).

Marginal cost is the addition to total cost as a result of increasing the use of variable factors of production to increase output. In our previous analysis we assumed that labor was the only variable factor of production. In this case the marginal cost of producing an additional unit of output was the money wage (W), the amount paid for an additional unit of labor, divided by the marginal product of labor (MPN). Marginal cost (W/MPN) increased as output increased because as more labor was hired, the marginal product of labor (MPN) declined. Additionally, in the variable-wage model of the preceding section, in order to get workers to supply additional labor, the money wage had to be increased, a further factor causing marginal cost to rise as output increased. These two factors, the declining marginal product of labor and increasing upward pressure on money wages as output and employment increase, explain why the aggregate supply schedule is upward-sloping.

A shift in the aggregate supply schedule—for example, a shift upward to the left, as in Figure 8.15*b*—means that after the shift, firms will produce less for a given price or, put differently, firms will find it optimal to continue to produce the same output, only at a higher price. From condition (8.7) it can be seen that any factor that causes marginal cost to increase *for a given output level* will cause such a shift upward and to the left in the aggregate supply schedule. If marginal cost increases for a given output, then to continue to meet condition (8.7) *at a given price*, the firm must decrease output. As output declines, marginal cost will decline (MPN will rise and W will fall) and equality (8.7) can be restored. Alternatively, price would have to rise by the amount of the increase in marginal cost for the firm to find it optimal to continue to produce the same level of output.

This is only half the story; the next question is to determine the factors that will change marginal cost for a given output level. Such factors are often termed *cost push* factors because they affect price independently of the level of demand, acting by shifting the supply curve. One set of such cost push factors are factors that affect the money wage demands on the part of labor at a given level of employment; these are factors that shift the labor supply curve as that schedule is drawn, for example, in Figure 8.11. So far we have considered one factor that shifts the labor supply schedule, a change in the workers' expectation about the aggregate level of price (P^e).

In the preceding section we assumed that the laborers' expected price level depended on the past behavior of prices and, hence, was given in the short run. Over time, however, as new information is received, the workers will adjust their price expectation. Figure 8.16 shows the effect on labor supply and on the aggregate supply curve of an increase in workers' expectation concerning the aggregate price level.

Suppose that as a result of observed past increases in the aggregate price level, workers' expectation of the current price level rises from P_0^e to P_1^e.

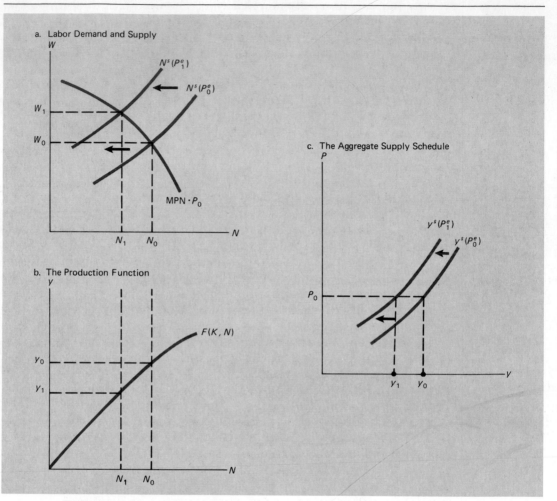

FIGURE 8.16 Shift in the Aggregate Supply Schedule with an Increase in the Expected Price Level

An increase in the expected price level shifts the labor supply schedule to the left from $N^s(P_0^e)$ to $N^s(P_1^e)$ in part a. At a given price level, P_0, employment declines from N_0 to N_1 and output falls from y_0 to y_1 (part b). This decline in output for a given price level is reflected in a shift to the left in the aggregate supply schedule from $y^s(P_0^e)$ to $y^s(P_1^e)$ in part c.

The labor supply schedule would then shift to the left in Figure 8.16a, from $N^s(P_0^e)$ to $N^s(P_1^e)$. Less labor will be supplied at each money wage because with the higher expectation about the aggregate price level, a given money wage corresponds to a lower real wage. Looked at from the firm's point of view, a higher money wage would have to be paid to obtain a given quantity of labor. At the initial price level P_0, the shift in the labor supply schedule will reduce employment (from N_0 to N_1). Consequently, output at price level P_0 falls (from y_0 to y_1), as can be seen in Figure 8.16b. The aggregate supply schedule shifts to the left in Figure 8.16c [from $y^s(P_0^e)$ to $y^s(P_1^e)$].

We see then that any factor that shifts the labor supply curve upward to the left, lowering labor supply for a given money wage or, what amounts to the same thing, increasing the money wage at which a given amount of labor will be supplied, shifts the aggregate supply schedule to the left. Such shifts in the labor supply function play an important part in our analysis of the longer-run adjustment of output and employment to policy changes.

If we broaden our analysis to allow for variable factors of production other than labor, it follows that an autonomous increase in the price of *any* variable factor of production will increase marginal cost for a given output level and shift the aggregate supply schedule to the left.

In particular, autonomous increases in the price of raw materials have this type of cost-push effect. Keynesians believe that increases during the 1970s in the world price of raw material inputs to the production process, primarily energy inputs, caused large increases in production cost for a given level of output and resulted in significant shifts to the left in the aggregate supply schedule, increasing the domestic aggregate price level and reducing real output.

In addition to the direct effects that increases in raw material prices have on the aggregate supply schedule, such supply shocks have indirect effects that come through an effect on labor supply. Increases in raw material prices, for example, the price of imported oil and other energy products, push up the domestic price level. As domestic prices rise and enough time passes for these price increases to be perceived by the suppliers of labor, the workers' expectation about the aggregate price level (P^e) will increase. As was just explained, such an increase in the expected price level will cause a shift to the left in the aggregate supply curve, further increasing the price level and causing an additional decline in real output.

The Keynesian explanation of the large price increases and output declines in the 1973–75 period and again in 1979–80 relies on such direct and indirect effects of supply shocks. The key supply shock in each case was a massive increase in the price of crude oil on the world market. Figure 8.17 shows the price of crude oil for the period since 1965, measured in both nominal and real (deflated by the price of U.S. exports) terms. The spikes in the series in 1974 and 1979–80 are evident. In 1974–75 there was a fourfold increase in the price of oil caused by the firming up of the OPEC (Organization of Petroleum Exporting Countries) pricing cartel. The 1979 disruption of the world oil market following the Iranian revolution again precipitated a huge increase in crude oil prices. The Keynesian view of the effects of such supply shocks is represented graphically in Figure 8.18. The initial increase in oil prices and increase in the price of other energy sources

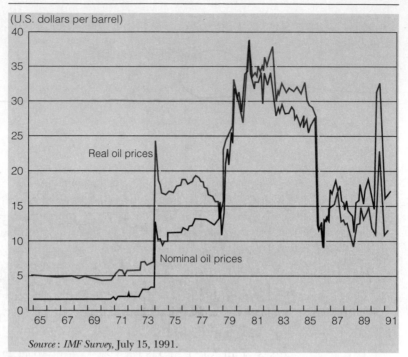

FIGURE 8.17   Two Decades of Volatile Oil Prices
Real prices are obtained by deflating nominal prices by unit values of manufactured goods exports.

(coal, natural gas, etc.), which results from the attempt of energy users to substitute other fuels for the higher-priced oil, cause a shift in the aggregate supply schedule from $y_0^s(P_0^e)$ to $y_1^s(P_0^e)$. Output declines from y_0 to y_1, and price rises from P_0 to P_1. This is the direct effect of the supply shock. As prices of energy-related products and of all products that use such energy inputs in the production process—a virtually all-inclusive category—rise, labor suppliers in time perceive the increase in price; the expected price level rises (from P_0^e to P_1^e). There is a further shift to the left in the aggregate supply schedule, from $y_1^s(P_0^e)$ to $y_1^s(P_1^e)$. Price increases further to P_2, and output declines to y_2.[7]

---

[7]This secondary shift in the supply schedule as a result of the adjustments in price expectations explains why supply shocks have inflationary effects that persist for a number of quarters rather than just causing a one-time rise in the price level. Such persistence may also be the result of accommodating increases in aggregate demand, as discussed in the next section.

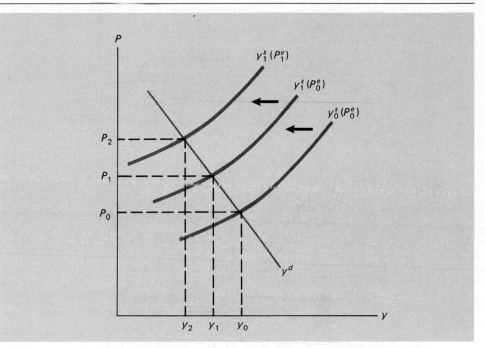

FIGURE 8.18   Effects of an Autonomous Increase in the World Price of Energy Inputs

An autonomous increase in the price of energy inputs shifts the aggregate supply schedule to the left from $y_0^s(P_0^e)$ to $y_1^s(P_0^e)$; output falls from y_0 to y_1 and the price level rises from P_0 to P_1. As labor suppliers perceive the rise in the price level, the expected price level rises from P_0^e to P_1^e. The aggregate supply schedule shifts farther to the left to $y_1^s(P_1^e)$. Output falls to y_2 and the price level rises to P_2.

Supply-Side Factors, 1981–91

As can be seen from Figure 8.17, the price of oil remained volatile during the post-1980 period. Oil prices fell sharply in the years from 1981 to 1986 as new sources of oil became available and the OPEC cartel weakened. This was in effect a favorable supply shock. By simply reversing the graphical analysis in Figure 8.18 we see that such a favorable shock would, in the absence of other changes, reduce the aggregate price level and increase output. In fact, during the first half of this time period there was a severe recession, which in the Keynesian view was caused by demand-side factors. The decline in the price of oil did contribute to the dramatic fall in the inflation rate during these years.

The next large change in oil prices came in August 1990, following Iraq's invasion of Kuwait. The price of oil shot up as Kuwaiti oil production was halted and the United Nations placed an embargo on Iraqi oil exports. The price of oil declined as rapidly as it had risen once a swift victory of UN forces was evident in early 1991. The effects of both the rise and fall of oil prices can be seen clearly in the behavior of the producer price index. The index rose by more than 15 percent (at an annual rate) between August and October 1990 and then fell by 5 percent (again at an annual rate) between December 1990 and March 1991. This brief episode again demonstrates the vulnerability of the U.S. economy to developments in the world oil market.

8.6 · SUPPLY SHOCKS AND AGGREGATE DEMAND POLICY

Unfavorable supply shocks, such as the energy price shocks experienced by the United States in the 1970s, create a dilemma for macroeconomic policymakers. The dilemma concerns the proper response of monetary and fiscal policy to such supply shocks. To see the nature of the policymaker's dilemma, first consider the case in which no response of monetary or fiscal policy occurs in the wake of an unfavorable energy price shock. In this case the situation is as illustrated in Figure 8.18. The supply shock would cause output to fall and prices to rise. In Figure 8.19 this outcome is shown as a fall in output from y_0 to y_1 and a rise in the price level from P_0 to P_1 as a result of a shift to the left in the supply schedule from y_0^s to y_1^s.

Instead, to avoid increased unemployment, the policymaker could offset some or all of the unfavorable output effect of the supply shock by increasing the level of aggregate demand through expansionary monetary and/or fiscal policies. To offset all of the unfavorable output effect of the supply shock, the policymaker expands demand by enough to shift the aggregate demand schedule from y_0^d to y_H^d in Figure 8.19, thereby restoring output to the initial level y_0. The policymaker *accommodates* the supply shock by increasing aggregate demand sufficiently to support the same level of output even with higher energy prices. Notice, though, that in doing so the policymaker exacerbates the inflationary effect of the supply shock. With an accommodating aggregate demand policy, the price level rises to P_2, a higher level than P_1, when there was assumed to be no accommodation.

An alternative policy response would be to offset the price rise caused by the supply shock by lowering aggregate demand through restrictive monetary and fiscal policies. Such policies could offset all the unfavorable price effects of the supply shock by shifting the aggregate demand schedule from y_0^d to y_L^d in Figure 8.19. Even given the new supply schedule y_1^s, with demand at this low level the initial price level P_0 is restored. Notice, however, that the effect of the restrictive aggregate demand policy is to worsen the output effect of the supply shock. Output falls to y_2 below y_1, the level of output with no demand response.

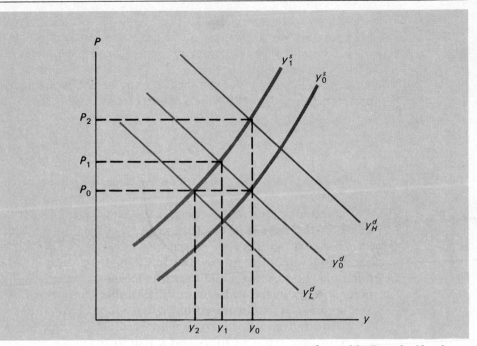

FIGURE 8.19 Aggregate Demand Responses to an Unfavorable Supply Shock
A supply shock shifts the aggregate supply schedule from y_0^s to y_1^s; output will fall
from y_0 to y_1 and the price level will rise from P_0 to P_1. The policymaker could
increase aggregate demand to y_H^d and offset the unfavorable output effect of the
supply shock, but then price would rise further to P_2. Alternatively, he could lower
demand to y_L^d to offset the price effect of the supply shock, but in this case output
would fall by more, to y_2.

We see, therefore, that accommodation of the supply shock can offset the
unfavorable output effect of the supply shock only by increasing the unfavorable price-level effect. On the other hand, restrictive aggregate demand
policies as a response to the supply shock, although they help reduce the
unfavorable price effect of the shock, do so only at the cost of worsening the
output effect. This is the dilemma of policymakers in the face of a supply
shock such as the oil price increase in 1974. In the Keynesian view, it is the
fact that, in the presence of supply shocks, aggregate demand policy alone
cannot prevent both price increases and declining output that explains why
even well-designed policy actions of the 1970s (and the Keynesians do not
claim that all policy actions were well designed) did not produce attractive
outcomes.

Of course, as we have seen, not all supply shocks are unfavorable. Favorable supply shocks make a policymaker's task easier. If the aggregate supply

curve is shifting to the right, aggregate demand policy can be more expansionary without pushing up the price level. Alteratively, inflation can
be reduced with less unfavorable effects on output and employment. During the early 1980s, for example, the favorable performance of energy and
other raw materials prices meant that the reduction in inflation during these
years was achieved with less output loss than would otherwise have occurred,
although the output loss was still large.

8.7 • CONCLUSION: KEYNES VERSUS THE CLASSICS

The last four chapters have analyzed the Keynesian view of macroeconomics.
What are the major differences between this Keynesian view and the classical macroeconomic theory that Keynes attacked? In this chapter we have
seen how the Keynesian system can be summarized by the aggregate supply
and aggregate demand relationships. The classical model can be expressed
in the same manner, as was done in Chapter 4. A convenient way to summarize the differences between the Keynesian and classical theories is to
examine the differences between the respective aggregate demand and aggregate supply relationships in the two models.

Keynesian Versus Classical Theories of Aggregate Demand

The classical model did not contain an explicit theory of aggregate demand.
The *quantity theory of money* provided an implicit classical theory of aggregate
demand. Using the quantity theory relationship

$$MV = Py \tag{8.8}$$

with the assumption that V is constant, we can determine Py for a given value
of M. This relationship gives the rectangular hyperbola $y^d(M_0)$ plotted in
Figure 8.20a for M equals M_0. This was the classical aggregate demand
curve. The nominal demand for goods (Py) depended on the quantity of
money.

The logic behind this relationship was clearest for the Cambridge form of
the quantity theory:

$$M = M^d = kPy \tag{8.9}$$

Since k is equal to $1/V$, (8.8) and (8.9) are equivalent. From (8.9) it can be
seen that an increase in M will, for a given value of Py and an assumed
constant k, cause an excess supply of money. The classical theory assumed
that this excess supply of money would be reflected in an excess demand for
goods.

Increases in demand by one sector of the economy, government demand
or autonomous investment demand, for example, would not affect aggregate

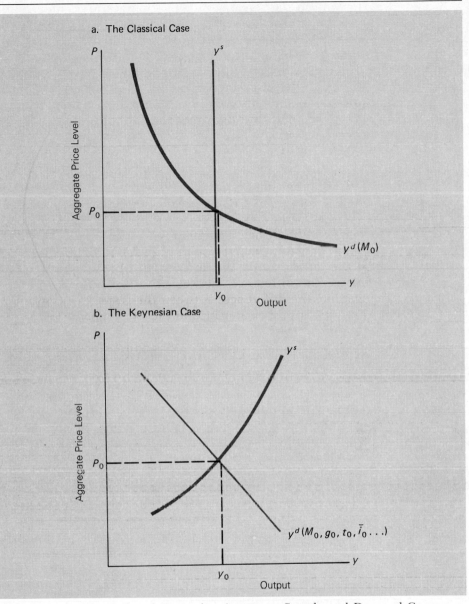

FIGURE 8.20 Classical and Keynesian Aggregate Supply and Demand Curves
The classical aggregate supply schedule is vertical while the Keynesian aggregate supply schedule slopes upward to the right. The classical aggregate demand schedule depends only on the level of the money stock (M_0), while in the Keynesian system aggregate demand also depends on the levels of fiscal variables (g_0, t_0), the level of autonomous investment ($\bar{i}_0$), and other variables as well.

demand in the classical system. Changes in sectoral demands would cause adjustments in the interest rate. The interest rate played a stabilizing role in the classical system and ensured that such changes in sectoral demands could not change aggregate demand. For example, in the classical model an increase in government spending financed by selling bonds to the public would cause the interest rate to rise until private spending had declined by just the amount of the increase in government spending. Aggregate demand would be unchanged (Section 4.3). *Only monetary factors shift the classical aggregate demand curve.*

The Keynesian aggregate demand curve is shown in Figure 8.20*b*. Although both the classical and Keynesian aggregate demand curves are downward-sloping schedules when plotted against price, there is an important difference between them. Whereas the classical aggregate demand schedule shifts only when the stock of money changes, the position of the Keynesian aggregate demand curve depends on variables such as the level of government spending (g_0), the level of tax collections (t_0), and the level of autonomous investment expenditures ($\bar{i}_0$) in addition to the quantity of money (M_0). As we have seen, the Keynesian aggregate demand function will shift when any of these other factors vary. The interest rate does not completely insulate aggregate demand from changes in sectoral demands in the Keynesian system. This difference in the determinants of aggregate demand in the Keynesian and classical models produces important differences in their respective explanations of the sources of instability in the economy and the usefulness of various stabilization policies.

Keynes believed that the instability of investment demand was the major cause of cyclical fluctuations in income. Autonomous changes in investment demand caused by changes in expectations cause shifts in the aggregate demand function and consequently instability in price and output. Fiscal policy could be used to cause offsetting changes in aggregate demand and potentially stabilize aggregate demand even though investment demand was unstable.

In the classical view there is no need for government policy to stabilize aggregate demand in the face of investment instability, nor would fiscal policy be able to perform such a function. For a given stock of money, the aggregate demand curve will be unaffected by either autonomous changes in investment or by changes in fiscal policy variables. To classical economists the only source of instability in aggregate demand is from changes in the quantity of money. The remedy is stable money. The business cycle is a "dance of the dollar," to use Irving Fisher's phrase.

Keynesian Versus Classical Theories of Aggregate Supply

The key difference between the classical and Keynesian aggregate supply functions concerns the slope of the function. The classical aggregate supply function, shown in Figure 8.20a, is vertical. The vertical supply function results from the classical assumptions about the labor market. Labor supply and demand are assumed to depend only on the real wage, which is known to all. The money wage is assumed to be perfectly flexible, adjusting quickly to equate supply and demand. Since the aggregate supply curve is vertical, output and employment are completely supply-determined. Aggregate demand plays no systematic role in determining output.

In the *short run* the Keynesian aggregate supply curve slopes upward to the right. We would expect the curve to be quite flat at levels of output well below full capacity and to become steeper as full capacity output is approached. The Keynesian view of aggregate supply (Sections 8.3 and 8.4) emphasizes the stickiness of the money wage and the failure of market participants to perceive the real wage correctly. As a consequence, the labor market will not be in continual equilibrium at full employment. Actual output and employment will not be completely determined by the supply factors that determine *full employment* output. Shifts in the aggregate demand function will move the economy along the upward-sloping supply function, causing output to change. In the Keynesian system the level of aggregate demand is an important factor determining the level of output and employment.

Classical economists recognized that a rigid money wage would result in an aggregate supply curve that was not vertical. With a rigid money wage, output would not be completely supply-determined. In such a situation, aggregate demand would affect output.

The fact that with a rigid money wage, output is affected by aggregate demand even in the classical model has led some economists to conclude that the only important difference between the classical and Keynesian models is that Keynes assumed the money wage was fixed, whereas classical economists assumed the money wage to be perfectly flexible. Such an interpretation underestimates the contribution of Keynesian economics. As we have seen, the Keynesian theory of aggregate demand differs considerably from that of the classical economists. Also, the Keynesian theory of aggregate supply does not rest *only* on the assumption of an institutionally rigid money wage, although, as we saw in Section 8.3, Keynesians *do* believe that wages are sticky in the downward direction. A Keynesian aggregate supply curve can also result where the money wage is flexible, but labor suppliers have imperfect information about the level of the real wage. Differing views of the labor market, however, certainly are an important source of the differing conclusions reached in the classical and Keynesian models.

The Keynesian aggregate supply curve in Figure 8.20b was termed a short-run supply curve, to emphasize that it pertained to a short period of time, not to a long-run equilibrium situation. Factors such as explicit long-term labor contracts, implicit contracts, and resistance to wage cuts seen as cuts in the relative wage would slow but not permanently prevent the necessary wage adjustment to return the economy to a full-employment level. Imperfect information about the real wage on the part of labor suppliers would also be a short-run phenomenon. Eventually, expectations would approach the actual value of the price level and, hence, of the real wage. The Keynesians do not deny that eventually the economy would approach full employment. But to the Keynesians such long-run "classical" properties of the economy are unimportant. They agree with Keynes that "this *long run* is a misleading guide to current affairs. *In the long run* we are all dead. Economists set themselves too easy, too useless a task if in tempestuous seasons they can only tell us that when the storm is long past the ocean is flat again."[8]

Keynesian Versus Classical Policy Conclusions

Given the differences in their models, it is not surprising that Keynesian and classical economists reach different policy conclusions. Classical economists stressed the self-adjusting tendencies of the economy. If left free from destabilizing government policies, the economy would achieve full employment. Classical economists were noninterventionist in that they did not favor active monetary and fiscal policies to stabilize the economy. Such policies, to affect aggregate demand, would have no effects on output or employment given the supply-determined nature of those variables in the classical system.

Keynesians view the economy as unstable as a result of the instability of aggregate demand, primarily the private-investment component of aggregate demand. Aggregate demand does affect output and employment in the Keynesian view. Consequently, swings in aggregate demand will cause undesirable fluctuations in output and employment in the short run. These fluctuations can be prevented by using monetary and fiscal policies to offset undesirable changes in aggregate demand. Keynesians are interventionists, favoring active policies to manage aggregate demand.

Review Questions and Problems

1. Explain why the Keynesian aggregate demand curve is downward-sloping when plotted against the price level.

2. Derive the Keynesian aggregate demand curve for the case where investment is completely interest-inelastic and therefore the *IS* schedule is

---

[8]John M. Keynes, *A Tract on Monetary Reform* (London: Macmillan, 1923), p. 80.

vertical (follow the procedure in Figure 8.2). Explain the resulting slope of the aggregate demand curve for this case.

3. In what sense is the classical theory of aggregate supply "fundamentally incompatible" with the Keynesian system?

4. Why are fiscal policy multipliers smaller in magnitude in the variable price-fixed wage version of the Keynesian model than in the fixed-price $IS-LM$ model? Why are these multipliers still smaller when we allow the money wage as well as the price level to be variable?

5. Analyze the effects of an increase in the money stock within the Keynesian model, where both the price level and money wage are assumed to be variable. Include in your answer the effects on the level of real income, the price level, the interest rate, and the money wage.

6. In the Keynesian system, increases in aggregate demand can lead to increases in output because the money wage rises less than proportionately with the price level in response to such increases in demand. This is necessary since firms will hire more workers only if the real wage (W/P) falls. Explain the possible reasons why the money wage does not adjust proportionately with the price level in the short-run Keynesian model.

7. Assume that there is an exogenous decline in the price of imported oil. Using the graphical analysis in this chapter, explain how such a shock would affect output and the price level. Explain the role that inflationary expectations play in this adjustment.

8. Explain the dilemma that is created for policymakers by unfavorable supply shocks.

9. "Money is more important in the Keynesian system than in the classical system." Do you agree? Or would you maintain that the opposite is true?

10. What do you see as the essential differences between the classical and Keynesian theories of aggregate supply?

11. What do you see as the essential differences between the classical and Keynesian theories of aggregate demand?

12. Compare the effects of an expansionary fiscal policy action, an increase in government spending financed by government bond sales to the public, for example, in the Keynesian and classical models. Include in your answer the effects of this policy shift on the level of real income, employment, the price level, and the rate of interest.

13. Within the variable price-variable wage version of the Keynesian model, analyze the effects that an unfavorable supply shock, such as a rise in the price of oil, would have on the rate of interest. Would the equilibrium rate of interest rise or fall?

Selected Readings

Baily, Martin Neil, "The Labor Market in the 1930s," in James Tobin, ed., *Macroeconomics: Prices and Quantities.* Washington, D.C.: The Brookings Institution, 1983.

Blinder, Alan S., *Economic Policy and the Great Stagflation.* New York: Academic Press, 1979.

Branson, William, *Macroeconomic Theory and Policy.* New York: Harper & Row, 1989, Chaps. 6–9.

Bruno, Michael, and Jeffrey Sachs, *The Economics of Worldwide Stagflation.* Cambridge, Mass.: Harvard University Press, 1985.

Gramlich, Edward, "Macro Policy Responses to Price Shocks," *Brookings Paper on Economic Activity,* No. 1 (1979), pp. 125–66.

Modigliani, Franco, "Liquidity Preference and the Theory of Interest and Money," *Econometrica,* 12 (January 1944), pp. 45–88. Reprinted in Friedrich Lutz and Lloyd Mints, *Readings in Monetary Theory.* Homewood, Ill.: Irwin, 1951.

Smith, Warren, "A Graphical Exposition of the Complete Keynesian System," *Southern Economic Journal*, 23 (October 1956), pp. 115–25.

9 The Monetarist Counterrevolution

9.1 • INTRODUCTION

The British news magazine *The Economist* defined a *monetarist* as someone "who thinks it more important to regulate the supply of money in an economy than to influence other economic instruments. This is thought very wicked by those who can't be bothered to find out what it means."[1] In the next two chapters we examine the monetarist position and see why monetarists place such importance on the money supply. First, let us look briefly at the historical background against which monetarism developed.

The Keynesian attack on the classical orthodoxy was successful. A debate continued between classical economists and Keynesians, but by 1950 Keynesian economics was well established as a new orthodoxy. After Keynes died in 1946, his successors took up the task of refining his theories and applying them to the policy questions facing Western nations as they converted to peacetime economies in the aftermath of World War II. As we have seen, one aspect of the Keynesian Revolution was an attack on the classical quantity theory of money. In fact, *early* Keynesian economists, though not later *neo-Keynesians,* attached very little macroeconomic importance to the money supply. Monetarism began as an attempt to reassert the economic importance of money and therefore of monetary policy.

Rather than attempt to give a capsule definition of monetarism, we instead list a number of propositions that characterize the monetarist position.

---

[1] *The Economist*, January 8, 1983, p. 4.

This strategy is not without risks. As Milton Friedman, the central figure in the early development of monetarism, notes: "One man's 'characteristic monetarist proposition' is not another's."[2] The characteristic monetarist propositions advanced here are the following:

1. The supply of money is the dominant influence on nominal income.
2. In the long run, the influence of money is primarily on the price level and other *nominal* magnitudes. In the long run, *real* variables, such as real output and employment, are determined by real, not monetary, factors.
3. In the short run, the supply of money does influence real variables. Money is the dominant factor causing cyclical movements in output and employment.
4. The private sector of the economy is inherently stable. Instability in the economy is primarily the result of government policies.

From these four propositions we see that two policy conclusions follow:

1. Stability in the growth of the money stock is crucial for stability in the economy. Monetarists believe that such stability is best achieved by adopting a rule for the growth rate in the money stock. Milton Friedman has long proposed a constant money growth rate rule. Other monetarists favor less inflexible rules, but monetarists generally favor rules rather than the discretion of policymakers for determining money growth.
2. Fiscal policy, by itself, has little systematic effect on either real or nominal income. Fiscal policy is not an effective stabilization tool.

The first of the monetarist propositions is that the level of economic activity in current dollars is determined primarily by the stock of money. An important element in this proposition is that the direction of influence or causation is assumed to be from money to income. For the most part, changes in the money stock are assumed to *cause* changes in nominal income. The level and rate of growth of the money stock are assumed to be determined primarily by the actions of the government central bank.

The second monetarist proposition asserts that in the long run the level of economic activity measured in real (inflation-corrected) dollars does not depend on the quantity of money. In the long run the level of real output is determined by real factors such as the stock of capital goods, the size and quality of the labor force, and the state of technology. If, in the long run, the level of real economic activity is not affected by the quantity of money

---

[2]An alternative list of monetarist propositions is given in Thomas Mayer, *The Structure of Monetarism* (New York: Norton, 1978).

while the level of economic activity in nominal terms is almost completely determined by the stock of money, it follows that the long-run effect of money is on the price level.

Proposition 3 states that, in the short run, real output and employment *are* strongly influenced by changes in the stock of money. Prices are influenced as well, but in the short run prices, including wage rates (the price of labor), are not perfectly flexible. Thus, when the quantity of money changes, in the short run, prices do not make the full long-run adjustment. Output and employment are also affected.

The fourth monetarist proposition asserts that the private sector (businesses and households) is not the source of instability in the economy. As one monetarist, Karl Brunner, put it, the private sector is "essentially a shock-absorbing, stabilizing and self-adjusting process. Instability is produced dominantly by the operation of the government sector." The government causes instability in the economy primarily by allowing instability in the growth of the money stock, the major determinant of the level of economic activity. In the monetarist view the government can also destabilize the economy by interfering with the normal adjustment mechanisms in the private economy. Mandatory controls on prices and wages are the most obvious example of government interference with such adjustment properties. Other examples are usury ceilings on interest rates, rent controls, and minimum wage laws.

The two policy corollaries follow from the four monetarist propositions. Given propositions 1 and 3, the importance of stable money growth for a stable economy is evident. The monetarists believe that adopting a rule (e.g., a law) is the best way to achieve stable money growth.

If monetary factors dominate the determination of nominal income and short-run real income, only a little role is left for other systematic influences. The term *dominate* does, however, allow for some ambiguity. Does it mean that movements in the money stock explain 55 percent of the systematic movement in income, or 95 percent? This question is important in assessing the role of fiscal policy (and other factors) in determining the level of economic activity. As stated, our second policy conclusion allows little independent role for fiscal policy. This seems consistent with the position of monetarists such as Milton Friedman. Other monetarists do not accept such a strong form of this policy proposition, but the general monetarist position has been that fiscal policy is not an effective stabilization tool.

In considering the basis for these monetarist propositions and policy conclusions, it is convenient to divide the analysis into two parts. First we examine the reasons why the monetarists ascribe such predominance to money (i.e., the basis of propositions 1 and 3). We postpone until Chapter 10 the question of what monetary policy cannot do, the basis for proposition 2. Although proposition 4 is not given separate consideration, it will be important at a number of points in our discussion of monetarism.

9.2 • THE REFORMULATION OF THE QUANTITY THEORY OF MONEY

The first stage in the development of monetarism centered on redefining the quantity theory of money in the light of Keynes's attack. The central monetarist in this period was Milton Friedman, a professor of economics at the University of Chicago from 1946 until his retirement in 1977 and since that time a senior research fellow at the Hoover Institution.

We have examined the quantity theory of money in our consideration of classical economics (Section 4.1). Friedman describes the quantity theory in the following way:

> In monetary theory, that analysis was taken to mean that in the quantity equation $MV = PT$ the term for velocity could be regarded as highly stable, that it could be taken as determined independently of the other terms in the equation, and that as a result changes in the quantity of money would be reflected either in prices or in output.[3]

This is proposition 1 of monetarism, as stated previously. (Notice that the stability of velocity means not only that changes in M will cause changes in PT, but that *only* changes in M can change PT.)

The quantity theory of money had come into disrepute, together with the rest of classical economics, as a result of the Great Depression of the 1930s. Friedman believed that the events of the 1930s had been improperly assessed and did not in fact offer evidence against the quantity theory of money. He did, however, see the need to restate the quantity theory in terms that took account of Keynes's contribution. His purpose in doing this was to reassert the importance of money. To see why he felt this was needed, it is best to start by considering the role (or lack of a role) that some early Keynesians attributed to money as a determinant of the level of economic activity.

Money and the Early Keynesians

Our analysis of the Keynesian system made clear that within that framework money was one of a number of important determinants of the level of economic activity. But velocity was not constant or independently determined; it was systematically determined within the system. Factors other than money could also affect the level of economic activity. Consider, for example, the response of the system to an increase in government spending, as depicted in Figure 9.1.

---

[3]Milton Friedman, *The Counter-revolution in Monetary Theory* (London: Institute of Economic Affairs, 1970).

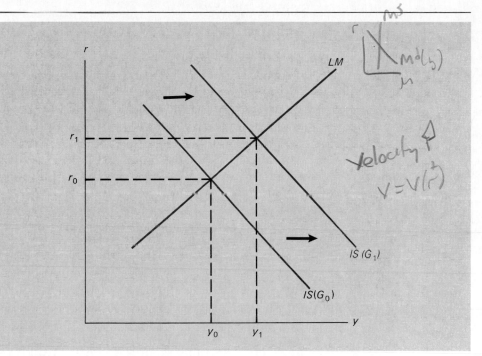

FIGURE 9.1   Effects of an Increase in Government Spending:
The Keynesian View

An increase in government spending shifts the IS schedule to the right. The equilibrium interest rate rises, and the equilibrium level of income rises. Since the money stock is unchanged and income has risen, the velocity of money, the ratio of income to the money stock, has increased.

The increase in government spending from G_0 to G_1 shifts the IS curve from IS (G_0) to $IS(G_1)$. Income rises from y_0 to y_1, and the interest rate increases from r_0 to r_1. The money stock is held constant here, with the increased government spending assumed to be financed by selling bonds to the public. The higher level of income causes a higher transactions demand for money. To bring money demand back into equality with the unchanged money supply, a rise in the interest rate is required. At the higher interest rate the speculative demand for money will have declined, and the demand for transaction balances *at a given level of income* will also have fallen. Thus, the same money stock can support a higher income level. Another way to express this finding is to say that velocity varies positively with the interest rate.

Since velocity is variable in the Keynesian system, there is no one level of income corresponding to a given level of the money stock. It is not even an approximately accurate statement of the Keynesian view that in the short run nominal or real income is determined solely by the level of the money supply. This is not to say that the Keynesians believe that money is unimportant; they do not. The quantity of money is *one* of the key determinants of income in the Keynesian system. As we saw in Chapter 7, an increase in the quantity of money, for example, would shift the *LM* curve to the right in Figure 9.1. Income would rise, and the interest rate would fall. There is no reason in the Keynesian system to view these changes as small.

Many *early* Keynesian economists (circa 1945–50) did, however, believe that money was of little importance and monetary policy of little use as a stabilization tool. Their view was based on empirical judgments about the slopes of the *IS–LM* curves, which, as we saw in our analysis of the Keynesian system, are important in determining the relative effectiveness of monetary and fiscal policy. Influenced by the experience of the Depression, they believed that the *LM* schedule was quite flat and the *IS* schedule quite steep—the configuration that would be characteristic of depression conditions such as those of the 1930s. The Depression was characterized by low levels of income and the interest rate. At such a low level of the interest rate the elasticity of money demand would be high, for reasons discussed in Chapter 6. Such a situation approaches the liquidity trap case; the *LM* curve becomes very flat. Further, in depression conditions the early Keynesian economists believed investment would be relatively inelastic, making the *IS* curve quite steep. The Depression was a period with a very low rate of utilization of existing plant and equipment. With such excess capacity, early Keynesian economists thought it unlikely that investment would respond much to changes in the interest rate.

Figure 9.2 shows this configuration of *IS–LM* curves and illustrates the ineffectiveness of an increase in the quantity of money that shifts the *LM* curve from LM_0 to LM_1. With the *LM* curve flat around the point of equilibrium, a given change in the money stock does very little in terms of lowering the interest rate, the first link in the chain connecting money and income in the Keynesian model. Further, with a steep *IS* curve, a drop in the interest rate would not increase investment very much. This combination of an assumed high interest elasticity of money demand and low interest elasticity of the demand for output led early Keynesian economists to the conclusion that the quantity of money was unimportant.

What role was there for monetary policy? During World War II much of the war expenditure had been financed by selling bonds to the public at relatively low interest rates. Keeping the interest rate on bonds low and stable would have the desirable effects of keeping the cost of interest payments on the debt low and protecting the capital value of the bonds for the investors (recall that bond prices and interest rates vary inversely). Low interest rates also mean that monetary policy would make whatever limited contribution it could to strengthening aggregate demand. Since early Keynesian economists feared a return to the severe depression conditions of the 1930s, this was

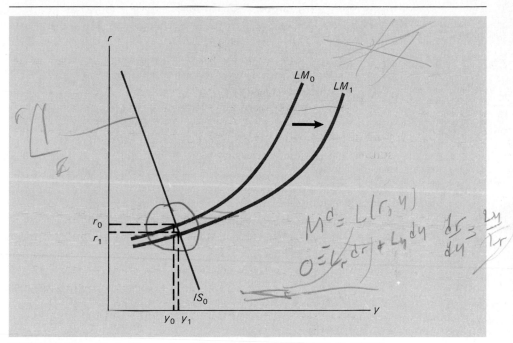

FIGURE 9.2 Early Keynesian View of Monetary Policy Ineffectiveness
With the IS curve quite steep and over the range where the LM schedule is nearly
horizontal, an increase in the quantity of money, which shifts the LM schedule from
LM_0 to LM_1, has little effect on income.

another desirable feature of low interest rates. Thus low and stable interest
rates became the goal of monetary policy. To achieve this goal, the monetary
authority cooperated with the Treasury to "peg" or fix the levels of interest
rates, and in doing so they surrendered control over the quantity of money.

There was a further element in the view of the early Keynesians that
made pegging the interest rate desirable. Following Keynes, they felt that
the demand for money was highly unstable. The LM curve was not only flat
(in the relevant range) but shifted around in an unpredictable way. These
shifts would lead to instability in financial markets. Such instability could be
avoided by pegging the interest rate.

It will be useful for our later analysis to examine just what the monetary
authority does when it pegs the interest rate and the implications of pegging
interest rates for money stock control. Consider the situation in which there is
one type of bond, a *perpetuity* paying a fixed amount per period.[4] In this case,

[4]Recall here that a perpetuity is a bond that pays interest each period but never pays back
principal—an infinitely lived bond.

as we saw in Section 6.1, the price of the bond is inversely related to the current market interest rate. The price of the bond (PB) can be expressed as

$$PB = \frac{CP}{r}$$

or, equivalently,

$$r = \frac{CP}{PB} \tag{9.1}$$

where CP is the number of dollars of interest the bond pays per period (the coupon payment) and r is the interest rate expressed as a decimal. If CP is $100 and r is 0.05 (5 percent), the bond will sell for $2000 (100 ÷ 0.05 = 2000).

If the monetary authority wished to peg the interest rate at 5 percent, it would maintain the price of the bond at $2000 by standing ready to buy or sell bonds at that price. As long as the monetary authority will sell the bond at $2000, no investor will pay a higher price to buy from a private bondholder. The interest rate cannot fall below 5 percent [from equation (9.1) note that $r = CP ÷ PB = 100 ÷ 2000 = 0.05$]. Similarly, since the monetary authority will buy bonds for $2000, no bondholder will sell for less to a private buyer. The interest rate will not rise above 5 percent. As long as the monetary authority has a sufficiently large holding of bonds, which in practice it does, it can fix the price of bonds and peg the interest rate.

But what happens to the quantity of money? The monetary authority buys or sells bonds by exchanging them for money. We consider the details of the process later, but for now assume that the monetary authority simply prints new money to pay for bonds it purchases from private bondholders and retires from circulation the money earned from sales of bonds. Since in order to peg the interest rate the monetary authority must stand ready to exchange money for bonds on demand, the quantity of money will be determined not by the monetary authority but by the desire of the private sector to hold bonds. *The monetary authority can peg the interest rate, but in doing so it surrenders to the private sector control of the quantity of money.*

To understand better the demand-determined nature of the quantity of money in a system where the monetary authority is pegging the rate of interest, consider our *IS–LM* graph in such a situation, as shown in Figure 9.3. The graph contains three possible *IS* curves, IS_0, IS_1, and IS_2, corresponding to successively higher levels of aggregate demand. We assume that the monetary authority pegs the interest rate at $\bar{r}$. This is represented in Figure 9.3 by the perfectly horizontal *LM* schedule, $\overline{LM}$, at interest rate $\bar{r}$. The *LM* curve in this case is flat, even though the interest elasticity of money demand is not infinite. We do not need to assume that there is a liquidity trap. With the interest rate pegged, it is the fact that the monetary

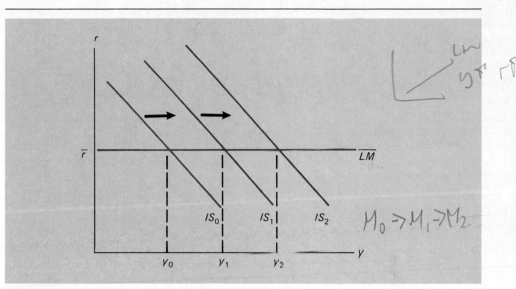

FIGURE 9.3 *IS–LM* with the Interest Rate Pegged

If the monetary authority pegs the interest rate at $\bar{r}$, the *LM* curve effectively becomes horizontal. Increases in aggregate demand that shift the *IS* schedule from IS_0 to IS_1, then to IS_2, will increase income from y_0 to y_1, then to y_2. The monetary authority supplies the additional money required for increased transactions balances as income rises. The quantity of money becomes demand-determined.

authority will buy and sell bonds—increase or decrease the money stock—to prevent any movements in the interest rate that makes the *LM* schedule flat. It is the money supply that is now perfectly interest-elastic.

Now we can see how the quantity of money in the system will be determined. Recall that in the Keynesian model, money demand is given by

$$M^d = L(y, r) \tag{9.2}$$

With r fixed at $\bar{r}$, money demand varies solely with income. With the interest rate pegged, the money stock will be determined by this demand for money and therefore by the level of income. Consider what happens as aggregate demand increases from IS_0 to IS_1, then to IS_2 in Figure 9.3. With the *IS* curve at IS_0, income will be at y_0 and money demand will be

$$M_0^d = L(y_0, \bar{r}) \tag{9.3}$$

With the increase in aggregate demand shifting the *IS* schedule to IS_1 and then to IS_2, income rises from y_0 to y_1 and then to y_2 in Figure 9.3. As a result of the increase in income, money demand increases to

$$M_1^d = L(y_1, \bar{r})$$

PERSPECTIVES

9.1 THE MONETARIST VIEW OF THE GREAT DEPRESSION

Both Friedman and the Keynesians agree that it was the Great Depression of the 1930s that put the classical theories, including the quantity theory of money, in disrepute. Friedman, however, believes that the Keynesians misread the evidence from the Depression.

Friedman does not deny that the experience of the United States and other industrialized countries in the 1930s contradicts the classical view of the labor market, where the money wage adjusts quickly to maintain full employment. On this issue the monetarists and Keynesians agree. Friedman does believe that Keynesians wrongly concluded that the Depression disproved the quantity theory of money. Let us look at some evidence.

Table 9.1 shows the level of several macroeconomic aggregates in 1929, at the start of the Depression, compared with their level in 1933, at the low point of the slump. From the table we see that nominal GNP fell 46.0 percent, and real GNP fell 29.6 percent. The rest of the drop in nominal GNP is accounted for by a fall in the aggregate price level. Column 3 shows that the narrowly defined money stock, M1 (currency plus checkable deposits), fell by 26.5 percent between 1929 and 1933. The M2 measure of the money supply, a broader measure that includes other bank deposits, fell by 33.3 percent.

We see that there *was* a large decline in the money stock as we fell into the Great Depression, which on the surface is consistent with the quantity theory. Velocity also fell, as evidenced by the larger percentage decline in nominal income relative to the fall in either money supply measure. But quantity theorists would expect this, since during the deflation of the Depression, the value of money (in terms of purchasing power) was rising. This would be likely to increase the demand for money for a given nominal income and therefore to lower velocity.

Keynesians dispute this monetary explanation of the Depression. They do believe that if the Federal Reserve had been able to prevent a decline in the money stock during the 1929–33 period, the Depression would have been less severe than it was. They believe, however, that the primary causes of the Depression were autonomous declines in several components of aggregate demand: consumption, investment, and exports, caused, in turn, by factors such as the stock market crash in 1929, overbuilding in the construction sector by the late 1920s, and the breakdown of the international monetary system. This has been called the "spending

TABLE 9.1   Selected Macroeconomic Aggregates (1929, 1933)

	Nominal GNP(Y)	Real GNP(y) (in 1982 dollars)	M1	M2
1929	$103.9 billion	$708.6 billion	$26.4 billion	$46.2 billion
1933	$56.0 billion	$498.5 billion	$19.4 billion	$30.8 billion
Percentage decline	46.0%	29.6%	26.5%	33.3%

---

hypothesis," in contrast to the "money hypothesis" advanced by Friedman and other monetarists.[1]

---

[1] For Friedman's analysis, see Milton Friedman and Anna J. Schwartz, *The Great Contraction* (Princeton, N.J.: Princeton University Press, 1965). Also on the subject of the causes of the Great Depression, see Peter Temin, *Did Monetary Forces Cause the Great Depression?* (New York: Norton, 1976), and the papers in Karl Brunner, ed., *The Great Depression Revisited* (Boston: Martinus Nijhoff, 1981).

---

and then

$$M_2^d = L(y_2, \overline{r}) \tag{9.4}$$

To increase its money holdings, the private sector must sell bonds. Normally, this would result in a fall in bond prices, but the monetary authority prevents this by buying any bonds the public wants to sell at existing bond prices. As income rises, the monetary authority supplies the additional money required for increased transaction balances. The quantity of money is determined by the demand for money.

To the early Keynesians this loss of control of the money stock was not considered important. The quantity of money was not considered important.

Read Perspectives 9.1.

Friedman's Restatement of the Quantity Theory: The Weak Form

Contrary to the view of early Keynesians, Friedman argued that the demand for money was stable. Contrary to the near-liquidity-trap characterization, Friedman maintained that the interest elasticity of money demand was certainly not infinite and was in fact "rather small." The quantity of money, far from being unimportant, was the dominant influence on the level of economic activity.

Friedman's conclusions rest on a restatement of the classical quantity theory of money. Friedman's version of the quantity theory is closest to the Cambridge approach we considered previously. That approach focused on the demand for money. The central relationship was

$$M^d = \overline{k}P y \tag{9.5}$$

expressing a proportional relationship between money demand (M^d) and the level of nominal income [price (P) times real income (y)]. The factor of proportionality (k) was taken as constant in the short run.

Friedman emphasizes the fact that the quantity theory was, as can be seen from equation (9.5), a theory of money demand. It is because k was treated as a constant by the Cambridge economists and the *nominal* supply of money

(M) was treated as being set exogenously by the monetary authority that the Cambridge equation can be transformed into a theory of nominal income,

$$M = M^d = \bar{k}Py$$

$$M\frac{1}{\bar{k}} = Py \tag{9.6}$$

or the alternative form (where V, the velocity of money, equals $1/k$).

$$M\bar{V} = Py \tag{9.7}$$

where the bar over k or V indicates that these magnitudes do not vary. Friedman examined the changes in the Cambridge theory of money demand that must be made in the light of Keynes's theory of money demand. Then he showed how this revised version of the Cambridge theory could be transformed into a theory of nominal income.

Keynes's theory of money demand stressed the role of money as an asset in addition to its role in transactions. In studying the factors that determined how much money people would hold, Keynes was naturally led to consider factors that determined the desirability of money relative to other assets. He made the simplifying assumption that other assets were a homogeneous enough group that he could lump them together under the category "bonds." He then considered how an individual allocated his wealth between money and bonds. The key factors that he thought determined the split were the level of income and the level of the interest rate. Put in terms of the Cambridge equation, Keynes focused on the interest rate as the primary determinant of k, the amount of money balances one would hold for a given level of income. A rise in the interest rate led to a fall in k or, equivalently, a rise in velocity; this is what we saw in the preceding subsection. Since k was a variable, not a constant, the Cambridge equation could not by itself provide a theory of nominal income.

Friedman accepted Keynes's emphasis on the role of money as an asset. With this as a basis, he sets out his own theory of the demand for money. Again income is one determinant of money demand and, as with Keynes, one can view Friedman's analysis as providing a theory of what determines the Cambridge k, money holdings as a proportion of nominal income. Friedman's money demand function can be written as follows:

$$M^d = L(P, y, r_B, r_E, r_D) \tag{9.8}$$

where P = price level

y = real income

r_B = nominal interest rate on bonds

r_E = nominal return on equities

r_D = nominal return on durable goods

Money demand is assumed to depend on nominal income, the product of the first two arguments in the demand function. An increase in nominal income would increase money demand.[5] For a given level of nominal income, Friedman assumes, as does Keynes, that the amount of money demanded depends on the rate of return offered on alternative assets. The money demand function given by equation (9.8) is a simplification of Friedman's equation and includes the rates of return on major alternatives to money as an asset. These are bonds, the asset Keynes focused on, equities (shares of stock in corporations), and durable goods such as consumer durables, land, and houses. Durable goods do not pay an explicit interest rate or dividend rate. Their return is the expected increase in the price of the good over the period for which it is held. Thus, the expected rate of inflation is also a determinant of money demand. An increase in the rate of return on any of these alternative assets causes the demand for money to decline.

Friedman's theory differs from Keynes's in several respects. First, Friedman views the money demand function as stable. The variables in the equation determine the quantity of money that will be demanded; the function is not assumed to shift erratically. Keynes's view was that the demand for money function was unstable, shifting with changes in the public confidence in the economy.

Second, Friedman does not segment his money demanded into components representing transaction balances, speculative demand, and a precautionary demand. Money, like other "goods," has a number of attributes that make it useful, but Friedman does not find it helpful to specify separate demands based on each of the uses of money.

The third difference between Keynes's and Friedman's money demand theories is that Friedman includes separate yields for bonds, equities, and durable goods. Keynes focused on the choice of money versus bonds. It is not clear how much of a substantive difference this is since what Keynes termed "bonds" can be considered more broadly as at least including equities. Often this has not been done, however, and Keynesian analysis has focused narrowly on the money-versus-bonds choice. Friedman makes explicit the possibility of other substitutions and also allows for a shift from money directly into commodities (durable goods) as rates of return change.

Friedman's money demand theory can be used to restate the Cambridge equation as follows:

$$M^d = k(r_B, r_E, r_D)Py \qquad (9.5')$$

---

[5]There is a difference between the concept of income in Keynes's theory and Friedman's income variable, which he called "permanent income." Friedman's permanent income concept is discussed in Chapter 14.

where instead of a constant k we now have k expressed as a function of the rates of return on the assets that are alternatives to holding money. A rise in the rate of return on any one of these alternative assets would cause k to fall, reflecting the increased desirability of the alternative asset. In these terms Friedman can be seen to have restated the quantity theory, providing a systematic explanation of k, an explanation that takes account of the Keynesian analysis of money's role as an asset.

If this is the restated quantity theory, how would we characterize a modern quantity theorist? How would he differ from a Keynesian? In Friedman's view, a quantity theorist must believe the following:

1. The money demand function is stable.
2. This demand function plays an important role in determining the level of economic activity.
3. The quantity of money is strongly affected by money supply factors.

In Friedman's version of the Cambridge equation, the equilibrium condition in the money market is

$$M = M^d = k(r_B, r_E, r_D)Py \qquad (9.9)$$

With a stable money demand function, an exogenous increase in the money stock must lead to a rise in Py or must cause declines in $r_B, r_E,$ and r_D (which will cause k to rise), with indirect effects on Py.[6] A quantity theorist must believe that the money demand function is in fact stable. He must believe that changes in the money stock do come mostly from the supply side as a result of central bank policies. Finally, he must believe that such changes in the quantity of money are important in determining nominal income; much of the effect of a change in M does come in the form of a change in Py.

In what way does a quantity theorist differ from a Keynesian? The answer to this question depends on whether the term *Keynesian* refers to the position of the *early* Keynesians described in the preceding subsection or, more generally, to the *neo-(or modern) Keynesian* theory. Friedman's theory, as outlined so far, is clearly antithetical to the early Keynesian position. Like Keynes, the early Keynesians believed that the money demand function was unstable; that the interest elasticity of money demand was extremely high; and that, as a consequence, changes in the quantity of money did not have important predictable effects on the level of economic activity. In Friedman's view the quantity theorist believes that the money demand function is stable and that the quantity of money is an important determinant of the level of

---

[6]Notice that a fall in the rates of return on the alternative assets to money (r_B, r_E, r_D) will increase money demand for a given income level and therefore raise k.

economic activity. Further, Friedman believes, as we will see shortly, that the interest elasticity of money demand is low.

Vis-à-vis the early Keynesians, it is hard with hindsight not to conclude that Friedman's view was more correct. Today few economists share the view of the early Keynesians that money is unimportant. In the United States the importance of money was demonstrated by the failure of the policy of pegging interest rates. The post–World War II period did not see a return to the Depression conditions of the 1930s, as many of Keynes's followers expected. Instead, inflation became a problem. Consumers forced to save during the war as a result of rationing and shortages satisfied a pent-up demand for consumer durables and semidurables from automobiles to baby carriages. Strong demand encouraged investment spending to convert plants from production of war materials to consumer goods.

With aggregate demand growing and the interest rate pegged at a low level, the situation was similar to that depicted in Figure 9.3 as the IS curve moves from IS_0 to IS_1, then to IS_2. At each step the monetary authority must increase the money stock to keep the interest rate from rising as the demand for transactions balances grows. This growth in the money stock can contribute to an inflationary spiral. In the United States such a process continued until the Federal Reserve stopped cooperating with the Treasury to peg interest rates at low levels and began to exert independent control over the money stock.

What about the differences between the quantity theory as outlined so far and the neo-Keynesian position? Neo-Keynesians believe that money is important. They believe that innovations in the financial sector during recent years have cast doubt on the stability of the money demand function especially for M1 (currency plus checkable deposits). This is in part a matter of how to define money as new types of deposits become available. The monetarists recognize these definitional problems as well. On the interest elasticity of money demand, estimates by neo-Keynesians are higher than suggested by Friedman's own research, but certainly not so high as to indicate the presence of a liquidity trap. Overall, if a quantity theorist or monetarist need only subscribe to the three propositions listed by Friedman, the neo-Keynesian and modern quantity theory positions would not be extremely far apart.

Friedman's Restatement of the Quantity Theory: The Strong Form

The quantity theory view embodied in these three propositions is, however, a *weak quantity theory* view—weak in at least two senses. First, it is not sufficient to establish the quantity theory postulate that we attributed to the classical quantity theory: that the price level would move proportionately with the money stock. Second, the weak quantity theory is not sufficient to establish the first and third of the monetarist propositions listed in the introduction: that the supply of money is the dominant influence on nominal income and in the short run on real income as well. The weak quantity theory position is that money matters for such variables but not that it is the *only* major systematic influence on them. Friedman and others offer a strong modern quantity theory position that is consistent with these two monetarist positions. In the short run, it is not consistent with the classical view of the proportionality of money and prices, although this proportionality is assumed to hold in the long run. It is this strong quantity theory position that differs sharply from the neo-Keynesian position.

The strong quantity theory position extends the quantity theory from a theory of money demand to one of nominal income. We have seen how the Cambridge quantity theorists did this with the assumption of a constant k [see equation (9.6) or (9.7)]. Friedman points out that his version of the quantity theory can also be turned into a theory of nominal income if the variables in his money demand function [equation (9.8)] other than nominal income (r_B, r_E, r_D) have little effect on money demand. This being the case, these variables will have little effect on k. Money holdings as a proportion of income (k) will be nearly constant. Since Friedman does not believe that money demand is completely independent of these rates of return, the theory of nominal income that results from assuming that k is a constant will only be an approximation. But *any* theory will hold only approximately. Friedman and others have done empirical work that convinces them that such a strong quantity theory position, which can be written as

$$Py = \frac{1}{k}M \qquad (9.10)$$

is a better approximation than that given by simple representations of the Keynesian view. It is this strong quantity theory that is required for statements by Friedman such as "I regard the description of our position as 'money is all that matters for changes in *nominal* income and for *short-run* changes in real income' as an exaggeration but one that gives the right flavor to our conclusions"; or "appreciable changes in the rate of growth of the stock of money are a necessary and sufficient condition for appreciable changes in the rate of growth of money income."[7]

This strong quantity theory position is a central element of monetarism. It is this strong quantity theory position that produces policy conclusions

---

[7]These two quotations are from Milton Friedman, "A Theoretical Framework for Monetary Analysis," in Robert Gordon, ed., *Milton Friedman's Monetary Framework* (Chicago: University of Chicago Press, 1974), p. 27; and Milton Friedman and Anna Schwartz, "Money and Business Cycles," *Review of Economics and Statistics,* 45 (February 1963), supplement, pp. 32–64, respectively.

sharply at odds with neo-Keynesian views, as we see in the next section. Prior to that, it is useful to represent this strong quantity theory position in terms of the *IS–LM* diagram and the aggregate supply–aggregate demand framework used to explain the Keynesian position. This will facilitate comparisons between monetarists and neo-Keynesians, and in the course of representing the strong quantity theory position in these terms, we will explain one further difference between monetarists and neo-Keynesians. In Figure 9.4 we have drawn the *IS–LM* curves as the strong quantity theorist would. The *LM* curve is nearly, but not quite, vertical, reflecting Friedman's view that the interest elasticity of money demand is quite low.

Another divergence from the Keynesian position concerns the slope of the *IS* curve. Here a flatter *IS* curve is consistent with the monetarist position that aggregate demand is quite sensitive to changes in the interest rate. Neo-Keynesians also believe that the interest rate affects aggregate demand and would not argue that the *IS* curve should be as nearly vertical as we drew it for the model of the early Keynesians (Figure 9.2). The difference

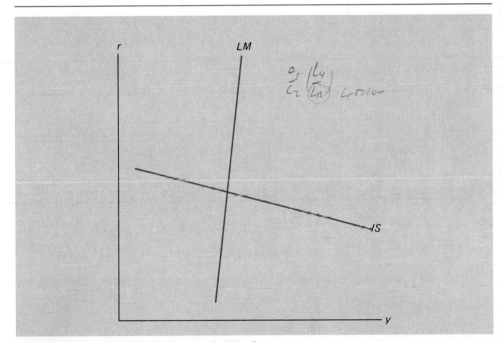

FIGURE 9.4 *IS–LM:* A Monetarist Version
In the monetarist view, the *IS* schedule is quite flat, reflecting a high interest elasticity of aggregate demand. The *LM* schedule is nearly vertical, reflecting a very low interest elasticity of money demand.

between neo-Keynesians and monetarists on this point is one of degree. Monetarists argue that Keynesians restrict channels by which the interest rate affects aggregate demand to an effect on investment by means of a change in the cost of borrowing funds. Monetarists argue that this is too narrow an interpretation of the effects of interest rates, resulting in part from the tendency of Keynesians to think of "bonds" as just one class of financial assets, rather than as all assets other than money.

In his theory of money demand, Friedman did not lump all nonmoney assets into one category. He separately considered bonds, equities, and durable goods, avoiding Keynes's simplification of aggregating to just "bonds" and money. Monetarists believe that if it is recognized that a change in *the* interest rate is really a change in all these yields, its effects go beyond the effects of a change in borrowing cost to firms that buy investment goods. In addition, a change in *the* interest rate means a change in the prices of corporate stock, the prospective return on real estate, and holding durable goods as well. Monetarists believe that the interest rate plays a more important role in determining aggregate demand than the neo-Keynesian model allowed.

Figure 9.4 adequately brings out several of the features of the monetarist view that differ from that of the neo-Keynesians, but it is deficient in one respect. We have generally used the *IS–LM* curves by themselves to show how real GNP and the interest rate were determined, with the price level held constant. A constant price level, even as a short-run approximation, is *not* an assumption made by the monetarists. Figure 9.5 shows how the monetarist view would be represented in the aggregate supply–aggregate demand framework of previous chapters.

Three positions for the aggregate demand curve are shown in the graph, $y^d(M_0)$, $y^d(M_1)$, and $y^d(M_2)$, corresponding to three values of the money stock, M_0, M_1, and M_2. Recalling the monetarist (strong quantity theory) formula, giving nominal income

$$Py = \frac{1}{\bar{k}}M \tag{9.10}$$

the monetarist position can be represented as asserting that changes in M are *required* for significant shifts in the aggregate demand curve. Money is the only important systematic influence on aggregate demand.

Left unanswered is the question of what determines aggregate supply. The real variables that determine the position of the aggregate supply curve will, in the monetarist view, be the determinants of the level of real output *in the long run* (see proposition 2). There is also the question of the slope of the aggregate supply curve and, consequently, the proportions of a money-induced rise in nominal income that go to increase output and price, respectively. This is the central question of the next chapter. First, we analyze the differing views of monetarists and neo-Keynesians on the relative effectiveness of fiscal and monetary policies. Here the issue is the effect

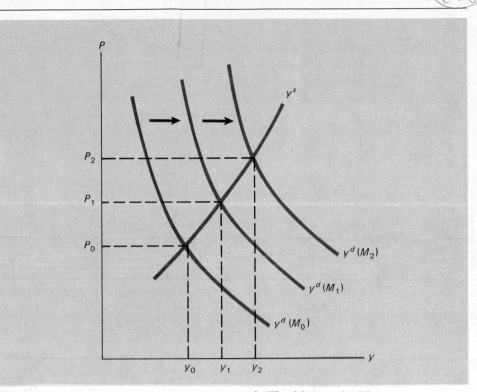

FIGURE 9.5 Aggregate Supply and Demand: The Monetarist View
In the monetarist view, the position of the aggregate demand schedule is determined primarily by the level of the money stock. Increases in the money stock from M_0 to M_1, then to M_2 shift the aggregate demand schedule from $y^d(M_0)$ to $y^d(M_1)$, then $y^d(M_2)$.

of these policies on aggregate demand. Whether the change in aggregate demand primarily affects prices or output is not crucial to this analysis, and we revert to the use of the *IS–LM* curve graph to illustrate these policy differences.

9.3 • MONETARY AND FISCAL POLICY: MONETARISTS VERSUS KEYNESIANS

Fiscal Policy

The monetarist and Keynesian frameworks produce quite different views about the effectiveness of fiscal policy changes. The monetarist view on the effectiveness of fiscal policy has been expressed by Milton Friedman as follows: "I come to the main point—in my opinion, the state of the budget by itself has no significant effect on the course of nominal income, on deflation, or on cyclical fluctuations."[8] In reference to the Keynesian proposition that fiscal policy was effective, Friedman wrote: "The 'monetarists' rejected this proposition and maintained that fiscal policy by itself is largely ineffective, that what matters is what happens to the quantity of money."[9] The most optimistic assessment he has given fiscal policy effects is that they are "certain to be temporary and likely to be minor."

When Friedman discusses the independent effects of fiscal policy, the question at issue, he means the effects of changes in the government budget *holding constant the quantity of money*. Consider an increase in government spending. If tax rates are not changed, which has been our usual assumption when we consider one policy change at a time, the new spending must be financed by printing money or by selling bonds. Similarly for a tax cut, if spending is to be unchanged, lost tax revenues must be replaced by sales of bonds to the public or by printing new money.

If a tax cut or spending increase is financed by printing new money, we have both a monetary policy action (M increases) and a fiscal policy action (G increases or T falls). In terms of the IS–LM framework, both the IS and LM curves shift. Monetarists *do not* argue that this type of policy change will be ineffective. They do argue that the policy effect will come mainly because the stock of money changes. The controversy is over what Friedman refers to, as stated previously, as the effect of a change in the federal budget *by itself*, meaning without an accompanying change in the quantity of money. This means, in the case of a tax cut or spending increase, that the deficit created by these actions would be financed completely by sales of bonds to the public. The monetarist position is that such policy actions will have little systematic effect on nominal income (prices or real output) over short-run periods of perhaps one to three years.

The reasons monetarists reach this conclusion can be seen from Figure 9.6. There we consider the effects of an increase in government spending when we accept the monetarist assumptions about the slopes of the IS and LM curves. An increase in government spending from G_0 to G_1 shifts the IS curve to the right, from IS_0 to IS_1. Recall from our analysis of the Keynesian system that the size of the change in government expenditure affects the size of the horizontal shift in the IS curve. The IS_0 and IS_1 curves have been drawn to reflect an increase in government spending of approximately the same amount as that depicted in Figure 9.1, the last time we analyzed an

---

[8] Milton Friedman and Walter Heller, *Monetary Versus Fiscal Policy* (New York: Norton, 1969), p. 51.

[9] Friedman, *Counter-revolution*, p. 18.

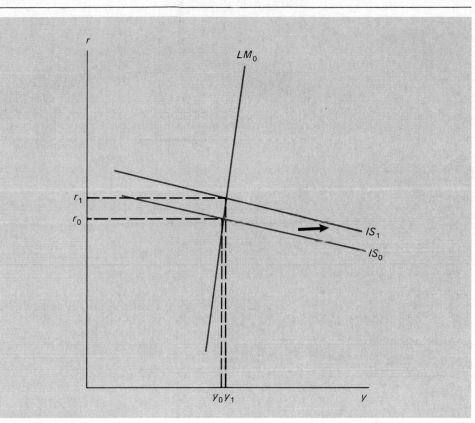

FIGURE 9.6   Effects of an Increase in Government Spending:
The Monetarist Case
As increase in government spending shifts the IS schedule from IS_0 to IS_1. With
the relatively flat IS schedule and nearly vertical LM schedule, this fiscal policy action
has little effect on income (y rises only from y_0 to y_1).

increase in government spending in the Keynesian model.[10] The effect of
the increase in government spending in the monetarist case (Figure 9.6) is
primarily to cause the interest rate to rise (from r_0 to r_1). The level of income
is changed only slightly (from y_0 to y_1). Why?

   In essence, the explanation for these results has already been supplied
in the discussion about the dependence of the relative effectiveness of
monetary and fiscal policy on the slopes of the IS and LM curves, in

---

[10]The horizontal shift in the IS curve will be equal to $\Delta G[1/(1 - b)]$, where b is the marginal
propensity to consume (see Section 6.2).

particular on the assumed magnitudes of the interest elasticities of money demand and of investment demand. Monetarists assume that the interest elasticity of money demand is small; the *LM* curve is steep. The increase in government spending increases aggregate demand initially. As income begins to rise, the demand for transactions balances increases. With the money stock fixed, this puts upward pressure on the interest rate, which rises until money supply and demand are again equal. If money demand is interest-inelastic, a large increase in the interest rate is required to reequilibrate money demand with the fixed money supply.

The *IS* curve is relatively flat in the monetarist view. Investment demand is highly sensitive to changes in the interest rate. Therefore, the rise in the interest rate required to keep the money market in equilibrium will cause private-sector aggregate demand to decline substantially as government spending begins to stimulate income. This reduction in private-sector aggregate demand is what we referred to earlier as "crowding out." In the monetarist model, such crowding out occurs almost dollar for dollar with an increase in government spending. On net, aggregate demand and, hence, income are increased very little by an increase in government spending.

Although the analysis so far provides sufficient reason for a monetarist to expect little increase in income as a result of an expansionary fiscal policy, it leaves out one key element in the monetarist analysis of crowding out.

We saw in our analysis of the Keynesian system that the equilibrium interest rate is that rate at which the public's demand for money is equal to the exogenously given money supply. Since total wealth is fixed, and wealth consists of bonds plus money, equilibrium in the money market guarantees equilibrium in the bond market. The *IS–LM* curve version of the Keynesian model ignores the effect on the interest rate of ongoing increments to wealth that result from new saving or changes in bond supply that come as a result of financing business investment *or a government deficit*. The important implication of this assumption for our analysis here is that the *IS–LM* curve model neglects any *direct* upward pressure on interest rates that would come as a result of the government selling bonds to the public to finance a budget deficit. This is not to say that the model neglects all sources of upward pressure on interest rates from deficit spending. As income increases, money demand increases, and with a fixed money stock the interest rate has to rise to restore equilibrium in the money market. What is meant here by *direct* effect is the upward pressure on interest rates that is created by the sale of the new bonds *at a given level of income*.

Monetarists argue that government bond sales will directly create upward pressure on interest rates, an additional source of crowding out. Monetarists believe that if the money stock is held constant, the public will be willing to buy new bonds, thus shifting their portfolio of assets more toward bonds and away from money, only if the interest rate they earn on bonds is increased. This *portfolio effect* can be illustrated as follows.

We rewrite the Keynesian money demand function to include a wealth variable, where we assume that an increase in wealth (Wh) would cause an increase in the demand for money,

$$M^d = L(y, r, \text{Wh}) \tag{9.11}$$

where, since wealth (Wh) equals bonds (B) plus money (M), we can equivalently write this demand function as

$$M^d = L(y, r, B + M) \tag{9.12}$$

At a given level of income and of the interest rate, an increase in wealth coming from an increase in the stock of bonds creates an increased demand for money to restore the initial proportions of money and bonds.

Now consider the effects that an increase in government spending financed by bonds would have on income perhaps eight quarters (two years) after the policy change was initiated. We depict this graphically in Figure 9.7. To be concrete, suppose that government spending is increased by 10 units at an annual rate and then is maintained at this new level. In Figure 9.7 the effect of this increase in government spending is shown by the rightward shift in the IS curve from IS_0 to IS_1. This results in an increase in y from y_0 to y_1. At the end of two years, if tax collections and the money stock were held constant, 20 units (10 per year for two years) of new bonds would have been sold to the public to finance this new spending.% [11] The increase in bond supply would increase wealth and, hence, increase the demand for money *at given levels of y and r*. This increase in the demand for money will shift the LM curve to the left from LM_0 to LM_1,[12] causing income to decline to y_2. The interest rate is pushed even farther, up to r_2. In the graph income is shown to have declined even relative to y_0, the equilibrium level of income in the absence of any fiscal policy action. This is not the necessary or even the most likely case. What is ensured is that this direct crowding out will cause income to decline relative to y_1. Since monetarists believe that the original increase from y_0 to y_1 is likely to be minor, they expect the net effect of a debt-financed fiscal policy action to be small, with even the direction of the effect uncertain.

As noted previously, the IS–LM curve version of the Keynesian model disregards this direct crowding out. In times when deficits are small relative to the existing stock of assets, Keynesians assume that any wealth effect of newly created bonds on money demand (the leftward shift in the LM curve

---

[11] Because in reality tax collections move with the level of income even if tax rates are unchanged, some of the new spending will be financed by increased tax collections. This means fewer bonds would have to be sold, and the magnitude of the direct crowding out discussed here would be lessened.

[12] The reasons an increase in the demand for money, for given levels of y and r, shifts the LM curve to the left are discussed in Section 6.2.

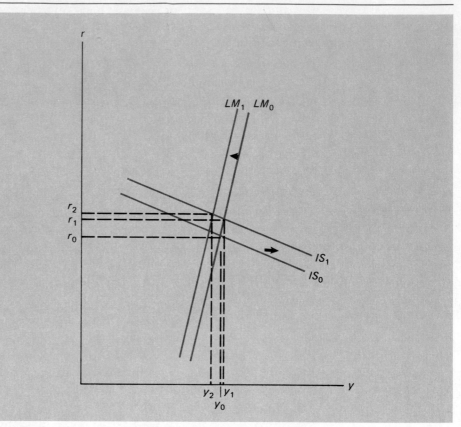

FIGURE 9.7 Direct Crowding Out in the *IS–LM* Model
An increase in government spending shifts the *IS* schedule from IS_0 to IS_1, which in the monetarist view has a small expansionary effect on income, which rises from y_0 to y_1. The sale of bonds to finance the increased government spending increases wealth and causes the *LM* schedule to shift to the left from LM_0 to LM_1, reducing income to y_2.

in Figure 9.7) would be negligible.[13] In the years since 1980, with persistent large deficits, Keynesians agree that the rapid growth in the stock of government bonds has put upward pressure on the interest rate *directly* as well as by increasing the level of income. Many Keynesian economists have been critical of the fiscal policy actions that resulted in such large deficits precisely because they believe that the resulting rise in interest rates has crowded out

---

[13]Recall here that the existing stock of nonmoney assets includes private bonds and corporate equities, as well as government bonds.

investment. To this extent monetarists and Keynesians have been in agreement. Still, Keynesians believe that increases in government spending or tax cuts financed by bond sales *will* have substantial, persistent effects on income; crowding out will not be so severe as to cancel out the direct effects of such fiscal policy actions on aggregate demand. The Keynesians do not like the *mix* of monetary and fiscal policy in recent years, but this has not changed their view that properly applied fiscal policy is a useful stabilization tool.

Monetary Policy

Both monetarists and neo-Keynesians believe that monetary policy actions have substantial and sustained effects on nominal income. The early Keynesians did, as we have seen, doubt the effectiveness of monetary policy. At one stage in the debate over monetarism and the quantity theory of money (perhaps circa 1945–50) it might have been correct to refer to Keynesians as "fiscalists" relying solely on fiscal policy, in contrast to the monetarist reliance on monetary policy. This is certainly not the case today. The difference between neo-Keynesians and monetarists over monetary policy concerns not *whether* monetary policy can affect income but *how* monetary policy should be used to stabilize income.

The Monetarist Position

Monetarists believe that changes in the quantity of money are the dominant influence on changes in nominal income and, for the short run, on changes in real income as well. It follows that stability in the behavior of the money stock would go a long way toward producing stability in income growth. Friedman in fact traces most past instability in the growth of income to unstable money growth. Because of the importance of money and because of what Friedman regards as past mistakes in money management, his position on monetary policy is as follows:

> My own prescription is still that the monetary authority go all the way in avoiding such swings by adopting publicly the policy of achieving a specified rate of growth in a specified monetary total. The precise rate of growth, like the precise monetary total, is less important than the adoption of some stated and known rate.[14]

To give an example, the monetary authority might announce and achieve a target rate of growth in M1 (currency plus checkable deposits) of 5 percent per year. Friedman believes that nominal income growth would then be approximately 5 percent per year. If the trend growth in real income were 3 percent per year, the price level would rise by about 2 percent per year. The

---

[14]Milton Friedman, "The Role of Monetary Policy," *American Economic Review,* 58 (March 1968), p. 16.

5 percent level is not crucial, but whatever level is picked, Friedman wants a *constant growth rate in the money stock.*

Other monetarists have recently proposed alternative rules for money growth that are less inflexible than Friedman's constant money growth rate rule. Reasons for these alternatives are considered in Section 9.4. The common element in the monetarist proposals, however, is that growth in the money stock is determined by a rule, not left to the discretion of policymakers. To see how monetarists believe monetary policy would work when conducted by a rule, we examine the case of Friedman's constant money growth rate rule.

A monetarist view of income determination with a constant money growth rate policy is illustrated in Figure 9.8. If a constant growth rate policy is followed, the level of the money stock at any one point in time (t) has been fixed exogenously. Since in the monetarist view the demand function for money is stable, this means that the position of the LM curve is fixed exogenously, at LM_{t0}. The IS curve may shift around due to other shocks to the economy. In Figure 9.8, depending on the values of these other shocks (fiscal policy, export demand, etc.), we assume that the IS curve may be at $IS_{t0}, IS_{t1},$ or IS_{t2}. If the LM curve is steep, as it is drawn in Figure 9.8 and as the monetarists assume, these shifts in the IS curve will, *for a given LM curve,* have little destabilizing effect on income. In Figure 9.8 such shocks would cause income to vary only between y_{t0} and y_{t2}. Further, recall that monetarists believe that, left to itself, the private sector is quite stable. This does not mean that there will be no shocks to the IS curve because of the private sector, but the fluctuations from this source should be minor.

To summarize, monetarists believe that money is the primary determinant of nominal income and of real income in the short run. Stabilizing money growth will remove the major source of instability in income determination. There are other sources of instability, but these are not major because, given the level of the money stock, a given shock will not have a great impact (the LM curve is steep). Further, shocks of large magnitude are not likely because of the essential stability of the private sector.

If one accepts the reasoning that one will do pretty well with such a monetary rule, such as the constant growth rate rule, the question still remains: "Why not the best?" Why not use monetary policy, which is very potent, to offset even minor shocks that affect income? Why not "fine tune" the economy? Friedman's answer to this question is "We simply do not know enough to be able to recognize minor disturbances when they occur or to be able to predict either what their effects will be with any precision or what monetary policy is required to offset their effects."[15] Friedman and other monetarists

---

[15] Ibid., p. 14.

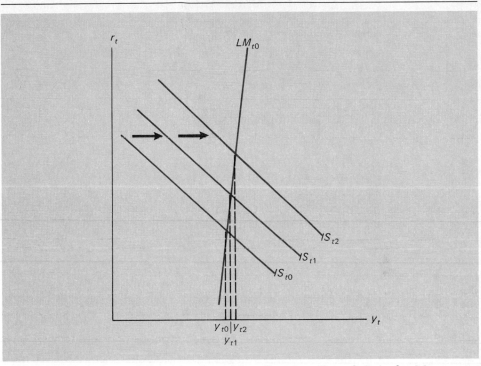

FIGURE 9.8   Income Determination with a Constant Growth Rate for Money:
The Monetarist View

If a constant money growth rate policy is followed, at a point in time, t, the position
of the LM schedule will be fixed at LM_{t0}. If the LM schedule is very steep, as the
monetarists believe, then even if there are shifts in the IS schedule (from IS_{t0} to
IS_{t1} to IS_{t2}), income will vary only over the narrow range y_{t0} to y_{t2}.

believe that changes in the money stock will have a strong effect on income,
but they believe that money affects income with a lag. The bulk of the effect
of a monetary action today will, they believe, come only after 6 to 18 months.
Thus, to offset a minor shock, one must be able to predict its size and when
it will affect the economy several quarters in advance. Friedman and other
monetarists do not think we know enough to do this.

Monetarist economist Allan Meltzer, on the basis of a study of the ac-
curacy of economic forecasts, concludes that "forecasts of main economic
aggregates are so inaccurate—so wide of the mark on average—that discretionary policies based on forecasts are unlikely to stabilize the economy."[16]

---

[16]Allan Meltzer, "Limits of Short-Run Stabilization Policy," *Economic Inquiry,* 25 (January 1987),
p. 1.

Monetarists believe that, in the past, in trying to offset minor shocks, the monetary authority has *destabilized* income more often than not. To again quote Milton Friedman, "There is a saying that the best is often the enemy of the good, which seems highly relevant. The goal of an extremely high degree of economic stability is certainly a splendid one; our ability to attain it, however, is limited."[17]

Contrast with the Keynesians

We have already examined the neo-Keynesian view of monetary policy. In this view monetary policy is one of the main tools that can be used by the policymaker to stabilize income. The neo-Keynesians believe that both monetary and fiscal policy variables should be actively adjusted to offset shocks to the economy that would otherwise be destabilizing. Franco Modigliani, a leading neo-Keynesian, expressed this view (which he characterized as non-monetarist) as follows:

> Nonmonetarists accept what I regard to be the fundamental practical message of *The General Theory:* that a private enterprise economy using an intangible money *needs* to be stabilized, *can* be stabilized, and, therefore, *should* be stabilized by appropriate monetary and fiscal policies.[18]

Neo-Keynesians favor active discretionary monetary as well as fiscal policy actions. They oppose the constant money growth rate policy espoused by Friedman and other monetarists. What are the reasons for the differing views of monetarists and Keynesians on this issue?

The first explanation for these differing views about the proper conduct of monetary policy is the disagreement between monetarists and neo-Keynesians concerning the need for active stabilization policies. Whereas monetarists view the private sector as stable and "shock-absorbing," neo-Keynesians see the private sector as shock-producing and unstable. This is not to say neo-Keynesians believe that without government stabilization policies we would constantly experience depressions and hyperinflations, but rather that shocks we experience would result in substantial prolonged deviations from conditions of full employment and price stability. They believe this would be the case even with a fixed rate of growth in the money stock.

---

[17]Milton Friedman, *The Optimum Quantity of Money and Other Essays* (Chicago: Aldine, 1969), p. 187.

[18]*The General Theory* was Keynes's major work on macroeconomics. Franco Modigliani, "The Monetarist Controversy, or Should We Forsake Stabilization Policies?" *American Economic Review,* 67 (March 1977), p. 1.

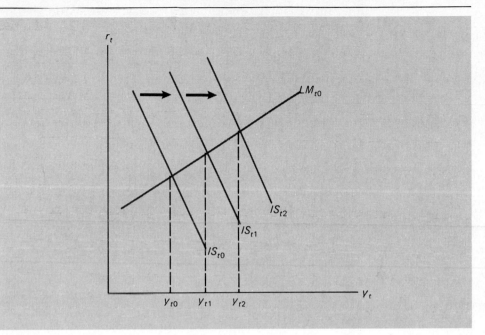

FIGURE 9.9 Income Determination with a Constant Growth Rate for Money: A Neo-Keynesian View
Even if a constant money growth rate policy is followed and the position of the LM schedule at time period t is fixed at LM_{t0}, the neo-Keynesians believe income can still vary over the range y_{t0} to y_{t2} in response to shocks to aggregate demand (shifts in the IS curve from IS_{t0} to IS_{t1} to IS_{t2}).

This type of situation is depicted in Figure 9.9. Shocks to the economy from sources such as autonomous changes in investment demand will, in the absence of offsetting monetary and fiscal policies, cause the IS curve to move among positions such as IS_{t0}, IS_{t1}, and IS_{t2}. This will cause income to vary substantially over the range of y_{t0}, to y_{t2}. Since Keynesians believe private-sector demand is unstable, they view such shifts in the IS curve as likely. They do not believe that money plays such a dominant role in income determination; thus in Figure 9.9 the LM curve is much less steep than in the monetarist case (Figure 9.8). Consequently, these shifts in the IS curve do produce large changes in income.

A second source of the differing views of monetarists and neo-Keynesians is also evident from Modigliani's statement. He believes that we *can* stabilize the economy. We can predict shocks that will hit the economy and design policies to combat them. To be sure, there will be (and have been) errors, but overall such policies will result in a more stable economic performance than we would have with fixed policy rules. Modigliani characterizes the fixed-rule policy as equivalent to

arguing to a man from St. Paul wishing to go to New Orleans on important business that he would be a fool to drive and should instead get himself a tub and drift down the Mississippi: that way he can be pretty sure that the current will eventually get him to his destination; whereas if he drives, he might take a wrong turn and, before he notices he will be going further and further away from his destination and pretty soon he may end up in Alaska, where he will surely catch pneumonia and he may never get to New Orleans.[19]

To Friedman and other monetarists, adopting the constant growth rate rule puts the economy on a safe route and does not sacrifice much. To the neo-Keynesians, viewing money as only one of the major determinants of income and the contribution of other factors such as investment decisions as unstable, the loss from such a constant growth rate rule is much greater, and they oppose such policy rules.

9.4 · SOME EVIDENCE ON THE MONETARIST–KEYNESIAN CONTROVERSY

Before going on to other aspects of monetarism, let us examine the degree to which data on the behavior of the actual economy help settle issues that divide neo-Keynesians and monetarists. The central issues in the Keynesian–monetarist controversy are *empirical* ones, meaning ones concerning the actual values of observed variables and parameters in the economy. Such issues, therefore, should be subject to tests on data from the economy.

Evidence from Statistical Models

In fact, both monetarists and Keynesians have tested their theories extensively using data from the United States and other economies.[20] But this statistical work has not definitely settled the controversy. Monetarist economists, including Milton Friedman, have focused their research on examining the money-to-income relationship in different historical periods. The research of Friedman and others has convinced the monetarists of the closeness and

---

[19]Ibid., p. 13.

[20]Examples of monetarist statistical work are Milton Friedman and David Meiselman, "The Relative Stability of Monetary Velocity and the Investment Multiplier in the United States, 1897–1958," in *Stabilization Policies,* Commission on Money and Credit, 1963; Milton Friedman and Anna Schwartz, *A Monetary History of the United States* (Princeton, N.J.: Princeton University Press, 1963); Milton Friedman, ed., *Studies in the Quantity Theory of Money* (Chicago: University of Chicago Press, 1956); and Milton Friedman and Anna Schwartz, *Monetary Trends in the United States and the United Kingdom, 1867–1965.* (Chicago: University of Chicago Press, 1982).

stability of this relationship. This monetarist research has also provided support for the monetarist belief in the effectiveness of monetary policy and the ineffectiveness of fiscal policy.[21]

The Keynesian model implies that numerous factors have important effects on short-run equilibrium real output. These include monetary factors, autonomous expenditure components (including fiscal policy variables), and supply-side factors (e.g., energy price shocks). Keynesian statistical analysis has focused on modeling the channels by which each of these factors affects output, the price level, and the interest rate. This has led to very complex empirical models, often including 100 or more equations, in contrast to the very simple (sometimes single-equation) monetarist models. These Keynesian models have produced results in line with Keynesian theory. On policy questions, for example, the Keynesian models imply that *both* monetary and fiscal policy will have significant effects on real output for periods of several years.[22]

The Recent Behavior of the Money–Income Relationship

Although statistical research over the years has produced conflicting results and therefore has not resolved the central issues in the monetarist–Keynesian controversy, some economists argue that the behavior of the U.S. economy over the 1980s provide dramatic evidence against the monetarist theoretical position and policy prescriptions.[23] Specifically, it is argued that money and income have not moved closely together over the past decade. Velocity has not been stable, but rather swings in velocity have been important to the cyclical behavior of output. With unstable velocity (Y/M), stable growth in money (M) does not mean stable growth in income (Y); hence, it is argued that the monetarist case for a constant money growth rate rule has been weakened.

---

[21] In addition to Friedman and Meiselman, "The Relative Stability of Monetary Velocity and the Investment Multiplier in the United States, 1897–1958," see Leonall Andersen and Jerry Jordan, "Monetary and Fiscal Actions: A Test of Their Relative Importance in Economic Stabilization," Federal Reserve Bank of St. Louis *Review*, 50 (November 1968), pp. 11–24. The Andersen and Jordan paper is reprinted, along with a number of related papers on the monetarists' statistical approach, in Federal Reserve Bank of St. Louis *Review*, 68 (October 1986).

[22] For examples of such Keynesian models, including discussion of policy effects, see Frank de Leeuw and Edward Gramlich, "The Federal Reserve–MIT Econometric Model," *Federal Reserve Bulletin*, 54 (January 1968), and "The Channels of Monetary Policy: A Further Report on the Federal Reserve–MIT Model," *Journal of Finance*, 24 (May 1969), pp. 265–90; Michael Evans, *Macroeconomic Activity: Theory, Forecasting and Control* (New York: Harper & Row, 1969); and Gary Fromm, "Survey of United States Models," in Gary Fromm and Lawrence Klein, eds., *The Brookings Model: Perspective and Recent Developments* (Amsterdam: North-Holland, 1975).

[23] Benjamin M. Friedman, "Lessons from the 1979–82 Monetary Policy Experiment," *American Economic Review*, 74 (May 1984), pp. 382–87; and Benjamin M. Friedman, "Monetary Policy Without Quantity Variables," *American Economic Review*, 78 (May 1988), pp. 440–45.

280

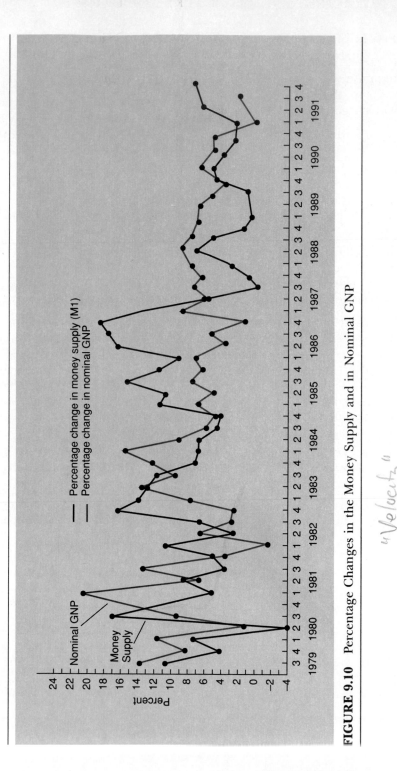

"Velocity"

FIGURE 9.10 Percentage Changes in the Money Supply and in Nominal GNP

Recent Instability in the Money–Income Relationship

Figure 9.10 shows quarterly percentage changes (at annual rates) for both the money supply and nominal GNP from the third quarter of 1979 through the end of 1991. As can be seen from the figure, this was a turbulent period with large changes in each series.

The figure indicates that there were times during this period when the money supply and nominal income moved closely together (e.g., 1979–80), as would be predicted by the monetarists. But at other times the movements in the two series are quite dissimilar. In early 1981, for example, money supply growth fell sharply while the rate of growth in nominal GNP rose. Again in early 1982, the two series moved in opposite directions. Then in 1985, 1986, and the first half of 1987, especially rapid growth in the money supply was accompanied by only modest growth in the nominal GNP; there was a dramatic fall in velocity (Y/M) during these years.

Table 9.2 shows the percentage change in velocity for each year from 1981 through 1990. In the monetarist view, changes in velocity should be only a minor factor in explaining the cyclical behavior of nominal GNP. If the money supply and nominal GNP move closely together, then velocity, which is the ratio of the two (Y/M), should be stable. The figures in Table 9.2 indicate, however, that velocity was subject to considerable instability during the 1980s. Especially notable are the sharp declines in velocity during 1982–3 and 1986–7.

Monetarist Reaction

Because of the instability in the money–income relationship, the *Economist* magazine was led to ask in 1986, "Is this the year monetarism vanishes?" The data from the 1980s have led monetarists to reconsider their position in some areas, but not to change their fundamental views. Milton Friedman, for example, assessing the experience of the 1980s, concludes that "The long and the short of it is that I remain convinced of a fundamental tenet

TABLE 9.2   Percentage Change in Velocity, 1981–90

Year	Change (%)	Year	Change (%)
1981	4.3	1986	−8.1
1982	−2.9	1987	−4.9
1983	−3.5	1988	3.7
1984	3.7	1989	5.7
1985	−2.6	1990	1.4

of monetarism: Money is too important to be left to central bankers."[24] Friedman continues to support a money growth rate rule.

Friedman and others view the instability of velocity in the 1980s as the result of a number of one-time events during the decade. One of these is the *disinflation* during the decade. Monetarists believe that this sharp drop in the inflation rate raised the demand for money for a given level of income and thus lowered velocity. Recall that in Friedman's money demand function, equation (9.8), the expected inflation rate entered by means of r_D, the rate of return on durable goods. Lower inflation in the 1980s resulted in lower expected inflation. The perceived return on durable goods as investments (gold, diamonds, real estate, BMWs) fell, the demand for money rose, and velocity fell. As monetarist Karl Brunner argued,

> Lower inflation makes it cheaper to hold cash balances, so people hold larger ones, thus bringing a drop in velocity. The same thing happened at the end of the German hyperinflation in 1923 and in Switzerland when that country switched to a noninflationary monetary policy in 1973. But the drop in velocity is a one-time event that should not affect the long-term trend.[25]

Another factor that monetarists believe explains the rise in money demand for a given level of income (and thus a fall in velocity) is the dramatic fall in interest rates in the 1980s. The rate of interest on three-month U.S. treasury bills, for example, fell from 14.0 percent in 1981 to 5.5 percent in 1991. Monetarists, as we have seen, assume that money demand is *not* very responsive to interest rates (including the return on durable goods), but they argued that such *large* movements did have significant impact.[26]

Finally, changes in the type of bank deposits that were available to the public and the phasing out of ceilings on deposit rates are other events the monetarists cite as sources of the instability of velocity. These changes in the deposit market are discussed in Chapter 15.

Monetarism has not vanished. But the events of the 1980s, even if they can be explained with hindsight, did reduce monetarist influence on economic policy. Whether that influence will be revived or further eroded depends, in large part, on the behavior of velocity in the 1990s. Was the experience of

---

[24]Milton Friedman, "M1's Hot Streak Gave Keynesians a Bad Idea," in Peter McClelland, ed., *Readings in Introductory Macroeconomics* (New York: McGraw-Hill, 1988), reprinted from *The Wall Street Journal*, p. 78.

[25]Karl Brunner, "Monetarism Isn't Dead," in Peter McClelland, ed., op. cit., p. 77.

[26]See, for example, the discussion in William Poole, "Monetary Policy Lessons of Recent Inflation and Disinflation," *Journal of Economic Perspective*, 2 (Summer 1988), pp. 73–100.

the 1980s a one-time event or will the money–income relationship continue to fluctuate erratically?

9.5 • CONCLUSION

In this chapter we examined the monetarist belief in the importance of money. According to the *strong quantity theory,* or monetarist position, money is the dominant determinant of nominal income. This position contrasts with the neo-Keynesian view that money is one of several variables with important effects on income. These different positions on the importance of money lead monetarists and neo-Keynesians to different conclusions about monetary and fiscal policy.

The monetarist view is that fiscal policy actions have little independent effect on the level of economic activity. This policy view is essentially a corollary to the monetarist proposition that money is the dominant factor determining nominal income. Keynesians believe that fiscal policy actions exert significant and sustained influence on the level of economic activity. They reject the strong quantity theory position. Fiscal policy variables are among the important nonmonetary factors that they believe also affect income.

On monetary policy, the difference between monetarists and neo-Keynesians is not about the potential of monetary policy to significantly affect the level of economic activity—both believe that monetary policy has strong effects. They differ on what they view as the proper role for monetary policy. Monetarists are *noninterventionists*. They favor a constant growth rate in the money stock that then creates an environment in which a stable private sector of the economy can function effectively. Neo-Keynesians are *interventionists* or policy *activists*. They see the need for active discretionary monetary and fiscal policies to keep an unstable private economy on track.

In Chapter 10, when we analyze the monetarist view of why money affects only nominal, and not real, variables in the longer run, we see additional reasons for the noninterventionist views of monetarists. Again neo-Keynesians will disagree. We will also see in Chapter 10, however, that there are areas of agreement between monetarists and neo-Keynesians.

Review Questions and Problems

1. Compare Keynesian and monetarist views on how the velocity of money is determined. How do their differing views on velocity affect their respective policy conclusions?

2. Why were early Keynesian economists so pessimistic about the effectiveness of monetary policy?

3. Compare Milton Friedman's formulation of the money demand function with the Keynesian specification in previous chapters.

4. How does the weak quantity theory position described in the text differ from what was termed the strong quantity theory or monetarist position?

5. Show how the *IS* and *LM* curves look in the monetarist view. Use these *IS* and *LM* curves to illustrate the monetarist conclusions about the relative effectiveness of monetary and fiscal policy.

6. Compare monetarist and Keynesian views on the proper conduct of fiscal policy. For both monetarists and Keynesians, explain not only the conclusion they reach concerning fiscal policy but also how that conclusion is related to their respective theories.

7. Compare monetarist and neo-Keynesian views on the proper conduct of monetary policy. For both monetarists and neo-Keynesians, explain not only the conclusion they reach concerning monetary policy but also how the conclusion is related to their respective theories.

8. Analyze the effects of a decrease in taxes from T_0 to T_1 in the monetarist framework. In your answer be sure to take account of the financing of the deficit that results from the tax cut. How are the equilibrium levels of income and the interest rate affected by the tax cut?

Selected Readings

Brunner, Karl, "The Role of Money and Monetary Policy," Federal Reserve Bank of St. Louis *Review,* 50 (July 1968), pp. 9–24.

Dewald, William, "Monetarism Is Dead: Long Live the Quantity Theory," Federal Reserve Bank of St. Louis *Review,* 70 (July/August 1988), pp. 3–18.

Friedman, Benjamain, "Lesson on Monetary Policy from the 1980s," *Journal of Economic Perspectives* 2 (Summer 1988), pp. 51–72.

Friedman, Milton, "The Quantity Theory of Money—A Restatement," in Milton Friedman, ed., *Studies in the Quantity Theory of Money.* Chicago: University of Chicago, 1956. Reprinted in Milton Friedman, *The Optimum Quantity of Money and Other Essays.* Chicago: Aldine, 1969.

Friedman, Milton, "A Monetary and Fiscal Framework for Economic Stability," *American Economic Review,* 38 (June 1948), pp. 245–64. Reprinted in Friederick Lutz and Lloyd Mints, eds., *Readings in Monetary Theory.* Homewood Ill.: Irwin, 1951.

Friedman, Milton, and Schwartz, Anna, "Money and Business Cycles," *Review of Economics and Statistics,* 45 (February 1963), supplement, pp.

32–64. Reprinted in Milton Friedman, ed., *The Optimum Quantity of Money and Other Essays*. Chicago: Aldine, 1969.

Friedman, Milton, and Schwartz, Anna, *Monetary Trends in the United States and United Kingdom*. Chicago: University of Chicago Press, 1982.

Gordon, Robert J., ed., *Milton Friedman's Monetary Framework*. Chicago: University of Chicago Press, 1974.

Makinen, Gail, *Money, the Price Level, and Interest Rates*. Englewood Cliffs, N.J.: Prentice-Hall, 1977, Chaps. 9 and 12.

Mayer, Thomas, *The Structure of Monetarism*. New York: Norton, 1978.

Meltzer, Allan, "Limits of Short-run Stabilization Policy," *Economic Inquiry*, 25 (January 1987), pp. 1–14.

Modigliani, Franco, "The Monetarist Controversy, or Should We Forsake Stabilization Policies?" *American Economic Review*, 67 (March 1977), pp. 1–19. Reprinted in Thomas Havrilesky and John Boorman, *Current Issues in Monetary Theory and Policy*. Arlington Heights, Ill.: AHM Publishing, 1980.

Poole, William, "Monetary Policy Lessons of Recent Inflation and Disinflation," *Journal of Economic Perspectives*, 2 (Summer 1988), pp. 73–100.

10 Output, Inflation, and Unemployment: Monetarist and Keynesian Views

The preceding chapter focused on the monetarist analysis of the importance of money. We examined the basis for the monetarist belief that money is the dominant influence on nominal income. We also saw that for the *short run*, monetarists believe that changes in the money stock are the primary determinant of fluctuations in real output and employment. In this chapter we consider a limitation that monetarists place on the importance of money, a limitation expressed in the second of the monetarist propositions given in Chapter 9.

> **2.** In the long run the influence of money is primarily on the price level and other *nominal* magnitudes. In the long run, *real* variables, such as real output and employment, are determined by real, not monetary factors.

The basis of this proposition is the theory of the **natural rate of unemployment** developed by Milton Friedman.[1]

In the first section of the chapter, Friedman's concepts of the natural rates of unemployment and output are explained. Then we consider the implications that the natural rate theory has for the inflation–unemployment relationship and the role of monetary policy in both the short and long run. The third section of the chapter considers the Keynesian positions on the natural

---

[1] The theory of the natural rate of unemployment was also developed independently by Edmund Phelps of Columbia University. See, for example, the contributions by Phelps and others in Edmund Phelps, ed., *Employment and Inflation Theory* (New York: Norton, 1970).

rate concept and the inflation–unemployment trade-off.[2] The chapter concludes with an overall comparison of the monetarist and Keynesian models.

10.1 • THE NATURAL RATE THEORY

According to the natural rate theory, there exists for any economy an equilibrium level of output and an accompanying rate of unemployment determined by the supply of factors of production, technology, and institutions of the economy (i.e., determined by real factors). This is Friedman's natural rate. Changes in aggregate demand, which Friedman believes are dominated by changes in the supply of money, cause temporary movements of the economy away from the natural rate. Expansionary monetary policies, for example, move output above the natural rate and move the unemployment rate below the natural rate for a time. The increased demand resulting from such an expansionary policy would also cause prices to rise. In the short run the price adjustment would not be complete, as in the classical theory where increases in demand cause prices to rise but do not affect output. *The monetarists do not agree with the classical position that output is completely supply-determined even in the short run.*

Friedman does believe that equilibrating forces cause the levels of output and employment to return to their natural rate over a longer period. It is not possible, in Friedman's view, for the government to use monetary policy to maintain the economy permanently at a level of output that holds the unemployment rate below the natural rate. It is at least not possible for the policymakers to do so unless they are willing to accept an ever-accelerating rate of inflation. The natural rate of unemployment is defined by Friedman as that rate of unemployment "which has the property that it is consistent with equilibrium in the structure of *real* wage rates."[3] Thus the natural rate of unemployment or the corresponding natural rate of employment will be a level such that labor demand equals labor supply at an equilibrium real wage. Such a situation is depicted in Figure 10.1*a*.

The labor-demand schedule in part *a* is the familiar marginal product of labor schedule (MPN). At *N**, the natural rate of employment, labor demand

---

[2]In differentiating the modern Keynesian position from that of the early Keynesians, it was convenient in Chapter 9 to use the term neo-Keynesian. This term was commonly used to describe the Keynesian view as it had developed by the late 1960s. From this point on, however, we will drop the prefix "neo" when referring to the modern Keynesian view. This will avoid confusion later when we discuss some very recent work within the Keynesian tradition which is being referred to as *new Keynesian economics.*

[3]Milton Friedman, "The Role of Monetary Policy," *American Economic Review,* 58 (March 1968), p. 8.

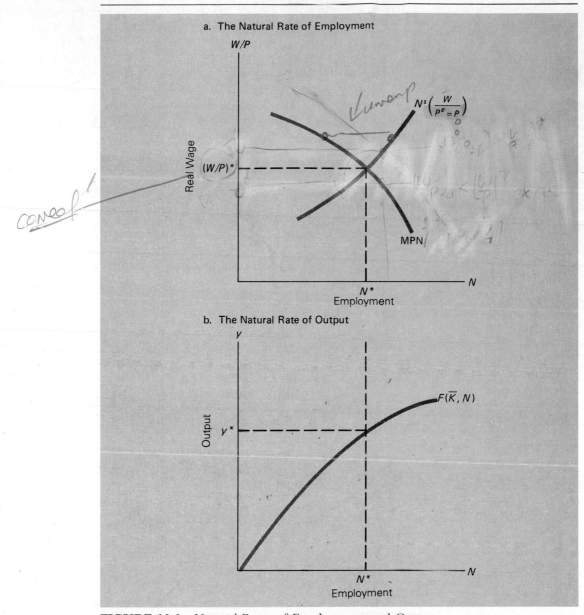

FIGURE 10.1 Natural Rates of Employment and Output
In part *a*, the natural rate of employment (N^*) is determined at the point where labor supply is equated with labor demand *and* with labor suppliers correctly evaluating the price level ($P^e = P$). The natural rate of output (y^*) is then determined in part *b* along the production function.

is equated with labor supply, where in drawing the labor-supply schedule, $N^s (W/(P^e = P))$, we stipulate that the price level expected by labor suppliers is equal to the actual price level ($P^e = P$). Only at this level of employment is there no tendency for the real wage to change. Labor demand and supply are equated. Moreover, labor suppliers have a correct expectation of the price level. If such were not the case, there would be a tendency for labor supply to change as workers perceive that their expectations are in error.

The natural rate of unemployment can be found simply by subtracting those employed from the total labor force to find the number unemployed and by expressing this number as a percentage of the total labor force. Using another familiar device, the production function in Figure 10.1b, we can find the level of output that will result from an employment level N^*. This is the natural level of output, y^*.

As can be seen from Figure 10.1, the natural rates of output and employment depend on the supply of factors of production and the technology of the economy—supply-side factors. The natural rates of output and employment do *not* depend on the level of aggregate demand. All this is much the same as in the classical system; the difference between the monetarists and the classical economists is that the monetarists do not assume that the economy is necessarily at these natural levels of employment and output in the short run.

Like the Keynesians, the monetarists assume that labor suppliers do not have perfect information about the real wage. They must base their labor supply decisions on the expected real wage (W/P^e). Therefore, in the short run, labor supply may not be given by the supply schedule in Figure 10.1a; P^e may not equal P. In this case, employment and hence output will not be at their natural rates, as we will see presently.

10.2 • MONETARY POLICY, OUTPUT, AND INFLATION: A MONETARIST VIEW

To see why Milton Friedman and other monetarists believe that output and employment diverge from their natural rates temporarily, but will eventually be drawn to these rates, we examine Friedman's analysis of the short-run and long-run consequences of an increase in the rate of growth in the money stock.

Monetary Policy in the Short Run

Let us suppose that we begin with a situation in which the economy is in equilibrium at the natural rate of unemployment and output. Also suppose that the money stock (and hence nominal income) has been growing at a rate equal to the rate of growth of real output. Thus the price level is assumed to have been stable for some time. Suppose now that the rate of growth in the money stock is increased above the rate consistent with price stability. For concreteness, assume that the rate of growth in the money stock rises from 3 percent to 5 percent.

The increase in the growth rate of the money stock will stimulate aggregate demand and, as a consequence, nominal income. The *short-run* consequences of this increase in aggregate demand are described by Friedman as follows:

> To begin with, much or most of the rise in income will take the form of an increase in output and employment rather than in prices. People have been expecting prices to be stable, and prices and wages have been set for some time in the future on that basis. It takes time for people to adjust to a new state of demand. Producers will tend to react to the initial expansion in aggregate demand by increasing output, employees by working longer hours, and the unemployed by taking jobs now offered at former nominal wages. This much is pretty standard doctrine.[4]

The *standard doctrine* to which Friedman refers is the notion of a **Phillips curve**. The Phillips curve is a negative relationship between the unemployment rate (U) and the inflation rate (P), such as that plotted in Figure 10.2. High rates of growth in aggregate demand stimulate output and hence lower the unemployment rate. Such high rates of growth in demand also cause an increase in the rate at which prices rise (i.e., raise the inflation rate). Thus the Phillips curve postulates a trade-off between inflation and unemployment; lower rates of unemployment can be achieved, but only at the cost of higher inflation rates.[5] In the description given previously of the immediate effects of an increase in the rate of growth in the money stock, Friedman is agreeing with this notion of a trade-off between inflation and unemployment *in the short run*. He is, in fact, arguing that the terms of the trade-off are rather good in the short run, since much of the increase in nominal income is in the form of an increase in *real* output with prices rising to a lesser extent.

Monetary Policy in the Long Run

The distinctive element in Friedman's analysis is his view of the long-run effects of monetary policy. It is here that the notion of the natural rate of unemployment comes into play. We have just considered the short-run effects of an increase in the rate of growth of the money stock from 3 percent

---

[4]Ibid., p. 10.

[5]The Phillips curve derives its name from the British economist A. W. H. Phillips, who studied the trade-off between unemployment and wage inflation (a key element in price inflation) in the British economy.

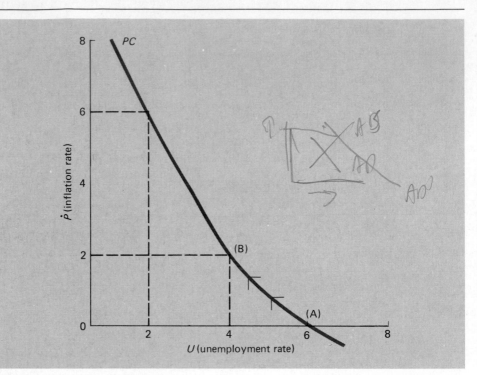

FIGURE 10.2   The Phillips Curve
In the short run, an increase in the rate of growth in the money stock moves the
economy from point A to point B along the short-run Phillips curve. Unemployment
declines, and inflation rises.

to 5 percent. In terms of Figure 10.2, the original equilibrium was with
stable prices ($\dot{P} = 0$) and unemployment equal to the natural rate assumed
to be 6 percent (point A in Figure 10.2). As a result of the increase in the
rate of growth in the money stock, we assume that the economy moves to
a new *short-run* equilibrium, with unemployment reduced to 4 percent and
an inflation rate at 2 percent (point B in Figure 10.2). The expansionary
aggregate demand policy succeeds in lowering the unemployment rate to a
level below the natural rate.

Friedman accepts this outcome:

> But it describes only the initial effects. Because selling prices of products typically
> respond to an unanticipated rise in nominal demand faster than prices of factors
> of production, real wages received have gone down—though real wages antic-
> ipated by employees went up, since employees implicitly evaluated the wages
> offered at the earlier price level. Indeed, the simultaneous fall *ex post* in real

wages to employers and rise *ex ante* to employees is what enabled employment to increase. But the decline *ex post* in real wages will soon come to affect anticipations. Employees will start to reckon on rising prices of the things they buy and to demand higher nominal wages for the future. "Market" unemployment is below the natural level. There is an excess demand for labor so real wages will tend to rise toward their initial level.[6]

Consider this explanation further. Friedman points out that in the short run, product prices increase faster than factor prices, the crucial factor price being the money wage. Thus the real wage (W/P) falls. This is a *necessary* condition for output to increase, for firms must be on their labor demand curve in Figure 10.1. Firms expand employment and output only with a decline in the real wage.

Friedman does not argue that workers are always on the labor supply curve shown in Figure 10.1. That curve expresses labor supply as a function of the *actual* real wage, and Friedman does not assume that workers know the real wage. In the short run, after a period of stable prices, workers are assumed to evaluate nominal wage offers "at the earlier price level." While prices have risen, workers have not yet seen this, and they will increase labor supply if offered a higher money wage *even if this increase in the money wage is less than the increase in the price level, even if the real wage is lower.* In the short run, labor supply increases because the *ex ante* or expected real wage is higher as a result of the higher nominal wage and unchanged view about the behavior of prices. Labor demand increases because of the fall in the *ex post* level of the actual real wage paid by the employer. Consequently, unemployment can be pushed below the natural rate.

This situation is temporary, for workers eventually observe the higher price level and demand higher money wages. In terms of Figure 10.1, the real wage has been pushed below $(W/P)^*$, the wage that clears the labor market once labor suppliers correctly perceive the price level and, hence, the real wage. At a lower real wage, there is an excess demand for labor, which pushes the real wage back up to its equilibrium level, and this rise in the real wage causes employment to return to the natural rate shown in Figure 10.1.

The implications for the Phillips curve of this long-run adjustment back to the natural rate are illustrated in Figure 10.3. The schedule labeled PC $(\dot{P}^e = 0)$ is the short-run Phillips curve from Figure 10.2. Here we have made explicit the fact that the curve is drawn for a given expected rate of inflation on the part of the suppliers of labor, in this case stable prices ($\dot{P}^e = 0$, where $\dot{P}^e$ is the expected rate of inflation). We have already analyzed the process whereby an increase in the rate of growth of the money stock from

---

[6] Friedman, "Role of Monetary Policy," p. 10.

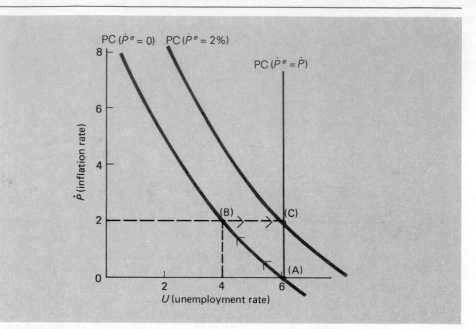

FIGURE 10.3 Short-Run and Long-Run Phillips Curves
As labor suppliers come to anticipate the higher inflation rate, the short-run Phillips curve shifts from PC($\dot{P}^e = 0$) to PC($\dot{P}^e = 2\%$). The unemployment rate returns to the natural rate of 6 percent; the inflation rate remains higher at 2 percent (we move from point B to point C).

3 percent to 5 percent moves the economy in the short run from point A to point B.

As suppliers of labor come to anticipate that prices are rising, the Phillips curve will shift upward to the right. Suppliers of labor will demand a higher rate of increase in money wages and, as a consequence, a higher rate of inflation will now correspond to any given unemployment rate. If money growth is continued at 5 percent, the economy will return to the natural rate of unemployment of 6 percent, but now with an inflation rate of 2 percent instead of the initial stable price level. In terms of Figure 10.3, this longer-run adjustment moves the economy from point B to point C.

The policymaker may not be content with this return to 6 percent unemployment (the natural rate) and may still pursue a target unemployment rate below the natural rate. In this case he will again increase the rate of growth in the money stock. Let us suppose that this time he increases money stock growth from 5 percent to 7 percent. The effects of this further expansion of aggregate demand are illustrated in Figure 10.4 and can be

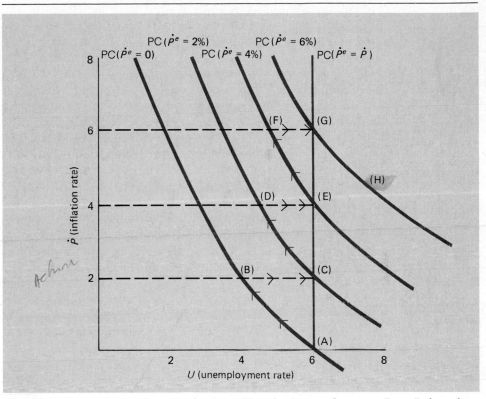

FIGURE 10.4   Effect of an Attempt to "Peg" the Unemployment Rate Below the
Natural Rate

Additional increases in money growth, to 5 percent, then 7 percent, then 9 percent,
in each case result in temporary reductions in unemployment (movements from C
to D and E to F, for example). But in the longer run we simply move up the vertical
Phillips curve (to points like E and G, for example).

analyzed as previously. Until the suppliers of labor come to anticipate the
further increase in the inflation rate, employment will expand. The economy
would move to a point such as D in Figure 10.4, with the unemployment
rate below the natural rate of unemployment.

Suppliers of labor after a time will come to anticipate the higher inflation
rate that corresponds to a 7 percent growth in the money stock. The short-
run Phillips curve will shift to the schedule labeled PC($\dot{P}^e = 4\%$), and the
economy will return to the natural rate of unemployment, with the inflation
rate increased to 4 percent (7 percent money growth minus 3 percent growth
in real income). In terms of Figure 10.4 we move from point D to point
E. If the policymaker persists in his attempt to "peg" the unemployment rate,

he will again increase money stock growth, for example, to 9 percent. This will move the economy in the short run to point F, but in the longer run to point G, with a still higher rate of inflation.

Eventually, one expects the policymaker will be led to conclude that inflation has become a more serious problem than unemployment (or he will be replaced by a different policymaker who has this view) and the acceleration of inflation will stop. Notice, however, that when inflation has persisted for a long time, inflationary expectations become built into the system. At a point such as point G in Figure 10.4, expansionary aggregate demand policies have increased the expected (and actual) inflation rate to 6 percent (9 percent money growth minus 3 percent growth in real income). An attempt to lower inflation by slowing the rate of growth in the money stock, let us suppose all the way back to the initial noninflationary 3 percent, will *not* immediately move the economy back to a point such as the initial point (A). In the short run we would move along the short-run Phillips curve that corresponds to an expected inflation rate of 6 percent, to a point such as point H in Figure 10.4, with high inflation and unemployment above the natural rate. Just as it took time for suppliers of labor to recognize that the rate of inflation had increased and, hence, to demand a faster rate of growth in money wages, it will take time for them to recognize that the inflation rate has slowed and for them to modify money wage demands to a level compatible with price stability. In the meantime, in the monetarist view, the economy must suffer from high inflation and high unemployment.

In the monetarist view, expansionary monetary policy can only temporarily move the unemployment rate below the natural rate. Put differently, there is a trade-off between unemployment and inflation only in the short run. In terms of Figures 10.3 and 10.4, the downward-sloping short-run Phillips curves *that are drawn for given expected inflation rates* illustrate the short-run trade-off between unemployment and inflation. The long-run Phillips curve showing the relationship between inflation and unemployment *when expected inflation has time to adjust to the actual inflation rate* ($\dot{P} = \dot{P}^e$)—*when inflation is fully anticipated*—is vertical, as shown in Figures 10.3 and 10.4.

Friedman's theory of the natural rate of unemployment and output is the theoretical foundation for the monetarist belief that in the long run the influence of the money stock is primarily on the price level and other nominal variables. Real variables such as output and employment have time to adjust to their natural levels in the long run. Those natural rates of output and employment depend on real variables such as factor supplies (labor and capital) and technology.

Policy Implications

The theory of the natural rate of unemployment implies that the policymaker cannot peg the unemployment rate at some arbitrarily determined target rate. Attempts to lower the unemployment rate below the natural rate by increasing the rate of growth in aggregate demand will be successful only in the short run. The unemployment rate will gradually return to the natural rate, and the lasting effect of the expansionary policy will be a higher inflation rate.

Monetarists believe that the natural-rate theory strengthens the case for noninterventionist policies—most important, their suggestion of a constant money growth rate policy. They believe that the record of the U.S. economy in the post–World War II years provides evidence that interventionist policies to affect unemployment resulted in only short-run gains and were responsible for increased inflation rates.

Consider, for example, the behavior of unemployment, inflation, and money growth rates for the United States from 1961 to 1971, as shown in Table 10.1.

According to the monetarist interpretation, the expansionary policies of the mid-1960s succeeded in temporarily lowering the unemployment rate from an average rate of 5.8 percent for the 1961–64 period to an average rate of 3.8 percent for the 1965–69 period. In the monetarist view, this decline in unemployment resulted from the increase in the rate of growth in the money stock beginning in 1964, which is evident in the table. The natural-rate theory suggests that at first the increased money growth would stimulate output and employment, the effect on prices coming with a longer lag. Consequently, the theory would have predicted the higher inflation rates observed in the table for the later 1960s. The natural-rate

TABLE 10.1 Unemployment, Inflation, and Money Growth Rates for the United States, 1961–71

Year	Unemployment Rate[a]	Inflation Rate[b]	Money Growth Rate[c]
1961	6.7	0.7	2.1
1962	5.5	1.2	2.2
1963	5.7	1.6	2.9
1964	5.2	1.2	4.0
1965	4.5	1.9	4.2
1966	3.8	3.4	4.7
1967	3.8	3.0	3.9
1968	3.6	4.7	7.2
1969	3.5	6.1	6.1
1970	4.9	5.5	3.8
1971	5.9	3.4	6.7

[a] Civilian unemployment rate (percent).

[b] Annual percentage rate of change in the consumer price index.

[c] Annual percentage rate of growth in M1 (currency held by the public plus checkable deposits).

theory would also have predicted the reversal of the downward movement in the unemployment rate, the average unemployment rate for 1970–71 being 5.4 percent, whereas the inflation rate remained high relative to the early 1960s.[7]

Friedman's analysis of the Phillips curve can also be used to explain the simultaneously high inflation and high unemployment later in the 1970s. Excessive monetary growth had eventually resulted in entrenched expectations of high inflation. These raised the average inflation rate corresponding to a given unemployment rate; the Phillips curve was shifted upward. When the Federal Reserve sometimes shifted toward a more anti-inflationary policy, the economy operated at points like H in Figure 10.4 with high inflation and unemployment.

In the 1980s, the monetarists saw the high unemployment early in the decade as again the result of previous excessive monetary growth that had created high inflationary expectations. As the Federal Reserve shifted to a more prolonged restrictive policy, at first we moved along a very unfavorable short-run Phillips curve. Only after the actual inflation rate fell did the expected inflation rate gradually fall, causing the short-run Phillips curve to shift downward. This eventual downward shift, in the monetarist view, enabled unemployment to decline in the late 1980s as the inflation rate remained low.

The monetarist view is, then, one explanation for many of the changes in the relationship between inflation and unemployment that were described in Chapter 1.

10.3 • A KEYNESIAN VIEW OF THE OUTPUT–INFLATION TRADE-OFF

Friedman's theory of the natural rate of unemployment is a theory that explains both the short-run and long-run relationship between inflation and unemployment. The Phillips curve expressing this relationship between inflation and unemployment is, according to Friedman, downward-sloping in the short run but vertical in the long run. What is the Keynesian view of the Phillips curve, and how does it differ from the natural-rate theory? How can Keynesians defend activist policies to affect output and employment if the natural-rate theory is correct and such policies have only a temporary effect on output and employment? These are the questions considered in this section.

---

[7]The inflation rate did fall from 5.5 percent in 1970 to 3.4 percent in 1971, but this was in part because of mandatory price and wage controls instituted on August 15, 1971. The inflation rate before controls were imposed was still in excess of 5 percent.

To anticipate our conclusions on these questions, we find the following:

1. Traditional Keynesian models, such as those considered in Chapter 8, also imply that once the economy has fully adjusted to a change in inflation (caused, for example, by a change in money supply growth), output and employment will be unaffected. These Keynesian models also imply a vertical Phillips curve.
2. Keynesians, however, will be seen to draw different policy conclusions from this absence of a long-run trade-off between inflation and unemployment.
3. Moreover, for reasons we consider later in this section, Keynesians question whether the natural rate of unemployment (or output) is a useful or meaningful concept.

The Phillips Curve: A Keynesian Interpretation

The Keynesian view of the relationship between the rate of inflation and the levels of employment and output follows directly from the theory of how price and output are determined. That theory was considered in Chapter 8. Here we relate it to the concept of the Phillips curve.

The Short-Run Phillips Curve

Figure 10.5 shows the effect on price, output, and employment of a sequence of expansionary policy actions increasing aggregate demand. The version of the Keynesian model here is the same as in Section 8.4. The money wage is flexible, and labor supply is assumed to depend on the expected real wage (W/P^e), the known money wage divided by the expected price level.

In the Keynesian system an expansionary aggregate demand policy might be a monetary policy action such as the increase in the rate of growth in the money stock analyzed in the preceding section, or it might be a fiscal policy action such as a series of increases in government spending. In either case the effect of the policy will be to produce a series of shifts in the aggregate demand schedule, as shown in Figure 10.5a. As can be seen from Figure 10.5, the effects of these increases in aggregate demand will be to increase output (from y_0, to y_1, to y_2, then to y_3) and employment (from N_0, to N_1, to N_2, then to N_3), as well as the price level (from P_0, to P_1, to P_2, then to P_3). As employment increases, the unemployment rate will decline. The level of the money wage will also increase.

These results can be interpreted in terms of a Phillips curve relationship. The more quickly aggregate demand grows, the larger the rightward shifts in the aggregate demand schedule, and, *ceteris paribus*, the faster will be the rate of growth in output and employment. For a given growth in the labor force, this means that the unemployment rate will be lower the faster the rate of growth in aggregate demand. As can also be seen from the example

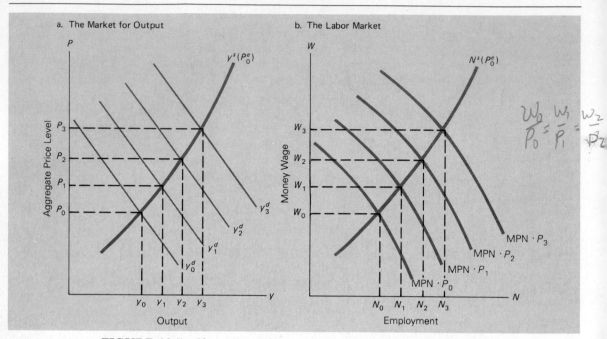

FIGURE 10.5   Short-Run Effects of Increases in Aggregate Demand in the Keynesian Model

An expansionary aggregate demand policy such as an increase in the rate of growth in the money stock will cause a series of shifts to the right in the aggregate demand schedule (from y_0^d to y_1^d to y_2^d to y_3^d). In the short run, output, the price level, and the level of employment all rise.

in Figure 10.5, increases in aggregate demand cause the price level to rise, so, again *ceteris paribus*, the faster the growth of aggregate demand is, the higher the rate of inflation will be.

The Keynesian model then implies a trade-off between inflation and unemployment. High rates of growth in demand correspond to low levels of unemployment and high rates of inflation. Slower growth in aggregate demand means a lower inflation rate but a higher rate of unemployment. The Phillips curve implied by the Keynesian model is downward-sloping.

But is this a short-run or a long-run relationship? Notice that so far we are holding the expected price level constant. We are considering the effects of increases in demand in the short run. As explained in Chapter 8, the Keynesians view the expected price level as depending primarily on the past behavior of prices. Thus, as successive periods go by with increases in the actual price level, the expected price level will rise. In the long run we must take account of the effects of such increases in the expected price level. Since

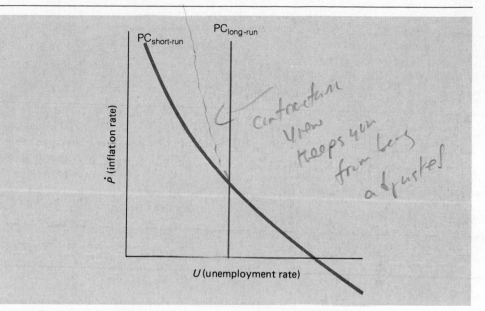

FIGURE 10.6 The Phillips Curve: The Keynesian Perspective
In the short run, the Phillips curve implied by the Keynesian model is downward-sloping. In the long run in the Keynesian model, as in Friedman's analysis, the Phillips curve is vertical.

we did not do so in Figure 10.5, our results there and the Phillips curve relationship derived from them pertain to the short run. To emphasize this, we have labeled the labor supply curve $N^s(P_0^e)$ and the aggregate supply curve $y^s(P_0^e)$, to indicate that these curves are drawn for the initial value of the expected price level. In Figure 10.6 we label the Phillips curve implied by the example in Figure 10.5 as the short-run Phillips curve, PC(short run).[8]

The Long-Run Phillips Curve

The long run differs from the short run in that in the long run the expected price adjusts to the actual price. The suppliers of labor perceive the inflation that has come as a result of the expansionary aggregate demand policy.

---

[8]The short-run nature of the downward-sloping Phillips curve was recognized, but perhaps not given sufficient emphasis, before Friedman's work. Paul Samuelson and Robert Solow wrote in this context:

All of our discussion has been phrased in short-run terms, dealing with what might happen in the next few years. . . . What we do in a policy way during the next few years might cause it [the Phillips curve] to shift in a definite way. [Paul Samuelson and Robert Solow, "Analytical Aspects of Anti-Inflation Policy," *American Economic Review,* 50 (May 1960), pp. 177–94.]

Notice that, as was the case in Friedman's description of the short-run effects of an increase in aggregate demand, employment increases in the Keynesian model only because the increase in price lowers the real wage and increases the demand for labor. The increase in price is not perceived by the labor suppliers as a fall in the real wage. Their expectation of the price level (P^e) is assumed not to have changed. In fact, the quantity of labor supplied increases as the money wage (W) rises (see Figure 10.5b). This situation changes in the longer run when the expected price adjusts to the actual price.

The longer-run adjustment of output and employment to an increase in aggregate demand is illustrated in Figure 10.7. Recall that in the Keynesian system, labor supply depends on the expected real wage:

$$N^s = t\left(\frac{W}{P^e}\right) \tag{10.1}$$

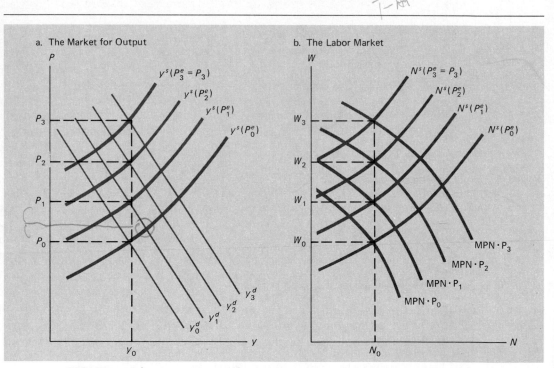

a. The Market for Output

b. The Labor Market

FIGURE 10.7 Long-Run Effects of Increases in Aggregate Demand in the Keynesian Model

In the long run, leftward shifts in the labor supply schedule and consequently leftward shifts in the aggregate supply schedule reverse the increases in output and employment that come as a result of the expansionary aggregate demand policy (represented by the shifts to the right in the aggregate demand schedule). Output and employment return to their initial levels, y_0 to N_0.

where the effect of the money wage on labor supply is positive and the effect of an increase in expected price is negative. As the expected price rises, the labor supply curve in Figure 10.5b shifts to the left. Less labor will be supplied at any money wage (W) since a given money wage corresponds to a lower expected real wage (W/P^e) after an increase in the expected price level. This shift in the labor supply curve is shown in Figure 10.7b. As the expected price level rises to P_1^e, to P_2^e, and then to P_3^e, the labor supply curve shifts to $N^s(P_1^e)$, to $N^s(P_2^e)$, then to $N^s(P_3^e = P_3)$.

As the labor supply curve shifts to the left, the level of employment for any given price level declines. We move back up on a given labor demand curve (which is drawn for a given price level). The increase in expected price lowers employment for any price level and, therefore, lowers output supplied at any price level. The aggregate supply curve also shifts upward to the left with each increase in expected price, reflecting this decline in output supplied at a given price level. These shifts in the supply curve are illustrated in Figure 10.7a.

The labor supply and aggregate supply curves will continue to shift to the left until expected price and actual price are equal. The *long-run* equilibrium position is shown in Figure 10.7, where the labor supply curve is $N^s(P_3^e = P_3)$ and the aggregate supply curve is $y^s(P_3^e = P_3)$. Notice that at this point income and employment have returned to their initial levels y_0 and N_0. This must be the case because output and employment can be maintained above y_0 and N_0 only as long as the expected price is below the actual price, that is, only as long as labor suppliers underestimate the inflation caused by the expansionary aggregate demand policy. Once the suppliers of labor correctly perceive the increases in the price level, they will demand increases in the money wage proportionate to the increase in the price level. At this point the real wage will have returned to its initial level ($W_3/P_3 = W_0/P_0$). Both labor supply and labor demand will have returned to their initial levels. Consequently, employment and output will be at their initial levels of N_0 and y_0.[9] We therefore arrive at a conclusion equivalent to Friedman's theory. An increase in the level of aggregate demand increases the level of output and employment and, as a consequence, lowers the unemployment rate only in the short run. As shown in Figure 10.6, the long-run Phillips curve is vertical in the Keynesian view as well as the monetarist.

---

[9]In this discussion of the *long-run* effects of an increase in aggregate demand, we are ignoring some elements of the Keynesian theory of labor supply that explain why the money wage is sticky in the *short run* (see Section 8.3). We are not, for example, allowing for the effects of implicit or explicit labor contracts, which prevent the money wage from adjusting to changes in demand conditions. Such factors are important in explaining the short-run behavior of the labor market. They are, however, factors that can slow but not ultimately prevent adjustment to the long-run equilibrium position.

Stabilization Policies for Output and Employment: The Keynesian View

Why does the Keynesian acceptance of the absence of a long-run effect of aggregate demand on output and employment not lead to an acceptance of the monetarist noninterventionist policy position? The reason is that in the Keynesian view, aggregate demand policies are aimed at stabilizing output and employment in the *short run*.

The goal of such stabilization policies is to keep the economy at its equilibrium level in the face of shocks to aggregate demand or supply. In other words, the aim of *stabilization* policies is, as the name implies, to offset what would otherwise be destabilizing influences on output and employment. The focus of such policies is on the short-run.

The monetarist noninterventionist policy conclusion is based, to a large extent, on the propositions discussed in Chapter 9. The private sector is basically stable if left to itself. Thus one would not expect large destabilizing shocks to private-sector demand for output. Even if there were such shifts in private-sector demand (undesired shifts in the *IS* schedule), they would have little effect on output if the money stock were held constant, because of the steepness of the *LM* schedule (see Figure 9.8). There may be small shocks that will cause output and employment to deviate somewhat from the natural rate, but Friedman and other monetarists do not believe that our knowledge of the economy allows us to predict such shocks and design policies with sufficient precision to offset them.

One could still argue that, left to itself, the private sector produces equilibrium levels of output and employment that are "undesirable." Unemployment might be "too high." It could then be proposed that the role of monetary policy was to ensure that unemployment and output were at "desirable" levels. The theory of the natural rate of unemployment shows that monetary policy cannot fulfill this role and indicates that attempts to achieve such arbitrary unemployment targets will have destabilizing effects on the price level in the long run. The natural-rate theory therefore buttresses the monetarist noninterventionist policy proposition.

If one does not accept the other propositions of the monetarists—and, as we have seen, Keynesians do not—there is still a possible short-run role for stabilization policies, whether monetary or fiscal. Keynesians believe that private-sector aggregate demand is unstable, primarily because of the instability of investment demand. Keynesians believe that *even for a given money stock*, such changes in private-sector aggregate demand can cause large and prolonged fluctuations in income. Consequently, they believe that monetary and fiscal policies should be used to offset such undesirable changes in aggregate demand and to stabilize income.

An example of the type of destabilizing shock the Keynesians would expect is illustrated in Figure 10.8. Here we assume that, as the result of an

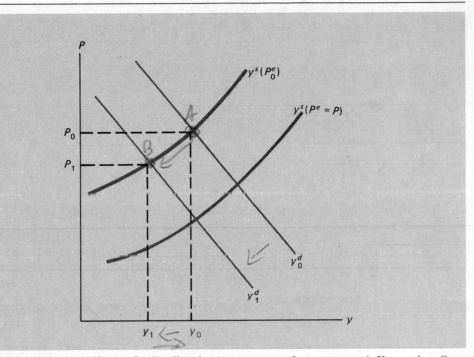

FIGURE 10.8 Effects of a Decline in Autonomous Investment: A Keynesian Case
A decline in autonomous investment will cause the aggregate demand schedule to shift from y_0^d to y_1^d. In the short run, output will fall below y_0 to y_1. In the long run, the aggregate supply schedule will shift out to $y^s(P^e = P)$ as labor suppliers come to expect a lower price level, corresponding to lower aggregate demand. Rather than wait for this adjustment, the Keynesians advocate aggregate demand management policies, in this case an expansionary policy, to restore the level of aggregate demand to y_0^d.

autonomous decline in investment demand, the aggregate demand schedule shifts from y_0^d to y_1^d. In the short run, output will fall below the initial level, y_0, to y_1. In the long run, suppliers of labor will make a downward adjustment of their expected price level as they observe the lower actual prices. Just as the aggregate supply curve shifted upward to the left when the expected price rose, it will now shift to the right as the expected price level declines. Workers now see a given money wage as representing a higher expected real wage. Labor supply and hence output and employment for a given price level will increase. The aggregate supply curve will eventually shift to position $y^s(P^e = P)$ in Figure 10.8, where output has returned to y_0. This adjustment will be slowed by the existence of implicit and explicit labor contracts and other factors that make the money wage sticky downward, because with a lower price level, the money wage must fall to restore employment to the initial level.

Keynesians do not deny that this supply adjustment will take place. They do believe, however, that the required fall in the money wage will come only after a relatively long and economically costly adjustment period—the costs being the lost output due to being at y_1 instead of y_0. In such a case Keynesians favor the use of monetary and fiscal policy to offset the decline in aggregate demand due to the fall in autonomous investment. An increase in government spending could, for example, shift the aggregate demand curve back to y_0^d and restore output and employment to their original levels.

Keynesian Doubts About the Natural-Rate Concept

We have seen that in both the Keynesian and monetarist views, there are, at any given point in time, levels of output and employment to which the economy will move given enough time. Friedman calls these *natural* rates. Keynesians question whether the natural-rate concept is useful or meaningful.

The Basic Objection

The term *natural rate* implies that the output, employment, or unemployment level referred to is determined by *intrinsic* elements of an economic system. The term also suggests that, whether "desirable" or not, these levels cannot be changed except by changing the intrinsic elements of the system.

Keynesians question whether output and employment levels toward which the economy tends at a point in time—levels that have what we might call *persistence*—are related to any such intrinsic elements in the economic system. They also question whether these levels are as hard to change as the term *natural* suggests.

To see the basis of these objections, consider the unemployment figures in Table 10.2. Shown in the table are average unemployment rates for selected European countries for four periods. The time periods range from 6 to 10 years. Averages over periods of this length should give reasonable approximations to the natural rate. In other words, if there is a tendency for unemployment to move toward one rate, then actual unemployment should fluctuate around that rate—sometimes above it, sometimes below. Averaging the unemployment rate over a number of years should provide an estimate of that rate.

If this is the case, then for most of the countries in the table, the natural rate has been rising over the past three decades. In the 1980s, the natural rate, using the average as an approximation, has risen to extremely high lev-

TABLE 10.2 European Unemployment Rates, Selected Periods (percent)

	1960–67	1968–73	1974–79	1980–89
Belgium	2.1	2.3	5.7	11.1
W. Germany	0.8	0.8	3.5	6.8
Spain	2.3	2.7	5.3	17.5
France	1.5	n.a.	4.5	9.0
United Kingdom	1.5	2.4	4.2	9.5
Italy	4.9	5.7	6.6	9.9
Denmark	1.6	1.0	n.a.[a]	9.0

Source: *Historical Statistics*, 1960–89 (Paris: Organization for Economic Cooperation and Development, 1991), p. 39.

[a] n.a. = not available.

els.[10] In the United States we have also seen (Table 1.2) that unemployment rates have, on average, been higher in the 1980s and 1970s in relation to the 1950–70 period. Keynesians object to attributing these variable and at times high unemployment rates to natural causes.

Hysteresis

Keynesians *do* believe that unemployment rates exhibit persistence, meaning that, during given periods, such as those in Table 10.2, unemployment tends to remain around a certain level. The unemployment rate in the 1960s, for example, tended to remain low, while in the 1980s, it was stuck at very high levels in some countries. Keynesians argue that, rather than this being the result of any intrinsic characteristics of the economic system, the unemployment rate in one period is strongly influenced by its past values. This property of a process is called **hysteresis**, which means that the history of a variable affects its present behavior. Thus, in many European countries, the recessions of the 1970s and early 1980s led to high *cyclical* unemployment. High unemployment rates later in the 1980s were in large part the result of the earlier unemployment. The economic processes that result in unemployment having the hysteresis property are considered in Chapter 12, which examines some recent directions in Keynesian research.

---

[10]There are other more sophisticated ways of estimating the so-called natural rate of unemployment. These other estimates also show sharp increases in the natural rates for many European countries. One estimate for Germany goes from 1.6 to 8.0 percent in 10 years; another for France goes from 3.3 to 9.0 percent in 5 years. See Robert Solow, "Unemployment: Getting the Questions Right," *Economica*, 33 (Supplement, 1986), p. S.32.

In sum, Keynesians do not believe the concept of a natural rate is useful. As Robert Solow expresses this view, A natural rate that hops around... under the influence of unspecified forces, *including past unemployment rates*, is not "natural" at all. "Epiphenomenal" would be a better adjective; look it up.[11]

10.4 • MONETARISTS VERSUS KEYNESIANS

This chapter and the preceding one have considered the basis for the several propositions of monetarism. We have also considered the Keynesian view on the issues raised by the monetarists. We conclude this discussion by summarizing the major differences between Keynesian and monetarist views. As with the Keynesian–classical dispute, it is useful to consider separately issues pertaining to aggregate demand and aggregate supply.

Monetarist Versus Keynesian Theories of Aggregate Demand

Monetarist and Keynesian views of aggregate supply and aggregate demand are displayed in Figure 10.9. For aggregate demand, the striking feature of the monetarist view is that the level of aggregate demand is determined primarily by the level of the money stock. Changes in the money stock are believed by the monetarists to be the major factors causing movements in aggregate demand and in nominal income.

As drawn, the aggregate demand curve in Figure 10.9a depends only on the quantity of money. Such a characterization reflects what Friedman termed an "exaggeration but one that gives the right flavor" to monetarist conclusions. This is the strong form of the monetarist position. Monetarists do not deny that there are some *nonsystematic* influences on aggregate demand. They do, however, argue that changes in money stock are the dominant factor causing appreciable systematic movements in aggregate demand and, therefore, nominal income.

Because they believe that changes in the money stock are the dominant factor causing changes in aggregate demand, monetarists believe that stable growth in the money stock is a requirement for economic stability. They advocate a growth rate rule for the money stock. Since movements in aggregate demand are dominated by monetary factors, monetarists deny the usefulness of fiscal stabilization policies.

The Keynesian aggregate demand schedule (y^d) is shown in Figure 10.9b. In the Keynesian view, the level of aggregate demand does not depend on the level of the money stock (M_0) alone. In addition, Keynesians believe that

---

[11]Robert Solow, "Unemployment: Getting the Questions Right," p. S.33.

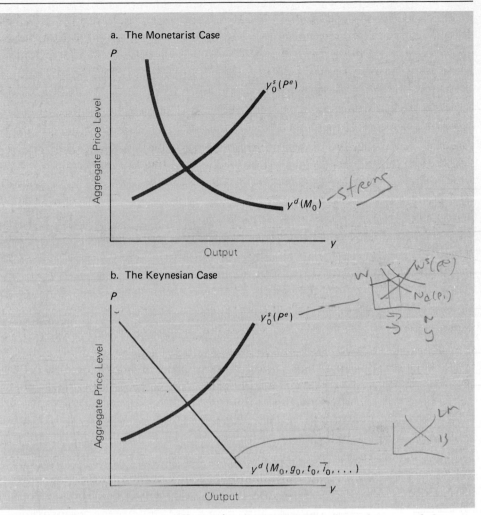

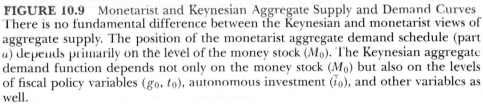

FIGURE 10.9   Monetarist and Keynesian Aggregate Supply and Demand Curves
There is no fundamental difference between the Keynesian and monetarist views of
aggregate supply. The position of the monetarist aggregate demand schedule (part
a) depends primarily on the level of the money stock (M_0). The Keynesian aggregate
demand function depends not only on the money stock (M_0) but also on the levels
of fiscal policy variables (g_0, t_0), autonomous investment ($\bar{i}_0$), and other variables as
well.

other variables have *important* and *systematic* effects on aggregate demand. These other influences include fiscal policy variables [the level of government spending (g_0) and taxes (t_0)], the level of autonomous investment demand ($\bar{i}_0$), and other factors that would cause autonomous changes in demand (exports, autonomous shifts in consumer demand, etc.). Keynesians believe that private-sector aggregate demand is unstable, primarily but not solely as a result of instability of investment demand. They favor activist fiscal and monetary policies to stabilize aggregate demand. Stable money growth alone will not produce economic stability because of the unstable behavior of the nonmonetary factors that are important in determining demand.

Monetarist Versus Keynesian Theories of Aggregate Supply

There is no difference between the monetarist aggregate supply curve, as drawn in Figure 10.9a, and the Keynesian counterpart, as drawn in Figure 10.9b. This similarity reflects the agreement between Keynesians and monetarists that the aggregate supply curve is upward-sloping in the short run. An increase in aggregate demand will increase both output and price in the short run in either model. Both groups believe that there is a trade-off between unemployment and inflation in the short run.

In both the monetarist and Keynesian cases, as indicated by the labeling of the curves, the upward-sloping aggregate supply function is drawn for a given value of the expected price. In the longer run, when the expected price level also has time to adjust, output will not be affected by changes in aggregate demand in either the monetarist or the Keynesian model. Shifts in the labor supply curve and therefore the aggregate supply curve (e.g., Figure 10.7) as the expected price level rises counterbalance the effect of the higher level of demand.

To monetarists, the fact that output can be influenced by aggregate demand only in the short run is seen as buttressing their case for a constant money growth rate. They emphasize the possible long-run destabilizing effects of government policies aimed at pegging the level of output at a rate below the natural rate. Since they believe that the private sector is inherently stable, they do not see a useful purpose for government policies aimed at stabilizing output and employment in the short run.

Keynesians, since they believe that private-sector aggregate demand is unstable, *do* see a need for stabilization policies. Although they are not unmindful of the possibility that government policies can be a source of instability in the economy, Keynesians are more optimistic than monetarists about the ability of the monetary and fiscal authorities to design effective stabilization policies. The long-run relationship between aggregate demand and output is not seen by Keynesians as relevant to questions of stabilization policy that pertain to the short run.

Review Questions and Problems

1. Explain the concept of the natural rate of unemployment. What are the implications of Milton Friedman's theory of the natural rate of unemployment for the effectiveness of economic stabilization policies?

2. Explain why monetarists believe that monetary policy affects output and employment in the short run but not in the long run. What is the crucial difference between the short run and the long run?

3. Contrast monetarist and Keynesian views of the relationship between real output (or employment) and aggregate demand in both the short run and the long run. Contrast the conclusions that monetarists and Keynesians draw from this analysis of the aggregate demand–output relationship for the usefulness of activist policies to stabilize output and employment. To what degree do differences in the theoretical analysis explain the differences in policy conclusions?

4. Explain the concept of the Phillips curve. Is there any difference between monetarist and Keynesian views of the Phillips curve?

5. Within the monetarist framework, would an expansionary fiscal policy action have short-run and long-run effects that are similar to those of the expansionary monetary policy analyzed in Section 10.1?

6. At the end of the inflationary decade of the 1970s, the Federal Reserve is widely perceived to have moved to a much more restrictive monetary policy. Use the Phillips curve framework of Figures 10.2 and 10.3 to provide a monetarist analysis of the effects this policy shift would have on inflation and unemployment.

7. Explain Keynesian objections to the concept of a *natural* rate of unemployment.

8. Summarize what you believe to be the essential differences between the monetarist and Keynesian positions.

9. A supply shock such as the exogenous increase in the price of oil analyzed in Section 8.5 would have no effect on real or nominal income within the monetarist model. This follows because such a supply shock would not affect the quantity of money that is the dominant factor determining nominal income and, in the short run, real income as well. Do you agree or disagree with this statement? Explain.

10. Contrast monetarist and classical views on the short-run effects of an increase in the quantity of money.

Selected Readings

Blanchard, Olivier, "Wage Bargaining and Unemployment Persistence," *Journal of Money, Credit and Banking,* 23 (August 1991), pp. 277–92.

Blanchard, Olivier, and Summers, Lawrence, "Hysteresis and the European Unemployment Problem," in Stanley Fischer, ed., *NBER Macroeconomics Annual.* Cambridge, Mass: MIT Press, 1986.

Blinder, Alan, "The Challenge of High Unemployment," *American Economic Review,* 78 (May 1988), pp. 1–15.

Branson, William *Macroeconomic Theory and Policy.* New York: Harper & Row, 1989, Chap. 20.

Friedman, Milton, "The Role of Monetary Policy," *American Economic Review,* 58 (March 1968), pp. 1–17. Reprinted in Milton Friedman, *The Optimal Quantity of Money and Other Essays.* Chicago: Aldine, 1969.

Humphrey, Thomas, "The Evolution and Policy Implications of Phillips Curve Analysis," Federal Reserve Bank of Richmond *Monthly Review* (March 1985), pp. 3–22.

Kahn, George A., "Inflation and Disinflation: A Comparison Across Countries," Federal Reserve Bank of Kansas City *Economic Review,* 70 (February 1985), pp. 23–42.

Rasche, Robert, "A Comparative Static Analysis of Some Monetarist Propositions," St. Louis Federal Reserve Bank *Review,* 55 (December 1973), pp. 15–23. Reprinted in Thomas Havrilesky and John Boorman, *Current Issues in Monetary Theory and Policy.* Arlington Heights, Ill.: AHM Publishing, 1980.

Santomero, Anthony, and Seater, John, "The Inflation–Unemployment Trade-off: A Critique of the Literature," *Journal of Economic Literature,* 16 (June 1978), pp. 499–544.

Solow, Robert M., Unemployment: Getting the Questions Right, *Economica,* 53 (Supplement: 1986), pp. S.23–S.34.

Vane, Howard, and Thompson, John, *Monetarism: Theory Evidence and Policy.* New York: Wiley, 1979, Chap. 4.

11 New Classical Economics

The next theoretical system we consider, the *new classical economics,* developed against the background of the high inflation and unemployment of the 1970s and the accompanying dissatisfaction with the prevailing Keynesian orthodoxy. Both monetarism and the new classical economics have their theoretical origins in aspects of classical economics, and both schools of economists reach similar noninterventionist policy conclusions. Robert Lucas, the central figure in the early development of the new classical economics, in an article entitled "Rules, Discretion, and the Role of the Economic Advisor," expressed his basic agreement with Milton Friedman's proposal for noninterventionist policy rules.[1] Also much in the spirit of Friedman, Lucas concluded of economists that "As an advice giving profession we are in way over our heads."[2] In fact, new classical economists are even more skeptical than monetarists about the usefulness of activist stabilization policies.

The new classical economics, however, is a more fundamental attack on the Keynesian *theoretical* system than is monetarism. Monetarists accept much of the theoretical contribution of Keynesian economics. Monetarists and Keynesians reach very different policy conclusions and differ on a number of empirical questions,[3] but in the preceding two chapters we presented no distinct monetarist theoretical models. New classical economists have attacked the Keynesian theoretical structure as "fundamentally flawed." These

---

[1] Robert Lucas, "Rules, Discretion, and the Role of the Economic Advisor," in Stanley Fischer, ed., *Rational Expectations and Economic Policy* (Chicago: University of Chicago Press, 1980).

[2] Ibid., p. 259.

[3] The stability of the private sector, the interest elasticity of money demand, and the importance of fiscal policy crowding out are a few.

economists argue that we must go back to the methodology of classical economics as a basis for constructing useful macroeconomic models.

This chapter first presents the new classical economists' critique of Keynesian macroeconomics, focusing especially on the differences in the policy conclusions of the two groups (Section 11.1). Next, we take a broader look at the new classical economics, indicating new classical economists' own suggestions of useful avenues for future research and examining the classical roots of their approach (Section 11.2). The next section considers the Keynesian response to the new classical economics (Section 11.3). The final section (11.4) contains concluding comments on the current state of the controversy between Keynesian and new classical economists.

11.1 • THE NEW CLASSICAL ATTACK

We have already had reason to quote Franco Modigliani's Keynesian view that a private-enterprise economy needs to be, can be, and should be stabilized by active government aggregate demand management. The monetarists' contrary view has also been examined. The central policy tenet of the new classical economics is that stabilization of *real* variables such as output and employment *cannot* be achieved by aggregate demand management. The values of such variables *in both the short run and the long run* are insensitive to *systematic* aggregate demand management policies. In other words, in the new classical view, systematic monetary and fiscal policy actions that change aggregate demand will not affect output and employment even in the short run. This is what has been termed the **new classical policy ineffectiveness postulate.**

Although monetarists question the necessity and desirability of activist policies to affect output and employment, and question the effectiveness of *fiscal* policy actions, they believe that systematic *monetary* policy actions have real effects in the short run. The new classical objection to the use of activist stabilization policies is thus more far-reaching than that of monetarists.

A Review of the Keynesian Position

To see the basis for this new classical policy position, we need to consider the new classical economists' critique of Keynesian macroeconomics. A good starting place is a review of the Keynesian analysis of the relationships among real output, employment, and aggregate demand, as discussed in Section 10.3. Consider the effects in the Keynesian model of an expansionary policy action, for example, an increase in the money stock. In the short run such a policy action would increase aggregate demand. The aggregate demand curve would shift to the right along the upward-sloping aggregate supply schedule (as illustrated, for example, in Figure 10.5a). The price level and level of real output would rise. Parallel to the increase in real output is a rise in employment as labor demand increases, with the rise in prices shifting the labor demand schedule to the right along the upward-sloping (drawn against the money wage) labor supply schedule (as illustrated, for example, in Figure 10.5b).

Crucial to these results was the fact that the positions of both the aggregate supply schedule and labor supply schedule were fixed in the short run. The position of both these schedules depended on the value of the expected price level (P^e), which was assumed to depend primarily on past prices and not to change with current policy actions.

In the longer run, the expected price level converged to the actual price level, and we saw that both the aggregate supply schedule and the labor supply schedule shifted to the left. The initial levels of employment and real output were restored, with only the price level and the money wage left permanently higher as a result of the increase in the money stock (see Figure 10.7). Output and employment remained above their long-run equilibrium levels only for as long as it took labor suppliers to perceive correctly the change in the price level that resulted from the expansionary policy action. As long as our attention is confined to monetary policy actions, monetarists would agree with the foregoing analysis of an increase in aggregate demand, although they draw different policy conclusions from this analysis than do Keynesians.

The Rational Expectations Concept and Its Implications

The new classical economists do not agree with this analysis. In particular, they do not accept the difference between the short-run and long-run results in this Keynesian or monetarist analysis of the effects of aggregate demand on output and employment. The focal point of their criticism is the Keynesian (and monetarist) assumption concerning the formation of price expectations. This formulation assumes that labor suppliers form an expectation of the current aggregate price level (or future inflation rate) on the basis of the past behavior of prices. In practice, Keynesians and monetarists have assumed that such price expectations adjust slowly and can be assumed to be fixed for the analysis of policy effects over relatively short periods. Thus, we previously *defined* the short run as that period of time over which such expectations were fixed.

New classical economists have criticized such formulations of expectations formation as "naive in the extreme." Why, they ask, would rational economic agents forming an expectation of the price level, for example, rely only on past values of the price level? Why especially would they do so when in general such behavior results in their being *systematically* wrong when aggregate demand shifts? We have been assuming that following changes in aggregate demand, the increase in the money stock considered in the preceding subsection, for example, labor suppliers fail to perceive the effect that the demand shift will have on price. New classical economists argue that economic agents will not persist in making such systematic errors.

The new classical economists propose that economic agents will form **rational expectations,** rational in the sense that they will not make avoidable systematic errors. According to the hypothesis of rational expectations, expectations *are formed on the basis of all the available relevant information concerning the variable being predicted.* Furthermore, the rational expectations hypothesis maintains that individuals *use available information intelligently; that is, they understand the way in which the variables they observe will affect the variable they are trying to predict.* According to the rational expectations hypothesis, then, expectations are, as the originator of the concept, John Muth, suggested, "essentially the same as the predictions of the relevant economic theory,"[4] based on available information. What does the rational expectations assumption imply about the way labor suppliers form price expectations?

If expectations are rational, then in forming a prediction of the value of the aggregate price level for the current period, labor suppliers will use all relevant past information, not just information about the past behavior of prices. In addition, they will use any information they have about the current values of variables that play a role in determining the price level. Most important from the standpoint of the effects of aggregate demand management policy, labor suppliers will take account of any anticipated (expected) policy actions in forming their price forecasts. Further, they are assumed to understand the relationship between such aggregate demand policies and the price level.

A useful contrast can be made between the *backward-looking* nature of expectations in the Keynesian model and the *forward-looking* nature of rational expectations. In the Keynesian model, expectations are backward-looking because the expectation of a variable such as the price level adjusts (slowly) to the past behavior of the variable. According to the rational expectations hypothesis, economic agents instead use all available relevant information and intelligently assess the implication of that information for the future behavior of a variable such as the price level.

If such forward-looking rational forecasts of the price level are in fact made by labor suppliers, then the analysis of the preceding subsection must be modified in an important way. To see this, we analyze the effects of the same expansionary policy action previously considered, a one-time increase in the money stock. To analyze the effects of such a change with the assump-

---

[4]John Muth, "Rational Expectations and the Theory of Price Movements," *Econometrica,* 29 (July 1961), p. 316.

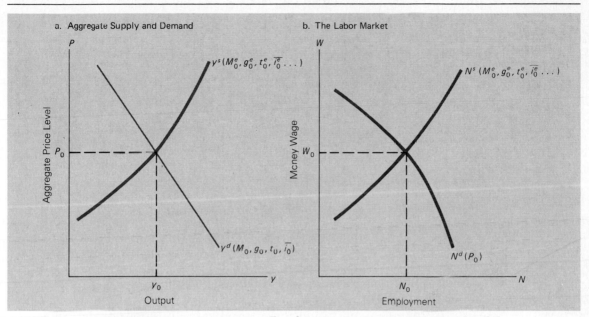

FIGURE 11.1 Output and Employment in the New Classical Model
The distinctive feature of the new classical model is that both the aggregate supply and labor supply schedules depend on the rationally formed expectations of current variables, including monetary and fiscal policy variables 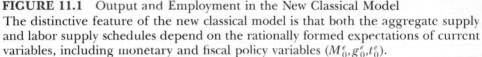.

tion that expectations are rational, we must begin by specifying whether or not the policy change was anticipated.[5] We will see that anticipated and unanticipated policy changes have very different effects when expectations are assumed to be rational. First, we assume that the policy change was anticipated. This might be because the policymaker announces the policy change. Alternatively, the public may anticipate the policy change because the policymaker is known to act in certain systematic ways. For example, if the policymaker systematically responds to an increase in unemployment in one period by increasing the money stock in the next period (to counteract unemployment), the public will come to anticipate an increase in the money stock for period t when they observe an increase in the unemployment rate of period $t - 1$.

To begin, consider the characterization of equilibrium output and employment in the new classical analysis, as illustrated in Figure 11.1. The crucial

---

[5] The terms *expected* and *anticipated* or *unexpected* and *unanticipated* are used interchangeably here. Generally, policy shifts are referred to as either *anticipated* or *unanticipated*, whereas we refer to *expected* levels of variables, including policy variables.

difference between the new classical case and the Keynesian case concerns the variables that determine the positions of the labor supply and the aggregate supply schedules. As in the Keynesian theory, we are assuming here that labor supply depends on the expected real wage, the known money wage divided by the expected price level:

$$N^s = t\left(\frac{W}{P^e}\right) \tag{11.1}$$

Consequently, the position of the labor supply schedule, and therefore the aggregate supply schedule, again depends on the expected price level. Increases in the expected price level will shift both schedules to the left.

In the new classical model, however, with the assumption of rational expectations, the expected price level depends on the expected levels of the variables in the model that actually determine the price level. These include the *expected* levels of the money stock (M^e), government spending (g^e) and tax collections (t^e), autonomous investment (i^e), and possibly other variables.[6] The dependence of the expected price level, and hence the positions of the labor supply and aggregate supply schedules on these variables, is indicated by the labeling of these curves in Figure 11.1. Especially important for the new classical policy conclusion is the fact that the positions of the labor supply and aggregate supply schedules depend on the expected levels of the policy variables (M^e, g^e, t^e).

Now consider the effect of a fully anticipated increase in the money stock from M_0 to M_1, as depicted in Figure 11.2.[7] Initially, assume that the aggregate demand, aggregate supply, and labor market supply and demand schedules are at the same positions as in Figure 11.1, with actual and expected variables subscripted zero (0). The increase in the money stock will shift the aggregate demand schedule out to $y^d(M_1, \ldots)$. If the supply schedule did not shift, output would rise from y_0 to y_1', and the price level would increase from P_0 to P_1'. With the rise in the price level, the labor demand curve shifts to the right (to the dashed schedule $N^d(P_1')$ in Figure 11.2). *If the labor supply curve did not also shift*, employment would rise (from N_0 to N_1'). In the Keynesian or monetarist frameworks, with the expected price level unrelated to the current level of policy variables, the positions of the aggregate supply curve and labor supply schedules *would* be fixed in the short run and our analysis would be complete.

---

[6] Expected changes in oil prices or other supply-side factors, for example, would also affect the expected price level.

[7] The positions for the aggregate demand schedule and other schedules continue to depend on all the variables discussed previously, including policy variables, but for notational simplicity the labels on the schedules in the graph contain only the variables that are assumed to change.

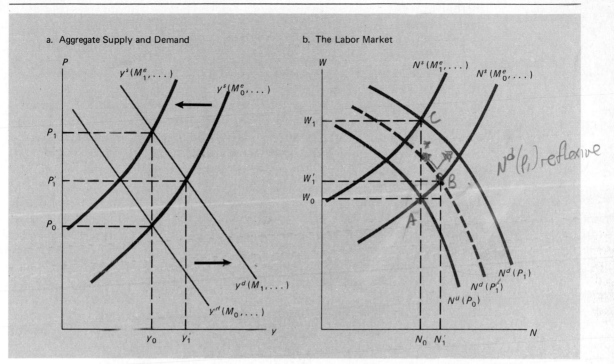

FIGURE 11.2 Effects of an Increase in the Money Stock: The New Classical View

The increase in the money stock shifts the aggregate demand curve from $y^d(M_0, \ldots)$ to $y^d(M_1, \ldots)$. By itself, this change would increase output to y_1' and the price level to P_1'. The increase in the price level would shift the labor demand schedule from $N^d(P_0)$ to $N^d(P_1')$ and employment would rise to N_1'. However, since the increase in the money stock was fully anticipated, there is also an increase in the *expected* money stock. This increase in the expected money stock shifts the aggregate supply schedule to the left from $y^s(M_0^e, \ldots)$ to $y^s(M_1^e, \ldots)$ and also shifts the labor supply schedule to the left from $N^s(M_0^e, \ldots)$ to $N^s(M_1^e, \ldots,)$. These shifts cause employment and output to fall back to their initial levels (y_0 and N_0).

But as can be seen in Figure 11.2, in the new classical case the positions of the labor supply and aggregate supply schedules are *not* fixed in the short run. The expansionary policy action was assumed to be fully anticipated. Therefore, the level of the *expected* money stock also increases. This will increase the *expected* price level since, with rational expectations, labor suppliers will understand the inflationary effect of the increase in the money stock. The labor supply schedule and, as a consequence, the aggregate supply schedule will shift to the left to the positions given by $N^s(M_1^e, \ldots)$ and $y^s(M_1^e, \ldots)$, as shown in Figure 11.2. As the decline in aggregate supply puts further upward pressure on the price level, the labor demand schedule shifts out to $N^d(P_1)$. The new equilibrium is where output and employment have returned to their initial levels, y_0, N_0, while the price level and the money wage are permanently higher at W_1, P_1, respectively. Notice that the return to the initial levels of output and employment takes place in the short run when expectations are rational.

The new classical analysis differs from the Keynesian or monetarist analysis in that, with the new classical assumption of rational expectations, labor suppliers are assumed to perceive correctly the increase in price that will be a consequence of the increase in the money stock. They demand proportionately higher money wages. The labor market will return to equilibrium only after the money wage and price level have increased in the same proportion, the real wage is unchanged, and consequently employment and output are back at their initial levels. Put differently, in the Keynesian or monetarist analysis the increase in the money stock leads to an increase in employment and output in the short run, that is, until labor suppliers correctly perceive the increase in the price level that comes as a result of the expansionary monetary policy action. In the Keynesian or monetarist view, since expectations about prices are backward-looking, depending on the past behavior of prices and adjusting only slowly to current conditions, this short-run period in which the increase in the money stock affects output and employment can be of considerable length. If expectations are rational, forward-looking labor suppliers thus cannot be systematically "fooled" by anticipated changes in aggregate demand policy. Such policy actions will not affect output and employment, even in the short run.

The new classical assumption of rational expectations thus has very dramatic implications for macroeconomic policy. If expectations are formed rationally, anticipated aggregate demand policy actions will not affect real output or employment, even in the short run. Notice that since the public will learn any systematic "rules" of policy action, such as the hypothetical response of the money stock to unemployment mentioned previously, any such set of systematic policy actions will come to be anticipated and will not affect the behavior of output or employment.[8] The values of real variables such as output and employment will be insensitive to systematic changes in aggregate demand management policies. This conclusion is extremely important because, if it is accepted, there is no useful role for aggregate demand policies aimed at stabilizing output and employment.

---

[8] That the public would learn systematic policy "rules" follows from the assumption of rational expectations. Estimates of such rules could be made on the basis of past policy behavior. Since such estimates would be helpful in predicting policy actions and consequently in predicting the behavior of prices and other variables, the rational economic agent would be assumed to use the information.

Thus far we have been assuming that the increase in the money stock was anticipated either because it was announced or because it was a systematic policy response that could be predicted. Now consider the effects of an *unanticipated* increase in aggregate demand. To be specific, we again consider the effects of an increase in the money stock from M_0 to M_1, but the analysis would be similar for an unanticipated increase in aggregate demand from another source. The short-run effects of this unanticipated increase in the money stock—what can be termed a *monetary surprise*—can also be explained with reference to Figure 11.2. As before, the increase in the money stock shifts the aggregate demand schedule from $y^d(M_0, \ldots)$ to $y^d(M_1, \ldots)$. As the price level rises to P_1', the labor demand schedule also shifts out to the right, to $N^d(P_1')$. If the increase in the money stock is unanticipated, these are the only curves that shift in the short run. The additional shift to the left in the labor supply curve and consequently the shift to the left in the aggregate supply curve shown in Figure 11.2, where the increase in the money stock was anticipated, does *not* occur for an unanticipated increase in the money stock. When the increase in the money stock is not anticipated, it does not affect the labor suppliers' expectation of the value the aggregate price level will take on over the current period. This is why the labor supply curve does not shift.

When the increase in the money stock is unanticipated, the new classical model indicates that output and employment will be affected. In Figure 11.2, output will rise from y_0 to y_1' and employment will increase from N_0 to N_1', results identical to those of the Keynesian or monetarist analysis of such an increase in aggregate demand. Since the increase in the money stock is unanticipated, it cannot affect even the rational expectation of the price level. For the short run, even assuming rational expectations, labor suppliers will not perceive the inflationary effect of the increase in aggregate demand. This was the assumption in the Keynesian or monetarist view *for any change in aggregate demand*. New classical economists deny that anticipated changes in aggregate demand can affect output and employment, but their view of the effects of unanticipated changes in aggregate demand does not differ from that of Keynesians or monetarists.

Note, however, that the results here are those for the short run. Even though the policy change was unanticipated, in future periods economic agents would find out that policy had in fact changed. In particular, labor suppliers would observe that the money stock had increased and would revise their price forecasts upward. In the long run the labor supply schedule, and consequently the output supply function, would shift left, as shown in Figure 11.2. Output and employment would return to their initial levels. Again, there is no fundamental difference here between the Keynesian (or monetarist) and new classical analyses of the effects of an *unanticipated* change in aggregate demand.

This analysis of the effects of an unanticipated monetary policy action illustrates an important difference between the new classical theory and the original classical theory explained in Chapters 3 and 4. In the new classical model, economic agents are assumed to be rational, but they do not have perfect information; they make mistakes in predicting the price level, and such mistakes cause short-run deviations of output and employment from their long-run equilibrium rates. In the classical model, economic agents were assumed to have perfect information. Labor suppliers knew the real wage. In effect, in the classical system there were no monetary (or other) surprises. There were no deviations from the supply-determined rates of output and employment.

The New Classical Policy Conclusions

We can now restate the new classical *policy ineffectiveness postulate* in a clearer manner. New classical economists believe that real output and employment are unaffected by systematic, and therefore predictable, changes in aggregate demand policy. In both Keynesian and monetarist models, changes in aggregate demand policies affect output and employment because labor suppliers fail to perceive correctly the effects on the price level of such policy changes. New classical economists assume that expectations are rational and consequently that labor suppliers will not make such systematic mistakes in their price forecasts. If the policy action is anticipated, the price effects of that policy will be also. Although new classical economists assume that expectations are rational, they do not assume that economic agents have perfect information. Unanticipated changes in aggregate demand, whether policy-induced or from other sources, will affect real output and employment. Labor suppliers will not be able to perceive the effects on the price level as a result of such unanticipated changes in aggregate demand.

The new classical view that unanticipated aggregate demand changes affect output and employment still does not provide any meaningful role for macroeconomic stabilization policy. To see this, consider the new classical economists' view of the proper policy response to a decline in private-sector demand, for example, an autonomous decline in investment demand. We have already analyzed the Keynesian view of the proper policy response to such a shock (Section 10.3). Keynesians argue that a decline in private-sector demand should be offset by an expansionary monetary or fiscal policy action to stabilize aggregate demand, output, and employment.

The effects of the decline in investment demand are depicted in Figure 11.3. The decline in investment demand shifts the aggregate demand schedule from $y^d(\bar{i}_0)$ to $y^d(\bar{i}_1)$ in Figure 11.3a. This causes output to decline from y_0 to y'_1. The price level will fall from P_0 to P'_1 and, as a result, the labor demand curve in Figure 11.3b will shift downward from $N^d(P_0)$ to $N^d(P'_1)$. Whether there are additional effects from the decline in investment demand

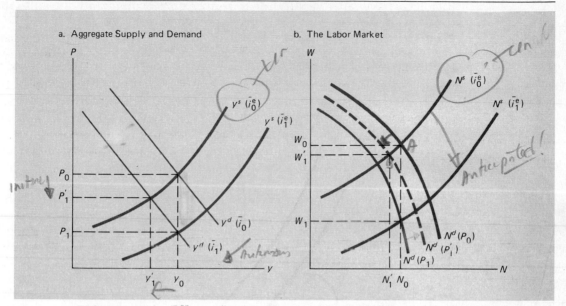

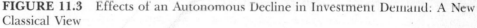

FIGURE 11.3   Effects of an Autonomous Decline in Investment Demand: A New Classical View

An autonomous decline in investment demand shifts the aggregate demand schedule from $y^d(\bar{i}_0)$ to $y^d(\bar{i}_1)$. This shift would reduce output from y_0 to y_1' and lower the price level from P_0 to P_1'. The fall in the price level shifts the labor demand schedule from $N^d(P_0)$ to $N^d(P_1')$, which causes employment to fall from N_0 to N_1'. These are the only effects if the decline in investment demand was not anticipated. If the decline in investment demand was anticipated, the expected level of autonomous investment ($\bar{i}^e$) will also fall (from $\bar{i}_0^e$ to $\bar{i}_1^e$). The aggregate supply schedule will shift from $y^s(\bar{i}_0^e)$ to $y^s(\bar{i}_1^e)$ and the labor supply schedule will shift from $N^s(\bar{i}_0^e)$ to $N^s(\bar{i}_1^e)$. Those shifts cause output and employment to return to their initial levels.

depends, in the new classical view, on whether the decline was or was not anticipated. To begin, we assume that it was anticipated.

In that case, labor suppliers will anticipate the decline in the price level that will result from the decline in aggregate demand. Labor suppliers, now expecting the price level to be lower, will supply more labor at a given money wage, since with the lower expected price level, a given money wage corresponds to a higher expected real wage. This fall in the expected price level shifts the labor supply curve to the right in Figure 11.3b [from $N^s(\bar{i}_0^e)$ to $N^s(\bar{i}_1^e)$]. As a consequence, the aggregate supply schedule shifts to the right in Figure 11.3a [from $y^s(\bar{i}_0^e)$ to $y^s(\bar{i}_1^e)$.] There is a further decline in the price level to P_1, and therefore a further downward shift in the labor demand schedule to $N^d(P_1)$. At the new *short-run* equilibrium, the money wage and price level have fallen sufficiently to restore employment and output to their initial levels, N_0 to y_0.

This analysis is just the reverse of our previous analysis of an anticipated increase in aggregate demand coming as a result of an increase in the money stock. In the new classical system, output and employment are not affected by anticipated changes in aggregate demand, even in the short run. Consequently, there is no need for a stabilization policy response to an anticipated demand change such as a decline in investment demand. In the new classical view, the economy is self-stabilizing with respect to such shocks.

But what if the decline in investment demand had not been anticipated? In that case the labor suppliers would not have foreseen the price decline that resulted from the decline in aggregate demand. The labor supply curve (Figure 11.3b) and the aggregate supply curve (Figure 11.3a) would have remained at $N^s(\bar{i}_0^e)$ and $y^s(\bar{i}_0^e)$, respectively. The decline in investment demand would have caused output and employment to decline to the levels given by y_1' and N_1'. Would not an offsetting policy action to raise aggregate demand back to its initial level be called for in this case?

The answer is that such a policy response would be desirable but not feasible. The decline in investment demand was by definition unanticipated. With the assumption of rational expectations, this means that the decline could not have been predicted by economic agents on the basis of *any* available information. The policymaker, like any other economic agent, would have been unable to foresee the investment decline in advance. He could not have acted to raise aggregate demand to offset the decline. Once the investment decline has occurred and has had its effect on output, the policymaker could act to raise aggregate demand if the low investment level was expected to be repeated in future periods. If low investment was *expected* to continue in future periods, however, there would be no need for a policy response since private agents would also hold this expectation. At this point the shift in the labor supply and aggregate supply schedules would take place. In other words, as long as the shock is unanticipated, the policymaker lacks the knowledge needed to act to offset the shock. Once the shock is anticipated by the policymaker, it is anticipated by other economic agents, including labor suppliers, and there is no need to offset the shock.

The foregoing analysis indicates that in the new classical view there is no useful role for aggregate demand policies aimed at stabilizing output and employment. New classical economists' policy conclusions are strongly noninterventionist, just as were those of classical economists. In this respect new classical economists agree with the monetarists, although, as a comparison of this chapter with the preceding two will show, new classical economists reach their noninterventionist policy conclusions for somewhat different reasons. Concerning monetary policy, many new classical economists arrive at the same position as monetarists, generally favoring a money growth rate rule such as the constant growth rate rule proposed by Milton Friedman.

Such a policy rule does away with unanticipated changes in the money stock, which can have little stabilization value and are likely to move the economy away from the natural rate of output and employment by causing economic agents to make price forecast errors. In addition, a constant rate of growth in the money stock would contribute to stability in the inflation rate, and if the constant money growth rate was low, to a low inflation rate as well.

In the case of fiscal policy, new classical economists favor stability and the avoidance of excessive and inflationary stimulus. Excessive and/or erratic government deficit spending should be avoided. New classical economists Thomas Sargent and Neil Wallace, for example, were critical of the large deficits that resulted from the Reagan administration's fiscal policy of the 1980s.[9]

Instability in fiscal policy causes uncertainty, making it difficult for even agents forming rational expectations to correctly anticipate the course of the economy. Moreover, Sargent and others believe that a *credible* policy to provide low stable money growth cannot coexist with a fiscal policy that generates large deficits. Huge deficits put great pressure on the monetary authority to increase money growth in order to help finance the deficit.[10] Sargent and other new classical economists believe that control of the government budget deficit is necessary for a credible, noninflationary monetary policy.[11]

11.2 • A BROADER VIEW OF THE NEW CLASSICAL POSITION

New classical economists are highly critical of Keynesian economics as a whole. In one summary of their position, new classical economists Robert Lucas and Thomas Sargent use terms such as "fundamentally flawed," "wreckage," "failure on a grand scale," and "of no value" to describe major aspects of the Keynesian theoretical and policy analysis.[12] The title of their paper, "After Keynesian Macroeconomics," suggests their view that a total

---

[9]Thomas Sargent and Neil Wallace, "Some Unpleasant Monetarist Arithmetic," Federal Reserve Bank of Minneapolis *Review* (Fall 1981).

[10]Recall that from the government's budget constraint it follows that deficits must be financed either by the sale of bonds or the creation of new money. Even if, at present, the deficit is financed only by bond sales, the new classical economists argue that the resulting upward pressure on the interest rate will eventually lead the monetary authority to deviate from a stable money growth rule. Rational economic agents will predict this and therefore will not believe that the monetary authority will stick to announced targets for money growth.

[11]See the discussion in Thomas Sargent, "Stopping Moderate Inflations: The Methods of Poincaré and Thatcher," in Rudiger Dornbusch and Mario Henrique Simonsen, eds., *Inflation, Debt, and Indexation* (Cambridge, Mass.: MIT Press, 1983).

[12]Robert Lucas and Thomas Sargent, "After Keynesian Macroeconomics," in *After the Phillips Curve: Persistence of High Inflation and High Unemployment* (Boston: Federal Reserve Bank of Boston, 1978).

restructuring of macroeconomics is required. The basis for such a restructuring, they believe, can be found in the classical economics.

Lucas, Sargent, and other new classical economists are critical of the theoretical foundations of the Keynesian system. They argue that Keynes's model was one where "rules of thumb" such as the consumption function and Keynesian money demand function replaced sounder classical functions based on individual optimizing behavior. Generally, they believe that the classical system was more carefully constructed from a theory of rational choices by individual households and businesses. The Keynesian model is, in their view, made up of more ad hoc elements, which were failed attempts at explaining the observed behavior of the economy in the aggregate. A good example of this failing of the Keynesian system is in the handling of expectations. The Keynesian system uses a rule of thumb whereby the expected current price is expressed as a function of the past behavior of prices. Such an assumption is not derived on the basis of individuals making optimal use of information and implies, in general, that economic agents choose to ignore useful information in making their price forecasts. New classical economists make the alternative assumption that expectations are rational, which they argue to be consistent with optimal use of information by the economic agents in the model.

New classical economists are also critical of Keynes's assumption that wages are "sticky," meaning, as they interpret this assumption, that wages "are set at a level or by a process that could be taken as uninfluenced by the macroeconomic forces he proposed to analyze." We have already considered the arguments that Keynesians advance in support of the assumption of wage rigidity. New classical economists do not find these arguments convincing. They favor the classical view that markets, including the labor market, "clear"; prices, including the wage rate, which is the price of labor, move to equate supply and demand.

New classical economists argue that fruitful macroeconomic models should rectify the failures of Keynesian economics by consistently adhering to the assumptions that

1. Agents optimize; that is, they act in their own self-interest. _RE!_
2. Markets clear.

New classical economists believe that the classical model adhered to these assumptions and is a basis for future work in macroeconomics.

Why, then, did Keynes dispense with these assumptions? In the new classical view, Keynesian economics was a response to the supposed failure of classical economics to explain the problem of unemployment and the relationship between unemployment and aggregate demand. Recall that the classical aggregate supply schedule was vertical. With such a vertical supply schedule, aggregate output was totally dependent on supply factors. The equilibrium classical model was abandoned by Keynes because it did not explain the prolonged deviations of output and employment from full-employment levels. The classical model also failed to explain why these deviations from full employment were often related to movements in the price level. Specifically, high levels of employment and output were in many cases associated with rising price levels, whereas low levels of employment and output were associated with declining price levels. Such behavior is explainable in the Keynesian system, in which increases in aggregate demand increase the price level as well as the levels of output and employment. The empirical evidence seems to support the notion of an upward-sloping, not a vertical, aggregate supply curve.

New classical economists argue that the classical model can explain both the deviations of employment from full-employment levels and a positive relationship between output and price changes if one incorporates the assumption of rational expectations into the classical system. Recall that the classical theory of the labor market, which was the basis for the classical vertical aggregate supply function, assumed that labor suppliers knew the real wage, implying that labor suppliers had *perfect information* about the value the aggregate price level would take on over the short run. New classical economists substitute the assumption that labor suppliers make a rational forecast of the aggregate price level. In this case, as we have seen, systematic, and hence anticipated, changes in aggregate demand will not affect output and employment, but unanticipated changes in aggregate demand will. Such unanticipated changes in aggregate demand can explain deviations of employment from the full-employment level. Notice also that unanticipated increases in aggregate demand will increase price as well as output and employment, with the reverse effect for unanticipated decreases in demand. Thus, with the rational expectations assumption, the classical system can explain the positive relationship between output changes and price changes.

This substitution of the assumption of rational expectations for the classical assumption of perfect information does not require substantive changes in the noninterventionist classical policy conclusions, for as we saw earlier in this chapter, meaningful aggregate demand management policies involve *systematic* variations in aggregate demand, and these have no effect on output and employment in the new classical view. New classical economists believe that the updated classical model, with the rational expectations assumption substituted for the perfect information assumption, provides a starting point for the construction of useful macroeconomic models.

11.3 • THE KEYNESIAN COUNTERCRITIQUE

The theme that runs through the Keynesian response to the new classical criticisms is that, although much is valid in the points they raise, especially concerning the weakness of the Keynesian treatment of expectations formation, it is still, as the Keynesian Robert Solow puts it, "much too early to tear up the *IS–LM* chapters in the textbooks of your possibly misspent youth."[13] Keynesians continue to believe that Keynes provided the basis for a useful framework in which to analyze the determinants of output and employment. They continue to believe in the usefulness of activist policies to stabilize output and employment.

The major areas in which the Keynesians have raised objections to the new classical view are as follows.

Persistence

The Question of Persistence

In the preceding section we saw that the new classical model, with the concept of rational expectations, could explain deviations of employment from the full-employment level. Unanticipated declines in aggregate demand would move output and employment below the full-employment levels. Keynesians argue that although such an explanation might be plausible for brief departures from full employment, it is not adequate to explain the persistent and substantial deviations from full employment that we have actually experienced. An unanticipated decline in investment demand, such as we considered previously (Figure 11.3), might well cause output and employment to decline over a short period, let us say one year. By the next year, however, this decline in aggregate demand would be seen to have taken place; it would no longer be unanticipated. Labor suppliers would recognize that the aggregate price level had declined. Consequently, the shifts to the right in the labor supply curve and the aggregate supply curve discussed previously (see Figure 11.3) would restore employment and output to their initial levels.

This being the case, how can the new classical model explain unemployment rates of 10 percent or more in Great Britain for the entire period 1923–39 or during the Great Depression of the 1930s in the United States, when the unemployment rate exceeded 14 percent for 10 consecutive years? In the more recent past, how can such a theory explain the movement of the unemployment rate during the deep and prolonged recessions of the mid-1970s and early 1980s?

Read Perspectives 11.1.

The response of new classical economists to this criticism is that although the source of the unemployment, the unanticipated change in aggregate demand, will be of short duration, as Keynesians point out, there is no reason why the effects of such a shock will not persist. Consider, for example,

---

[13] Robert Solow, "Alternative Approaches to Macroeconomic Theory: A Partial View," *The Canadian Journal of Economics* (August 1979). Another useful paper in this area by Solow is "On Theories of Unemployment," *American Economic Review* (March 1980), pp. 1–11.

the response to an unanticipated decline in aggregate demand. Assume that after one year or so, everyone recognizes that demand has fallen, so that the change is no longer unanticipated. Declines in output and employment will have occurred. New classical economists argue that it will take time before such declines are reversed. Firms that have already cut output levels will not find it optimal to restore production immediately to the levels before the shock because of the cost of adjustments in output levels. Moreover, firms will have accumulated excess inventory stocks over the period during which output was in decline. It will take time to run off such stocks; in the meantime, production and therefore employment will remain depressed. On the labor supply side, workers who have become unemployed will not find it optimal to take the first job offer that comes along, but will engage in a search for the best job opportunity. As a consequence of such adjustment lags, new classical economists argue that lengthy deviations from full employment, such as the United States experienced during the mid-1970s and early 1980s, can be explained even though the shocks that cause such deviations are short-lived.

What about the depressions in Great Britain and the United States in the 1930s? One proponent of the new classical position, Robert Barro, has tentatively explained the severity of at least the U.S. experience by the extent of the largely unanticipated monetary collapse during the early years of the Depression, when the money stock fell by one third. The slow recovery is viewed as a result of the massive government intervention during the New Deal period that subverted the normal adjustment mechanisms of the private sector.[14] Other new classical economists, such as Sargent and Lucas, agree at least in part with Keynesians that the Great Depression is not well explained by their theory, but also do not find the Keynesian explanation convincing.

On this question of persistence, Keynesians remain unconvinced that adjustment lags provide a sufficient explanation of prolonged and severe unemployment. They believe that if one accepts the classical or new classical framework, one can explain episodes such as the Great Depression only as a result of factors on the supply side, which in their view are the only factors in these models that could cause prolonged unemployment. If markets clear and there is no involuntary unemployment, then as Modigliani puts it, to the classical or new classical economists "what happened to the United States in the 1930s was a severe attack of contagious laziness."[15]

---

[14]See Robert Barro, "Second Thoughts on Keynesian Economics," *American Economic Review*, 69 (May 1979), p. 57. Examples of such New Deal interventions include NRA codes to fix prices and wages, agricultural policies to restrict output and raise prices, and increased regulation of the banking and securities industry, which might have hindered the raising of funds for investment. (*See Perspectives 11.2.*)

[15]Franco Modigliani, "The Monetarist Controversy, or Should We Foresake Stabilization Policies?" *American Economic Review,* 67 (March 1977), p. 6.

PERSPECTIVES

11.1

The New Classical Economics and the Disinflation of the 1980s

As was noted previously, in the early 1980s the U.S. economy experienced a costly *disinflation*—costly in terms of foregone output and high unemployment. Table 11.1 shows unemployment and inflation rates for the period. Keynesians argue that this experience with disinflation provided a decisive test of the new classical economics—and the theory failed.[1]

Critics of the new classical economics argue that the disinflation of the early 1980s was the result of a well-publicized restrictive

monetary policy; that is, a restrictive policy, "probably about as well anticipated as such a policy is ever likely to be."[2]

Consequently, these critics argue that in the new classical framework the monetary-policy–induced disinflation of 1981–82 should have been relatively costless in terms of output and employment effects. In the new classical theory, an anticipated decline in money growth should not affect output and employment. But the disinflation was not costless. Instead, the recession of 1981–82 was the most severe since the Great Depression. As can be seen from Table 11.1, the unemployment rate rose to 9.7 percent for 1982 (10.8 percent in November of that year). Benjamin Friedman therefore questioned, "If the new classical macroeconomic

[1] See Benjamin Friedman, "Recent Perspectives in and on Macroeconomics," in George Feiwel, ed., *Macroeconomics and Distribution* (London: Macmillan, 1985); and Robert J. Gordon, "Using Monetary Control to Dampen the Business Cycle: A New Set of First Principles," National Bureau of Economic Research Working Paper, No. 1210 (October 1983).

[2] Benjamin Friedman, "Recent Perspectives in and on Macroeconomics," p. 278.

TABLE 11.1   Inflation, Unemployment, and the Federal Budget Deficit, 1979–85

	Inflation Rate[a]	Unemployment Rate[b]	Federal Budget Surplus (+) or Deficit (−) ($ billions)
1979	13.3	5.8	−16.1
1980	12.4	7.1	−61.3
1981	8.9	7.6	−63.8
1982	3.9	9.7	−145.9
1983	3.8	9.6	−176.0
1984	4.0	7.5	−169.6
1985	3.8	7.2	−196.9

[a] Annual percentage change in CPI.

[b] Civilian unemployment rate (percent).

analysis of anticipated monetary policy is not relevant during this period, then it is not clear when—or if ever—that analysis is likely to be relevant."[3] Robert Gordon concludes that "In the end the 1981–82 recession may prove to have been as fatal to the Lucas–Sargent–Wallace proposition as the Great Depression was to pre-Keynesian classical macroeconomics."[4]

This is not the view of new classical economists. Thomas Sargent, for example, *in 1981* argued that costless disinflation was possible in the new classical framework, but only under very stringent conditions. A policy that would work in this respect "would be a once-and-for-all widely understood and widely agreed upon change in the monetary and fiscal regime," which must also be viewed as "unlikely to be reversed."[5] In short, to be relatively costless, a disinflation policy must be *credible* to the public.

In Sargent's view, as explained in Section 11.1, one requirement for a credible disinflation policy is that monetary restraint be accompanied by gaining control of the government budget deficit. Suppose the monetary authority tightens but fiscal policy is such that there are large current and prospective future deficits. Sargent believes that rational economic agents will predict that the monetary authority will reverse course in the future and increase money growth to help finance the deficits. Describing his own research on previous disinflation, Sargent concludes that "The theoretical doctrines and historical evidence...provide little reason for being optimistic about the efficacy of a plan for gradual monetary restraint which is simultaneously soft on the government deficit."[6] As can be seen from Table 11.1, the disinflation in the United States in the early 1980s was accompanied by rapidly growing deficits. Projections were for the deficit to grow even higher later on in the 1980s. Sargent and other new classical economists therefore would not have expected the tight monetary policy of 1980–81 to have reduced inflationary expectations quickly enough to produce a relatively costless disinflation.

---

[3] Ibid.

[4] Robert J. Gordon, "Using Monetary Control to Dampen the Business Cycle: A New Set of First Principles," p. 25. The Lucas–Sargent–Wallace proposition to which Gordon refers is the new classical policy ineffectiveness postulate explained in Section 11.1.

[5] Thomas Sargent, "Stopping Moderate Inflations: The Methods of Poincaré and Thatcher," p. 57.

[6] Ibid., p. 90.

The Extreme Informational Assumptions of Rational Expectations

Policy Makers have Info advantge

Keynesians accept the new classical economists' criticism of price expectations formulations which assume that economic agents use only information about past prices in making price forecasts. Such rules are naive because they assume that economic agents neglect other available and potentially useful information in making their forecasts. Such naive assumptions about expectations came into use in the 1950s and early 1960s when the inflation rate was both low and stable. In these circumstances such naive price-forecasting rules might have been reasonable approximations of the way people made forecasts, since good forecasts could in fact have been based on the past behavior of prices. With the volatile and often high inflation of the post-1970 period, it is harder to believe that economic agents did not find it worthwhile to make more sophisticated forecasts.

Still, many Keynesians argue that the rational expectations assumption errs in the direction of assuming that economic agents are unrealistically sophisticated forecasters, especially when rational expectations are assumed for the individual suppliers of labor. Keynesians criticize the assumption that individuals use *all* available relevant information in making their forecasts. Such an assumption ignores the costs of gathering information.

The rational expectations theory also presumes that individuals use available information intelligently. They know the relationships that link observed variables with the variables they are trying to predict. They are also able to estimate the systematic response pattern of policymakers. For example, if the monetary policymaker typically responds to rising unemployment by increasing the money stock, the public will come to anticipate such policy actions. They will also be able to predict the price effects of such anticipated monetary policy actions. Many Keynesians deny that individual labor suppliers possess such knowledge of both the working of the economy and the behavioral patterns of policymakers.

If the economy, including the behavior of policymakers, had been stable and subject to little change for a long period of time, it is perhaps not unreasonable to believe that economic agents would come to know the nature of the underlying relationships that govern policy variables and economic aggregates. The rational expectations assumption might be realistic in a long-run equilibrium model, but Keynesians argue that it is not realistic in the short run. In the short run the cost of gathering and processing information may be high enough that labor suppliers making forecasts of the aggregate price level or inflation rate do not find it worthwhile to use much information over and above the past behavior of prices. Keynesians do not make an unqualified defense of such naive rules and agree that more research is needed on expectations formation. Many Keynesians, however, given the current state of knowledge, regard such naive rules as better approximations than the rational expectations hypothesis.

If expectations are not rational, there is a role for aggregate demand management policy aimed at stabilizing output and employment. Even systematic changes in aggregate demand will affect output and employment in this case since they will not be predicted by economic agents. If private-sector aggregate demand is unstable, as Keynesians believe it is, a stabilization policy is needed. Further, the monetary and fiscal policymaking authorities can be assumed to be able to forecast systematic changes in private-sector aggregate demand. These policymaking authorities *do* gather what they consider to be all the available and important information on variables they wish to forecast and control. They also invest considerable resources in trying to estimate the relationships that characterize the economy. Keynesians regard the rational expectations assumption as reasonably correct when applied to the policymakers. The policymakers can design policy changes to offset what to the public are unanticipated changes in private-sector aggregate demand. Notice that these stabilization policies, *even though they are systematic,* do affect output and employment. Since the expectations of private-sector economic agents are not rational, the actions of the policymakers will not be anticipated. In essence this role for stabilization policy stems from an *information advantage* on the part of the policymaker.

Keynesians conclude that

> macroeconomic models based on the assumptions of the rational expectations hypothesis do not demonstrate the short-run ineffectiveness of policy, therefore, because they are not really short-run models. The information availability assumption of the rational expectations hypothesis implicitly places such models in a long-run equilibrium context in which their classical properties...are not surprising.[16]

In rebuttal, new classical economists have defended the rational expectations assumption. They admit that the rational expectations hypothesis is "unrealistic," but as Bennett McCallum argues, "All theories or models are 'unrealistic' in the sense of being extremely simplified descriptions of reality....So the true issue is: of all the simple expectational assumptions conceivable, which one should be embodied in a macroeconomic model to be used for stabilization analysis."[17] New classical economists favor the rational expectations assumption over formulations that assume that individuals form price expectations on the basis of the past history of prices because the rational expectations hypothesis is consistent with individual optimizing behavior—a property they feel all relationships in economic models should have.

---

[16]Benjamin Friedman, "Optimal Expectations and the Extreme Informational Assumptions of 'Rational Expectations' Macromodels," *Journal of Monetary Economics* (January 1979), pp. 39–40.

[17]This quotation is from McCallum's useful nontechnical exposition, "The Significance of Rational Expectations Theory," *Challenge Magazine* (January–February 1980), p. 39.

Auction Market Versus Contractual Views of the Labor Market

In the new classical view, as in the original classical theory, the money wage is assumed to adjust quickly to clear the labor market—to equate labor supply and demand. This is an *auction market* characterization. In contrast, in the Keynesian *contractual* view of the labor market "wages are not set to clear markets in the short run, but rather are strongly conditioned by longer-term considerations involving . . . employer–worker relations."[18] The money wage is sticky in the downward direction. In Arthur Okun's phrase, the labor market functions more by the *invisible handshake* than by the *invisible hand* of a competitive market mechanism. Most of the response to a decline in aggregate demand and, consequently, the demand for labor comes in the form of a reduction in employment rather than in a drop in the money wage. The reasons advanced by Keynesians to explain the downward rigidity of the money wage were discussed in Chapter 8. These include laborers' reluctance to accept money wage cuts that will be viewed by each group of workers as declines in their wages relative to other groups of workers. Also important are explicit and implicit contracts in the labor market that fix, or at least limit the flexibility of, the money wage over considerable periods of time.

The Keynesian view of the labor market is one in which long-term arrangements are made between buyers and sellers and, further, in which long-term relationships develop between *particular* buyers and sellers. Generally, the form of such relationships has been to fix the money wage paid to labor while leaving the employer free to adjust hours worked over the course of the explicit or implicit contract. Layoffs or hours reductions are considered an "acceptable" response on the part of the employer to a fall in demand. Applying pressure for wage cuts or replacing current workers with unemployed workers who will work for lower wages is not acceptable. This contractual Keynesian view of the labor market explains wage stickiness on the basis of the institutional mechanisms that characterize the labor market. Much work is currently under way to investigate the theoretical reasons for such labor market institutions to have developed. Even without such theoretical foundations, the Keynesians argue that institutional mechanisms of this nature *do exist,* and they criticize new classical economists for ignoring these elements of reality which their model cannot explain.

---

[18] Arthur Okun, *Price and Quantities* (Washington, D.C.: The Brookings Institution, 1981), extends this contractual view to product markets, with resulting price stickiness. New Keynesian models of this type are examined in Chapter 12.

New classical economists agree that the labor market is, at least in part, characterized by long-term contracts. They deny, however, that the existence of such contracts has, of itself, any implication for whether the labor market will clear—that is, for whether or not there will be involuntary unemployment. They deny that the terms of labor contracts are so rigid that employers and employees cannot effect changes that are desirable to both parties. For example, if the money wage specified is too high to maintain the market clearing level of employment, workers could give up other provisions in the contract, increase the work done per hour, or in extreme cases allow revision of the wage in some fashion. New classical economists would probably not deny that fixed-money-wage labor contracts cause some deviation of employment from the market clearing levels, but they do not believe this deviation is significant.

Read Perspectives 11.2.

11.4 • CONCLUSION

The new classical economics presents a very fundamental challenge to Keynesian orthodoxy. On the theoretical level new classical economists question the soundness of the Keynesian model, arguing that many of its relationships are not firmly based on individual optimizing behavior. As an example, new classical economists point to the naive treatment of price expectations in the Keynesian model. Further, they criticize what they consider arbitrary assumptions of Keynesians concerning wage stickiness and consequent involuntary unemployment.

New classical economists believe that useful macroeconomic models can be constructed by modifying the classical model, which they believe was based on individual optimizing behavior, to incorporate the rational expectations concept in place of the classical assumption of perfect information. With this change, they believe that the classical model is capable of explaining fluctuations in output and employment while retaining the assumption that markets clear.

On policy questions, new classical economists maintain that output and employment are independent of systematic and, therefore, anticipated changes in aggregate demand. This is the new classical policy ineffectiveness postulate. Since meaningful aggregate demand management policies to stabilize output and employment consist of such systematic changes in aggregate demand, new classical economists see no role for these policies. They arrive at noninterventionist policy conclusions similar to those of the original classical economists.

Keynesians criticize the new classical theory on several grounds. They argue that the new classical model cannot explain the prolonged and severe

PERSPECTIVES

11.2

The Great Depression: New Classical Views

The world Depression of the 1930s was such a pivotal event in the development of our thinking about macroeconomic questions that it is of interest to examine how each of the theories we consider explains this phenomenon. As we have seen, Keynesian economists do not believe that new classical economists can convincingly account for the Great Depression.

Let us examine what several leading proponents of the new classical view have had to say about the Depression. First, Robert Lucas:

> If you look back at the '29 to '33 episode, there were a lot of decisions made that, after the fact, people wished that they had not made. There were a lot of jobs people quit that they wished they had hung onto; there were job offers that people turned down because they thought the wage offer was crappy. Then three months later they wished they had grabbed. Accountants who lost their accounting jobs, passed over a cab driver job, and now they're sitting on the street while their pal's driving a cab. So they wish they'd taken the cab driver job. People are making this kind of mistake all the time. Anybody can look back over the '30's and think of decisions he could have taken to make a million. Stocks I would have bought. All kinds of things. I don't see what's *hard* about this question of people making mistakes in the business cycle.[1]

Lucas is pointing to misperceptions—unanticipated changes in prices—having real effects. Lucas sees unanticipated declines in the price level as the result of the sharp (unanticipated) decline in the money supply, as Milton Friedman suggests (see Perspectives 9.1).[2]

Robert Barro also sees monetary and other government policies as key factors in the 1929–33 experience: "The unprecedented monetary collapse over this period accords quantitatively with the drastic decline in economic activity."[3] In addition to the effects that the rapid decline in the money supply may have had, Barro points to a real (or supply-side) effect from the collapse of much of the banking system during this period. (Nine thousand banks failed between 1923 and 1933.) As banks failed, for example, crops might not be produced because farmers could not get loans to buy farm machinery. Generally, a decline in the availability of financial services may have reduced overall output supply in the 1929–33 period.[4]

As a further alternative to Keynesian explanations of the Depression, Barro suggests that "the government interventions associated with the New Deal, including the volume of public expenditures and direct price

[1] Arjo Klamer, *The New Classical Macroeconomics: Conversations with the New Classical Economists and Their Opponents* (Totowa, N.J.: Rowman and Allanheld, 1983), p. 41.

[2] Ibid., p. 42.

[3] Robert J. Barro, "Second Thoughts on Keynesian Economics," *American Economic Review,* 69 (May 1979), p. 58.

[4] Robert J. Barro, "Rational Expectations and Macroeconomics in 1984," *American Economic Review,* 74 (May 1984), p. 180.

regulations, retarded the recovery of the economy, which was nevertheless rapid after 1933."[5]

But both Barro and Lucas still find parts of the Depression phenomenon puzzling and would, at least in some respects, agree with new classical economist Thomas Sargent that

"I do not have a theory, nor do I know somebody else's theory that constitutes a satisfactory explanation of the Great Depression. It's really a very important, unexplained event and process, which I would be very interested in and would like to see explained.[6]"

[5]Robert J. Barro, "Second Thoughts on Keynesian Economics," p. 57.

[6]Arjo Klamer, *The New Classical Macroeconomics*, p. 69.

unemployment experienced by the United States and other industrialized countries. They claim that the rational expectations assumption ascribes an extreme and unrealistic availability of information to market participants. Finally, and most important, they criticize the auction market characterization of the labor market in the new classical model. Keynesians believe that the labor market is much more a contractual market and that the nature of these contractual arrangements leads to wage rigidities and consequent involuntary unemployment.

The new classical critique has, however, stimulated new avenues of Keynesian research on the causes of unemployment. The new Keynesian models emerging from this research effort are considered in the next chapter, in which we also examine the development of a second generation of new classical models—the so-called real business cycle models.

Review Questions and Problems

1. Explain the concept of *rational expectations*. How does this view of how expectations are formed differ from the assumption made in previous chapters that workers formed expectations of current and future price levels based on past information about prices?

2. Explain the implications of the rational expectations assumption for the effectiveness of economic stabilization policy.

3. Contrast the new classical and Keynesian views of the way in which labor markets function.

4. Within the new classical framework, how could you explain a sustained departure from high-employment output such as that experienced by the United States in the early 1990s?

5. Compare the new classical and monetarist positions concerning the usefulness and effectiveness of aggregate demand management policies to stabilize output.

6. Even within the new classical model, anticipated policy actions such as an increase in the money stock will affect *nominal* income. Explain why the adjustment of economic agents' expectations, which offsets the real effects of such a policy change, does not offset the nominal effects as well.

7. Why attach the adjective *new* to *classical* to describe the model in this chapter? How does this analysis differ from the classical model presented in Chapters 3 and 4?

8. Comment on the following statement. Do you agree or disagree with the view expressed concerning the effectiveness of systematic or anticipated fiscal policy actions within a new classical economic framework? Explain.

> The new classical economics or rational expectations theory provides a convincing explanation of the inability of systematic monetary policy to affect real income or employment. The situation is quite different, however, with fiscal policy actions such as increases in government spending, which will affect real output and employment whether they are anticipated or not—the difference between monetary and fiscal policy being that monetary policy affects aggregate demand and, hence, output by *inducing* private economic agents to change their demands for output. With rational expectations this effect will be offset. An increase in government spending affects aggregate demand directly and there is no way for the private sector to offset its effects on income and employment.

9. How would a supply shock such as the exogenous increase in the price of oil that was analyzed in Section 8.5 affect the aggregate price level and the level of real output in the new classical model?

Selected Readings

Attfield, C. L. F., Demery, D., and Duck, N. W., *Rational Expectations in Macroeconomics.* Oxford: Basil Blackwell, 2nd ed. 1991.

Blinder, Alan, "Keynes, Lucas and Scientific Progress," *American Economic Review,* 77 (May 1987), pp. 130–36.

Hoover, Kevin, *The New Classical Macroeconomics.* Oxford: Basil Blackwood, 1988.

Lucas, Robert, "Methods and Problems in Business Cycle Theory," *Journal of Money, Credit and Banking,* 12 (November 1980, Part 2), pp. 696–714.

Lucas, Robert, "Understanding Business Cycles," in Karl Brunner and Alan Meltzer, eds., *Stabilization of the Domestic and International Economy.* Amsterdam: North-Holland, 1977.

Lucas, Robert, and Sargent, Thomas, "After Keynesian Macroeconomics," in *After the Phillips Curve: Persistence of High Inflation and High Unemployment.* Boston: Federal Reserve Bank of Boston, 1978. See also the "Comment on Lucas–Sargent" by Benjamin Friedman and the "Summary and Evaluations" by Robert Solow and William Poole in this volume.

McCallum, Bennett, "The Significance of Rational Expectations Theory," *Challenge Magazine* (January–February 1980), pp. 37–43.

McCallum, Bennett, "Postwar Developments in Business Cycle Theory: A Moderately Classical Perspective," *Journal of Money, Credit and Banking,* 20 (August 1988, Part 2), pp. 460–71.

Okun, Arthur, *Prices and Quantities.* Washington, D.C.: The Brookings Institution, 1981.

Sargent, Thomas, and Wallace, Neil, "Rational Expectations and the Theory of Economic Policy," *Journal of Monetary Economics,* 2 (April 1976), pp. 169–83.

Solow, Robert, "On Theories of Unemployment," *American Economic Review,* 70 (March 1980), pp. 1–11.

Solow, Robert, "Alternative Approaches to Macroeconomic Theory," *Canadian Journal of Economics,* 12 (August 1979), pp. 339–54.

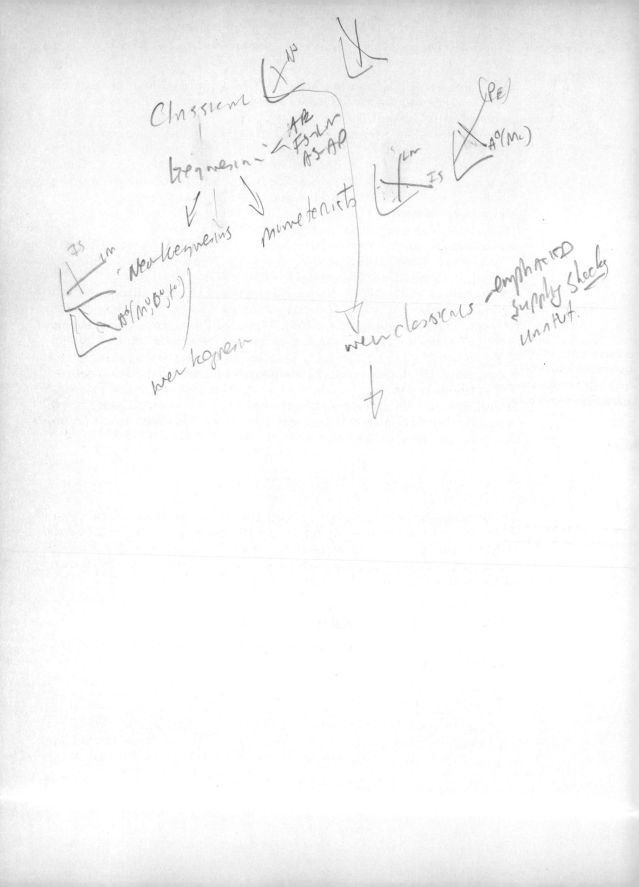

12 New Classical and New Keynesian Directions

Quick change in supply side (handwritten note)

The controversy between Keynesian and new classical economists spawned two new directions in macroeconomic research. One, very strongly rooted in the classical tradition, is the **real business cycle theory**. The second, the **new Keynesian theory**, as its name suggests, follows in the Keynesian tradition. Both are recent developments in macroeconomics, with research beginning only in the 1980s, and consequently, any evaluation of this literature is preliminary. Still, current research in both areas is active and deserves attention. The real business cycle theory is discussed in Section 12.1. We then turn to the new Keynesian theory in Section 12.2.

12.1 • REAL BUSINESS CYCLE MODELS

The real business cycle theory is an outgrowth of the new classical theory, which in turn built on the original classical economics. In fact, real business cycle models are sometimes referred to as the second generation of new classical models. Real business cycle models share several important features with new classical models.

Central Features of Real Business Cycle Models

Recall that new classical economists believe that useful macroeconomic models should have two characteristics:

1. agents optimize.
2. markets clear.

Real business cycle theorists agree. A hallmark of real business cycle models is the careful attention paid to the microeconomic foundations of the model—the individuals' optimizing decisions. Real business cycle theorists also believe

341

that the business cycle is an *equilibrium* phenomenon, in the sense that all markets clear. This contrasts with the Keynesian view that the labor market does not clear. The Keynesian model includes involuntary unemployment. In real business cycle models, as in new classical models, all unemployment is voluntary.

Where the real business cycle theorists part company with new classical economists is on the question of the causes of fluctuations in output and employment. Real business cycle theorists see these fluctuations as "arising from variations in the real opportunities of the private economy."[1] Factors that might cause such changes include shocks to technology, variations in environmental conditions, changes in the real (relative) prices of imported raw materials (e.g., crude oil), and changes in tax rates. Fluctuations in output would also occur with changes in individuals' preferences, for example, a change in the preference for goods relative to leisure. These are the same factors that determined output in the original classical model presented in Chapter 3. But the classical economists believed that for the most part these factors changed only slowly over time. In the short run they were taken as given.[2] They were the factors that would determine long-run growth in the model. The real business cycle theorists argue that these supply-side variables are also the source of short-run fluctuations in ouput and employment.

This view distinguishes the real business cycle theorists from new classical economists, who regarded unanticipated changes in aggregate demand, resulting, for instance, from "monetary surprises," as the main source of fluctuations in output and employment. Nothing in the new classical framework precludes an important role for supply-side variables, such as the oil price shocks of the 1970s or changes in tax rates, in the short run. Still, unanticipated changes in demand were viewed as the major source of cyclical fluctuations in output. Factors such as technology shocks or changes in individual preferences were not emphasized.

The view that changes in real supply-side factors determine short-run fluctuations in output and employment also differentiates real business cycle models from Keynesian models. As we saw in Chapter 8, Keynesian models can incorporate the effects of supply-side shocks, but it is a central tenet of the Keynesian theory that aggregate demand is an important factor in determining output and employment in the short run.

---

[1] Robert G. King and Charles Plosser, "Money Credit and Prices in a Real Business Cycle Model," *American Economic Review*, 74(June 1984), p. 363.

[2] Tax rates could, of course, change in the short run, with effects that we considered in Section 4.3. As noted there, however, classical economists gave little attention to the effect of changes in tax rates due to the low level of tax rates at the time they wrote.

Before we consider an example of a real business cycle model, there are two more general points to make. First is the question of why real business cycle theorists reject the new classical explanation of the source of short-run fluctuations in output, while in other respects the two approaches are so similar. One reason is that the empirical evidence on the role of unanticipated changes in aggregate demand in determining output is quite mixed. Probably more important, real business cycle theorists believe that the view that errors in predicting aggregate demand can explain large and costly fluctuations in output ultimately violates the postulate that agents optimize. As Robert Barro expresses this view, "If information about money and the general price level mattered much for economic decisions, people could expend relatively few resources to find out quickly about money and prices."[3] If they don't, they are not optimizing.

Finally, we should note that there are two possible interpretations of the real business cycle theory. One views it as proposing that real supply-side factors are simply more important than nominal demand-side influences. In this interpretation, however, real business cycle models are just versions of the new classical model which, as explained previously, can also incorporate supply-side shocks. When real business cycle theorists differentiate their models from new classical models such as the one considered in Chapter 11, they assert a much stronger position—that is, that monetary and other nominal demand-side shocks have *no* significant effect on output and employment. Many real business cycle models do not even include money as a variable.

A Simple Real Business Cycle Model

In the words of one of their developers,

> Real business cycle models view aggregate economic variables as the outcomes of the decisions made by many individual agents acting to maximize their utility subject to production possibilities and resource constraints. As such the models have an explicit and firm foundation in microeconomics.[4]

In this section we construct a simple model of this type. Having constructed the model, we consider how optimizing economic agents respond to changes

---

[3] Robert J. Barro, *Modern Business Cycle Theory* (Cambridge, Mass.: Harvard University Press, 1989), p. 2.

[4] Charles Plosser, "Understanding Real Business Cycles," *Journal of Economic Perspectives,* 3 (Summer 1989), p. 53.

in economic conditions and the implications of their actions for the behavior of aggregate economic variables.

A usual assumption in real business cycle models is that the economy is populated by a group of identical individuals. The behavior of the group can then be explained in terms of the behavior of one individual, called a *representative agent.* We will call the agent Robinson Crusoe.

Robinson's goal is to maximize his utility in each period of his life. He gets utility from two sources: consumption and leisure. We will assume that he has the following utility function (*U*):

$$U_t = U(c_t, le_t) \tag{12.1}$$

where *c* is consumption and *le* is leisure. To consume, Robinson must first work to produce output. In doing so he forgoes leisure. Thus, as in the earlier models we considered, there is a labor–leisure trade-off. Output in the model is generated by the production function

$$y_t = z_t F(K_t, N_t) \tag{12.2}$$

Equation (12.2) is similar to the aggregate production function in the original classical model discussed in Chapter 3. The production function specifies the amount of output (*y*) that will result from employing given amounts of capital (*K*) and labor (*N*) in time period *t*. There are, however, two differences between equation (12.2) and our earlier production function. Equation (12.2) contains the additional term z_t, which represents "shocks" to the production process. By shocks to the production process we mean events that change the level of output forthcoming for given levels of the labor and capital inputs. Real business cycle theorists include a number of factors in this category. Among the important ones are: shocks to technology, environmental factors, changes in government regulations that affect productivity, and changes in the availability of raw materials.

The second difference between equation (12.2) and our earlier version of the production function is the absence of a bar over the *K* in (12.2). In the real business cycle the capital stock is not taken as given but rather is chosen for each period by the representative agent, in a manner discussed presently.

Robinson does not have to consume all the output he produces each period. The young Robinson might want to save to provide for when he is an old Robinson or for a future generation of Crusoe Jrs. What is required is that

$$y_t = c_t + s_t \tag{12.3}$$

Saving (*s*) plus consumption (*c*) must equal income, ignoring the existence of taxes. Equation (12.3) indicates that in addition to a labor–leisure trade-off the representative agent faces a trade-off between consumption today and saving to increase future consumption. Saving today will increase consumption in the future because saving is assumed to be invested to increase the capital stock in the next period

$$K_{t+1} = s_t + (1 - \delta)K_t \qquad (12.4)$$

The capital stock in period $t + 1$ is equal to saving in period t plus the portion of the capital stock $(1 - \delta)$ left over from period t, where δ is the depreciation rate for capital (the fraction of the capital stock that wears out in each period).

In this representative agent framework, the behavior of aggregate output, employment, consumption, and saving are described in terms of the choices made by Robinson Crusoe. We now consider how those choices are affected by a change in the economic environment Robinson confronts.

Effects of a Positive Shock to Technology

Let us suppose that in a given time period there is a favorable shock to technology. For now we will assume that the shock is temporary, lasting only one period; later we will consider shocks that are more long-lived. This shock is assumed simply to occur exogenously and is represented in our model by a rise in the z_t term in equation (12.2), let us say from an initial level z_{0t} to a higher value z_{1t}. Given K_t and N_t, there is an exogenous rise in y_t.

The effect of this shock is illustrated in Figure 12.1. Initially, with z_t equal to z_{0t} the production function is given by $z_{0t}F(K_t, N_t)$. Let us suppose that, faced with this set of production possibilities, Robinson chooses N_0 as the optimum amount of work to perform, and as a result output is at y_0. The positive technology shock shifts the production function upward to $z_{1t}F(K_t, N_t)$. In addition to this upward shift, the nature of the shock is assumed to be such that the production function becomes steeper for any level of the labor input. Recall from Chapter 3 that the slope of the production function is the marginal product of labor—here Robinson Crusoe's labor. So we are assuming that the shock increases Robinson's productivity.

Even at the same level of labor input (N_0), this would cause a rise in output, to y_1' in the figure. The favorable shock has, however, changed the production possibilities facing Robinson. If he observes the change, which we will assume to be the case, he will react. In the figure we assume that he reacts to the increase in his productivity by working more. The level of the labor input rises to N_1 in Figure 12.1, and output rises to y_1.

Now Robinson must decide what to do with the increased level of output. Equation (12.3) tells us that the increase in output will go to consumption or saving. He could just consume it all. But particularly in the case of a temporary shock, it is likely that he will save a portion of the increase in output to allow consumption to also be higher throughout the future.

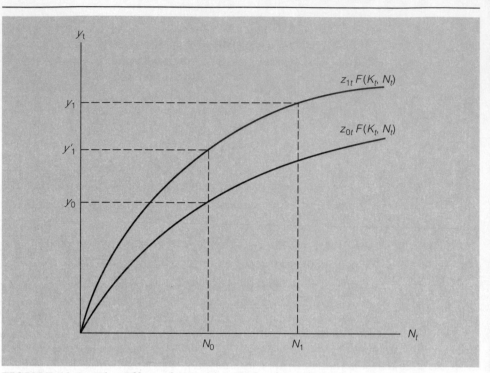

FIGURE 12.1 The Effect of a Positive Technology Shock in a Real Business Cycle Model

If this is the case, then equation (12.4) tells us that the higher saving, which in turn means higher investment, will cause the capital stock to be higher in the next period than it otherwise would be. Because of a higher capital stock, output in the next period as well as other future periods will also be higher than it would have been in the absence of the technology shock. This is true even though the *direct* effect of the shock lasted for only one period.

Had the shock lasted for a number of periods or been permanent in its effects, Robinson's responses would have been somewhat different. Since he would know that output would be high for a longer period, his incentive to save would be reduced and his incentive to consume increased. Also, since he would know his productivity would be higher for a number of periods, because of the direct effect of the shock, he might increase his work effort in each period by less. Long-lived productivity shocks will, however, also result in changes in output, the capital stock, and employment that persist for many periods.

It is important that the effects of technology shocks last for many periods. A key Keynesian criticism of the new classical model, which shares the equilibrium approach taken by the real business cycle theorists, is that it cannot explain the *persistence* of real world business cycles. Real business cycle theorists argue that the dynamic responses of optimizing agents to changes in economic conditions will, as just explained, have long-lasting effects. These responses can explain periods of persistently high or low economic activity.

We have focused on shocks to technology because they are central to real business cycle theorists' explanation of economic fluctuations. As noted earlier, however, other factors considered in real business cycle models include changes in environmental conditions, relative prices of raw materials, variations in tax rates, and changes in preferences. All these shocks are additional causes of cyclical movements in output and employment.

Macroeconomic Policy in a Real Business Cycle Model

In a real business cycle model, fluctuations arise from individuals' responses to changes in the economic environment. These responses are the result of optimizing behavior. In these models it would be suboptimal for policymakers to eliminate the business cycle if they could actually do so. What role is there then for macroeconomic policy in a real business cycle model? Let us start with monetary policy, then turn to fiscal policy.

Monetary Policy

The defining feature of real business cycle models is that real, not monetary factors are responsible for fluctuations in output and employment. As we mentioned earlier, many real business cycle models do not even include money as a variable and therefore have nothing to say about the way monetary policy should be conducted. In real business cycle models that do consider money, its role is to determine the price level, much the same as in the original classical model. Changes in the quantity of money result in proportionate changes in the price level with no change in output or employment.[5]

---

[5] Here we are considering a model in which all money is issued by the government: a world of only currency. Were we to consider bank deposits as well, the role of money in a real business cycle model becomes considerably more complex. This is because banks that issue deposits also provide credit and other services to firms. These services can affect the productivity of firms. Thus, changes in banking industry—bank failures, for example—can have real effects in a real business cycle model. It remains true, however, that changes in the quantity of money do not affect output and employment. For a real business cycle model that includes both currency and bank deposits, see Robert G. King and Charles Plosser, "Money, Credit and Prices in a Real Business Cycle Model."

It follows, then, that monetary policy should focus on control of the price level. One desirable monetary policy would be one that resulted in slow, steady growth in the money supply and thus stable prices, or at least a low rate of inflation. When we consider fiscal policy, however, we will see that an alternative view of the optimal conduct of monetary policy emerges from the real business cycle theory. In any case there is certainly no role for activist monetary stabilization policy of a Keynesian type. Monetary policy cannot affect output and employment, and even if it could it would be suboptimal to try to eliminate the business cycle.

Fiscal Policy

Many fiscal policy actions will affect output and employment in a real business cycle model. The effect will not be by means of an effect on nominal aggregate demand, as in the Keynesian model, but via supply-side effects. Changes in tax rates on labor income or the return to capital will affect the choices of optimizing agents. Moreover, these effects will be distortionary. A tax on labor income, for example, will cause an individual to choose too much leisure in relation to employment (with resulting consumption). Even a lump sum tax will affect individual behavior because it will affect wealth over the planning horizon.

The task of fiscal policy in the real business cycle framework is to minimize these tax distortions subject to providing needed government services (e.g., defense). This is where an alternative role for monetary policy emerges (alternative to simply keeping inflation low through slow, steady money growth). Recall from our previous discussion of the government budget constraint (Section 4.3) that an alternative to financing government spending by taxation is to finance it by printing money.[6] Policymakers can then reduce the distortion due to taxation by financing a portion of government spending with creation of new money. The term economists use for this is *seigniorage*—the government gets real resources through money creation. Seigniorage, however, also has costs since the faster the rate of growth in the money supply is, the higher will be the inflation rate. In the real business cycle model, it follows that the optimal use of monetary and fiscal policy is to combine them so as to minimize the total costs from inflation and tax distortion. This is far different from the Keynesian view of optimal monetary and fiscal *stabilization* policy.

---

[6]Borrowing from the public by the sale of government bonds is another way to pay for government spending. In real business cycle models, however, the government is constrained to repay all borrowing at some point. Thus bond sales can affect only the timing of taxation or money financing, not their amount.

Questions About Real Business Cycle Models

Real business cycles have been an active research area in recent years, but the approach is not without its critics. These critics argue that "real business cycle theory does not provide an empirically plausible explanation of economic fluctuations."[7] Critics have raised a number of issues concerning the realism of the real business cycle theory's explanation of economic fluctuations. We will consider two that appear to be central: the question of whether technology shocks are of sufficient magnitude to explain observed business cycles and the related question of whether observed changes in employment can actually be explained as the voluntary choices of economic agents facing changing production possibilities (or changing tastes).

The Importance of Technology Shocks

Critics of the real business cycle approach question whether there are shocks to technology that are large enough to cause economic fluctuations of the type and size we observe. First, these critics point out that many technology shocks are likely to be specific to individual industries. In any given year, while some industries might be experiencing negative shocks, others will have positive shocks. But in a real-world recession, for example, the decline in output is widespread across industries of very diverse structure. Although the critics do not deny that some technology shocks affect many industries (e.g., the information transmission revolution), they do not believe there are enough of these to explain recessions where output falls to as much as 10 percent below potential output.

Technology shocks are, of course, only one type of shock considered in the real business cycle theory—though they have received the most emphasis. Concerning the other shocks (and technology shocks as well) that are included in real business cycle models, critics do not argue that real supply-side shocks are unimportant, only that they are not all important. Many economists who do not accept the real business cycle explanation of economic fluctuations do believe that the sharp rise in the relative price of

---

[7]N. Gregory Mankiw, "Real Business Cycles: A New Keynesian Perspective," *Journal of Economic Perspectives*, 3(Summer 1989), p. 79. Additional surveys of the real business cycle literature, from a number of viewpoints, include Bennett T. McCallum, "Real Business Cycle Models," in Robert J. Barro, ed., *Modern Business Cycle Theory* (Cambridge, Mass.: Harvard University Press, 1989); Lawrence H. Summers, "Some Skeptical Observations on Real Business Cycle Theory," Federal Reserve Bank of Minneapolis *Quarterly Review*, 10(Fall 1986), pp. 23–27; Carl Walsh, "New Views of the Business Cycle: Has the Past Emphasis on Money Been Misplaced," Federal Reserve Bank of Philadelphia *Business Review* (January/February 1986), pp. 3–13; and Alan C. Stockman, "Real Business Cycle Theory: A Guide, an Evaluation and New Directions," Federal Reserve Bank of Cleveland *Economic Review*, 24(1988 Quarter 4), pp. 24–47.

PERSPECTIVES

LABOR MARKET
FLOWS

Critics of the real business cycle approach argue that the nature of labor market flows is inconsistent with a theory in which cyclical unemployment is voluntary. Figure 12.2 shows the share of total unemployment accounted for by job leavers and job losers for the years 1984–91. Job leavers are those who quit their jobs. These are the workers that would be classified as voluntarily unem-

ployed. Job losers are those who were laid off or fired.

Notice that during the long recovery following the 1981–82 recession the proportion of job losers fell and that of job leavers rose. This is consistent with a pattern: as economic activity picked up, layoffs fell, and as other job opportunities were created, the number of job quits rose. Then, in the recession that

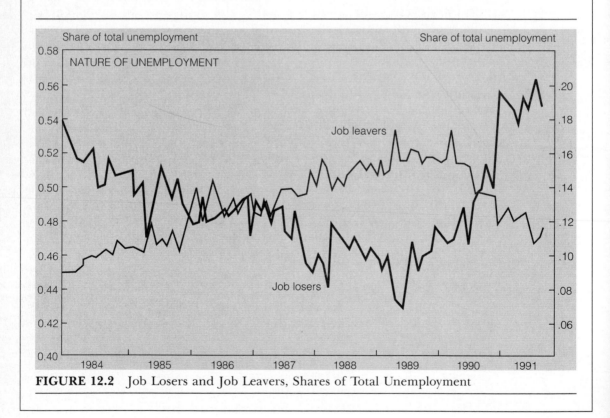

FIGURE 12.2 Job Losers and Job Leavers, Shares of Total Unemployment

began in 1990, the proportion of job losers rose sharply while fewer workers quit their jobs.

The pattern of labor market flows in Figure 12.2 is not, however, easily explained from a real business cycle perspective. If cyclical unemployment is voluntary, then job leavers should rise, not fall, during a recession. Moreover a real business cycle explanation of Figure 12.2 must somehow account for job losers. Did they voluntarily lose their jobs? On the face of it, these data seem more consistent with an explanation of cyclical unemployment as involuntary.

imported oil was the central cause of the deep recession in the United States and other industrialized nations in the mid-1970s. Other recessions, such as the one in the United States in the early 1980s, the critics believe are better explained by changes in aggregate demand—in this case by a restrictive Federal Reserve monetary policy.

Voluntary Employment Changes

In real business cycle models, changes in employment come as economic agents respond to changes in economic conditions. In our discussion of the effects of a positive shock to technology, we saw that the shock made Robinson Crusoe more productive and he responded by working more. Output rose because of both the direct effect of the shock and the increase in Crusoe's labor input. A negative technology shock would have the opposite effect— both output and employment would decline. In each case the changes in employment would be voluntary and desirable (agents are optimizing).

Another way of putting this is that individuals are moving along their labor supply curves in response to changes in their marginal productivity and, therefore, their real wage. This was the analysis of employment changes in the original classical model, presented in Chapter 3. Critics of the real business cycle approach argue that to explain real-world fluctuations in this manner requires an implausibly high response of labor supply to changes in the real wage—a very flat labor supply curve. This follows because, although swings in employment over the business cycle are large, changes in the real wage are small. Critics argue that studies show only small responses of hours worked to changes in the real wage (a steep labor supply curve).[8] They argue that the data are more consistent with the Keynesian explanation in which workers are assumed to be thrown off their labor supply curves; unemployment is involuntary.

Read Perspectives 12.1.

---

[8]See for example, Joseph G. Altongi, "Intertemporal Substitution in Labor Supply: Evidence from Micro Data," *Journal of Political Economy*, 94 (June 1986), Part 2, pp. S176–S215.

Concluding Comment

Real business cycle theorists remain convinced that the business cycle can be explained as an equilibrium phenomenon. Fluctuations in output come as optimizing economic agents respond to real shocks that affect production possibilities. Policies to try to prevent these fluctuations are unnecessary and misguided. Critics of the real business cycle approach, many of whom view the business cycle from a Keynesian perspective, find this explanation implausible. They see business cycles as the result of changes in nominal aggregate demand, as well as changes in real supply-side variables. Economists who view the business cycle from this Keynesian perspective believe that the policy prescription of the real business cycle theory wrongfully calls for inaction in the face of costly deviations from potential output.

12.2 • NEW KEYNESIAN ECONOMICS

Keynes wanted to explain the existence of involuntary unemployment—at times mass involuntary unemployment. He set out to show how aggregate demand affected output and employment. The Keynesian models we have considered can explain unemployment and a role for aggregate demand in determining output and employment. A key element in these models is money wage rigidity. A fall in aggregate commodity demand, for example, leads to a fall in labor demand. As a result of the existence of fixed-wage labor contracts and workers' backward-looking price expectations, the money wage will not fall sufficiently in the short run to maintain the initial employment level. Employment and output will fall. Unemployment will rise.

In recent years, economists working within the Keynesian tradition have pursued additional explanations of involuntary unemployment. The models emerging from this research effort are called *new Keynesian* models. In part, this new research is a response to the new classical critique of the older Keynesian models. N. Gregory Mankiw and David Romer, both of whom have made important contributions to the new Keynesian economics, state that "The new classical economists argued persuasively that Keynesian economics was theoretically inadequate, that macroeconomics must be built on a firm microeconomic foundation."[9] Perhaps not all new Keynesians are this critical of the earlier Keynesian models, but their main task has been to im-

---

[9]N. Gregory Mankiw and David Romer, eds., *New Keynesian Economics* (Cambridge, Mass.: MIT Press, 1991), p. 1. This two-volume collection of articles is a good sample of the new Keynesian research effort. An excellent critical survey of the new Keynesian literature is Robert J. Gordon, "What Is New Keynesian Economics," *Journal of Economic Literature*, 28(September 1990), pp. 1115–71.

prove the microeconomic foundations of the Keynesian system. Because they see wage and price rigidities as central to Keynes's explanation of involuntary unemployment, much effort has gone to show that these rigidities can arise from the behavior of optimizing agents; that is, they can be given a solid microeconomic basis.

New Keynesian economists have not tried to develop one rationale for all price and wage rigidities. Rather they believe that a number of features of the wage and price setting process explain such rigidities. In fact, the new Keynesian literature is characterized by what has been called a "dizzying diversity" of approaches. They have, however, the following common elements:

1. In new Keynesian models, some form of imperfect competition is assumed for the product market. This contrasts with the earlier Keynesian models which assumed perfect competition.

2. While the key nominal rigidity in earlier Keynesian models was that of the money wage, new Keynesian models also focus on product price rigidity.

3. In addition to factors that cause nominal variables (e.g., the money wage) to be rigid, new Keynesian models introduce real rigidities — factors that make the real wage or firm's relative price rigid in the face of changes in aggregate demand.

We consider three types of new Keynesian models: sticky price (menu cost) models, efficiency wage models, and insider–outsider models.

Sticky Price (Menu Cost) Models

As explained in the beginning of this section, earlier Keynesian models viewed the money wage as the variable which failed to adjust to changes in aggregate demand; output and employment had to adjust. The product market in those models was characterized by perfect competition. Keynesian economists did not necessarily believe that most real-world product markets were perfectly competitive. The assumption of perfect competition was made for simplicity and reflected the view that money wage rigidity was the real culprit in explaining unemployment.

A crucial element in new Keynesian **sticky price** models is that the firm must *not* be a perfect competitor.[10] With perfect competition, prices are simply set by the forces of supply and demand. Individual firms have no

---

[10]Sources for the models considered in this section(see suggested readings) include Mankiw (1985), Rotemberg (1987), and Akerloff and Yellen (1987).

power over their product price; they face horizontal demand schedules. The perfectly competitive firm, a dairy farm, for example, can sell all it wants to at the going market price of, say one dollar per gallon. If, due to a drop in aggregate demand, the market price declines to 80 cents per gallon, the firm can sell all it wants at this new price. If in the face of the fall in demand the perfectly competitive firm maintained its original product price, it would sell no output—no room for sticky prices here.

If, however, there is a monopolistic competitor or oligopolistic firm, the situation is different.[11] If La Residence, a Chapel Hill restaurant, did not lower prices in the face of a general fall in the demand for restaurant meals, it would lose some but not all its customers. Similarly, during a recession, when the demand for automobiles declines, Ford Motor Company can continue to sell cars even if its prices remain unchanged. Monopolistic competitors and oligopolies have some control over the price of their products. In fact, the incentive to lower prices may be fairly weak for these types or firms. If they hold to their initial price when demand falls, they will lose sales, but the sales they retain will still be at the relatively high initial price. Also, if all firms hold to the initial price, no individual firm will lose sales to its competitors.

Still, in the face of a fall in demand, the profit maximizing price will decline even for a firm in a setting of imperfect competition. Though the gain in profits from lowering price may be small, there is some gain. Why, then, might firms still not lower prices? Firms would hold product prices constant even as demand fell if there was a perceived cost to changing prices that outweighed the benefit of the price cut. Such costs of price changes are called *menu costs*. The name stems from the fact that if restaurants change prices, they must print new menus. More generally, when firms change prices, new price sheets must be made up and customers notified of the new prices. Such explicit costs of price changes by themselves may be too small to explain significant price stickiness, but there are possible additional, less direct costs of price changes.

One is potential loss of consumer goodwill. Of course consumer goodwill would be lost only through price increases, but firms that cut prices in recessions must raise them in recoveries. Firms may instead find it optimal to change prices when their costs change, the necessity of which customers will understand, but not to vary prices with changes in demand. They will thus

---

[11]Recall from microeconomics that monopolistic competition is a situation in which many firms provide differentiated products, for example, different types of food at different restaurants. Oligopoly refers to situations in which, due to substantial costs to enter the market, there are only a few firms. The product may be standarized or differentiated (e.g., aluminum or automobiles).

not be considered "price gougers" in periods of high demand and will not lower prices when demand falls off.

A second possible perceived cost of a price reduction in a recession is that it may set off competitive rounds of price cuts or even lead to a price war as other firms respond. This potential cost is most relevant for oligopolistic markets, where firms are cognizant of other firms' reactions to their pricing decisions.[12]

If these perceived costs or price changes are high enough, price stickiness will exist. Declines in aggregate demand will result in falls in output and employment, not simply price reductions. Of course, not all prices need to be sticky. As long as the number of industries in which prices are rigid constitutes a significant segment of the economy, the declines in output and employment may be substantial.

Efficiency Wage Models

In 1914 Henry Ford instituted the five-dollar day for his workers. At the time, the going competitive wage rate was between two and three dollars. Ford decided to pay this above-market wage because he thought it would discourage absenteeism, reduce turnover in Ford's labor force, and improve worker morale; productivity would therefore increase. Modern **efficiency wage** models have the same premise: the efficiency of workers depends positively on the real wage they are paid.[13]

The efficiency wage idea can be formalized by defining an index of worker efficiency, or productivity, (e) such that

$$e = e\left(\frac{W}{P}\right) \tag{12.5}$$

Worker efficiency is a positive function of the real wage. This being the case, we now write the aggregate production function as

$$y = F\left(\overline{K}, e\left(\frac{W}{P}\right)N\right) \tag{12.6}$$

---

[12] Proponents of sticky price models point to some real-world examples of price rigidity. The price of tin remained constant from 1929 to 1937 in spite of the Great Depression. *Reader's Digest* magazine changed its newsstand price only six times between 1950 and 1980. These examples are from Julio Rotemberg, "The New Keynesian Microfoundations," pp. 75–76.

[13] Ford's experiment with the five-dollar day is analyzed from the viewpoint of the modern efficiency wage theory in Daniel M. G. Ruff and Lawrence H. Summers, "Did Henry Ford Pay Efficiency Wages," *Journal of Labor Economics,* 5(October 1987, Part 2), pp. S57-S86. Readings on efficiency wage models (see selected readings) are Akerlof and Yellin (1986; 1987) and Katz (1988).

As before, output (y) depends on the amount of capital (K).[14] Output also depends on the amount of the labor input, which we now measure in efficiency units. The number of efficiency units of labor equals the number of physical units (N), measured in manhours per period, for example, multiplied by the index of efficiency. Output increases when either more units of labor are hired (N increases) or the efficiency of the existing labor force improves (e is increased by a rise in W/P).

With the production function as given by equation (12.6), the goal of the firm is to set the real wage so that the cost of an efficiency unit of labor is minimized or, to say the same thing in reverse, to maximize the number of efficiency units of labor bought with each dollar of the wage bill. This is accomplished by increasing the real wage to the point where the elasticity of the efficiency index ($e(W/P)$) with respect to the real wage is equal to 1.

Let's use an example to see why this is the case. First, recall that elasticity is the percentage change in one variable (here the efficiency of labor) per 1 percent change in another (here the real wage). So we are saying that the condition that determines the optimal level of the real wage, which in the literature is called the efficiency wage, $(W/P)^*$, is

$$\frac{\text{percentage change in } e\left(\dfrac{W}{P}\right)}{\text{percentage change in}\left(\dfrac{W}{P}\right)} = 1 \tag{12.7}$$

Suppose that, beginning at a low level, a 1 percent increase in the real wage leads to a 2 percent increase in the efficiency of labor. The firm will benefit from this increase because it will result in each dollar of the wage bill buying more efficiency units of labor. (Wage bill up 1 percent, number of efficiency units up 2 percent.) With further increases in the wage bill, efficiency gains begin to decline. At the point where a 1 percent increase in the real wage produces only a 1 percent increase in efficiency, the firm will not find it optimal to increase the real wage any further—the efficiency wage has been reached.[15]

Proponents of the efficiency wage theory argue that in many industries real wages are set on such efficiency grounds. Real wages do not adjust

---

[14] Here we have gone back to the specification of the aggregate production function in earlier chapters, where the stock of capital is fixed, as indicated by the bar over K. We also ignore the technology shock introduced in the previous section on real business cycle models and for simplicity omit the time (t) subscripts used earlier in the chapter.

[15] If, for example, the firm increases the real wage further to the point that a 1 percent increase in the real wage resulted in a 1/2 percent increase in efficiency, the number of efficiency units per dollar of the wage bill would have fallen.

to clear labor markets. In fact, the rationales that underlie efficiency wage models imply that firms will set the real wage *above* the market clearing level. Persistent, involuntary unemployment will result. Our next task is to examine these rationales for efficiency wages, some of which were anticipated by Henry Ford.

The key element in efficiency wage models is an explanation of why the efficiency (or productivity) of workers depends on the real wage—a rationale for equation (12.5) and thus for the way the labor argument appears in equation (12.6). Several rationales have been offered:

1. *The shirking model* By setting the real wage above going market levels (i.e., a worker's next best opportunity), a firm gives a worker an incentive not to shirk or loaf on the job. If he does, he may be fired, and he knows it would be hard to get another job at such a high wage. If firms can monitor job performance only imperfectly and with some cost, such a high-wage strategy may be profitable.

2. *Turnover cost models* By paying an above-market wage, firms can reduce quit rates and thus recruiting and training costs. The high wage also allows them to develop a more experienced, and therefore productive, workforce.

3. *Gift exchange models* Another rationale for efficiency depending on the real wage centers on the morale of a firm's workers. According to this argument, if the firm pays a real wage above the market clearing wage, this will improve morale and workers will put forth more effort. The firm pays the workers a *gift* of the above-market wage, and the workers reciprocate with higher efficiency.[16]

None of these rationales is intended to apply to all parts of the labor market. None, for example seems likely to apply to counter attendants at fast food restaurants. If, however, efficiency wage considerations are important and therefore real wage rates are set above market clearing levels in many sectors, substantial involuntary unemployment may result. Workers will continue to seek jobs in the high-wage sector, working, for example, when demand is high, rather than take low-paying jobs.

Notice that it is the real wage that is fixed on efficiency grounds (to meet condition (12.7)). Efficiency wage models explain a *real* rigidity. We have just seen how this real rigidity can explain involuntary unemployment. By itself, however, the rigidity of the *real* wage due to the payment of efficiency

---

[16] A different argument for the positive relationship between worker efficiency and the real wage is one more applicable to developing counties. A higher real wage allows for a higher consumption level, which provides better nutrition and health. These in turn reduce absenteeism and make workers more energetic and productive. An early model of this relationship is Harvey Leibenstein, "The Theory of Underemployment in Densely Populated Backward Areas," in *Economic Backwardness and Economic Growth* (New York: Wiley, 1963), though a similar argument can be found in the work of Alfred Marshall in the nineteenth century.

wages does not explain why changes in aggregate demand affect output and employment and therefore the level of involuntary unemployment. If there was a fall in nominal aggregate demand, resulting, for example, from a decline in the money supply, firms could lower their prices sufficiently to keep output (sales) unchanged and lower the *money* wage by the same amount to keep the real wage at the efficiency wage, $(W/P)^*$. If, however, firms do not lower prices because of menu costs, as explained in the previous section, then to keep the real wage at the efficiency wage requires the money wage also to be fixed. In this case, when aggregate demand declines, output and employment will fall and involuntary unemployment will rise. Thus, a combination of a nominal rigidity, the menu cost, and the real wage rigidity due to efficiency wages combine to explain changes in involuntary unemployment.

Insider–Outsider Models and Hysteresis

The last of the new directions in Keynesian research that we consider is the one most closely related to the persistent high unemployment rates in Europe since 1980 (see Table 10.2). Such persistent high unemployment contrasts sharply with the low unemployment rates for the same countries from the late 1950s to the early 1970s. These patterns have led to the hypothesis that unemployment at present is strongly influenced by past unemployment. Economies can, as it were, get stuck in *unemployment traps*. The term for this we used in Chapter 10 is *hysteresis*. A variable exhibits hysteresis if, when shocked away from an initial value, it shows no tendency to return even when the shock is over. In terms of unemployment, hysteresis models try to explain why high unemployment persists even after its initial cause is long past.

There are a number of explanations for hysteresis in the unemployment process. The discussion here is limited to one model that has received considerable attention—**the insider–outsider model**.[17] Rather than present the model formally, we will explain it with an example.

As with the sticky price model, versions of the insider–outsider model require imperfect competition. In the case of the insider–outsider model, it is assumed that both the product and the labor market are imperfectly competitive. So we will consider a situation with a labor union on the employee side and a few firms as employers; for example, the German steel industry. The union members, whom we will call *insiders*, are assumed to have bargain-

---

[17]An early version of the insider–outsider model is Olivier J. Blanchard and Lawrence Summers, "Hysteresis and the European Unemployment Problem," in Stanley Fischer, ed., *NBER Macroeconomics Annual* (Cambridge, Mass.: MIT Press, 1986). See also Assar Lindbeck and Dennis Snower, "Wage Setting Unemployment and Insider–Outsider Relations," *American Economic Review*, 76(May 1986), pp. 235–39; and Robert M. Solow, "Insiders and Outsiders in Wage Determination," *Scandinavian Journal of Economics*, 87(1985), pp. 411–28.

ing power with employers because it is costly to replace them with *outsiders* (nonunion members). The cost of replacing them is a recruiting and training cost for new workers. Union members may also impose costs on outsiders who attempt to underbid them for jobs, for example, by setting up picket lines.

The insiders are assumed to use their bargaining power to push the real wage above the market clearing level, resulting in an unemployed group of outsiders. Insiders will only push the real wage up to a certain point, however, because the higher the real wage, the fewer insiders will be employed. This follows because employment is equal to the firms' demand for labor, which depends negatively on the real wage. If in our example the insiders number 200,000, we will assume they bargain for a level of the real wage that they *believe* will result in all (or almost all) of them being employed. They may not, however, end up being employed, since if economywide aggregate demand slackens unexpectedly, output and employment will fall. A portion of the insiders will be laid off.

Thus, in the insider–outsider model unemployment results from a real wage set above the market clearing level (outsider unemployment) as well as from a cyclical response to changes in aggregate demand. A novel feature of these models is the interrelationship of these two types of unemployment.

To see this interrelationship, consider the effect of several prolonged recessions such as those in the 1970s and early 1980s. During the recessions some layoffs are permanent, and some workers drift out of the union. *Some insiders become outsiders.* Exactly how quickly this happens depends on union rules. With the pool of insiders reduced, let us say to 160,000 workers, when an economic recovery takes place, the union will bargain for a higher real wage than previously (before the recessions when there were 200,000 insiders). There are now fewer insiders whose employment prospects matter. (Notice here the assumption that insiders are unconcerned about outsiders.) With a higher real wage, employment will remain lower than in the prerecession period.

Past unemployment, then, causes current unemployment by turning insiders into outsiders; this is the hysteresis phenomenon. Once this has happened, a sort of unemployment trap occurs. The outsiders do not exert downward pressure on real wages because they are irrelevant to the wage-bargaining process.[18] Insider–outsider models thus explain why high

---

[18] There are extensions of the basic insider–outsider model, in which the unemployed outsiders do have some influence on the wage bargain. In these extended models, the higher the rate of unemployment, the less bargaining power the insiders are able to exert. This is because their fear of becoming unemployed is greater, since they know their prospect of finding another job is poorer, and the employers' threat to replace them with unemployed workers is more credible. In these extended models, however, there is still persistent unemployment. See the discussion in Oliver J. Blanchard, "Wage Bargaining and Unemployment Persistence," *Journal of Money, Credit, and Banking,* 23(August 1991), pp. 278–92.

unemployment has persisted in some European countries for such long periods—periods too long to be the result of fixed money-wage contracts or backward-looking price expectations.

12.3 • CONCLUSION

Real business cycle theory and the new Keynesian economics are extensions of two conflicting traditions in macroeconomics. The real business cycle theory is a modern version of the classical economics. The business cycle is an equilibrium phenomenon. It is the result of the actions of optimizing agents in the face of changes in the economic environment (e.g., productivity shocks) or in preferences. Macroeconomic stabilization policies are counterproductive. The real business cycle theorists therefore reach noninterventionist policy conclusions, as did the original classical economists.

The new Keynesian economics is set firmly in the diametrically opposed tradition of John Maynard Keynes. New Keynesian economists believe that much unemployment is involuntary. They believe that the deviations of output below potential output during recessions are socially costly. There is a potential role for stabilization policy in preventing such output shortfalls and alleviating the additional personal costs of involuntary unemployment. The new Keynesian economics is an attempt to improve the microeconomic foundations of the traditional Keynesian models, not to challenge their major premises.

We have looked at some criticisms of the real business cycle explanation of economic fluctuations. New Keynesian economics also has its critics. Some doubt that menu costs, efficiency wage considerations, or bargaining models are of much substantive importance in the real world. The challenge to the new Keynesian economists is to provide empirical support for their theoretical models. A large research effort with this aim is underway. A similarly large research effort on the part of real business cycle theorists is attempting to show that their model can explain real-world business cycles.

Review Questions and Problems

1. Compare the real business cycle theorists' view of the causes of fluctuations of output and employment with the view of new classical economists.

2. Within the simple real business cycle model presented in Section 12.1, analyze the effect of a negative shock to technology (a negative shock to z_t) that lasts for one period.

3. Explain the real business cycle theorists' views on the proper conduct of monetary and fiscal policy.

4. Suppose there was a change in preferences in a real business cycle model such that the representative agent valued leisure more and consumption goods less. How would output and employment be affected by the change?

5. Explain why the assumption of imperfect competition is important within each of the new Keynesian models considered in Section 12.2.

6. Suppose that you observe in wage data that workers with identical skills are paid very different wage rates in different industries. Is this consistent with the assumption that the labor market is competitive? Is it consistent with the efficiency wage model?

7. Explain how the insider–outsider model accounts for the persistent high unemployment in a number of European countries during the post-1980 period.

8. New classical economists believe that useful macroeconomic models are those where (1) agents optimize and (2) markets clear. Do the models that emerge from the new Keynesian research effort have either or both of these properties? Explain.

9. Explain the relationship of the new Keynesian models to the Keynesian models we considered in Chapters 5 through 8.

Selected Readings

Real Business Cycle Models

Attfield, C.L.F., Demery, D., and Duck, N., *Rational Expectations in Macroeconomics*, 2nd ed. Oxford: Basil Blackwell, 1991, Chap. 8.

King, Robert G., and Plosser, Charles I., "Money, Credit and Prices in a Real Business Cycle Model," *American Economic Review,* 74 (June 1984), pp. 363–80.

Kydland, Finn E., and Prescott, Edward C., "Business Cycles: Real Facts and a Monetary Myth," Federal Reserve Bank of Minneapolis *Quarterly Review,* 14 (Spring 1990), pp. 3–18.

McCallum, Bennett T., "Real Business Cycle Models," in Robert J. Barro, ed., *Modern Business Cycle Theory*. Cambridge, Mass.: Harvard University Press, 1989.

Mankiw, N. Gregory, "Real Business Cycles: A New Keynesian Perspective," *Journal of Economic Perspectives,* 3(Summer 1989), pp. 79–90.

Plosser, Charles, "Understanding Real Business Cycles," *Journal of Economic Perspectives,* 3(Summary 1989), pp. 51–77.

Rush, Mark, "Real Business Cycles," Federal Reserve Bank of Kansas City *Review,* 72(February 1987), pp. 20–32.

Stockman, Alan C., "Real Business Cycle Theory: A Guide, an Evaluation and New Directions," Federal Reserve Bank of Cleveland *Economic Review,* 24(1988 Quarter 4), pp. 24–47.

Summers, Lawrence H., "Some Skeptical Observations on Real Business Cycle Theory," Federal Reserve Bank of Minneapolis *Quarterly Review,* 10(Fall 1986), pp. 23–27.

Walsh, Carl, "New Views of the Business Cycle: Has Past Emphasis on Money Been Misplaced," Federal Reserve Bank of Philadelphia *Business Review* (January/February 1986), pp. 3–13.

New Keynesian Economics

Akerlof, George, and Yellin, Janet, *Efficiency Wage Models of the Labor Market,* New York: Cambridge University Press, 1986.

Akerlof, George, and Yellin, Janet, "Rational Models of Irrational Behavior," *American Economic Review,* 77 (May 1987), pp. 137–42.

Ball, Laurence, Mankiw, N. Gregory, and Romer, David, "The New Keynesian Economics and Output Inflation Tradeoff," *Brookings Papers on Economic Activity,* 1(1988), pp. 1–65.

Blanchard, Olivier J., "Why Does Money Affect Output: A Survey," in Frank H. Hahn and Benjamin M. Friedman, eds., *Handbook in Monetary Economics,* Vol. 2. Amsterdam: North Holland, 1990.

Blanchard, Olivier J., "Wage Bargaining and Unemployment Persistence," *Journal of Money, Credit and Banking,* 23(August 1991), pp. 277–92.

Blanchard, Olivier J., and Summers, Lawrence H., "Hysteresis and the European Unemployment Problem," in Stanley Fischer, ed., *NBER Macroeconomics Annual.* Cambridge, Mass.: MIT Press, 1986.

Gordon, Robert J., "What Is New Keynesian Economics?," *Journal of Economic Literature,* 28 (September 1990), pp. 1115–71.

Katz, Lawrence, "Some Recent Developments in Labor Economics and Their Implications for Macroeconomics," *Journal of Money, Credit and Banking,* 20(August 1988, Part 2), pp. 507–22.

Mankiw, N. Gregory, "Small Menu Costs and Large Business Cycles: A Macroeconomic Model of Monopoly," *Quarterly Journal of Economics,* 100 (May 1985), pp. 529–38.

Mankiw, N. Gregory, and Romer, David, *New Keynesian Economics,* Vols. 1 and 2. Cambridge, Mass.: MIT Press, 1991.

Okun, Arthur, *Prices and Quantities.* Washington D.C.: The Brookings Institution, 1981.

Rotemberg, Julio J., "The New Keynesian Microfoundations," in Stanley Fischer, ed., *NBER Macroeconomics Annual.* Cambridge, Mass.: MIT Press, 1987.

13 Macroeconomic Models: A Summary

We have now completed our analysis of the major schools of macroeconomic theory. The original classical macroeconomic model was presented. Then the Keynesian attack on the classical economics was discussed. The Keynesian macroeconomic model, which dominated macroeconomic analysis from the early post–World War II era until the late 1960s, was considered in detail. Next, we analyzed challenges to the Keynesian orthodoxy by the monetarists and new classical economists. Finally, we examined two very recent lines of research on macroeconomic fluctuations: real business cycle models and the new Keynesian economics.

This chapter gives an overview of the theories considered in earlier chapters, with an attempt to clarify areas of agreement and controversy among these various schools of macroeconomic theory.

13.1 • THEORETICAL ISSUES

It is again convenient to center our discussion on the aggregate supply–aggregate demand framework we have used to characterize the various economic models. The first of the models we considered, the classical model, views output as completely determined by supply factors. This view is embodied in the *vertical aggregate supply schedule* shown in Figure 13.1*a*.

Central to the classical theory of output and employment are the classical labor market assumptions. Both labor supply and demand depend only on the real wage, which is known to all market participants. The money wage is perfectly flexible and moves to equate demand and supply in the labor market. Increases in aggregate demand cause prices to rise which, other things being equal, is a spur to production. To clear the labor market, however, the

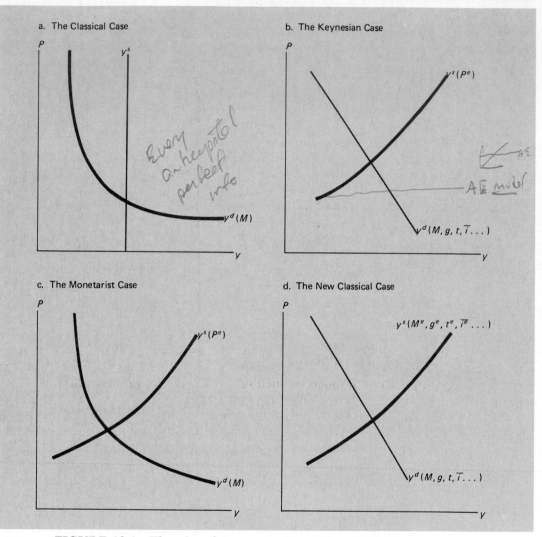

FIGURE 13.1   Theories of Aggregate Demand and Supply

money wage has to rise proportionately with the price level. The real wage is then unchanged, and consequently the levels of employment and output are unchanged in the new equilibrium.

In the classical system, then, the role of aggregate demand is to determine the price level. The classical theory of aggregate demand is an implicit theory based on the quantity theory of money. The quantity theory provides a proportional relationship between the exogenous quantity of money and the level of nominal income. In the Cambridge form this relationship is

$$M = kPy \tag{13.1}$$

With k treated as a constant, changes in the quantity of money result in proportional changes in nominal income (Py). With real income (y) fixed, the full adjustment comes in the level of prices.

This relationship provides the classical aggregate demand schedule drawn in Figure 13.1a. The economic process behind this theory of aggregate demand is that if, for example, there is an excess supply of money ($M > kPy$), a corresponding excess demand for commodities will drive up the aggregate price level. Equilibrium between money demand and supply implies that there is no spillover to the commodity market causing a change in the price level. The classical model has *a monetary theory of aggregate demand.*

The real business cycle theory is a modern version of the classical theory. As in the classical model, output and employment in the real business cycle model are determined completely by real supply-side variables. The labor market is always in equilibrium; all unemployment is voluntary. The role of money in the real business cycle model, again as in the classical model, is solely to determine the price level.

In its simplest and most extreme form, the Keynesian model is the antithesis of the classical theory. In a simple Keynesian model, such as that discussed in Chapter 5, supply plays no role in output determination. The aggregate supply curve implied by such simple Keynesian models would be horizontal, indicating that supply is no constraint on the level of production, an assumption appropriate, if ever, only to situations where production is well below capacity levels. On the demand side, the simple Keynesian model (again see Chapter 5) concentrates on the determinants of autonomous expenditures: government spending, taxes, and autonomous investment demand. Monetary factors are neglected. This simple model highlights a central notion in Keynesian economics, the importance of aggregate demand in determining output and employment.

But this simple Keynesian model is an incomplete representation of Keynes's work. Additionally, the Keynesian theory has been modified and refined over the period since Keynes wrote. The modern Keynesian model allows for the influence of both supply factors on output and monetary factors on aggregate demand. Still, the model remains "Keynesian" in that aggregate demand is important in determining the level of output.

On the supply side, the Keynesian view is illustrated by the aggregate supply schedule shown in Figure 13.1b. In contrast to the vertical classical supply curve, the Keynesian aggregate supply function slopes upward to the right. Increases in aggregate demand that shift the aggregate demand schedule out to the right will increase both price and output. In the short run, an increase in the price level will cause firms to supply a higher level of output because the money wage will not rise proportionately with price.

The money wage is assumed to adjust only incompletely as a result of institutional factors in the labor market, the most important being fixed-money wage contracts, as well as labor suppliers' imperfect information about the aggregate price level and, hence, about the real wage. Much of the research effort of the new Keynesian economists is directed toward providing additional rationales for wage and also price stickiness—toward improving the microeconomic foundation of the Keynesian aggregate supply function in Figure 13.1.

On the demand side (the y^d schedule in Figure 13.1b) the modern Keynesian model provides a role for monetary factors (M) as well as fiscal policy variables (g and t) and other autonomous elements of aggregate demand (e.g., autonomous investment, $\bar{\imath}$). The Keynesian theory of aggregate demand is an *explicit* theory, in contrast to the *implicit* theory of the classical economists, in that the level of aggregate demand is found by first determining the level of the components of aggregate demand: consumption, investment, and government spending. Then we sum these to find aggregate demand. Money affects aggregate demand, primarily the investment component of aggregate demand, by influencing the level of the interest rate. There is no reason to believe that such monetary effects on aggregate demand are small. Neither is there reason to believe that monetary influences are dominant. Money is one of several important influences on aggregate demand in the Keynesian system.

There are, thus, two important differences between the Keynesian and classical frameworks.

1. In the classical model output and employment are completely supply-determined, whereas in the Keynesian theory in the short run, output and employment are determined jointly by aggregate supply and demand. In the Keynesian system, aggregate demand is an important determinant of output and employment.
2. Aggregate demand in the classical model is determined solely by the quantity of money. In the Keynesian system, money is one of a number of factors that determine aggregate demand.

These two issues, the role of aggregate demand in determining output and employment and the relative importance of monetary and other factors as determinants of aggregate demand, are also the ones that divide the Keynesians from the monetarist and the new classical economists.

The major controversy between monetarists, whose view of aggregate supply and demand is represented in Figure 13.1c, and Keynesians has centered on point 2, the degree to which monetary forces dominate the determination of aggregate demand. Monetarists have taken the Cambridge version of the quantity equation [equation (13.1)] as the basis for their own strong quantity theory view that money is the dominant influence on aggregate demand and, therefore, nominal income.

On the supply side there is no fundamental difference between the monetarist and the Keynesian theories. In both monetarist and Keynesian models, the aggregate supply schedule slopes upward to the right in the short run and approaches the vertical classical formulation only in the long run. In both models changes in aggregate demand will affect output in the short run. But agreement on this issue has not kept monetarists and Keynesians from reaching substantially different conclusions about the usefulness of aggregate demand management policies to stabilize output and employment in the short run.

The new classical view of the determination of aggregate supply and demand is illustrated in Figure 13.1d. The issue dividing new classical economists and Keynesians concerns point 1, the degree to which aggregate demand plays a role in determining the level of real output. New classical economists believe that systematic and, therefore, predictable changes in aggregate demand will not affect the level of real output. Such changes will be anticipated by rational economic agents. The aggregate demand curve and the aggregate supply schedule will shift symmetrically, changing the price level but leaving real output unchanged. To reflect this dependence of the aggregate supply schedule on expected changes in the determinants of aggregate demand and consequently the rational expectation of the price level, the aggregate supply schedule in Figure 13.1d is shown as depending on the expected level of the money stock (M^e) as well as expected values of fiscal policy variables and other possible determinants of aggregate demand (g^e, t^e, $\bar{i}^{re}$, . . .).

Unanticipated changes in aggregate demand—for example, an increase in the money stock (M) that could not have been predicted (M^e is unchanged)—will shift the aggregate demand curve without shifting the aggregate supply schedule. Such unanticipated changes in aggregate demand will cause labor suppliers to make price forecast errors and will therefore affect output and employment. In this respect the new classical model is a modification of the original classical model, in which there was *no* role for aggregate demand in determining output and employment. The modification is the substitution of the rational expectations assumption in the new classical analysis for the classical assumption of perfect information. In the classical analysis there were no price forecast errors on the part of labor suppliers. Labor suppliers and demanders both had perfect information about the price level. In effect, there were assumed to be no unanticipated shifts in aggregate demand.

On the demand side, there is no clear difference between the new classical and Keynesian positions (compare the y^d schedules in Figures 13.1b and d). Differences may emerge as more work is done to develop a complete new classical model, since, as we have seen, the new classical economists do not believe that the Keynesian theory of aggregate demand is based on a sound choice theoretic basis. Note also that there is no reason why a new classical economist might not take a monetarist position on the determinants of aggregate demand.

From the foregoing it should be clear that the monetarist–Keynesian dispute and the Keynesian–new classical dispute revolve around the same issues that separate Keynesians from classical economists and real business cycle theorists. The Keynesian revolution was an attack on the classical supply-determined, full-employment theory of output and employment, as well as on the quantity theory of money. New classical economists and monetarists have modified these two aspects of classical economics and have used these modified versions of the classical model to attack the Keynesian system. The two issues listed as points 1 and 2, which in terms of Figure 13.1 concern the slope of the short-run aggregate supply function and the determinants of the position of the aggregate demand function, have been the central issues in the macroeconomic controversies of the past 60 years.

13.2 • POLICY ISSUES

Given the classical roots of the real business cycle, monetarist, and new classical theories, it is not surprising that these modern theories share the non-interventionist policy conclusions of the original classical model. In contrast, Keynesians are policy interventionists who favor aggregate demand management to stabilize output and employment.

In the classical system, output and employment are self-adjusting to the supply-determined level of full employment. There is clearly no role for interventionist aggregate demand stabilization policies. This is also the case in real business cycle models, where any fluctuations in output and employment result from optimal responses of economic agents to changes in the economic environment. In the new classical model, unanticipated shifts in aggregate demand do affect output and employment. Sensible stabilization policies, however, would have to consist of systematic reaction patterns to the state of the economy. Such systematic shifts in aggregate demand would be anticipated by the public and, therefore, would not affect output or employment. Consequently, new classical economists also view aggregate demand stabilization policies as ineffective.

Monetarists believe that *monetary* policy actions, whether anticipated or not, affect output and employment in the short run. Still, they arrive at the same noninterventionist policy conclusions as the classical and new classical economists. Like classical economists, monetarists believe that the private sector is stable if left free from destabilizing government policy actions. Further, since in the monetarist view aggregate demand is determined predominantly by the money stock, the best way to stabilize aggregate demand is to provide stable growth in the money stock. Rather than interventionist stabilization policies, monetarists favor a constant growth rate or other simple rule for the money stock.

Ranged against this noninterventionist view is the Keynesian position that a private-enterprise monetary economy is unstable in the absence of government policies to regulate aggregate demand. Keynesians favor activist monetary and fiscal policies to offset shocks to private aggregate demand. In years when substantial unfavorable supply shocks to the economy have occurred, Keynesians have favored the use of aggregate demand policies to try to offset the output and employment effects of these shocks as well.

Thus, although we have considered several different schools of macroeconomic theory, on the major policy issue the controversy is between two positions—the noninterventionist position, with roots in the original classical system, and the Keynesian interventionist position. On this policy issue, as with the theoretical issues discussed previously, the controversy is a long-standing one. In modern form it extends back over the 60 years since the Keynesian attack on the classical orthodoxy. But there were heretics before Keynes, and the origins of the policy and theoretical controversies discussed here date back to the early 1800s.

How can such controversies proceed for so long without resolution? In economics we have no opportunity for controlled laboratory experiments aimed at settling such controversies. We cannot, for example, construct an economy, let the money stock grow for 10 years at a constant rate, and then see if the monetarist predictions are verified. As Milton Friedman has written on this issue of why economists disagree,

> Controlled experiments permitting near isolation of one or a few forces are virtually impossible. We must test our propositions by observing uncontrolled experience that involves a large number of people, numerous economic variables, frequent changes in other circumstances, and, at that, is imperfectly recorded. The interpretation of the experience is further complicated because the experience affects directly many of the observers, often giving them reasons, irrelevant

from a scientific view, to prefer one rather than another interpretation of the complex and ever-changing course of events.[1]

Or as Keynes wrote earlier, "In economics you cannot *convict* your opponent of error—you can only convince him of it." [2]

Failure to resolve the continuing controversies in macroeconomics is unsettling even if it is not surprising. This failure contributes to the popular (mis?) conception of macroeconomists as a quarrelsome group, who must not know all that much if they can agree on so little. This and preceding chapters in Part II present areas of agreement as well as controversy. An attempt has been made to show that the controversies center on well-defined issues based in theoretical differences in the underlying models. Still, the student of macroeconomics is left with the choice of which view of the macroeconomy he or she finds to be the most plausible.

Review Questions and Problems

1. Suppose that investment demand in a given economy is predicted to be weak next year, let us say 10 percent below this year's level, because of an exogenous shock. All other components of aggregate demand are predicted to be at levels comparable to this year's. These levels were consistent with high employment and relatively stable prices. For each of the following macroeconomic systems, explain the effects of this exogenous fall in aggregate demand and explain the proper policy response implied by the model; that is, what action should the policymaker take?

  a. The classical model.
  b. The Keynesian model.
  c. The monetarist model.
  d. The new classical model.

2. The question of what information market participants possess at any point in time and how quickly they learn—what can be termed the information structure of the model—is a distinguishing feature of the different macroeconomic systems we dealt with. With reference to the classical, Keynesian, monetarist, and new classical models, explain the differing assumptions about the information that market participants possess and the degree to which these

---

[1]Milton Friedman, "Why Economists Disagree," in Milton Friedman, *Dollars and Deficits* (Englewood Cliffs, N.J.: Prentice Hall, 1968), pp. 15–16.

[2]Quoted from, Paul Davidson, *Money and the Real World* (New York: Wiley, 1978), p. ix.

differing assumptions account for the different policy conclusions one derives from these models.

3. Within the classical, real business cycle, Keynesian, monetarist, and new classical models, analyze the effect of an autonomous fall in the price of imported oil. Explain the effect of this change on output employment and the aggregate price level within each framework.

4. Which of the frameworks that we have considered do you view as the most useful in explaining the behavior of the economy and providing proper policy prescriptions? Defend your choice.

III Extensions of the Models

The chapters in Part III consider refinements and extensions of the models in Part II. We begin in Chapter 14 with a further examination of the determinants of the private sector's demand for output: consumption spending and investment spending. In Chapters 15 and 16 we take a more detailed look at money demand and money supply. Chapter 17 extends our previous models to analyze a long-run horizon. In this chapter we also consider economic growth over intermediate-run periods of perhaps a decade.

14 Consumption and Investment

I n this chapter we look in detail at the private sector's demand for output. First we consider household consumption (Section 14.1). Then we turn to investment (Section 14.2), which consists of fixed business investment, residential construction expenditures, and the change in business inventories. Under the heading of investment we also discuss purchases of consumer durable goods—a type of investment by households.

14.1 • CONSUMPTION

Early Empirical Evidence on the Keynesian Consumption Function

Household consumption expenditures account for approximately two thirds of gross national product. In Part II we saw that the consumption to income relationship—the consumption function—is a key element in the Keynesian theory of income determination. The starting point for Keynes's theory of consumer behavior is the following concept:

> The fundamental psychological law, upon which we are entitled to depend with great confidence both *a priori* from our knowledge of human nature and from the detailed facts of experience; is that men are disposed, as a rule and on the average, to increase their consumption as their income increases, but not by as much as the increase in their income.[1]

---

[1] John M. Keynes, *The General Theory of Employment, Interest and Money* (New York: Harcourt, Brace and Company, Inc., 1936), p. 96.

This psychological law translates into the Keynesian consumption function:

$$C = a + bY_D \qquad a > 0, \quad 0 < b < 1 \tag{14.1}$$

where C is real consumption and Y_D is real disposable income, which equals real GNP minus taxes. The parameter b is the marginal propensity to consume (MPC), which measures the increase in consumption per unit increase in disposable income ($\Delta C / \Delta Y_D$). The *intercept, a,* measures consumption at a zero level of disposable income. The consumption function (14.1) is shown graphically in Figure 14.1.

Because of the intercept, the Keynesian consumption function is not a proportional relationship between consumption and income; that is, consumption is not a constant fraction of disposable income. The ratio of consumption to income is termed the *average propensity to consume,* APC, which from equation (14.1) can be seen to be given by

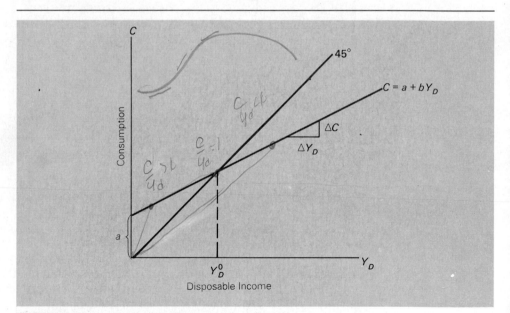

FIGURE 14.1 Keynesian Consumption Function
The Keynesian consumption function shows consumption as a function of disposable income. The intercept (a) gives the level of consumption corresponding to a zero level of disposable income. The slope of the consumption function (b) is the marginal propensity to consume ($\Delta C / \Delta Y_D$).

$$APC = \frac{C}{Y_D} = \frac{a}{Y_D} + b \tag{14.2}$$

The APC is greater than the MPC, by the amount a/Y_D. It also follows from equation (14.2) that the APC declines as the level of income increases. This implies that as income rises, households consume a smaller fraction of income, which is to say that they save a larger fraction of income. The ratio of saving to income is termed the *average propensity to save* (APS) and is equal to $(1 - APC)$, or

$$APS = 1 - \frac{a}{Y_D} - b = \frac{-a}{Y_D} + (1 - b) \tag{14.3}$$

which can be seen to increase as disposable income rises. In Figure 14.1, below the income level Y_D^0, consumption exceeds disposable income. In this range the APC is greater than 1 and the APS is negative. Above the income level Y_D^0, the APC is less than 1 and the APS is positive. Total consumption increases less than proportionately with Y_D, so the APC declines and the APS rises as we move to higher-income levels in the graph.

The version of the consumption function just described has been called the *absolute income hypothesis*; consumption is assumed to react rather mechanically to actual current levels of income. Keynes advanced this hypothesis about consumption, as we have seen, on the basis of "knowledge of human nature" and "detailed facts of experience." Early followers of Keynes attempted to provide a stronger empirical basis for this form of the consumption function, with mixed results.

Using statistical techniques and annual data for a short period, 1929–41, Keynesian economists obtained the following type of estimate for the consumption function[2]:

$$C = 26.5 + 0.75Y_D \tag{14.4}$$

In equation (14.4) the estimate of the MPC (b) is 0.75, and the estimate of the intercept (a) is \$26.5 billion. The positive value of the intercept (a) confirmed the Keynesian view that the average propensity to consume ($a/Y_D + b$) exceeded the marginal propensity to consume (b). Equation (14.4) implies that the APC declines as income rises. At a level of disposable income equal to \$100 billion, the APC estimated from equation (14.4) would be 1.015

---

[2]This estimate is taken from Gardner Ackley, *Macroeconomic Theory* (New York: Macmillan, 1961), p. 226. Data for the equation are in 1954 constant dollars.

(26.5/100 + 0.75), implying that the APS is negative (−0.015), but at an income level of 200, the APC would be 0.883 (26.5/200 + 0.75). An estimated consumption function such as equation (14.4) seemed to predict annual levels of consumer expenditures during this period (1929–41) reasonably well.

Further support for the Keynesian form of the consumption function came from comparative studies of family budgets. As one looked at budgets for families at progressively higher income levels, the absolute amount of consumption increased ($b > 0$), but by less than the increase in income ($b < 1$). Also, families at higher income levels consumed a smaller proportion of income, indicating that the APC declined as income rose.

The fact that the proportion of income that is saved apparently increased as income rose led some early Keynesians to worry about secular stagnation in the economy. As the ratio of saving to income increased, these economists worried that aggregate demand would fall short of output. Recall that saving is a *leakage* from the circular flow of income and expenditure. Aggregate demand would be inadequate unless the fall in the C/Y_D ratio (rise in the S/Y_D ratio) were balanced by growth in the other components of aggregate demand: government spending and investment. In the absence of such growth, these economists feared that aggregate demand would fall short of full-employment output, resulting in stagnation.[3] Whether such a secular decline in the ratio of consumption to income would have led to chronically deficient levels of aggregate demand is a matter of conjecture. It turns out that, although there has been continued growth in real GNP in the United States and other industrialized countries, there has been no tendency for the APC to decline and the APS to rise. The shares of consumption and saving in income have been relatively constant for over a century, as became apparent when estimates of GNP and output shares extending back into the nineteenth century became available in the early post–World War II period.

Data from an early study by Simon Kuznets for real national income (Y), real consumption (C), and the ratio of the two (C/Y) are given in Table 14.1. The data are overlapping decade averages of annual figures. As can be seen from the table, there was no downward trend in the ratio of consumption to income even though national income grew from an average of $9.3 billion in the 1869–78 decade to $72.0 billion in the 1929–38 decade. Nor is there evidence of a downward trend in the average propensity to consume in more recent years. The APC (C/Y_D) was 0.93 in 1950, 0.89 in 1970, and 0.93 in 1990. The Kuznets data, as well as later estimates, strongly suggest that the

---

[3] For an example of this stagnationist thesis, see Alvin Hansen, "Economic Progress and Declining Population Growth," *American Economic Review,* 29 (March 1939).

TABLE 14.1   Consumption and National Income, 1869–1938[a]

Years	Y	C	C/Y
1869–78	9.3	8.1	0.87
1874–83	13.6	11.6	0.85
1879–88	17.9	15.3	0.85
1884–93	21.0	17.7	0.84
1889–98	24.2	20.2	0.83
1894–1903	29.8	25.4	0.85
1899–1908	37.3	32.3	0.87
1904–13	45.0	39.1	0.87
1909–18	50.6	44.0	0.87
1914–23	57.3	50.7	0.88
1919–28	69.0	62.0	0.90
1924–33	73.3	68.9	0.94
1929–38	72.0	71.0	0.99

[a] Y, national income, billions of dollars; C, consumption expenditure, billions of dollars.

Source: Simon Kuznets, *National Product Since 1869* (New York: National Bureau of Economic Research, 1946), p. 119.

secular or long-run relationship between consumption and income is a proportional one, as Figure 14.2 illustrates.

Additionally, data from the early post–World War II period showed that quarter-to-quarter changes in consumption were not well explained by quarter-to-quarter movements in income. Gardner Ackley, for example, examined 22 quarter-to-quarter changes in consumption and income. He found that in five quarters the changes in consumption and income were in opposite directions. In 10 of the cases in which consumption and income did change in the same direction, the change in consumption *exceeded* the change in income. In only 7 of the 22 quarters were the movements in consumption and income consistent with a short-run marginal propensity to consume ($\Delta C / \Delta Y_D$) which is positive and less than 1.[4] This erratic short-run behavior of consumption indicated that either the relationship of consumption to current income in the short run was not as mechanical as predicted by the absolute income hypothesis or that other variables were influencing consumption behavior.

We can summarize the early evidence about the consumption function as follows. Evidence from short-run annual time series data (e.g.,

---

[4] See Ackley, *Macroeconomic Theory*, pp. 253–54.

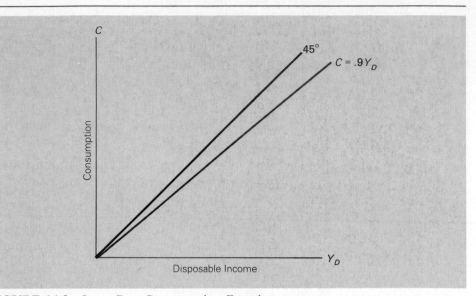

FIGURE 14.2   Long-Run Consumption Function
As indicated by the data going back to the nineteenth century, the long-run consumption function is shown as a proportional relationship with an MPC = APC, both approximately 0.9.

1929–41) and family budget studies seemed to support the Keynesian hypothesis about consumption—the absolute income hypothesis—as represented by (14.1). Time series data for a longer time period (e.g., 1869–1938) suggest that the consumption–income relationship is proportional rather than the nonproportional relationship given by (14.1). There is therefore a need to reconcile long-run evidence on the consumption function with the short-run time series evidence and cross-sectional evidence from family budget studies. Finally, the erratic quarter-to-quarter movements of consumption relative to income that were noted previously cast doubt on the closeness of the consumption–income relationship in the short run. Resolving these puzzles posed by the early empirical evidence on consumer behavior has been the task of the modern theory of the consumption function.

The Life Cycle Theory of Consumption

To see how post-Keynesian consumption theories have tried to reconcile the somewhat disparate implications from different data sources, we consider one of these theories, the **life cycle theory** of consumption, in detail. We then compare the conclusions of this theory with another explanation of the same phenomena, Milton Friedman's **permanent income hypothesis**.[5]

The Life Cycle Hypothesis

The life cycle hypothesis was developed by Franco Modigliani, Albert Ando, and Richard Brumberg.[6] As stated by Modigliani:

> The point of departure of the life cycle model is the hypothesis that consumption and saving decisions of households at each point of time reflect a more or less conscious attempt at achieving the preferred distribution of consumption over the life cycle, subject to the constraint imposed by the resources accruing to the household over its lifetime.[7]

An individual's or household's level of consumption depends not just on current income but also, and more importantly, on long-term expected earnings. Individuals are assumed to plan a lifetime pattern of consumer expenditure based on expected earnings over their lifetime.

To see the implications of this theory for the form of the consumption function, we first look at a simplified example. Consider an individual of a given age who is in the labor force, has a life expectancy of T years, and plans to remain in the labor force for N years. Our representative consumer might, for example, be 30 with a life expectancy of 50 (additional) years, plan to retire after 40 years, and, therefore, have expected years in retirement equal to $(T - N)$, or 10. We make the following assumptions about the individual's plans. The individual is assumed to desire a constant consumption flow over his lifetime. Further, we assume that he intends to consume the total amount of his lifetime earnings plus current assets; he plans no bequests. Finally, we assume that the interest paid on his assets is zero; current saving results in dollar-for-dollar future consumption. These assumptions are purely to keep the example simple and are relaxed later.

---

[5] For another reconciliation of the long-run and short-run evidence on the consumption function, see James Duesenberry, *Income, Saving, and the Theory of Consumer Behavior* (Cambridge, Mass.: Harvard University Press, 1949).

[6] Two early papers on the life cycle hypothesis are Franco Modigliani and Richard Brumberg, "Utility Analysis and the Consumption Function: An Interpretation of Cross Section Data," in K. Kurihara, ed., *Post-Keynesian Economics* (New Brunswick, N.J.: Rutgers University Press, 1954), pp. 388–436; and Albert Ando and Franco Modigliani, "The Life Cycle Hypothesis of Saving: Aggregate Implications and Tests," *American Economic Review*, 53 (March 1963), pp. 55–84. For an evaluation of the performance of the life cycle theory by one of its orginators, see Franco Modigliani, "Life Cycle, Individual Thrift and the Wealth of Nations," *American Economic Review*, 76 (June, 1986), pp. 297–313.

[7] Franco Modigliani, "The Life Cycle Hypothesis of Saving, the Demand for Wealth and the Supply of Capital," *Social Research*, 33 (June 1966), pp. 160–217, 162.

These assumptions imply that consumption in a given period will be a constant proportion, $1/T$, of expected *lifetime* resources. The individual plans to consume his lifetime earnings in T equal installments. The consumption function implied by this simple version of the life cycle hypothesis is

$$C_t = \frac{1}{T}[Y_t^1 + (N-1)\overline{Y}^{1e} + A_t] \qquad (14.5)$$

C_t is consumption in time period t. The term in brackets is expected lifetime resources, which consist of

Y_t^1 = the individual's labor income in the current time period(t)

$\overline{Y}^{1e}$ = the average labor income expected over the future ($N-1$) years during which the individual plans to work

A_t = the value of presently held assets

It can be seen from equation (14.5) that, according to the life cycle hypothesis, consumption depends not only on current income but also on expected future income and current asset holdings (i.e., current wealth). In fact, the life cycle hypothesis suggests that consumption would be quite unresponsive to changes in current income (Y_t^1) that did not also change average expected future income. From equation (14.5), for example, we can compute

$$\frac{\Delta C_t}{\Delta Y_t^1} = \frac{1}{T} = \frac{1}{50} = 0.02$$

An increase in income that was expected to persist through the work years would mean that $\overline{Y}^{1e}$ also rose, and the effect on consumption would be much greater:

$$\frac{\Delta C_t}{\Delta Y_t^1} + \frac{\Delta C_t}{\Delta \overline{Y}^{1e}} = \frac{1}{T} + \frac{N-1}{T} = \frac{N}{T} = \frac{40}{50} = 0.8$$

A one-time or transient change in income of, say, $100 will have the same effect as a change in wealth (note that $\Delta C_t/\Delta Y_t^1 = \Delta C_t/\Delta A_t = 1/T$) of the same amount. Lifetime resources will go up by $100, and this will be spread out in a planned consumption flow of $100/T = 100/50 = 2$ per period in our example, where the individual expects to live for 50 additional years. A permanent increase in income of $100 will lead to an increase of consumption of $80 in each of the remaining periods, including the 10 planned periods of retirement. The increase of $80 in each of these 10 retirement years, a total of $800, is financed by a saving of $20 ($100 - 80$) in each of the 40 remaining working years.

The life cycle hypothesis attempts to account for the dependence of consumption and saving behavior on the individual's position in the life cycle. Young workers entering the labor force have relatively low incomes and low (possibly negative) saving rates. As income rises in middle-age years, so does the saving rate. Retirement brings a fall in income and might be expected to begin a period of *dissaving* (negative saving rates). This time profile of consumption and saving is depicted in Figure 14.3. Here the desired pattern of consumption is taken to rise mildly with time instead of maintaining the constant desired consumption pattern assumed in our individual example. The pattern of income rises more sharply, though, and the typical individual smooths out his consumption flow by a short period of early dissaving, a period of positive saving, then a somewhat longer period of dissaving in retirement.

The general form of the aggregate consumption function implied by the life cycle hypothesis is

$$C_t = b_1 Y_t^1 + b_2 \overline{Y}^{1e} + b_3 A_t \tag{14.6}$$

where the variables $C_t, Y_t^1, \overline{Y}^{1e}$, and A_t are as defined for equation (14.5) but should now be interpreted as economywide averages. If the simplifying assumptions made previously of no bequests, zero interest on saving, and a uniform consumption pattern over time are relaxed, the parameters b_1, b_2, and b_3 will no longer be simply functions of N and T as were the coefficients in equation (14.5). Still, in the aggregate consumption function (14.6), as in the case of equation (14.5), consumption depends not just on current labor income (Y_t^1), but also on future expected labor income ($\overline{Y}^{1e}$) and wealth

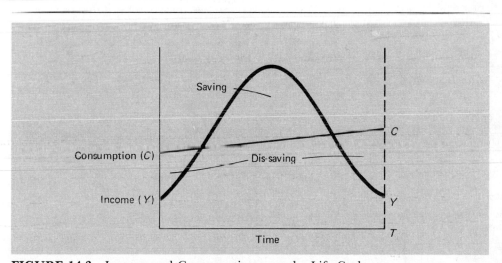

FIGURE 14.3 Income and Consumption over the Life Cycle
Consumption is shown as rising gradually over the life cycle. Income rises sharply over the early working years, peaks, and then declines, especially with retirement. This pattern of consumption and income results in periods of dissaving in the early working years and the late stage of the life cycle, with positive saving over the high-income middle period of the life cycle.

(A_t). It will also be true in the aggregate, as in the simplified individual example, that the response to a *transient* or one-time increase in labor income (an increase in Y_t^1) will be quite small, much less than the response to a permanent income change (an increase in Y_t^1 and $\overline{Y}^{le}$).

To use equation (14.6) to study actual consumer behavior, some assumption must be made about the way in which individuals form expectations concerning lifetime labor income. In a study for the United States, Ando and Modigliani make the simple assumption that expected average future labor income is just a multiple of current labor income:

$$\overline{Y}^{le} = \beta Y_t^1 \qquad \beta > 0 \tag{14.7}$$

According to this specification, individuals revise their expectation of future expected labor income $\overline{Y}^{le}$ by some proportion β of a change in current labor income. Substitution of equation (14.7) for $\overline{Y}^{le}$ in the aggregate consumption function (14.6) yields

$$C_t = (b_1 + b_2\beta)Y_t^1 + b_3A_t \tag{14.8}$$

A representative statistical estimate of the equation based on the work of Ando and Modigliani is the following:

$$C_t = 0.72Y_t^1 + 0.06A_t \tag{14.9}$$

An increase in current labor income of $100 *with the assumed effect on future labor income* will increase consumption by $72. An increase in wealth of $100 will increase consumption by $6. As noted previously, an increase in income that was known to be temporary and therefore would *not* affect future expected labor income would have the same effect as an increase in wealth. Thus, according to this estimate, the marginal propensity to consume out of such a transient income flow is on the order of 0.06, the marginal propensity to consume out of wealth.

The life cycle hypothesis can explain the puzzles that emerged from the early empirical work on consumption functions. According to the life cycle hypothesis, the relationship between consumption and current income would be nonproportional, as seems to be the case in *short-run* time series estimates [see equation (14.4)]. The intercept of the function measures the effect of wealth [$0.06A_t$ in equation (14.9)]. But the intercept is not constant over time; such short-run consumption functions shift upward over time as wealth grows. Such upward shifts in the short-run consumption function (SCF) are illustrated in Figure 14.4. The shifting short-run consumption functions trace out a long-run consumption function (LCF).

If the ratios of wealth and labor income to disposable personal income are relatively constant over time, the life cycle consumption function [equation (14.9)] is also consistent with the evidence from long-run time series data that the long-run consumption–income relationship (LCF in Figure 14.4) is proportional, with the APC(C/Y_D) relatively stable in the neighborhood

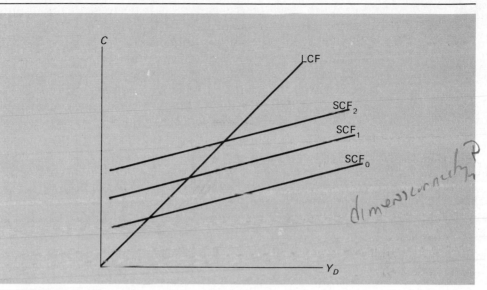

FIGURE 14.4   Short-Run and Long-Run Consumption Functions
As wealth increases over time, the nonproportional short-run consumption function shifts upward (from SCF_0 to SCF_1, then to SCF_2) to trace out the long-run
proportional consumption income relationship (LCF)

of 0.9. To see this, first note that the ratio of labor income to disposable
personal income has been approximately 0.88, that is, $Y_t^1 = 0.88Y_D$. The
ratio of wealth to disposable income is approximately 4.75; $A_t = 4.75Y_D$.
Substitution of these expressions for A_t and Y_t^1 in the estimated aggregate
consumption function (14.9) yields

$$C_t = 0.72(0.88Y_D) + 0.06(4.75Y_D)$$
$$= 0.63Y_D + 0.29Y_D$$
$$= 0.92Y_D$$

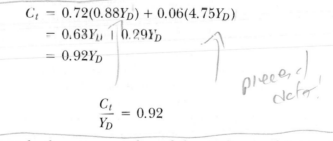

or

$$\frac{C_t}{Y_D} = 0.92$$

which is approximately the average value of the APC over the post–World
War II period.
    The life cycle hypothesis also explains the evidence from cross-sectional
family budget studies showing that higher-income families consume a
smaller proportion of income (have a lower APC) than do lower-income
families. A larger proportion of high-income families might be expected to

be those in their peak earning years, that is, in the "humped" portion of Figure 14.3. It is in this range that, according to the life cycle hypothesis, income should exceed consumption by the greatest amount and the APC should therefore be lowest. Conversely, a sample of low-income families would have a high proportion of new entrants to the labor market and retirees, groups that tend to dissave. These groups with high APCs would push up the APC for the sample of low-income families.

Finally, the life cycle hypothesis explains why quarter-to-quarter movements in consumption do not closely mirror quarter-to-quarter movements in income, the other anomalous finding of early research on the consumption function. The change in income from any given quarter to the next will be the result, in large part, of one-time factors that will not affect individuals' perceptions of lifetime average income. We have seen that such transient income changes have little impact on consumer behavior according to the life cycle hypothesis. It is not surprising, therefore, that quarter-to-quarter changes in consumption and income are not closely related.

Critics of the Life Cycle Hypothesis

Although the life cycle hypothesis explains several puzzling features of the consumption–income relationship, the approach is not without its critics. Gardner Ackley, for example, points out that the life cycle theory assumes that each household, in making consumption decisions, has at all times "a definite, conscious vision"

> of the family's future size and composition, including the life expectancy of each member;
> of the entire lifetime profile of the income from work of each member—after the then applicable taxes;
> of the present and future extent and terms of any credit available to it;
> of the future emergencies, opportunities, and social pressures which will impinge upon its consumption spending.[8]

Further, each household must hold such a vision with enough certainty that it would be worthwhile to use this vision as a basis for rational planning of consumption decisions. Ackley finds these assumptions to be unrealistic. In essence, Ackley will not accept the point of departure for the life cycle hypothesis, Modigliani's statement that consumption and saving decisions of households "reflect a more or less conscious attempt at achieving the preferred distribution of consumption over the life cycle."

Another criticism of the life cycle approach is that it fails to recognize the presence of *liquidity constraints*. Even if a household or individual possessed

---

[8]Gardner Ackley, "Discussion" of a paper by James Tobin and Walter Dolde, in *Consumer Spending and Monetary Policy: The Linkages* (Boston: Federal Reserve Bank of Boston, 1971).

a concrete vision of future income, there is very little opportunity in real world capital markets for borrowing for any long period on the basis of this future income. As a result, consumption may be much more responsive to changes in current income, whether temporary or not, than would be predicted on the basis of the life cycle hypothesis. The response of consumption to current income, however, may not be the simple mechanical one predicted by the "absolute income" hypothesis. The consumption pattern of younger households whose consumption is limited by liquidity constraints may be very responsive to changes in current income. The consumption of older households with more accumulated wealth may not be responsive to temporary variations in current income. Small temporary changes in income may be financed out of a buffer of liquid assets, but larger changes may cause liquidity constraints to become binding and begin to affect consumption behavior. Consideration of liquidity constraints on households therefore leads one to believe that current income may be a more important influence on consumption than would be predicted on the basis of the life cycle hypothesis, but the consumption-to-current-income relationship may be more complex than that implied by Keynes's absolute income hypothesis. Recent statistical work does in fact suggest the importance of liquidity constraints as an explanation of a considerable response of consumption to current income.[9]

Other recent research emphasizes the importance of bequests in determining saving—rather than the life cycle motive, which emphasizes saving to finance consumption in retirement. A study by Laurence Kotlikoff and Lawrence Summers concluded that the desire to make bequests was the most important motive for saving.[10]

Whether saving is for bequests or to support consumption in retirement years has important implications for a number of issues. To take an example, consider the effect on the saving rate as a result of recent legislation to add insurance for catastrophic illness to Medicare. If saving is to finance consumption during retirement (life cycle saving), one would expect the saving rate to fall as a result of the additional insurance. Individuals need to save less to finance possibly very large medical expenses. If saving is for bequests, the effect of the legislation is less clear. This is because we know very little about the factors that determine the size of bequests people make.

[9]See Marjorie Flavin, "Excess Sensitivity of Consumption to Current Income," *Canadian Journal of Economics*, 18 (February 1985), pp. 117–36; and "The Adjustment of Consumption to Changing Expectations About Future Income," *Journal of Political Economy*, 89 (October 1981), pp. 974–1009.

[10]Laurence J. Kotlikoff and Lawrence H. Summers, "The Role of Integenerational Transfers in Aggregate Capital Accumulation," *Journal of Political Economy*, 89 (August 1981), pp. 706–32.

PERSPECTIVES

Declining U.S.
Personal Saving

Whether saving is primarily for life cycle reasons or for the bequest motive, the fact is that the U.S. personal (household) saving rate fell during the 1980s. This can be seen from Table 14.2, which shows U.S. personal saving as a percentage of disposable income for the 1970s and the years 1981–90. The decline in U.S. personal saving has been a concern, since saving provides funds required to finance investment and consequently capital formation. The decline in saving has also been surprising because Reagan administration tax policies contained several features aimed at strengthening the incentives to save.

Several explanations have been offered for the decline in the saving rate.[1] One consistent with the life cycle hypothesis is that increased Social Security benefits have reduced the need to save for retirement years. Another explanation is that increased access to borrowing (e.g., credit card borrowing, home equity loans) has decreased saving for future purchases of durable goods. A third explanation is that the growing number of two-income families, in which the chance of both wage earners becoming unemployed is small, has reduced saving for a "rainy day."

Whatever the cause, the decline in the saving rate has been worrisome, especially to those who thought that, even with the higher 1970s rate, the United States saved too little.[2]

TABLE 14.2 U.S. Personal Saving Rate (percentage of disposable income)

1971–80	7.8
1981	7.5
1982	6.8
1983	5.4
1984	6.1
1985	4.4
1986	4.1
1987	2.9
1988	4.2
1989	4.6
1990	4.5

[1]See the discussion in Lawrence Summers and Chris Carroll, "Why Is U.S. National Saving So Low?" *Brookings Papers on Economic Activity* (1987:2), pp. 607–35.

[2]See Martin Feldstein, "Does the United States Save Too Little?" *American Economic Review*, 67 (February 1977), pp. 116–21.

Franco Modigliani has disputed the Kotlikoff and Summers evidence. To him, the data suggest that only 15 to 20 percent of saving is for bequests. The bulk is life cycle saving. Controversy and research on this issue continue.[11]
Read Perspectives 14.1.

[11]See Franco Modigliani, "The Role of Integenerational Transfers and Life Cycle Saving in the Accumulation of Wealth;" and Laurence Kotlikoff, "Intergenerational Transfers and Savings," *Journal of Economic Perspectives* 2 (Spring 1988), pp. 15–58.

Policy Implications of the Life Cycle Hypothesis

As mentioned at the beginning of this section, the consumption function is an important element in Keynesian macroeconomic theory. Fluctuations in the unstable investment component of private aggregate demand are assumed to be amplified and transmitted throughout the economy by the induced consumption response to the initial income change; this is the multiplier process. A change in government spending would have multiplier effects, again with induced effects on consumption. A change in taxes in the Keynesian system would affect disposable income and therefore consumption, but this effect was also predicated on the absolute income hypothesis about consumer expenditures. In this subsection we examine the changes required in the Keynesian analysis of the multiplier process and the effects of fiscal policy when consumption is assumed to be determined according to the life cycle hypothesis instead of the absolute income hypothesis. We also consider the implications of the life cycle hypothesis for the effectiveness of monetary policy.

Fiscal Policy and the Multiplier Process

The key element in the Keynesian analysis of the multiplier effects of changes in investment or fiscal policy variables is the response of consumption to current income. According to the life cycle hypothesis, consumption is determined primarily by expected lifetime income and wealth. A change in current income of itself has little influence on consumer behavior. In the empirical work of Ando and Modigliani discussed previously, expected future income is assumed to be proportional to current income. If this is correct, we would expect a strong response of consumption to current income, since changes in current income cause proportional changes in expected lifetime income as well. Ando and Modigliani's estimate of the consumption function [equation (14.9)] implies that the marginal propensity to consume out of current labor income is 0.72. This value is high enough to be consistent with the earlier Keynesian multiplier analysis and to imply strong effects for changes in taxes and government spending. In other empirical work by Modigliani, expected lifetime income is assumed instead to depend on a weighted average of the past 12 quarters' income levels.[12] With this assumption as well, the response of consumption to income was strong enough to produce results consistent with earlier Keynesian analysis. For example, there were strong effects for tax and government spending changes within a year. The life cycle hypothesis does not therefore seem to imply an essential modification of the general Keynesian multiplier or fiscal policy analysis.

---

[12] See Franco Modigliani, "Monetary Policy and Consumption," in *Consumer Spending and Monetary Policy: The Linkages* (Boston: Federal Reserve Bank of Boston, 1971).

One modification is required in the Keynesian view of fiscal policy effects if the life cycle hypothesis is adopted in place of the absolute income version of the consumption function. According to the life cycle hypothesis, current income has a strong effect on consumption only because of the assumption that changes in current income affect expected average lifetime income. This is clearly not the case when the change in current income is known to be transient, as it would be with a change in tax rates or government transfer payments that is explicitly temporary. In the second quarter of 1975, for example, $8 billion was paid out to taxpayers as a one-time rebate in order to stimulate aggregate demand. According to the life cycle theory, such a one-time payment does *not* affect expected future income and therefore has very little effect on consumption.

Even temporary tax changes may have strong effects, however, if liquidity constraints are important in determining consumption, as discussed previously. If a household would choose a higher level of consumption if it were not constrained by the amount that can be borrowed, then a $200 rebate, such as was received in 1975, would increase consumption by up to $200. The rebate would reduce the liquidity constraint. On the question of the efficacy of temporary tax changes as a stabilization tool, therefore, it appears that the crucial issue is the importance of liquidity constraints as a determinant of aggregate consumption.

Monetary Policy and Consumption

In our analysis of monetary policy effects, the main focus was on investment. The life cycle hypothesis implies that monetary policy may have important direct effects on consumption as well. According to the life cycle hypothesis, household wealth is one of the main determinants of consumption. Monetary policy affects household wealth and therefore consumption. Monetary policy actions affect wealth both directly by changing the quantity of money which is a component of household net wealth and by affecting interest rates and consequently the market value of other assets, such as government and private bonds and corporate equities (stocks). In Chapter 6 we analyzed the relationship between the interest rate and the market value of bonds. An increase in the interest rate resulting from a tight money policy will cause bond prices to fall and, hence, cause households to suffer capital losses on bonds. A decline in interest rates resulting from an expansionary monetary policy will cause bond prices to rise, with resulting capital gains on bonds. Equity prices would also be expected to move inversely with interest rates. Equities pay streams of dividends, and with higher market interest rates, the price investors will be willing to pay for an equity with a given dividend flow will fall.

Tight money policies therefore reduce wealth and consumption, whereas expansionary policies have the opposite effects. Empirical work by Modigliani, mentioned previously, indicates that monetary policy effects on consumption are a large component of the overall effects of monetary policy. In the Federal Reserve–Massachusetts Institute of Technology statistical model developed by Modigliani (and many others), this wealth effect on consumption accounts for 34 percent of the effects of a monetary policy action in the first year after the policy shift and 45 percent of the effect after four years.

The hypothesis that liquidity constraints are important in the determination of consumption provides an additional channel by which monetary policy might affect consumption. Tight money policies result in larger downpayment requirements and stricter credit standards for consumer credit and increase the severity of the liquidity constraint facing many households. Expansionary monetary policies make credit more available and reduce liquidity constraints. A graphic illustration of how consumption may be affected by liquidity constraints, whether real or only perceived, came in the spring of 1980. The Federal Reserve, in an effort to reduce the growth of consumer credit, instituted a number of credit controls. There are indications that the public overreacted and feared that credit would simply become unavailable. Owing in part to this expected liquidity constraint, real consumer expenditure fell by 10.5 percent at an annual rate in the second quarter of 1980.

The Permanent Income Hypothesis

An alternative explanation of consumer behavior is the permanent income hypothesis suggested by Milton Friedman.[13] This hypothesis has in common with the life cycle hypothesis the property that long term income is assumed to be the primary determinant of consumption.

Friedman's Consumption Function

Friedman postulates that consumption is proportional to permanent income:

$$C = \kappa Y^p \qquad (14.10)$$

where Y^p is permanent income and κ (Greek kappa) is the factor of proportionality ($\kappa > 0$). Permanent income is expected average long-term income from both "human and nonhuman wealth," that is, both expected labor income (the return to human wealth or human capital) and expected earnings from asset holdings (nonhuman wealth).[14]

---

[13] Milton Friedman, *A Theory of the Consumption Function* (Princeton, N.J.: Princeton University Press, 1957).

[14] Although here we drop the D subscript, which indicates disposable income, each of the income concepts discussed is net of taxes.

Friedman does not expect this consumption equation to predict consumption perfectly because, in addition to the part of consumption determined on the basis of permanent income, in any period there is a random element to consumption that Friedman terms "transitory" consumption. Similarly, in any period, there is a transitory component of income; measured income generally will not equal permanent income for the individual or in the aggregate. We can then write measured income (Y) as

$$Y = Y^p + Y^t$$

where Y^t is transitory income, which may be either positive or negative, causing measured income to exceed or fall short of permanent income. According to the permanent income hypothesis, it is only the permanent component of income that influences consumption. Consumption, even the transitory component of consumption referred to previously, is independent of transitory income.

As with the life cycle theory, in order to implement the permanent income hypothesis, some assumption must be made about how individuals form long-term expectations about income. In applications of the permanent income hypothesis, Friedman and other researchers have assumed that, given an initial estimate of permanent income, individuals revise this estimate from period to period in the following manner:

$$Y_t^p = Y_{t-1}^p + j(Y_t - Y_{t-1}^p), \qquad 0 < j < 1 \tag{14.11}$$

Equation (14.11) states that in each period individuals adjust their estimate of permanent income by a fraction j of the discrepancy between actual income in the current period and the prior period's estimate of permanent income. For example, suppose $j = 0.40$. Then, coming into 1992, assume that an individual estimated his or her permanent income to be $30,000 (Y_{t-1}^p), but actual income in 1992 turned out to be $40,000 (Y_t). From equation (14.11), we compute

$$Y_t^p = \$30,000 + 0.40(\$40,000 - \$30,000)$$
$$= \$34,000$$

The individual assumes that 40 percent ($4000) of the deviation of actual income from the previous estimate of permanent income represents a change in permanent income, whereas the other 60 percent ($6000) is regarded as transitory income.

The permanent income hypothesis can also explain the puzzles about the consumption–income relationship that were discussed earlier. The permanent income hypothesis is consistent with the proportional long-run consumption function (APC constant) and the nonproportional short-run consumption function (APC declines as Y increases) found in the time-series data. In the long run, income growth is dominated by changes in permanent income, with positive and negative transitory changes in income canceling out. The long-run consumption–income relationship will therefore be approximately the proportional relationship given by equation (14.10) with constant APC equal to κ. In the short run, years of high income will generally be years when the transitory component of income is positive. Since consumption rises only with increases in permanent income, in these high-income years the ratio of consumption to measured income [APC = $C/Y = C/(Y^p + Y^t)$] will be low. In low-income years when transitory income is generally negative, permanent income will be above measured income and the ratio of consumption, which depends on permanent income, to measured income will be high (the APC will be high).

These implications of the permanent income hypothesis can be illustrated a little more formally using equations (14.10) and (14.11). Substituting equation (14.11) into equation (14.10), we have

$$C_t = \kappa\left[Y^p_{t-1} + j(Y_t - Y^p_{t-1})\right]$$

$$C_t = \kappa Y^p_{t-1} + \kappa j(Y_t - Y^p_{t-1}) \qquad (14.12)$$

$$C_t = \kappa(1 - j)Y^p_{t-1} + \kappa j Y_t$$

The consumption–income relationship implied by equation (14.12) is nonproportional in the short run, with the first term on the right-hand side $(\kappa(1 - j)Y^p_{t-1})$ providing an intercept in the consumption function. Dividing equation (14.12) by Y_t, we can express the APC as

$$APC = \frac{C_t}{Y_t} = \kappa(1 - j)\frac{Y^p_{t-1}}{Y_t} + \kappa j \qquad (14.13)$$

When actual income is low relative to permanent income ($Y_t < Y^p_{t-1}$), from equation (14.13) we can see that the APC will be relatively high. Conversely, when current income is higher than permanent income ($Y_t > Y^p_{t-1}$), the APC will be low.

Over the long run, permanent (Y^p) and actual (Y) income will *on average* be equal, let us say, to some level $\overline{Y}$, and equation (14.13) simplifies to

$$APC = \frac{C}{Y} = \kappa(1 - j)\frac{\overline{Y}}{\overline{Y}} + \kappa j$$

$$\frac{C}{Y} = \kappa - \kappa j + \kappa j = \kappa$$

The long-run consumption function is a proportional relationship.

The evidence from the cross-sectional budget studies that high-income families have a lower APC than low-income families is also consistent with the permanent income hypothesis. A sample of high-income families at a given time is likely to contain more than a proportionate number of families experiencing positive transitory income flows ($Y^t > 0$). Since the consumption levels of these families depend only on their permanent incomes, the measured APCs for these families will be low, bringing down the average APC for the high-income group. On the other hand, a group of families with a low income at a given point in time will contain a disproportionate share of families with a negative transitory income component and hence a high measured APC. This will push up the average APC for the low-income group. In terms of equation (14.13), many of the high-income families will, as a result of positive transitory shocks to income, have *low* ratios of Y^p_{t-1} to Y_t and therefore low APCs. Many low-income families, as a result of negative transitory shocks to income, will have high ratios of Y^p_{t-1} to Y_t and hence high APCs.

Finally, the permanent income hypothesis is consistent with the failure of quarter-to-quarter movements of consumption to follow closely such short-run movements in income. Quarter-to-quarter income changes will contain many transitory income changes to which consumption does not respond. Likewise, according to Friedman's hypothesis, there is a transitory component to consumption that is not related to income.

The policy implications that follow from the permanent income hypothesis are similar to those that follow from the life cycle hypothesis in many respects. Generally, however, advocates of the permanent income hypothesis have been more pessimistic about the efficacy of fiscal policy, especially tax policy, as an instrument for controlling aggregate demand.[15] It is easy to understand the source for this pessimism in the case of explicitly temporary tax cuts or tax increases. Such policy shifts will cause changes only in the transitory component of income and therefore will be ineffective in controlling consumption and aggregate demand. Pessimism about the effectiveness of permanent changes in tax policy appears to stem not from any implications of the permanent income hypothesis itself but from the assumption made about how quickly individuals adjust their estimates of permanent income.

From equation (14.12) the short-run MPC, the change in consumption per unit change in *current* income, can be seen to be

$$\frac{\Delta C_t}{\Delta Y_t} = \kappa\, j \tag{14.14}$$

that is, the long-run MPC out of permanent income ($\Delta C / \Delta Y^p$), κ, multiplied by the fraction by which the individual's estimate of permanent income

---

[15] See, for example, Robert Eisner, "What Went Wrong," *Journal of Political Economy*, 70 (May–June 1971), pp. 629–41.

is adjusted to a change in actual income, j (see equation 14.11). If individuals adjust their estimates of permanent income only slowly over time to changes in current income, j, and therefore the MPC out of current income, will be small. For example, if κ is 0.9 but j is 0.3, the MPC out of current income will be

$$\frac{\Delta C_t}{\Delta Y_t} = \kappa j = 0.9 \times 0.3 = 0.27$$

With a low MPC, a change in tax policy, even if perceived as permanent, will not cause a large consumption response. In the Keynesian system, tax policy works by means of an effect on current (disposable) income and therefore consumption (by means of the MPC). If the response of consumption to income is weak, even permanent changes in tax policy will be ineffective. If, however, the estimate of permanent income is more responsive to a change in current income (j is high), or if a change in tax rates, perceived as permanent, independently causes such an estimate to be revised, there is no reason why tax policy should not be effective, even accepting the permanent income hypothesis.

Rational Expectations and the Permanent Income Hypothesis

As formulated by Friedman, the permanent income hypothesis assumes that individual estimates of permanent income are formed in a *backward-looking* manner. This is implied by equation (14.11), which states that individuals revise their estimates of permanent income based on how *last* period's actual income differed from last period's estimate of permanent income. This type of backward-looking expectation is consistent with Friedman's treatment of expectations of inflation in his Phillips curve analysis (Section 10.2).

We saw in Chapter 12, however, that the new classical economists criticized the assumption of backward-looking expectations as naive. They proposed instead that expectations were *rational* (or forward-looking). Expectations were formed using all available relevant information and using it intelligently. What implications does the rational expectations assumption have for the permanent income hypothesis?

If expectations are rational, then all information available prior to the current period will already have been used to estimate permanent income. This implies that changes in consumption will come only as the result of *unanticipated* changes in income that cause changes in estimated permanent income.[16] Changes in consumption should come only with income surprises.

---

[16]The first linking of the rational expectations hypothesis and the permanent income hypothesis was Robert Hall, "Stochastic Implications of the Life Cycle–Permanent Income Hypothesis: Theory and Evidence," *Journal of Political Economy*, 86 (December 1978), pp. 971–87.

As with the implications of rational expectations discussed in Chapter 11, the joint hypothesis of the permanent income consumption function and rational expectations has been tested extensively but with mixed results.

Some early research suggested that surprises in income explain changes in consumption better than actual changes in income. Later studies, however, were not favorable to this joint hypothesis. Consumption seems to respond too much to actual changes in income to be consistent with a response only to revisions in permanent income. This "excessive sensitivity" of consumption to changes in *actual* income may be due to liquidity constraints, which we discussed earlier. Households that were unable to borrow previously, for example, will increase consumption if income increases, whether or not the increase was anticipated. On the other hand, research has shown that consumption responds less to unanticipated changes in income than is consistent with the rational expectations and permanent income hypothesis. Consumption is "excessively insensitive" to *unanticipated* changes in income.[17]

14.2 • INVESTMENT SPENDING

Next, we consider investment demand. Investment in the national income accounts includes business fixed investment (purchases of durable equipment and structures), residential construction investment, and changes in business inventories. Additionally, our discussion of consumption in Section 14.1 is most appropriately applied to household expenditures on nondurable consumer goods, services, and the *service flow* from consumer durable goods. These categories measure the flow of goods used up by the household sector in a given period, and it is this quantity that the theories discussed in Section 14.1 are intended to explain. Consumer *expenditures* as measured in the national income accounts, however, include purchases of consumer durable goods (automobiles, refrigerators, televisions, etc.), not the service flow from these goods. Therefore, we also deal briefly in this chapter with the factors that determine the timing of such consumer durable goods purchases, which are a form of household investment.

We deal first with business fixed investment, the largest component of investment. The other components of investment are discussed later.

---

[17]On these issues see Alan Blinder and Angus Deaton, "The Time Series Consumption Function Revisited," *Brookings Papers on Economic Activity*, 16:2 (1985), pp. 465–521; Marjorie Flavin, "Excess Sensitivity of Consumption to Current Income," *Canadian Journal of Economics*, 18 (February 1985), pp. 117–36; and John Campbell and Angus Deaton, "Why Is Consumption So Smooth," *Review of Economic Studies*, 56 (July 1989) pp. 357–74.

Business Fixed Investment

Business fixed investment is important in two respects. First, investment spending is a significant component of total aggregate demand ($550.4 billion in 1991, 10 percent of GNP). The importance of investment to cyclical movements in income is even more than in proportion to its size as a share in GNP because it is one of the more volatile components of GNP. This fact was recognized by Keynes, among others, and variations in fixed business investment are an important element in many theories of the cyclical behavior of output.

Figures for (gross) business fixed investment both in absolute terms and as a share of GNP are given in Table 14.3. The variability of business fixed investment as a share of GNP is evident from the table, although in the post–World War II period this variability is considerably less than it was prior to the war. Over this postwar period, business fixed investment has ranged between 9 and 12 percent of GNP.

TABLE 14.3 Business Fixed Investment, 1929–91, Selected Years

Year	Business Fixed Investment	Business Fixed Investment as Share of Total Output
1929	10.6	0.103
1933	2.4	0.043
1939	5.9	0.065
1940	7.5	0.075
1943	5.0	0.026
1945	10.1	0.048
1950	27.3	0.095
1955	38.5	0.096
1960	48.5	0.096
1965	72.7	0.105
1970	103.9	0.105
1975	157.7	0.101
1980	308.8	0.117
1985	442.9	0.110
1986	435.2	0.103
1987	444.9	0.098
1988	488.4	0.100
1989	511.9	0.098
1990	524.3	0.096
1991	550.4	0.097

Source: Economic Report of the President, 1985, 1991, 1992.

The second important macroeconomic role for business fixed investment follows from the fact that net fixed business investment measures the amount by which the stock of capital increases in each period; that is,

$$K_t - K_{t-1} = I_{n,t} \qquad (14.15)$$

where K is the capital stock and $I_{n,t}$ is *net* fixed investment. Business fixed investment is therefore important in the process of longer-run economic growth. In this chapter we focus primarily on the role of investment as a component of aggregate demand, although the growth role of investment cannot be ignored completely. In Chapter 17 the role of investment in the growth process—the role of investment in changing aggregate supply over time—is examined.

In previous chapters, investment was assumed to depend negatively on the interest rate,

$$I = I(r) \qquad (14.16)$$

Investment was also assumed to depend positively on the expected future profitability of investment projects. In the discussion here we explain the effect on investment of changes in output. The role of the interest rate, as well as other factors that influence the cost of capital to the firm, are also discussed in more detail.

Investment and Output: The Accelerator Relationship

As noted previously, net investment measures the change in the capital stock. (In the remainder of this section the term *investment* is used to mean business fixed investment.) Most investment theories therefore first explain the desired stock of capital. Investment is then explained as a response to deviations of the actual capital stock from the desired level. It is not hard to see that the desired capital stock depends on the level of output. Higher levels of output lead firms to demand a larger stock of capital, one of the factors used to produce output. The **accelerator model** is a simple representation of this relationship.

The accelerator model specifies the desired capital stock as a multiple of the level of output:

$$K_t^d = \alpha Y_t \qquad \alpha > 0 \qquad (14.17)$$

In the simplest form of the accelerator model, net investment is assumed to be equal to the difference between the desired capital stock and the stock of capital inherited from the preceding period. If we ignore depreciation of the existing capital stock for the moment, we have

$$I_{n,t} = K_t^d - K_{t-1} \qquad (14.18)$$

$$I_{n,t} = .5((\alpha Y_t - K_{t-1}))$$

The stock of capital inherited from the last period will be the desired capital stock based on income in the last period:

$$K_{t-1} - K_{t-1}^d = \alpha Y_{t-1} \tag{14.19}$$

Therefore, we can rewrite (14.18) as

$$I_{n,t} = K_t^d - K_{t-1} = \alpha Y_t - \alpha Y_{t-1} = \alpha(Y_t - Y_{t-1})$$

$$\tag{14.20}$$

$$I_{n,t} = \alpha \Delta Y_t \qquad I = I(y) \quad C = C(y)$$

The level of investment spending depends on the *rate of change* in output.

This simple version suggests a crucial feature of the accelerator model. From (14.17), α can be seen to be the desired capital/output ratio:

$$\alpha = \frac{K_t^d}{Y_t} \tag{14.21}$$

Assume, for example, that this ratio is 2. In this case every one-dollar change in the rate of growth in output (ΔY_t) will cause a two-dollar change in investment. Investment would then be expected to exhibit considerable instability over the business cycle. Further, recall from our discussion of the Keynesian model in Chapter 5 that changes in investment (in this case as a result of changes in ΔY) have multiplier effects on income. Thus the simple accelerator theory, together with the multiplier process, can explain cyclical fluctuations in output.[18] A shock to output growth would cause investment to change, with resulting multiplier effects on the level of equilibrium output and therefore further effects on investment via the accelerator. As with the simple theory of the Keynesian multiplier in Chapter 5, however, considerable modification of the accelerator theory of investment is required before we can use it to explain the investment process in the real economy.

A first modification that would make the simple accelerator model more realistic is to allow for lags in the adjustment of the actual capital stock to the level of the desired capital stock. Suppose that the period to which we apply the model is a calendar year. Also assume that, because of an increase in output, there is an increase in the desired capital stock. Investment projects will be planned to eliminate this discrepancy between the actual and desired capital stock. In addition to what we may call the direct cost of the investment projects, there will be *adjustment costs*, which it is reasonable to assume will rise quickly as the rate of investment is increased. Examples of such costs of adjustment include plant shutdowns or hiring of overtime labor to install

Lags:

Adjustment Cost

---

[18] An early model of the interaction of the accelerator and the Keynesian multiplier was constructed by Paul Samuelson, "Interactions Between the Multiplier Analysis and the Principle of Acceleration," *Review of Economics and Statistics,* 21 (May 1939), pp. 75–78.

equipment, extra cost of speeding plant construction (overtime, etc.), and disruption of production if management concentrates solely on expediting investment projects. If such costs of adjustment do rise rapidly as the pace of investment is quickened, it will be optimal for firms to adjust the actual capital stock to the desired capital stock slowly over time, closing only a portion of the gap between the two within one period.

To reflect this adjustment lag, we modify (14.18) as follows:

$$I_{n,t} = \lambda (K_t^d - K_{t-1}) \qquad 0 < \lambda < 1 \tag{14.22}$$

Using (14.17), we have

$$I_{n,t} = \lambda (\alpha Y_t - K_{t-1}) \tag{14.23}$$

where, since the actual capital stock is not equated to the desired capital stock in each period, K_{t-1} will *not* generally equal K_{t-1}^d. Equation (14.23) specifies a *partial adjustment* mechanism where a fraction, λ (lambda), of the gap between the desired and actual capital stock is filled each period by investment. Since only a portion of the desired change in the capital stock is accomplished within one period, in a given period investment will be responding to changes in income during a number of previous periods. Equation (14.23) implies a slower response of investment to changes in current income and hence implies that investment will be less volatile in the short run than would be the case with the simple accelerator relationship [equation (14.20)]. Equation (14.23), which is termed the *flexible accelerator* model of investment, appears more consistent with the observed behavior of investment. Although investment is volatile, it is not as volatile as the simple accelerator model predicts.

The flexible accelerator model can also be modified to allow for variations in the speed with which investment is undertaken to fill the gap between the desired and actual capital stock (the λ parameter). This is a choice variable to the firm and may be influenced by credit conditions, including the level of the interest rate, tax considerations, and other variables. One would expect, for example, that, other things being equal, less investment would be undertaken to eliminate discrepancies between the actual and desired capital stock when the interest rate (cost of borrowing) was high than when the interest rate was low. Thus the flexible accelerator model is not inconsistent with the assumption made in Part II that investment is negatively related to the interest rate. In the following subsection we see an additional role for the interest rate, and other factors influencing the cost of capital to the firm, in determining investment.

Investment and the Cost of Capital

Even the flexible version of the accelerator theory of investment assumes that the desired capital stock is a fixed multiple of output ($K^d = \alpha Y$). This specification ignores the fact that different levels of output can be produced with the same level of capital by varying the labor input, that is, by varying the capital/labor ratio (K/N) and therefore the desired capital/output ratio (α). The optimal choice of a capital–labor mix to produce a given output depends on the ratio of the two factor costs, the ratio of the cost of capital to the real wage. We would expect the amount of capital used to produce a given output to be positively related to the real wage and negatively related to the cost of capital. The relevant real wage for the investment decision is not the current real wage but the average real wage expected over the lifetime of the capital goods being purchased. If it is assumed that this variable does not change significantly in the short run, then the only modification we need to make to the flexible accelerator model is to take account of the relationship between the cost of capital and the desired capital stock.

In our discussion of the flexible accelerator model, it was pointed out that the timing of investment would be expected to depend on credit conditions, including the level of the interest rate. The previous argument indicates that it is the overall level of investment, not just the timing of investment, that is expected to depend on the interest rate and, more broadly, on all factors that affect the cost of capital. This follows since the desired capital/labor and therefore capital/output ratio (α) depend on the cost of capital. We would therefore expect an investment function of the general form

$$I_{n,t} = I(Y_t, CC_t, K_{t-1}) \tag{14.24}$$

where CC is a measure of the cost of capital, which we now consider in more detail.

In deciding on its desired capital stock, the firm is comparing the marginal productivity of additional units of capital with what may be termed the *user cost of capital*, the cost to the firm of employing an additional unit of capital for one period.[19] What elements comprise this user cost of capital? If the firm must borrow to finance the purchase of capital goods, the interest rate is the cost of borrowing. If the capital goods are purchased with previously earned profits that have not been distributed to stockholders (retained earnings), the interest rate represents the opportunity cost of the investment project, since alternatively the firm could have invested its funds externally and earned

---

[19] The firm's choice of the optimal capital stock is made in a manner analogous to the firm's choice of the level of labor input in the short run. For the case of the labor input, the firm employs labor to the point where the marginal product of labor is equated with the real wage — the user cost of labor. For the case of capital, the desired capital stock is the level that equates the marginal product of capital with the user cost of capital. In the case of capital, though, we assume that because of costs of adjustment, the actual capital stock adjusts to the desired capital stock with a lag.

that interest rate. In either case the interest rate is an element of the user cost of capital.

So far in our discussion we have assumed that investment depends on the nominal rate of interest, simply the rate observed in the market. If inflation is expected, however, we need to distinguish between the *nominal* interest rate (r) and the real interest rate, where the *real* interest rate, ϕ (phi), is defined as the nominal rate minus the expected inflation rate ($\dot{p}^e$), that is,

$$\phi = r - \dot{p}^e \qquad \text{(14.25)}$$

It is the real rate of interest on which the level of investment depends. If, for example, the firm borrows at a nominal rate of 10 percent, then at the end of one year, it will have to repay \$110 for each \$100 borrowed. If over the year the firm expects the average price level to rise by 10 percent, then the expected real value of the sum to be repaid, its expected value in terms of goods and services at the end of the year, will be just equal to the value of the \$100 the firm borrowed. The real interest rate will be zero ($r = \dot{p}^e = 10$ percent $-$ 10 percent $= 0$). Looked at slightly differently, the expected amount of output the firm would have to sell to repay \$110 at the end of one year is just equal to the amount that would generate \$100 at the beginning of the year if prices (including the firm's product price) are expected to rise 10 percent during the year. Therefore, real borrowing costs would be zero if the nominal rate were 10 percent.

If inflation rates are low and steady, as they were in the United States from 1953 to 1966, the nominal interest rate will not be seriously misleading as a measure of the cost of capital. The real and nominal rates will differ only by a small, fairly constant amount. It is when inflation rates are variable and at times very high, and when people come to anticipate inflation, as was certainly the case in the later U.S. experience, that it becomes important to distinguish between the nominal and real interest rate. In such circumstances, it is important to remember that the *real* interest is the relevant borrowing cost for the investment decision.

An additional element of the user cost of capital is the depreciation rate. A certain proportion, δ (delta), of the capital stock is used up (worn out) in the production process during each period, and this depreciation rate is a cost to the firm of using capital goods.

To this point, then, we can express the user cost of the capital as

$$\text{"user cost"} \quad CC = \phi + \delta = r - \dot{p}^e + \delta \qquad \text{(14.26)}$$

Equation (14.26) requires one further modification, because of the effects of tax programs on the cost of capital. A number of government tax programs offset a portion of the user cost of capital. We summarize the effects of these programs by assuming that the government subsidizes investment purchases of capital goods at the rate τ (tau), where τ is a positive proportion of the

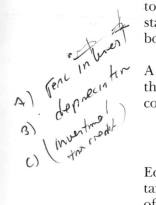

cost of the investment good ($0 < \tau < 1$). The effective cost of capital to the firm is then

$$CC = (1 - \tau)(r - \dot{p}^e + \delta) \qquad (14.27)$$

Perhaps the most obvious form of such a subsidy is an *investment tax credit.* The Kennedy administration, for example, instituted an investment tax credit in 1962 whereby a corporation's tax liability to the federal government was reduced by 7 percent of the amount of its fixed investment expenditure.[20] The government was, in effect, paying a 7 percent subsidy for investment purchases ($\tau = 0.07$). The effective user cost of capital to the firm is 93 percent of the cost without the tax credit ($1 - \tau = 0.93$).

Tax programs other than investment tax credits can also affect the user cost of capital. The corporate income tax reduces the after-tax profits generated by an investment project. If each of the items that comprise the cost of capital (interest costs and depreciation) is fully tax deductible, then the after-tax cost of capital is also reduced proportionately. For example, with a 28 percent corporate tax rate, each dollar in pretax profits will bring only $.72 in after-tax profits; each dollar of interest expense or depreciation will reduce tax liabilities by $.28 and, effectively, cost the firm $.72. Thus if all elements of the cost of capital are fully deductible, we would expect the effect of the corporate income tax on investment to be neutral. An additional way of reducing the effective user cost of capital to the firm is to make a part of the cost of capital *more* than 100 percent deductible in the early years after the investment is undertaken. This is the idea behind *accelerated depreciation allowances*. For example, in the United Kingdom 100 percent of the cost of an investment project can be deducted from a corporation's taxable income as depreciation in the year the investment is made. Actual depreciation will occur only over the course of many years. In the United States, a substantial shortening of the time period over which plant and equipment could be depreciated for tax purposes was an important element of the Reagan administration's tax policy. By giving firms such early tax savings, governments reduce the effective user cost of capital and hope to encourage investment.

To summarize our discussion of fixed investment to this point, we have developed an investment function of the following general form:

$$I_{n,t} = I(Y_t, r_t, \dot{p}^e, \tau_t, K_{t-1}) \qquad (14.28)$$

Net investment (I_n) depends on income and the variables r, $\dot{p}^e$, and τ, which represent elements of the user cost of capital, where we have omitted the depreciation rate δ, which we assume to be constant over time. Given the level of the lagged capital stock, an increase in income (Y), the expected

---

[20] The tax credit was only 3 percent for utilities, and the full 7 percent was only for equipment with a life of eight years or more. The details of the program are not crucial to the discussion.

rate of inflation ($\dot{p}^e$), or the tax subsidy to investment (τ) will all increase net investment. Increases in the nominal interest rate will cause investment expenditures to decline.

Monetary and Fiscal Policy and Investment

In Part II we analyzed the effects of monetary and fiscal policies on the level of investment. Here we consider some modifications and extensions of that analysis suggested by the investment theory in the previous subsections. First we reexamine fiscal policy effects.

Fiscal policy effects on investment were indirect and perverse in our analysis in Part II. For example, we found that an increase in government spending to increase aggregate demand would raise the interest rate and *crowd out* private investment expenditures. Tax cuts, where all taxes in Part II were taxes on households, would do the same. This crowding out was an offset to the intended effects of the policy. The analysis in this chapter suggests that by combining an expansionary fiscal policy—for example, a cut in the personal income tax—with a tax policy such as an investment tax credit to stimulate investment, these unfavorable effects of fiscal policy on investment can be prevented. The personal income tax cut stimulates aggregate demand, pushing up both income and the nominal interest rate. The rise in the nominal interest rate increases the user cost of capital. The role of the investment tax credit is to offset this rise in the user cost of capital. Additionally, the previous analysis suggests that tax policy toward investment (setting τ) provides an alternative tool to monetary policy as a means of stabilizing investment demand. Both types of policy work by changing the effective cost of capital to the firm.

Another implication of our analysis in this chapter is that expansionary fiscal policy actions may, on net, stimulate rather than crowd out private investment expenditures, even ignoring changes in the tax treatment of investment. This is because expansionary fiscal policies will increase Y and therefore stimulate investment by means of the accelerator mechanism. This effect may be quantitatively more important than any negative effect by means of a fiscal policy-induced increase in interest rates. Which effect dominates clearly depends on the importance of output growth versus the cost of capital as determinants of investment.

Regarding monetary policy, the modification of our previous analysis results from the distinction that we previously ignored between the nominal and the real rates of interest. Since it is the latter rate that is relevant for the investment decision, monetary policy must affect the real rate of interest in order to affect the level of investment. In the Keynesian or monetarist system, where the expected inflation rate depends primarily on the past history of inflation and, further, is assumed to change only slowly over time, changes in the nominal rate will mean changes in the real rate in the short run. The expected inflation rate, which is the difference between the two interest-rate concepts, is relatively constant in the short run. Thus our previous analysis is substantively unchanged. Within the new classical view, anticipated monetary policy actions will quickly affect price expectations and will not affect the real rate of interest, even in the short run. This is one further aspect of the new classical view that anticipated monetary policy actions do not affect real variables, and it is consistent with our earlier analysis.

Other Components of Investment

We turn now to the other components of investment: residential construction investment and inventory investment. We will also discuss the determinants of consumer durable goods expenditures. Residential construction investment and inventory investment, although they are relatively small as components of GNP, are important in explaining the cyclical variation of income. The determinants of residential construction investment and inventory investment are somewhat different from those of fixed business investment, and therefore we discuss these categories of investment separately. Consumer durable goods expenditures, especially new automobile purchases, are also important to the explanation of the cyclical behavior of income.

Residential Construction Investment

Residential construction investment is expenditure for the construction of new housing units. In recent years residential construction investment has varied between 3.0 and 5.4 percent of GNP, as can be seen from Table 14.4.

TABLE 14.4 Residential Construction
(percentage of total output)

1965	4.5	1979	4.9
1966	5.8	1980	3.9
1967	3.6	1981	3.5
1968	4.0	1982	3.0
1969	4.1	1983	4.0
1970	3.7	1984	4.2
1971	4.7	1985	4.8
1972	5.4	1986	5.2
1973	5.1	1987	5.1
1974	4.0	1988	5.0
1975	3.6	1989	4.5
1976	4.2	1990	4.2
1977	5.0	1991	3.4
1978	5.1		

In considering the determinants of residential construction investment, two features of the housing market should be kept in mind:

1. Houses have an average life of 40 to 50 years. As a consequence, the *stock* of existing housing units at a point in time is very large relative to the *flow* supply of new housing units.
2. There is a well-developed resale market for housing units.

These two properties require that we analyze residential construction investment—construction of new houses—within the context of the overall market for houses—new and previously existing.

Figure 14.5 illustrates the determination of the price of houses and the quantity of new housing units supplied. In Figure 14.5a the *stock* supply of houses (H_s^s), which includes *all* existing houses, is plotted as a vertical

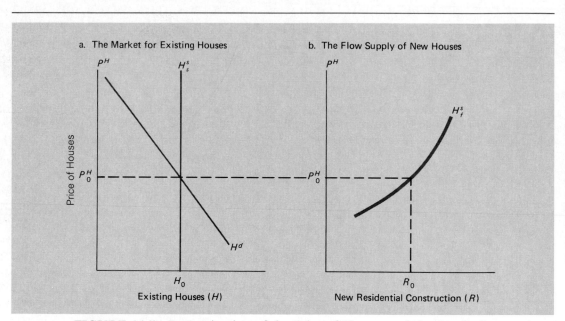

FIGURE 14.5 Determination of the Price of Houses and the Level of Residential Construction

The equilibrium price of houses, P_0^H, is determined in part *a* at the point where the demand for houses is equal to the fixed supply of existing houses. At price P_0^H, the flow supply of houses, which is residential construction investment, is shown in part *b* to equal R_0.

schedule against the price of houses (P^H).[21] The schedule is vertical because the stock of existing houses at any point in time is given. The demand for houses is plotted as a downward-sloping function of the price of houses. The price of houses is determined at the intersection of the supply and demand curves, P_0^H in the graph. In Figure 14.5b the supply of *newly constructed* houses, the *flow* supply of houses, is shown to depend positively on the price of houses. It is this flow supply of new houses that is counted as residential construction investment (R) in the national income accounts. At a price level of P_0^H, the level of residential construction investment would be R_0, as shown in Figure 14.5b.

For a given stock of existing houses, the price of houses and quantity of new houses produced depend on the state of housing demand, the H^d schedule in Figure 14.5a, as well as on factors that affect the position of the flow supply schedule for houses (II_f^s) in Figure 14.5b.

In the long run the demand for houses depends largely on demographic factors such as the rate of growth in the population and the rate of formation of new households. The coming to adulthood of the post–World War II baby boom generation and the tendency toward one-member households in the post–1970 period, for example, were strong stimuli to housing demand. Housing demand also depends on income, where, as in our discussion of consumption, the appropriate income variable is a smoothed measure of expected lifetime average income or permanent income. Although demographic factors and income are the major long-term determinants of housing demand, the primary variables that cause short-run swings in housing demand and consequently in residential construction investment are credit market conditions.

Most housing purchases are financed by long-term (20- to 30-year) mortgage borrowing. Thus, the mortgage rate of interest has an important effect on the effective cost of the house, as measured by the monthly mortgage payment the homeowner will have to make. Here again, though, it needs to be recognized that the appropriate interest measure is a real interest rate, the nominal rate minus the expected inflation rate. In this case the relevant expected inflation rate is the expected increase in the price of houses. If, for example, the mortgage rate is 12 percent and the expected rate of price increase for houses is 10 percent, the real borrowing cost would be 2 percent.[22] Increases in mortgage interest rates for given rates of expected

---

[21] We are ignoring the differences in the prices of new and existing houses, as well as among different types of houses.

[22] The mortgage will be for a long term. The expected rate of appreciation in housing prices, which is subtracted from the mortgage rate, must be for the time horizon over which the borrower expected to hold the mortgage, which may not be for the full term.

appreciation in housing prices would decrease housing demand and therefore the price of houses. Consequently, the level of residential construction investment (new housing construction) would decline.

During "tight-money" periods in the 1970s and early 1980s, in addition to high interest rates, a scarcity of mortgage funds, and consequently *credit rationing* in the mortgage market, also lowered housing demand. During those periods the largest proportion of mortgage lending was done by savings and loan associations and mutual savings banks. These financial intermediaries raise their funds primarily from depositors. The interest rates they paid to their depositors were constrained by federally imposed rate ceilings, called regulation Q ceilings after the regulation imposing them. As a result of regulation Q ceilings, during periods of high *market* rates, the interest rates paid by savings and loans and mutual savings banks were not competitive. Investors withdrew funds and put them directly into money market instruments such as short-term government bonds. Consequently, the savings and loans and mutual savings banks had to curtail mortgage lending. They did this in part through credit rationing by means of setting high down-payment ratios, refusing loans to only marginally qualified buyers, refusing to lend for construction of nonowner-occupied housing, and at times simply staying out of the market completely. As a result, in times of high market interest rates, mortgage money was not only expensive, but to many it became unavailable.

Regulation Q ceilings were removed gradually in the 1980s. Credit rationing should therefore be much less important in the current environment. Now, it is mainly through its effect on the mortgage interest rate that restrictive monetary policy discourages residential construction.

The effects on the housing market of a period of "tight" money, meaning a period of high interest rates and possibly reduced availability of mortgage funds, are illustrated in Figure 14.6. The tight-money conditions reduce the overall demand for houses, as illustrated by the shift of the demand schedule from H_0^d to H_1^d in Figure 14.6a. As a consequence, the price of houses falls from P_0^H to P_1^H. Additionally, as shown in Figure 14.6b, the high interest rates cause a shift to the left in the flow supply schedule, from $H_{f,0}^s$ to $H_{f,1}^s$. This shift reflects the fact that builders must borrow funds to finance the building of houses. High interest rates on these construction loans add to the cost of building houses. This is a shift to the left in the flow supply function. Because of the effect on both overall housing demand and the flow supply of new houses, residential construction investment declines from R_0 to R_1 in Figure 14.6b.

Credit rationing, due to regulation Q, and the direct effect of high interest rates caused the housing market to be very sensitive to restrictive monetary policies in the 1970s and early 1980s. Housing starts (new houses put under construction) fell 43 percent between 1973 and 1975 as monetary policy became more restrictive. Following a later move toward tighter money in 1979,

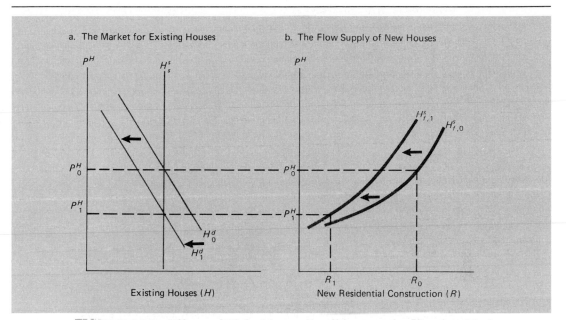

FIGURE 14.6 Effects of Tight-Money Conditions on the Housing Market
High interest rates and possible reduced availability of mortgage funds shift the demand schedule for the existing stock of houses down from H_0^d to H_1^d (part a). The price of existing houses declines from P_0^H to P_1^H. The tight-money conditions also shift the supply schedule for new houses to the left, from $H_{f,0}^s$ to $H_{f,0}^s$ (part b). As a result of this shift in the flow supply schedule for new houses and of the movement down the supply schedule due to the price fall, residential construction declines from R_0 to R_1.

housing starts fell by nearly 50 percent over a three-year period. With regulation Q ceilings gone and therefore credit rationing much less of a factor, the housing industry is somewhat less sensitive to shifts in monetary policy. Still, the long-term nature of mortgage loans continues to make residential construction one of the most interest-rate-sensitive components of aggregate demand.

Inventory Investment

Firms hold inventories both of goods that will be used in the production process and of finished goods awaiting sale. Changes in the stock of business inventories comprise inventory investment, a small but cyclically volatile component of total output. In the United States during the post–World War II period, inventory investment has, in fact, been so volatile that it has accounted for a very substantial portion of the decline in output during recessions. In the 1981–82 recession, negative inventory investment (the decline in the level of inventories) constituted 41 percent of the decline in output; for the 1973–75 recession the figure was 65 percent.[23]

The starting point for the standard theory of inventory investment is the assumption that a firm's desired level of inventories depends on the level of the firm's sales. In the aggregate, desired inventories (IN^d) are generally assumed to be proportional to expected sales (S^e), that is,

$$IN_t^d = \gamma S_t^e \qquad \gamma > 0 \tag{14.29}$$

where γ (gamma) is the factor of proportionality.

If we assume that actual inventories are adjusted to the desired level with a lag, as a result of costs of adjustment, we can specify inventory investment (ΔIN) as

$$\Delta IN_t = IN_t - IN_{t-1} = \lambda_1(IN_t^d - IN_{t-1}) \qquad 0 < \lambda_1 < 1 \tag{14.30}$$

We can rewrite equation (14.30) as

$$\Delta IN_t = \lambda_1(\gamma S_t^e - IN_{t-1}) \tag{14.31}$$

From equation (14.31) we expect a *positive* relationship between inventories and expected sales or the general level of economic activity. There is, however, another aspect to the inventory–sales relationship.

In our discussion of the Keynesian model, we made a distinction between *intended* and *unintended* inventory investment or accumulation. As discussed there, when aggregate demand falls short of output, the difference shows up as an unintended accumulation of business inventories that is counted in the national income accounts as inventory investment. This suggests a *negative* relationship between sales and inventory investment to the degree that sales differed from the expected level of sales, the sales level on which the firms' production decisions were based. Taking account of this additional relationship results in the following specification for inventory investment:

$$\Delta IN_t = \lambda_1(\gamma S_t^e - IN_{t-1}) + \lambda_2(S_t^e - S_t) \qquad 0 < \lambda_1 < 1; 0 < \lambda_2 < 1 \tag{14.32}$$

The first term is as in the preceding equation. The second term specifies that at least a portion of the amount by which sales (S) fall short of (or exceed) expected sales (S^e) shows up as an unintended increase (decrease) in business inventories.

---

[23]These figures are from Alan S. Blinder and Louis J. Maccini, "Taking Stock: A Critical Assessment of Recent Research on Inventories," *Journal of Economic Perspectives*, 5 (Winter 1991), pp. 73–96.

From equation (14.32) we would expect that as sales vary over the business cycle, the following pattern of inventory investment would emerge. As sales start to fall off in a downturn, to the degree that the change was unanticipated, business inventory investment would increase. This would be an unintended inventory accumulation [the second term in equation (14.32)]. In the later stages of the downturn, as the drop in sales becomes anticipated (S^e falls), we would expect to observe a rather sharp drop in inventory investment or even to see inventory disinvestment, as firms try to cut inventories. A reverse pattern will be evidenced following an upturn. Thus inventory investment would move in a procyclical way but lagging the cycle somewhat.

This cyclical pattern of inventory investment is illustrated in Table 14.5, which shows the behavior of real income and inventory investment during three periods of recession and recovery. As can be seen from the table, inventory investment remained positive (the level of inventories continued to increase), whereas real GNP declined throughout 1974. Inventory investment then turned sharply negative in 1975, as firms tried to restore desired inventory sales ratios. Inventory investment turned strongly positive again only after the recovery was well under way in 1976. In the 1979–80 period, there were also signs of unintended inventory accumulation, when GNP declined in the second quarter of 1979 and again, though to a lesser extent, in the second quarter of 1980. There was a sharp run-off of inventories just as GNP growth resumed in the third quarter of 1980. In the 1981–82 recession, it again appears that unintended inventory accumulation occurred during the first part of the downturn in 1981. This was followed by a sharp decline in inventories that continued well after the beginning of the economic recovery in the fourth quarter of 1982.

Table 14.5 also shows the instability of inventory investment. For example, inventory investment averaged $21 billion in the last three quarters of 1981, then swung to an average of *minus* $24.6 billion for 1982. Such fluctuations in inventory investment form a major part of the fluctuation in GNP over the business cycle.

Read Perspectives 14.2.

Consumer Durable Goods Expenditures

Consumer durable goods include items such as automobiles and household appliances. Consumer durable goods expenditures have averaged 8 to 10 percent of GNP in recent years. The proper durable goods variable for the consumption theories considered in Section 14.1 is the service flow from durable goods, sometimes measured as depreciation of the stock of consumer durables. Because of the difficulty of accurate measurement of depreciation of consumer durables, the national income accounts include all expenditures on durables under consumption. Still, from a theoretical standpoint,

TABLE 14.5 Inventory Investment During Three Recessions and Recoveries (billions of dollars at an annual rate)

Year:Quarter	Inventory Investment and the Change in Real GNP (1974:I–1976:II)									
	1974:I	1974:II	1974:III	1974:IV	1975:I	1975:II	1975:III	1975:IV	1976:I	1976:II
Change in real GNP	−12.4	−5.7	−7.6	−17.2	−29.9	18.4	32.5	9.1	26.2	15.5
Inventory investment	13.7	12.9	2.3	6.8	−22.0	−25.1	4.9	−3.6	14.5	18.3

Year:Quarter	Inventory Investment and the Change in Real GNP (1979:I–1980:IV)							
	1979:I	1979:II	1979:III	1979:IV	1980:I	1980:II	1980:III	1980:IV
Change in real GNP	14.1	−6.5	14.8	2.4	11.3	−38.6	8.6	13.7
Inventory investment	24.3	33.1	13.3	−0.8	2.5	7.4	−16.0	−17.4

Year:Quarter	Inventory Investment and the Change in Real GNP (1981:II–1983:III)									
	1981:II	1981:III	1981:IV	1982:I	1982:II	1982:III	1982:IV	1983:I	1983:II	1983:III
Change in real GNP	−1.8	8.6	−20.8	−17.8	−3.0	−3.4	1.7	12.2	33.9	25.4
Inventory investment	15.0	33.6	14.3	−25.7	−11.2	−4.9	−56.4	−39.4	−14.5	8.5

Source: Economic Report of The President, 1982, 1984.

PERSPECTIVES

Inventories
in the Recent Recession

As this is being written, it is not known whether or not the recession which began in July 1990 is over. So the full profile of inventory investment over recession and recovery cannot yet be described. So far, however, the behavior of inventory investment in this recession seems to be following the same pattern as that in the previous three recessions.

Figure 14.7 plots the inventory-to-monthly-sales ratio from 1989 to 1991. The hatch marks show the period of recession.

Notice how the inventory sales ratio shoots up during the early part of the recession, then declines sharply as the recession proceeds. This is the same pattern as in the earlier recessions, as seen in Table 14.5. The graph reflects the fact that inventory investment was a positive 3.4 percent between June and December 1990, which was likely due to sales falling below firms' expectations, and then a negative 3.4 percent over the first eight months of 1991 as expectations adjusted (both figures at an annual rate).

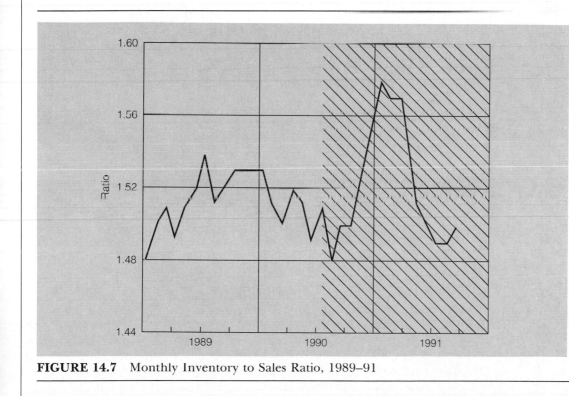

FIGURE 14.7   Monthly Inventory to Sales Ratio, 1989–91

expenditure on consumer durables net of depreciation of the stock of durables should be viewed as a form of investment by households.

One reason it is important to distinguish consumer durable expenditures from the service flow from durables is that, whereas the service flow, as part of consumption, depends on expected lifetime or permanent income, the timing of expenditures on durables is much more responsive to current income. Fluctuations in consumer expenditures on durable goods, especially automobiles, have been a prime factor in recent recessions in the United States. In the 1980 recession, for example, consumer expenditures on durable goods fell by 11 percent between the first and second quarters. This drop in consumer expenditures of $24.5 billion at an annual rate constituted approximately 70 percent of the total drop in GNP.

Both the 1974–75 and 1980 recessions followed large increases in energy prices, including the price of gasoline. In early 1974 and in the spring and summer of 1979, there were also gasoline shortages. The high price of gasoline and supply disruption led to a fall in consumer demand for new domestically produced automobiles as consumers cut overall automobile purchases and also switched to more fuel-efficient imports. *Real* (1982 dollars) expenditures on new domestic automobiles in 1974–75 averaged only 79 percent of the 1973 level. During the second quarter of 1980, real expenditures on automobiles were running at 66 percent of the level of 1978, although in this latter period tight credit conditions were probably more important in explaining the drop than were conditions in the energy market. High interest rates during 1982 led to another sharp decline in automobile sales, even as energy prices fell. Declines in the demand for domestically produced automobiles have contributed substantially to past recessions. Unemployment in the automobile industry and the industries that are suppliers of the automobile industry have risen much more than the national average in each of the last three U.S. recessions.

If consumer durable goods expenditures are responsive to changes in current income, changes in tax rates could be used to regulate aggregate demand even if consumption (purchases of consumer nondurables, services, and the service flow from consumer durables) did not respond strongly to tax-induced changes in disposable income. Consumption might not respond if the tax change were temporary and consumption depended on expected lifetime or *permanent* income, but even a temporary tax change could have a strong effect on the timing of consumer durable expenditures. Additionally, monetary policy might be used to affect the level of consumer durable expenditures. Empirical research in the United States for the 1950s and 1960s did not reveal much evidence of a systematic negative relationship between interest rates and the level of consumer durable expenditure. More recent work, however, does suggest that monetary policy affects consumer durable goods expenditure both through interest rates and, more broadly, by affecting the overall liquidity position of households.[24] Tight-money policies, for example, will, as we have seen, lower the values of long-term bonds and corporate equities, causing a decline in household wealth and therefore in willingness to borrow to finance purchases of durables. This research indicates that effects on consumer durable expenditures are an additional way in which monetary policy affects aggregate demand.

14.3 • CONCLUSION

It would be satisfying to close this discussion of aggregate demand by drawing some definite conclusions as to whether private-sector demand is unstable, as the Keynesians believe, or , as the monetarists believe, the private sector is "shock-absorbing." Clearly, several components of aggregate demand—business fixed investment, residential construction investment, inventory investment, and consumer durable goods expenditures—exhibit considerable variability over the cycle. But is the source of this variability inherent within these expenditure functions, or are these categories of expenditure simply responding for the most part to policy-induced shocks? The data themselves reveal little about the relative quantitative importance of policy-induced shocks versus shocks originating with private-sector demand itself. Monetarists and Keynesians have quite different interpretations of the cyclical instability of aggregate demand described in this chapter.

Review Questions and Problems

1. Explain the essential elements of the life cycle theory of consumer behavior.

2. Explain why the existence of "liquidity constraints" facing certain households would have an important implication for the life cycle theory of consumption.

3. What are the implications of the life cycle theory of consumer behavior for the effectiveness of fiscal policy actions?

4. Explain the permanent income theory of consumer behavior. Compare the permanent income hypothesis with the life cycle theory of consumption.

---

[24] See, for example, two papers by Frederick S. Mishkin, "Illiquidity, Consumer Durable Expenditure, and Monetary Policy," *American Economic Review,* 66 (September 1976), pp. 642–53, and "What Depressed the Consumer? The Household Balance Sheet and the 1973–75 Recession," *Brookings Papers on Economic Activity,* No. 1, 1977, pp. 123–64.

5. How do the life cycle hypothesis and the permanent income hypothesis resolve the apparent contradiction between the short-run data, which suggest a nonproportional relationship between consumption and income, and the long-run data, which suggest a proportional relationship?

6. Do the more detailed specifications of consumption in this chapter lead you to believe that monetary policy would be more or less effective than was suggested by our previous analysis? Do they indicate that fiscal policy is likely to be more or less effective, again relative to our previous analysis?

7. Suppose that the level of Social Security benefits were substantially cut for those retiring after the year 2015. What effect would this have on the saving rate, assuming either (a) saving is primarily life cycle saving or (b) saving is primarily for bequests to a future generation? Explain.

8. Explain the relationship between output and investment implied by the *accelerator* theory. How do costs of adjustment affect the model?

9. What elements are comprised in the cost of capital relevant to the firm's investment decision? Explain how this cost of capital can be influenced by monetary and fiscal policy actions.

10. Explain the channels by which an expansionary monetary policy would affect the level of residential construction activity.

11. Distinguish between consumption of durables and consumer purchases of durable goods. Why might it be important to make this distinction?

12. Explain the way in which you would expect inventory investment to respond to an increase in sales during a period when GNP rises rapidly.

13. Do the more detailed specifications of fixed business investment and the other components of investment lead you to believe that monetary policy will be more or less effective than was suggested by our previous analysis? Do they indicate that fiscal policy is likely to be more or less effective, again relative to our previous analysis?

Selected Readings

Consumption

Ackley, Gardner, *Macroeconomic Theory and Policy*. New York: Macmillan, 1978, Chaps. 16 and 17.

Ando, Albert, and Modigliani, Franco, "The Life Cycle Hypothesis of Saving: Aggregate Implications and Tests," *American Economic Review*, 53 (March 1963), pp. 55–84.

Blinder, Alan S., and Deaton, Angus, "The Time Series Consumption Function Revisited," *Brookings Papers on Economic Activity,* 16:2 (1985), pp. 465–521.

Campbell, John, and Deaton, Angus, "Why is Consumption So Smooth," *Review of Economic Studies,* 56 (July 1989), pp. 357–74.

Duesenberry, James, *Income, Saving and the Theory of Consumer Behavior.* Cambridge, Mass.: Harvard University Press, 1949.

Friedman, Milton, *A Theory of the Consumption Function.* Princeton, N.J.: Princeton University Press, 1957.

Hall, Robert, "Stochastic Implications of the Life Cycle–Permanent Income Hypothesis: Theory and Evidence," *Journal of Political Economy,* 86 (December 1978), pp. 971–87.

Keynes, John M., *The General Theory of Employment, Interest and Money.* New York: Harcourt, Brace and Company, 1936, Chaps. 8–10.

Kotlikoff, Laurence, "Intergenerational Transfers and Savings," *Journal of Economic Perspectives,* 2 (Spring 1988), pp. 41–58.

Modigliani, Franco, "The Life Cycle Hypothesis of Saving, the Demand for Wealth and the Supply of Capital," *Social Research,* 33 (June 1966), pp. 160–217.

Modigliani, Franco, "Monetary Policy and Consumption," in *Consumer Spending and Monetary Policy: The Linkages.* Boston: Federal Reserve Bank of Boston, 1971.

Modigliani, Franco, "Life Cycle, Individual Thrift and the Wealth of Nations," *American Economic Review,* 76 (June 1986), pp. 297–313.

Modigliani, Franco, "The Role of Intergenerational Transfers and Life Cycle Saving in the Accumulation of Wealth," *Journal of Economic Perspectives,* 2 (Spring 1988), pp. 15–40.

Tobin, James, and Dolde, Walter, "Wealth Liquidity and Consumption," in *Consumer Spending and Monetary Policy: The Linkages.* Boston: Federal Reserve Bank of Boston, 1971.

Fixed Business Investment

Ackley, Gardner, *Macroeconomic Theory and Policy.* New York: Macmillan, 1978, Chaps. 18 and 19.

Bischoff, Charles, "Business Investment in the 1970's: A Comparison of the Models," *Brookings Papers on Economic Activity,* No. 1, 1971, pp. 13–63.

Clark, Peter K., "Investment in the 1970's: Theory, Performance and Prediction," *Brookings Papers on Economic Activity,* No. 1, 1979, pp. 73–113.

Eisner, Robert, and Strotz, R. H., "Determinants of Business Investment," in Commission on Money and Credit, *Impacts of Monetary Policy.* Englewood Cliffs, N.J.: Prentice-Hall, 1964. Reprinted (in part) in N. F. Keiser, ed.,

Readings in Macroeconomics. Englewood Cliffs, N.J.: Prentice-Hall, 1970, pp. 133–40; and in Arnold Zellner, ed., *Readings in Economic Statistics and Econometrics*. Boston: Little Brown, 1968, pp. 463–516.

Evans, Michael, *Macroeconomic Activity.* New York: Harper & Row, 1969, Chaps. 4 and 5.

Fazzari, Steven; Hubbard, R. Glen; and Petersen, Bruce C., "Financing Constraints and Corporate Investment," *Brookings Papers on Economic Activity,* (1988:1), pp. 141–95.

Samuelson, Paul, "Interactions Between the Multiplier Analysis and the Principle of Acceleration," *Review of Economics and Statistics,* 21 (May 1939), pp. 75–78. Reprinted in M. G. Mueller, ed., *Readings in Macroeconomics.* New York: Holt, Rinehart and Winston, 1966.

Other Components of Investment

Biven, David G., "Inventories and Interest Rates," *American Economic Review,* 76 (March 1986), pp. 168–76.

Blinder, Alan S., "Inventories and the Structure of Macroeconomic Models," *American Economic Review,* 71 (May 1981), pp. 11–16.

Blinder, Alan S., and Maccini, Louis J., "Taking Stock: A Critical Assessment of Recent Research on Inventories," *Journal of Economic Perspectives,* 5 (Winter 1991), pp. 73–96.

Evans, Michael, *Macroeconomic Activity.* New York: Harper & Row, 1969, Chaps. 6–8.

Feldstein, Martin, and Auerbach, Alan, "Inventory Behavior in Durable-Goods Manufacturing: The Target Adjustment Model," *Brookings Papers on Economic Activity,* No. 2, 1976, pp. 351–96.

Hymans, Saul H., "Consumer Durable Spending: Explanation and Prediction," *Brookings Papers on Economic Activity,* No. 2, 1970, pp. 173–99.

Jaffe, Dwight M., and Rosen, Kenneth T., "Mortgage Credit Availability and Residential Construction," *Brookings Papers on Economic Activity,* No. 2, 1979, pp. 336–76.

Juster, Thomas F., and Wachtel, Paul, "Inflation and the Consumer," *Brookings Papers on Economic Activity,* No. 1, 1972, pp. 71–114.

15 Money Demand

We have considered the demand for money in our discussion of the classical, Keynesian, and monetarist theories. The treatment of money demand in those chapters, however, was limited to the simplest money demand specifications. The discussion of these specifications was confined to issues of general importance for the overall model. In this chapter we take a more detailed look at the demand for money.

As a starting point, let us review our previous analysis of money demand. Classical economists concentrated on the role of money as a medium of exchange (i.e., a generally accepted means of payment). They confined their attention to what Keynes termed the *transactions* demand for money. With uncertain as well as planned transactions taken into account, this medium-of-exchange function of money can also incorporate what Keynes called the *precautionary* demand for money.

In the form developed by the Cambridge economists (Section 4.1), the classical money demand function can be expressed as

$$M^d = kPy \qquad (15.1)$$

Money demand (M^d) was proportional to nominal income (the price level P times real income y). The proportion of income held in the form of money (k) was considered to be relatively stable as long as we were considering equilibrium positions. In the alternative Fisherian version of the classical theory,

$$MV = Py \qquad (15.2)$$

the velocity of money, equal to $1/k$, was assumed to be stable. An important feature of this classical analysis is that the interest rate was not considered to be an important determinant of money demand.

Keynes's theory of money demand considered the role of money as a *store of value* in addition to its role as a medium of exchange. The store-of-value

419

function of money means simply that money is one possible asset in which one can hold wealth. In analyzing the store-of-value function of money, Keynes was led to view money as one asset in an individual's portfolio and to consider the manner in which an individual divides his wealth between money and alternative assets. Keynes lumped all these assets that were alternatives to holding money into one category, which he termed "bonds." The important variable that Keynes believed would determine the split of an individual's portfolio between money and bonds was the interest rate, the return on bonds. At a high rate of interest the foregone interest payments that would result from holding money instead of bonds would be high. Further, in Keynes's view, when the interest rate was high relative to some reasonably fixed view of the normal level of the interest rate, the public would expect a future decline in the interest rate. Such a decline in the rate of interest would mean a capital gain on bonds.[1] Both because of the high foregone interest payments and the fact that at a high interest rate a future capital gain on bonds was likely, Keynes believed that a high interest rate would result in a low demand for money as a store of value. As the interest rate declined, the demand for money as an asset would increase. Thus, according to Keynes's theory, the demand for money would vary inversely with the rate of interest. This is Keynes's theory of the speculative demand for money.

Keynes also considered the transaction demand for money and the precautionary demand for money. Both of these demands grew out of the means-of-payment function of money, as noted previously. Keynes viewed income as the primary variable determining the amount of money held because of both the transactions and precautionary motives, higher values of income increasing the amount of money held for each purpose.

The Keynesian money demand function can be expressed as

$$M^d = L(y, r) \tag{15.3}$$

Money demand depends on both the level of income *and the interest rate*. The fact that in the Keynesian view money demand was a function of the interest rate as well as the level of income was of considerable importance in explaining the differences in policy conclusions between the classical and Keynesian models. If the demand for money is simply proportional to income, as in equations (15.1) and (15.2), then nominal income is completely determined by the supply of money. With k fixed in equation (15.1), for example, an increase in the money stock (M) in equilibrium must result in a proportional increase in nominal income, as can be seen by writing the equilibrium condition

$$M = M^d = kPy \tag{15.4}$$

---

[1]The relationship between bond prices and interest rate changes is discussed in Section 6.1.

from which it follows that

$$\Delta M = k\,\Delta P\,y$$
$$\frac{1}{k}\Delta M = \Delta P\,y \tag{15.5}$$

Note that with k fixed, nominal income can change *only* when the quantity of money changes, as can be seen from equation (15.5). Factors such as fiscal policy actions or autonomous changes in investment demand have no role in income determination. In terms of the IS–LM analysis of Chapters 6 and 7, this is the classical case of the vertical LM schedule, where fixing the supply of money fixes the level of income, with shifts in the IS schedule affecting only the interest rate.

With the Keynesian form of the money demand function, income is no longer proportional to the quantity of money. Factors other than changes in the quantity of money, including fiscal policy changes and autonomous shifts in investment demand, can cause changes in income. Again in terms of the IS–LM analysis, the LM curve is upward-sloping, not vertical. Shifts in the IS curve change the level of income. The relative importance of monetary factors and the other determinants of income (factors that shift the IS curve) depend on the slopes of the IS and LM schedules, as discussed previously (see Table 7.2).

In the monetarist view, the interest rate theoretically belongs in the money demand function. Empirically, the monetarists do not believe that the interest elasticity of money demand is high. They believe that the LM schedule, although not vertical, is quite steep. For this reason, among others, they believe that money is the dominant influence on nominal income.

The role of the interest rate in determining money demand is thus a question with important policy implications. Keynes's followers have not been satisfied with Keynes's own theory of the relationship between the interest rate and money demand—his theory of the speculative demand for money. They have advanced additional reasons for the dependence of money demand on the interest rate. This modern-Keynesian theory of money demand also extends Keynes's analysis of the transactions demand for money. These extensions of the Keynesian theory are discussed in Sections 15.2 and 15.3. Beginning in the mid-1970s, money demand functions constructed on the basis of this theory began to "misbehave." The actual behavior of money demand began to diverge seriously from the predictions of the theory. Specifically, for a time beginning in the mid-1970s, the public was holding much less money than the theory of money demand predicted. This event was termed the "Case of the Missing Money." Then during the 1980s, the growth in money demand exceeded the rate predicted by theory. Possible reasons for this instability in money demand are discussed in Section 15.4.

Prior to presenting theories of money demand, we consider the definition of *money*.

15.1 · THE DEFINITION OF MONEY

The Functions of Money

The standard definition of money is whatever performs monetary functions, and there are three widely accepted functions of money:

Means of Exchange.   Money serves as a medium for transactions. You can buy goods or services with money. You receive money for sales of goods or services. We don't often think about it, but this function of money contributes greatly to economic efficiency. Exchange without money would mean swaps of goods for goods—what is called *barter*. Some barter transactions exist even in a monetary economy. You might trade babysitting services for a free room in a house near campus, for example.

But barter as the predominant means of trade is very inefficient. The problem is that barter transactions require a *double coincidence of wants*. Ms. Jones wants to buy shoes and sell jewelry. Ms. Smith wants to sell shoes but wants to buy a computer. No trade takes place, and both must take time to look for trading partners whose buying *and* selling desires coincide with theirs. In a monetary economy, Ms. Jones buys the shoes from Ms. Smith with money. Ms. Smith can then use the money to buy a computer from *anyone* selling one. Ms. Jones needs only to find someone who wants to buy jewelry (without necessarily wanting to sell shoes).

Store of Value.   Money functions as a store for wealth, a way to save for future spending. Money is one type of financial asset. Other stores of value (e.g., a corporate or government bond) are not money because they do not perform the other monetary functions. They cannot be used as a means of exchange or as a unit of account, the third central function of money.

Unit of Account.   Prices are measured in terms of money. In Albania prices (and debts) are measured in terms of the lek, in Poland the zloty, in Britain the pound. In the United States, as you already know, prices and debts are measured in dollars and cents. As with the means-of-exchange function, money provides great conveniences as a unit of account. Merchants, for example, simply post one price in dollars, not in terms of each possible commodity that might be traded for their goods.

Components of the Money Supply

The money supply is composed of those financial assets that serve the preceding functions. Which assets are these in the United States? This question is harder to answer than it might at first appear. In fact, there are several different measures of the money supply. All are composed of currency and deposits at commercial banks and other depository institutions (e.g., savings and loan associations).

One measure, called **M1**, is the narrowest of the money measures in the United States. It consists of currency plus *checkable* deposits.

Checkable deposits are those on which you can write checks, that is, those on which you can direct the bank in writing to make payments to another party.[2] Currency clearly fulfills the three monetary functions previously discussed. So do bank deposits, as long as you can write checks on them.[3] Checks on deposits can be used to buy things (means-of-exchange function); deposits are a store of value, and currency or deposits are a unit of account.

Two other measures, **M2** and **M3**, are broader. They include the components of M1 plus additional bank deposits that have no or only limited provisions for checks.

M2, for example, includes money market mutual fund accounts, which allow only checks for amounts above some minimum (e.g., $500), and regular savings and time deposits on which no checks can be written.[4] M3 is an even broader measure of money, which includes large deposits, termed *certificates of deposit (CDs)*, on which no checks can be written. Details of the composition of each of these measures of money, as well as figures for the level of these measures for October 1991, are given in Table 15.1.

The rationale for the broader money measures is that the additional deposit categories included in them relative to M1 are very similar to checkable deposits or are easily converted to checkable deposits. Balances in regular saving accounts, for example, can be converted into checkable deposits (or currency) simply by going to the bank. If these additional deposit types are sufficiently close substitutes for checkable deposits and currency, we may want to consider them as money.

---

[2]Another small item included in M1 is travelers' checks. Our discussion here ignores a number of small items in the different definitions of money. For detailed definitions, see notes Table 15.1.

[3]Often in the discussion it is convenient to refer to deposits as *bank* deposits, but keep in mind that other institutions such as savings and loans and credit unions, which are not, strictly banks, provide some of these deposit accounts.

[4]Balances in regular savings accounts are, in practice, available on demand. Time deposits, however, are for a specified time period (e.g., one year), and there may be penalties for early withdrawal.

TABLE 15.1 Money Supply Measures (billions of dollars), October 1991

M1	$ 879.4	Averages of daily figures for
		(1) currency outside the Treasury, Federal Reserve Banks, and the vaults of commercial banks;
		(2) travelers' checks on nonbank issuers;
		(3) demand deposits at all commercial banks other than those due to domestic banks, the U.S. government, and foreign banks and official institutions less cash items in the process of collection and Federal Reserve float; and
		(4) negotiable order of withdrawal (NOW) and automatic transfer service (ATS) accounts at banks and thrift institutions, credit union share draft accounts (CUSD), and demand deposits at mutual savings banks.
M2	3398.8	M1 plus savings and small-denomination time deposits at all depository institutions, overnight repurchase agreements at commercial banks, overnight Eurodollars held by U.S. residents other than banks at Caribbean branches of member banks, money market mutual fund shares, and money market deposit accounts (MMDAs).
M3	4146.4	M2 plus large-denomination time deposits at all depository institutions and term repurchase agreements at commercial banks and savings and loan associations.

15.2 · THE THEORY OF THE TRANSACTIONS DEMAND FOR MONEY

Money is a medium of exchange, and individuals hold money for use in transactions. The fact that not only is money *used* in transactions, but positive sums of money are being held at any point in time for transaction purposes is the result of the imperfect synchronization in income receipts and expenditures. Money is held to bridge the gap between receipts and expenditures. Theories of the transactions demand for money have generally assumed that income is a good measure of the volume of transactions and, as a consequence, that the transactions demand for money varies positively with income. In the classical theory, income was the only systematic determinant of the transactions demand for money. Since the transactions motive, stemming from the role of money as a medium of exchange, was the major role of money considered in the classical theory, the classical money demand function ($M^d = kPy$) expressed money demand simply as a function of income.

We saw that the Keynesian money demand function [$M^d = L(y, r)$] expressed money demand as a function of both income and the interest rate, an increase in the interest rate being expected to reduce money demand for a given income level. Keynes's own theory of the relationship of money demand and the interest rate was the *speculative demand for money*, which concerned money's role as a store of value. It was previously noted that the transactions demand might also be expected to be negatively related to the level of the interest rate. Individuals would economize on their holdings of transactions balances at higher interest rates. Extensions of Keynes's theory of the demand for money developing this relationship between the transactions demand for money and the interest rate are the subject of this section. In the next section we discuss extensions of Keynes's theory of the demand for money as a store of wealth.

Before beginning our discussion of these theories of the demand for money, two points are worth noting. First, as we just explained, there is no unique definition of money. For the purposes of the transactions demand for money, the relevant concept of money is the narrow definition confined to those assets actually used in transactions—the M1 definition of money. When we turn to consideration of money as a store of wealth, a broader definition of money such as M2 or M3 will be relevant. Second, many of the theories of money demand are often stated in terms of the behavior of households. But money is also held by firms and by the government sector. In recent years, for example, the government and business sectors accounted for approximately one third of money (M1) holdings.

The Inventory-Theoretic Approach to Money Demand

Extensions of Keynes's theory of the transactions demand have followed an **inventory-theoretic approach**. The transactions demand for money has been regarded as the inventory of the medium of exchange (money) that will be held by the individual or firm. The theory of the optimal level of this inventory has been developed by William Baumol and James Tobin along the lines of the theory of the inventory holdings of goods by a firm.[5]

To explain the inventory-theoretic approach, we consider first the example of an individual who receives an income payment of Y dollars *in cash* at the beginning of the period ($t = 0$). To be concrete, suppose that the individual has a monthly income payment of $1200. We further assume that the individual spends this income at a uniform and perfectly predictable rate throughout the period. By the end of the monthly period ($t = 1$), cash holdings have fallen to zero. This time profile of money holdings is depicted in Figure 15.1. The average inventory of money held during the period will equal $Y/2$, in this case $600 ($1200/2), which is also the amount that will be held at the midpoint of the period ($t = 1/2$). This follows from the assumption that expenditures take place at a uniform rate over the period.

---

[5]William Baumol's article "The Transactions Demand for Cash: An Inventory-Theoretic Approach" appeared in the *Quarterly Journal of Economics* 66 (November 1952), pp. 545–56. James Tobin's article "The Interest-Elasticity of the Transactions Demand for Cash" appeared in the *Review of Economics and Statistics*, 38 (August 1956), pp. 241–47.

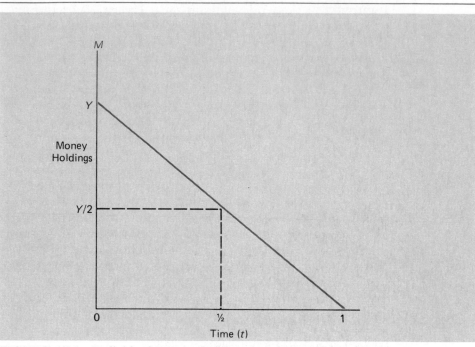

FIGURE 15.1 Individual Money Holdings (No Bond Market Transactions)
The individual receives income in cash of Y dollars at the beginning of the period.
The income payment is spent at an even rate over the period. Average holdings of
cash equal the holdings at the midpoint of the period $Y/2$.

From Figure 15.1 the relationship between the level of income and the
average level of money holdings can be seen. The higher the initial income
payment, the higher is the average level or inventory of money holdings.
The inventory-theoretic approach also suggests that the level of the inventory holding of money depends on the carrying cost of the inventory. In the
case of money, the relevant carrying cost is the interest foregone by holding
money and not bonds, net of the cost to the individual of making a transfer
between money and bonds, which we will call the *brokerage fee*.[6] The time

---

[6] As explained in Chapter 6, some components of M1—the definition of money relevant for
transactions demand—pay interest. The interest rates paid on these M1 deposits are, however,
lower than those on non-M1 assets, for example, on treasury bills or actual bonds. The interest
foregone by holding the M1 deposits that pay some interest is then the differential between
the rate on non-M1 assets and M1 deposits. It will simplify our analysis, without changing our
conclusions, to neglect interest payments on deposits in our discussion.

profile of money holdings shown in Figure 15.1 assumes that throughout the month the individual holds all of the unspent income payment received at the beginning of the month in the form of money. Alternatively, he could invest a proportion of the initial income payment in bonds and then sell the bonds when additional money was needed for transactions.[7]

If the individual invested half of the income payment in bonds at the beginning of the month and then sold the bonds when cash holdings were exhausted at midmonth, the time profile of money holdings would be as depicted in Figure 15.2. At the beginning of the month, money holdings are $Y/2$ (Y minus bond purchase of $Y/2$). Money holdings are then run down to zero by the midpoint of the period at a uniform rate. Average money holdings for the first half of the period are therefore $Y/4$. At the midpoint of the period, the bonds are sold. Money holdings return to $Y/2$ and are then spent at a uniform rate over the last half of the period. The average money holding for the second half of the period is again $Y/4$. Thus the average money holding for the period as a whole is $Y/4$, which is lower than $Y/2$ for the case where no bonds are held. The average bond holding for the period is $Y/4$ (the average of $Y/2$ for the first half of the period and zero for the second). If the monthly interest rate on bonds is r percent and there is a fixed brokerage fee for each transaction in the bond market of b dollars, then the net profit (Pr) from the one bond purchase and one sale (number of transactions, n, equals 2) is

$$Pr(n = 2) = r\frac{Y}{4} - 2b \tag{15.6}$$

The first term is the interest earning on the average bond holding. The second term is the transactions cost, which equals the brokerage fee times the number of bond market transactions.

If, instead, the individual chose to engage in three transactions ($n = 3$) in the bond market, the optimal strategy would be to buy an amount of bonds equal to $\frac{2}{3}Y$ at the start of the period, sell bonds equal to $\frac{1}{3}Y$ when initial money holdings of $\frac{1}{3}Y$ are exhausted at $t = \frac{1}{3}$, and then sell the remaining amount of bonds, $\frac{1}{3}Y$, when money holdings are again

---

[7]Notice that since money here is defined to be actual transactions balances (M1), such assets as savings deposits or money market mutual funds are *not* considered as money. These assets are then included in "bonds," so the choice the individual faces can be thought of as one between holding transactions balances or, for example, holding a money market fund account that pays interest but requires periodic trips to the bank to deposit funds in a checking account. The "brokerage" cost in this case is a time cost. For the wealthy individual or business firm, the interest-earning asset, which is the alternative to holding money, might be a short-term government security, and the brokerage cost is an actual broker's fee for buying or selling the security.

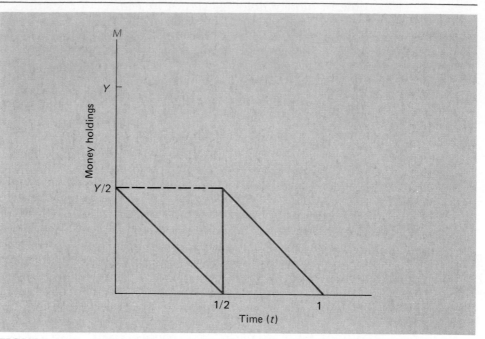

FIGURE 15.2 Individual's Money Holdings (Two Bond Market Transactions)
The individual receives Y dollars at the beginning of the period, half of which $(Y/2)$ is used to purchase bonds. The other half is spent at an even rate over the first half of the period. The bonds are sold at t = one half, and the cash received $(Y/2)$ is spent at an even rate during the second half of the period. Average cash holdings are $Y/4\,(Y/2 \div 2)$ in each half of the period and, therefore, for the period as a whole.

exhausted at $t = \frac{2}{3}$.[8] The time profile of money holdings over the period in this case would be as shown in Figure 15.3. From the preceding example and the figure, it can be seen that average money holdings are equal to $Y/6$ $(Y/3 \div 2$ for each third of the time period). Average bond holdings equal $Y/3$ ($\frac{2}{3}Y$ for the first third of the period, $\frac{1}{3}Y$ over the second third, zero for the last third) and net profit from the bond transactions equals

$$Pr(n = 3) = r\frac{Y}{3} - 3b \qquad (15.7)$$

---

[8]Notice that a specific strategy of purchases and sales is being considered here, namely, a strategy whereby, after the initial bond purchase, sales are evenly spaced across the time period. Such a strategy can be shown to be the optimal one in the sense that it enables the individual to maximize his average holdings of bonds and, hence, interest earnings for a given number of transactions. For a proof of this, see Tobin, "Interest-Elasticity."

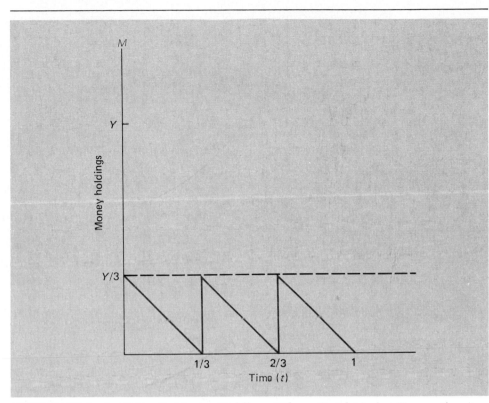

FIGURE 15.3 Individual's Money Holdings (Three Bond Market Transactions) In this case ($n = 3$) two thirds of the income payment is invested in bonds at the beginning of the period. The remaining one-third Y ($Y/3$) is spent at an even rate over the first third of the period. Bond sales of $Y/3$ are made at $t = \frac{1}{3}$ and $t = \frac{2}{3}$ with cash receipts again spent at even rates. Average money holdings are $Y/6$ ($Y/3 \div 2$) for each third of the period and, therefore, for the period as a whole.

Average money holdings, average bond holdings, and net profit can be expressed in terms of the number of bond market transactions (n).

In the general case, average money holdings (M) will be

$$M = \frac{1}{2n}Y \tag{15.8}$$

In the examples, for $n = 2$, money holdings were $Y/4$ ($= Y/2(2)$) and for $n = 3$ money holdings were $Y/6$ ($= Y/2(3)$). Average bond holdings (B) can be expressed as

$$B = \frac{n-1}{2n}Y \tag{15.9}$$

For the cases considered previously, average bond holdings were

$$\frac{Y}{4}\left(=\frac{2-1}{2(2)}Y\right) \text{ for } n = 2 \quad \text{and} \quad \frac{Y}{3}\left(=\frac{3-1}{2(3)}Y\right) \text{ for } n = 3$$

The general expression for net profits is

$$Pr = r\frac{n-1}{2n}Y - nb \tag{15.10}$$

The first term in this expression is the interest earnings on bonds equal to the interest rate (r) times average bond holdings $((n-1)/2n)Y$, which is given by equation (15.9). The second term is transaction costs, the brokerage fee (b) times the number of transactions (n). By substituting $n = 2$ and $n = 3$ into equation (15.10), we can get equations (15.6) and (15.7) from our previous examples.

From these results it can be seen that, for a given income payment, the choice of how much money (or how many bonds) to hold is determined by the choice of n. Determining the optimum n determines the optimal money and bond holdings for the individual. Economic theory tells us that the individual will choose n such that net profits from bond transactions (Pr) are maximized. He will increase the number of transactions in the bond market until the point is reached where the marginal interest earnings from one additional transaction are just equated with the constant marginal cost, which will be equal to the brokerage fee.

The determination of the optimal number of bond transactions to undertake is depicted in Figure 15.4. The marginal cost (MC) of an additional transaction, which is the brokerage fee (b), is assumed to be constant, hence the horizontal marginal cost schedule in Figure 15.4.

What about the marginal revenue schedule? When we previously considered going from zero bond market transactions to one purchase and sale, we found that interest earnings increased from zero to $r(Y/4)$. A further increase to three bond market transactions increased average bond holdings from $Y/4$ to $Y/3$, and therefore interest earnings rose from $r(Y/4)$ to $r(Y/3)$, a further, though smaller, increase in interest earnings of $r(Y/12)$ [note that $r(Y/12) = r(Y/3) - r(Y/4)$]; the marginal revenue of the third transaction is then $r(Y/12)$. Now consider the marginal revenue from a fourth bond market transaction. Using the formula given [equation (15.9)] for average bond holdings, we can compute bond holdings that result from four bond market transactions,

$$B = \frac{n-1}{2n}Y = \frac{4-1}{2(4)}Y = \frac{3}{8}Y$$

Therefore, interest earnings will be $r(^3/_8)Y$ for four bond market transactions. The marginal revenue of the fourth transaction will be $r(Y/24)$ [note

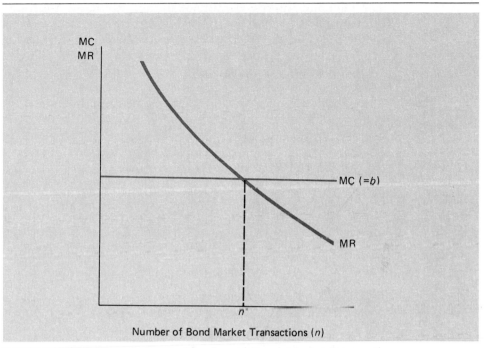

FIGURE 15.4 The Optimum Number of Bond Market Transactions
The optimum number of bond transactions (n^*) is chosen to equate the declining marginal revenue of additional bond market transactions (MR) with their constant marginal cost (MC).

that $r(Y/24) = r(\frac{3}{8})Y - r(Y/3)$]. The marginal revenue from the fourth bond market transaction is positive but is *less* than the marginal revenue from the third transaction [$r(Y/24) < r(Y/12)$]. This is the general case. The increment to interest earnings from an additional bond market transaction declines as the number of bond market transactions increases. The marginal revenue schedule is downward-sloping, as shown in Figure 15.4.

The optimal number of bond market transactions is determined at the point where the marginal revenue schedule intersects the horizontal marginal cost schedule, at n^* in Figure 15.4. Beyond this point the marginal gain in interest earned from increasing the number of bond market transactions is not sufficient to cover the brokerage cost of the transaction.

The choice of n determines the split of money and bond holdings *for a given income payment*. We can see how various factors affect the demand for money and bonds by seeing how they affect n. Factors that increase (decrease) n will, for a given income, increase (decrease) average bond holdings and decrease (increase) average money holdings. Figure 15.5a shows the effect on n of an increase in the interest rate from r_0 to r_1. This increase in the interest rate shifts the marginal revenue schedule upward from $MR(r_0)$ to $MR(r_1)$ in Figure15.5a. At a higher interest rate, an additional bond market transaction will increase bond holdings by the same amount as before but will increase interest earnings on the bond holding by a greater amount. The individual responds by engaging in more bond market transactions; the optimum number of bond market transactions rises from n_0^* to n_1^* The average bond holding over the period increases. The average money holding declines. This is the effect referred to in previous chapters as economizing on transactions balances at higher interest rates. The inventory-theoretic approach to the transactions demand for money provides a theoretical basis for this negative relationship between money demand and the interest rate.

The inventory-theoretic approach to the transactions demand for money also suggests that the demands for money and bonds depend on the cost of making a transfer between money and bonds, what we have termed the brokerage fee (b). Figure 15.5b illustrates the effect on the optimum number of bond transactions (n) as a result of an increase in the brokerage fee from b_0 to b_1. The increase in the brokerage fee increases the marginal cost of bond market transactions and consequently lowers the number of such transactions, from n_0^* to n_1^* in Figure 15.5b. The increase in the brokerage fee increases the transactions demand for money and lowers the average bond holding over the period. This follows since an increase in the brokerage fee makes it more costly to switch funds temporarily into bond holdings.

Changes in the interest rate or brokerage fee affect the split of a given income payment between money and bond holdings. What is the effect of changing the level of income (Y)? We have already mentioned one effect. For a given n that determines the split between money and bonds, an increase in Y increases both the demand for money and bonds. For the cases considered—for example, with n equals 2—the average money and bond holdings are both $Y/4$ and clearly depend positively on Y. However, an increase in Y will *not* leave n unchanged. As Y rises, the marginal revenue from each additional bond transaction will increase, since each bond transaction will be for a greater amount and will therefore result in a greater increase in interest earnings. With the assumption of a fixed brokerage fee, the marginal cost of a transfer will be constant. The increase in income will then increase n. Graphically, this effect is the same as for the increase in the interest rate in Figure 15.5a; the MR schedule shifts to the right along a fixed MC schedule. Given the assumptions made here, it can be shown that the increase in n will not be so great as to cause money holdings to decline on net as income rises. *An increase in income will increase the holdings of both bonds and money.* With the increase in n, the split between the two assets will move toward a higher proportion of bonds and lower proportion of money.

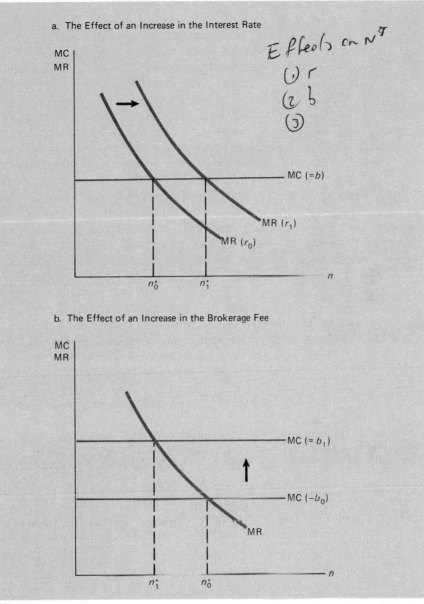

FIGURE 15.5 Factors Determining the Optimum Number of Bond Market Transactions (n^*)

Part a: An increase in the interest rate from r_0 or r_1 shifts the marginal revenue curve to the right from $MR(r_0)$ to $MR(r_1)$. The optimal number of bond market transactions increases from n_0^* to n_1^*. Part b: An increase in the brokerage fee from b_0 to b_1 shifts the marginal cost schedule up from $MC(= b_0)$ to $MC(= b_1)$. The optimal number of bond market transactions falls from n_0^* to n_1^*.

As a consequence, the transactions demand for money will rise less than proportionately with income.

There is one qualification to the foregoing analysis. We have so far not constrained n to be an integer, but clearly it must be. You cannot engage in 6.89 bond market transactions and, more important, you cannot engage in any number less than 2. If a comparison of marginal cost and marginal revenue indicates that the optimal level of transactions is less than 2, no transactions will be undertaken. For individuals with modest incomes, this situation seems quite likely. The brokerage cost will be high enough (even if it is just a time cost of switching between savings deposits and checkable deposits) that the individual will simply hold money needed for transactions throughout the whole period. In our example in which the pay period is 1 month and monthly income is $1200, if the *monthly* interest rate is $1/2$ of 1 percent (0.005, as a decimal), then for $n = 2$, average bond holdings would be $300 ($Y/4$), and interest earnings would be $1.50 ($300 \times 0.005$). It is easy to see that the brokerage cost may exceed this amount and cause the individual to forgo any bond market transactions. For those with relatively low incomes, the transactions demand for money may, therefore, simply be proportional to income and independent of the interest rate and brokerage fee. For wealthier individuals and especially for firms, however, brokerage costs will not prohibit bond market transactions.

The Inventory-Theoretic Approach Continued: The Case of Uncertainty

In the preceding subsection we derived an expression for the transactions demand for money under the assumption that the stream of transactions the individual will undertake can be perfectly predicted at the beginning of the period. Here we relax that assumption and recognize that there is an element of uncertainty concerning the expenditures that will have to be undertaken over a given period. By doing so, we provide a rationale for Keynes's precautionary demand for money. In addition, we will see the effect that changes in the degree of uncertainty about necessary future expenditures have on the demand for money.

The standard type of example used to explain the precautionary motive for holding money is that of a man starting on a business trip. He has a certain amount of money with him for planned transactions but also carries some additional money in case of unexpected expenditures, such as car repairs. If he did not do so, he might incur some cost, such as a missed business appointment, while he tried to arrange to obtain money to pay for car repairs or other unexpected expenditures. The modern business man or woman probably carries so many credit cards that the story has become unrealistic, but the point it makes is relevant. We hold money over and above that required for planned expenditures because of uncertainty about the volume of expenditures that will prove necessary. We do so because there is a cost to being without the money needed to finance unforeseen expenditures—what can be termed the cost of being *illiquid*. The higher our money holdings, the less likely it is that we will incur such a cost.

The level of uncertainty about the future stream of expenditures is therefore one factor determining the level of money demand. For one class of money holders, business corporations, uncertainty concerning both receipts and expenditures provides the *primary* motive for holding money. Rather than receiving an income payment on the first of a given month and making payments over the month, a typical corporation is continually receiving income and making expenditures. If there is a significant nonsynchronization of receipts and expenditures, for a reasonably large corporation the gain in holding bonds instead of keeping idle money balances is likely to be large, even net of brokerage fees. The major factor causing corporations to hold transactions balances in the form of money is uncertainty about the pattern of receipts and expenditures. It is to guard against the costs of illiquidity resulting from an unexpected excess of expenditures over receipts that corporations have a large transactions demand for money. An implication of this that will be important later is that any changes that enable the corporation to reduce the uncertainty about future receipts and expenditures will reduce the corporate transactions demand for money.

The role of uncertainty in determining the transactions demand for money can be illustrated by modifying the graphical analysis in Figure 15.4. With uncertainty about the level of expenditures over the course of the period, putting more funds into bonds and less into money will increase the probability of becoming illiquid and incurring some cost. We can model this as an additional marginal cost to increasing the number of bond market transactions (n) and therefore lowering money holdings.

Specifically, let the probability of illiquidity (i.e., the probability that the individual or firm will not have sufficient money to finance a necessary expenditure) be given by $p(M, \mu)$. M is the amount of money held, which will negatively affect the probability that an individual will become illiquid. The term μ (mu) is a measure of the uncertainty of expenditures. The higher the value of μ, the more likely it is that expenditures will deviate greatly from the predicted pattern, and for a given holding of money, the more likely it is that an individual will become illiquid. The last element to be specified is the cost of becoming illiquid. For simplicity let us assume this cost is equal to b, the brokerage cost. If the firm or individual becomes illiquid, an unplanned sale of bonds has to be made and an extra brokerage cost is incurred.

With these modifications, the marginal cost of engaging in an additional bond market transaction (increasing n) can be expressed as

$$MC = b + \Delta p(M, \mu)b \qquad (15.11)$$

The marginal cost includes the fixed brokerage fee (b), as before. Additionally, in the presence of uncertainty an increase in the number of bond market transactions will decrease the holdings of money, and thus increase the probability of illiquidity [$\Delta p(M, \mu)$ will be positive]. This increase in the probability of becoming illiquid times the cost of becoming illiquid (b) is an additional marginal cost of a bond market transaction.

The determination of the optimal number of bond market transactions in the presence of uncertainty is depicted in Figure 15.6. The marginal cost curve is higher than the corresponding schedule for the case of no uncertainty, where marginal cost is simply the brokerage fee b. The marginal cost schedule is upward-sloping, since we assume that the *increase* in the probability of illiquidity that comes from each additional bond transaction will become greater the higher the value of n, and hence the further money holdings have been drawn down.

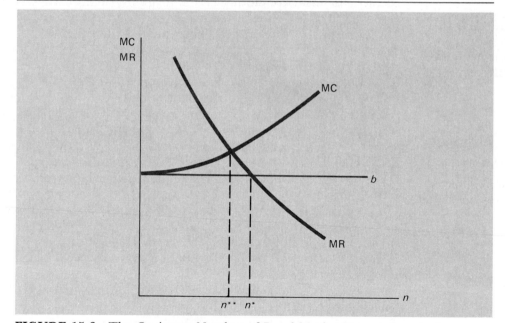

FIGURE 15.6 The Optimum Number of Bond Market Transactions in the Presence of Uncertainty

With uncertainty about the stream of transactions and the resulting chance of becoming illiquid, the marginal cost of each transaction exceeds the brokerage fee. Because of the higher marginal cost of an additional bond market transaction, the optimal number of bond market transactions in the presence of uncertainty (n^{**}) will be lower than in the case of no uncertainty (n^*).

The optimum number of bond market transactions is now given by n^{**}, where the new MC schedule intersects the MR schedule. Compared with the case in which no uncertainty exists about the pattern of expenditures (MC $= b$), the number of bond market transactions is reduced, which means that average bond holdings are lower and average money holdings are higher. This increase in money holdings resulting from the decline in the number of bond market transactions from n^* to n^{**} is the *precautionary* demand for money.

Finally, consider the effects of a change in μ, the degree of uncertainty about the stream of expenditures that will have to be undertaken. It seems reasonable to assume that an increase in μ will shift the MC schedule upward, as shown in Figure 15.7. With more uncertainty about the pattern of expenditures (a higher value of μ), any increase in n can be expected to cause a greater increase in the probability of illiquidity. If this is the case, then an increase in μ (from μ_0 to μ_1) will lower n^{**} from n_0^{**} to n_1^{**} in Figure 15.7 and increase the demand for money. Correspondingly, any reduction in the uncertainty of the pattern of expenditures for individuals or firms will

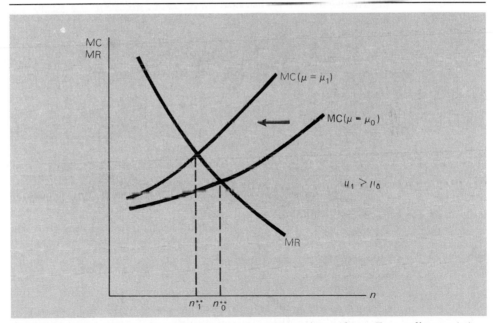

FIGURE 15.7 **Effect of an Increase in the Uncertainty About Expenditures (μ)**
An increase in uncertainty about the pattern of expenditures (from μ_0 to μ_1) shifts the marginal cost schedule upward. The optimal number of bond market transactions falls (from n_0^{**} to n_1^{**}).

enable them to increase their holdings of bonds and reduce their demand for money.

Summary

Our analysis to this point results in a demand for money function subsuming Keynes's transactions and precautionary demand for money, which is of the following form:

$$M^d = L(y, r, b, \mu) \tag{15.12}$$

The demand for money depends positively on the level of income (y), the level of the brokerage fee (b), and the uncertainty about the pattern of expenditures (μ). Money demand depends negatively on the rate of interest. The money demand functions used in previous chapters omitted the last two arguments in (15.12). Implicitly, these were assumed to be constant in the short run and thus not to affect the analysis. This has also been the usual assumption in empirical work on money demand. But in the 1970s and 1980s there were systematic changes in both μ and b, and such changes are one element in the puzzles concerning money demand instability that we will consider in Section 15.4. First, we explain some modifications that have been made in Keynes's theory of the demand for money as a store of wealth.

15.3 • EXTENSIONS OF KEYNES'S THEORY OF THE DEMAND FOR MONEY AS A STORE OF WEALTH

Keynesian economists working in the 1950s followed Keynes's approach to the theory of the demand for money in that they considered the function of money as a store of wealth (or value) in addition to the means-of-payment function. They modified and extended Keynes's analysis, however, to remedy what they saw as weaknesses in his theory of the speculative motive for money demand.

Keynes's theory of the speculative demand for money had been criticized on two grounds. First, recall that Keynes's theory implies that the individual investor would hold *all* of his wealth in bonds (other than the amount of money held as transaction balances) as long as the interest rate is above the "critical rate," a rate below which the expected capital loss on bonds outweighed the interest earnings on bonds. If the interest rate fell below this critical rate, the investor would transfer all his wealth to money.[9] Keynes's

---

[9]See the discussion in Section 6.1.

theory therefore cannot explain why an individual investor holds both money balances *and* bonds as stores of wealth, but such *portfolio diversification* does occur.

Second, according to Keynes's theory, investors hold money as an asset when the interest rate is low because they expect the interest rate to rise—returning to a *normal* level. A crucial element of Keynes's theory is the existence of a fixed or at least only slowly changing *normal* level for the interest rate, around which the actual interest rate fluctuates. The assumption of a normal level of interest rates around which the actual rates fluctuate is more consistent with interest-rate behavior for the period before Keynes wrote *The General Theory* in 1936 than afterward. In the period since 1950, there has been a pronounced upward trend in interest rates. In such a circumstance, Keynes's particular assumption that investors always expect a return of interest rates to some normal level requires modification. At a minimum, the normal level itself has to be assumed to be changing over time. Keynesian economists have modified Keynes's original theory in a way that explains why portfolio diversification takes place and that does not depend on Keynes's particular assumption about investor expectations of a return of the interest rate to a "normal" level. The starting point of this portfolio theory of money demand is the work of James Tobin.[10]

The Demand for Money as Behavior Toward Risk

Tobin analyzes the individual's allocation of his portfolio between money holdings and bond holdings. The transactions demand for money is assumed to be determined separately along the lines of the analysis of the preceding section, and the demand for money considered here is solely the demand for money as a store of wealth.

In Tobin's theory the individual investor has no fixed normal level to which he always expects interest rates to return. We can assume that the individual believes capital gains or losses to be equally likely; that is, the *expected* capital gain is zero. The best expectation of the return on bonds is simply the interest rate (r). But note that this interest rate is only the *expected* return on bonds. The actual return generally includes some capital gain or loss, since the interest rate generally does not remain fixed. Thus bonds pay an expected return of r, but they are a risky asset—their actual return is uncertain.

Money, in contrast, is a safe asset. Money's nominal return of zero is lower than the expected return on bonds, but there are no capital gains or

---

[10]Tobin's original article on this subject, "Liquidity Preference as Behavior Towards Risk," appeared in the *Review of Economic Studies*, 25 (February 1958), pp. 65–86.

losses when money is held.[11] Tobin argues that an individual will hold some proportion of his wealth in money because by doing so he lowers the overall riskiness of his portfolio below what it would be if he held all bonds. The overall expected return on the portfolio would be higher if the portfolio were all bonds, but if the investor is *risk averse*, he will be willing to sacrifice higher return, to some degree, for a reduction in risk. The demand for money as an asset is explained as aversion to risk.

Tobin's theory can be explained more precisely by referring to Figure 15.8. In the upper quadrant on the vertical axis we measure the expected return to the portfolio; the horizontal axis measures the riskiness of the portfolio. The expected return on the portfolio is the total interest earning on bonds, which depends on the interest rate and the proportion of his portfolio that the individual places in bonds. The total risk the individual takes depends on the uncertainty concerning bond prices—the uncertainty concerning future interest-rate movements—as well as on the proportion of the portfolio placed in bonds, the risky asset. We denote the expected total return R and the total risk of the portfolio σ_T. If the individual holds all his wealth (Wh) in money and none in bonds, the portfolio will have zero expected return and zero risk. This portfolio allocation is shown at the origin (point O) in Figure 15.8. As the proportion of bonds in the portfolio increases, expected portfolio return and risk both rise. The terms on which the individual investor can increase the expected return on the portfolio (R) at the cost of increasing risk (σ_T) are represented by the line C.[12] As the investor moves along C, more bonds and less money are being held.

The lower quadrant of Figure 15.8 shows the allocation of the portfolio between bonds and money, which results in each risk–return combination. Bond holdings (B) are measured on the vertical axis. The amount of bonds held in the portfolio increases as we go *down* the vertical axis to a maximum of Wh, the total amount of wealth. The difference between bond holdings and total wealth is the demand for money as an asset (M). The schedule B in the lower portion of the graph shows the relationship between total

---

[11] Again, here we are ignoring the interest rate paid on deposits. To assume a positive deposit rate, but one less than the interest rate on bonds (r) will not affect our analysis as long as we assume that, because of costs to the bank of providing deposits, as r rises the deposit rate does not rise by the same amount—in other words, as long as we assume that as r rises, the *relative* return on bonds rises.

[12] Let σ be a measure of the uncertainty about the price of a given bond, the total risk on the portfolio can be measured by $\sigma_T = \sigma B$. Total expected return is $R = rB$, so the slope of the C line is $\Delta R/\Delta \sigma_T = r/\sigma$. Note that the C schedule here bears no relationship to the consumption function in previous chapters, which was also denoted by the letter C.

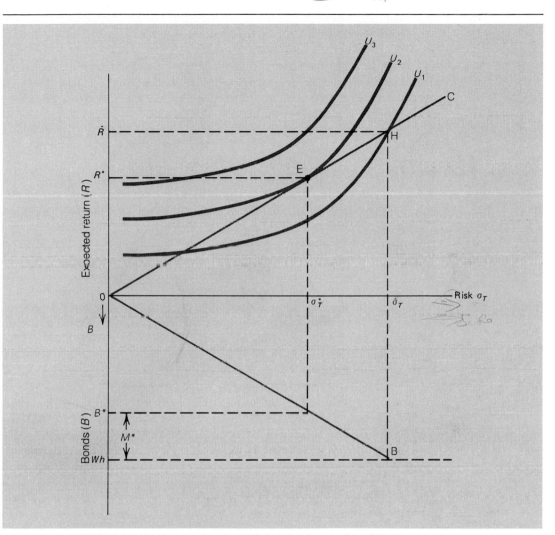

FIGURE 15.8   Determination of the Optimum Portfolio

The upper quadrant of the figure shows the individual's optimum portfolio allocation. At point E the risk-expected return trade-off the individual faces in the market,
reflected in the slope of the line C, is just equal to the terms on which he is willing
to accept increased risk in return for an increase in expected return, given by the
slope of his indifference curve (U_2). The lower quadrant shows the bond and money
holdings (B^*, M^*) that correspond to this choice of risk and expected return.

risk of the portfolio (σ_T) and the proportion of the portfolio held in bonds, with higher levels of risk associated with higher proportions of bonds in the portfolio.

To find the optimum portfolio allocation, we need to consider the preferences of the investor. We assume that the investor is risk averse; that is, whereas he wishes to receive a higher return on the portfolio, he also wants to avoid risk. He will accept a higher level of risk only if compensated by an increase in expected return. Formally, we assume that the investor's utility function is

$$U = U(R, \sigma_T) \tag{15.13}$$

where an increase in expected return (R) increases utility and an increase in risk (σ_T) decreases utility. On the basis of this utility function, we can draw indifference curves for the investor, U_1, U_2, U_3 in Figure 15.8, showing the terms on which he is willing to accept more risk if compensated by receiving a higher expected return. Each point along one of these curves represents a given level of utility. As we move from U_1 to U_2 to U_3, we are moving to higher levels of utility—higher levels of R and lower levels of σ_T. The curves are drawn sloping upward to represent a risk-averse investor who will take on more risk only if compensated by a higher return. Further, the curves become steeper as we move to the right, reflecting the assumption of *increasing risk aversion*, meaning that the more risk the individual has already taken on, the greater the increase in expected return he will require before he is willing to accept an additional increase in risk.

We now have all the elements needed to determine the optimal portfolio allocation between money and bonds. The individual investor will move to the point along the C schedule where that schedule is just tangent to one of his indifference curves. At this point the terms on which he is *able* to increase expected return on the portfolio by accepting more risk, given by the slope of the C schedule, will be equated to the terms on which he is *willing* to make this trade-off, given by the slope of his indifference curve. This is the point of utility maximization. In Figure 15.8 this tangency occurs at point E, with expected return R^* and total risk on the portfolio of σ_T^*. From the lower quadrant it can be seen that this risk–return combination is achieved by holding an amount of bonds equal to B^* and by holding the remainder of wealth M^* in the form of money.

The demand for money is then what Tobin terms "behavior toward risk"—the result of attempting to reduce risk below what it would be if all wealth were held in bonds. In Figure 15.8 such an all-bonds portfolio would incur risk of $\hat{\sigma}_T$ and earn expected return of $\hat{R}$, point H in the graph. This portfolio yields a lower level of utility than that represented by bond holdings of B^* and money holdings of M^*. The reason for this can be seen from the graph. As we move farther along the C schedule past point E, the incremental expected return on the portfolio from holding additional bonds is insufficient to compensate the investor for the additional risk he incurs (the slope of the C schedule is lower than that of the U_2 schedule). Movement to point H takes him to a lower indifference curve, U_1 in Figure 15.8.

Money Demand and the Rate of Interest

Tobin's theory implies that the amount of money held as an asset depends on the level of the interest rate. This relationship between the interest rate and asset demand for money is depicted in Figure 15.9. The effect of an increase in the interest rate will be to improve the terms on which the expected return on the portfolio can be increased by accepting greater risk. At a higher interest rate a given increase in risk, which corresponds to a given increase in the amount of bonds in the portfolio, will result in a greater increase in expected return on the portfolio. In Figure 15.9, increases in the interest rate from r_0 to r_1, then to r_2, will rotate the C schedule in a counterclockwise direction from $C(r_0)$ to $C(r_1)$, then to $C(r_2)$.[13] The point of portfolio optimization shifts from point E to point F and then to point G in the graph. In response to the increase in the interest rate, the individual will increase the proportion of his wealth held in the interest-bearing asset, bonds (from B_0 to B_1 to B_2), and will decrease his holding of money (from M_0 to M_1 to M_2).

Tobin's theory implies, as did Keynes's, that the demand for money as a store of wealth depends negatively on the interest rate.[14] Within Tobin's framework an increase in the rate of interest can be considered an increase in the payment received for undertaking risk. When this payment is increased, the individual investor is willing to undertake more risk by putting a greater proportion of his portfolio into the risky asset, bonds, and thus a smaller proportion into the safe asset, money.

---

[13] As explained in footnote 12, the slope of the C schedule is r/σ; thus an increase in r will increase the slope of the C schedule.

[14] The conclusion that an increase in the interest rate will result in a decline in money demand does require one additional assumption. As explained in the text, a rise in the interest rate on bonds improves the terms of the trade-off between risk and return, making bonds more desirable. This corresponds to the usual *substitution* effect in consumer demand theory. There is also an *income* effect, however, which may work in the opposite direction. With a higher interest rate, a given return can now be achieved with a lower proportion of bonds in the portfolio. This income effect may lead the investor to lower the demand for bonds and increase the security gained from holding money. In the terms of consumer demand theory, risk may be an inferior good. In the text we make the typical assumption that the substitution effect dominates any possible negative income effect.

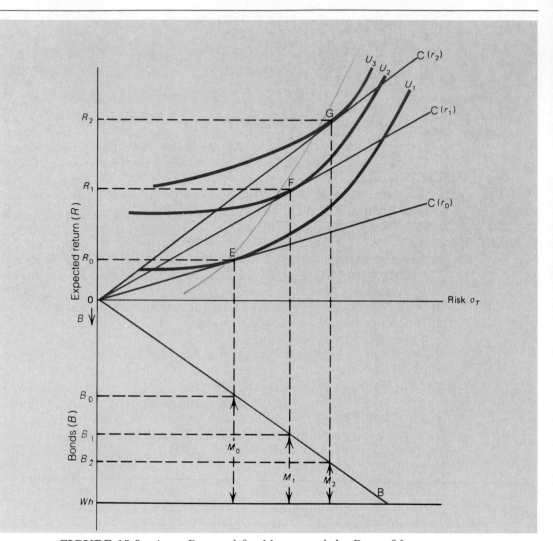

FIGURE 15.9　Asset Demand for Money and the Rate of Interest
Increases in the interest rate (from r_0 to r_1 and then r_2) make the C schedule steeper by increasing the expected return that can be gained by undertaking increased risk. The individual responds by undertaking more risk and earning higher expected returns (the equilibrium point moves from point E to F, then to G). Holdings of the risky asset, bonds, increase (from B_0 to B_1, then to B_2); money holdings decline (from M_0 to M_1 then to M_2).

15.4 • INSTABILITY OF MONEY DEMAND

Our analysis of the transactions and precautionary demands for money (Section 15.2) left us with the following specification for money demand:

$$M^d = L(y, r, b, \mu) \qquad (15.14)$$

where y is the level of income, r is the interest rate, b the brokerage cost, and μ a measure of the uncertainty concerning transactions that will have to be undertaken in the current period. Our consideration of the role of money as a store of wealth—Tobin's portfolio theory (Section 15.3)—suggests an additional reason for including the interest rate in the money demand function, since his analysis implies that the demand for money as a store of wealth will decline with an increase in the interest rate. Tobin's analysis also indicates that uncertainty about future changes in bond prices, and hence the risk involved in buying bonds, may be an additional determinant of money demand.

In practice, a simplification of equation (15.14) has become the conventional specification of the money demand function. This simple form is that used in the earlier Keynesian theoretical models in Part II:

$$M^d = L(y, r) \qquad (15.15)$$

Money demand has been taken to depend on income and on an interest rate, usually a short-term interest rate. Although the preference for this specification has never been unanimous, this type of money demand function performed well in predicting actual money holdings up until 1973, and it was widely used for empirical work and in policy formation.

Evidence on the Instability of Money Demand

Beginning in 1974, equations such as (15.15) began to "misbehave." First, over the 1974–79 period such equations, when estimated by statistical procedures and used to predict the public's holding of money, began to seriously overpredict the amount of money the public was holding. Given the level of income and the interest rate, the public was holding less money than these equations predicted. The question of why this was happening has been called, as noted previously, the "Case of the Missing Money." Later, during the 1980s, the situation was reversed, and the conventional money demand function began to seriously underpredict the public's money demand.[15]

---

[15] For recent discussions of the instability of the U.S. money demand function, see Stephen M. Goldfeld and Daniel E. Sichel, "The Demand for Money," in Frank H. Hahn and Benjamin M. Friedman, eds., *Handbook of Monetary Economics* (Amsterdam: North-Holland, 1990); and John A. Leventakis and Sophocles N. Brissimus, "Instability of the U.S. Money Demand Function," *Journal of Economic Surveys*, 5(2:1991), pp. 131–61.

TABLE 15.2 Underprediction of Money Demand
(1982–83), Percentage Growth Rate in M1

Year	Quarter	Actual	Predicted
1982	1	10.3	5.4
1982	2	2.2	1.8
1982	3	6.1	4.3
1982	4	15.4	6.7
1983	1	12.8	6.9
1983	2	11.6	6.7
1983	3	9.5	6.9
1983	4	4.8	7.7

Source: Thomas Simpson, "Changes in the Financial System: Implications for Monetary Policy," *Brookings Papers on Economic Activity* (1984:1), Table 2, p. 253. Predictions are from what Simpson terms the "Standard Model."

Both the overprediction of money demand in the 1970s and the subsequent underprediction in the early 1980s were large. By 1979, the conventional money demand function was overpredicting money demand by $55.7 billion, or 15.5 percent.[16]

Table 15.2 documents the *underprediction* of money demand in 1982 and 1983. In the table the comparison is between the predicted and actual percentage growth (at an annual rate) in money demand (M1 definition). Over the whole of 1982, the conventional money demand function predicted growth in money demand of 4.6 percent, compared to actual growth of 8.5 percent; for 1983, predicted growth was 7.1 percent, compared to actual growth of 9.7 percent (averages of four quarterly figures).

The failure of the conventional money demand function indicates a possible instability in money demand, and such instability would have important theoretical and policy implications. Clearly an unstable money demand function would be a matter of importance to the monetarists. A central proposition of monetarism is that there is a stable relationship between money demand and income, ensuring that changes in the *supply* of money will have predictable effects on nominal income. But it is not only to the monetarists that unstable money demand would be important. In the Keynesian view as well, monetary factors—factors determining the position of the *LM* schedule—are an important determinant of income. If the demand for money is unstable, there are unpredictable shifts in the *LM* schedule that

---

[16]See Richard Porter, Thomas Simpson, and Eileen Mauskopf, "Financial Innovations and the Monetary Aggregates," *Brookings Papers on Economic Activity* (1979), p. 214, Table 1.

need to be offset by monetary or other policy actions.[17] Finally, we see in a later chapter that instability in money demand has important implications for the proper conduct of monetary policy by the central bank.

Explanation of Instability of Money Demand

A number of possible explanations have been offered for the difficulty in predicting money demand. Consider first the underprediction of the 1974–79 period—the so-called "Case of the Missing Money." Two factors that may have caused money (M1) demand to fall short of predicted levels over this period are (1) declines in the brokerage fee for moving from demand deposits to other interest-bearing assets (b) and (2) improvements in cash management practices on the part of firms, which lower the uncertainty about expenditures that will have to be made (μ).[18] These two variables, the brokerage fee and a measure of the uncertainty of transactions, are not included in the conventional money demand function [equation (15.15)], even though the theory of the transactions demand for money implies that these variables will have a role in money demand. If brokerage costs declined in the 1970s and firms reduced the uncertainty about their transactions through better cash management practices—both changes that would reduce money demand—it should not be surprising that the conventional money demand function, which did not take account of these changes, overpredicted money demand.

There is evidence that brokerage fees did decline during the 1970s as a result of the development of new substitutes for checkable bank deposits. To give an example, money market mutual funds grew rapidly in the 1970s. These funds sell shares to the public, invest in short-term liquid assets, and then let shareholders withdraw money (redeem their shares) by writing checks drawn on a designated bank. The individual's investment in the fund is equivalent to a checkable deposit, although typically with a fairly high minimum for each check ($250 to $500). The brokerage cost of buying a government bond might make it unprofitable for an individual to economize on demand deposits by temporarily transferring funds into such a bond. There is no explicit "brokerage" fee for shifting funds in and out of a money market fund, however, and the time cost of such transactions is low.

Money market mutual funds were not included in the monetary aggregates in the 1970s. (They are now in M2, but not M1.) Therefore, as interest rates rose in the 1970s, individuals increasingly shifted from checkable bank

---

[17]The effect on the *LM* schedule of a shift in the money demand function is explained in Section 6.2.

[18]Demand deposits are checkable deposits at commercial banks on which no interest is paid. Until the 1970s, these were the only available checking accounts.

deposits, which paid zero interest, to money market mutual funds, which could pay market-determined interest rates; and the demand for money fell well below predicted levels.

There is also evidence that cash management practices on the part of both large and small businesses improved over the mid- and late-1970s. This development was in response to the high levels of short-term interest rates during this period. These high interest rates increased the incentives for cash managers to economize as much as possible on the holding of non–interest-bearing checkable deposits. To do this, they have made investments in cash management techniques that enable them to forecast their short-term cash flows (receipts and expenditures) more accurately, to process receipts as quickly as possible, and in some cases to delay disbursements as long as possible.[19] With these reductions in the uncertainty about their cash flow (μ), firms were able to reduce their transactions demand for money—holding, instead, short-term bonds and other interest-bearing assets. Once the initial investment had been made to institute such cash management procedures, they continued to be used even when short-term interest rates declined.

This combination of lower brokerage fees and improved cash management techniques on the part of firms can explain the bulk of the overprediction of money demand by conventional money demand functions, which neglected both phenomena.

What changed so that, rather than overpredicting, the conventional money demand function began to underpredict money demand in 1982 and 1983? Again, at least part of the explanation has to do with innovations in the financial sector. When the separate components of money demand are examined, the bulk of the underprediction of money demand during this period is in the NOW (negotiated order of withdrawal) account component.[20]

NOW accounts are a type of checkable deposit, introduced nationwide at the beginning of 1981, on which, unlike the situation with demand deposits, banks can pay interest. At first, however, there were legal ceilings on the interest banks could pay on these accounts. Super NOW accounts, which did not have such legal ceilings, were offered for the first time in 1983. The presence of this new deposit type may explain the faster-than-predicted growth in money demand in 1983, especially the bulge in the first several months of that year.

Even in 1982, growth in money demand may have been the result of financial innovation. As just noted, regular NOW accounts had been allowed

[19] Examples of such cash management procedures are given in Porter, Simpson, and Mauskopf, "Financial Innovations."

[20] See Thomas Simpson, "Changes in the Financial System: Implications for Monetary Policy."

nationwide only beginning in January 1981. At that time the short-term interest rate (3-month Treasury bill rate) was 14.7 percent, whereas regular NOW accounts paid the legally imposed ceiling rate, which was then 5 percent. But by the end of 1982, the short-term interest rate had fallen to 8 percent, compared to the NOW ceiling then of 5.25 percent. The conventional function would have predicted an increase in money demand produced by the decline in the short-term interest rate, but estimates of the interest sensitivity of money demand were from a period before the existence of NOW accounts. These estimated money demand functions may have understated the substitution that would take place into NOW accounts as the opportunity cost of holding such accounts fell dramatically.

Adjustments in the 1980s

Later in the 1980s, given the previous errors in predicting money demand, much effort went into constructing better empirical money demand functions. The Federal Reserve was especially interested in this subject because of its importance for monetary policy.

One focus of this research was careful modeling of the returns on the various components of the monetary aggregates. This required models of how banks and other depository institutions set deposit rates. Modeling deposit-rate setting led in turn to studying disaggregated demands for the components of monetary aggregates, because banks appear to set deposit rates differently on different types of deposits.

These new approaches produced a money demand function for the M2 aggregate that had reasonably low prediction errors for the 1980s.[21] M1 demand remains unstable and difficult to predict. Even for M2, there are doubts whether estimated money demand functions will remain stable as further changes in the deposit market occur. Overall, the instability and unpredictability of money demand have led monetary policymakers to place less emphasis on monetary aggregates, as we will see in Chapter 19.

15.5 • CONCLUSION

A summary of the state of the theory of money demand in the early 1970s would have approached the subject as one in which a reasonable consensus

---

[21] See, for example, George Moore, Richard Porter, and David Small, "Modeling the Disaggregated Demands for M2 and M1 in the 1980s: The U.S. Experience." Board of Governors of the Federal Reserve, mimeo (May 1988).

had been reached. Money demand had been shown theoretically and empirically to depend on income and the interest rate. The conventional form of the money demand function discussed in the preceding section performed well. The recent failure of this conventional money demand function has led to renewed interest in the money demand function.

The recent problems in predicting money demand have not led most economists to view the existing theory of money demand as fundamentally flawed. As the preceding discussion illustrates, the source of these recent difficulties can be found in the effects of innovations in the financial sector—the growth of new substitutes for bank deposits, the development of new cash management techniques, and deregulation, which allows depository institutions to pay market-determined deposit rates. In terms of the theory of money demand, more attention needs to focus on previously neglected determinants of money demand: brokerage fees and the uncertainty of transactions flows. Moreover, in a world of market-determined deposit rates for many categories of deposits, the opportunity cost of holding money is more complex to measure.

Review Questions and Problems

1. Explain the composition of each of the main monetary aggregates: M1, M2, and M3.

2. What is the most important difference between the classical and Keynesian theories of money demand?

3. According to the inventory-theoretic approach to the transactions demand for money, how would you expect the amount of money an individual demanded for transactions purposes to be affected by:

   a. An increase in the interest rate paid on bonds.
   b. An increase in the brokerage fee for bond market transactions.
   c. An increase in income.
   d. An increase in the length of the payment period, for example, from a week to a month.

4. Explain the modifications of the inventory-theoretic approach to the transactions demand for money that are required when we assume that the stream of transactions faced by the individual is uncertain.

5. Show how James Tobin's theory explains the demand for money as an asset as "behavior towards risk." How does Tobin's theory differ from Keynes's formulation of the asset demand for money; Keynes's theory of the speculative demand for money? In what respects are Tobin's and Keynes's theories similar?

6. Within Tobin's theory of the demand for money, explain how the optimal portfolio (the choice of money and bond demand) would be affected by an increase in uncertainty about the price of bonds.

7. Explain the nature of the difficulties in predicting money demand in the post-1974 period. How would you explain the source of these difficulties?

Selected Readings

Baumol, William, "The Transaction Demand for Cash: An Inventory-Theoretic Approach," *Quarterly Journal of Economics*, 66 (November 1952), pp. 545–56.

Branson, William, *Macroeconomic Theory and Policy*, 3rd ed. New York: Harper & Row, 1989, Chap. 14.

Goldfeld, Stephen M., "The Case of Missing Money," *Brookings Papers on Economic Activity*, No. 3, 1976, pp. 683–730.

Goldfeld, Stephen M., and Sichel, Daniel E., "The Demand for Money," in Frank H. Hahn and Benjamin M. Friedman, eds., *Handbook of Monetary Economics*. Amsterdam: North-Holland, 1990.

Judd, John, and Scadding, John, "The Search for a Stable Money Demand Function," *Journal of Economic Literature*, 20 (September 1982), pp. 993–1023.

Laidler, David, *The Demand for Money*, 2nd ed. New York: Dun-Donnelley, 1977, Chaps. 2–5.

Porter, Richard, Simpson, Thomas, and Mauskopf, Eileen, "Financial Innovations and the Monetary Aggregates," *Brookings Papers on Economic Activity*, No. 1, 1979, pp. 213–29.

Simpson, Thomas, "The Redefined Monetary Aggregates," *Federal Reserve Bulletin*, 66 (February 1980), pp. 97–114.

Simpson, Thomas, "Changes in the Financial System: Implications for Monetary Policy," *Brookings Papers on Economic Activities*, No. 1 (1984), pp. 249–65.

Surrey, M. J. C., *Macroeconomic Themes*. London: Oxford University Press, 1976, Chap. 4.

Trehan, Bharat, and Walsh, Carl E., "Portfolio Substitution and Recent M1 Behavior," *Contemporary Policy Issues*, 5 (January 1987), pp. 54–63.

Wenninger, John, "Responsiveness of Interest Rate Spreads and Deposit Flows to Changes in Market Rates," *Federal Reserve Bank of New York Quarterly Review*, 11 (Autumn 1986), pp. 1–11.

16 The Money Supply Process

So far we have been assuming that the supply of money is exogenously determined by the central bank. In this chapter we consider the money supply process in more detail. The structure of the central bank in the United States, the **Federal Reserve System**, is discussed, and the Federal Reserve is shown to have a pivotal role in determining the supply of money. The banking system and the nonbank public will, however, also be seen to play a part in determining the money stock. The realism of our previous assumption that the money stock was exogenous will be seen to depend on the behavior of the Federal Reserve. Since it is in the power of the Federal Reserve to offset in large part the actions of the other participants in the money supply process (the banking system and the nonbank public), the money stock is *potentially* an exogenous policy variable. For reasons explained in this chapter, the Federal Reserve has not always chosen to offset such private-sector actions, and the actual determination of the money stock has resulted from both private-sector and Federal Reserve actions. In this chapter we restrict ourselves to a consideration of the way the money supply is determined under different assumptions about the way the Federal Reserve behaves. In a later chapter we consider the question of how the Federal Reserve *should* behave—the question of *optimal* monetary policy.

We begin in Section 16.1 with a discussion of the structure of the Federal Reserve system and the tools that the Federal Reserve uses for monetary control. In Section 16.2 we consider the relationship between bank reserves and deposits, a vital linkage in the process of Federal Reserve control over the money stock. In Section 16.3 we return to the question raised previously concerning the relative roles of the nonbank public, the banking system, and the Federal Reserve in determining the money stock. Section 16.4 concludes our analysis of the money supply process.

16.1 • THE FEDERAL RESERVE SYSTEM

The Structure of the Central Bank

The U.S. system of central banking was established by the Federal Reserve Act of 1913. Unlike the European countries, which have a single central bank, the United States has a system of Federal Reserve Banks, one for each of 12 Federal Reserve districts. Each Federal Reserve Bank is named for the city in which it is located: the Federal Reserve Bank of New York, the Federal Reserve Bank of Chicago, the Federal Reserve Bank of San Francisco, and so forth. For some of the functions of central banking this regional character of our system is important, but the making of macroeconomic policy has become centralized in Washington in two policymaking groups.

The first of these groups is the board of Governors of the Federal Reserve. The board is composed of seven members (governors) appointed by the President of the United States with the advice and consent of the Senate for a term of 14 years. One member of the board is appointed by the president as chairman of the board. When this post has been held by forceful individuals, the chairman has been the dominant figure in monetary policy formation.

The second monetary policymaking group is the Federal Open Market Committee. The most important method by which the Federal Reserve controls the money stock is the purchase and sale of government securities in the "open market," that is, the market of dealers in government securities located in New York City. We will see how the Federal Reserve uses open-market purchases or sales of securities to increase or decrease the *legal reserves* of the banking system. Since banks are required to hold fixed proportions of their deposits in the form of legal reserves, such **open-market operations** can be used to control the deposit component of the money stock. The Open Market Committee controls open-market operations. The Open Market Committee is composed of 12 voting members: the seven members of the Board of Governors and five of the presidents of the regional Federal Reserve Banks. The presidents of the regional banks serve on a rotating basis, with the exception that the president of the New York Bank, the bank charged with actually carrying out open-market operations, is always a voting member of the Open Market Committee.

Federal Reserve Control of the Money Stock

Recall that the monetary aggregates discussed in Chapter 15 consisted of currency held by the public plus various classes of bank deposits. To simplify our discussion, let us assume that only one type of deposit represents all the different types of deposits on which checks can be written, what we will refer to as *checkable* deposits. These include demand deposits, NOW accounts, and credit union share drafts. Savings and time deposits are brought into our discussion at a later point. For now the term *deposits* refers to the assumed one type of checkable deposit. Currency in the United States consists primarily of Federal Reserve notes—paper money issued by the Federal Reserve.

To control the deposit component of the money stock, the Federal Reserve sets legal reserve requirements on deposits. Federal Reserve legal reserve requirements specify that banks must hold a certain percentage of their deposit liabilities either in the form of vault cash (currency) or as deposits at regional Federal Reserve Banks. Given the existence of legal reserve requirements, the Federal Reserve can control the money stock by regulating the supply of legal reserves. Technically, setting reserve requirements and fixing the level of reserves only sets a ceiling on the level of deposits. If, for example, the required reserve ratio is 10 percent and reserves are set at $60 billion, then the maximum amount of deposits would be $600 billion. In fact, since legal reserves (currency or deposits at regional Federal Reserve Banks) do not pay interest, banks will hold few reserves beyond those required by Federal Reserve regulations. Thus the actual level of deposits will be close to the maximum value supportable by a given reserve level.

A convenient starting point for an analysis of Federal Reserve control of bank deposits by means of control of legal reserves is the balance sheet summarizing the assets and liabilities of the Federal Reserve System. A simplified version of this balance sheet is shown in Table 16.1. The primary assets held by the Federal Reserve are U.S. government securities. A much smaller item on the asset side of the balance sheet, but one that we return to later in the discussion, is the amount of loans to commercial banks; these are the *borrowed reserves* of the banking system. On the liability side, the two important items are Federal Reserve notes outstanding, which make up the bulk of U.S. paper currency, and bank reserve deposits. This latter item consists of the deposits held at the Federal Reserve Banks by the banking system to satisfy legal reserve requirements.

These two items on the liability side of the Federal Reserve balance sheet (currency plus bank reserve deposits) form what is termed the **monetary**

TABLE 16.1 Balance Sheet of Federal Reserve Banks, October 1991 (billions of dollars)

Assets		Liabilities	
U.S. government securities	257.4	Federal Reserve notes	274.4
Loans to commercial banks	0.3	Bank reserve deposits	34.9
Other assets	66.1	Other liabilities and capital	14.5
Total assets	323.8	Total liabilities and capital	323.8

Source: Federal Reserve Bulletin, January 1992.

base, since together they provide the foundation for the money stock.[1] Currency is directly included in the money stock if held by the (nonbank) public. The portion of currency held as bank reserves plus bank reserve deposits provides the reserves supporting the deposit component of the money stock. The Federal Reserve controls the quantity of its liabilities, which means that it can control the monetary base and therefore control bank reserves and the money stock.

The Tools of Federal Reserve Control

In this section we discuss the major tools the Federal Reserve uses to control bank reserves.[2] In Section 16.2 the process by which changes in bank reserves affect the level of bank deposits is explained. One point should be noted before proceeding. When the Federal Reserve takes some action changing the monetary base—an action increasing the base, for example—the net effect on bank reserves depends on how much of the increase in the base goes into increased currency holding by the (nonbank) public. The behavior of the public's currency holdings, then, influences the ultimate effect of Federal Reserve actions on the level of bank reserves and, hence, deposits. This influence is explained in the next section, but for now we assume that the public's holding of currency is fixed. With this assumption, changes in the monetary base produce dollar-for-dollar changes in the quantity of bank reserves.

The Federal Reserve uses three major tools to control the reserve position of banks.

Open-Market Operations

The first of these, *open-market operations*, was referred to previously. To see how an open market action by the Federal Reserve affects bank reserves, consider the example of an open-market purchase of a government security worth $1000.

Government securities constitute the major part of Federal Reserve assets, as can be seen from Table 16.1. The purchase of the additional security will increase the government security item on the asset side of the Federal Reserve's balance sheet by $1000. To pay for this security, the Federal Reserve writes a check on itself, drawn on the New York Federal Reserve Bank. A key point to note here is that the Federal Reserve, by writing this check, does not reduce the balance in *any* account. The Federal Reserve simply creates a new liability against itself. What happens to the check? Let us suppose that some

---

[1] The monetary base is often referred as the stock of *high-powered money*, since a given base supports a much larger money stock.

[2] Hereafter we drop the adjective *legal* when referring to bank reserve assets that satisfy reserve requirements.

TABLE 16.2 Effect on the Federal Reserve's Balance Sheet of a $1000 Open Market Purchase

Assets		Liabilities	
Government securities	+1000	Bank reserve deposits	+1000

individual investor sold the security to the Federal Reserve. He will take the check he receives and deposit it in his account at a commercial bank, Chase Manhattan Bank in New York, for example.

Chase Manhattan will then present the check to the New York Federal Reserve Bank for payment. The Federal Reserve will credit the Chase Manhattan account balance at the New York Federal Reserve Bank by $1000. The open-market purchase results in an increase of an equal amount in bank reserve deposits with the Federal Reserve. The effects of the open-market purchase on the balance sheet of the Federal Reserve are summarized in Table 16.2.

In a similar manner, a sale of government securities in the open market will reduce bank reserve deposits by an equal amount. In this case the Federal Reserve receives a check drawn on a commercial bank by the individual who purchased the security. The Federal Reserve lowers that bank's deposit balance at a regional Federal Reserve Bank by the amount of the check. Such open-market purchases and sales of securities provide a flexible means of controlling bank reserves. Open-market operations are the most important of the Federal Reserve's tools of monetary control.

The Discount Rate

The Federal Reserve Open Market Committee oversees open-market operations. The remaining tools of monetary control are administered by the Board of Governors of the Federal Reserve System. The first of these is the Federal Reserve **discount rate**, the interest rate charged by the Federal Reserve on its loans to banks. The Federal Reserve raises or lowers this rate to regulate the volume of such loans to banks. To see the effect on bank reserve deposits of changes in the volume of loans from the Federal Reserve, consider the effect of a loan of $1000 from the Federal Reserve to a bank. The effects on the Federal Reserve's balance sheet are shown in Table 16.3.

TABLE 16.3 Effect on the Federal Reserve's Balance Sheet of a $1000 Loan to a Bank

Assets		Liabilities	
Loans to banks	+1000	Bank reserve deposits	+1000

The asset item "loans to banks" increases by $1000. The proceeds from the loan are credited to the account of the borrowing bank at the Federal Reserve. At this point bank reserve deposits increase by $1000. By lowering the discount rate, the Federal Reserve can encourage banks to borrow and increase the borrowed component of bank reserve deposits. Raising the discount rate has the reverse effect.

The Required Reserve Ratio

The third tool the Federal Reserve uses to control the bank's reserve position is the level of the **required reserve ratio**—the percentage of deposits banks must hold as reserves. Changes in this policy instrument do not change the level of total bank reserves, but by changing the required reserve ratio on deposits, the Federal Reserve changes the quantity of deposits that can be supported by a given level of reserves. Increases in the required reserve ratio reduce the quantity of deposits that can be supported by a given amount of reserves. Consider our previous example, where reserves were set at $60 billion, so that with a 10 percent reserve requirement, the maximum level for checkable deposits was $600 billion. If the required reserve ratio were increased to 15 percent, the maximum level of deposits, with reserves unchanged at $60 billion, would be $400 billion. The increase in the required reserve ratio from 10 percent to 15 percent would have the same effect as a reduction in reserves (e.g., through an open-market sale of securities) from $60 billion to $40 billion ($40 = 0.10 \times 400$).

16.2 · BANK RESERVES AND BANK DEPOSITS

Thus far we have seen how the Federal Reserve can use open-market operations, changes in discount rate, and changes in the required reserve ratio on deposits to affect the reserve position of banks. In this section we examine the process whereby changes in reserves affect the level of deposits in the banking system. Again a convenient starting point is a balance sheet, in this case one for the commercial banking system.[3]

A simplified form of the consolidated balance sheet for all commercial banks is shown in Table 16.4. On the asset side, the first item is cash assets of commercial banks. Reserves (vault cash plus deposits at the Federal Re-

---

[3] To simplify the discussion, we focus on deposit creation by the commercial banking system and neglect other depository institutions (e.g., savings and loans, mutual savings banks, and credit unions). The reserve to deposit linkages for other depository institutions are quite similar to those for commercial banks.

TABLE 16.4 Consolidated Balance Sheet for the Commercial Banking System October 1991 (billions of dollars)

Assets		Liabilities	
Cash assets, including reserves	210.3	Checkable deposits	628.0
Loans	2255.9	Time and savings deposits	1815.7
U.S. Treasury securities	522.1	Other liabilities and capital	1017.9
Other securities	159.8		
Other assets	313.5		
Total assets	3461.6	Total liabilities and capital	3461.6

Source: Federal Reserve Bulletin, January 1992.

serve) come under this category, but other items are included as well (e.g., bank deposits at other banks). Reserves as of the time period for which the table was computed (October 1991) totaled $56.3 billion, of which all but $1.0 billion were required reserves. As explained previously, banks hold few excess reserves, since reserve assets do not pay interest. The other major items on the asset side of the ledger are loans by the commercial banks, which include loans to consumers and businesses and the banks' holdings of both government and private securities. The major liabilities of the commercial banks are deposits, both checkable and savings plus time deposits.[4]

A Simple Model of Deposit Creation

Now consider the effects on the bank of an increase in reserves. Let us return to our example of the Chase Manhattan Bank. Recall our assumption that the Federal Reserve has purchased a $1000 security from an individual, making payment with a check drawn on the New York Federal Reserve Bank. The individual had deposited the check in his account at the Chase Manhattan Bank. When the check is presented for payment at the New York Federal Reserve Bank, Chase Manhattan's reserve deposits at the New York Federal Reserve increase by $1000. To this point, the effects on Chase Manhattan's balance sheet as a result of this open-market purchase by the Federal Reserve are as shown in Table 16.5. Checkable deposits and reserves have both increased by $1000. For simplicity, we continue to assume that there is a uniform reserve requirement of 10 percent. In that case, the increase in reserves will consist of an increase of $100 in required reserves $(0.10 \times 1,000)$ and an increase of $900 in excess reserves, as shown in Table 16.5.

---

[4]There is a significant "other liabilities" category. This contains funds borrowed by banking corporations.

TABLE 16.5   Initial Effect on Chase Manhattan Bank's Balance Sheet from a $1000 Open-Market Purchase

Assets			Liabilities	
Reserves		+1000	Checkable deposits	+1000
Required reserves	+100			
Excess reserves	+900			
Total assets		+1000	Total liabilities	+1000

Table 16.5, however, gives only the initial effects of the open-market purchase on Chase's balance sheet. The position described in Table 16.5 will *not* be an equilibrium for Chase because the bank will not, in general, wish to increase *excess* reserves. Since reserves do not pay interest, the bank will convert the excess reserves, which are in the form of deposits at the New York Federal Reserve, into interest-earning assets. This sets in motion a process of deposit creation whereby the initial increase in reserves of $1000 causes deposits to increase by a multiple of that initial increase.

In describing this process it is convenient to begin by making some simplifying assumptions. First, we continue to assume that the public's holdings of currency remain unchanged. None of the initial increase in the monetary base, which was in the form of bank reserves, is siphoned off into increased currency holdings by the public. Second, we assume that the quantities of time and savings deposits are fixed. We continue to focus only on checkable deposits. Finally, the banking system's *desired* level of excess reserves is assumed to be constant. The effect of altering these assumptions is examined later.

Having made these assumptions, we are ready to describe the process of deposit creation. The Chase Manhattan Bank in our example has $900 in excess reserves, which it wants to convert into interest-earning assets. The bank can do this by either increasing loans or purchasing additional securities. Neither of these actions will produce any lasting effect on the liability side of the ledger; there is no effect on the *equilibrium* level of Chase Manhattan's deposits. If the bank buys a new security, this clearly does not change deposits. If the bank makes a loan, temporarily it may credit the amount of the loan to the checking account of the customer, and this would increase deposits. But the customer would not borrow just to increase his checking account balance. Suppose that the loan was to a consumer who used the proceeds to buy a new boat. The consumer pays for the boat with a check drawn on Chase Manhattan, and when this transaction is completed, deposits at Chase will have returned to their initial level (before the loan).

TABLE 16.6 Final Effects on Chase Manhattan Bank's Balance Sheet from a $1000 Open-Market Purchase

Assets			Liabilities	
Reserves		+100	Checkable deposits	+1000
Required reserves	+100			
Loans		+900		
Total assets		+1000	Total liabilities	+1000

The consumer's check will be deposited in the account of the firm that sold him the boat. This firm's checking account balance, let us suppose at Citibank, increases by $900. Citibank presents the check to Chase for payment—the check clears through the Federal Reserve System—which results in a transfer of funds from Chase's account at the New York Federal Reserve Bank to the account of Citibank at that Federal Reserve Bank. At this point the $900 in excess reserves is eliminated from the Chase Manhattan Bank's balance sheet—the bank's reserve deposits have declined by $900. The Chase Manhattan Bank's balance sheet is now at its final position, where the effects of the open-market operation are shown in Table 16.6. On the liability side, deposits are higher by the $1000 deposit of the original individual who sold a government security to the Federal Reserve. Required reserves are higher by $100(= 0.10 × 1000). Earning assets of the bank, loans in our example, have risen by $900.

Although we are now finished with Chase Manhattan's balance sheet, the process of deposit creation is not complete. Table 16.7 shows the effects on Citibank's balance sheet to this point. Because of the deposit by the boat manufacturer, checkable deposits are up by $900. After the check has cleared through the Federal Reserve System, $900 has been transferred to Citibank's reserve account. Thus reserves are increased by $900, of which only $90(0.10 × 900) is required to back the increase in deposits. Citibank, finding itself with $810 of excess reserves, will attempt to convert them into interest-earning assets by proceeding in the same manner as did Chase

TABLE 16.7 Initial Effects on Citibank's Balance Sheet

Assets			Liabilities	
Reserves		+900	Checkable deposits	+900
Required reserves	+90			
Excess reserves	+810			
Total assets		+900	Total liabilities	+900

TABLE 16.8   Final Effects on Citibank's Balance Sheet

Assets			Liabilities	
Reserves		+90	Checkable deposits	+900
Required reserves	+90			
Securities		+810		
Total assets		+900	Total liabilities	+900

Manhattan. The bank will increase its volume of loans or buy additional securities.

Suppose in this case that the bank uses the $810 of excess reserves to purchase a security, a corporate bond, for example. The final position of Citibank will be as shown in Table 16.8. Deposits remain up by $900, increasing required reserves by $90. As soon as Citibank pays for the security with a check drawn upon itself and that check clears the Federal Reserve System, the bank's excess reserves will be zero. Earning assets will be increased by $810, and the bank will be in equilibrium.

The process of deposit creation continues beyond this point, however, because the individual who sold the corporate bond to Citibank has deposited the proceeds of the check he received for $810 in his account at some other commercial bank. That bank now has excess reserves of $729, the $810 minus the $81 of reserves required to back the deposit. Another round of deposit creation will ensue.

The initial increase of $1000 in reserves began a process of deposit creation whereby deposits of $1000, then $900, then $810, then $729 resulted from the banking system's attempts to convert what were initially excess reserves into earning assets. The individual bank's attempt to rid itself of excess reserves, under the assumptions made to this point, simply transfers the reserves to another bank, together with creating a deposit at that bank. The newly created deposits increase required reserves by 10 percent of the increase in deposits; thus at each round in the process the newly created deposit is 10 percent smaller than for the previous round. The process will stop when all the new reserves have been absorbed in required reserves. With a $1000 increase in reserves and a required reserve ratio of 10 percent, the new equilibrium will be reached when the quantity of deposits has increased by $10000($1000 = 0.10 × $10000). At this point required reserves will have increased by $1000. There will no longer be any excess reserves in the system. The expansion of bank credit and the resulting creation of new bank deposits will come to an end.

More generally, an increase in reserves (R) of ΔR will cause deposits to increase until required reserves have increased by an equal amount. The increase in required reserves is equal to the increase in checkable deposits times the required reserve ratio on checkable deposits; that is,

$$\text{increase in required reserves} = \text{rr}_d \, \Delta D \tag{16.1}$$

where rr_d is the required reserve ratio and ΔD is the increase in deposits. For equilibrium, then,

$$\text{increase in reserves} = \text{increase in required services} \tag{16.2}$$

$$\Delta R = \text{rr}_d \, \Delta D \tag{16.3}$$

Therefore,

$$\Delta D = \frac{1}{\text{rr}_d} \, \Delta R \tag{16.4}$$

The increase in deposits will be a multiple $(1/\text{rr}_d)$ of the increase in reserves. In our previous example, with ΔR equal to 1000 and rr_d equal to 0.1 (a 10 percent reserve requirement), we have, from equation (16.1),

$$\Delta D = \frac{1}{0.1}(1000) = 10000 \tag{16.5}$$

the result reached previously.

From equation (16.4) we can also define a *deposit multiplier*, giving the increase in deposits per unit increase in bank reserves:

$$\frac{\Delta D}{\Delta R} = \frac{1}{\text{rr}_d} \tag{16.6}$$

The deposit multiplier for the simple case considered so far is equal to the reciprocal of the required reserve ratio on checkable deposits. For rr_d equal to 0.1 in our example, the deposit multiplier would be 10. Deposits increase by ten dollars for each one-dollar increase in reserves.

This simple form of the deposit multiplier results from the simplifying assumptions made previously and will have to be modified when we relax those assumptions. What follows generally is that, given the system of fractional legal reserve requirements, an increase in reserves will cause deposits to increase by a multiple of the reserve increase. All of our analysis can, of course, be reversed to consider the effects of an open-market sale of securities, which will lower bank reserves and begin a process of deposit contraction. Also note that a similar process of deposit creation would result from a reduction in the Federal Reserve discount rate, which would increase borrowed reserves, or from a lowering of reserve requirements, which, although it would not change total reserves, would create excess reserves in the banking system at the initial level of deposits. The balance sheet changes for such policy actions would be somewhat different from those shown in

Tables 16.5 to 16.8, but the general effect would be the same. Both of these alternative expansionary policies would cause both bank credit and bank deposits to increase.

The relationship just derived between reserves and deposits can be restated as a relationship between the monetary base (MB) and the money supply (M^s). The monetary base is equal to currency held by the public plus bank reserves. Thus far we are assuming that currency holdings of the public are constant, so that the change in the monetary base equals the change in reserves ($\Delta\text{MB} = \Delta R$). In this case the change in the *money supply* will be just equal to the change in bank deposits, again since currency held by the public is held constant ($\Delta D = \Delta M^s$). As a consequence, we can write a **money multiplier**, giving the increase in the money supply per unit increase in the monetary base:

$$\frac{\Delta M^s}{\Delta\text{MB}} = \frac{\Delta D}{\Delta R} = \frac{1}{\text{rr}_d} \qquad (16.7)$$

which in this simple case is just equal to the deposit multiplier. This expression will also require modification when we relax some of our simplifying assumptions, and generally the money multiplier will not be equal in value to the deposit multiplier. Generally, however, a given increase in the monetary base will cause the money stock to rise by a multiple of the increase in the base.

As described so far, the process of deposit or money creation must seem somewhat mechanical. New doses of reserves are converted by simple multipliers into new deposits, and the money supply increases. Simple models such as that developed in this section are helpful in explaining the close relationship between bank deposits and bank reserves but tell us little about the economic processes behind deposit and money creation. Before going on to more complex models of deposit creation, it is worthwhile to stop and consider the nature of these processes.

When banks find themselves with excess reserves following a Federal Reserve open-market purchase of securities, they attempt to convert those excess reserves into interest-earning assets. They attempt to expand bank credit by making more loans and purchasing securities. To increase the volume of its lending, a bank offers lower interest rates on loans and perhaps adopts lower standards of creditworthiness. In buying securities, banks bid up the prices of such securities; they bid down the interest rate on securities. Among the earning assets banks buy are mortgages; thus in times of credit expansion, mortgage interest rates will also fall. Federal Reserve open-market purchases, as well as other expansionary policy actions that increase bank reserves, will therefore lead to credit expansion and a general decline in interest rates. This is the other side of the process of deposit and money creation.

Deposit Creation: More General Cases

In addition to possibly obscuring the economic process involved, simple models such as that in the preceding section overstate the degree of precision in the relationship between Federal Reserve policy actions and resulting changes in the stock of deposits or money. In this section we take note of some of the complexities involved in this relationship.

First, consider the effect of modifying our assumption that the public's currency holdings are constant throughout the process of deposit creation. Instead, assume, as seems likely to be the case, that as the quantity of deposits grows, the public also chooses to hold an increased amount of currency. In this case some of the increase that occurs in the monetary base as a result of an open-market purchase will end up not as increased bank reserves, but as an increase in the public's holding of currency.

Suppose for simplicity that the public holds a fixed ratio of currency to checkable deposits, for example, one dollar in currency per four dollars in checkable deposits ($CU/D = 0.25$, where CU denotes currency). Now, the individual who in our example sold the $1000 bond to the Federal Reserve will not deposit the full $1000 in his checking account. He will deposit only $800, keeping the remaining $200 as currency ($200/800 = 0.25 = CU/D$). Bank reserves will increase by only $800 as a result of the $1000 open-market operation. Further, at each stage in the deposit creation, as checkable deposits rise, the public's demand for currency will increase in order to maintain a constant currency/checkable deposit ratio. At each stage there will be a further leakage from bank reserves into currency.

As a consequence of the fact that reserves will increase by less, the increase in deposits for a given increase in the monetary base will be lower when the public's holding of currency rises than when it is fixed. The increase in the money stock will also be lower. This follows because each dollar of the base that is part of bank reserves backs a multiple number of dollars in deposits—ten in our example of a 10 percent reserve requirement—whereas each dollar of the monetary base that ends up as currency held by the public is simply *one* dollar of the money stock. The more of the increase in the base that goes into bank reserves, the higher will be the money multiplier.

Relaxing our assumption that banks do not change their desired holdings of excess reserves provides an additional reason to expect that the expression derived in the preceding subsection ($1/rr_d$) is an overstatement of the true money multiplier. It appears likely that as deposits rise, banks will increase their excess reserves. Excess reserves are held as a buffer against unexpected deposit flows, and as deposits increase, so does the potential volume of deposit flows. Additionally, as we have discussed, the process of deposit expansion leads to a drop in the level of interest rates. The cost of holding excess reserves is the interest foregone by not using these funds to purchase interest-bearing assets. As the interest rate falls, this cost becomes lower. Banks are likely to respond by holding more excess reserves.

If some of the increase in bank reserves ends up as new excess reserves, the quantity of deposits created by a given increase in reserves will be smaller than when excess reserves are constant. Generally, the higher the bank's desired excess reserve/checkable deposit ratio (ER/D), the lower will be the money multiplier.

Next, consider the effect of modifying the assumption that the public's holdings of time and savings deposits are fixed. Again, a more realistic assumption would be that the public increases its time and savings deposits together with its holdings of checkable deposits. The way in which the increase in time and savings deposits affects the money multiplier depends on whether there are legal reserve requirements on these deposits and on which of the monetary aggregates we are considering. First, suppose that there are legal reserve requirements for time and savings deposits.

If the money stock is narrowly defined to include only currency plus checkable deposits (M1), then the money multiplier will be *smaller* when time deposits and savings deposits increase than when they are fixed. This follows because, with some reserves now going to satisfy reserve requirements on new time and savings deposits, fewer are available to support an increase in checkable deposits. As a consequence, the increase in checkable deposits and in the narrowly defined money stock per unit increase in the base is reduced. If, however, we define money more broadly to include time and savings accounts (M2, for example), then the larger the proportion of the increase in deposits going into time and savings deposits, the *larger* will be the value of the money multiplier (defined as $\Delta M2/\Delta MB$). The reason for this is that the required reserve ratios for time and savings deposits are typically lower than for checkable deposits. The larger the proportion of the increase in deposits that occurs in the deposits with the lowest required reserve ratio, the greater is the increase in deposits that can be supported by a given increase in the monetary base.

Now consider the case in which there are no legal reserve requirements on time or savings deposits. If we are considering the M1 multiplier for this case, the increase in time and savings deposits has no effect. This follows because no reserves are needed to satisfy reserve requirements on these deposits. If we are considering the M2 multiplier, however, this multiplier will still be larger the larger the proportion of the increase in deposits that comes in time plus savings deposits. This again follows because they have the lower reserve requirement, in this case zero.

In the United States there were legal reserve requirements on time and savings deposits for most of the post–World War II period. Therefore, we will derive the money multiplier for this case. The last of these reserve requirements was phased out in 1991, however, so they are not presently a factor that affects the money multiplier.

The discussion in this subsection leads to the conclusion that the expression for the money multiplier will be more complex than the one derived in the preceding subsection. We would instead expect the money multiplier (*m*) *for the narrowly defined money stock* (M1) to be a function of the following form:

$$m = \frac{\Delta M^s}{\Delta MB} = m\left(rr_d, \frac{CU}{D}, \frac{ER}{D}, \frac{SD + TD}{D}, rr_{sd}, rr_{td}\right) \qquad (16.8)$$

The money multiplier (*m*) would depend negatively on the required reserve ratio on checkable deposits (rr_d) as before, but on the following additional factors as well:

1. The public's desired currency/checkable deposit ratio (CU/D); as explained previously, the higher the currency/checkable deposit ratio, the lower the money multiplier.
2. The excess reserve/checkable deposit ratio (ER/D); as also explained previously, the higher the bank's desired excess reserve/checkable deposit ratio, the lower the money multiplier.
3. The public's desired ratio of savings plus time deposits to checkable deposits [(SD + TD)/D]; the higher the public's desired ratio of savings plus time deposits to checkable deposits, the greater the proportion of the increase in the monetary base that will become required reserves for time and savings deposits and, hence, not be available to support an increase in checkable deposits. Since we are defining the money multiplier for the narrowly defined money stock, any increase in this variable lowers the money multiplier.[5]
4. The required reserve ratios for savings and time deposits (rr_{sd}, rr_{td}); the higher the required reserve ratios on savings and time deposits, the more reserves will be needed to support any increase in savings or time deposits and, hence, not be available to back an increase in checkable deposits. Thus an increase in either rr_{sd} or rr_{td} will lower the money multiplier.

If the value of the money multiplier (*m*) in (16.8) were known, the Federal Reserve could then predict the change in the money stock that would result from a given change in the monetary base:

$$\Delta M^s = m \, \Delta MB \qquad (16.9)$$

---

[5]As just discussed, this assumes that there are legal reserve requirements on time and savings deposits.

The same information can be expressed slightly differently by defining a *money supply function* giving the supply of money corresponding to a given level of the monetary base:

$$M^s = m \cdot \text{MB} \tag{16.10}$$

Equation (16.10) would replace our previous assumption that the money stock was given exogenously. Prior to introducing the complications discussed in this subsection, a money supply function in the form of equation (16.10) would still imply that the money stock was exogenously set by the Federal Reserve as long as the monetary base was controlled by the Federal Reserve. This is true because, prior to our discussion in this section, the money multiplier (m) depended only on the required reserve ratio on checkable deposits, which was set exogenously by the Federal Reserve. With both the monetary base and the money multiplier set by the Federal Reserve, there would be no role for the public or the banking system in determining the money supply. The more complicated expression for the money multiplier given by equation (16.8) contains variables determined by the (nonbank) public [CU/D and $(SD + TD)/D$] and by the banking system (ER/D), implying that even if the Federal Reserve set the monetary base exogenously, the level of the money supply would not be exogenous; it depends to a degree on the behavior of the public and banking system.

16.3 • WHO CONTROLS THE MONEY STOCK

What, then, can be said about the relative importance of the Federal Reserve, the banking system, and the nonbank public in determining the money stock? To begin with, let us continue to assume that the monetary base is set exogenously by the Federal Reserve. In that case, the reason that the Federal Reserve would not have perfect control over the money stock is because, as just explained, the value of the money multiplier depends to some extent on the behavior of the banking system and the public. How great is the loss of control resulting from these sources?

If we are considering a short period of time, one to two months, for example, uncertainty about the money multiplier results in a serious loss of money stock control for the Federal Reserve. The variables that affect the money stock and are outside the direct control of the Federal Reserve—the currency/deposit ratio, the excess reserve/deposit ratio, and the saving plus time deposit/checkable deposit ratio—cannot be predicted with great precision in the short run. Notice that although in our discussion we made simplifying assumptions such as a fixed currency/deposit ratio, in fact the currency, excess reserve, and savings plus time deposit/checkable deposits ratios are *variables* that depend on the decisions of the banking system and public. These decisions depend in turn on the behavior of other economic variables. To give some examples, the excess reserve/deposit ratio depends on the cost of holding such reserves—the interest rate that could be earned on loans and securities. The savings plus time deposit/checkable deposit ratio depends on the interest rates paid on savings and time deposits relative to other market rates, as well as on various factors affecting the growth of new types of deposits. With the introduction in the 1980s of accounts which pay a market-determined interest rate, there is the added complication that the currency/checkable deposit ratio will fluctuate with movement in this rate. Precise control of the money stock would require highly accurate predictions of these variables, among others. Although no one would deny that movements in the monetary base are an important determinant of money growth from month to month, uncertainty concerning short-run variations in the money multiplier makes precise monetary control quite difficult over such a time horizon.[6]

When considering a longer period, six months to one year, for example, difficulties in monetary control caused by uncertainty about the money multiplier are less serious. Although the Federal Reserve may not be able to predict in a given month the response of the money stock to a given change in the monetary base, the policymakers can monitor the month-to-month behavior of the money stock and make the adjustments in the monetary base required to achieve the desired *average* rate of growth in the money stock over a period of several months. To see how this might be done, consider the following example.

Suppose that the Federal Reserve wished to achieve a growth rate for the money stock (M1) of 5 percent for a given calendar year. If no change in the money multiplier was expected, the Federal Reserve could attempt to achieve this target by increasing the monetary base at an annual rate of 5 percent. Assume that in February of the year in question, the data received show that for January, with a 5 percent growth (all growth rates expressed at annual rates) in the monetary base, the money stock grew by only 1 percent. There had been a fall in the money multiplier. The Federal Reserve could then, in February and the following months, cause the monetary base to

---

[6]One additional difficulty in short-run control of the money stock should be mentioned. Even if the Federal Reserve is trying to control the monetary base—the assumption we are making here—it will not be possible to do so with absolute precision on a month-to-month basis. One reason for this is that the monetary base includes borrowed reserves. Although the Federal Reserve can influence bank borrowing by means of changes in the discount rate and can offset any undesired changes in borrowed reserves through open-market operations, there will be some time lags before such adjustments are made. As a consequence, month-to-month movements in the monetary base will depend to some extent on the borrowing behavior of banks as well as on the policy actions of the Federal Reserve.

grow by more than 5 percent to offset this fall in the money multiplier. If the action taken in one month was insufficient to get the money stock back on the 5 percent growth path, a further adjustment to the growth rate in the monetary base could be made. P. T. Barnum once said that the trick to keeping a lamb in a cage with a lion is to have a large reserve supply of lambs. Federal Reserve control over the money stock rests on a supply of actions that can be taken to offset any undesired movements stemming from other sources. Even over periods as long as six months or one year, such control is not perfect. If the Federal Reserve set a target growth rate for the money stock of 5 percent and concentrated all its policy actions on achieving that target, we might end up with growth of 4.8 percent or 5.2 percent. We would not, however, end up with 2 percent or 8 percent.

In actual historical experience the Federal Reserve has announced growth-rate targets for 6- to 12-month periods and has ended up wide of the mark. If, as argued previously, the Federal Reserve *can* control the money stock with a reasonable degree of precision, what explains the failure of the Federal Reserve to hit its own preannounced money growth targets? Why in practice has the Federal Reserve often not closely controlled the money stock?

We previously assumed that the Federal Reserve controlled the monetary base and *concentrated its policy actions* on achieving a money stock target. The reason monetary growth targets are not achieved in practice is that the Federal Reserve is unwilling to concentrate all its efforts on this one policy goal. The Federal Reserve has also been interested in the behavior of other financial market variables, the most important being interest rates. Conflicts arise between hitting target levels of money stock growth and achieving desirable behavior of these other variables. When such conflicts arise, the Federal Reserve has sometimes chosen to miss the money growth target rather than accept what is viewed as the cost of hitting such targets, the resulting undesirable behavior of interest rates. We consider this choice between money stock targets and interest-rate targets at greater length in Chapter 19, but the essence of the conflict between achieving target levels of the money stock and desirable behavior of the interest rate can be explained at this point.

Figure 16.1*a* reproduces an earlier graph showing the demand and supply schedules (M^s and M^d) for money intersecting to determine the equilibrium interest rate r^*. We assume, as we did earlier, that the money supply is exogenous. In terms of the analysis of this chapter, we assume that the Federal Reserve uses control of the monetary base to achieve its money stock target (M^*). Also suppose that the equilibrium interest rate r^* shown in Figure 16.1*a* is regarded by the Federal Reserve as the desired level of the interest rate.

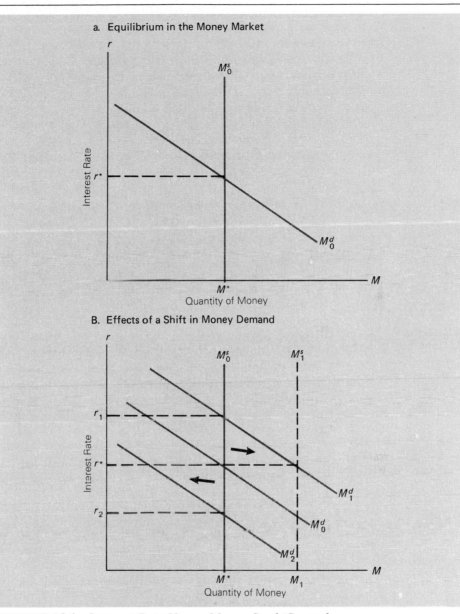

FIGURE 16.1 Interest Rate Versus Money Stock Control

Part a shows money market equilibrium with interest rate r^* and money stock M^*. If, however, as shown in part b, the money demand function shifts from M_0^d to either M_1^d or M_2^d, then if the Federal Reserve keeps the money stock at M_0^s, the interest rate must diverge from the target level r^*. Alternatively, the Federal Reserve could accommodate the shift in money demand, to M_1^d, for example, by raising the money stock to M_1^s. In this case the money stock target, M^*, will not be achieved.

Now consider the effects of shifts in the money demand schedule, as shown in Figure 16.1*b*. Such shifts could result from changes in income, which change money demand for a given interest rate. Alternatively, such shifts could represent the effects of actual shifts in the money demand *function* — changes in the amount of money demanded at given levels of both income and the interest rate. Such changes in the demand for money might shift the money demand schedule to positions such as M_1^d (an increase in money demand) or M_2^d (a decline in money demand) in Figure 16.1*b*. What will the Federal Reserve do in response to such shifts? If they stick to their money stock target and maintain the money stock at M^*, the interest rate will move away from r^*, the Federal Reserve's desired level for the interest rate. A decline in money demand (a shift in the money demand schedule from M_0^d to M_2^d) would cause the interest rate to fall to r_2; an increase in money demand (a shift in the money demand schedule from M_0^d to M_1^d) would cause an undesirable rise in the interest rate to r_1.

The Federal Reserve can prevent or mitigate these movements in the interest rate only by changing the monetary base, and, hence, the money supply. In the case of an increase in money demand, the Federal Reserve could, by increasing the monetary base, move the money supply to the level given by the M_1^s schedule in Figure 16.1*b*. This increase in the money stock would produce equilibrium in the money market at the desired interest rate r^*. The Federal Reserve would, however, miss the money stock target; the money stock would be M_1, which is above M^*. This is a case in which the Federal Reserve is *accommodating* the public's increased demand for money. The Federal Reserve supplies new money balances in order to keep the increased demand for money from pushing up the interest rate. Notice that with such accommodation, neither the money supply nor the monetary base are any longer being set exogenously. They are responding to the behavior of the public.

To the degree that the Federal Reserve engages in such accommodation, the public will have a large role in determining the value of the money stock even over periods of six months to a year. In the extreme case where the Federal Reserve pegs the interest rate at a fixed level for a long period of time, as was done in the United States in the early post–World War II period,[7] the monetary authority plays a completely passive role in the money supply process, having to supply whatever amount of money is required to maintain the desired level of the interest rate.

Read Perspectives 16.1.

---

[7]See the discussion in Section 9.2.

PERSPECTIVES

16.1

The Money Supply During the Great Depression

The monetary collapse during the Great Depression demonstrates the potential importance of banks and the (nonbank) public in the money supply process. This is illustrated in Figure 16.2.

Part *a* of the figure charts the behavior of two of the factors that determine the value of the money multiplier (*m*): the currency/deposit ratio (CU/*D*) and the excess reserve/deposit ratio (ER/*D*). The first of these

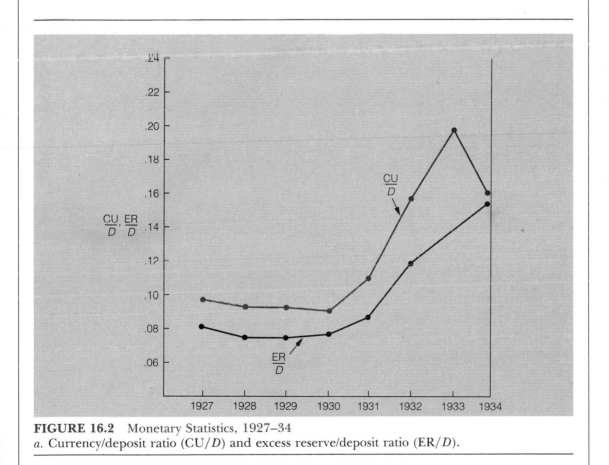

FIGURE 16.2   Monetary Statistics, 1927–34
a. Currency/deposit ratio (CU/*D*) and excess reserve/deposit ratio (ER/*D*).

is determined by the public and the second by banks. Both of these ratios can be seen to have risen sharply in the early 1930s. The cause of the rise in both ratios was the large number of bank failures during the period; more than 9000 banks failed between 1929 and 1933. The bank failures caused a loss of confidence in bank deposits. As a consequence, the public held more of their money balances in the form of currency. Banks that did not fail held more excess reserves to ward off "runs" by depositors that could result in the bank's insolvency.

As discussed in the text, a rise in either the currency/deposit ratio or the excess reserve/deposit ratio causes the money multiplier to fall. This effect can be seen from the plot of the money multiplier (m) in part b of Figure 16.2. Besides the multiplier, the other fact determining the money supply is the monetary base (MB). Part b of the figure shows that the monetary base increased over this period. As can be seen from part c, however, the increase in the base was too small to keep the M1 measure of the money supply from declining sharply. Between 1929

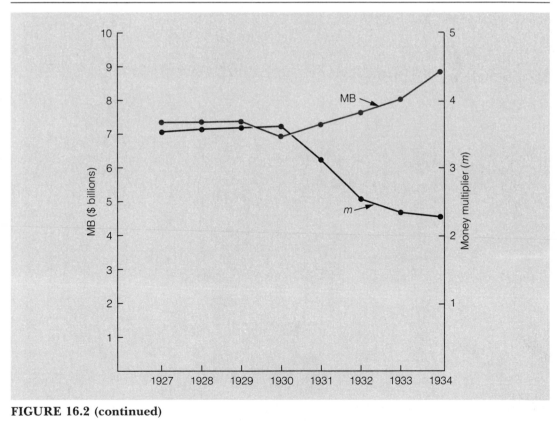

FIGURE 16.2 (continued)
b. The monetary base (MB) and the monetary multiplier (m).

and 1933 M1 fell by 26.5 percent. The decline in M2 was even larger (33.3 percent).

The behavior of the Federal Reserve during this period has been criticized, especially by monetarists who see the decline in the money supply as the cause of the Depression. There is, however, a question of whether the Federal Reserve in the early 1930s had adequate tools to prevent the collapse.[1] In any case the fall in the money multiplier and consequent fall in monetary aggregates in the early 1930s do indicate that the public and the banks can be major players in the money supply process.

[1]On these issues see Milton Friedman and Anna Schwartz, *A Monetary History of the United States* (Princeton: Princeton University Press, 1963); and Peter Temin, *Did Monetary Forces Cause the Great Depression?* (New York: Norton, 1976).

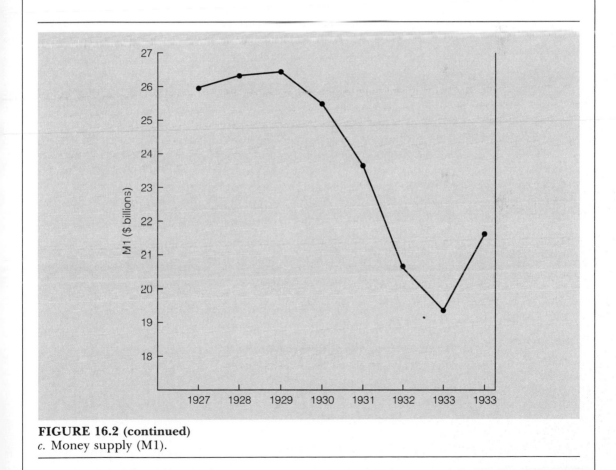

FIGURE 16.2 (continued)
c. Money supply (M1).

16.4 • CONCLUSION

Before this chapter we assumed that the money supply was set exogenously by the monetary authority. In the first sections of this chapter we considered the way in which the U.S. monetary authority, the Federal Reserve, controls the monetary base (currency plus bank reserve deposits) and the linkages between control of the monetary base and control of the money stock. What we have seen is that, because of uncertainty about the value of the money multiplier, precise Federal Reserve control of the money stock in the very short run (one or two months) is quite difficult. The behavior of the public and the banking system will have a substantial influence on such short-term variations in the money stock. Over longer periods (six months to a year, for example), the Federal Reserve can control the money stock with reasonable precision by altering the monetary base to offset any undesirable changes in the money stock as a result of the behavior of the banking system or (nonbank) public. When the Federal Reserve does not control the money stock over such longer periods, the failure to do so is one of will rather than ability.

The reason why the Federal Reserve does not always concentrate solely on controlling the money stock is that to do so would result in what the Federal Reserve regards as undesirable fluctuations in the interest rate. To prevent such undesirable interest-rate movements, the Federal Reserve at times accommodates changes in the public's demand for money with the effect that the monetary base and the money stock are no longer exogenous. The reasons for the Federal Reserve's concern over fluctuations in interest rates and the relative desirability of controlling interest rates or the money stock are topics we return to in Chapter 19, when we analyze the Federal Reserve's operating procedures in more detail.

Review Questions and Problems

1. What are the major policymaking bodies within the Federal Reserve System? Explain their composition and functions.

2. Suppose that the Federal Reserve wants to increase bank reserves. Explain the various measures that could be taken to achieve that end. In each case illustrate the linkage between the Federal Reserve's policy action and the level of bank reserves.

3. What is the maximum amount of the increase in checkable deposits that can result from a $1000 increase in legal reserves if the required reserve ratio for checkable deposits is 10 percent? Explain exactly how this increase comes about in a commercial banking system. Give several reasons why the actual increase may fall short of the theoretical maximum.

4. Suppose that the level of the required reserve ratio on checkable deposits were 0.10. Also assume that the public's holdings of currency and savings plus time deposits are constant, as are bank's desired excess reserves. Analyze the effects on the money stock of a $1000 open-market sale of securities by the Federal Reserve. In your answer, explain the role of the commercial banking system in the adjustment to this monetary policy action.

5. Explain the concept of the money multiplier. What factors determine the size of the money multiplier?

6. Within the *IS–LM* curve model used in Chapters 6 and 7, show how income and the interest rate will be affected by each of the following changes.

    a. An increase in the required reserve ratio for checkable deposits.
    b. An open-market sale of securities by the Federal Reserve.
    c. A decrease in the Federal Reserve discount rate.

7. In the text it was argued that the Federal Reserve would find it very difficult to exert close control of the rate of growth in the money stock over very short periods but would be able to achieve much greater control over somewhat longer periods. What are the nature of the difficulties in short-run monetary control, for example, on a month-to-month basis? Why are these difficulties less serious over longer periods?

8. Within the *IS–LM* curve model, illustrate the nature of the conflict the Federal Reserve faces between trying to control the money stock and trying to achieve "desirable" levels of the interest rate.

Selected Readings

Balbach, Anatol, and Burger, Albert, "Derivation of the Monetary Base," Federal Reserve Bank of St. Louis *Review*, 58 (November 1976), pp. 2–8. Reprinted in Thomas Havrilesky and John Boorman, *Current Issues in Monetary Theory and Policy*, 2nd ed. Arlington Heights, Ill.: AHM Publishing Corp., 1980.

Branson, William, *Macroeconomic Theory and Policy*, 3rd ed. New York: Harper & Row, 1989, Chap. 15.

Cacy, J. A., "The Choice of a Monetary Policy Instrument," Federal Reserve Bank of Kansas City *Economic Review* (May 1978), pp. 17–35.

Chandler, Lester, and Goldfeld, Stephen, *The Economics of Money and Banking* New York: Harper & Row, 1977, Chaps. 8 and 9.

Jordan, Jerry, "Elements of Money Stock Determination," Federal Reserve Bank of St. Louis *Review*, 51 (October 1969), pp. 10–19. Reprinted in Thomas Havrilesky and John Boorman, *Current Issues in Monetary Theory and Policy*, 2nd ed. Arlington Heights, Ill.: AHM Publishing, 1980.

Meek, Paul, *U.S. Monetary Policy and Financial Markets*. New York: Federal Reserve Bank of New York, 1982.

Meulendyke, Ann-Marie, *U.S. Monetary Policy and Financial Markets*. New York: Federal Reserve Bank of New York, 1990.

Mishkin, Frederick, *The Economics of Money Banking and Financial Markets*, 3rd ed. Boston: Little, Brown and Company, 1992, Chaps. 12–19.

Ritter, Lawrence S., and Silber, William L., *Money*, 7th ed. New York: Basic Books, 1990.

17

The Supply Side: Intermediate- and Long-Term Economic Growth

The changes in output discussed in previous chapters were short-run changes in actual output for a given level of potential output. In this chapter we consider the determinants of output movements over longer periods of time. First, we examine the determinants of the long-run equilibrium rate of growth in output. Next, we look at factors that determine the time path of output in what can be called the intermediate run, a period too long to be accurately represented by the short-run models of Part II, but not necessarily characterized by the assumptions we will make about long-run equilibrium growth. This intermediate period analysis might, for example, ask which factors will be important in determining the growth rate for the United States economy over the 1990s. Issues concerning economic growth in such intermediate-run periods have been central to recent controversies over **supply-side economics**.

When dealing with the short run, we have seen that there is much controversy over the relative importance to be attached to aggregate supply and demand as determinants of output. In the case of long-run equilibrium economic growth, it is clear that supply factors—factors determining the growth of potential output—are of predominant importance. Substantial output growth over long periods has been the result of growth of factor supplies (the labor force and capital stock) and changes in technology that increase output per unit of factors employed. When we consider periods of intermediate length, we will see that there are again differences of opinion between those who believe that demand factors play a role and those who emphasize the importance of the supply side.

We begin with an analysis of long-run equilibrium growth, what is called "steady-state growth" (Section 17.1), and then consider output determination over intermediate-run periods (Section 17.2). This chapter concludes with an analysis of the Reagan and Bush administrations' supply-side policies to influence economic growth over such intermediate-run periods (Section 17.3).

17.1 • LONG-RUN STEADY-STATE GROWTH

Growth and the Aggregate Production Function

Over the period 1870–1990, national income in the United States increased at an annual rate of 3.5 percent. Per capita output increased at an annual rate of 1.8 percent. What factors account for such sustained growth? One way to approach this question employs the notion of the *aggregate production function* seen in previous chapters. The aggregate production function relates the level of output to the level of factor inputs.

For the purposes of this chapter, the aggregate production function can be written as

$$Y = A(t)F(K, N) \tag{17.1}$$

Equation (17.1) differs from expressions for the short-run aggregate production function in two respects. First, there is the additional term $A(t)$. This term represents technological change, which is taken simply to depend on time; that is, as time passes, the $A(t)$ term increases, meaning that more output will be produced for a given amount of factor inputs. In equation (17.1) the $A(t)$ term enters multiplicatively. With this specification, technological change is assumed not to affect the relative marginal productivities of the two factors, as determined by the $F(K, N)$ part of the production function. In other words, technological change results in equal increases in the productiveness of both factors. Such technological change is termed *neutral* (favoring neither capital nor labor) technological change. Robert Solow, in a study of shifts in the aggregate production function over time, found evidence that for the United States, technological change had in fact been neutral. We restrict our analysis to this case.[1]

A second difference between equation (17.1) and previous specifications of the production function is the absence of the bar over the K variable in equation (17.1), indicating that here we are not assuming the capital stock is constant. This reflects the fact that we are now dealing with the long run.

---

[1] See Robert Solow, "Technical Change and the Aggregate Production Function," *Review of Economics and Statistics*, 39 (August 1957), pp. 312–20. Also relevant to the discussion here are Chaps. 1 and 2 of Solow's book, *Growth Theory* (London: Oxford University Press, 1970).

On the basis of equation (17.1) we follow Solow's method in the previously mentioned study and write the following specification for the growth in output over time:

$$\frac{\dot{Y}}{Y} = \frac{\dot{A}}{A} + w_k \frac{\dot{K}}{K} + w_n \frac{\dot{N}}{N} \tag{17.2}$$

where the dot over a variable indicates the time rate of change in that variable (e.g., $\dot{N}$ is the rate at which the labor force is increasing). Equation (17.2) specifies the proportional rate of increase in output ($\dot{Y}/Y$) as depending on the proportional rate of technological change ($\dot{A}/A$) and the proportional rates of change in the capital stock and number of workers employed ($\dot{K}/K$ and $\dot{N}/N$). The weights (w_k, w_n) attached to these latter two variables are their shares in national output, reflecting their importance in the production process. From equation (17.2), the growth in output can be seen to depend on the rate at which technological progress occurs over time and the rate at which factor supplies are growing over time.

If the production function given by equation (17.1) exhibits what are termed **constant returns to scale**, it can be written in an alternative form that will provide some insights into the way in which each factor enters in the growth process. Constant returns to scale mean that if all inputs rise in some proportion, output will increase in the same proportion. A doubling of the amount of both capital and labor used in production would, for example, just double the amount of output produced. In essence, we assume that the productivity of the inputs is not affected by scale. With constant returns to scale, it follows that for a given technology, fixing $A(t)$, output per worker (Y/N) will depend only on the amount of capital employed per worker, the capital/labor ratio.[2] Letting q equal output per worker (Y/N) and k equal capital per worker (K/N), we can rewrite (17.1) as

$$\frac{Y}{N} = A(t)f\left(\frac{K}{N}\right)$$

or

$$q = A(t)f(k) \tag{17.3}$$

where $f(k)$ is the function relating output per worker to the capital/labor ratio, for a given technology—what is called the *intensive* form of the aggregate production function.

The relationship given by equation (17.3) is shown in Figure 17.1. The state of technology is assumed to be given by $A(t_0)$, which fixes the position

---

[2]With constant returns to scale, output per worker (Y/N) does not depend on the level of output. Therefore, with technology fixed, once we fix the capital/labor ratio (K/L), there is no other variable that affects output per worker; Y/N is also fixed.

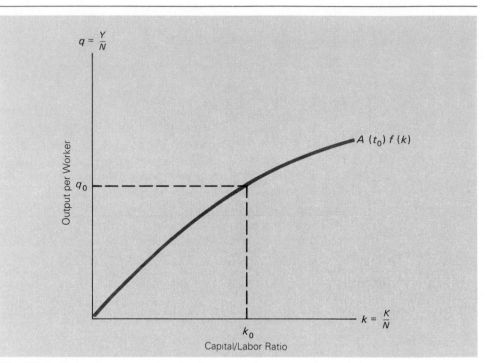

FIGURE 17.1   Aggregate Production Function: Equation (17.3)
The intensive form of the production function shows the level of output per worker ($q = Y/N$) corresponding to each capital/labor ratio ($k = K/N$) for a given technology ($A(t_0)$). As the capital/labor ratio rises, output per worker increases but at a declining rate, reflecting diminishing returns to increases in capital per worker.

of the production function relating output per worker to capital per worker. As we move out to the right along the production function, output per worker increases with the increase in capital per worker (k). The shape of the production function in Figure 17.1 reflects the assumption that there are diminishing returns to increases in capital per worker. The increment to output per worker declines with successive increases in capital per worker.[3] At an assumed initial capital/labor ratio of k_0, output per worker would be q_0 in the figure.

---

[3]Notice this assumption of diminishing returns to increases in capital intensity is not at odds with our assumption that the production process exhibits constant returns to scale. The latter assumption refers to the effect of proportional increases in *all* factors of production. Diminishing returns to increases in capital intensity refer to the effects of increases in the amount of one factor (capital) per unit of the other factor (labor).

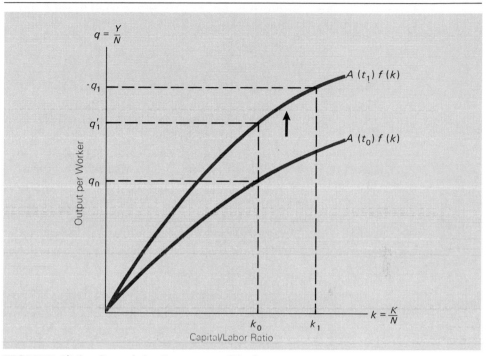

FIGURE 17.2   Growth in Output per Worker

Output per worker increases from q_0 to q_1' as the result of technological progress as the production function shifts upward from $A(t_0)f(k)$ to $A(t_1)f(k)$. There is a further increase in output per worker from q_1' to q_1 as a result of an increase in the capital/labor ratio from k_0 to k_1.

Figure 17.2 illustrates the process of growth in output per worker between two points of time, t_0 and t_1. Technological change causes the production function to shift upward from $A(t_0)f(k)$ to $A(t_1)f(k)$. By itself, this technological change would increase output per worker, at the initial capital/labor ratio k_0, from q_0 to q_1' in Figure 17.2. Additionally, however, we assume that the capital/labor ratio increases over time, a process called *capital deepening*. This is illustrated in the graph by a movement to a capital/labor ratio of k_1. As a result, output per worker increases further, to q_1.

The framework illustrated in Figure 17.2 [the graph of equation (17.3)] suggests that the growth of output per worker is the result of two factors:

1. Technological change, which increases output per worker for a given capital/labor ratio.
2. Capital deepening, as the capital/labor ratio increases.

If we are considering the growth rate in total output, as opposed to output per worker, growth in the labor force is an additional source of growth.

Sources of Economic Growth

The analysis in the preceding subsection indicates that the economic factors that determine a country's long-run equilibrium growth rate will be those that affect the rate of technological change, labor force growth, and rate of capital formation. Influences on these magnitudes are the ultimate sources of economic growth. We begin with a somewhat paradoxical result, namely, that, *within the framework we are considering*, the *long-run equilibrium* growth rate does not depend on a nation's saving rate ($s = S/Y$).

The independence of a nation's growth rate from the saving rate is at first surprising, since one would expect the saving rate to affect the rate of capital formation and therefore the equilibrium growth rate. To see why the equilibrium growth rate does not depend on the saving rate, let us analyze the effect of an increase in the saving rate within the production function framework of the preceding section.

In Figure 17.3, assume that initially the saving rate is s_0 and that the economy is in equilibrium with the capital/labor ratio k_0 and output per worker equal to q_0. Consider the ray marked $1/\alpha_0$ coming from the origin and intersecting the production function at a level of output per worker equal to q_0. Each point along the line corresponds to a constant ratio of the variable on the vertical axis Y/N to the variable on the horizontal axis K/N, that is, a constant output/capital ratio, since

$$\frac{Y}{N} \div \frac{K}{N} = \frac{Y}{K} = \frac{1}{\alpha}$$

where α is the capital/output ratio (K/Y). Initially, then, the capital/output ratio is α_0 in Figure 17.3.

Now consider the effect of an increase in the saving rate to some higher value s_1 (say, 15 percent of income as opposed to 10 percent of income). Initially, the economy was assumed to be in equilibrium at the capital/labor ratio k_0, which means that capital and labor were growing at the same rate. With the increase in the saving rate, the rate of capital formation will initially increase. To see this clearly, we need to specify the relationship between capital formation and the saving rate. The rate of capital formation can be written as

$$\frac{\dot{K}}{K} = \frac{I}{K} - \frac{D}{K} \tag{17.4}$$

where I is gross investment and D is depreciation. Since in long-run equilibrium output will grow as supply grows, we ignore the problem of inadequate

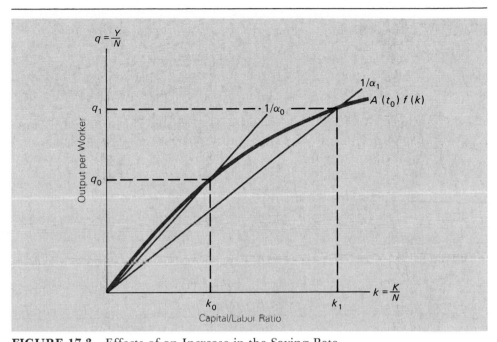

FIGURE 17.3   Effects of an Increase in the Saving Rate.
As a result of an increase in the saving rate, the capital/labor ratio increases from k_0 to k_1. Output per worker increases from q_0 to q_1. The capital/output ratio rises from α_0 to α_1. Once q_1 is reached, there is no further increase in output per worker. The initial equilibrium growth rate in output is restored.

demand. We assume that all saving (S) is channeled into investment ($I - S$). Also assume that depreciation is a constant fraction (δ) of the capital stock. Using these facts, we can rewrite equation (17.4) as

$$\frac{\dot{K}}{K} = \frac{S}{K} - \frac{\delta K}{K} = \frac{sY}{K} - \frac{\delta K}{K} \tag{17.5}$$

where the second equality follows from the fact that saving is equal to the saving rate times the level of income. From equation (17.5) it follows that an increase in the saving rate (s) will initially increase the rate of capital formation.

Since the rate of capital formation has increased with no change in the rate of growth in the labor force, the capital/labor ratio will rise. A new equilibrium will be reached, as shown in Figure 17.3, at capital/labor ratio k_1 and with higher output per worker q_1. Once this adjustment is made, however, there will be no further increase in output per worker and, since labor force growth is unchanged, the equilibrium growth rate returns to its initial level.

To see why this has happened, look at the ray labeled $1/\alpha_1$, originating at the origin and crossing the production function at the new level of output per worker q_1 in Figure 17.3. As explained previously, each point along such a ray corresponds to a fixed capital/output ratio. The $1/\alpha_0$ ray is flatter than the initial $1/\alpha_0$ ray, indicating that the ratio of Y/N to K/N, the output/capital ratio, is lower after the increase in the saving rate. The capital/output ratio (K/Y) is therefore *higher*. At a higher capital/output ratio, a larger saving rate $(s = S/Y)$ is required just to maintain a constant growth rate in the capital stock. Once the capital/output ratio reaches α_1, capital formation will have returned to the initial equilibrium rate equal to the growth rate in the labor force. There will be no further increases in either output per worker or the capital/labor ratio.

The effect on the rate of economic growth will be as shown in Figure 17.4. Assume that the equilibrium growth rate for income is g. If the rise

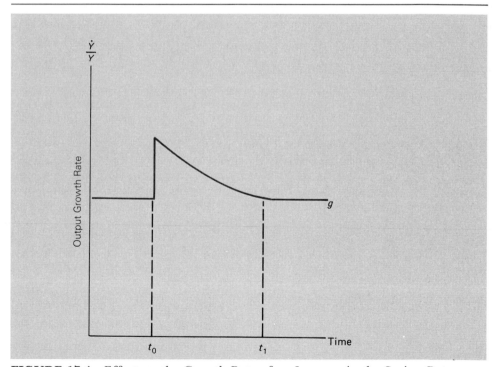

FIGURE 17.4   Effect on the Growth Rate of an Increase in the Saving Rate
At the time t_0, the saving rate increases. Initially the rate of growth in output rises. This is the period where output per worker is increasing from q_0 to q_1, as shown in Figure 17.3. At time t_1, when output per worker has reached q_1 in Figure 17.3, the initial equilibrium growth rate g has been restored.

in the saving rate occurs at time t_0, the growth rate ($\dot{Y}/Y$) will rise temporarily as the economy moves from the initial level of output per worker q_0 to the higher level of output per worker q_1. As this new higher level of output per worker is reached, the growth rate will return to g, as shown at time t_1 in Figure 17.4. The increase in the saving rate causes a temporary period of faster growth but does not affect the equilibrium growth rate.

None of the preceding implies that the saving rate is unimportant in the growth process. The temporary period during which a change in the saving rate does affect the growth rate (from t_0 to t_1 in Figure 17.4) may be a substantial period in calendar time. Also, notice that even after the full adjustment to a change in the saving rate (after we reach t_1 in Figure 17.4 and k_1 and q_1 in Figure 17.3), the higher saving rate has resulted in a *permanent* increase in capital per worker and output per worker. An economy with a higher saving rate will therefore have a higher standard of living as the result of a more capital-intensive production process.

Recent Developments in the Theory of Economic Growth

After an active period in the 1950s and 1960s, interest in the theory of long-run economic growth declined in the 1970s. The latter part of the 1980s witnessed a resurgence of interest in growth theory. Interest in the theory had declined because of doubts about whether it really told us much about growth. The theory certainly explained the dynamics of the growth process, but ended up telling us that the long-run equilibrium growth rate depended on two exogenous variables: the rate of population growth and the rate of technological change. Since these were exogenous, the theory did not really isolate the fundamental sources of long-run growth. For this reason few policy conclusions came out of the traditional theory of long-term growth. As Paul Romer, one of the developers of the new growth theory, states this view, "From the point of view of policy advice, growth theory had little to offer. In models with exogenous technological change and exogenous population growth, it never really mattered what the government did."[4]

Endogenous Growth Models

Recent research in growth theory extends the traditional analysis by making the rates of technological change and/or population growth endogenous.

---

[4] Paul Romer, "Capital Accumulation and Long-Run Growth," in Robert J. Barro, ed., *Modern Business Cycle Theory* (Cambridge, Mass.: Harvard University Press, 1989), p. 51. Keep in mind here that we are discussing the long run. In the previous subsection we saw that the saving rate could affect the growth rate, perhaps for a substantial period of time. There are certainly government policies that can influence saving. It was only the long-run equilibrium growth rate that was exogenous.

PERSPECTIVES
Accounting for U.S. Economic Growth, 1929–82

Economist Edward Denison has carefully studied economic growth in the United States. Table 17.1 summarizes his findings concerning the sources of growth in U.S. output for 1929–82. As the table indicates, real output grew at an *annual* rate of 2.9 percent over this period. The other numbers in the table show the percentage (proportion of the total) contribution to the growth rate of a number of factors. These factors are broken into two groups.

The first group, containing one factor, is growth in labor input. This is simply growth in output due to the increase in the quantity of labor. Denison estimates that 32 percent, approximately one third, of the growth in output between 1929 and 1982 came from this source.

The other sources of growth are factors that increase the amount of output per unit of labor input (what we referred to as output per worker in the previous section), factors that increase **labor productivity**. Let's consider each in turn.

EDUCATION PER WORKER

The first of these other sources of growth listed in Table 17.1 is education per worker. As explained by Denison:

> Educational background decisively conditions both the types of work an individual is able to perform and his proficiency in any particular occupation. The distribution of American workers by highest school grade completed has shifted upward continuously and massively, and this shift has been a major growth source.[1]

Denison estimates that 14 percent of U.S. economic growth is due to increased education of the labor force.

CAPITAL FORMATION

Denison estimates that capital formation was responsible for 19 percent, just less than one fifth, of U.S. economic growth between 1929 and 1982.

TECHNOLOGICAL CHANGE

The next factor in Table 17.1 is **technological change**. This includes changes in technological knowledge (e.g., ways to employ robots in the production process), as well as new knowledge about how to organize

TABLE 17.1 Sources of U.S. Economic Growth, 1929–82 (percent)

Annual growth rate of output (percent)	2.9
Percentage of growth due to:	
Growth in labor input	32
Growth in labor productivity	
Education per worker	14
Capital	19
Technological change	28
Economies of sale	9
Other factors	−2

Source: Edward F. Denison, *Trends in American Economic Growth, 1929–82* (Washington, D.C.: The Brookings Institution, 1985), p. 30.

[1] Edward F. Denison, *Trends in American Growth 1929–82* (Washington, D.C.: The Brookings Institution, 1985), p. 15.

businesses (managerial strategies). In Denison's estimates, technological change accounts for 28 percent of growth and is the most important influence on labor productivity.

ECONOMIES OF SCALE

Denison finds that, rather than the constant return to scale we assumed in the previous section, the United States has experienced **economies of scale**; even given the state of technology, an increase in the quantity of inputs has resulted in a more than proportional increase in output. Denison estimates that 9 percent of US growth results from this source

OTHER FACTORS

Denison considers a number of other factors that either stimulate or retard the growth process (e.g., changes in allocation of resources across industries, effects of weather on farm output, work stoppages). Taken together, these factors had a net negative effect equal to 2 percent of economic growth.

Overall, Denison's estimates indicate that the main sources of U.S. growth from 1929 to 1982 were *growth in the quantity of the labor input* and four other factors that cause labor productivity to grow: *education per worker, capital formation, technological change,* and *economies of scale*.

Having done so, we can ask what factors will speed up or impede the growth process. How will various government policies affect the growth in these variables? The new growth theory is not an attack on the traditional theory. It is, rather, an extension of it, to go more deeply into the question of the ultimate sources of growth. To see the lines along which this research is proceeding, we will examine a model of endogenous technological change.[5] To consider an endogenous technology, we modify the production function in (17.1) as follows[6]

$$Y_t = F(K_t, N_t, A_t) \tag{17.6}$$

As before, the level of output (Y) depends on the levels of the capital (K) and labor (N) inputs. Output also depends on the level of technology (A), which now appears inside the production function as one of the endogenous inputs. The relationship between output and technology is, however, different from that with the other inputs. This can be seen by looking at the production function for an individual firm, denoted by the subscript i.

$$Y_{i,t} = F(K_{it}, N_{it}, A_t) \tag{17.7}$$

---

[5] For a model of endogenous population growth see Becker, Gary, Murphy, Kevin, and Tamua, Robert, "Human Capital, Fertility and Economic Growth," *Journal of Political Economy*, 98 (October 1990), pp. 512-537.

[6] This specification is taken from the Arrow–Romer model described in Paul M. Romer, "Capital Accumulation and Long Run Growth," pp. 98–100.

The firm's output depends on its own level of capital (K_{it}) and labor (N_{it}), but on the economy wide level of technology (A_t). Advances in the state of knowledge are therefore assumed to increase the productivity of all firms.[7]

The level of technology is not assumed to grow exogenously. In one type of endogenous growth model, the growth of technology is assumed to depend on the growth of capital. New investment fosters inventions and improvements in the machines that comprise the stock of capital. There is also assumed to be momentum to advances in knowledge. Inventions and productivity advances themselves lead to more knowledge by what is termed a "learning by doing" process.

In other models, increases in the labor input also increase the stock of knowledge, by a process one author describes as follows: "the greater the level of the labor input, the greater is the scope for learning and acquisition of new skills. A higher level of labor input also requires more intensive use of factors fixed in the short run, thus raising the incentive to eliminate waste and bottlenecks."[8] This is, again, a process of learning by doing.

Policy Implications of Endogenous Technological Change

Consider the effects of an increase by all firms in their employment of the labor and capital inputs in a model with endogenous technological change. Suppose, for example, firms increase capital and labor by 5 percent. We will assume that this increase by itself would cause output to rise proportionately by 5 percent. This is the assumption made in the traditional theory—constant returns to increases in capital and labor. As just discussed, however, the increases in capital and labor will advance the economywide technology (A_t rises). This leads to an additional rise in output. Models with endogenous technological change therefore exhibit increasing returns to scale, once we take account of the effects that increases in capital and labor have on technology.[9] Increasing returns to scale has important policy implications.

With increasing returns, changes in the saving rate and therefore in the rate of capital formation can have permanent effects on the long-run equilibrium growth rate. This result contrasts with the traditional growth theory

---

[7]Some models do allow for technological advances, the benefit of which accrues only to the firm that finances them. This could occur because of patents. Still there are at least some advances where the benefits are available to all firms.

[8]George Stadler, "Business Cycle Models with Endogenous Technology," *American Economic Review*, 80 (September 1990), pp. 763–768.

[9]Notice that this is consistent with Denison's finding of economies of scale in the U.S. growth experience. (See Perspectives 17.1.)

in which the effect of changes in the saving rate on the growth rate is temporary (see Figure 17.4).

In the traditional model, an increase in the rate of capital formation causes a less than proportionate increase in the growth rate of output. This is because, with constant returns to scale, the growth rate in the labor input would also have to increase by the same amount as that of capital for output growth to rise proportionately. We are assuming the growth rate in the labor input to be fixed. While the growth rate in output rises less than in proportion to the increase in the growth rate in capital, depreciation rises proportionately. This is because, in both the traditional and newer growth models, depreciation is simply a fraction of the stock of capital, δ in the previous subsection. With the growth rate in output rising less than proportionately while the growth rate in capital and the depreciation rate are rising proportionately, depreciation becomes a larger fraction of output and eventually absorbs the higher saving. The rate of capital formation and the growth rate in output return to their initial levels.

With increasing returns, it is possible that *taking account of the positive effect which capital formation has on the level of technology (A),* an increase in the saving rate and, therefore, in the rate of capital formation will result in a proportionate increase in the growth rate in output. If so, depreciation will not increase as a fraction of output and will not absorb the higher level of saving. The rate of capital formation and the growth rate in output will be permanently higher.

It follows, then, that with endogenous technological change and therefore increasing returns to scale, policies that affect the saving rate and rate of capital formation will affect the long-run equilibrium growth rate. Since many government policies have potential effects on the variables, what the government does now matters for long-run growth.

We consider a number of such policies when we turn to the subject of growth over the intermediate run, for in the past this was the time frame over which they were thought to be relevant. It should be kept in mind, however, that in the presence of endogenous technological change, these policies are also relevant for long-run equilibrium growth.

17.2 · DETERMINANTS OF OUTPUT GROWTH IN INTERMEDIATE-RUN PERIODS

In this section the factors that determine the growth of output over periods longer than the short-run periods analyzed in Part II, but not necessarily periods in which the economy is in long-run equilibrium, are examined. The short-run period in our earlier analysis was characterized by the assumptions of a constant capital stock, a fixed labor force, and an unchanged technology. Output changes came as the level of employment varied. When considering changes in output in the intermediate run, perhaps over 10 to 15 years rather than over a cycle of 2 to 4 years, we are not entitled to these assumptions. Variations in the rates of capital formation, growth in the labor force that results from growth in the working age population as well as changes in labor force participation rates, and variations in the rate of technological change are factors that determine growth rates of output in the intermediate run. What about the importance of demand? Economists who accept the classical, real business cycle or new classical views see little direct role for aggregate demand as a significant factor in determining the growth path of output over periods of intermediate length. In the classical or real business cycle theories, aggregate demand does not even play a role in determining output in the short run. In the new classical model, only unanticipated demand changes affect output. Therefore, only deviations of demand growth from the average rather than the average rate of growth in demand over a period of 10 to 15 years itself would affect output.

The situation is somewhat different with respect to the monetarist and Keynesian (or new Keynesian) views. As we have explained, the long-run equilibrium growth rate is supply-determined, but both monetarists and Keynesians believe that changes in demand affect output over periods of several years. If we look at any 10- to 15-year period, the average rate of growth may be affected by demand-induced recessions or expansions within that period. Demand factors might be used to explain why the growth rate of output was approximately zero for the 1929–39 decade of the Great Depression. Unstable growth in aggregate demand might also be used by a monetarist or Keynesian to explain why growth in real output averaged 3.1 percent in the decade from 1969 to 1979, a period during which there were two recessions, compared with an annual growth of 4.3 percent in the 1960s, where there was a sustained expansion from February 1961 to December 1969.

Thus, as with analysis of the short run, there is considerable disagreement over the relative importance of supply and demand in explaining the determination of output over intermediate-run periods. One position, which we call the "supply-side" view, ascribes predominance to supply-side factors as determinants of the behavior of output. The other position, which can be termed the Keynesian position, maintains, as James Tobin has said, that God gave us two eyes so that we could watch both supply and demand.

The supply-side position, what has been termed *supply-side economics*, was the subject of much controversy in the late 1970s and throughout the 1980s. The ideas of supply-side economics played an important role in the redirection of monetary and especially fiscal policy during the Reagan presidency.

Before examining the supply-side position and its critics, we consider the growth performance of the economy in recent decades.

U.S. Economic Growth, 1960–91

The growth experience for the United States for the 1960–91 period is summarized in Table 17.2. As can be seen from the table, the rate of growth in output and labor productivity has slowed over the past two decades. The rate of capital formation has also declined. Growth in the labor force increased as the post–World War II baby-boom generation came to adulthood in the late 1960s and into the 1970s, then returned to its earlier level in the 1980s.

The facts that supply-side and Keynesian economists must explain are, therefore, the following:

1. The growth rate in U.S. output slowed markedly in the post-1970 period
2. There has been a sharp decline in the growth rate in labor productivity in the past two decades.
3. The rate of capital formation has also slowed relative to pre-1970 years.

Read Perspectives 17.2.

The Supply-Side Position

The theoretical origins of supply-side economics lie in the classical theories examined in Chapters 3 and 4. In particular, for the intermediate run, economists favorable to the supply-side position accept the classical view that output is determined by real variables on the supply side of the economy—growth of factor supplies and changes in technology. They also adhere to a classical view of the saving–investment process, where the interest rate is a crucial variable. Most fundamentally, the supply-side economists share the

TABLE 17.2 U.S. Growth Experience 1960–91

	Average Annual Percentage Growth Rate			
Item	**1960–68**	**1968–73**	**1973–79**	**1979–91**
Gross domestic output	4.5	3.2	2.4	2.5
Labor productivity	2.6	1.0	0.0	1.0
Total labor force	1.6	2.4	2.6	1.7
Capital formation	5.0	3.7	1.9	2.3

Source: Historical Statistics, 1960–89, Paris: OECD, 1991; *Economic Report of the President*, 1992.

PERSPECTIVES

GROWTH AND PRODUCTIVITY SLOWDOWNS IN OTHER INDUSTRIALIZED ECONOMIES

Table 17.3 shows growth rates for output and labor productivity for six major industrialized countries. The data are average annual percentage growth rates for time periods similar to those considered for the United States in Table 17.2. The striking feature in the table is a marked slowdown in output growth and productivity growth in the post-1970 period in *all* these countries.

The data in the table are for large industrial economies, but data for the smaller ones tell the same story. The growth and productivity slowdown of the 1970s, with relatively slow growth continuing in the 1980s, affected virtually every industrialized economy. In seeking explanations of the slowdown, this suggests that we should look for causes that could have such broad international effects.

TABLE 17.3 Growth Rate in Output and Labor Productivity, Selected Countries, Annual Average

Country	Item	1960–68	1968–73	1973–79	1979–89
Canada	Output	5.5	5.4	4.2	3.1
	Labor productivity	4.0	3.2	1.4	1.2
France	Output	5.4	5.9	3.0	2.1
	Labor productivity	4.9	4.7	2.7	2.0
Italy	Output	5.7	4.6	2.6	2.5
	Labor productivity	6.3	4.9	1.7	2.1
Japan	Output	10.4	8.4	3.6	4.1
	Labor productivity	8.8	7.3	2.9	3.0
W. Germany	Output	4.1	4.9	2.3	1.8
	Labor productivity	4.2	4.1	2.9	1.7
United Kingdom	Output	3.1	3.2	1.5	2.3
	Labor productivity	2.7	3.0	1.3	1.7

Source: Historical Statistics, Paris: OECD, 1988,1992.

classical economists' faith in the free-enterprise capitalist system and dislike of government intervention in the economy. To analyze these ideas in more depth, we begin by stating some propositions of supply-side economics. We then explain each proposition in terms of its classical roots and show how each applies to current U.S. economic problems and policies. In the next subsection we examine the Keynesian critique of supply-side economics.

The following four propositions are important elements of supply-side economics.[10]

1. Output growth in the intermediate run is predominantly supply-determined by rates of growth in factor supplies and the rate of technological change.
2. The rate of growth of the capital input is determined primarily by the incentives for saving and investment, the incentives being the *after-tax* returns to saving and investment.
3. The rate of growth in the labor input, although in the long run determined by demographic factors, can also be affected significantly by incentives, in this case by changes in the after-tax real wage.
4. Excessive government regulation of business has discouraged capital formation, contributed to the slowdown in the growth of labor productivity, and reduced the U.S. growth rate.

Intermediate-Run Output Growth Is Supply-Determined

It was pointed out in Section 17.1 that in the long run, economic growth depends on supply factors. The supply-side economists believe that this is also true of growth in the intermediate run. Clearly, this follows in the classical model, where even in the short run output is supply-determined. Intermediate-run growth in the classical model is illustrated in Figure 17.5. Output increases from y_0 to y_1 to y_2 as the supply curve shifts to the right, reflecting growth in factor supplies and changes in technology. If the aggregate demand schedule remains at y_0^d in Figure 17.5, prices will fall succes-

---

[10]Elements of the supply-side position may be found in George Gilder, *Wealth and Poverty* (New York: Basic Books, 1981), especially Chaps. 4, 15–16; Paul Craig Roberts, *The Supply-Side Revolution* (Cambridge, Mass.: Harvard University Press, 1983); Arthur B. Laffer and Jan P. Seymour, eds., *The Economics of the Tax Revolt: A Reader* (New York: Harcourt Brace Jovanovich, 1979) and Laurence Meyer, ed., *The Supply-Side Effects of Economic Policy* (St. Louis: Center for the Study of American Business, 1981). The last two sources also contain critiques of the supply-side positions. Two useful analyses of supply-side economics are James Barth, "The Reagan Program for Economic Recovery: Economic Rationale (A Primer on Supply-Side Economics)," Federal Reserve Bank of Atlanta *Review* (September 1981), pp. 4–14; and John Tatom, "We Are All Supply-Siders Now!" Federal Reserve Bank of St. Louis *Review*, 63 (May 1981), pp. 18–30. Later evaluations are Martin Feldstein, "Supply-Side Economics: Old Truths and New Claims," *American Economic Review*, 76 (May 1986), pp. 26–30; and Lawrence Chimerine and Richard Young, "Economic Surprises and Messages of the 1980s," *American Economic Review*, 76 (May 1986), pp. 31–36.

sively to P_1 and then to P_2. If, instead, demand is increased as a result of growth in the money stock proportional to the growth in output, the price level will be maintained at P_0. Whichever is the case, the growth in output is determined solely by shifts in the supply curve.

It would be overly restrictive to say that Figure 17.5 represents the supply-side view of intermediate-run growth. Some, perhaps most, supply-side economists accept that demand plays a role in the *short-run* determination of income; the very short-run aggregate supply curve is upward-sloping to the right rather than vertical, as the classical economists would have drawn it. Consequently, to avoid short-run disruptions, many supply-side economists would favor a policy strategy in which demand was raised sufficiently to avoid the need for deflation (the fall in prices from P_0 to P_2 in Figure 17.5).

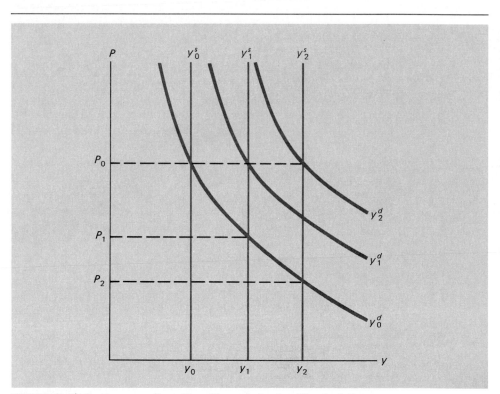

FIGURE 17.5   Intermediate-Run Growth in the Classical System
Growth in factor supplies shifts the supply curve to the right (from y_0^s to y_1^s, then y_2^s). If demand is unchanged, the price level falls (from P_0 to P_1, then to P_2). Appropriate increases in the quantity of money would increase demand sufficiently (from y_0^d to y_1^d, then to y_2^d) to maintain the initial equilibrium price level (P_0).

Still, a central element in the supply-side position is that for *intermediate-run* periods, growth in output is supply- and not demand-determined.[11]

A final element of the supply-side economists' view of the role of aggregate demand in the intermediate-run growth process is their belief that overexpansion of aggregate demands *retards* growth. They believe that the inflation caused by excessive aggregate demand growth inhibits investment and saving and weakens the work incentives to labor suppliers. As we will see later, in the supply-side economists' view, these negative growth effects of inflation are the result of the fact that the U.S. tax system, especially as it was set up in the 1970s, did not adjust adequately for inflation.

The Levels of Saving and Investment Depend on After-Tax Rates of Return to These Activities

Supply-side economics stresses the importance of the after-tax rate of return to investment as a primary determinant of investment and therefore the rate of capital formation. The after-tax rate of return is the pretax profit rate multiplied by 1 minus the rate at which profits are taxed. Similarly, the after-tax return for saving is believed by supply-side economists to be an important influence on the saving rate. Here the relevant rate of return is the after-tax *real* rate of interest, which equals the after-tax nominal interest rate (the nominal rate multiplied by 1 minus the rate at which interest payments are taxed) minus the expected inflation rate.[12]

This view of saving and investment is a classical notion. Recall our discussion of the theory of interest in the classical model, as illustrated in Figure 17.6. The equilibrium (real) interest rate is shown to be determined by the intersection of the saving and investment schedules. This reflects the assumption we make for the moment that the government deficit $(g - t)$ is zero. Otherwise, government deficit bond financing would be an additional demand for loanable funds. The position of the investment schedule is shown to depend on cp, the pretax corporate profit rate, and t^{cp}, the effective tax

---

[11]On this issue and on those discussed later, one can distinguish between a moderate and an extreme supply-side position. On many of these issues moderate supply-side economists differ from the Keynesians only in ascribing more importance to supply-side factors. The more extreme supply-side positions virtually ignore the demand side. Martin Feldstein, former chairman of the Council of Economic Advisors under President Reagan, for example, whose work on incentives for investment is described later, is an economist who has emphasized the importance of supply-side variables, but who has at times been at odds with more extreme supply siders.

[12]In Section 14.2 we defined the real rate of interest (ϕ) as the nominal interest rate (r) minus the expected rate of inflation (p^e). Here for simplicity we represent the *real* interest rate by the symbol r.

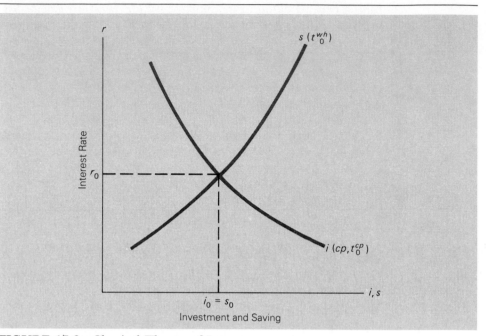

FIGURE 17.6   Classical Theory of Interest
The position of the saving schedule depends on the tax rate for interest and dividend income (t_0^{wh}). The position of the investment schedule depends on the effective tax rate on corporate profits (t_0^{cp}) as well as on the pretax corporate profit rate (cp). These tax rates, t_0^{wh} and t_0^{cp}, will, therefore, affect the value of the equilibrium real interest rate (r).

rate on corporate profits, to be explained later. The position of the saving schedule depends on t^{wh}, the rate of taxation of individual income earned on accumulated savings (wealth). In the simple classical model, income earned from accumulated savings would simply be interest income on bonds. In the real economy, t^{wh} would also represent tax rates on dividend income and tax rates on capital gains produced by changes in asset prices. In our earlier analysis we were interested in establishing that the real interest rate (r) was determined by what the classical economists called the forces of productivity and thrift, productivity being reflected in the profit rate and therefore the position of the investment schedule, thrift reflected in the position of the saving schedule (both for a given structure of taxes). Here the important point is that in the classical view productivity and thrift, *as well as the structure of taxes,* are the determinants of saving, investment, and consequently the determinants of the rate of capital formation.

Supply-side economists need not accept the particular specification of the saving and investment functions in our simple version of the classical system. In trying to predict the level of investment spending for the United States in a particular year in the 1990s, for example, supply-side economists would use a much more complex investment function than that plotted in Figure 17.6. They would take account of factors such as lags and adjustment costs discussed in our more detailed analysis of investment (Section 14.2). The essentially classical feature in supply-side economists' view of the saving–investment process is their stress on the importance of rates of return as influences on the rates of saving, investment, and thus capital formation. Where else might one put the emphasis? The answer is on income and, hence, on aggregate demand; we will see that Keynesians believe that the level of income is the most important determinant of investment. Investment can best be kept high according to this Keynesian view by keeping the economy at a high rate of capacity utilization. Keynesians do not ignore rates of return, nor do supply-side economists ignore income as a determinant of saving or investment. It is a matter of emphasis, and supply-side economists emphasize rates of return as incentives for saving and investment.

If one stresses the importance of incentives for saving and investment, one is led to seek the source of the decline in the rate of U.S. capital formation in the post-1970 period in factors that weakened these incentives. One is led to seek the solution to slow capital formation in increased incentives for savers and investors. Martin Feldstein and a number of other economists claim that the interaction of inflation and the U.S. tax system weakened these incentives over the course of the 1970s. They have argued that increases in the inflation rate raise the effective tax rate on corporate income and, therefore, lower the after-tax rate of return on investment in two important ways.[13]

The first of these effects that inflation has on the effective tax rate on corporate income is the result of the standard inventory procedure followed by many firms in the 1970s, the so-called first in–first out system (FIFO). Under FIFO, as items are used up from an inventory of raw materials, or finished goods are sold from inventory, it is assumed that goods are being used or sold in the order in which they were purchased or produced; first in are first out. The true costs to the firm of using up materials or selling finished goods is the *replacement cost*, not the cost when they were originally acquired. When inflation is taking place, FIFO *understated* true costs of production, overstates profits, and hence resulted in an increase in the firm's corporate tax liability.

---

[13] See Martin Feldstein and Lawrence Summers, "Inflation and the Taxation of Capital Income in the Corporate Sector," *National Tax Journal*, 32 (December 1979), pp. 445–70.

Inflation also raises the effective tax rate on corporate income as a result of depreciation laws. Firms can deduct depreciation of capital investments only at *original* costs. In inflationary periods, as with inventories, the true cost of depreciating capital is the replacement cost. This cost is understated by depreciation at original or "historic" cost, so profits are overstated, and, through this channel, too, the effective corporate tax liability was increased in the inflationary 1970s.

Supply-side economists also argue that the combination of inflation and the U.S. tax system reduced the incentives to save during the 1970s. The income tax that an individual pays is based on the *nominal* interest, dividends, or capital gains that he earns on his invested savings. Two examples will illustrate how increased inflation and taxation of nominal interest payments or capital gains lower the real return on saving. Suppose that initially the nominal interest rate is 6 percent and the rate of inflation is 2 percent (a pretax real rate of 4 percent). At a 50 percent marginal tax rate, an individual investor would have an after-tax *nominal* return of 3 percent [6 percent $\times$ $(1 - t^{wh})$ = 6 percent $\times$ $(1 - 0.5)$] and an after-tax real return of 1 percent (3 percent $-$ 2 percent). Now suppose that the nominal interest rate were 16 percent with an inflation rate of 12 percent (again a pretax real rate of 4 percent). The after-tax nominal return will be 8 percent [16 percent $\times$ (1 $-$ 0.5)], which means that the after-tax real return is now -4 percent.

Or consider the case of taxation of nominal capital gains, on corporate equities, for example. Suppose that an individual purchased a share of stock at a price of $100 in 1967 and sold it in 1980 for $200. Since the price level rose by over 150 percent in this period while the price of the stock doubled, or rose 100 percent, the individual's real return is negative even before taxes. Still, he must pay a capital gains tax on the nominal capital gain (of $100), increasing the size of his real loss. Supply-side economists argue that taxing of nominal capital gains and interest earnings during inflationary periods results in an increased effective tax rate on real returns and will retard saving.

The effects of overtaxing both corporate profits and the return to saving during inflationary time periods are illustrated in Figure 17.7. Suppose that we move from a period of relatively low inflation rates such as the 1950s and 1960s to a period of higher inflation rates such as the 1970s. Because of use of the FIFO inventory accounting system and historic cost depreciation, this results in an increase in the effective tax rate on corporate profits from t_0^{cp} to t_1^{cp} in Figure 17.7. For a given before-tax profit rate cp, this increase in the effective tax rate will shift the investment schedule to the left as shown in the graph. Further, due to the taxing of nominal interest payments and capital gains, the effective tax on the return to saving is increased from t_0^{wh} to t_1^{wh}, which shifts the saving schedule to the left in Figure 17.7. After the adjustment to a new equilibrium, saving and investment are reduced from the levels i_0 and s_0 to the levels shown as s_1 and i_1 in Figure 17.7. The rate of capital formation is reduced by the interaction of inflation and the tax system.

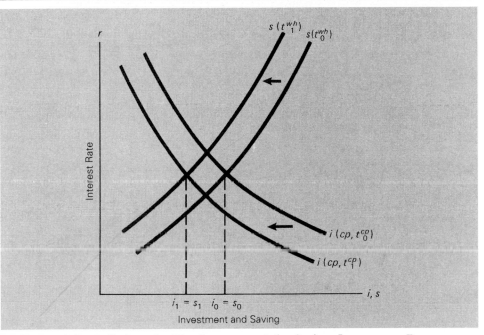

FIGURE 17.7 Inflation, the Tax System, and the Saving–Investment Process
An increase in the effective corporate tax rate due to increased inflation causes the investment schedule to shift leftward from $i(cp, t_0^{cp})$ to $i(cp, t_1^{cp})$. An inflation-induced increase in the effective tax rate on interest income and capital gains shifts the saving schedule leftward from $s(t_0^{wh})$ to $s(t_1^{wh})$. The equilibrium levels of saving and investment fall from $i_0 = s_0$ to $i_1 = s_1$.

Labor Supply Is Responsive to Changes in the After-Tax Real Wage

Supply side economists argue that labor supply is responsive to changes in *after-tax* real wages. Here again the supply-side view is rooted in classical economics—in this case building on the classical analysis of the supply-side effects of changes in the marginal income tax rate (Section 4.3). Figure 17.8 illustrates the determination of equilibrium employment in the classical system and the effect of a change in the after-tax real wage as a result of a change in the marginal income tax rate t^y. Initially assume that the income tax rate is set at t_0^y. The labor supply curve is given by $N^s(t_0^y)$ and intersects the labor demand curve at N_0, the equilibrium level of employment.

Now assume that the income tax rate is raised to a higher level, t_1^y. According to the supply-side view, labor supply depends on the after-tax real wage, which will equal $(1 - t^y)W/P$. For example, with a marginal tax rate of 0.20, the after-tax real wage will be 0.80 times the pretax real wage. The marginal income tax rate thus forms a "wedge" between the wage paid by

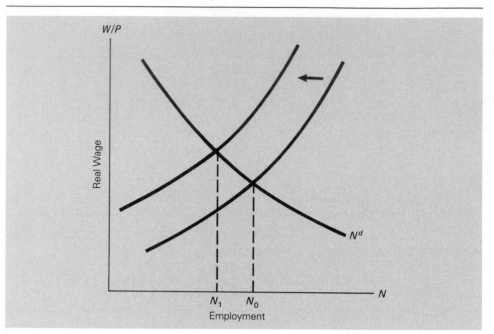

FIGURE 17.8 Taxes and Labor Supply in the Classical System
An increase in the income tax rate from t_0^y to t_1^y reduces the after-tax real wage and causes the labor supply schedule to shift to the left. The level of employment declines from N_0 to N_1.

the employer W/P and the wage received by the worker $(1 - t^y)W/P$. An increase in the tax rate from t_0^y to a higher level t_1^y would cause the labor supply schedule to shift to the left from $N^s(t_0^y)$ to $N^s(t_1^y)$ Less labor would be supplied at each level of the pretax real wage because with a higher tax rate a given pretax real wage represents a *lower* after-tax real wage. Employment declines from N_0 to N_1.

The supply-side economists believe that rising marginal tax rates in the United States during the 1970s increased the size of this "wedge," which the income tax creates between the real wage paid by the employer and the (after-tax) wage received by the employee (see Perspectives 4.2). They claim that work incentives were reduced, with negative effects on employment and output. Here again inflationary aggregate demand policies and a tax system not well designed to cope with the effects of inflation deserve much of the blame. The U.S. income tax system in the 1970s was progressive, so as *nominal* incomes went up as a result of inflation, individuals moved into higher marginal tax brackets.

Read Perspectives 17.3.

Government Regulation Contributed to the Slowdown
in the U.S. Growth Rate

Supply-side economists argue that the proliferation of government regulation of business contributed significantly to the slowdown in U.S. growth
during the 1970s. There was a new wave of government regulatory activity
that began in the 1960s. New agencies were set up and laws passed for such
purposes as pollution control, protection of worker safety, consumer product
safety, and pension reform. Supply-side economists argue that this increase
in government regulatory activity slowed economic growth in two ways.

First, complying with such regulations increases the cost of producing a
given output. Increases in government regulation therefore have the same
effects as the supply shocks considered in Chapter 8. The aggregate supply
curve shifts to the left, reducing output. Note that some of the increase in
cost comes from having to employ workers not directly for production of
output, steel, for example, but having them clean smokestacks to comply
with pollution controls, eliminate on the job safety hazards, or otherwise
comply with regulations. Thus, the increase in government regulation is a
possible factor explaining the decline in the growth of labor productivity.

Second, supply-side economists argue that government regulatory activity retarded capital formation, at least capital formation that contributes to
increased productivity in terms of measured output. According to one estimate, expenditures on pollution control absorbed approximately 20 percent
of net investment in 1970.[14]

The Keynesian Critique of Supply-Side Economics

We have stressed the classical roots of the supply-side economics. The supply-
side economics can be regarded as the intermediate-run counterpart to the
monetarist and new classical attacks on the Keynesian orthodoxy that had become dominant by the mid-1960s, those attacks also being based on classical
notions. In this section we analyze the Keynesian critique of the supply-side
position. We examine the Keynesian view of each of the supply-side propositions discussed in the preceding section.

The Supply-Determined Nature of Intermediate-Run Growth

As noted previously, the Keynesian position is that for periods of a decade
or so, both supply and demand factors are important in determining output
growth. In explaining the lower growth in the United States in the 1970s,
for example, James Tobin sees as the primary causes supply shocks, the most
important from the energy sector, and monetary policy "overkill," meaning overly restrictive monetary policy actions that were imposed to slow the

---

[14]See Lawrence Summers, "Tax Policy and Corporate Investment," in Meyer, *Supply-Side Effects*.

PERSPECTIVES

THE LAFFER CURVE

17.3

A "simplified" income tax form circulated as a joke reads

Form "1040"

This year's income_____.

SEND IT IN.

A tax system represented by this form, that of a 100 percent tax rate, would not collect any revenue. Who would work and report income? At the other end of the tax rate spectrum, a rate of 0 percent would also obviously yield no revenue. Therefore, we know that if we plot a relationship between tax *revenue* and the tax *rate*, with revenue on the vertical axis, the curve will first rise as the tax rate moves up from zero, but at some point, before the tax rate hits one, it will decline. For example, the relationship might be as shown in Figure 17.9.

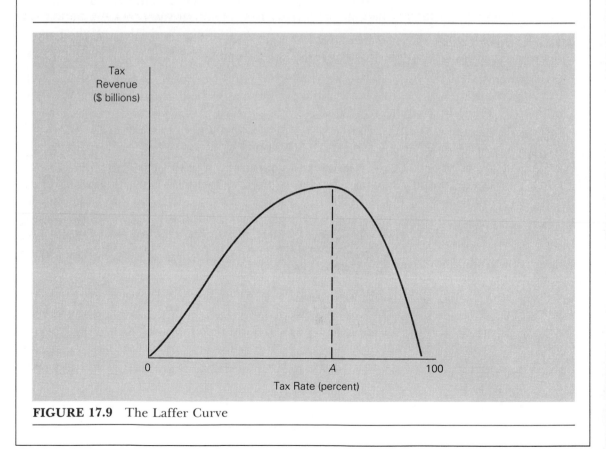

FIGURE 17.9 The Laffer Curve

This curve showing tax revenue collected at each tax rate (or overall level of tax rates) is called the Laffer curve. The curve is named after its popularizer, Arthur B. Laffer, who supposedly first drew the curve on a cocktail napkin in a Washington, D.C. restaurant. Whatever its origin, the Laffer curve has received much attention because it illustrates the possibility that increases in tax rates may *reduce* tax revenue. Conversely, a cut in tax rates may *increase* revenue. This will happen if tax rates are initially in the range to the right of point A in Figure 17.9.

A number of supply-side economists, including Laffer, argued that this was the case for the United States in the early 1980s. Tax cuts would expand the economy through the supply side. This would increase the tax base. Moreover, supply-siders argued that tax avoidance (e.g., through the use of tax shelters) and tax evasion (e.g., failure to report taxable income) could decline. Together, it was argued, these effects would lead to increased tax revenues even at lower tax rates.

Economists of other than the supply-side persuasion, and many moderate supply-siders, did not believe the U.S. economy was on the downward-sloping portion of the Laffer curve. They saw the huge deficits that emerged in the 1980s after tax cuts as support for their view

economy when a slowdown was already under way. Tobin blames such mistimed monetary actions in part for the severity of the recessions of the 1970s, which resulted in the lower growth rate for the decade.[15]

Saving and Investment and After-Tax Rates of Return

On the question of whether depressed rates of return have lowered saving, investment, and capital formation, there are areas of agreement and disagreement between the supply-side economists and the Keynesians.

Keynesian economists do not deny that capital formation is important to growth or that the slowdown in net capital formation was one cause of the growth slowdown of the 1970s. Nor do the Keynesians oppose policies to improve investment incentives. Tobin points out, for example, that it was during the Kennedy administration, a highpoint of Keynesian influence, that the first investment tax credit was passed.

Still, in the Keynesian view, the primary explanation for the slowdown in net capital formation in the 1970s lies in the low levels of output growth during that period, which caused investment demand to lag. In the Keynesian view, then, *for the most part* causation runs from low output to low investment rather than in the reverse direction. The low output levels are ascribed, as explained previously, to supply shocks and, at times, overly restrictive monetary policies.

---

[15]See James Tobin, "Stabilization Policy Ten Years After," *Brookings Papers on Economic Activity* 1 (1980), pp. 19–71.

What about the role of incentives for saving and investment? Although not ignoring the effects of changes in after-tax returns on investment demand, many Keynesians seem to accept the evidence from studies such as Peter Clark's, that output is the key variable determining investment.[16] The best way to encourage investment, then, is to keep the economy near the full-capacity level of output. In the case of saving, the Keynesians would not deny that the rate of return (after taxes) is a determinant of saving. Nor would most Keynesians deny that a decline in this rate of return may have caused the decline in the saving rate that did occur in the late 1970s. They believe, however, as Tobin states, that "an explanation of the slowdown in business capital formation in the 1970s may be sought in investment demand rather than saving supply."

In explaining the continued weakness of capital formation over the decade of the 1980s, Keynesian economists see a larger role for saving. Not only did the saving rate decline in the 1980s (see Perspectives 14.1), but a larger portion of saving went to finance the large deficits that emerged during the Reagan administration. We return to this point in Chapter 18.

The Effect of Income Tax Cuts on Labor Supply

Keynesian economists do not believe that "vast increases" in labor supply will result from lowering marginal income tax rates. They do not believe that current income tax rates are a serious impediment to labor supply. As evidence of this, Keynesian economists cite the high labor-force-participation ratios in Western European countries (Germany, for example), where marginal tax rates are substantially higher than in the United States. Further, they point out that although with a progressive income tax, inflation will push individuals into higher tax brackets, actual tax rates paid will increase only if the tax schedule is unchanged. If, instead, Congress periodically lowers tax rates to offset the effects of inflation (or for some other reason), actual marginal tax rates may not rise. According to estimates cited by James Tobin, the federal marginal rate of personal income tax averaged over all brackets was actually lower in 1975 than in 1960—18.0 percent, compared with 18.8 percent. In the 1975–80 period there does appear to have been some "bracket creep" because of inflation, with the average marginal tax rate increasing to 21.6 percent. But Tobin finds no evidence of a weakened "propensity to supply labor."[17]

In rebuttal, supply-side economists point to the large increase in payroll taxes over recent years. Payroll (social security) taxes are an additional el-

---

[16] Peter Clark, "Investment in the 1970's: Theory, Performance and Prediction," *Brookings Papers on Economic Activity* 1 (1979), pp. 73–113.

[17] See James Tobin, "The Reagan Economic Plan—Supply-Side, Budget and Inflation," in *The Reagan Economic Plan* (San Francisco: Federal Reserve Bank of San Francisco, 1981).

ement in the "wedge" between the wage paid by the employer and that received by the worker. Additionally, the supply-side economists point to empirical studies indicating that, given secular trends that have increased labor force participation rates, income and payroll tax rates have negative effects on labor supply.[18]

The issues, then, appear to be the empirical ones of whether increases in marginal tax rates have been of a magnitude sufficient to create an important work disincentive and, further, whether reductions in marginal tax rates affect labor supply strongly enough to increase employment and output substantially.

Regulation as a Source of Inflation and Slow Growth

With regard to the effects of government regulation on inflation and growth, the issues are broad ones, and it is incorrect to argue that there is *a* Keynesian position that contrasts with the supply-side position. As stated previously, there was no doubt a tremendous growth in government regulation in the period from the late 1960s to 1980. There is also no doubt that complying with many of these regulations was quite costly to firms and that much of the cost is passed on to consumers. Nor is it doubtful that many of the regulations are cost ineffective, in that more efficient ways exist to achieve the same benefits.

Economists who would not go as far as the supply-siders in massive dismantling of the regulatory structure that arose since the 1960s believe either the benefits are greater than the supply-side economists believe or the costs, in terms of lost growth, are lower. Additionally, they may be more optimistic about the possibility for improvement in regulatory effectiveness. The prospective benefits from these new regulations include cleaner air, cleaner water, safer workplaces, and safer consumer products. These are, of course, desirable to all, but there are differences of opinion as to the degree to which government intervention in the economy is needed to achieve them.

As for the cost of regulation in terms of intermediate-run growth, there is also room for a divergence of opinion. Edward Denison, whose study of the sources of U.S. economic growth was cited earlier, estimates that mandated expenditures for pollution abatement, together with required spending to improve water safety and health, cut the U.S. growth rate by between 0.1 and 0.2 percentage points over the 1970s and early 1980s.[19] This is a modest

---

[18]See, for example, Jerry Hausman, "Income and Payroll Tax Policy and Labor Supply," in Meyer, *Supply-Side Effects*; Jerry Hausman, "Labor Supply," in Henry Aaron and Joseph Pechman, eds., *How Taxes Affect Economic Behavior* (Washington, D.C.: The Brookings Institution, 1981); and Jerry A. Hausman and James M. Poterba, "Household Behavior and the Tax Reform Act of 1986," *Journal of Economic Perspectives*, 1 (Summer 1987), pp. 101–20.

[19]Edward Denison, *Trends in American Economic Growth*, p. 66.

though not insignificant part of the growth slowdown. But Denison also finds that much of the slowdown in growth cannot be explained by *any* of the factors he considers. He finds a large unexplained "residual" drop in the growth rate because of factors not measured explicitly. One cannot rule out overregulation by government in many areas, in addition to pollution control and worker safety (the areas measured by Denison), as factors responsible for the otherwise unexplainable portion of the decline in the growth rate.

17.3 • SUPPLY-SIDE ECONOMICS AND THE POLICIES OF THE REAGAN AND BUSH ADMINISTRATIONS

After the high inflation and unemployment of the 1970s, voters in the United States were ready in 1980 for an experiment with supply-side economics. To be sure, the Reagan economic proposals and, to an even greater degree, his policies as enacted contained elements based on theories other than those of the supply-siders. Still, the central novel elements of what became known as Reaganomics were supply-side proposals. George Bush was at first highly critical of supply-side economics, terming it "voodoo economics." Still many of the initiatives of the Bush administration have been in line with supply-side prescriptions.

Economic Redirection in Reagan's First Term

President Reagan came into office in 1981, proclaiming that the United States was "in the worst economic mess since the Great Depression." The major elements of President Reagan's economic recovery plan that was proposed as a cure for the country's economic ills were based on the supply-side propositions we have discussed.

Personal Income Tax Reductions

As enacted by Congress, the Reagan tax cut bill reduced marginal income tax rates, in three stages, by a total of 23 percent. The bill also lowered the top rate on income earned from capital from 70 to 50 percent. Beginning in 1985, the tax bill indexed tax brackets to inflation to prevent "bracket creep." As discussed in Section 17.2, in the view of supply-side economists, such income tax cuts should increase labor supply and therefore output (supply-side proposition 3).

Personal income tax cuts should also increase personal saving. The reduction in the maximum tax bracket from 70 to 50 percent was especially aimed at increasing saving. Additionally, to encourage saving, the tax act extended the opportunity to use IRA accounts to all households. IRA accounts allow for deposit of $2000 per year ($4000 for a two-worker couple) to a retirement account. Contributions to these accounts are deductible from taxable income, with taxes paid as withdrawals are made after retirement. Accumulated interest on IRA accounts is also tax-free until withdrawal.[20]

Reductions in Business Taxes

The Reagan administration's tax act had several features aimed at encouraging business investment by increasing the after-tax return to investment. The most important of these was the *accelerated cost recovery system* (ACRS), which was a set of accelerated depreciation allowances for business plants and equipment. To give an example, a piece of industrial equipment that could have been depreciated over an 8.6-year period before the tax act could be depreciated over a 5-year period under the act's provisions.

Accompanying these accelerated depreciation allowances was a leasing system whereby firms without taxable income (e.g., firms with losses, not profits) could, through leasing arrangements, in return for compensation, transfer their tax deductions under the new tax act to profitable firms. Finally, with regard to business taxation, the investment tax credit for certain types of equipment was increased.

These business tax cuts were aimed at offsetting the inflation-induced increase in the effective tax rate on business profits, which was discussed in Section 17.2. Such tax cuts are consistent with the supply-side view (proposition 2) that the way to encourage capital formation is by increasing the after-tax return to investment.

Reductions in Nondefense Government Spending

According to the supply-side view, personal and business tax cuts should increase aggregate supply and, therefore, produce noninflationary real output growth. Also, it was hoped that such growth would increase the tax base and therefore increase tax revenues to offset, in large part (or completely), the loss in revenue caused by the lower tax rates. However, to ensure that demand was not overly stimulated, and to keep the budget deficit as small as possible, the Reagan program proposed cuts in nondefense government spending. Cuts were proposed in areas such as housing, education, and income maintenance programs. Such cuts in nondefense spending were also needed, in part, to finance a proposed increase in defense spending. In addition to the tax cuts, therefore, the Economic Recovery Act of 1981 cut 1982 nondefense spending by an amount on the order of $30–40 billion.

After this early success, cuts in nondefense spending met more resistance. Given the increase in defense spending, the overall lack of much success in cutting nondefense spending meant that government spending as a

---

[20]The tax reform act of 1986 established an income threshold above which IRA contributions were nondeductible from taxable income. Interest was still tax-free until withdrawal, regardless of income. In 1992, President Bush proposed further modifications in the IRA program.

percentage of GNP *rose* rather than fell during President Reagan's first term. Failure to cut spending, together with tax reduction, led to high government budget deficits, the consequences of which are examined in Chapter 18.

Reductions in Governmental Regulation

Consistent with the supply-side view that government regulation of the economy in areas such as air quality, worker safety, and consumer product safety has been overly costly and has retarded growth (proposition 4), the Reagan administration began a regulatory review. The aim was to eliminate "wasteful or outdated regulation and to make necessary regulation more efficient and more flexible." Some specific regulatory initiatives in the first Reagan administration were a shift in some responsibilities for air pollution control to the states, decontrol of petroleum markets, proposals to abolish the Departments of Energy and Education, and an Executive Order calling for a cost-benefit analysis before issuing any new federal regulation.

The Second Reagan Administration

On the spending side, the second Reagan administration continued the policy of the first with attempts to increase defense expenditures and reduce nondefense expenditures. As in the first term, many politically popular domestic programs proved impossible to cut. Moreover, as huge deficits continued, Congress became reluctant to increase defense spending substantially.

On the tax side, the centerpiece was *tax reform*—touted by President Reagan as a "second American Revolution." The aims of tax reform were, first, to broaden the tax *base* by eliminating many deductible items and, second, to reduce *marginal tax rates*. The combination of these actions was to be offsetting, so that total revenues would neither rise nor fall. Lower marginal tax rates would, however, improve incentives for labor supply, saving, and investment.

Congress passed a tax reform act in August 1986 that reflected not only the president's wishes but also the goals of tax reformers in Congress from both political parties. The act lowered the highest tax rate from 50 percent to 28 percent—the lowest top rate since 1931. Moreover, it created only two tax rates, 15 percent (on income up to approximately $30,000 on a joint return) and 28 percent.[21] The act also raised personal exemptions so that approximately 6 million low-income recipients were removed from the tax rolls. To keep tax reform from reducing tax revenues, the act removed many deductions and eliminated a number of tax shelters.

---

[21]There is, in effect, a third marginal rate of 31 percent on incomes between $43,000 and $90,000 due to a phase-out of the benefits of personal exemptions over this income range.

Initiatives in Bush's First Term

As noted earlier, George Bush had at one time been skeptical about supply-side economics. Also, when he took office both houses of Congress had substantial Democratic majorities that had always been skeptical of supply-side policy prescriptions. Still, a number of Bush's proposals were certainly consistent with supply-side positions.

When he ran for president in 1988, a central plank in Bush's economic platform was his pledge of "no new taxes." This pledge conformed to the supply-side view of the disincentive effects of higher taxes. Unfortunately, from a supply-sider's view, as the budget deficit ballooned in 1990 and 1991, Bush abandoned this pledge to reach a deficit reduction compromise with Congress. A second Bush initiative, was a proposal to lower the capital gains tax. The supply-side analysis suggests that such a reduction would have a favorable effect on saving and thus on capital formation.

Bush also carried on with the Reagan administration's attempt to cut government spending. With the dissolution of the Soviet Union and consequent end of the Cold War, the major issue came to be one of what to do with the "peace dividend"; as defense spending declined, should overall spending fall or should the funds be transferred to domestic spending?

17.4   CONCLUSION

It is still too early for a definitive evaluation of the economic effects of Reaganomics, but some things are clear. One is that Reagan administration officials promised too much. According to administration public forecasts in 1981, inflation was supposed to decline without a recession. Growth in real GNP in 1982, for example, was forecast to be 4.2 percent; actual growth turned out to be *minus* 2.5 percent. The federal budget was supposed to be balanced by 1985; the actual budget deficit was just short of $200 billion in that year. The Bush administration had similar difficulties with deficit projections. On coming into office, the administration projected that the deficit would be reduced from $136 billion in fiscal 1989 to $30.6 billion by fiscal 1992. The actual figure for 1992 was nearly $400 billion.

But the fact that Reaganomics was oversold does not mean that the program or Bush's follow-up program was a failure. One area in which there was considerable success was in reducing the inflation rate.

One area, however, in which the Reagan–Bush program has yet to bear fruit is in encouraging saving and investment. Despite programs to provide incentives, the overall U.S. saving rate (corporation and household) has not increased. The household (personal) saving rate actually *fell* markedly in the 1980s (Perspectives 14.1). Net fixed business investment, and therefore the rate of capital formation, also failed to increase markedly in the 1980s.

The growth slowdown was not reversed. The growth rate in labor productivity did rise modestly, but remained low relative to the pre-1970 level.

This failure of saving and investment to respond to the policy changes in the 1980s did not surprise the more moderate (or traditional) supply-side economists, who

> were content to claim that the pursuit of such tax, spending, and monetary policies would, over the long run, lead to increased real incomes and a higher standard of living. We recognized that the key to this process was increased saving and investment and knew that it would take a long time to have a noticeable effect.[22]

If these more moderate supply-side economists are correct, the policies of the Reagan years may favorably affect saving, investment, and economic growth in the 1990s. The prolonged recession that began in the summer of 1990 has not, however, gotten the 1990s off to a good start as a high growth decade.

Review Questions and Problems

1. Explain why it is that in the traditional growth model with exogenous technological change, the long-run equilibrium rate of growth in output is independent of the saving rate (S/Y).

2. Explain why, in a model with endogenous technological change, a rise in the saving rate may lead to a permanent rise in the long-run growth rate in output.

3. According to Denison's estimates, which factors were the most important in accounting for the growth in real output over the 1929–82 period?

4. Outline the main features of a supply-sider's prescription for policies to foster noninflationary economic growth. How do these policy prescriptions differ from those of the Keynesians?

5. Compare the Keynesian and supply-siders' positions on the effects of a tax cut.

6. Compare the Keynesian and supply-siders' positions on the determinants of saving, investment, and capital formation.

7. Within the supply-side theory, what is the proper role for aggregate demand management policies?

8. An investment tax credit allows firms to deduct a portion of investment spending from their corporate tax liability. Analyze the effect on output of such a tax credit in the Keynesian model and, alternatively, within the supply-side framework.

---

[22]Martin Feldstein, "Supply-Side Economics: Old Truths and New Claims," p. 27.

Selected Readings

Long-Run Growth

Branson, William, *Macroeconomic Theory and Policy,* 3rd ed. New York: Harper & Row, 1989, Chaps. 22–27.

Denison, Edward, *Trends in American Economic Growth: 1929–82.* Washington, D.C.: The Brookings Institution, 1985.

Dixit, A. K., *The Theory of Equilibrium Growth.* London: Oxford University Press, 1976.

Jones, Hywel, *An Introduction to Modern Theories of Economic Growth.* New York: McGraw-Hill, 1975.

Lucas, Robert E., "On the Mechanics of Economic Development," *Journal of Monetary Economics,* 22(July 1988), pp. 3–42.

Romer, Paul, "Capital Accumulation in the Theory of Long-Run Growth," in Robert J. Barro, ed., *Modern Business Cycle Theory.* Cambridge, Mass.: Harvard University Press, 1989.

Intermediate-Run Growth

Blanchard, Olivier J., "Reaganomics," *Economic Policy,* 2 (October 1987), pp. 17–56.

Bosworth, Barry, and Burtless, Gary, "Effects of Tax Reform on Labor Supply, Investment and Saving," *Journal of Economic Perspectives,* 6 (Winter 1992), pp. 3–25.

Feldstein, Martin, "Supply Side Economics: Old Truths and New Claims," *American Economic Review,* 76 (May 1986), pp. 26–30.

Feldstein, Martin, and Summers, Lawrence, "Inflation and the Taxation of Capital Income in the Corporate Sector," *National Tax Journal,* 32 (December 1979), pp. 445–70.

Jorgenson, Dale W., "Productivity and Postwar U.S. Economic Growth," *Journal of Economic Perspectives,* 2 (Fall 1988), pp. 23–41.

Laffer, Arthur B., and Seymour, Jan, eds., *The Economics of the Tax Revolt: A Reader.* New York: Harcourt Brace Jovanovich, 1979.

Meyer, Laurence H., ed., *The Supply-Side Effects of Economic Policy.* St. Louis: Center for the Study of American Business, 1981.

Modigliani, Franco, "Reagan's Economic Policies: A Critique," *Oxford Economic Papers,* 40 (September 1988), pp. 397–426.

Niskanen, William A., *Reaganomics.* New York: Oxford University Press, 1988.

Roberts, Paul Craig, *The Supply-Side Revolution.* Cambridge, Mass.: Harvard University Press, 1983.

Tobin, James, "Stabilization Policy Ten Years After," *Brookings Papers on Economic Activity* 1 (1980), pp. 19–71.

IV Economic Policy

CHAPTER OUTLINE

The two chapters in this part extend our discussion of macroeconomic stabilization policy. The macroeconomic effects of monetary and fiscal policies were analyzed in the previous chapters on macroeconomic models, but in those chapters the policy actions we considered were simple and in some cases unrealistic policy shifts, a "lump-sum" change in the level of tax collections, for example. In the next two chapters, we take a more detailed look at the policymaking process. We examine the goals of macroeconomic policy and the optimum ways in which the policy process should be designed to achieve these goals—questions of optimal economic policy. In dealing with these questions, we return to the issue of whether policy should be conducted by rules (e.g., the constant money growth rule of the monetarists) or by discretion (e.g., the activist policy prescription of the Keynesians).

Chapter 18 examines fiscal policy, and Chapter 19 considers monetary policy. Chapter 19 is followed by a historical appendix that provides a listing, along with a brief description, of major macroeconomic policy actions for the period since the Great Depression of the 1930s.

18 : Fiscal Policy

Part *a* of Table 18.1 shows the budget projections President Bush submitted to Congress in January 1989. According to these projections, the federal budget deficit was to decline substantially in each year of his administration. By 1993 there was to be a small surplus. (The most recent U.S. federal budget surplus was in 1969.) Table 18.1*a* also shows the Gramm–Rudman–Hollings deficit targets. These are target levels for deficits set in the (amended) Gramm–Rudman–Hollings deficit control bill—targets the planned Bush budgets had to meet. The Gramm–Rudman–Hollings Act, originally passed in 1985 and amended in 1987, is an example of conducting fiscal policy by *rules*, in this case deficit ceilings.

In the fall of 1990, the Gramm–Rudman–Hollings ceilings, which had by then clearly become unreachable, were superceded by the Deficit Reduction agreement between Congress and President Bush; decisions on the deficit were back to being made by *discretion*, rather than fixed rules. The agreement was to trim $500 billion from the budget deficit over 5 years. These targets also seem unlikely to be achieved. Part *b* of Table 18.1 shows projected deficits for 1992–96 as of early 1992. Notice that while in 1989 the budget was expected to be in balance or show a slight surplus by 1993, the current projected deficit for that year is over $350 billion.

One of the key issues we consider in this chapter is whether fiscal policy is best conducted by fixed rules, such as the Gramm–Rudman–Hollings Act, or left to the discretion of policymakers. We also try to determine why, with either kind of policy, the federal budget deficit has been so difficult to control.

fixed rules vs. discretion

517

TABLE 18.1   U.S. Budget Summary[a]: President Bush's budget proposals (billions U.S. dollars)

	1989	1990	1991	1992	1993
a. Projections as of 1989					
Receipts	979.3	1065.6	1147.6	1218.6	1286.6
Outlays	1149.5	1160.4	1211.8	1249.2	1284.1
Deficit (−) or surplus	−170.2	−94.8	−64.2	−30.6	2.5
Gramm–Rudman–Hollings deficit targets[b]	−136.0	−100.0	−64.0	−28.0	0.0

	1992	1993	1994	1995	1996
b. Projections as of 1992					
Receipts	1075.7	1164.8	1263.4	1343.5	1427.5
Outlays	1475.1	1516.7	1474.8	1535.5	1607.5
Deficit (−) or surplus	−399.4	−351.9	−211.4	−192.0	−180.0

[a] Fiscal years ending September 30. Data include on- and off-budget totals.

[b] Deficit targets under the 1987 amendment to the Balanced Budget and Emergency Deficit Control Act (Gramm–Rudman–Hollings Act). Asset sales cannot be counted toward meeting these targets.

Source: IMF *Survey,* February 20, 1989; February 17, 1992.

We begin by examining the goals of macroeconomic policy and the possibility that the goals of policymakers diverge from those of the public. Such a divergence is used by some economists as an argument in favor of a *rule*, for example, one mandating a balanced federal budget, to constrain fiscal policymakers. Next we consider the behavior of the federal budget over the post–World War II period and the relationship between the budget and the state of the economy. With this background, we examine Keynesian objections to balanced-budget rules. The last section considers some economic implications of federal government budget deficits, in particular, the implications of the especially large deficits of the 1980s and early 1990s.

18.1 · THE GOALS OF MACROECONOMIC POLICY

What are the goals of macroeconomic policy? Low unemployment and price stability seem to be agreed upon as policy goals, although, as we saw in Part II, there is considerable disagreement concerning the ability of policymakers to achieve these goals by means of aggregate demand management. There are also differences of opinion about the relative weights that should be assigned to each of these goals. Economic growth is a third policy goal—one that is closely related to the unemployment goal, because the creation of new jobs requires a growing economy.

Suppose we agree that the goals of macroeconomic policy should be to achieve target levels of inflation, unemployment, and economic growth. The question of optimal conduct of macroeconomic policy would then be one of how to set the policy *instruments*, variables such as the levels of government spending and various tax rates in the case of fiscal policy, in order to come as close as possible to achieving the target levels for these goal variables. One way of formulating this problem in theory is to assume that the policymaker minimizes a social-loss function of the following form:

$$L = a_1(U - U^*)^2 + a_2(\dot{P} - \dot{P}^*)^2 + a_3(\dot{y} - \dot{y}^*)^2 \quad (18.1)$$
$$a_1, a_2, a_3 > 0$$

[handwritten margin notes: "Social Loss Formulation"; "relative wts"]

In this equation, L is the social welfare loss that comes as a result of deviations of the macroeconomic goal variables from the target levels, the costs of excessively high unemployment, for example. The goal variables themselves are the level of unemployment (U), the inflation rate ($\dot{P}$), and the rate of growth in real income ($\dot{y}$). The target levels for these variables are U^*, $\dot{P}^*$, and $\dot{y}^*$, respectively. In the particular form given by equation (18.1) the loss in social welfare depends on the squared deviations of the goal variables from the target levels. This implies that the welfare loss from a given increase in the deviation of a goal variable from the target level increases as we get further from the target level; large deviations from desired levels receive especially heavy weights. The coefficients (a_1, a_2, and a_3) in equation (18.1) represent the relative weights attached to the different targets.

[handwritten margin notes: "MACRO targets"; "U, P, y"]

Equation (18.1) is only one possible representation of the social-loss function that is relevant to macroeconomic policies. The key assumption for this type of formulation of the optimal policy problem is simply that the policymaker minimizes some social-welfare-loss function. The problem is, then, to find the setting of the instruments that results in the minimum loss. One can further investigate whether various rules, such as the constant money growth rule, outperform more activist policy prescriptions.

18.2   THE GOALS OF MACROECONOMIC POLICYMAKERS

There is a growing literature questioning the realism of the preceding formulation of the optimum policy question. We examine two strands in this critical literature: the **public-choice** view and the **partisan theory.** A common element in both these criticisms is that politics plays a much more important role in macroeconomic policymaking than was suggested in the previous section.

The Public-Choice View

Economists and political scientists who espouse the public-choice view argue that macroeconomic policymakers act to maximize their own welfare or utility rather than for the social good.[1] As Gordon Tullock, a proponent of the public-choice view, puts it: "Bureaucrats are like other men.... If bureaucrats are ordinary men, they will make most (not all) their decisions in terms of what benefits them, not society as a whole." [2] Rather than a social-loss function such as that given by (18.1), the relevant loss function is one that measures variables of direct importance to policymakers. In the case of elected officials making fiscal policy decisions, this alternative approach to the policymaking problem emphasizes votes as the central goal variable motivating policymakers.

Within the public-choice framework, one representation of the appropriate loss function that the policymaker seeks to minimize is

$$L = b_1 \text{VL} \qquad b_1 > 0 \qquad (18.2)$$

where VL is vote loss and b_1 is the weight given to votes lost. Equivalently, the policymaker could be assumed to maximize votes gained. Macroeconomic goal variables enter the picture because the behavior of the economy affects votes.

For example, vote loss might be represented as

$$\text{VL} = c_0 + c_1(U - U^*)^2 + c_2(\dot{P} - \dot{P}^*)^2 + c_3(\dot{y} - \dot{y}^*)^2 \qquad (18.3)$$

The macroeconomic goal variables and their target levels are the same as in equation (18.1). The parameters c_1, c_2, and c_3 represent the loss of votes resulting from deviations of the macroeconomic goal variables from target levels. This particular representation assumes that vote loss depends on the squared deviation from the target level, assuming as before that an especially heavy weight is given to large deviations from desired target levels. The c_0 parameter represents all other influences on voter behavior (e.g., foreign policy questions, other domestic issues).

---

[1]More generally, the term *public choice* can be defined as the application of choice theoretic economic analysis to political decision making. See, for example, Dennis Mueller, *Public Choice II* (Cambridge: Cambridge University Press, 1989).

[2]Gordon Tullock, *The Vote Motive* (London: Institute of Economic Affairs, 1976).

Let us suppose that vote loss is given by equation (18.3) and the policymaker acts to minimize vote loss; the relevant loss function is equation (18.2). Will policy actions differ from those that would result from the policymaker acting more altruistically and minimizing the social-loss function given by equation (18.1)? Advocates of the public-choice view of policymaker behavior argue that they would. To see why, we first examine the condition necessary for behavior in the two cases to be the same and then explain why the advocates of the public-choice view do not believe that this condition will be met in practice.

First assume that voter behavior is governed by what we may call *collective rationality*, by which is meant that vote loss because of *macroeconomic concerns* is proportional to social-welfare loss. This means simply that where macroeconomic variables affect voting behavior, voters reward or punish incumbent politicians depending on their performance in minimizing social-welfare loss. In this case, the optimal strategy to minimize vote loss [equation (18.2)] is to minimize social-welfare loss [equation (18.1)].[3] As has been recognized in the public-choice literature, it is when this type of collective rationality does not exist that the behavior of the vote-maximizing policymaker will deviate from social-welfare-maximizing behavior.

The following hypotheses about voter behavior have been advanced in the public-choice literature.[4]

1. *Voters are myopic.* Advocates of the public-choice view argue that voting behavior will be heavily influenced by the state of the economy over the few quarters before the election and that the level of economic activity, not the inflation rate, will be the variable whose recent performance determines votes. "Incumbent politicians desire re-election and they believe that a booming preelection economy will help to achieve it."[5] As a consequence, we have a "political business cycle," in which aggregate demand is overly stimulative in the preelection period, with inflation following after the election.

2. *Unemployment is more likely to result in vote loss than is inflation.* The inflation process is presumed to be sufficiently complex and ill understood that

---

[3]Mathematically, in this case, c_1, c_2, and c_3 in equation (18.3) are proportional to a_1, a_2, and a_3 in equation (18.1). Therefore, the same setting of the policy instruments that minimizes equation (18.1) will minimize (18.3).

[4]See, for example, James M. Buchanan and Richard E. Wagner, *Democracy in Deficit* (New York: Academic Press, 1977); and Edward R. Tufte, *Political Control of the Economy* (Princeton, N.J.: Princeton University Press, 1978).

[5]Tufte, ibid., p. 5.

politicians can avoid blame for inflation more easily than they can in the case of unemployment: "At any moment of time the inflation is blamed on events which are not under the control of the political party in power, but ideally on the political party previously in power."[6] As a consequence, advocates of the public-choice view argue that elected officials will rarely respond to inflation with restrictive policies but will respond to unemployment with expansionary policies. The fiscal policy process will have an inflationary bias.[7]

3. *Deficit bias of the budget process.* This inflationary bias is reinforced by the inherent bias toward budget deficits that public-choice writers believe to be characteristic of democratic government fiscal policies. For example, as James Buchanan and Richard Wagner argue:

> Elected politicians enjoy spending public monies on projects that yield some demonstrable benefits to their constituents. They do not enjoy imposing taxes on these same constituents. The pre-Keynesian norm of budget balance served to constrain spending proclivities so as to keep governmental outlays roughly within the revenue limits generated by taxes. The Keynesian destruction of this norm, without an adequate replacement, effectively removed the constraint. Predictably politicians responded by increasing spending more than tax revenues, by creating budget deficits as a normal course of events.[8]

Various groups of voters, in Buchanan and Wagner's view, perceive the direct benefits to them from the spending programs but put little weight on the indirect costs that come through the inflationary effects of government deficit spending.

If we accept the public-choice characterization, how can this inflationary bias in the fiscal policy process be corrected? Buchanan and Wagner, from whose book we quoted, believe that we must restore the "pre-Keynesian norm of budget balance"; we must avoid *all* deficit spending. They favor an amendment to the U.S. Constitution that would require Congress and the president to balance the budget. A balanced budget amendment would, they believe, eliminate the inflationary effects of federal deficit spending.

---

[6] Morris Perlman, "Party Politics and Bureaucracy in Economic Policy," in Tullock, *Vote Motive*, p. 69.

[7] In terms of (18.1) and (18.3), these public-choice writers argue that, although inflation does cause significant social-welfare loss [a_2 in (18.1) may be large], inflation does not result in much of a vote loss [c_2 is small (18.3)]. Therefore, the vote-maximizing policymaker does not respond.

[8] Buchanan and Wagner, *Democracy in Deficit*, pp. 93–94.

Bush's Gamble –
Cut Taxs for the Rich –
Investors/wealth Holder

Also, since new or expanded government spending programs would have to be financed by new taxes in a balanced-budget system, the growth of the government sector would be curtailed by such an amendment. In the public-choice view, optimal fiscal policy is not a question of designing policies to stabilize the macroeconomy. It is, rather, imposing rules on the policymakers that eliminate the destabilizing effects of deficit spending. As might be expected, Keynesian economists do not agree with this policy prescription. Their criticisms of such a budget-balancing amendment are considered later.

The Partisan Theory

In the partisan (or partisan party) theory, political factors also affect macroeconomic policy. The partisan theory, however, views politicians as *ideologically* motivated leaders of competing parties.[9] The parties in turn represent different constituencies with different preferences concerning macroeconomic outcomes. In the most common specification of the partisan party model, there is a liberal (or labor) party and a conservative party. The liberal party places primary emphasis on full employment and income redistribution, whereas the conservative party values price stability most highly.

Rather than a political business cycle, the partisan theory predicts *party cycles* as macroeconomic policy varies, depending on which party is in power. In the case of fiscal policy, for example, the partisan model predicts that if the liberal party gained office, government spending would rise (or tax rates fall) as politicians tried to stimulate demand and, hence, employment. Government outlays might also rise as transfer payments were increased to redistribute income. In most circumstances the more expansionary fiscal policy would also increase the rate of inflation. If the liberal party lost office at a later point, fiscal policy would become more restrictive as the conservatives sought to combat inflation. Unemployment would rise, and a recession might result.

As with political business cycles, partisan party cycles would be prevented or at least mitigated by a fiscal policy rule, such as a constitutional balanced-budget amendment. A rule for fiscal policy would limit the ability of each party to pursue its goals by manipulating aggregate demand. Also,

---

[9]An early contribution to the partisan party theory is Douglas Hibbs, "Political Parties and Macroeconomic Policy," *The American Political Science Review,* 71 (December 1977), pp. 1467–87. See also Thomas Havrilesky, "A Partisan Theory of Fiscal and Monetary Regimes," *Journal of Money, Credit and Banking,* 19 (August 1987), pp. 308–25; and Alberto Allesina, "Macroeconomics and Politics," NBER *Macroeconomics Annual,* 1988, pp. 13–61.

PERSPECTIVES

18.1

RATIONAL EXPECTATIONS
AND THE PARTISAN THEORY

The original forms of the political business cycle model and the partisan model did not assume that expectations were *rational*, and therefore forward-looking. In fact, the myopic behavior of voters in the political business cycle model is clearly inconsistent with rational expectations.

The partisan model of fiscal policy has been modified to assume rational expectations in a paper by Alberto Alessina and Jeffrey Sachs.[1] As before, assume that there are two parties—one liberal, whose constituency is most concerned about unemployment, and one conservative, with a constituency most concerned about inflation.

The economic environment assumed by Alessina and Sachs is consistent with the new classical model, in that expectations are rational, but it has the Keynesian element that money wages are set by contracts of several years' duration. In such a framework, elections create uncertainty concerning the future behavior of the inflation rate, and therefore the money wage demands workers (or their unions) should make.

Consider the situation in the year before a general election. Workers might presume

that if the liberals win, the inflation rate will be high, let's say 7 percent, while if the conservatives win, it will be low, say 3 percent. Even if expectations are rational, the best the workers can do is form an expectation of inflation that is a weighted average of the two possible outcomes. If they view the election of each party as equally likely, then in the previous example, the rational expectation of inflation would be 5 percent. Firms and workers would set money wages accordingly.

Now consider what happens after the election. If the liberals win, the inflation rate (7 percent) will exceed the expected inflation rate (5 percent) on the basis of which money wages were set. This will cause rapid expansion of output as firms hire additional workers. This follows because the real wage will be unexpectedly low for firms. On the other hand, if conservatives win, actual inflation (3 percent) will be below expected inflation (5 percent), and money wages will have been set too high. This will cause unemployment to rise, and a recession may ensue.

Party cycles are then possible in the partisan party model even if expectations are rational. The theory predicts that recessions are most likely in the first couple of years following the election of a conservative President—a prediction borne out in 1981–82 and again in 1990.

[1]Alberto Alesina and Jeffrey Sachs, "Political Parties and the Business Cycle in the United States, 1948–84," *Journal of Money, Credit and Banking*, 20 (February 1988), pp. 63–82.

redistribution efforts by the liberal party would be hampered if any increased transfer payments required new taxes. Whether or not one favored such an amendment would then be influenced by one's views concerning income redistribution.

Read Perspectives 18.1.

18.3 • THE FEDERAL BUDGET

Two fiscal policy variables, the levels of government spending and tax collections, were included in the theoretical models considered in Part II. The government spending variable there (*G*) was the government spending component in national income, which includes both federal and state and local government spending on *currently produced goods and services.* The tax variable (*T*) included federal, state, and local tax collections. Fiscal stabilization policy is conducted by the federal government. States and localities have limited abilities to run budget deficits. The levels for both their expenditures and revenues are determined by local needs and the state of the economy rather than being set to influence macroeconomic goals. Therefore, our discussion here focuses on federal budget policy.

Table 18.2 gives figures for total federal government receipts and outlays (expenditures) and for the federal deficit (receipts minus outlays). The figures reveal rapid growth in both outlays and revenues, as well as rapid growth in the deficit in recent years. But the economy has been growing as well. Figure 18.1 shows some budget items expressed as percentages of GDP. There you can see a clearer picture of how the government has grown relative to the economy as a whole.

In 1929 the federal government was quite small as a portion of the economy. Total federal outlays were less than 3 percent of GDP. Fiscal policy changes typically represented minor budget adjustments and were of little significance to the overall economy. Both outlays and revenues rose modestly during the 1930s. Outlays rose more than revenues, with a resulting budget deficit. World War II brought a huge expansion in government military spending, only partly paid for with increasing tax revenues. Budget deficits in the early 1940s rose as high as 25 percent of GDP, the equivalent of a deficit of over $1200 billion in terms of GDP in the early 1990s. These huge wartime deficits were financed by massive sales of bonds to the public.

After the war, both expenditures and tax revenues declined as proportions of GDP. Yet federal government outlays did not sink back to the level of the 1920s. By the mid-1950s, both outlays and revenues were about 17–18 percent of GDP. The federal government had taken on a number of new domestic functions in the 1930s: regulatory agencies, the social security system, price supports for agricultural products, and rural electrification, among others. Also, with the onset of the cold war in the late 1940s, defense spending remained high even in peacetime.

From Figure 18.1 it can be seen that in recent decades outlays have grown as a percentage of GDP, from 17 percent in 1955 to 23 percent in 1991. Tax revenues have grown as well, but beginning in the late 1960s, growth in spending outpaced revenue growth, resulting in persistent deficits. The budget deficit grew rapidly during the first half of the 1980s as the upward trend in outlays continued, while revenues declined slightly as a percentage

TABLE 18.2 Receipts and Outlays of the Federal Government (billions of dollars at an annual rate), Selected Years[a]

	Receipts	Outlays	Surplus or Deficit (−) (Receipts −Outlays)
1929	3.8	2.7	1.2
1933	2.7	4.0	−1.3
1939	6.8	9.0	−2.2
1941	15.5	20.5	−5.1
1945	42.7	84.7	−42.1
1950	50.4	41.2	9.2
1955	93.1	88.6	4.4
1960	97.0	93.4	3.5
1965	125.8	124.6	1.3
1970	195.2	208.5	−13.3
1975	294.8	364.2	−69.4
1980	553.0	613.1	−60.1
1981	639.0	697.8	−58.8
1982	635.4	770.9	−135.5
1983	660.0	840.0	−180.1
1984	725.8	892.7	−166.9
1985	788.6	969.9	−181.4
1986	827.2	1028.2	−201.1
1987	913.8	1065.6	−151.8
1988	972.3	1109.0	−136.6
1989	1055.2	1179.4	−124.1
1990	1104.8	1270.1	−165.3
1991	1119.1	1319.8	−200.7

[a] Figures may not sum to total due to rounding.

Source: Economic Report of the President, 1989; 1992.

of GDP. By 1986 the budget deficit was roughly 5 percent of GDP ($201.1 billion). The deficit declined in absolute terms between 1987 and 1990, but then turned sharply upward in the early 1990s. As could be seen from Table 18.1, large deficits are projected for well into the 1990s.

The causes of the growing federal budget deficit can be traced more precisely by considering data for several expenditure categories, shown in Figure 18.2. Each is a percentage of GDP.

The schedule marked "Federal government purchases of goods and services" is a narrower category than total federal government outlays. Federal government purchases of goods and services include only purchases of currently produced output. This is the government spending variable that appears in the national income accounts and in the macroeconomic models of Part II. Total federal outlays include, in addition to purchases of current output, transfer payments to persons (social security payments, veterans'

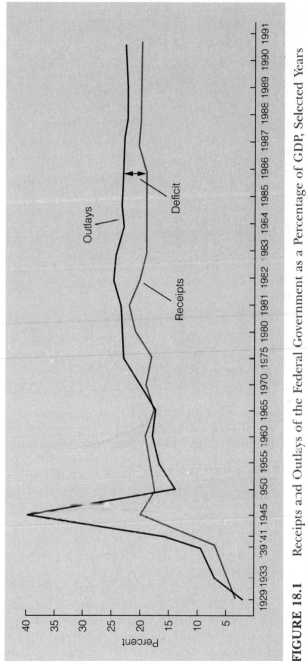

FIGURE 18.1 Receipts and Outlays of the Federal Government as a Percentage of GDP, Selected Years

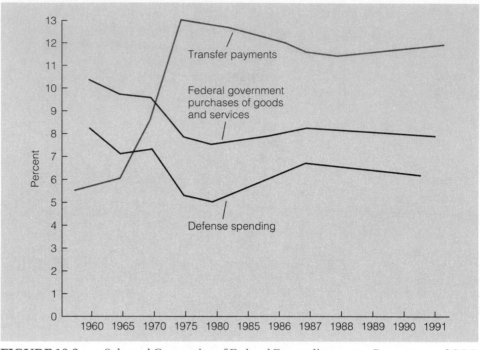

FIGURE 18.2   Selected Categories of Federal Expenditures as a Percentage of GDP

benefits, food stamps, aid to families with dependent children, etc.), transfer payments (grants) to state and local governments, and interest payments on the government debt (securities issued to finance previous deficits).

From the graph it can be seen that federal purchases of goods and services have not been rising as a proportion of GDP over recent decades. Looking at the schedule marked "Defense spending," one can see that the pattern of overall purchases has closely followed the pattern of purchases for national defense. That pattern was generally downward (as a percentage of GDP) over the years from 1960 to 1980, with one upward interruption in the late 1960s during the Vietnam War. During the Reagan administration, defense spending rose as a percentage of GDP, and as a consequence overall purchases also rose. By the end of the 1980s, however, both series had begun to decline as defense spending fell, with the easing of cold war tensions. In 1991, government purchases totaled only 7.8 percent of GDP, compared to 10.6 percent in 1960. Growth in total government *outlays* has not come because the government sector now purchases a larger fraction of output.

The schedule marked "Transfer payments" in Figure 18.2 shows the area of fastest growth in outlays since 1960. Transfer payments to persons and transfers (grants) to state and local governments rose from 5.5 percent of

GDP in 1960 to 13 percent in 1980. There were some cuts in these programs during the first Reagan administration, but in 1991 transfer payments still totaled 12 percent of GDP, 6.5 percent higher *as a percentage of GDP* than in 1960. In the 1980s, interest payments on the national debt also began to rise rapidly. This component of government outlays increased from 1.3 percent to 3.3 percent of GDP between 1980 and 1991.

We see, then, that the increase in total federal outlays (as a percentage of GDP) has come mostly from rising transfer payments to persons and to state and local governments. Additionally, in the 1980s, interest payments on the national debt rose rapidly. Tax revenues have not kept pace. The result has been that beginning in the 1980s, federal budget deficits rose to levels much higher than in our earlier peacetime experience.

18.4 THE ECONOMY AND THE FEDERAL BUDGET: THE CONCEPT OF AUTOMATIC FISCAL STABILIZERS

Viewed from the standpoint of stabilization policy, the federal budget contains three types of items that can be varied to affect macroeconomic goal variables: government purchases of goods and services, government transfer payments (including grants to state and local governments), and government tax receipts. In Part II we analyzed the effects of changes in government spending, which in those models was spending on goods and services only, and changes in tax receipts. In the models in Part II, tax receipts were net of transfers (taxes minus transfer payments); therefore, an increase in transfer payments would have the same effects in those models as a reduction in taxes. In this section we reverse the question and, instead of asking how changes in taxes or government expenditures affect income, we examine how the level of income affects items in the federal budget. In doing so, we see the way in which changes in the government budget work as an **automatic stabilizer** for the level of economic activity.

To consider how the level of economic activity affects the government budget, we need to modify our assumption that the level of net tax receipts (gross tax receipts minus government transfer payments) is exogenous. An assumption more in line with reality is that the schedule of tax *rates* is exogenously set, but the level of net tax collections depends on the level of income.[10] With this assumption, we can specify *net* tax collections (T) as determined by the following *net tax function*

$$T = t_0 + t_1 Y, \qquad t_0 < 0, \quad t_1 > 0 \tag{18.4}$$

---

[10] Even this assumption is only an approximation. The level of tax collections will also depend on the composition of income, since different components of income (profits and wages, e.g.) are taxed at different rates. Additionally, current marginal income tax rates rise with income; therefore, even tax rates are not truly exogenous.

where t_0 and t_1 are parameters that represent the tax structure. The parameter t_1 is the marginal net income tax rate, giving the increase in taxes (net of transfers) per unit increase in income ($t_1 = \Delta T / \Delta Y$). If the tax system were proportional, the other parameter in the tax function t_0 would be zero; tax collections would simply be equal to $t_1 Y$. Notice that in this case the marginal tax rate $\Delta T / \Delta Y$ would be equal to the average tax rate T/Y, both being given by t_1. The negative term t_0 allows the average tax rate, which from equation (18.4) would be $(t_0 / Y + t_1)$, to be less than the marginal rate (t_1). The negative term t_0 also allows for transfers, negative net taxes, which are independent of income.

From the net tax function given by equation (18.4) it follows that as income rises, net tax collections increase and the government budget surplus increases (or the deficit declines). This follows since at higher levels of economic activity, more tax revenue will be collected at any given set of tax rates. The positive relationship between *net* tax revenues and the level of economic activity also results from the fact that transfer payments, especially payments for unemployment compensation, decline as the level of economic activity rises. On the expenditures side of the budget, in the absence of discretionary policy shifts there is no reason to expect government spending (G) to respond to changes in the level of economic activity.[11] Our previous assumption that government spending was exogenous can be maintained.

Consequently, the net effect of a rise in the level of income will be to increase the federal budget surplus or to decrease the size of an existing deficit. An expansion in the level of economic activity therefore causes fiscal policy, as measured by the budget surplus, to become more restrictive. This works to dampen the expansion. Similarly, a shock that causes the level of economic activity to fall will automatically result in a decline in the federal budget surplus or a rise in the deficit, which will cushion the fall in income. This is the essence of the concept of *automatic fiscal stabilizers.*

To examine the functioning of automatic fiscal stabilizers in more detail, we return to the multiplier analysis of the Keynesian model in Chapter 5. In that chapter we considered the way in which aggregate demand responded to exogenous shocks such as changes in autonomous investment demand or government spending. In effect, automatic fiscal stabilizers work by reducing the response of aggregate demand, and hence income, to such exogenous shocks. To show this, we analyze the effects on the multiplier expressions, the expressions giving the aggregate demand response to these shocks, which come as a result of allowing for endogenous changes in net tax revenues.

The equilibrium condition for income from Chapter 5 is

$$Y = C + I + G \tag{18.5}$$

---

[11] Here and later, the term *government spending* refers to federal government purchases of goods and services only, with transfer payments included in the net tax variable.

Consumption (C) was assumed to be given by

$$C = a + bY_D \tag{18.6}$$

where Y_D is disposable income, defined as national income minus net tax collections ($Y - T$). Investment, government spending, and the level of tax collections were all taken to be exogenous in that simple version of the Keynesian system. Similar to the procedure followed in Chapter 5, we can substitute equation (18.6) into the equilibrium condition for income given by equation (18.5), and using the definition of Y_D, we can compute an expression for equilibrium income ($\overline{Y}$):

$$\overline{Y} = \frac{1}{1 - b}(a - bT + I + G) \tag{18.7}$$

From equation (18.7) we can compute the effects on equilibrium income of exogenous changes in investment (I), government spending (G), and *exogenous* tax collections (T) as follows:

$$\frac{\Delta Y}{\Delta I} = \frac{1}{1 - b}, \qquad \frac{\Delta \overline{Y}}{\Delta G} = \frac{1}{1 - b}, \qquad \frac{\Delta \overline{Y}}{\Delta T} = \frac{-b}{1 - b} \tag{18.8}$$

The task here is to see how these expressions are modified when the net tax function given by equation (18.4) is substituted for the assumption that tax collections are exogenous.

To begin, consider the form of the consumption function given by equation (18.6) with our new assumption about taxes. Using the definition of disposable income ($Y_D = Y - T$) and with T defined by equation (18.4), we can write the consumption function as

$$\begin{aligned}
C &= a + b(Y - T) \\
&= a + bY - bt_0 - bt_1 Y \\
&= a - bt_0 + (b - bt_1)Y \\
&= a - bt_0 + b(1 - t_1)Y
\end{aligned} \tag{18.9}$$

Substituting equation (18.9) into the condition for equilibrium income given in equation (18.5), we can derive the revised expression for the equilibrium level of income as follows:

$$\overline{Y} = \overbrace{a - bt_0 + b(1 - t_1)Y}^{C} + I + G$$

$$\overline{Y}[1 - b(1 - t_1)] = a - bt_0 + I + G$$

$$\overline{Y} = \frac{1}{1 - b(1 - t_1)}(a - bt_0 + I + G) \tag{18.10}$$

As with the previous expression (18.7), equation (18.10) specifies equilibrium income as determined by an autonomous expenditure multiplier, in this case $1/[1 - b(1 - t_1)]$, and the autonomous influences on income given by $a - bt_0 + I + G$. As before, we can compute the effects on equilibrium income of a change in investment or in the level of government spending.

$$\frac{\Delta \overline{Y}}{\Delta I} = \frac{\Delta \overline{Y}}{\Delta G} = \frac{1}{1 - b(1 - t_1)} \tag{18.11}$$

Note that the autonomous expenditure multiplier and hence the effect on income from a change in autonomous expenditures (changes in I or G, for example) is *smaller* when tax collections depend on income than when the level of tax collections is exogenous; that is,

$$\frac{1}{1 - b(1 - t_1)} < \frac{1}{1 - b}$$

To give an example, if b, the marginal propensity to consume, were equal to 0.8, and t_1, the marginal tax rate, were 0.25, we would have

$$\frac{1}{1 - b} = \frac{1}{1 - 0.8} = 5$$

$$\frac{1}{1 - b(1 - t_1)} = \frac{1}{1 - 0.8(1 - 0.25)} = \frac{1}{1 - 0.6} = 2.5$$

In this example the marginal tax rate of 0.25 cuts the value of the multiplier in half.

The presence of a marginal net income tax rate lowers the effect on equilibrium income of shocks to autonomous expenditure, such as an autonomous change in investment demand. It is in this sense that the income tax functions as an automatic stabilizer. This stabilizing effect of an income tax can be explained with reference to our earlier discussion of the multiplier process (Section 5.5). An initial shock to investment demand, for example, will change income and have an induced effect on consumption spending. It is this induced effect on consumption demand that causes equilibrium income to change by a multiple of the original change in investment demand. With a marginal income tax rate of t_1, each one-dollar reduction in GNP will reduce an individual's disposable income, the determinant of consumption, by only $(1 - t_1)$ dollars, since the individual's tax liability will fall by t_1 dollars. Since disposable income will be affected less per unit change in GNP, the induced effects on consumer demand will be smaller at each round of the multiplier process. The total effect on income of a change in autonomous investment, which consists of the original shock to investment plus the induced effects on consumption, will therefore be smaller where there is a marginal income tax rate than where tax collections are assumed to be exogenous.[12]

The automatic response of taxes and transfers to the level of economic activity has been a substantial stabilizing force in the U.S. economy over the post–World War II period, generally moving the budget sharply into deficit during recessions, with falling deficits or at times (in the 1950s) surpluses during expansionary periods. The increased size of the federal budget in the postwar period relative to the prewar period has increased the effectiveness of automatic fiscal stabilizers; in terms of our tax function, the marginal net tax rate is higher now than it was in a period such as the 1920s, and thus the multiplier is lower.

Substituting the net tax function given by equation (18.4) for the assumption that the level of tax collections is exogenous also requires a modification of the analysis of the effects of discretionary tax changes in the model. In the revised expression for equilibrium income given by equation (18.10), tax policy is represented by two variables: t_0, the intercept of the tax function, and t_1, the marginal income tax rate.

The closest analog to a lump-sum change in tax collections in the revised income equation is a change in t_0. Such a change could represent a lump-sum tax rebate to each taxpayer, for example, or a lump-sum change in transfer payments. From equation (18.10) the effects of a change in t_0 can be computed as

$$\frac{\Delta \overline{Y}}{\Delta t_0} = \frac{1}{1 - b(1 - t_1)}(-b) = \frac{-b}{1 - b(1 - t_1)} \tag{18.12}$$

Taking account of the change in the autonomous expenditure multiplier, this expression is the same as the tax multiplier where tax collections were exogenous [see equations (18.8)]. Again, the effect of a tax change, here a change in the intercept of the tax function, will be opposite in sign from the effect of a change in government spending or autonomous investment given by equation (18.11). An increase in t_0, for example, will cause equilibrium income to fall. Also, the effect of a one-dollar change in t_0 is smaller in absolute value than the effect of a one-dollar change in I or G. This is because, as in the earlier case, at a given level of GNP (Y), a one-dollar change in taxes will change autonomous expenditures [the term in parentheses in equation (18.10)] by only b (< 1) dollars, with the remaining $(1 - b)$

---

[12]Suppose, for example, that the fall in autonomous investment is 100 units. With tax collections exogenous, this initial drop in GNP would reduce disposable income by 100 units. In our previous example with the MPC(b) equal to 0.8, the first-round induced decline in consumption would be 80 units. With a marginal tax rate of 0.25, the decline of 100 units in GNP would reduce disposable income by only 75 units; the first-round decline in consumption would be only 60 units (0.75 × 0.8).

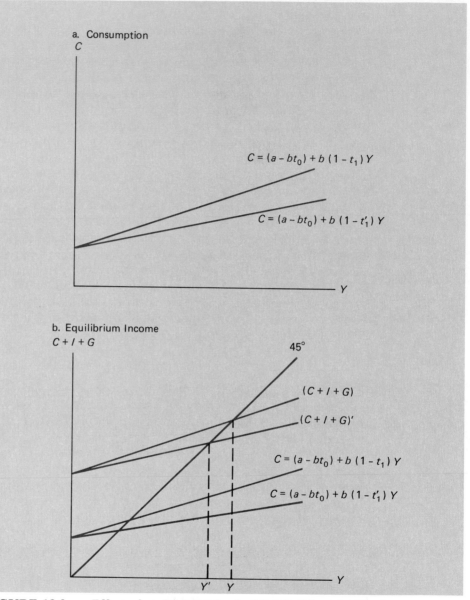

FIGURE 18.3   Effect of an Increase in the Marginal Income Tax Rate (t_1)
An increase in the income tax rate from t_1 to t_1' rotates the consumption function
downward in part a. Consequently, the $C + I + G$ schedule in part b also rotates
downward from $(C + I + G)$ to $(C + I + G)'$. Equilibrium income declines from Y
to Y'.

dollars absorbed by a change in saving. A one-dollar change in government spending or autonomous investment will change autonomous expenditures by one full dollar.

By inspection of equation (18.10), equilibrium income can also be seen to depend on the marginal tax rate t_1. An increase in t_1 will lower the autonomous expenditure multiplier, and therefore lower equilibrium income, given the values of the autonomous expenditure components. The way in which equilibrium income is affected by a change in the marginal income tax rate can perhaps best be seen graphically. Figure 18.3 illustrates the effects of an increase in the marginal tax rate from t_1 to t_1'. Figure 18.3a shows the effect of the increase in the tax rate on the consumption function.

With an income tax, consumption is given by equation (18.9). Before the increase in the marginal tax rate, the consumption line is $C = (a - bt_0) + b(1 - t_1)Y$ in the graph. The increase in the income tax rate rotates the function downward to the schedule $C = (a - bt_0) + b(1 - t_1')Y$. The new consumption line is flatter, indicating that a given increase in Y will cause consumption to rise by less with the higher tax rate. This follows, since with a higher tax rate, a given increase in Y, national income, will cause a smaller increase in disposable income and hence in consumption. Figure 18.3b shows the effect on equilibrium income from the rise in the tax rate. Since the consumption function rotates downward, as in Figure 18.3a, the $C + I + G$ line also rotates downward, from $(C + I + G)$ to $(C + I + G)'$. The effect of this is to cause equilibrium income to fall from Y to Y' in the figure. The higher tax rate lowers aggregate demand (at any positive level of income) and causes equilibrium income to fall.

18.5 KEYNESIAN OBJECTIONS TO BALANCED-BUDGET RULES

In his final economic report to Congress in 1989, President Reagan renewed his call for a constitutional amendment that would mandate a balanced federal budget. By 1992, with actual and projected deficits soaring, the amendment had gained considerable support in Congress. In Section 18.2 we saw that economists who accept the public-choice view of the budget process also favor an amendment to the constitution to require a balanced budget.

The main opponents to fiscal policy rules including a balanced-budget amendment and the deficit ceilings that were enacted in the Gramm–Rudman–Hollings act are Keynesians. Keynesians oppose such rules because they believe the rules impede the important stabilization role that fiscal policy should play—a role that at times *requires* budget deficits.

The role of the tax-transfer system as an automatic fiscal stabilizer, which was explained in Section 18.4, requires that the budget be allowed to go into deficit (or surplus) at appropriate points in the business cycle. During a recession, as the level of economic activity falls, in the Keynesian view, the budget *should* go into deficit. To raise tax rates or cut expenditures at such a time would only exacerbate the recession. Keynesians cite the 1932 tax increase as an example of the misguided fiscal policies that result from pursuing the goal of a balanced budget. The Hoover administration raised tax *rates* substantially in 1932 to try to balance the budget at a time when tax *revenues* were falling because of the Depression. The tax-rate increase came at a time when the unemployment rate was 24 percent. The policy did not succeed in balancing the budget because of the sharp decline in income, the result in part of the tax increase. During the 1974–75 recession, the federal budget deficit soared to nearly $70 billion. Keynesians believe we would have risked a rerun of the Great Depression had we tried to balance the budget or seriously limit the size of the deficit under such conditions.

In addition to impeding the working of automatic stabilizers, a balanced-budget rule would limit the ability of policymakers to take *discretionary* countercyclical fiscal actions. These are changes in government spending and in tax rates aimed at stabilizing private-sector aggregate demand—the real economy equivalents of the fiscal policy shifts discussed in previous chapters. Keynesians do not deny that there are examples in the past of ill-timed and at times destabilizing discretionary fiscal policy actions, as well as stabilizing ones. Moreover, Keynesians would no doubt agree that some of the failures of discretionary fiscal policy stem from interactions between the political process and macroeconomic policymaking. Keynesians opposed to constitutional budget-balancing amendments or other rules for fiscal policy argue, however, that the record for discretionary policy is not uniformly bad and that the cost of interfering with the functioning of automatic fiscal stabilizers through such amendments is great.[13]

18.6   WHAT ABOUT THE DEFICIT?

In 1963, when Senator Harry Byrd, Sr., asked Budget Director Kermit Gordon, a Keynesian economist, what balancing the budget would do for the country, Gordon replied, "It probably would add about 2.5 million people to the rolls of the unemployed, delay the recovery about four years, and knock 10 percent off U.S. output."[14] Walter Heller called this "an answer that will live in infamy—among fiscal troglodytes, that is." By the mid-1980s, Keynesian economists (including Heller) were among the harshest critics of the large budget deficits that emerged in the Reagan years. What had changed?

---

[13] See, for example, James Tobin, "Comment from an Academic Scribbler," *Journal of Monetary Economics* 4 (August 1978).

[14] Walter Heller, "Kermit Gordon," *Brookings Papers on Economic Activity*, 2 (1976), pp. 283–87.

Cyclical Versus Structural Deficits

To understand the differing Keynesian positions on the deficits of the early 1960s versus those of the mid-1980s, one useful distinction is that between **cyclical** and **structural deficits**. We have seen that the federal budget deficit depends in part on the level of economic activity. The *cyclical* deficit is the portion of the deficit that results from the economy being at a low level of economic activity. In the Keynesian view, cyclical deficits that reflect the working of automatic stabilizers are desirable.

The portion of the deficit that would exist even if the economy were at its potential output is called the *structural* deficit. A structural deficit is not directly attributable to the behavior of the economy and is part of the deficit for which policymakers are directly responsible. In other words, the structural deficit is the result of decisions policymakers have made about tax rates, the level of government spending, and benefit levels for transfer programs.

To break the deficit into cyclical and structural components, we need a measure of potential output—the level of output achieved when both capital and labor are utilized at their highest sustainable rates. We can then compute the changes in tax revenues and transfer payments that would have taken place if the economy had moved from actual to potential output. Using these figures, we can find the structural deficit. To give an example, suppose the actual deficit is $100 billion, but the economy is below potential output. If the level of economic activity increased to the potential level, tax revenues would rise, let us assume by $30 billion. Transfer payments would fall, say by $10 billion, because unemployment compensation payments would decline as employment rose. The structural deficit—the deficit at potential output—is then $60 billion (100 − 30 − 10). As discussed in Chapter 2, to compute the level of potential output requires choosing a benchmark *high-employment* unemployment rate. As also discussed there, considerable disagreement has arisen concerning the appropriate level for this benchmark rate. Table 18.3 shows the breakdown of federal government deficits for selected recent years into cyclical and structural components using 6 percent for the benchmark high employment rate—a figure proposed by a number of economists and government officials.

Note that in recession periods, such as 1975, 1980, and 1981–82, a substantial fraction of the deficit was cyclical. By the mid-1980s, however, the federal deficit had become mostly structural. In fact, in the later years of the decade, with the unemployment rate below 6 percent, this measure of the structural deficit exceeded the actual deficit. With the onset of another recession, the cyclical portion of the deficit is again substantial in 1991.

While Table 18.3 does not go back that far, earlier estimates reveal that the deficits of the early 1960s were cyclical deficits. In 1963, for example, when Kermit Gordon gave his previously quoted response to Senator Byrd,

TABLE 18.3 Cyclical and Structural Federal Budget
Deficits, Selected Years

	Actual Deficit	Structural Deficit	Cyclical Deficit
1974	−11.6	−10.4	−1.2
1975	−69.4	−43.0	−26.4
1976	−52.9	−33.5	−19.4
1977	−42.4	−34.7	−7.7
1980	−60.1	−37.4	−22.7
1981	−58.8	−27.9	−30.9
1982	−135.5	−60.7	−74.8
1983	−180.1	−101.6	−78.5
1984	−166.9	−142.3	−24.6
1985	−181.4	−172.0	−9.4
1986	−201.1	−187.9	−13.2
1987	−151.9	−151.4	−0.5
1988	−136.6	−162.5	25.9
1989	−124.2	−164.1	39.9
1990	−165.5	−174.9	9.6
1991	−200.7	−166.1	−34.6

Source: Economic Report of the President, 1988; and *Survey of Current Business,* various issues.

rather than a deficit measured at potential output (as it was estimated at the time), the budget showed a surplus of $13 billion; there was a structural *surplus.*[15] Gordon and other Keynesians opposed balancing the budget in 1963, because the deficit simply reflected the working of beneficial automatic fiscal stabilizers at a time when the economy was operating substantially below potential output.

The Keynesian View of Deficits in the 1980s

In one way, the Keynesian view of deficits has not changed over the years. In an early statement of the Keynesian view of fiscal policy, Abba Lerner argued in 1944 that the instruments to prevent unemployment and inflation are "not available until it is recognized that the size of the national debt is relatively unimportant."[16] This is the basis of the Keynesian objection

[15] Keith Carlson, "Estimates of the High-Employment Budget 1947–67," Federal Reserve Bank of St. Louis *Review,* 49 (June 1967), p. 11.

[16] Abba Lerner, *The Economics of Control* (New York: Macmillan, 1944), p. 302.

to rules mandating a balanced budget—such rules will interfere with the stabilization goals of fiscal policy. Keynesians do not object to deficits per se.

In the 1980s, Keynesians were critical of Reagan policy because they believed the large structural deficits reflected a mistaken *mix* of fiscal and monetary policies. Specifically, they believe that the deficits resulted from an overly expansionary fiscal policy. This fiscal policy was composed of the Reagan administration's large tax cuts and increased defense spending that more than counterbalanced cuts in nondefense spending. The overly expansionary fiscal policies, in the view of Keynesians, meant that, throughout much of the 1980s, monetary policy had to be especially restrictive to keep the level of aggregate demand from growing too quickly.

Keynesians believe that this mix of an easy fiscal and tight monetary policy had unfavorable effects on *the composition* of output in the following ways.

The Deficit and the Interest Rate

Figure 18.4 illustrates the relationship between the monetary–fiscal policy mix and the rate of interest. Part *a* of the figure shows the determination of output and the price level. We assume that y^* is the policymakers' desired level of output and is consistent with a price-level target of P^*. We assume that a higher output level would not be desired because the gain from an increase in output above y^* would not balance the cost in terms of the increase in the price level above P^*. To achieve y^* and P^*, we assume that the policymakers can use monetary and fiscal policy to manipulate the level of aggregate demand, as measured by the position of the y^d schedule in Figure 18.4a.

The position of the aggregate demand schedule consistent with y^* and P^*, as shown in Figure 18.4a, can be achieved with various policy mixes, as shown in Figure 18.4b. One mix, consisting of a tight fiscal and easy monetary policy, is given by the IS_0 and LM_0 schedules. Another mix consists of a more expansionary fiscal policy that results in a shift to the right in the IS curve to IS_1, accompanied by a more restrictive (tighter) monetary policy that shifts the LM schedule left to LM_1. For both policy combinations, the IS and LM schedules intersect at y^*, consistent with the position of the y^d schedule in Figure 18.4a; *both combinations produce the same level of aggregate demand.*

The difference between the two policy mixes is the resulting equilibrium interest rate. The tight fiscal–easy monetary policy mix produces the lower interest rate, r_0. Moving to the easy fiscal–tight monetary policy means shifting both the IS and LM schedules upward, increasing the interest rate to r_1.

The interest rate in our IS–LM graphs has been the nominal rate, but notice that the *real* rate of interest, defined as the nominal interest rate minus the expected inflation rate, also rises. Since both policy mixes produce the same price level in any period, there is no reason why the actual inflation rate and therefore the expected inflation rate over time will be affected by

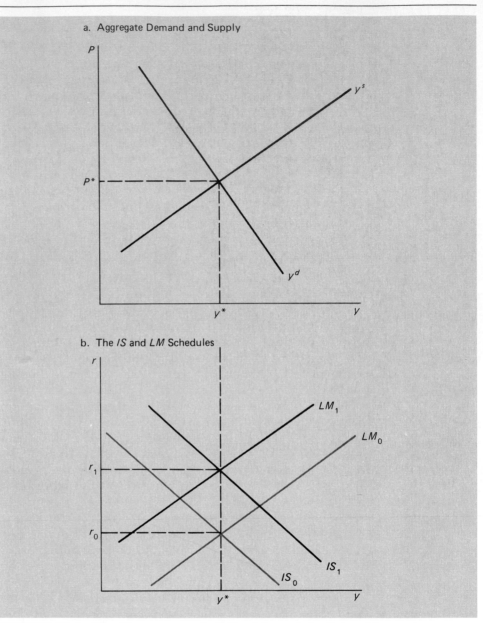

FIGURE 18.4 The Macroeconomic Policy Mix and the Rate of Interest
The y^d schedule in part a shows the level of aggregate demand consistent with the policymakers' desired income (y^*) and price level (P^*) goals. This level of aggregate demand can be achieved by an easy monetary—tight fiscal policy combination, represented by LM_0 and IS_0 in part b. Alternatively, the same level of aggregate demand can be achieved by an easy fiscal—tight monetary policy combination, represented by LM_1 and IS_1. The easy fiscal—tight monetary policy combination will, however, produce a higher real interest rate (r_1, compared to r_0).

the choice of policy mix. The higher nominal interest rate with the easy fiscal–tight monetary policy mix results in a higher real rate.

The Keynesians believe that an overly expansionary fiscal policy in the Reagan administration required a very tight monetary policy on the part of the Federal Reserve. They believe that the result was a very high real rate of interest. A high real rate of interest, they believe, lowered the investment component of GDP and hurt capital formation.

Budget Deficits and Trade Deficits

Keynesian economists have advanced a second criticism of the *policy mix* in the Reagan administration that also concerns the resulting *composition* of output. They believe that an easy fiscal–tight monetary policy mix will affect the composition of output by encouraging imports of foreign goods and discouraging U.S. exports. They believe that the easy fiscal–tight monetary policy of the Reagan administration contributed to the record U.S. foreign trade deficits of the 1980s—that is, the excess of imports over exports.

A link between the government budget deficit (the result of expansionary fiscal policy) and the trade deficit is suggested by the data in Table 18.4, which show both deficits rising sharply in the mid-1980s. The link between the budget deficit and the trade deficit is the level of U.S. interest rates.

In the Keynesian view, expansionary fiscal policies that produced the budget deficits, together with a relatively tight monetary policy, caused U.S. interest rates to be high over the first half of the 1980s. In turn, the high interest rates caused foreign investors to buy our securities—government bonds and bills and private bonds. To buy U.S. securities, however, foreign investors had to exchange their currency for U.S. dollars. For example, a

TABLE 18.4 Federal Government Budget Deficit and Foreign Trade Deficit (billions of dollars)

	Federal Government Budget Deficit	Foreign Trade Deficit
1980	−60.1	−25.5
1981	−58.8	−28.0
1982	−135.5	−36.4
1983	−180.1	−67.1
1984	−166.9	−112.5
1985	−181.4	−122.1
1986	−201.1	−145.1
1987	−151.8	−159.5
1988	−136.6	−127.0
1989	−124.2	−115.9
1990	−165.3	−108.1
1991	−200.7	−66.2

German resident who wanted to buy a U.S. Treasury bond first exchanged German marks for dollars and then used the dollars to buy the bond.

This demand for U.S. dollars to purchase U.S. securities pushes up the value of the dollar relative to other currencies (e.g., the mark, the British pound, etc.). Keynesians believe that the demand for dollars by foreign investors was the main cause of the rise of over 50 percent in the value of the dollar (relative to an average of foreign currencies) that took place between 1980 and 1985.

The rise in the value of the dollar makes U.S. goods (exports) expensive to foreigners. If the dollar rises in value in relation to the German mark, for example, German residents must pay more marks to buy U.S. goods. Due to this price rise, the demand for U.S. exports falls. On the other hand, the rising value of the dollar means that U.S. residents can buy foreign currencies, and therefore foreign goods, more cheaply. Our demand for imports will rise. The fall in exports and the rise in imports show up as a U.S. foreign trade deficit—an excess of imports over exports. As can be seen in Table 18.4, by 1985 the trade deficit reached $122.1 billion.

After 1985, the dollar began to decline in value relative to foreign currencies and had, by 1988, returned approximately to its 1980 value. The possible reasons for this reversal are discussed in Chapter 20. The relevant point for our discussion here is that the U.S. trade balance was slow to improve even as the value of the dollar fell. In fact, as can be seen from Table 18.4, the trade deficit continued to rise for a time, peaking at $159.5 billion in 1987.

There is a final point to note before we leave Table 18.4. Looking at the last two lines of the table, it can be seen that during 1990 and 1991 the trade deficit continued to decline while the budget deficit turned upward. We have seen in Table 18.1 that high deficits are also projected well into the 1990s. Should we therefore expect the recent improvement in the trade balance to be reversed? It is too early to tell, but there is a crucial difference between the current situation and that in the 1980s. In the 1980s, the Federal Reserve believed that the expansionary fiscal policy required a tight monetary policy and therefore high interest rates. In the early 1990s, in the midst of a protracted recession, the Federal Reserve has been working hard at reducing interest rates. Therefore, the link between the budget deficit and the trade deficit (through a high interest rate and consequent high value of the dollar) has been severed in the current situation.

Still, the Keynesians believe that the Reagan administration's monetary–fiscal policy mix in the 1980s did hurt U.S. export industries. Moreover, as a result of financing an excess of imports over exports by a capital inflow—in essence, by borrowing from abroad over the course of the decade—the United States went from being the world's largest creditor nation in 1980 to the largest debtor by 1990. We return in Chapter 20 to discuss this growing foreign debt.

Other Views of the Budget Deficit

Supply-side economists dispute the Keynesian view of the deficits in the 1980s. To a supply-side economist, the *source* of the deficit is important. If the deficit results from tax cuts that improve economic incentives and stimulate supply, then its effects need not be harmful.

In the case of the deficits of the 1980s, supply-side economists believe that the business tax cuts enacted in the 1980s work to offset the effects that high real interest rates might have on investment. In time, the supply-side economists have argued, Reagan tax cuts, if left in place, will produce rapid enough economic growth, and therefore revenue growth, to eliminate the deficit. In the meantime, supply-side economists argue that the "primary cost of the deficits is government spending itself, not how that spending is financed."[17]

What about the new classical and monetarist views on the deficit? The new classical economists were highly critical of Reagan administration fiscal policy. As discussed in Chapter 11, they believe that the large deficits have made it more difficult for the Federal Reserve to conduct a credible disinflation policy. Economic agents, seeing the large deficits, expect the Federal Reserve eventually to increase money growth in order to lower interest rates and help finance the deficit (both directly and by generating higher nominal income growth and therefore tax revenues). The new classical economists also believe that the deficits have caused an increasingly uncertain economic environment with consequent negative effects on economic activity. Thomas Sargent concludes that "The idea of coupling a very loose fiscal policy with a very tight monetary policy is a big mistake."[18]

In the monetarist model, as in the Keynesian model, we would expect a combination of tight monetary and easy fiscal policy to result in a rise in the real interest rate. As discussed in Section 9.3, bond-financed changes in fiscal policy in the monetarist model had their main effect on the interest rate. Therefore, monetarists as well as Keynesians have been concerned about the effects that the expansionary fiscal policy of the 1980s and the resulting large deficits would have on investment. Some monetarists, including Milton Friedman, have argued in agreement with the supply-siders, that it is the growth in government spending that is ultimately at fault for the deficit. They have, therefore, favored spending cuts rather than tax increases to resolve the problem.

Read Perspectives 18.2.

---

[17] Paul Craig Roberts, "The Deficit: Coming to Terms with the Real Issues," *Business Week* (April 9, 1984), p. 13.

[18] Arjo Klamer, *Conversations with Economists* (Totowa, N.J.: Rowman and Allenheld, 1983, p. 70). See also Thomas Sargent and Neil Wallace, "Some Unpleasant Monetarist Arithmetic," Federal Reserve Bank of Minneapolis, *Quarterly Review* (Fall 1981), pp. 1–17.

PERSPECTIVES

Ricardian Equivalence

Within the Keynesian, monetarist, and some new classical models, if government spending is financed by a deficit and thus by bond sales to the public, the interest rate will be higher than it would be if such spending were financed by taxation. This would also be the case in the classical model discussed in Chapter 4. A strand in the classical thought, however, suggested that the means of financing government spending did *not* affect the interest rate. This notion is called *Ricardian equivalence* after David Ricardo, who originated the idea, though he had doubts about its

validity.[1] Some new classical economists have revived the notion of Ricardian equivalence in recent years.[2] If Ricardian equivalence in fact held, then the supply-side economists would be right. Only the level of

[1]See Gerald O'Driscoll, "The Ricardian Nonequivalence Theorem," *Journal of Political Economy,* 85 (February 1977), pp. 207–10.

[2]Robert Barro's work is central in this regard. See his *Macroeconomics* (New York: Wiley, 1984), Chap. 15.

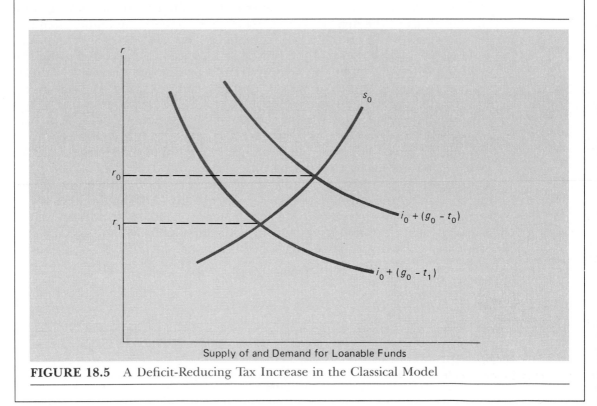

Supply of and Demand for Loanable Funds

FIGURE 18.5   A Deficit-Reducing Tax Increase in the Classical Model

government spending would matter; whether such spending were financed by taxation or borrowing would not affect the interest rate.

To understand Ricardian equivalence, we consider the effects of a shift from bond financing to tax financing. In the current context, think of this as reducing the budget deficit by a tax increase. First, we consider this shift in the standard classical model, then we show a change in the model that produces Ricardian equivalence.

Figure 18.5 shows the effects of a deficit-reducing tax increase in the standard classical model. Assume that tax collections rise from t_0 to t_1. The levels of investment and government spending are unchanged (at i_0 and g_0). The deficit is reduced, and the demand

for loanable funds falls from $i_0 + (g_0 - t_0)$ to $i_0 + (g_0 - t_1)$. The interest rate declines from r_0 to r_1.

Ricardo suggested, however, that private saving depended on the size of the deficit. The public was assumed to believe that the debt would be paid off eventually, and in the meantime interest payments would have to be made on it. Private saving was therefore assumed to depend positively on the deficit, as the public set aside funds to pay their *future* tax liability (or to bequeath wealth to their descendants for that purpose). Figure 18.6 shows the effects of the same deficit-reducing tax increase with this Ricardian assumption. Now, in addition to the decline in the demand for loanable funds, there is a decline in the

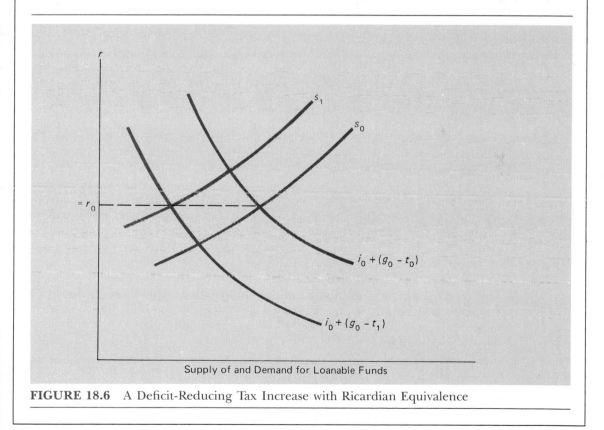

Supply of and Demand for Loanable Funds

FIGURE 18.6 A Deficit-Reducing Tax Increase with Ricardian Equivalence

supply of loanable funds (a shift in the saving function from s_0 to s_1). Private saving, in fact, decreases dollar for dollar with the fall in the deficit. This follows since, for each dollar's worth of bonds not sold by the government, the public stops saving one dollar, which was earmarked for future tax liabilities. The shifts in the supply and demand for loanable funds counterbalance one another, and the interest rate is unchanged.

If Ricardian equivalence holds, tax increases to reduce the deficit will not lower interest rates. Tax cuts that cause government deficits will not raise interest rates. Only the level of government spending matters.

Clearly, accepting Ricardian equivalence would change the way we view the current fiscal situation. Keynesians, as well as many monetarist and new classical economists, reject the idea as attributing too much foresight

to the public, as well as relying on several other highly restrictive assumptions.[3] As *The Economist* noted, concerning Ricardian equivalence, "This theory, like much of the debate about the new classical economics, seems to divide economists into those who think it is obviously true and those who think it too preposterous for words."[4]

---

[3] See, for example, the discussion in Willem Buiter and James Tobin, "Debt Neutrality: A Brief Review of Doctrine and Evidence," in *Social Security Versus Private Saving,* George M. von Furstenberg, ed. (Cambridge, Mass.: Ballinger Publishing Co., 1980), pp. 39–63. Keynesian critics also point out that if Ricardian equivalence held, the deficits of the 1980s should have increased the saving rate. In fact, as we saw in Chapter 14 (Perspectives 14.1), the U.S. saving rate declined markedly in the 1980s.

[4] *The Economist,* November 3–9, 1984, p. 66.

18.7   CONCLUSION

The issue of the deficit dominated the debate over fiscal policy in the 1980s and continues to do so into the 1990s. One implication of this is that the potential stabilization role for fiscal policy is complicated by concern over the deficit. In 1992, for example, during a recession, both President Bush and Democrats in Congress favored expansionary fiscal policy actions to stimulate the economy. But both wished to do so without raising the deficit. This sharply reduced their options to programs such as lowering middle-class taxes, while raising those of the rich or paying for tax cuts with spending cuts—all proposals that cancel out at least part of their own effect. Overall, the restrictions placed on fiscal policy by the attention focused on the deficit have increased the importance of the stabilization role for monetary policy, to which we now turn our attention.

Review Questions and Problems

1. Some economists who accept the public-choice view of the fiscal policy-making process have concluded that a constitutional amendment to mandate

a balanced federal budget would be desirable. Summarize their arguments in favor of such an amendment.

2. Explain the central element of the *partisan* theory of fiscal policymaking. Contrast the implications of the partisan theory concerning the relationship of fiscal policy to the business cycle with those of the public-choice view.

3. Summarize the trends in the level and composition of federal government expenditures during the period 1960–91.

4. Explain the concept of an automatic fiscal stabilizer. Give examples.

5. Suppose that, within the simple Keynesian model used in Section 18.4, the level of government spending (G) was 100, the level of investment spending (I) was 75, and consumption (C) was given by

$$C = 25 + 0.8Y_D$$

Net taxes are initially given by the tax function

$$T = 50 + 0.30Y$$

Calculate equilibrium income. Now suppose the tax rate is decreased from 0.30 to 0.25. Find the new level of equilibrium income. Compute the values of the autonomous expenditure multiplier before and after the tax cut.

6. Explain the objections that Keynesian economists have to fixed rules for fiscal policy, such as a constitutional amendment that would mandate a balanced federal budget.

7. Suppose that, within the simple Keynesian model used in Section 18.4, the level of government spending (G) was 100, the level of investment (I) was 75, and consumption (C) was given by

$$C = 25 + 0.8Y_D$$

Net taxes (T) are given by the tax function

$$T = 50 + 0.30Y$$

Calculate equilibrium income $(\overline{Y})$. Now suppose that the intercept of the net tax function (t_0) decreases from 50 to 40. Find the new level of equilibrium income.

8. Contrast the Keynesian and supply-side economists' views of the effects that the Reagan administration's policies had on capital formation in the 1980s (also draw on the material in Section 17.3 for your answer). Use graphs where helpful in your analysis.

Selected Readings

Abrams, Richard K., Froyen, Richard T., and Waud, Roger N., "The State of the Federal Budget and the State of the Economy," *Economic Inquiry*, 21 (October 1983), pp. 485–503.

Alesina, Alberto, "Macroeconomics and Politics," in Stanley Fischer, ed., NBER *Macroeconomics Annual*, 1988.

Barth, James R., Iden, George, and Russek, Frank S., "Do Federal Deficits Really Matter?" *Contemporary Policy Issues* (September 1984), pp. 79–95.

Benavie, Arthur, and Froyen, Richard, "A Balanced-Budget Constraint in Modern Stochastic Macromodels," *Southern Economic Journal*, 53 (July 1986), pp. 247–58.

Blanchard, Olivier J., "Reaganomics," *Economic Policy*, 2 (October 1987), pp. 15–56.

Blinder, Alan, *Economic Policy and the Great Stagflation.* New York: Academic Press, 1981, Chap. 7.

Buchanan, James M., and Wagner, Richard E., *Democracy in Deficit.* New York: Academic Press, 1977.

Buiter, Willem, "A Guide to Public Sector Debt and Deficits," *Economic Policy*, 1 (November 1985), pp. 13–79.

Evans, Paul, "Do Large Deficits Produce High Interest Rates?" *American Economic Review*, 75 (March 1985), pp. 68–87.

Modigliani, Franco, "Reagan's Economic Policies: A Critique," *Oxford Economic Papers*, 40 (September 1988), pp. 397–426.

Musgrave, Richard, *The Theory of Public Finance.* New York: McGraw-Hill, 1959, Chaps. 1–4 and 17–22.

Okun, Arthur M., "Rules and Roles for Fiscal and Monetary Policy," in James Diamond, ed., *Issues in Fiscal and Monetary Policy*. Chicago: DePaul University Press, 1971.

Rock, James M., ed., *Debt and the Twin Deficits.* Mountain View, Calif.: Mayfield Publishing Company, 1991.

Schultze, Charles, "Is There a Bias Toward Excess in U.S. Government Budgets or Deficits?" *Journal of Economic Perspectives*, 6 (Spring 1992), pp. 25–43.

19 Monetary Policy

In this chapter we focus on the conduct of monetary policy. We are especially concerned with the question of the optimal way in which monetary policy should be carried out. What should the Federal Reserve do?

19.1 • THE MONETARY POLICYMAKING PROCESS

The structure of the Federal Reserve System was discussed in Chapter 16. For purposes of macroeconomic policy, the key bodies within the Federal Reserve system are the Board of Governors of the Federal Reserve and the Open Market Committee. The Board of Governors is composed of seven governors, appointed by the president of the United States with Senate confirmation to terms of 14 years, with one of the governors designated by the president as chairman for a 4-year term. The Open Market Committee has 12 voting members, the 7 governors and 5 of the presidents of the 12 regional Federal Reserve banks. The presidents of the regional Federal Reserve banks serve on a rotating basis, with the exception that the president of the New York Federal Reserve Bank is a permanent voting member.

As discussed in Chapter 16, open-market operations are the major tool used by the Federal Reserve in conducting monetary policy, and our discussion in this chapter focuses on the behavior of the Open Market Committee. Adjustments in the Federal Reserve discount rate and the levels of reserve requirements are made by the Board of Governors to supplement, or at times substitute for, open-market operations.

In light of our discussion in Chapter 18 concerning the interaction of macroeconomic policymaking and democratic politics, it is worthwhile to consider the relationship of the Federal Reserve and other government policymaking bodies. The striking feature of the Federal Reserve's situation is the considerable degree of independence given to the monetary policy-making authority. The 14-year terms for which the governors are appointed and the fact that they cannot be reappointed provide insulation from the political process. The chairman of the Board of Governors is appointed for a 4-year term, but this term is not concurrent with that of the president of the United States. Therefore, an incoming president does not immediately get to appoint his choice of chairman. The other members of the Open Market Committee, the regional bank presidents, are appointed by the directors of the regional banks with the approval of the Board of Governors.

In the 1970s, Congress passed legislation requiring periodic reports from the Federal Reserve on the conduct of policy, but monetary policy decisions, such as the target growth rate in the money supply or the target level for interest rates, are not subjects on which Congress legislates. These decisions are made by the Open Market Committee. Further, the Federal Reserve has a degree of independence from the budget appropriations process because its expenses are paid by its interest earnings on holdings of government securities.

All this is not to say that the Federal Reserve is completely autonomous or that monetary policy is conducted in an apolitical setting. The chairman of the Board of Governors comes up for reappointment (as chairman) during the course of a president's term. For example, President Carter declined to reappoint Arthur Burns as chairman in 1978, replacing him with G. William Miller. In 1983 President Reagan did reappoint Paul Volcker (who was appointed by Carter in 1979 when Miller became Secretary of the Treasury), but only after much speculation that Reagan would prefer his own nominee. In 1987, when Volcker asked not to be considered for a third term as chairman and was replaced by Alan Greenspan, there was speculation that he did so because President Reagan failed to signal directly that he wanted Volcker to stay. Also, since board members often resign before the end of their terms, a president can sometimes make several appointments to the board and, therefore, perhaps change the course of monetary policy. By 1987, for example, President Reagan had appointed all the members of the board.

Furthermore, the Federal Reserve's independence is itself the result of congressional legislation, and the Federal Reserve recognizes that new legislation could weaken this independence. In fact, at times when there is a severe conflict between the Federal Reserve and the administration or Congress over the proper course of monetary policy, bills to limit Federal Reserve independence are often proposed in Congress. The Federal Reserve recognizes this threat and the fact that there are limits on how far it can go in pursuing goals that deviate from those of Congress and the president. Even taking account of these constraints, however, the degree of independence of the Federal Reserve is sufficient that in our following discussion we consider how the monetary policy authority itself makes policy decisions and determines optimal policy.

The Open Market Committee meets approximately eight times per year. At these meetings they review the current domestic and international economic situation. They also consider forecasts of the Federal Reserve staff concerning future economic events. On the basis of this information, they formulate a "directive" to the *Open Market Desk* at the New York Federal Reserve Bank, explaining how open-market operations should be conducted over the next month. The question of an optimal monetary policy strategy can then be viewed as the choice of a directive by the Open Market Committee.

19.2 • A STRATEGY FOR MONETARY POLICY: INTERMEDIATE TARGETING ON MONETARY AGGREGATES

In one sense, what the Federal Reserve should do is clear. Monetary policy should be conducted in a way that leads to stable growth in aggregate demand. The Federal Reserve should keep demand from growing too rapidly, with resulting inflation, or too slowly, with resulting high unemployment and slow economic growth. But what procedures are likely to result in desirable outcomes in an uncertain world? This is the question of what strategy should guide monetary policy. In this section we explain one strategy that the Federal Reserve has employed, that of **intermediate targeting on monetary aggregates**. In the next section we consider an alternative strategy, which focuses on interest rates.

The ultimate *targets* that the monetary authority attempts to control are macroeconomic goal variables such as the unemployment rate, inflation rate, and growth in real GNP. Rather than simply adjusting monetary policy instruments, primarily the level of open-market operations, on the basis of past observations on these variables and forecasts of their future behavior, in the short run the Federal Reserve has tried to influence these ultimate targets by influencing intermediate target variables.

An *intermediate target* is a variable that the Federal Reserve controls not because the variable is important in its own right but because by controlling the variable the policymakers believe they are influencing the ultimate policy targets in a predictable way. With a monetary aggregate as an intermediate target, the implicit assumption in Federal Reserve strategy is that, other things being equal, higher rates of growth in the money stock will increase inflation while lowering unemployment (raising the level of economic activity) in the short run. Slower monetary growth rates will, again *ceteris paribus*, be associated with lower inflation rates and higher short-run rates of unemployment.

What is the rationale for such intermediate targeting? Even if there is a predictable relationship between money growth rates and ultimate economic targets that the Federal Reserve wants to control, why use an intermediate target rather than control the ultimate targets directly? To understand the possible usefulness of the intermediate targeting approach, we must recognize the fact that monetary policy must be made under conditions of imperfect information and, therefore, uncertainty about the behavior of the economy. If the ultimate targets of policy can be observed at less frequent intervals than financial market variables such as interest rates, bank reserves, and monetary aggregates, then as information about such financial market variables becomes available, it can be used to adjust the previous policy setting. The intermediate targeting approach is one way of employing such financial market information.

As implemented by the Federal Reserve, intermediate targeting on a monetary aggregate proceeds as follows. At the beginning of each calendar quarter, the Open Market Committee chooses the money growth rate target that it views as consistent with its ultimate policy goals for the next year. The committee makes this choice on the basis of past data and staff forecasts of the behavior of the economy for given money growth rates. After this choice is made, monetary policy during the quarter proceeds *as if the chosen money growth target is the ultimate target of monetary policy.* Policy actions within the quarter are aimed at hitting this money target. At the beginning of the next quarter, the money target is reviewed and adjusted on the basis of new forecasts and the experience within the quarter.

To see how this process works, recall from Chapter 16 that the money stock (M1 definition) can be expressed as the monetary base (MB) times the money multiplier (m):

$$M^s = m \cdot \mathrm{MB} \tag{19.1}$$

where

$$m = m\left(\mathrm{rr}_d, \frac{\mathrm{CU}}{D}, \frac{\mathrm{ER}}{D}, \frac{\mathrm{SD} + \mathrm{TD}}{D}, \mathrm{rr}_{sd}, \mathrm{rr}_{td}\right) \tag{19.2}$$

The money multiplier depends on a number of variables, such as the required reserve ratio on checkable deposits (rr_d) and the currency/deposit ratio (CU/D) (see Section 16.2). The variables that determine the money multiplier are themselves functions of other economic variables, such as interest rates and the level of income. If the Federal Reserve is using a monetary aggregate such as M1 as an intermediate target, then within the quarter, open-market operations will be aimed at providing sufficient growth in the monetary base to achieve the target growth rate in the money stock. The Federal Reserve will monitor weekly money stock figures and offset the effects on the money stock of unpredicted changes in the money multiplier or in the monetary base (by changes in bank borrowing of reserves, for example). The financial market information they react to is, then, the weekly money stock figures, and they use this information in a particular way—to adjust open-market operations in order to hit the money stock target.

19.3 • EMPHASIS ON INTEREST RATES

There are a number of alternatives to the strategy of intermediate targeting on a monetary aggregate. In practice, the main alternative has been for the Federal Reserve to focus on the level of interest rates in place of monetary aggregates.

Interest Rate Targeting

An example will help clarify how a Federal Reserve strategy of focusing on interest rates would work. While at times policy has not been so mechanical, the strategy described will be one in which the Federal Reserve sets explicit interest rate targets. The Open Market Committee could, for example, set a range for the coming month of 5 to 6 percent for the rate on three-month Treasury bills. As with money supply targets, the range for the target interest rate would be chosen to hit the ultimate policy targets (inflation rate, unemployment rate, and growth rate of the economy). The interest rate would replace the money stock as an *intermediate target*.

Once the target range was set, the Open Market Desk would monitor the market where Treasury bills trade, which is part of the open market. If the interest rate on Treasury bills rose above the 6 percent ceiling of the target range, the desk manager would begin open-market purchases. These could involve Treasury bills or other government securities. The effect of open-market purchases, as we have seen, is to expand credit and lower interest rates. The desk would carry out enough open-market purchases to reduce the Treasury bill rate below 6 percent.

Alternatively, if the Treasury bill rate temporarily fell below 5 percent, the Open Market Desk would begin to *sell* securities in the open market—reducing bank reserves, restricting credit, and raising interest rates—until the Treasury bill rate rose back above 5 percent.

Thus, the Open Market Desk would keep the average Treasury bill rate between 5 and 6 percent for the month.

Implications for the Money Stock

Note that in carrying out open-market purchases or sales, the Open Market Desk increases or decreases bank reserves, bank deposits, and therefore the money stock. For example, keeping the interest rate in the target range might require large open-market purchases or sales, and therefore large changes in the money stock. The point of this is that a focus on the interest rate is in fact *an alternative* to targeting a monetary aggregate. The Federal Reserve cannot, in general, do both. Given this fact, which is the better strategy?

19.4 • IMPLICATIONS OF INTERMEDIATE TARGETING ON A MONETARY AGGREGATE

To answer the question just posed, we first consider how a strategy of intermediate targeting on a monetary aggregate would work in practice. In Section 19.5 we do the same for the case of interest rate targeting. Section 19.6 then evaluates the relative merits of each strategy.

To summarize our conclusion in advance, we find that, rather than one strategy being preferable under all circumstances, there are circumstances in which each is preferred. Recall that the rationale for any strategy of intermediate targeting depends on the fact that the Federal Reserve acts under uncertainty about exactly what is going on in the economy. Whether targeting interest rates or monetary aggregates is the preferable strategy will be seen to depend on the source of that uncertainty, though there are some other considerations as well.

The Ideal Case for Targeting on a Monetary Aggregate

We first consider the ideal case for targeting on a monetary aggregate, the case in which this is clearly the optimal strategy. This case is depicted within the *IS–LM* framework in Figure 19.1. For simplicity, suppose that the Federal Reserve has only one ultimate target, the level of real income (y), the desired level of which is (y^*).[1] Also assume that in a given quarter, based on its forecasts, the monetary policy authority concludes that the target level of income will be achieved if the money stock is set at M^*.[2]

The *LM* schedule in Figure 19.1 is vertical, reflecting an assumption that the demand for money is totally interest-inelastic. Money demand depends

---

[1] We assume that the Federal Reserve does not want income to fall below y^* because this would cause excessive unemployment. Levels of income above y^* are undesirable because of their future inflationary consequences.

[2] An important early analysis of the relative merits of an interest rate versus a monetary aggregate as a target under conditions of uncertainty is William Poole, "Optimal Choice of Monetary Policy Instruments in a Simple Stochastic Macro Model," *Quarterly Journal of Economics*, 84 (May 1970), pp. 197–216.

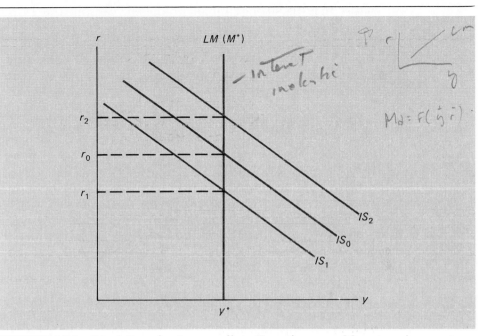

FIGURE 19.1 Ideal Case for Intermediate Targeting on a Monetary Aggregate
If the demand for money function is totally interest-inelastic and perfectly stable, then by hitting the money stock target M^*, the Federal Reserve will fix the vertical LM schedule at $LM(M^*)$. Income will be at the target level y^* regardless of the position of the IS schedule.

only on income. Further, we assume that the demand-for-money function is perfectly stable. There are no shifts in the function—no changes in the amount of money demanded for a given income level. On the supply side, the Federal Reserve is assumed to offset changes in the money supply that come as a result of the behavior of the public and the banking system. Thus, if the Federal Reserve achieves its target level of the money stock (M^*), the LM schedule will be perfectly stable at $LM(M^*)$ in Figure 19.1. This means that successfully hitting the intermediate target for the money stock will in fact mean successfully hitting the ultimate income target (y^*).

To see this, consider the situation depicted in the figure. We assume that the Federal Reserve cannot predict with certainty the position of the IS schedule. Assume that the predicted position for the curve is IS_0. Real sector demand factors such as exports, autonomous investment, and government spending may turn out to be weaker than predicted, causing the IS schedule to be to the left of IS_0, at IS_1. Alternatively, such real sector demand factors may be stronger than predicted, causing the *IS* schedule to be at a position such as IS_2, to the right of IS_0. By targeting the money stock, the Federal Reserve assures that the vertical *LM* schedule will be fixed at $LM(M^*)$, and consequently income will be at y^*, regardless of the position of the *IS* schedule. We said previously that when the Federal Reserve uses a money aggregate as an intermediate target, then within the quarter, policy proceeds as if the chosen money stock target *were* the ultimate target of monetary policy. In the case depicted in Figure 19.1, hitting the money stock target guarantees hitting the income target. The implicit assumption behind intermediate targeting on the money stock is indeed valid. This is the optimal case for such intermediate targeting.

Notice that while hitting the money stock target guarantees that we will hit the income target, unpredicted shocks that shift the *IS* schedule will cause volatility in the interest rate. If the actual position of the *IS* schedule is IS_1 or IS_2 instead of the Federal Reserve's predicted position IS_0, the interest rate will be r_1 or r_2 instead of the predicted level r_0. If the Federal Reserve also has a desired level for the interest rate, for example r_0, the Federal Reserve would miss this interest rate target. The interest rate must be free to adjust depending on the position of the *IS* curve. This illustrates the point made earlier that the Federal Reserve cannot generally hit both interest rate and money stock targets. Generally, interest rate volatility will be one result of adhering to money stock targets.

A final point to note about this ideal case for targeting a monetary aggregate is that it is very close to the *monetarist* case. Monetarists believe that the *LM* curve is quite steep and that, at least in most circumstances, money demand is stable—almost the conditions in Figure 19.1. It should then not be surprising that the monetarists favor targeting on monetary aggregates. Milton Friedman's proposal for a constant money growth rate rule is a form of targeting on a monetary aggregate, one where the target growth rate is set and never varied.

Less Than Ideal Cases for Intermediate Targeting on a Monetary Aggregate

Figure 19.2 illustrates cases in which achieving the money stock target will not generally mean that the income target will be achieved. In Figure 19.2*a* we still assume that if the Federal Reserve hits its money-stock target, it will fix the position of the *LM* curve. For this to be the case, we must still assume that the money demand function is perfectly stable. There are no unpredictable shifts in money demand that will shift the *LM* schedule for a given value of the money stock. In Figure 19.2*a*, we do not assume that money demand is totally interest-inelastic; the *LM* schedule is therefore not vertical.

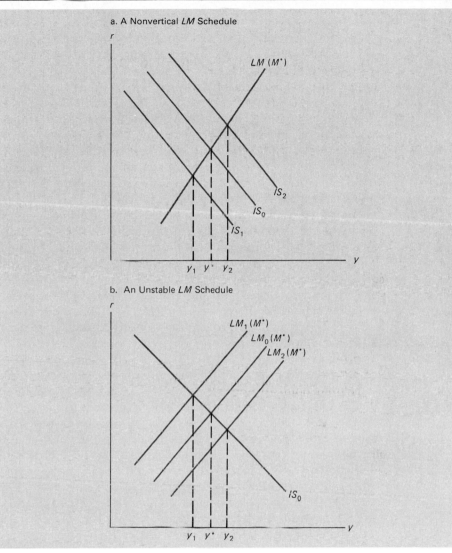

FIGURE 19.2 Less Than Ideal Cases for Targeting Money

Part *a:* A nonvertical *LM* schedule. If money demand is not totally interest-inelastic and the *LM* schedule is upward-sloping to the right, then hitting the money stock target will cause income to be at the target level y^* only if the *IS* schedule is at the predicted position IS_0. If, because of unpredicted shocks, the *IS* schedule is instead at IS_1 or IS_2, income will be away from y^*, at y_1 or y_2, even though M is at M^*. Part *b:* An unstable *LM* schedule. We assume that the Federal Reserve hits the money stock target M^*, which, based on its forecast of money demand, should set the *LM* schedule at $LM_0(M^*)$ and hit the income target y^*. If, because of an unpredicted shock to the money demand function, the *LM* curve shifts to either $LM_1(M^*)$ or $LM_2(M^*)$, income will be at y_1 or y_2 and the income target will be missed even if the money stock is at the target level M^*.

In this case, notice that even though the Federal Reserve achieves its target level of the money stock, it will hit the ultimate income target only if the *IS* curve is at the predicted position, IS_0—only if the Federal Reserve's real sector forecast, on which the choice of the money stock target was predicated, was correct. If real-sector demand was weaker than predicted and the *IS* schedule was at IS_1 in Figure 19.2a instead of IS_0, income would be at y_1, below y^*. If real-sector demand was stronger than predicted and the *IS* schedule was at IS_2, income would exceed the target level. In both cases the income target is missed even though the Federal Reserve hits the money stock target M^*. With a nonvertical *LM* schedule, fixing the money stock does not fix the level of income.

In Figure 19.2b we consider a case in which the money demand function is not perfectly stable. There are unpredicted shifts in money demand for given levels of income and the interest rate. Such shocks to money demand shift the *LM* schedule. In this case, even if the Federal Reserve hits its money stock target, the *LM* schedule will not be fixed. In Figure 19.2b, assume that, based on a forecast of money demand, the Federal Reserve predicts that the *LM* schedule will be at $LM_0(M^*)$. To isolate the effects of uncertainty about money demand more clearly, let us assume that the Federal Reserve's forecast about the real sector is correct: the predicted and actual position of the *IS* curve is IS_0.

If the Federal Reserve is using the money stock as an intermediate target and hits the money stock target (M^*), it will hit the income target (y^*) only if the prediction of money demand is correct—only if the *LM* schedule is at $LM_0(M^*)$ as predicted. This can be seen in Figure 19.2b. If there is an unpredicted shock that increases the demand for money above the predicted level and the *LM* schedule is at $LM_1(M^*)$ instead of $LM_0(M^*)$, the level of income (y_1) will fall short of the target level.[3] In the reverse case, when an unpredicted shock reduced money demand below the predicted level and the *LM* curve was at a position such as $LM_2(M^*)$, the level of income would be y_2 above the target level. Again, hitting the money stock target does not guarantee that the income target will be hit.

19.5 • IMPLICATIONS OF TARGETING THE INTEREST RATE

Next consider the implications of a monetary policy strategy of targeting the rate of interest. Here we will ignore the range within which the interest rate

---

[3]A shock that reduces (or increases) money demand means a shift in the money demand function that reduces (or increases) the quantity of money demanded for a given level of income and the rate of interest. The way in which shifts in the money demand function shift the *LM* schedule is explained in Section 6.2.

might be targeted (5–6 percent in the previous example) and simply assume that there is a single target level, r^*, for the interest rate. As with a money stock target, the policymaker is assumed to have one ultimate target, that of keeping real income (y) at a desired level (y^*).

As we saw in Section 9.2, if the Federal Reserve targets (or pegs) the interest rate, then in the *IS–LM* framework the *LM* schedule becomes horizontal. The *LM* schedule depicts equilibrium in the money market. To peg the interest rate, the Federal Reserve supplies whatever amount of money is necessary for money market equilibrium at the target interest rate.[4]

To see how well a strategy of targeting the interest rate works, we consider the same cases as we did for a money stock target in the previous section.

Uncertainty About the *IS* Schedule

In the first two cases the only uncertainty is assumed to be about the position of the *IS* schedule. Figure 19.3a depicts the situation in which, as in Figure 19.1, the predicted position of the *IS* schedule is IS_0. But positions IS_1 and IS_2 might occur, respectively, if demand is weaker or stronger than expected. In addition to the horizontal *LM* schedule, which is relevant when the interest rate is pegged (solid line), we also show (as a dashed line) the position of the *LM* schedule that would have resulted if we targeted the money supply (at M^*). In Figure 19.3a we assume that money demand is totally interest-inelastic (zero interest elasticity). Therefore, if the money stock were the intermediate target, the *LM* schedule would be vertical.

We see from the figure that with the interest rate targeted at r^*, we will hit the income target, y^*, only if the *IS* schedule turns out to be in the predicted position IS_0. If, for example, business investment demand were lower than predicted and the *IS* schedule were at IS_1, income would fall below the desired level (to $y_{r,1}$). In the case depicted in Figure 19.3a, we are certainly better off with a money stock target, where we stay at y^* regardless of the position of the *IS* schedule.

Part *b* of Figure 19.3 depicts the case in which we still allow only for uncertainty about the *IS* schedule, but no longer assume that money demand is completely interest-inelastic. (This is the case depicted previously in Figure 19.2a.) The assumption about the interest elasticity of money demand has no effect on the *LM* schedule when the interest rate is the (intermediate) target. That *LM* schedule (the solid *LM* line in the figure) is horizontal because the Federal Reserve supplies whatever level of money is required to keep the interest rate at r^*. The *LM* schedule with a money stock target, shown as

[4]As explained in Section 19.3, the Federal Reserve does not actually print or directly supply money, but rather carries out open-market operations to move the money supply to the level of money demand at r^*.

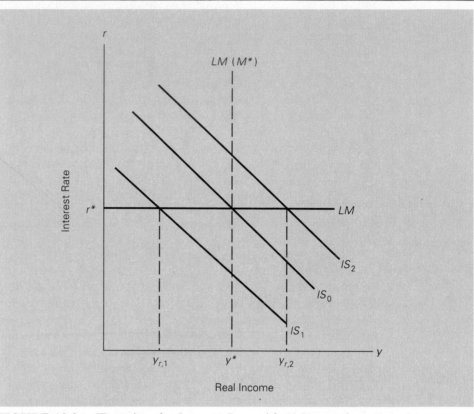

FIGURE 19.3a Targeting the Interest Rate with *IS* Uncertainty: Zero Interest Elasticity of Money Demand

a dashed line in Figure 19.3*b*, *LM*(*M**), will now be upward-sloping, not vertical.

Again, the predicted position of the *IS* schedule is IS_0, but the schedule may turn out actually to be at IS_1 or IS_2, respectively, if private-sector demand is weaker or stronger than predicted. As in part *a*, it can be seen that the money stock target is superior to the interest rate in keeping income close to y^* when the *IS* schedule is not at the predicted level. If the *IS* schedule turns out to be at IS_1 or IS_2, income will be at y_1 or y_2, respectively, with a money stock target. With an interest rate target, income would be at $y_{r,1}$ or $y_{r,2}$, respectively, for the same positions of the *IS* schedule; both levels are farther from y^*.

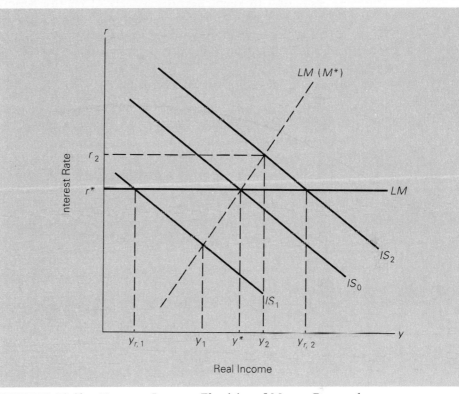

FIGURE 19.3b Nonzero Interest Elasticity of Money Demand

We see then that, regardless of whether the *LM* curve is vertical or upward-sloping, *a money stock target is superior to an interest-rate target when the uncertainty facing the policymaker concerns the IS schedule.* The reason for this is that when the *IS* schedule shifts away from its predicted position, the movement in the interest rate *dampens* (or reduces) the effect of the shift on income. When the interest rate is targeted, this *monetary dampener* is shut off.

To see this, consider the effects of an autonomous rise in investment demand (e.g., a shift from IS_0 to IS_2 in Figure 19.3b). If the money stock is the target, as the rise in investment causes income to rise, money demand rises and, with a fixed money stock, the interest rate must rise (to r_2 in Figure 19.3b). The rise in the interest rate will work against the autonomous rise in demand and cause overall investment to rise by less than it otherwise would. If the Federal Reserve is targeting the interest rate, this will not happen. As income increases, to keep the interest rate at r^*, the Federal Reserve must carry out open-market purchases to expand the money stock by enough to satisfy the increased demand for money. The dampening effect on the expansion is lost, and income moves farther from the target level, y^*.

Uncertainty About Money Demand

Figure 19.4 depicts the case where the money demand function is not perfectly stable (the case shown previously in Figure 19.2b). With the interest rate as a target, the LM schedule remains horizontal and stable (the solid LM line), and it does *not* shift when there is a shift in the money demand function. If, for example, a positive shock (a desirable new type of bank deposit) increases the demand for money at a given level of income and the interest rate, the Federal Reserve simply increases the money supply. Shocks to money demand will therefore *not* affect income with an interest rate target. Real income will remain at the target level y^*.

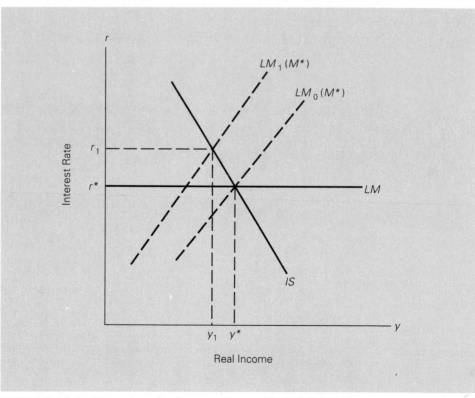

FIGURE 19.4   Targeting the Interest Rate with LM Uncertainty

With a money supply target, however, a positive shock to money demand *will* shift the position of the *LM* schedule away from the predicted level, even if the target level of the money supply is achieved. If with the money target, M^*, the expected position of the *LM* schedule were the dashed line $LM_0(M^*)$, then a positive shock to money demand would shift the schedule to $LM_1(M^*)$. The interest rate would be pushed up to r_1, and real income would fall to y_1 below y^*.

We see, then, that *if uncertainty centers on instability in money demand, an interest rate target is preferable to a money stock target.* If the interest rate is the target, the real sector (output market) is *insulated* from the effect of shocks to money demand. This is because the money supply adjusts to maintain the target level of the interest rate. In the case of a money stock target, the shock to money demand *does* affect the interest rate, and therefore aggregate demand and real income are displaced.

19.6 • MONEY STOCK VERSUS INTEREST RATE TARGETS

This section summarizes the relative advantages and disadvantages of using a monetary aggregate versus an interest rate as intermediate target for monetary policy.

The Sources of Uncertainty and the Choice of a Monetary Policy Strategy

The analysis in the previous section indicates that one important consideration in choosing between the money stock (monetary aggregate) and the interest rate as an intermediate target is the source of the uncertainty faced by the monetary policymaker. If the predominant sources of uncertainty are unpredictable shifts in the *IS* schedule, a money stock target is superior to an interest rate target. The implication for the actual economy of this result is that, when uncertainty comes from sources such as unpredictable shifts in the business sector's investment spending, residential construction investment, and consumer durable purchases—all private-sector demands for output—the money stock target is preferable.

The interest rate target was seen to be superior when uncertainty stems from shifts in the *LM* schedule due to unstable money demand. In the *IS–LM* model, assets are split into two groups, one termed *money* and one composite nonmoney asset termed *bonds*. Any factors that change the relative desirability of the two assets shift the model's *LM* schedule. The implication of this for the actual economy is that when the predominant source of uncertainty centers on shifts in asset demands (for bonds and money), the interest rate is the superior intermediate target.

When we discuss choices that the Federal Reserve has made, we will see that the consideration of the type of uncertainty that is greatest *has* been an important element in the choice of a monetary policy strategy. There are, however, other relative advantages and disadvantages of money stock targets compared to interest rate targets.

Other Considerations

One additional advantage for a money stock target is that a strong commitment to keep the money stock growing in a target range ensures control over inflation for medium-term periods (e.g., three to five years). Virtually all economists (not just monetarists) believe that sustained high inflation requires accommodating money stock growth. Strict adherence to money stock targets severely limits monetary accommodation, unless the targets are themselves high. The latter is highly unlikely in the current U.S. environment. A Federal Reserve chairman would have rough going explaining to Congress why target money growth for 1993 was 15 percent.

Advocates of targeting monetary aggregates argue that by setting low, noninflationary money stock targets, *and hitting them,* the Federal Reserve can build up anti-inflationary *credibility*; the public starts to believe the Federal Reserve will carry out announced policies. This has the advantage that inflationary expectations are kept at a low level.

An interest rate target provides no such anti-inflationary guarantee, and repeatedly hitting interest rate targets does not necessarily build up credibility of the monetary authority's anti-inflation policy. If the central bank targets the interest rate, it must increase the money supply to accommodate any increases in money demand. If a potentially inflationary boom begins, money demand will be increasing (higher transactions demand). The Federal Reserve may then unwittingly be led to fuel the inflationary boom by an accommodating increase in the money supply. This is not inevitable; the Federal Reserve may instead observe the potential for inflation and raise the target level of the interest rate. The point here is simply that hitting a particular interest rate target does not provide the inflation protection that targeting monetary aggregates (with low target growth rates) does.

There are, however, considerations that favor an interest rate target. For one thing, interest rates are not subject to the measurement problems that have arisen concerning monetary aggregates (e.g., new deposit types). Interest rate stability, at least in the short run, is another advantage cited for an interest rate target. To hit a money stock target, the Federal Reserve must be willing to let the interest rate fluctuate freely (Figure 19.2a). Some, though by no means all, economists and central bankers worry that this will cause instability in financial markets. Recall, for example, that sharp rises in interest rates cause significant capital losses on bonds. These losses may, in turn, lead to instability of financial institutions that hold large quantities of bonds.

19.7 • THE EVOLUTION OF FEDERAL RESERVE STRATEGY

In the years since 1970, the Federal Reserve has varied between an emphasis on interest rate control and targeting of monetary aggregates. Twice during this time period, the Federal Reserve dramatically shifted from one strategy to another. Actual Federal Reserve strategy, as well as the reasons for these shifts, can be best explained by looking at three subperiods.

1970–79: Federal Funds Rate Targeting

During the 1970s, the Federal Reserve targeted a short-term interest rate. The particular rate they chose was the *federal funds rate,* which is the interest rate charged on loans from one bank to another. When one bank lends to another, deposits at a regional Federal Reserve bank are transferred from the lending bank to the borrowing bank. These deposits are bank reserves, so loans in the federal funds market are transfers of reserves.

On a month-to-month basis during the 1970s, the Federal Reserve targeted the weekly average for the federal funds rate within a narrow range of one half to three fourths of a percentage point (e.g., 8.25–9.00 percent). They did this through open-market operations, as described in Section 19.3 (where we assumed the Treasury bill rate was the target rate). If, for example, the rate went above the upper end of the target range, the Open Market Desk at the Federal Reserve Bank of New York would purchase Treasury securities in the open market. This increases bank reserves. With more reserves in the system, there would be fewer banks trying to borrow reserves from other banks—fewer borrowers in the federal funds market. There would also be more lenders. This would cause the federal funds rate to fall. The Open Market Desk would create enough additional reserves to drive the federal funds rate down to within the target range. Conversely, if the federal funds rate fell below the lower boundary of the target range, the Open Market Desk would sell securities and reduce bank reserves.

Federal Reserve strategy in the 1970s was not to *peg* the interest rate near any one value for a long period of time. The target range of the federal funds rate was to be moved around from month to month. The target range would be increased if the Federal Reserve wanted to tighten monetary policy and lowered if it wished to move to a more expansionary policy.

Monetary aggregates were not neglected in the 1970s. Though on a month-to-month basis the interest rate target was given precedence, the Federal Reserve attempted to hit annual targets for the growth in several money stock measures. Still, at a number of points in the 1970s, the Federal Reserve allowed money stock targets to be missed in order to achieve the desired interest rate target.

1979–82: Targeting Monetary Aggregates

The first of the two dramatic switches in Federal Reserve policy came on October 6, 1979, when the Federal Reserve abandoned the strategy of targeting the federal funds rate. They instead adopted a strategy of directly controlling bank reserves to increase their ability to hit target ranges for growth in the monetary aggregates (M1 and M2), basically the strategy outlined in Section 19.2. Our earlier analysis in this chapter is helpful for an understanding of the reasons for this shift.

In 1979 the inflation rate was accelerating rapidly. The recession that many had expected during the year had not materialized. There was a great deal of uncertainty about the strength of private-sector demand. This is the situation (uncertainty about the *IS* schedule) when a monetary aggregate is superior to an interest rate as an intermediate target.[5]

We have also seen that a commitment to achieving low money growth targets virtually guarantees that high inflation rates will not be sustained, while a nominal interest rate target provides no such guarantee. With the inflation rate over 13 percent in 1979, this was a considerable advantage.

1982–?: Current Federal Reserve Strategy

While the Federal Reserve was not entirely successful in hitting money stock targets during the 1979–82 period, most observers credit the shift toward a more restrictive monetary policy in 1979 for the decline in inflation to around the 4 percent level by 1982, albeit with the cost of a serious recession in 1981–82.

The Federal Reserve, however, abandoned the strategy of intermediate targeting on monetary aggregates in the summer of 1982, the second of the policy shifts referred to earlier. Although it later returned to specifying target growth rates for the M2 aggregate, and in some years the M1 aggregate as well, these targets did not assume as much importance in the post-1982 period as during 1979–82. Although the Federal Reserve has not returned to formal interest rate targeting, it has placed more emphasis on interest rates in the post-1982 period than in the 1979–82 period. Overall,

---

[5]This is not to say that there was no uncertainty about money demand in 1979. As discussed previously in Section 15.4, there was evidence of considerable instability in money demand during this period. But by October 1979, uncertainty about the strength of inflationary pressure in the output market was the dominant concern.

monetary policy in recent years has been conducted more on a judgmental (or discretionary) basis than according to any formal strategy. The Federal Reserve has concentrated at times on monetary aggregates, at times on interest rates, and at times on other variables—including, as we see in Chapter 20, on foreign exchange rates.

The reason for the deemphasis of monetary aggregates in the post-1982 period, especially of the M1 aggregate, was the breakdown of the money–income relationship that occurred in the 1980s. There was substantial instability in money demand during this period, as we saw in Section 15.4. Swings in money demand often did not reflect underlying economic conditions, but were more heavily influenced by innovations in the deposit market as deregulation took place and banks offered many new types of deposits. In such conditions, stabilizing money growth would not stabilize the economy.

Read Perspectives 19.1.

Instability of money demand, and consequently uncertainty about the *LM* schedule, is the condition that favors the interest rate as an intermediate target. The Federal Reserve has been reluctant to go all the way back to the strategy of targeting the federal funds rate, partly because of fears that, as in the 1970s, this strategy would provide insufficient protection from an acceleration in inflation. Monetary policymakers have opted instead for the judgmental, less formal monetary policy procedure just described.

PERSPECTIVES

INSTABILITY IN THE MONEY–INCOME RELATIONSHIP

Figure 19.5 provides an illustration of the breakdown in the money–income relationship during parts of the 1980s. The figure shows growth rates for the money stock and nominal GNP from 1985 through the fourth quarter of 1990. The money measure is the M1 aggregate, the behavior of which was the most unpredictable during the decade.

Notice in the figure that the two surges in M1 growth in 1985 and 1986 did not correspond to increases in the growth in nominal GNP in those years. In fact, in 1986 growth in nominal GNP slowed, as M1 growth rose to over 15 percent. Then in 1987, GNP growth rose, and M1 growth plummeted.

M1 growth also fell sharply during the first half of 1989, while there was no large fall in the GNP growth rate. Not all the variability in M1 growth was due to unpredictable shifts in money demand. In the Keynesian view, for example, the fall in nominal interest rates in 1985–86 was an important fact causing the increase in the money growth rate. Still, these wide swings in the M1 growth rate were in large part unpredicted and unrelated to the underlying state of the economy. As a result, the Federal Reserve did not even set target ranges for M1 growth in the years after 1987.

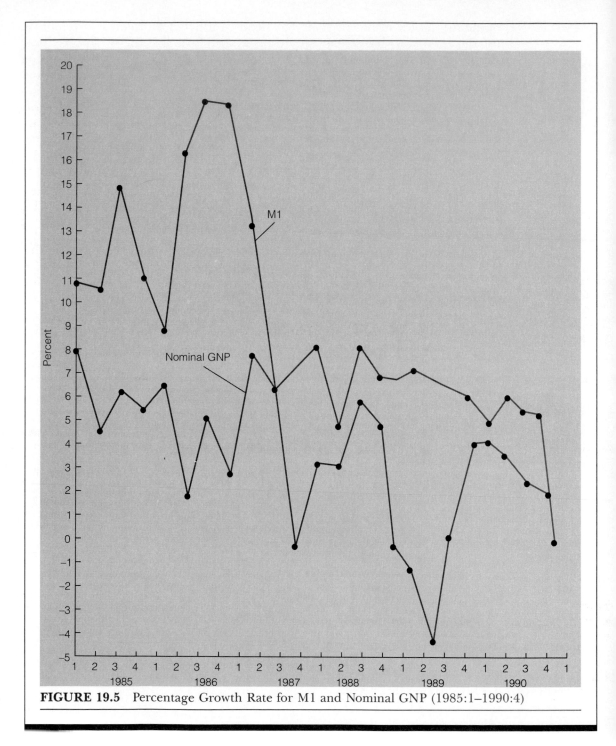

FIGURE 19.5 Percentage Growth Rate for M1 and Nominal GNP (1985:1–1990:4)

19.8 • CONCLUSION

Economists who prefer policy by rules rather than discretion, especially monetarists, who favor a money growth rate rule, have been critical of the Federal Reserve's operating procedure since 1982. Federal Reserve Board chairmen in this period have argued, however, that, under present circumstances, there is no alternative. In 1985, former Chairman Volcker defended the Federal Reserve's procedures as follows:

> The uncertainties surrounding M1, and to a lesser extent the other aggregates, in themselves imply the need for a considerable degree of judgment rather than precise rules in the current conduct of monetary policy—a need that, in my thinking, is reinforced by the strong crosscurrents and imbalances in the economy and in the financial markets. That may not be an ideal situation for either the central bank or for those exercising oversight—certainly the forces that give rise to it are not happy. But it is the world in which, for the time being, we find ourselves.[6]

The sentiments were echoed in current Federal Reserve Board Chairman Alan Greenspan's testimony before Congress:

> The Fed chairman also said he "sympathized" with several panel members who asked if there was some type of rule the Fed could devise to guide monetary policy, rather than relying solely on the discretion of the chairman and other board members. But he said: "I've been seeking that rule for a very long time, and I've somewhat concluded it is probably in the Don Quixote area."[7]

Review Questions and Problems

1. What is the Open Market Committee? What role does this committee play in formulating monetary policy?

2. Evaluate the arguments for and against the strategy of intermediate targeting on a monetary aggregate.

3. Why is it natural for a monetarist economist to favor the policy strategy of intermediate targeting on a monetary aggregate?

4. Using the *IS–LM* curve framework, analyze whether an increase in the instability of the money demand function would increase or decrease the desirability of intermediate targeting on a monetary aggregate.

---

[6] Federal Reserve *Bulletin* (September 1985), p. 694.

[7] *The Wall Street Journal* (December 21, 1987), p. 4.

5. Explain the shift that took place in Federal Reserve policy in 1979. Explain the reasons for this shift.

6. Why does the Federal Reserve often use intermediate target variables? Why not just focus on the ultimate policy objectives, such as inflation and unemployment?

7. Suppose that the Federal Reserve is using an interest rate as an intermediate target, while real income is the ultimate policy target, and there is an autonomous drop in business investment that the Federal Reserve had not predicted. Use the *IS–LM* model to show the effects of the shock. Would income have been affected less or more if the Federal Reserve were using a money stock target?

Selected Readings

Alesina, Alberto, "Macroeconomics and Politics," in Stanley Fischer, ed., NBER *Macroeconomics Annual*, 1988.

Dewald, William G., "Monetarism Is Dead; Long Live the Quantity Theory," Federal Reserve Bank of St. Louis *Review*, 70 (July/August 1988), pp. 3–18.

Friedman, Benjamin, "The Inefficiency of Short-Run Monetary Targets for Monetary Policy," *Brookings Papers on Economic Activity*, 2 (1977), pp. 293–318.

Friedman, Benjamin, "Lessons from the 1979–82 Monetary Policy Experiment," *American Economic Review* 74 (May 1984), pp. 382–87.

Friedman, Benjamin, "Monetary Policy Without Quantity Variables," *American Economic Review*, 78 (May 1988), pp. 440–45.

Friedman, Benjamin, "Lessons on Monetary Policy from the 1980s," *Journal of Economic Perspectives* 2 (Summer 1988), pp. 51–72.

Friedman, Milton, "Lessons from the 1979–82 Monetary Policy Experiment," *American Economic Review*, 74 (May 1984), pp. 394–400.

Friedman, Milton, "Monetary Policy: Theory and Practice," *Journal of Money, Credit and Banking*, 14 (February 1982), pp. 98–118.

Heller, H. Robert, "Implementing Monetary Policy," *Federal Reserve Bulletin*, 74 (July 1988), pp. 419–29.

Lombra, Raymond E., "Monetary Control: Consensus or Confusion," *Controlling Monetary Aggregates*. Boston: Federal Reserve Bank of Boston, 1981.

Modigliani, Franco, "The Monetarist Controversy, or Should We Forsake Stabilization Policies?" *American Economic Review*, 67 (March 1977), pp. 1–19.

Meulendyke, Ann Marie, *U.S. Monetary Policy and Financial Markets*. New York: Federal Reserve Bank of New York, 1990.

Poole, William, "Monetary Policy Lessons of Recent Inflation and Disinflation," *Journal of Economic Perspectives*, 2 (Summer 1988), pp. 73–100.

Poole, William, "The Making of Monetary Policy: Description and Analysis," *Economic Inquiry*, 13 (September 1975), pp. 253–65.

Tobin, James, "Monetary Policy: Rules, Targets and Shocks," *Journal of Money, Credit and Banking*, 15 (November 1983), pp. 506–18.

Wooley, John, *Monetary Politics*. Cambridge, Cambridge University Press, 1984.

Selected Macroeconomic Policy Actions, 1929–91

Throughout the book we have discussed actual macroeconomic policy actions in the context of the theories we were considering. Here, as background for that discussion, a number of important macroeconomic policy actions taken by the U.S. government during the period since the Great Depression are listed and briefly described. References are given to the sections of the text where these policy episodes are discussed further.

- ## 1929–33

Monetary Collapse During the Depression

Over the period 1929–33, the Federal Reserve allowed the money stock (M1) to decline by 27 percent. This monetary collapse is viewed by the monetarists as *the* cause of the Depression. Keynesians certainly regard it as an important contributing factor to the sharp decline in economic activity during this period (Perspectives 9.1).

- ## 1932

The Hoover Tax Increase

In 1932, with the unemployment rate at 24 percent, President Hoover initiated large increases in both excise and income taxes. Taxes were increased in order to balance the federal budget in the wake of falling tax revenues that occurred during the Depression (Sections 5.1, 18.5).

- ## 1933

Launching the New Deal

Upon taking office the Roosevelt administration enacted a broad program to combat the Depression. Included in the early stages of the program were efforts to raise prices, or at least to stem the decline in prices, such as the Agricultural Adjustment Act (AAA) and National Recovery Act (NRA). Public works programs, such as the Tennessee Valley Authority (TVA) and Works Progress Administration (WPA), were a second part of the program. A third part of the program was financial sector reform including initiating a system of deposit insurance and regulation of security markets.

• 1933

The United States Leaves the Gold Standard

As part of his plan to raise the U.S. domestic price level, Roosevelt took the United States off the gold standard, breaking the link of the dollar price to gold. The move prompted one of his economic advisors to assert, "this is the end of Western civilization." Great Britain had left the gold standard in 1931. Several continental European countries, led by France, remained on the gold standard for a few more years, but the classical gold standard was to collapse completely during the 1930s. Western civilization survived the demise of the gold standard, but international economic relations were badly disorganized in the 1930s.

• 1937–38

Restrictive Monetary and Fiscal Policies

The economic recovery in the United States had been proceeding from 1933 to 1937, with the unemployment rate dropping from 25.2 percent in 1933 to 14.3 percent in 1937. In 1937–38, however, both monetary and fiscal policies became highly restrictive. There followed a sharp decline in economic activity, with the unemployment rate rising to 19.1 percent in 1938. Fiscal policy became restrictive with tax increases and spending reductions aimed at balancing the federal budget. Roosevelt had never been comfortable with the notion of deficit spending and thought that by 1937 the recovery had proceeded far enough to allow a more *conventional* balanced budget policy to be followed. The Federal Reserve tightened monetary policy by doubling the required reserve ratios on deposits. The reason for the Federal Reserve's action was that the level of excess reserves in the system had gotten quite high, and the policymakers feared that their ability to control the money stock through control of bank reserves (Sections 16.2 and 16.3) had been weakened.

- ## 1940–42

  ### World War II Defense Buildup

  Federal government purchases of goods and services for national defense increased from $1.2 billion in 1939 to $49.4 billion in 1942. This massive defense buildup finally ended the Great Depression. The unemployment rate fell to 4.7 percent in 1942, then to 1.9 percent in 1943.

- ## 1942

  ### Wartime Wage and Price Controls

  Following a sharp rise in both wholesale and retail prices in 1940–42, general wage and price controls were instituted in 1942. The controls remained in effect until the second half of 1946.

- ## 1945

  ### The Bretton Woods Agreements

  The international monetary agreements signed at Bretton Woods, New Hampshire, near the end of World War II set up a fixed exchange rate system in which the dollar's value was fixed in terms of gold and convertible into gold. Other currencies had par values in terms of the dollar and were convertible into dollars. This international monetary system was to last until 1973 (Section 20.3).

- ## 1946

  ### The Employment Act

  Congress explicitly took responsibility for maintaining high levels of employment and production while also maintaining the purchasing power of the dollar (limiting inflation) by passage of the Employment Act.

- ## 1951

  ### Korean War Price and Wage Controls

  The beginning of the Korean War, in 1950, triggered a wave of panic buying by consumers and firms recalling the shortages of World War II. Prices rose quickly and price and wage controls, along with restrictive fiscal policy actions, were put into effect in 1951.

- ## 1951

Federal Reserve–Treasury Accord

Beginning in 1942 the Federal Reserve had been pegging the level of interest rates on government securities in order to help the Treasury market debt. In March 1951, the Treasury and Federal Reserve reached an accord whereby the Federal Reserve would no longer agree to peg interest rates, though it would still cooperate in marketing federal government debt (Section 9.2). The accord allowed the Federal Reserve to pursue an independent monetary stabilization policy.

- ## 1953–60

Fiscal Policy in the 1950s

The record of fiscal policy in the 1950s illustrated the importance of *automatic fiscal stabilizers* (Section 18.4) as the budget went into deficit during recessions and surplus with peaks in economic activity. Such fiscal stabilizers had become more important because of the larger size of the federal government budget in this period relative to the pre–World War II period. Discretionary fiscal policy actions were used during this period to a lesser extent than in later years.

- ## 1961–64

The New Economics of the Kennedy–Johnson Period

The Kennedy administration came into office with a program to speed recovery from the recession that had begun in 1960. Included in the program were an investment tax credit (Section 14.2), an increase in government spending, and tax cuts for persons and businesses (Section 17.2). The anti-inflationary part of the program was a set of voluntary wage and price guidelines. By the first half of 1965 the unemployment rate had declined to 4.8 percent (from 6.9 percent for the first half of 1961).

- ## 1965–67

Inflationary Vietnam War Spending

With the beginning of the Vietnam War, government spending on national defense rose from $49.4 billion in 1965 to $71.5 billion in 1967. Since this increase was not adequately financed by higher tax revenues, the federal deficit rose by approximately $14 billion over this period. With the economy already at a high employment level, the rate of inflation increased.

• 1966

A Credit Crunch

The expansionary fiscal policy and higher inflation rate in 1965–66 put in-creased pressure on the Federal Reserve. The resulting tightening of mon-etary policy led to a "credit crunch." Credit demand exceeded supply and interest rates rose sharply. With ceilings on deposit rates paid by financial intermediaries, deposits declined, with resulting credit rationing in the hous-ing market (Sections 6.1, 14.2).

• 1968

The Income Tax Surcharge

Finally, in the spring of 1968, a 10 percent income tax surcharge was leg-islated to aid in financing the Vietnam War. Passage of the surcharge had been held up because of a disagreement between President Johnson, who favored the surcharge, and some congressional leaders, who favored cuts in nondefense spending to fund the war.

• 1971

President Nixon's "New Economic Policy"

The Nixon administration came into office pledged to reduce the inflation rate. Restrictive monetary and fiscal policies in 1969–70 led to increased unemployment but did little to slow inflation. In August 1971 President Nixon announced several policy actions. First was a system of wage and price controls, beginning with a three-month freeze on prices and wages. Second was a series of moderately expansionary fiscal policy shifts. Finally, convertibility between the dollar and gold was suspended and a 10 percent surtax on imports imposed to deal with a growing international balance of payments deficit (Section 20.2).

• 1973

The Move to Floating Exchange Rates

After an attempt to establish a viable new set of fixed exchange rates in 1972 (the Smithsonian Agreements), the dollar was allowed to *float* in 1973. The Bretton Woods system of fixed exchange rates had been replaced by a managed floating of major world currencies (Sections 20.2 and 20.4).

- ### 1975

The Antirecession Tax Cut

A large tax cut, consisting of a one-time rebate and a reduction in personal income tax rates, was passed at just the low point of the severe 1974–75 recession. Both the rebate portion of the 1975 tax cut and the temporary income tax surcharge in 1968 gave rise to a controversy over the effectiveness of temporary changes in tax policy (Sections 14.1 and 14.2).

- ### 1979

Shift in the Federal Reserve's Operating Procedure

On October 6, 1979, the Federal Reserve announced a shift in the tactics of monetary policy. Previously the Federal Reserve had attempted to control the money stock through control of the federal funds rate. As of 1979, the Federal Reserve shifted to total reserves as an instrument through which it would seek to control the money stock (Section 19.7).

- ### 1981

The Reagan Economic Recovery Program

The Reagan administration's program consisted of a set of business and personal tax cuts, cuts in nondefense spending, increases in defense spending, and regulatory reform (Section 17.3) aimed at fostering noninflationary economic growth. The rationale for much of the program came from the theories of the supply-side economists (Section 17.2), but questions have been raised about whether as implemented the program was in fact supply-side economics in practice.

- ### 1983–88

Large Structural Deficits

The Reagan administration's tax cuts lowered federal government revenues as a percentage of GNP. Government expenditures, however, continued to increase as a percentage of GNP during the first Reagan administration. The result was the emergence of huge government deficits. In 1983 the federal deficit reached 5.0 percent of GNP. Large budget deficits persisted throughout the 1980s and into the 1990s (Sections 17.3, 18.6).

- ## 1985

Gramm–Rudman–Hollings Act

In 1985 Congress passed the Balanced Budget and Emergency Deficit Reduction Control Act mandating a move to a balanced federal budget in steps over five years, by automatic spending cuts if Congress failed to balance the budget by legislation. In 1987 the Supreme Court ruled that a key provision of the act was unconstitutional. Congress then passed an amended version. The amended version mandated a balanced budget (also to be achieved by steps) by 1993 (Section 18.1).

- ## 1985

The Plaza Accord

In September of 1985, finance ministers and central bankers from the United States, Japan, France, West Germany, and the United Kingdom met at the Plaza Hotel in New York. They agreed to intervene in foreign exchange markets to lower the value of the U.S. dollar. This was the first of several agreements among the major industrialized nations to coordinate exchange rate policies. The *Louvre Accord* in February 1987 was an agreement to stabilize the dollar in the wake of a sharp fall in its value between 1985 and early 1987 (Section 20.5).

- ## 1986

The Tax Reform Act of 1986

Congress passed a tax reform act in August 1986. The act lowered the highest tax rate from 50 to 28 percent—the lowest top rate since 1931. Moreover, it created only two tax rates, 15 percent (on incomes up to approximately $30,000 on a joint return) and 28 percent. The act also raised personal exemptions so that approximately six million low-income recipients were removed from the tax rolls. To keep tax revenue from falling due to the lower tax rates, the act also removed many deductions and eliminated a number of tax shelters (Section 17.3).

- ## 1990

Omnibus Budget Reconciliation Act

By the fall of 1990 it became evident that the deficit ceilings in the amended Gramm–Rudman–Hollings Act could not be achieved. The act was replaced by the Budget Reconciliation Act, which included a package of tax increases and spending cuts. The cuts were projected to reduce the deficit by $500 billion over five years.

Selected Readings

Bach, George L., *Making Monetary and Fiscal Policy.* Washington, D.C.: The Brookings Institution, 1971.

Blinder, Alan S., *Economic Policy and the Great Stagflation.* New York: Academic Press, 1981.

Feldstein, Martin, ed., *The American Economy in Transition.* Chicago: University of Chicago Press, 1980.

Friedman, Milton, and Schwartz, Anna, *A Monetary History of the United States, 1867–1960.* Princeton, N.J.: Princeton University Press, 1963.

Gordon, Robert A., *Economic Instability and Growth: The American Record.* New York: Harper & Row, 1974.

Kettl, Donald F., *Leadership at the Fed.* New Haven, Conn.: Yale University Press, 1986.

Kindleberger, Charles P., *The World in Depression, 1929–39.* Berkeley: University of California Press, 1973.

Stein, Herbert, *The Fiscal Revolution in America.* Chicago: University of Chicago Press, 1969.

Temin, Peter, *Lessons From the Great Depression,* Cambridge, Mass.: MIT Press, 1990.

Tew, Brian, *The Evolution of the International Monetary System, 1945–77.* London: Hutchison and Company, 1977.

Triffin, Robert, *Our International Monetary System: Yesterday, Today, and Tomorrow.* New York: Random House, 1968.

Open Economy Macroeconomics

P art V examines U.S. international economic relations. Both trade flows and capital movements are considered. We analyze how exchange rates are determined in different international monetary systems and consider the relative merits of these systems. Recent proposals to change the current international monetary system are explained. An appendix to this part develops an open economy version of the *IS–LM* curve model. The model is then used to study the effects of monetary and fiscal policy in the open economy under both fixed and flexible exchange rates.

Exchange Rates and the International Monetary System

In 1960 imports of goods and services totaled 4.4 percent of GDP. By 1991 this figure was 10.9 percent of GDP. Exports rose from 4.9 in 1960 to 10.5 percent of GDP in 1991. Financial markets in the United States and other nations have also become much more closely linked over the past three decades. Overall the U.S. economy has become much more *open* in the sense of having more extensive trade and financial dealings with other economies.

In previous chapters a number of examples and *Perspectives* have been chosen to emphasize the interrelations of the U.S. economy and the economies of other nations.[1] This chapter focuses explicitly on the macroeconomics of open economies which brings these interrelations to center stage. Among the topics considered are the determination of exchange rates, the current international monetary system as well as the system it replaced, and the interactions between the domestic economy and our international economic transactions.

Exchange rates are central to the focus of this chapter. An exchange rate between two currencies is the price of one currency in terms of the other. The price of the British pound in terms of the U.S. dollar on March 18, 1992, was $1.74 (i.e., $1.74 = 1 pound); the price of the French franc was 18 U.S. cents; the price of the German mark was 61 U.S. cents. Exchanges between the dollar and other currencies take place when U.S. residents want to purchase foreign goods or assets, as well as when foreign residents want to purchase U.S. goods and assets. A look at the nature of these transactions between the United States and other countries is a first step in studying how the relative values of national currencies are determined. The U.S. **balance of payments accounts** summarize our foreign economic transactions.

---

[1] Additionally, the Appendix to Chapter 5 contains an open economy macroeconomic model which is extended in the Appendix to this part.

20.1 • THE U.S. BALANCE OF PAYMENTS ACCOUNTS

The U.S. Department of Commerce records foreign economic transactions in the balance of payments accounts. On one side of the accounts, all earnings from the foreign activities of U.S. residents and the U.S. government are recorded as credits, whereas on the other side, expenditures abroad are reported as debits. A point to notice is that, by the usual principles of double-entry bookkeeping, each credit must be matched by an equal debit, and vice versa. Each expenditure on foreign goods, for example, must be financed somehow; the source of financing is recorded as a credit. A first conclusion, then, before we even look at the numbers, is that if *all* transactions are counted, the balance of payments always balances.

We will, however, want to consider subcategories of our foreign transactions, and for such subcategories there is no reason to believe that receipts from abroad will equal earnings from abroad. In recent years, for example, expenditures on our merchandise exports by foreign residents (a credit in our balance of payments) have fallen far short of our expenditures on imported goods (a debit in our balance of payments). This *deficit* in our **merchandise trade balance** has been a matter of concern, for reasons to be discussed.

Table 20.1 summarizes the U.S. balance of payments accounts for 1990.

The Current Account

The first group of items in the table are what are called **current account** transactions. Among these, the first items listed are *merchandise exports and imports,* to which we have just referred. Examples of merchandise exports are the sale of a U.S. computer system to a British firm or the sale of U.S. grain to Russia. Purchases of Japanese cars, German cameras, or Honduran bananas by U.S. residents are examples of U.S. imports. In 1990, U.S. merchandise imports exceeded exports by $108.2 billion. We had a merchandise trade deficit of that amount.

The next category in the table is imports and exports of *services.* In the table we enter only the net value of such transactions. Examples of transactions in the service category are financial, insurance, and shipping services. Also in this category are dividends and interest earned by U.S. residents from their assets abroad (a credit) and interest and dividends paid to foreign residents who hold U.S. assets (a debit). The net item in the table, $38.3 billion, indicates that in 1990 we exported more of such services than we imported. The last transactions in the current account are *net transfers.* Recorded here are private and government transfer payments made between the United States and other countries. Such payments include U.S. foreign aid payments (a debit) and private or government pension payments to persons living abroad (a debit). Any such transfer to a U.S. resident from abroad would be a credit on this line.

TABLE 20.1   U.S. Balance of Payments, 1990 (billions of dollars)

	Credit (+)	Debit (−)	Balance (−) Deficit (+) Surplus
Current account			
Merchandise exports (+) and imports (−)	389.5	−497.7	−108.2
Service transactions (net)	38.3		
Transfers (net)		−22.2	
Current account balance			−92.1
Capital account			
Capital inflows (+) and outflows (−)[a]	53.9	−55.5	
Capital account subbalance			−1.6
Statistical discrepancy			+63.5
Official reserve transactions			
Reduction in U.S. official reserve assets			−2.2
Increase in foreign official assets in the			
United States			32.4
Total official reserve transactions			30.2

[a] Includes increases in U.S. government foreign assets other than official reserve assets.

Source: Federal Reserve Bulletin, February 1992. Data are on a slightly different basis (coverage and timing) from U.S. census data shown elsewhere in the book.

If we stop or draw the line at this point, we can compute the *current account balance.* The table indicates that in 1990 the current account was in deficit by $92.1 billion. Overall, just considering current account transactions, U.S. residents spent over $92.1 billion more abroad than was earned.

The Capital Account

The next entries in the table record **capital account** transactions.[2] Capital inflows (credits) are purchases of U.S. assets by foreign residents. Such capital inflows include purchases by foreigners of U.S. private or government bonds, stocks, and bank deposits. Additionally, foreign direct investments in the United States, such as Honda's building of a plant in Ohio, are capital inflows in the balance of payments. Purchases by U.S. residents of financial assets

---

[2] In previous chapters the term *investment* has been used exclusively to refer to purchases of physical capital goods. The term *capital* referred to those physical goods themselves. In the discussion of international economic relations, the term *capital flows* refers to exchanges of financial assets involving individuals in different countries, as well as direct investment such as the purchase of a plant in another country.

or direct investments in foreign countries are capital outflows (debits) in the balance of payments. During the 1980s, the United States had large surpluses in the capital account which partly balanced out large deficits in the current account. In 1988, for example, when the U.S. current account deficit was $135 billion, the surplus on the capital account was $83 billion. Overall, during the years from 1983 to 1989 the cumulative surplus in our capital account was approximately $620 billion. In 1990, however, as can be seen from Table 20.1, there was a small deficit in the U.S. capital account. Recorded capital outflows exceeded capital inflows by $1.6 billion.

This figure may, however, be misleading, for the following reason. Notice the next item as we move down the balance of payments table, the item marked statistical discrepancy. Not all items in the balance of payments are properly recorded, and the statistical discrepancy, or errors and omissions term, is the amount that must be added to make the total balance of payments balance. In 1990 this amount was positive and especially large; there were large unrecorded U.S. earnings. One explanation of such earnings is that they represent *unrecorded* capital inflows. Foreigners may avoid recording their investments in the United States if such investments violate their countries' laws or in order to evade taxes. If the especially large statistical discrepancy in 1990 in large part represents an unreported capital inflow, then the true capital account (recorded plus unrecorded capital flows) may in fact have had a substantial surplus in that year.

An important point to note concerning the U.S. capital account is that foreign purchases of our assets largely represent U.S. borrowing from foreign residents. The large capital inflows of the 1983–89 period, for example, included $250 billion of foreign purchases of U.S. government securities and more than $300 billion of foreign loans or purchases of private U.S. securities. During this period, large excesses of merchandise imports over exports (trade deficits) were, in effect, financed by borrowing from abroad.

Official Reserve Transactions

Let us stop and examine the point we have now reached in considering U.S. foreign economic transactions. Suppose we draw a line below the statistical discrepancy.

All the items above the line represent international economic transactions undertaken by private U.S. residents or the U.S. government for some independent motive. By this we mean a motive other than the effect the transaction will have on the balance of payments, or, as we see presently, on the value of the U.S. dollar relative to other currencies. A U.S. resident buys a Japanese car or a share of stock in a German company because he prefers them to their domestic counterparts. The U.S. government may give foreign aid to another government to stabilize the political situation in that country. All the items above the line are what, from the point of view of the balance of payments accounts, can be termed *autonomous* or independently motivated transactions.

In contrast, the official reserve transactions below this line are carried out by central banks, either the U.S. Federal Reserve System or foreign central banks (e.g., the Bank of England or German Bundesbank) in pursuit of international policy objectives. Here we simply explain the nature of these transactions. The motivation for them is explained later in the chapter.

The first item below the statistical discrepancy in Table 20.1 is the *reduction in U.S. official reserve assets*. Official reserve assets are holdings of gold, special drawing rights (a reserve asset created by the International Monetary Fund),[3] and foreign currency holdings. If this item were positive, it would indicate that a portion of our official reserve assets were used to finance expenditures abroad. In fact, the negative sign on this item indicates that the United States *increased* holdings of reserve assets in 1990; so rather than financing our expenditures, this increase in reserves was a debit in the balance of payments—an expenditure that had to be financed. Reductions in U.S. official reserve assets are a credit in the balance of payments.

The next and last item in the balance of payments table is the *increase in foreign official assets in the United States*. Foreign central banks hold a portion of their reserve assets in the form of dollars. Dollars are an important reserve asset because the dollar is commonly used in international transactions and because of the central role the dollar has played in the international monetary system since World War II. If foreign central banks buy dollars, that is a credit in our balance of payments (a capital inflow), since they are investing in the United States.[4] In 1990 foreign central banks increased the amount of official reserve assets held in the United States by $32.4 billion, hence the positive item in this line of our balance of payments accounts.

20.2 • EXCHANGE RATES AND THE MARKET FOR FOREIGN EXCHANGE

The demand for foreign currencies by domestic residents is called the demand for **foreign exchange.** The foreign exchange market is the market in which national currencies are traded for one another. It is in this market, for example, that U.S. residents sell dollars to purchase foreign exchange

---

[3]The International Monetary Fund is an agency that was set up near the end of World War II to administer the international monetary agreements signed at that time. These agreements, the Bretton Woods agreements, are discussed in Section 20.4. Special drawing rights will also be discussed further.

[4]They need not hold actual U.S. currency. After buying the dollars, they can use them to purchase U.S. government or private securities.

(foreign currencies). In the United States, the central market for foreign exchange is composed of a number of brokers and bank foreign exchange departments in New York.

To see the link between the balance of payments accounts and transactions in the foreign exchange market, we begin by recognizing that all expenditures by U.S. residents on foreign goods, services, or assets and all foreign transfer payments (debits in the balance of payments accounts) also represent demands for foreign currencies, that is, demands for *foreign exchange*. The U.S. resident buying a Japanese car pays for it in dollars, but the Japanese exporter will expect to be paid in yen. So dollars must be exchanged for yen in the foreign exchange market. To take another example, if a U.S. resident wants to buy a share of stock on the London stock exchange, a broker must convert the buyer's dollars into British pounds before actually making the purchase. *Thus, the total U.S. residents' expenditures abroad represents a demand for foreign exchange.* Looked at from the point of view of the dollar, we can also state that the *total foreign expenditure of U.S. residents represents an equal supply of dollars in the foreign exchange market.*

Conversely, all foreign earnings of U.S. residents reflect equal earnings of foreign exchange. American exporters, for example, will expect to be paid in dollars, and to buy our goods, foreigners must sell their currency and buy dollars. *Total credits in the balance of payments accounts are then equal to the supply of foreign exchange or, what is the same thing, the demand for dollars.*

Demand and Supply in the Foreign Exchange Market

It is in the foreign exchange market that exchange rates among national currencies are determined. In our discussion of this process we make the following simplifying assumptions. Initially, we exclude official reserve transactions by central banks. In the jargon of international economics, we assume that central banks do not *intervene* in the foreign exchange market. We relax this assumption later in this section. Also for simplicity, we assume that there are only two countries, the United States, whose domestic currency is the dollar, and Germany, with the mark as the domestic currency unit. The *exchange rate* in this simple situation is the relative price of the two currencies, which we express as *the price of the mark in terms of dollars.* If, for example, the price of the mark is 0.25 dollar, then four marks trade for 1 dollar; at 0.40 dollar the exchange rate (price of the mark) is higher and 2.5 marks equal 1 dollar. It is important to remember that with the exchange rate expressed in this manner, a higher exchange rate means that the price of foreign currency (or foreign exchange) has risen. When the exchange rate rises, we say that the foreign currency has *appreciated* or the dollar has *depreciated*. Alternatively, a fall in the exchange rate means that the price of foreign exchange (price of the marks) has declined. The mark has *depreciated* while the dollar has *appreciated*.

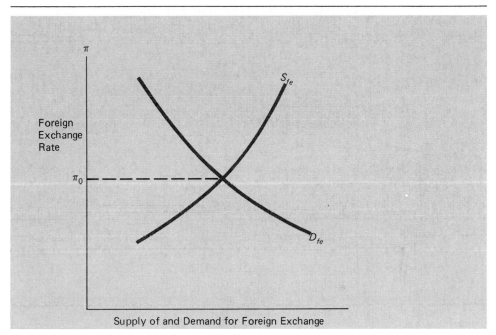

FIGURE 20.1 Foreign Exchange Market
The demand schedule for foreign exchange is downward-sloping plotted against the exchange rate (π), since the demand for foreign exchange to finance imports will fall as the exchange rate rises, making foreign goods more expensive. The supply schedule for foreign exchange is upward-sloping, reflecting the assumption that the foreign exchange proceeds from export sales rise as the exchange rate rises, making domestic goods less expensive to foreign buyers. The equilibrium value of the exchange rate is π_0, the rate which equates demand and supply.

In Figure 20.1 we represent graphically the supply and demand curves for foreign exchange plotted against the exchange rate (π). As was explained, all foreign expenditures by U.S. residents (imports, purchases of foreign assets, and foreign transfers) are demands for foreign exchange. How will this demand for foreign exchange vary with the price of foreign exchange? As drawn in Figure 20.1, the demand curve (D_{fe}) is downward-sloping, indicating that as the price of foreign exchange (price of marks) rises, the demand for foreign exchange falls. This is because a rise in the price of foreign exchange will increase the cost *in terms of dollars* of purchasing foreign goods. Imports will therefore decline and less foreign exchange will be demanded. Note that here we are holding all prices other than the exchange rate constant. Suppose that you are considering the purchase of a German camera that costs 200 marks. If the exchange rate, the price of the mark in terms of dollars, is 0.25, the camera will cost \$50 (200 marks = \$50 at 4 marks to the dollar). If the exchange rate rises to 0.5, the camera will cost $100 (200 marks = $100 at 2 marks to the dollar). The higher the exchange rate, the higher the dollar cost of imported goods and the lower the demand for foreign exchange.

What about the demand for foreign exchange for the purchase of foreign assets and for foreign transfers? With respect to the latter, there is no reason for a definite relationship between the amount of foreign transfers and the exchange rate. It is not clear what effect the change in the exchange rate would have on foreign aid programs, pension payments to persons living abroad, or gifts to foreign nationals. In the case of purchases of foreign assets, an increase in the exchange rate will, as in the case of imported goods, push up the price in dollars of the foreign stocks or bonds. The rise in the exchange rate will, however, also result in a proportional increase in the interest or dividend payment on the foreign bond or stock, again as measured in dollars. For example, a German bond costing 1000 marks and paying interest of 100 marks per year will cost $250 and pay interest of $25 per year at an exchange rate of 0.25 (4 marks = 1 dollar). At an exchange rate of 0.5 (2 marks = 1 dollar), the bond will cost $500 and pay interest of $50 per year. In either case the bond represents an asset that pays a return of 10 percent per year. Consequently, we would not necessarily expect any effect on the demand for foreign assets as a result of a change in the exchange rate.[5] The downward slope of the demand for foreign exchange schedule therefore results only from the fact that imports decline as the exchange rate rises.

The supply schedule for foreign exchange is drawn with a positive slope in Figure 20.1, which reflects the assumption that the supply of foreign exchange increases as the exchange rate rises. As the exchange rate (price of marks) rises, U.S. export goods become less expensive to Germans in terms of marks. Again here we are holding all other prices, including the dollar price of U.S. exports, fixed. Thus U.S. wheat, for example, which sells for $4 a bushel would cost a German 16 marks per bushel at an exchange rate of 0.25 (4 marks = 1 dollar) but only 8 marks at an exchange rate of 0.5 (2 marks = 1 dollar).

The demand for our exports should therefore increase as the exchange rate rises. Notice, however, that a given *dollar* volume of exports earns less foreign exchange (fewer marks) at the higher exchange rate. If, for example, the exchange rate rose by 10 percent and as a result the *dollar* volume of

---

[5]It is the expectation of a change in the exchange rate that would trigger changes in the demands for foreign versus domestic assets. If, for example, you expected the price of the mark to rise from 0.25 dollar today to 0.50 dollar next week, you would buy the German bond discussed in the text now for $250 and could sell it next week for $500. For now, however, we are not allowing for expected changes in the foreign exchange rate.

exports rose 10 percent, earnings of foreign exchange would be unchanged. The United States would be selling 10 percent more but earning 10 percent fewer marks on each sale.

For the supply of foreign exchange to increase as the exchange rate rises, the foreign demand for our exports must be more than *unit elastic*, meaning simply that a 1 percent increase in the exchange rate (which results in a 1 percent decline in the price of the export good to Germans) must result in an increase in demand of more than 1 percent. If this condition is met, the dollar volume of our exports will rise more than in proportion to the rise in the exchange rate and earnings of marks (the supply of foreign exchange) will increase as the exchange rate rises. This is the assumption we make in Figure 20.1.[6]

Exchange Rate Determination: Flexible Exchange Rates

So far we have excluded intervention (official reserve transactions) by central banks. The supply and demand schedules in Figure 20.1 are for only autonomous transactions in the balance of payments accounts. Let us continue with this assumption and see how the exchange rate is determined in the absence of intervention. In this case we would expect the exchange rate to move to clear the market, to equate the demand for and supply of foreign exchange. In Figure 20.1, this equilibrium exchange rate is π_0. The autonomous elements in the balance of payments account, those above the lines where the official reserve transactions are recorded, are equated by the adjustment of the exchange rate. Such a system of exchange rate determination where there is no central bank intervention is a *flexible exchange rate system* or, as it is sometimes called, a *floating rate* system. An exchange rate system or regime is a set of international rules governing the setting of exchange rates. A completely flexible or floating rate system is a particularly simple set of rules for the central banks of different countries to follow; they do nothing to directly affect the level of their exchange rate. The exchange rate is market determined.

To better understand the workings of a flexible exchange rate system, we examine the effect of a shock that increases the demand for foreign exchange. Suppose that there is an increase in the U.S. demand for imported goods. For example, assume that an increase in energy prices causes an increased demand for fuel-efficient foreign cars. The effect of this increase

---

[6]Empirical support for this assumption is provided by Hendrik Houthakker and Stephen Magee, "Income and Price Elasticities in World Trade," *Review of Economics and Statistics*, 5 (May 1969), pp. 111–25. A more recent estimate by Jaime Marquez, "Bilateral Trade Elasticities," *Review of Economics and Statistics*, 72 (February 1990) pp.75–76, indicates a just unit-elastic foreign demand for U.S. exports. This implies a vertical supply of foreign exchange. To assume a vertical supply curve would not change our analysis.

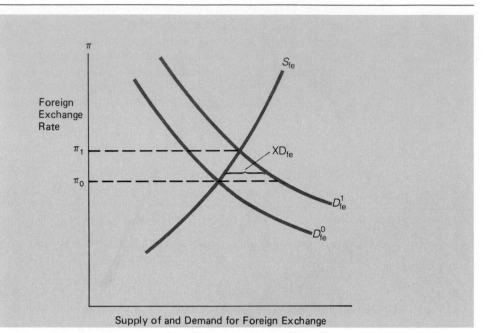

FIGURE 20.2   Effect in the Foreign Exchange Market of an Increase in the Demand for Imports
An autonomous increase in import demand shifts the demand schedule for foreign exchange from D_{fe}^0 to D_{fe}^1. At the initial equilibrium exchange rate there is now an excess demand for foreign exchange (XD_{fe}). The exchange rate rises to π_1 to reequilibrate supply and demand in the foreign exchange market.

in import demand would show up in the foreign exchange market as a shift to the right in the demand schedule for foreign exchange, for example, from D_{fe}^0 to D_{fe}^1 as illustrated in Figure 20.2. At a given exchange rate, there is a greater demand for imports in the United States and correspondingly a greater demand for foreign exchange to finance the increase in imports. At the initial equilibrium exchange rate π_0, there is now an excess demand for foreign exchange (shown as XD_{fe} in Figure 20.2). To clear the market, the exchange rate must rise to the new equilibrium value π_1. The rise in the exchange rate will cause the quantity of imports demanded to decline, since the dollar price of imported goods rises with the exchange rate. Also, the quantity of exports demanded will increase since the rise in the exchange rate makes U.S. exports less expensive to foreigners. At the new equilibrium with the higher exchange rate (π_1), the supply and demand for foreign exchange are again equal. The increase in import demand leads to a depreciation of the dollar.

In 1973, the United States moved toward greater flexibility in the exchange rate, as did other industrialized countries. Over the post-1970 period, however, the United States has not had a *completely* flexible exchange rate system. To varying degrees over this period, central banks, including the U.S. central bank, have intervened in the foreign exchange market to influence the values of their currency. The features of the current international monetary system are discussed later. Before we begin this discussion, it is useful to examine the working of the foreign exchange market under the polar opposite of a completely flexible rate system, a system of *fixed* or *pegged* exchange rates.

Exchange Rate Determination: Fixed Exchange Rates

An international monetary system is a set of rules organizing exchange rate determination and agreeing on which assets will be official reserve assets. An example of a fixed exchange rate system is the post–World War II Bretton Woods system. The international monetary agreements that comprise this system were negotiated near the end of the war (at Bretton Woods, New Hampshire). The International Monetary Fund (IMF) was set up to administer the Bretton Woods system. According to IMF rules, the United States was to set a parity or *par value* for its currency in terms of gold. Other nations would set parities for their currencies in terms of dollars, which with the dollar tied to gold also fixed the gold value of these other currencies. The United States agreed to maintain convertibility between the dollar and gold at the fixed price (originally $35 per ounce). Other countries agreed to maintain convertibility (after a period of postwar adjustment) with the dollar and other currencies but not with gold. The other countries agreed to maintain their exchange rates vis-à-vis the dollar within a 1 percent range on either side of the parity level. The differential responsibility of the United States as against other IMF members concerning convertibility into gold seemed sensible in that at the time the United States had approximately two thirds of the official world gold reserves.

Pegging the Exchange Rate

To see how a system of fixed exchange rates functions, we examine the way in which a country can "peg" or fix the level of its exchange rate. To do so we return to our two-country example and assume that the United States wants to fix its exchange rate against the mark, which we are using to represent the currencies of the rest of the world. We ignore the 1 percent margin just mentioned and assume that the U.S. central bank wishes to fix an exact par value for the dollar; let us say at an exchange rate of 1 mark equals 0.4 dollar (2.5 marks = 1 dollar). The working of the foreign exchange market with this fixed exchange rate system is illustrated in Figure 20.3.

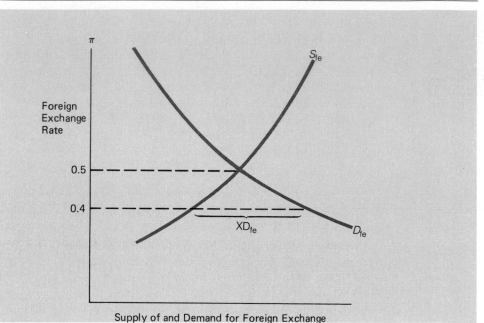

Supply of and Demand for Foreign Exchange

FIGURE 20.3   Foreign Exchange Market with Fixed Exchange Rate
If, in a fixed exchange rate system, the official exchange rate ($\pi = 0.4$) is below
the market equilibrium rate ($\pi = 0.5$), there will be an excess demand for foreign
exchange, XD_{fe}. To keep the exchange rate from rising, domestic or foreign central
banks must supply an amount of foreign exchange equal to XD_{fe}.

We assume that this official fixed exchange rate, 0.4 (1 mark = 0.4 dollar), is below the equilibrium exchange rate in a flexible rate system, the
equilibrium rate in Figure 20.3 being 0.5 (2 marks = 1 dollar). At the fixed
exchange rate in such a situation, the dollar would be said to be *overvalued*
and the mark *undervalued*. This means that, if the exchange rate were market
determined, the price of the mark relative to the dollar (the exchange rate)
would have to rise to clear the market. What prevents this from happening?

Recall that the demand and supply schedules that we constructed for the
foreign exchange market measure only *autonomous* transactions; they do not
take account of accommodating transactions undertaken by central banks to
finance payments imbalances. It is precisely such *intervention* by central banks
that is required to peg the exchange rate at a nonequilibrium value such as
0.4 dollar in Figure 20.3. To keep the rate at 0.4, the United States must stand
ready to buy and sell dollars at that exchange rate. If the U.S. central bank will
buy marks for 0.4 dollar the exchange rate cannot fall below that point since
no one would sell elsewhere for less. Similarly, the exchange rate cannot rise
above 0.4 since the central bank will be willing to sell marks at that price.

In the situation depicted in Figure 20.3, with the exchange rate below the equilibrium rate, there is an excess demand for foreign exchange (marks), shown as XD_{fe} in the figure. To keep the exchange rate from rising, the U.S. central bank must supply foreign exchange, that is, it must exchange marks for dollars in the foreign exchange market.

Alternatively, the German central bank (the Bundesbank) might be the one to intervene. This bank would supply marks (sell marks and buy dollars) to satisfy the excess demand for marks and keep the price of the mark at the official exchange rate of 0.4 dollar.

Implications of Intervention

There are two points to note concerning central bank intervention. The first concerns the effect on the U.S. balance of payments as a result of intervention in the foreign exchange market. Suppose it is the U.S. central bank that intervenes. Where does it get the marks that it sells to keep the exchange rate (price of the mark) from rising? (The Germans would be quite upset if we just printed some up.) Our central bank must use up its international reserve assets to buy marks from the German central bank in order to sell them in the foreign exchange market. This would show up in Table 20.1 as a reduction in U.S. official reserve assets.

If, alternatively, the German central bank supplied the marks directly in the foreign exchange market to satisfy the U.S. excess demand for foreign exchange, it would end up with increased holdings of dollars. In the U.S. balance of payments (Table 20.1), this would show up as an increase in foreign official assets in the United States. The sum of these two items (a reduction in U.S. official reserve assets and an increase in foreign official assets in the United States) equals the U.S. balance of payments *deficit*. This is a deficit because it is the amount by which our spending abroad (demand for foreign exchange) exceeds our earnings from abroad (supply of foreign exchange), taking account of only autonomous transactions (those reflected in the D_{fe} and S_{fe} curves). This deficit must be financed by central bank intervention if the official exchange rate is to be maintained.

Conversely, if, at the official exchange rate, the supply of foreign exchange exceeds the demand (there is an excess supply of foreign exchange), a country will have a surplus in the balance of payments. In this case, earnings from sales to foreign residents that produce the supply of foreign exchange exceed U.S. residents' expenditures abroad. When this is true for the United States, our official reserve assets increase or foreign official reserve assets in the United States decrease.

The second point to note about central bank intervention is that countries that must intervene continually to finance deficits will run out of official reserve assets. In our example, it is clear that if the United States financed its deficits by reductions in U.S. official assets, it would eventually exhaust its reserve holdings. But what if the deficit were financed by the German central bank, increasing its reserve assets in the United States by buying dollars? If the Germans continued to hold dollars, it would not affect our reserves. Under the Bretton Woods agreement, however, if they wished, the Germans could request that the U.S. buy back the dollars, using reserve assets (gold and SDRs). If they do, our reserves then fall.

To an extent, the United States was able to run continual balance of payments deficits during the Bretton Woods period because foreign central banks did not ask us to buy back dollars they had acquired in foreign exchange market interventions. At first, they did not do so because they wanted the dollars, which served as a reserve asset for them. (Remember, they were committed to maintaining the convertibility between their currency and the dollar.) Later on they did not ask us to redeem our dollars because they knew we couldn't do it; foreign dollar holdings far exceeded our reserves. This situation contributed to the collapse of the system, as we will see.

Countries other than the United States—Belgium, for example—could not run persistent deficits without losing their reserves more quickly. Since their currency, the Belgian franc, was not used as a reserve asset, other central banks would expect the Belgian government to buy back the francs they obtained in foreign exchange market intervention. To do so, Belgium would have to use up its official reserves (gold, SDRs, and U.S. dollars).

20.3 • THE CURRENT EXCHANGE RATE SYSTEM

The Bretton Woods system of fixed exchange rates collapsed in 1971. The current world system of exchange rate determination is best described as a *managed float* for major industrialized countries. Developing nations often have fixed exchange rate systems, although some allow exchange rate flexibility of varying degrees. A managed, or dirty float contains elements of a flexible exchange rate system (the float part) and a fixed rate system (the managed part). For a country with a managed float, the exchange rate is allowed to move in response to market forces. At times, however, the central bank does intervene to prevent *undesirable* or *disruptive* movements in the exchange rate. The question of how an undesirable or disruptive movement in the exchange rate has been defined in practice, and therefore when central banks choose to intervene in foreign exchange markets, will be considered presently. The factors that led to the breakdown of the Bretton Woods system are also discussed.

Current Exchange Rate Arrangements

Table 20.2 summarizes the exchange rate arrangements of the countries that are members of the IMF. As can be seen from the table, there is no one

TABLE 20.2   Exchange Rate Arrangement of IMF Members

Number of Fund Member Countries Whose Currencies:	March 31, 1990	
	(number)	(percent)
Are pegged to a single currency	53	35.1
Of which:		
U.S. dollar	34	22.5
French franc	14	9.3
Participate in the exchange rate mechanism	9	6.0
Are pegged to a composite of other currencies	41	27.2
Of which:		
SDR	7	4.6
Other	34	22.5
Managed floating and float independently or jointly	48	31.8
Total	151	100.0

Source: Jacob Frenkel and Morris Goldstein, "The Macroeconomic Policy Implications of Trade and Currency Zones," in Federal Reserve Bank of Kansas City, *Policy Implications of Trade and Currency Zones* (1991).

system of exchange rate determination. A number of countries, mostly the developing countries, peg their exchange rate to one currency, some to the U.S. dollar, some to the French franc. Others peg their exchange rate to a composite of other currencies. Nine European countries (including France, Germany, Italy, and the United Kingdom) participate in the European Monetary System. They maintain their exchange rates within a fixed range, one relative to the other, but these rates float as a group in relation to other world currencies. Japan, Canada, and the United States are among the group of countries listed as having floating exchange rates.

How Much Managing? How Much Floating?

In a managed float, central banks intervene in foreign exchange markets to prevent undesirable or disruptive movements in their exchange rates. Otherwise their exchange rates float. In the 1970s and 1980s, the degree to which the major industrialized countries intervened in the foreign exchange market varied significantly.

In the United States during the 1970s, there were frequent interventions in the foreign exchange market by the U.S. central bank. For example, in November 1978 there was a massive support program for the price of the dollar coordinated by the U.S. government. In 1981 the Reagan administration announced that central bank intervention would occur only when necessary to prevent disorder in the foreign exchange market initiated by crisis situations. Such situations were precipitated by events such as the shooting of President Reagan, the assassination of Egypt's President Sadat, or the declaration of martial law in Poland. Following this shift in the interpretation of what constituted a disruptive movement in the exchange rate, there was a marked decline in U.S. intervention in the foreign exchange market. During the first Reagan administration, there were periods of several quarters in which *no* intervention took place.

Even in the absence of U.S. central bank intervention, the price of the dollar does not float freely with the current exchange rate system. This is true because foreign central banks buy or sell dollars to influence the price of their currencies relative to the dollar. For example, in 1981 and again in 1984, European central banks sold dollars from their reserve holdings to slow the rise in the price of the dollar, which would have meant a fall in the price of their currencies (a rise in their exchange rate relative to the dollar). Then with the Plaza Accord in September of 1985, central banks of the large industrialized countries began concerted intervention with the aim of lowering the value of the dollar (raising the U.S. exchange rate). In 1987, for reasons that will be explained later, these central banks reversed course and intervened, again in concert, to prop up the dollar.

In the years since 1988, frequent intervention in the foreign exchange market by the Federal Reserve and other major central banks has continued. There have also been periodic meetings where *appropriate* levels for exchange rates have been discussed.

The Breakdown of the Bretton Woods System

We see from Table 20.2 that the current international monetary system is quite disorganized. Some call it a *nonsystem* and suggest a new Bretton Woods–type conference to reorganize it. How did this disorganization come about? In other words, what process led to the breakdown of the Bretton Woods fixed exchange rate system?

Central to the Bretton Woods system was the set of fixed exchange rates and the key currency role of the dollar. Par values set for currencies were not assumed to be fixed for all time; the Bretton Woods system was to be one of adjustable pegs. A country was to be able to change its exchange rate if it found that there was a "fundamental disequilibrium" in its balance of payments. Such changes were to be made in consultation with the IMF. Countries with chronic deficits would be expected to *devalue* their currencies, which means to lower the par value of the currency in terms of the dollar, and since the dollar's value in terms of gold was fixed, to also lower the currency's value in terms of gold. Countries with persistent surpluses would *revalue* their currencies at higher par values in terms of the dollar and gold.

In fact, adjustments in exchange rates proved extremely difficult. Countries with persistent surpluses were under no pressure to revalue their currencies. Governments of countries with persistent deficits found it politically difficult to devalue, since a decline in the value of the currency was taken as a sign of the failure of a government's economic policy. Also, rumors that a currency was to be devalued led to waves of speculation against the currency, as speculators sold the currency with an eye to buying it back after it had been devalued. Because of these difficulties in adjusting the par values of currencies, over the Bretton Woods period some countries (e.g., Great Britain) developed chronic balance of payments deficits and others (e.g., Germany), developed chronic surpluses.

Most damaging to the system, the United States developed into a chronic deficit country, an indication that the dollar was overvalued. To devalue the dollar, which since the dollar was convertible into gold at the fixed par value, meant a rise in the price of gold, presented special difficulties because of the key currency role played by the dollar within the Bretton Woods system. But the growing deficits in the U.S. balance of payments were creating a glut of dollars on the market. The problem became acute in the late 1960s and especially in 1971. Throughout the 1960s the United States had had deficits on the official reserve transactions balance. As long as such deficits were not too large, foreign central banks were willing to hold the dollars created by these deficits since the dollar served as a reserve currency. In this process, as described previously, foreign central banks intervened in the foreign exchange market. They sold their currency, obtained dollars, and held them as an official reserve asset. Such dollar reserves, which constituted claims on the United States, rose from $21.0 billion in 1960 to $38.5 billion in 1968. To some extent the deficits of the 1960s were also financed by a decline in U.S. official reserve assets. The U.S. official gold stock fell from $17.8 billion in 1960 to $10.9 billion in 1968.

In the late 1960s, the U.S. balance of payments position worsened. Severe inflationary pressure developed in the United States as a result of government spending on the Vietnam War, which was not adequately financed by increased taxes. This increased inflation worsened the U.S. balance of payments in the following way. Prices in the United States rose faster than prices in other industrial countries. With the exchange rate fixed, this meant that U.S. export goods became more expensive to foreigners while the price of foreign imports fell relative to domestic goods prices in the United States. As a consequence, the demand for U.S. exports fell and U.S. demand for imports rose; the U.S. balance of payments deficit increased. In 1971 the deficit on the official reserve transaction balance was $29.8 billion!

Foreign central banks could not continue to absorb so many dollar reserves. Nor could they demand payment from the United States in gold since the U.S. gold stock had fallen to $10.9 billion by 1968. The glut of dollars and the presumption that eventually the dollar would have to be devalued led to a lack of confidence in the dollar as reserve asset.

In 1972 the dollar was devalued, and the price of gold increased to $38. A new set of par values for other IMF member currencies was established. Attempts to defend the new set of par values had collapsed, however, by 1973. Again an upward surge of inflation in the United States and loss of confidence in the dollar were proximate causes of the problems in maintaining a set of fixed currency values. Also, beginning in 1973–74, huge increases in oil prices led to large balance of payments deficits for the industrialized oil-consuming nations and surpluses for the oil-producing countries. Exchange rate adjustments were required to restore equilibrium. The system of a managed float that emerged in the 1970s was the mechanism by which exchange rate adjustments necessitated by the declining strength of the dollar and rising oil prices were achieved.

20.4 • ADVANTAGES OF EXCHANGE RATE FLEXIBILITY

How has managed floating worked in practice? Should there be another Bretton Woods–type conference to reinstate a fixed exchange rate system? Or should we, as some propose, set up a system more organized than the current one but with more flexibility than a fixed exchange rate system such as the Bretton Woods system? To analyze these questions we begin by considering the arguments that were given in the early 1970s (and before) in favor of greater flexibility of exchange rates; what was expected from a managed float? Then we turn to a description of the U.S. experience with a floating exchange rate; what have we learned from nearly two decades of managed floating? With this as background we turn to a discussion of the relative merit of different exchange rate systems.

Two advantages cited for greater flexibility of exchange rates were[7]

1. Flexibility of exchange rates would allow policymakers to concentrate on domestic goals, free of worries about balance of payments deficits. Exchange rate flexibility would remove potential conflicts that arise between *internal balance* (domestic goals) and *external balance* (balance of payments equilibrium).

2. Flexible exchange rates would insulate the domestic economy from economic shocks that originate abroad.

---

[7]A classic statement of the advantages of flexible exchange rates is Milton Friedman, "The Case for Flexible Exchange Rates," in *Essays in Positive Economics* (Chicago: University of Chicago Press, 1957).

Policy Independence and Exchange Rate Flexibility

Our earlier analysis indicated that if a nation's central bank intervened in the foreign exchange market to finance a balance of payments deficit, it would lose official reserve assets. Continuing deficits would then lead eventually to the central bank running out of reserves. Before this happened the central bank would have to take policy actions with an aim to eliminating the balance of payments deficit. This is where the possible conflict comes between domestic goals and balance of payments equilibrium.

To see the nature of the conflict more clearly we examine how the main balance of payments items are related to the level of domestic economic activity.

The Trade Balance and the Level of Economic Activity

Figure 20.4 plots imports (Z) and exports (X) on the vertical axis and the level of domestic national income on the horizontal axis.

The import schedule is drawn sloping upward since the demand for imports depends positively on income. This follows because consumption

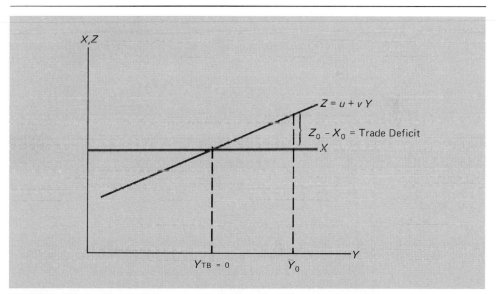

FIGURE 20.4 Trade Balance and the Level of Economic Activity
The level of income which equates imports (Z) with the exogenous level of exports (X) is $Y_{TB=0}$. There is no reason to believe that the equilibrium level of income is equal to $Y_{TB=0}$. For example, if $\overline{Y}_0$ is the equilibrium level of income, imports will exceed exports and there will be a deficit in the trade balance ($Z_0 - X_0$).

depends positively on income. As income rises consumption of imported goods as well as domestic ones increases. Also, as domestic national income increases more imported inputs will be needed (e.g., imported crude oil).

In contrast, the export schedule is horizontal. The demand for U.S. exports will be a part of the foreign demand for imports. The foreign demand for imports will depend on the level of *foreign* income. From the point of view of this country, foreign income and, hence, the demand for our exports is exogenous.

Additional variables that one would expect to influence both U.S. demand for imports and foreign demand of U.S. exports are the relative price levels in the two countries and the level of the exchange rate. These variables will determine the relative costs of the two countries' products to citizens of either country. Note that for now we are assuming that price levels and the exchange rate are fixed. The effects on imports and exports of changes in the domestic price level or exchange rate are examined later.

As shown in Figure 20.4, exports and imports will be equal if income is at the level $Y_{TB=0}$ (the trade balance will be zero). This level of income generates import demand just equal to the exogenous level of exports. But, notice that there is no reason to expect that $Y_{TB=0}$ will be an equilibrium level of income. The equilibrium level of income will be determined by aggregate demand and supply in the economy, not by the foreign sector alone. For example, in Figure 20.4 assume that the equilibrium level of income is at $\overline{Y}_0$, above $Y_{TB=0}$. At income level $\overline{Y}_0$, imports exceed exports and there is a trade deficit.

We have seen in earlier chapters how aggregate demand management policies can, at least in the Keynesian view, be used to affect equilibrium income. Such policies could then in principle be used to move equilibrium income to the level $Y_{TB=0}$, where exports equal imports. If the other current account items and the capital account were in balance, this would be a position of what we call *external balance* for the economy, which, in a fixed exchange rate system, means balance of payments equilibrium (official reserve transactions deficit equals zero). In terms of Figure 20.4, the policymaker could, for example, use a restrictive fiscal policy such as a tax increase to reduce income from $\overline{Y}_0$ to $Y_{TB=0}$.

But policymakers also have domestic goals. Within the Keynesian framework, aggregate demand management policies are to be used to pursue unemployment and inflation goals—to achieve *internal balance*. The problem, and the important point to note here, is that there is no reason to believe that the level of income which produces external balance is the optimal level with regard to domestic goals. Suppose, for example, that in Figure 20.4, the optimal level from the point of view of domestic goals is $\overline{Y}_0$. If a restrictive fiscal policy were used to lower income $Y_{TB=0}$, an undesirably high unemployment rate would result and internal balance would be disturbed. But if income is maintained at $\overline{Y}_0$, there will be a trade deficit; the economy will not have external balance.

We see then that *under a fixed exchange rate system, potential conflicts arise between the goals of internal balance and external balance.* In particular, countries may find that expansionary policies, which might be desirable from the point of view of reducing the unemployment rate, lead to income levels too high to balance the trade account and may therefore lead to balance of payments problems.

Capital Flows and the Level of Economic Activity

The primary determinants of the level of capital flows between nations are expected rates of return on assets in each of the countries. With a fixed exchange rate system the effects of expected exchange rate movements on asset returns can be ignored (except at times when there is speculation that the official exchange rate is to change). Interest rates in the various countries will be measures of relative rates of return. If we take the rate of return in other countries as given, the level of the capital flow into a particular country will depend positively on the level of its interest rate (r); that is,

$$F = F(r) \qquad (20.1)$$

where F is the net capital inflow (a negative value of F represents a net outflow or deficit on capital account).[8] The way in which changes in the level of economic activity affect the balance on the capital account will therefore depend on how the interest rate varies with the change in economic activity.

Consider, first, increases in economic activity caused by expansionary monetary policies. An expansionary monetary policy will stimulate aggregate demand and, hence, income by *lowering* the rate of interest. The effect of the lower rate of interest will be unfavorable to the balance on capital account. The amount of investment in the United States by foreigners will decline and U.S. investment abroad will increase as foreign assets become relatively more attractive. (Remember here that the foreign interest rate is assumed to be unchanged.) In the preceding section we saw that increases in income for any reason increased imports while leaving exports unchanged and therefore worsened the trade balance. If the increase in income is the result of an expansionary monetary policy, it follows that both the trade balance and the capital account will deteriorate.

---

[8]Capital flows include purchases of shares of stock in other countries and direct investments as well as purchases of bonds, the asset that earns the interest rate (r). Thus, other variables that influence the expected returns on stocks and direct investments might be included in a more complex specification of the capital flow function. For simplicity, we restrict our attention here to the simple function (20.1).

Now suppose, alternatively, that the increase in economic activity was the result of an expansionary fiscal policy or another nonmonetary shock to aggregate demand such as an autonomous increase in (domestic physical) investment. As income rises there is a consequent increase in the demand for money, and with a fixed money stock the interest rate will rise (see Section 7.1). In this case the increase in income is accompanied by an increase in the interest rate. Consequently, while the balance of trade worsens, the rise in the interest rate will stimulate a capital inflow. Whether the overall effect on the balance of payments is favorable or unfavorable depends on the relative strength of these two effects of the fiscal policy–induced expansion: the favorable effect on the capital account or the unfavorable effect on the trade balance.

We therefore find that in a fixed exchange rate system, conflicts may arise between domestic goals such as low unemployment and the goal of external balance as measured by balance of payments equilibrium. The conflict is especially severe with respect to monetary policy, where expansionary policy actions have unfavorable effects on both the trade balance and the capital account. Expansionary fiscal policies may also lead to balance of payments problems if their unfavorable effect on the trade balance outweighs their favorable effect on the capital account.

A final linkage between the balance of payments and the level of economic activity is through the price level. Unless the economy is far from full employment, expansionary aggregate demand policies, whether monetary or fiscal in nature, will cause the price level to rise. With a fixed exchange rate, an increase in the domestic price level will, for a constant foreign price level, increase imports and cause exports to decline. Foreign goods will be relatively cheaper to U.S. citizens and U.S. exports will be more expensive to foreign buyers. This *price effect* on the balance of trade reinforces the directly unfavorable effect that an economic expansion has on the trade balance for *both* monetary and fiscal policies.

Flexible Exchange Rates and Insulation from Foreign Shocks

The alleviation of conflicts that arise between internal and external balance in a fixed exchange rate system is one advantage that has been cited for a flexible exchange rate system. A further and related advantage claimed for a flexible exchange rate system is that it will insulate an economy from certain shocks. To see the reasoning behind this claim, consider the example of a country that is initially in a state of macroeconomic bliss, with an optimal level of unemployment, an optimum price level, and equilibrium in the balance of payments. Now suppose there is a recession abroad and foreign income declines. Since import demand by foreigners, which is the demand for this country's exports, depends on foreign income, it will fall with the foreign recession. In the foreign exchange market this decline in export

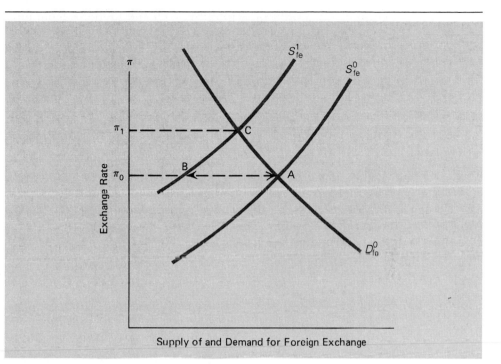

FIGURE 20.5   Insulation of the Domestic Economy in a Flexible Exchange Rate System
A foreign recession results in a fall in exports and a shift to the left in the supply of foreign exchange schedule from S_{fe}^0 to S_{fe}^1. With a fixed exchange rate system there will be a balance of payments deficit (A − B). In a flexible exchange rate system, the exchange rate will rise to π_1 to clear the foreign exchange market.

demand will show up as a shift to the left in the supply of foreign exchange schedule. As shown in Figure 20.5, the supply curve shifts from S_{fe}^0 to S_{fe}^1 as a result of the foreign recession.

In a fixed exchange rate system, the country would find itself with a balance of payments deficit equal to distance A−B in Figure 20.5. Also, since export demand is a portion of aggregate demand (the foreign demand for domestic output), the recession abroad will have contractionary effects on the domestic economy; aggregate demand falls and income declines.[9]

In a system of flexible exchange rates the excess demand for foreign exchange (equal to the balance of payments deficit A−B), which resulted from the foreign recession would cause the exchange rate to rise. The new

---

[9]This is a good point at which to review the appendix to Chapter 5, which explains the effects that changes in imports and exports have on aggregate demand.

equilibrium would be at point C with the higher exchange rate π_1. The increase in the exchange rate eliminates the balance of payment deficit. Notice another aspect of the adjustment to a new equilibrium. As we go to point C, the increase in the exchange rate stimulates export demand and lowers import demand. This increase in exports induced by the rise in the exchange rate will have an expansionary effect by increasing aggregate demand. The reduction in imports that is caused by the rise in the exchange rate will also be expansionary; domestic aggregate demand will increase as residents switch from buying imports to buying domestic goods.

In the flexible exchange rate case, we see then that the adjustment in the exchange rate works to offset *the contractionary effect on the domestic economy that comes as the result of a foreign recession.* It is in this sense that a system of flexible exchange rates works to insulate an economy from certain external shocks.

20.5 • U.S. EXPERIENCE WITH FLOATING EXCHANGE RATES

How has the system of floating exchange rates worked during the post-1973 period? To consider this question, let us start by looking at the behavior of the U.S. exchange rate over these years. Figure 20.6 plots the price of the German mark measured in U.S. cents over the 1973–91 period. The price of the mark is the analog to π in previous graphs, where π was the price of foreign

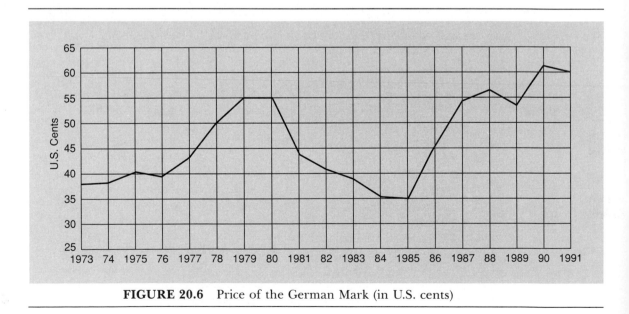

FIGURE 20.6 Price of the German Mark (in U.S. cents)

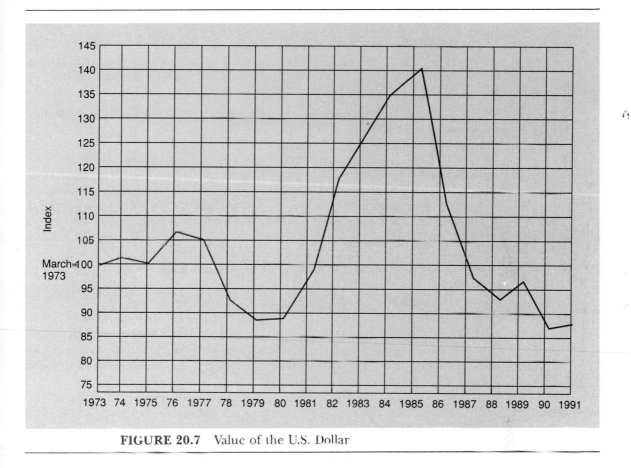

FIGURE 20.7   Value of the U.S. Dollar

exchange in our two-country (Germany and the United States) model. Figure 20.7 shows a more comprehensive measure of the relative price of U.S. currency, the *effective exchange rate,* which measures the *value of the U.S. dollar* relative to a weighted average of other currencies. The weights given to the currencies of other countries depend on their importance in U.S. foreign trade. It is important to note here that what we are measuring in Figure 20.7 is the *value of the dollar,* which is the inverse of the *price of foreign exchange,* for example, when the value of the dollar rises, π (the price of foreign exchange) falls.

From Figures 20.6 and 20.7, it can be seen that the U.S. exchange rate has been quite volatile during the floating rate period. Were we to look at monthly instead of annual values we would also observe substantial variations in exchange rates, with changes in excess of 2 percent per month the norm rather than the exception. This volatility of exchange rates in both the short and medium run is one argument used against flexibility of exchange rates, as we will see in the next section.

It can also be seen, looking at either figure, that there were three sharp swings in the value of the dollar during these years. There was a substantial fall in the value of the dollar (rise in the exchange rate) in the late 1970s. The 1980s then witnessed a spectacular rise in the value of the dollar (1981–85) followed by a sharp fall (1985–88).

The Dollar in Decline, 1976–80

An important factor determining the behavior of exchange rates among the industrialized countries in the mid- to late-1970s was their different responses to the oil price shocks of the period. As we saw in Chapter 8, countries confronted with an unfavorable supply shock, such as the fourfold increase in the price of oil in 1973–74, had to choose the degree to which their aggregate demand policy would *accommodate* the shock. To accommodate, in this context, means to expand aggregate demand to try to offset the unfavorable output and employment effects of the supply shocks. The cost of such accommodation is higher inflation.

Although other factors were certainly at work during the 1975–80 period, the currencies of countries that chose more accommodation, especially through expansionary monetary policy, tended to depreciate relative to those that had little or no accommodation. To see why, let us examine the effects that an expansionary monetary policy has in the foreign exchange market in a flexible exchange rate system, as illustrated in Figure 20.8.[10]

In the figure we assume that the initial position of the supply and demand curves for foreign exchange are given by S_{fe}^0 and D_{fe}^0, respectively. The initial equilibrium exchange rate is therefore at π_0 where these curves intersect.

Now consider the effects of an expansionary monetary policy. The expansionary monetary policy will reduce the domestic interest rate and increase domestic income and the price level. As discussed previously, the demand for imports will rise as a result of both the increase in income and the increase in the domestic price level. Further, the decline in the domestic interest rate will make domestic assets less attractive and domestic investors will shift to foreign assets. The increase in both the demand for imported goods and foreign assets represents increased demand for foreign exchange. In terms

---

[10] It is true that the U.S. exchange rate was not completely flexible during these years. There was a managed float and, as discussed previously, the U.S. central bank did intervene frequently in the foreign exchange market in the 1970s. Still, during the 1970s and 1980s, while intervention by the U.S. and foreign central banks may have affected the exchange rate over short periods, over periods of several years such as those we are considering, market forces determined the movements of exchange rates.

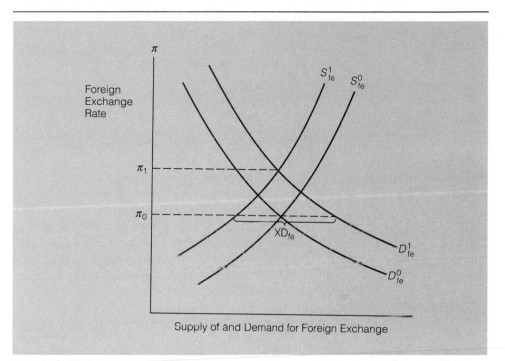

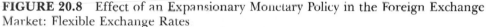

FIGURE 20.8 Effect of an Expansionary Monetary Policy in the Foreign Exchange Market: Flexible Exchange Rates
An expansionary monetary policy shifts the demand curve for foreign exchange to the right from D_{fe}^0 to D_{fe}^1 and shifts the supply curve for foreign exchange to the left from S_{fe}^0 to S_{fe}^1. The exchange rate rises to π_1 to clear the foreign exchange market and therefore eliminate the excess demand for foreign exchange (XD_{fe}).

of Figure 20.8, the demand schedule for foreign exchange will shift from D_{fe}^0 to D_{fe}^1 as a result of the expansionary monetary policy. The expansionary monetary policy will also affect the supply of foreign exchange. The monetary policy–induced decline in the interest rate will cause foreign investors to buy fewer of the country's assets, and the rise in the domestic price level will reduce export demand. The supply of foreign exchange schedule in Figure 20.8 will shift from S_{fe}^0 to S_{fe}^1.

With a flexible exchange rate system, the increase in demand and decline in supply in the foreign exchange market as a result of the expansionary monetary policy will cause the exchange rate to rise. As the exchange rate rises, the quantity of foreign exchange demanded will fall and the quantity of foreign exchange supplied will increase. A new equilibrium will be reached at exchange rate π_1, where the demand and supply for foreign exchange are again equal.

We see, then, that in a flexible exchange rate system, an expansionary monetary policy causes the exchange rate to rise (the value of the domestic currency to fall). Figure 20.8 considers the action of one country in isolation. Applied to the behavior of the major industrialized countries in the late 1970s, this analysis suggests that those countries which followed the more accommodative and therefore more expansionary monetary policies would have caused their exchange rates to rise (their currencies to depreciate). Those that accommodated less would have seen their exchange rates fall (their currencies appreciate).

The rise in the U.S. exchange rate, measured as the price of the German mark (see Figure 20.6), over the 1976–80 period can be attributed to a higher degree of accommodative aggregate demand policy in the United States relative to Germany. The fall in the value of the dollar measured more generally against other trading partners during this period indicates that U.S. policy was among the more expansionary ones in these countries. Switzerland, for example, showed no indication of accommodating the supply shocks of the 1970s by means of an expansion in demand, and the Swiss franc appreciated by 54 percent relative to the dollar between 1975 and 1980. At the opposite end of the spectrum, Italy followed a more expansionary monetary policy than the United States, and the Italian lira depreciated by 24 percent relative to the dollar during this period.[11]

The Rising Dollar, 1981–85

Beginning in 1981, the dollar reversed course and began to rise sharply in value relative to other major currencies, as can be seen in Figure 20.7. This meant that our exchange rate *fell* over this period, as can be seen from Figure 20.6. Between 1980 and the peak in the dollar's value in early 1985, the mark fell from a price of 55 cents (fewer than 2 per dollar) to 31 cents (more than 3 per dollar), a drop of 44 percent. Against the trade-weighted average of foreign currencies (Figure 20.7), the dollar rose by 64 percent.

If a relatively expansionary aggregate demand policy was important to the declining value of the dollar in the late 1970s, what explains the reversal in the early 1980s? Did aggregate demand policy in the United States become restrictive relative to the policies of Germany and its other trading partners?

Although there is considerable disagreement about the factors causing the rise in the value of the dollar, one explanation does see restrictive *monetary*

---

[11]The relative inflation rates for these four countries provide evidence on the differing degrees to which they accommodated the supply shocks of the period. The German and Swiss inflation rates for the 1975–80 period averaged 4.1 and 2.3 percent, respectively. The average U.S. inflation rate was 8.9 percent whereas the Italian inflation rate was still higher at 16.3 percent.

policy, and the resulting high interest rates, as the primary cause of the dollar's rise in value. Especially beginning with the recovery from the 1981–82 recession in 1983, however, aggregate demand policy in the United States was not, on the whole, less expansionary than in the other industrialized countries. This was because U.S. *fiscal* policy was very expansionary. This policy *mix,* a combination of tight monetary policy and easy fiscal policy, is seen as the cause of the rising dollar at a time when the recovery in the United States was more rapid than in other major industrialized countries. How might a tight-monetary, easy-fiscal policy mix lead to a rising dollar even with a strong U.S. expansion? The restrictive monetary policy would lead to a rise in the value of the dollar (fall in the U.S. exchange rate). The analysis here would be just the reverse of that in Figure 20.8. High U.S. interest rates would increase the net capital inflow. Moreover, the restrictive monetary policy would lower the level of income, thereby lowering imports. Finally, other things being equal, a more restrictive monetary policy would lead to a lower domestic inflation rate, further discouraging imports and encouraging exports.

Clearly these changes indicate that the demand for foreign exchange will fall and the supply rise; therefore, the exchange rate should fall and the value of the dollar should rise. But just as clearly, other things being equal, a country with a more restrictive monetary policy than its trading partners will have less robust rates of economic expansion.

The other unequal factor is fiscal policy. An expansionary fiscal policy will, because of positive effects on income and the domestic price level, encourage imports and discourage exports (through the price level effect). The expansionary fiscal policy will, however, result in higher interest rates and therefore increase the net *inflow* of capital. Consequently, whether an expansionary fiscal policy will, on balance, cause an excess demand for foreign exchange (through the import and export effects) or a net excess supply (through the increase in the capital inflow) is uncertain. Of itself, an expansionary fiscal policy may raise or lower the exchange rate (with the opposite effect on the value of the dollar).

The U.S. experience over the first half of the 1980s is consistent with a pattern in which either the expansionary fiscal policy contributed to the rise in the value of the dollar or, if it would by itself have lowered the value of the dollar, this effect was overwhelmed by the restrictive monetary policy. Although monetary policy effects are assumed to have been predominant in pushing up the price of the dollar, domestically, fiscal policy effects were sufficiently strong to have generated a fairly robust recovery.

One additional factor which may be important in explaining the rise in the dollar's value, especially near its peak in late 1984 and early 1985 is *speculative* buying of U.S. financial assets. In Section 20.2 it was pointed out that the demand for foreign assets does not depend on the *level* of

PERSPECTIVES
20.1

THE WORLD'S LARGEST DEBTOR

To say that foreign investors purchase our assets is to say that we borrow from abroad. The federal government raises funds, for example, by selling bonds. When those bonds are purchased by foreign investors, they become part of our external (foreign) debt.

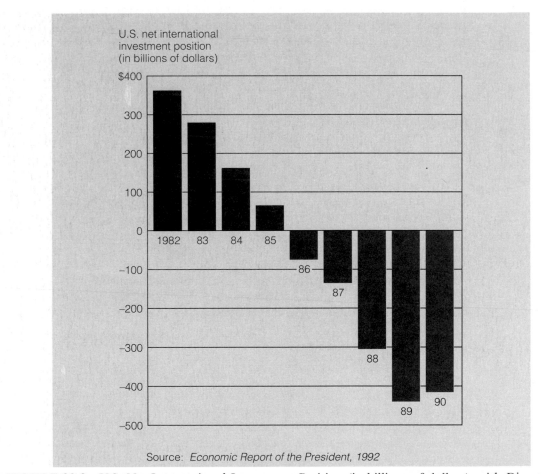

Source: *Economic Report of the President, 1992*

FIGURE 20.9 U.S. Net International Investment Position (in billions of dollars), with Direct Investment Valued at Current Cost

U.S. corporations raise funds for investment by selling bonds and stocks (equities). If these are sold to foreign investors, they are also part of our external debt. Interest and dividends must be paid to foreign investors by both the government and U.S. corporations.

During the 1980s, foreign investors greatly increased their holdings of U.S. assets. U.S. investors did continue to buy foreign assets, but not as fast as foreign investors bought U.S. assets. As a result, our net investment position (U.S. holdings of foreign assets minus foreign holdings of our assets) went from one of a net creditor nation to that of a net debtor. This transition is charted in Figure 20.9. By the end of 1990 foreign holdings of our assets (our debt) exceeded U.S. holdings of foreign assets by $412 billion. The United States had become the world's largest debtor.

Should we worry? While few see cause for panic, many observers are concerned about the size of the U.S. external debt. The debt is still relatively small compared to the size of the U.S. economy. At the end of 1990, it was approximately 8 percent of GDP. This compares to an external debt of 50 percent of GDP or more for large debtors among developing nations such as Brazil, Argentina, and Mexico. One concern about the debt is that foreign investors will at some point pull out of U.S. assets. If there were a *sudden shift* to foreign assets, our exchange rate would rise rapidly (as investors sold dollars) and there would be upward pressure on our interest rate (as U.S. firms and the government sought domestic lenders). Even in the absence of such a shift, there is the belief that foreign investment on the scale of the 1980s will not be available in the 1990s. The introduction of market economies in Eastern Europe and the Soviet Union has resulted in huge demands for capital in these regions. As capital flows elsewhere, less investment in the United States by countries such as Germany and Japan is expected. With projected continued high U.S. government deficits, this is another factor that would put upward pressure on U.S. interest rates.

the exchange rate. If, for example, the exchange rate rose from one level to a higher level, say 10 percent higher, then the foreign asset would cost 10 percent more in domestic currency, but the interest payment on the asset would be 10 percent higher, again expressed in the domestic currency. The percentage return on the asset would be the same at either *level* of the exchange rate.

What would matter for asset demands, however, are *expected changes* in the exchange rate. If the U.S. exchange rate were expected to fall (the value of the dollar were expected to rise), foreign investors would want to buy U.S. financial assets now. A German investor, for example, would buy U.S. financial assets now because he expects the dollar to rise relative to the mark, enabling him to sell the asset later and receive more marks. In buying dollars with which to purchase the U.S. assets the German investor is *speculating* on a future rise in the dollar's value. Some believe that, near its peak in early 1985, such speculative buying of dollars was the only factor explaining its continued rise.

Read Perspectives 20.1.

The Dollar's Slide (1985–88)

In October 1985, the finance ministers of five of the largest free market economies (the so-called G-5, or group of five) met at the Plaza Hotel in New York. At the meeting they agreed jointly to intervene in the foreign exchange market to bring down the value of the dollar. The central banks in these countries would do so by selling dollars from their reserve stocks (buying their own currencies) in the foreign exchange market, therefore increasing the supply of dollars (reducing the supply of foreign currencies) and driving the price of the dollar down.

Other factors were driving down the value of the dollar as well. Just as speculative buying of dollars had contributed to the rise of the dollar, with fear of central bank intervention and other signs of weakness, speculative selling began in 1986 to contribute to the dollar's fall. The dollar had risen so high that few believed its value was sustainable. Additionally, as the economic expansion in the United States slowed, monetary policy here became less restrictive and the U.S. interest rate fell. Relative to those of some European countries, U.S. financial assets were no longer so attractive.

By 1987, relative to the weighted average of foreign currencies (Figure 20.7), the value of the dollar had fallen 32 percent from its peak in 1985. In February the finance ministers met again, this time in Paris, and reached what has been called the *Louvre Accord*. They decided that the dollar had fallen far enough. They agreed to use foreign exchange market intervention to try to maintain their exchange rates within ranges around their then current values. At first these efforts were not successful, and the value of the dollar continued to fall throughout 1987. In 1988, however, as central bank intervention continued, the value of the dollar stabilized.

The Dollar Since 1988

The period since 1988 has not seen another dramatic swing in the U.S. exchange rate. The value of the dollar has fallen over these years (the exchange rate has risen), but by a modest amount. Relative to the German mark, for example, the cumulative fall in the value of the dollar between 1988 and 1991 was 8 percent. Of relevance to our discussion in the next section, however, is the fact that on a month-to-month basis the value of the dollar continued to show considerable volatility.

20.6 • FIXED VERSUS FLEXIBLE EXCHANGE RATES

The relative merits of fixed versus flexible exchange rates have long been debated by economists and central bankers. To provide a context in which to discuss this question, it was first necessary to explain the interrelationships between the balance of payments and the level of economic activity as well as the potential conflicts between the goals of internal and external balance that can arise in a fixed exchange rate system. Also necessary was some information about how the floating rate system has worked in practice. With this background, let us assess the arguments on each side of the issue. First, we consider the arguments advanced in favor of flexible exchange rates in light of the post-1973 experience with greater exchange rate flexibility. Then we examine arguments offered in favor of a fixed exchange rate system.

Greater Policy Independence

As discussed previously, a major advantage cited in favor of flexible exchange rates is that such a system will eliminate the conflicts that arise in a fixed rate system between internal and external balance. In a flexible rate system, the exchange rate will adjust to clear the foreign exchange market. Monetary and fiscal policy can be used to pursue domestic goals free from balance of payments constraints.

The post-1973 experience does show some evidence of flexibility on the part of nations to try to pursue independent domestic policies. These different domestic policies resulted in sustained movements in the countries' exchange rates. For example, we saw that industrialized countries *accommodated* the supply shocks of the 1970s to varying degrees, necessitating large changes in the relative values of their currencies. Also, in the 1980s, the Reagan administration mix of a tight-monetary–easy-fiscal policy deviated sharply from the policies of other industrialized nations. The result was a sharp rise in the value of the dollar.

Countries can, however, conduct policy without considering policy effects in the foreign exchange market only if they are indifferent to the behavior of their exchange rate.

For a number of reasons, governments have not been indifferent to exchange rate movements. A rising exchange rate (falling value of the domestic currency), for example, will fuel inflation by making imports more expensive (including imported raw materials). This rising exchange rate also indirectly fuels inflation by reducing the degree of competition faced by domestic producers of import competing goods. In the other direction, a falling exchange rate (rising value of the domestic currency) reduces the competitiveness of a country's exports on the world market. This was the situation in the United States during the first half of the 1980s. By 1985, with a burgeoning trade deficit, the Reagan administration was cooperating with other countries with the aim of lowering the dollar's value; the exchange rate had itself become a policy target.

None of this is to say that the move to greater exchange rate flexibility has not resulted in greater independence for countries in pursuing domestic goals; it has. However, the degree of independence achieved has been limited.

Greater Insulation from Foreign Shocks

The second prospective advantage for flexible exchange rates discussed in Section 20.4 was insulation from foreign shocks. As with policy independence, the experience of the post-1970 period demonstrated that there were limits to the benefits a system of flexible exchange rates provides in this area as well.

The inflationary recession that affected all industrialized, oil-consuming nations after the 1974 oil price shock showed that greater exchange rate flexibility would not shield countries from such *real* or supply-side shocks. The greater insulation from foreign shocks is limited to the type of *demand*-side shocks that come from a foreign recession in the manner analyzed in Figure 20.5. Even on the demand side, the recession of the early 1980s, which most (not all) economists believe originated on the demand side, spread to all the major industrialized countries.

Overall, considering both greater policy independence and insulation from some foreign shocks, an advocate of flexible rates might agree with international economist Richard Cooper's assessment:

> I conclude that the experience under floating exchange rates has been a reasonably good one. It is worth keeping in mind that the smoothness of a ride depends on the size of the bumps in the road as well as on the quality of the shock absorbers. If we abstract from sharp day-to-day movements, floating exchange rates performed about as well as one would have expected, given the disturbances.[12]

Arguments for a Return to a Fixed Rate System

Not all economists and certainly not all central bankers view the current system so favorably. In recent years there have been calls for a new Bretton Woods–type conference to set up a system with less flexibility in exchange rates. Given the at least limited advantages of a flexible exchange rate system in freeing domestic policy instruments from a balance-of-payments constraint and insulating an economy from certain foreign shocks, what case can be made for the alternative of a fixed rate system?

---

[12]Richard Cooper, "Flexible Exchange Rates 1973–80" in Richard Cooper, *The International Monetary System: Essays in World Economics* (Cambridge, Mass.: MIT Press, 1987).

Advocates of fixed exchange rates believe that such a system will provide a more stable environment for growth in world trade and international investment. They also argue that the combination of a fixed exchange rate system and increased policy coordination among industrialized economies will lead to increased macroeconomic stability.

After the breakdown of a previous fixed exchange rate system early in the 1930s, the world economy went through a period of freely fluctuating exchange rates. On the basis of that experience Norwegian economist Ragnar Nurkse made the case against flexible exchange rates as follows:

> Freely fluctuating exchange rates involve three serious disadvantages. In the first place they create an element of risk which tends to discourage international trade. The risk may be covered by "hedging" operations where a forward exchange market exists; but such insurance, if obtainable at all, is obtainable only at a price....
>
> Secondly, as a means of adjusting the balance of payments, exchange fluctuations involve constant shifts of labor and other resources between production for the home market and production for export. Such shifts may be costly and disturbing; they tend to create frictional unemployment, and are obviously wasteful if exchange-market conditions that call for them are temporary....
>
> Thirdly, experience has shown that fluctuating exchanges cannot always be relied upon to promote adjustment. A considerable if continuous movement of the exchange rate is liable to generate anticipations of a further movement in the same direction, thus giving rise the speculative capital transfers of a disequilibrating kind.[13]

Let's consider each of these purported flaws in light of the post–1973 experience with fluctuating exchange rates.

Exchange Rate Risk and Trade

In addition to the broad swings in exchange rates, such as those shown for the dollar in Figures 20.6 and 20.7, exchange rates have also been volatile in the short run, with changes of 5 percent in a month or 20 percent in a year quite common. This poses a risk, for example, to a domestic exporter or an investor who plans a foreign investment, such as a plant, in another country. Some such risks can be hedged in the *forward market* for foreign exchange. A U.S. exporter who is to receive Japanese yen in three months can contract to trade those yen for dollars at a price that is set today.

But not all exchange risk in foreign trade and investment can be easily hedged. If a U.S. firm is deciding whether to enter the export market, which

---

[13] Quoted in Peter Kenen, "Macroeconomic Theory and Policy: How the Closed Economy Was Opened," in Ronald Jones and Peter Kenen, eds., *Handbook of International Economics*, Vol. II. (Amsterdam: North Holland, 1985).

involves costs such as establishing foreign business contacts and foreign advertising, it must consider the future prospects of the dollar. A future rise in the value of the dollar may, for example, make the firm's product noncompetitive in the export market. Fluctuations in the exchange rate are then an additional source of risk. Similarly, a U.S. firm planning to build a plant in a foreign country to produce for the foreign market would want to know the exchange rate to know what the plant would earn in terms of dollars. Exchange rate risk would again be a factor.

Fluctuating exchange rates do add risks to foreign trade and investment, not all of which can be easily hedged. Whether these risks seriously discourage such activities is a question that has not yet been definitely answered.

Exchange Rate Swings and Adjustment Costs

Nurkse's second argument was that exchange rate fluctuations, such as those shown in Figures 20.6 and 20.7, would cause resources to be shifted in and out of export industries, with consequent adjustment costs including frictional unemployment. As the value of the U.S. dollar rose in the early 1980s our export performance did suffer. Then as the value of the dollar fell and our export performance improved, problems arose for German and Japanese exporters.

The adjustment costs that accompanied the wide swings in the value of the U.S. dollar in the 1980s were probably the most important source of the growing discontent with flexible exchange rates.

Speculation and Exchange Rate Instability

The last of Nurkse's arguments was that freely fluctuating exchange rates would lead to destabilizing speculation in foreign exchange markets. We saw in the previous section that this type of speculation is thought by some to have been a factor in the height to which the dollar rose in 1985. Investors in financial assets saw the dollar rising, and believing it would rise even more, they demanded dollar-denominated assets. This demand put further upward pressure on the value of the dollar. To the degree that such speculation magnifies exchange rate movements, it exacerbates the problems discussed in the previous two subsections.

Alternatives to Flexible Exchange Rates

The most widely discussed proposals to change the current system of exchange rates are of two types. One is a new explicit system of fixed exchange rates. The other is a more flexible system of adjustable *target zones* for exchange rates. To be specific we will outline one proposal of each type: Ronald

McKinnon's fixed rate proposal and Edison, Miller, and Williamson's target zone proposal.[14]

The McKinnon Standard

The heart of McKinnon's proposal is an agreement among the United States, Japan, and Germany to fix the dollar, mark, yen exchange rates within a 10 percent range. Once these exchange rates are fixed they would not be changed. McKinnon's proposal is for permanently fixed rates, not adjustable pegs as originally envisioned for the Bretton Woods system. With these key exchange rates fixed, McKinnon sees other countries pegging their exchange rates to the dollar, mark, or yen. All three of these currencies would be used as international reserves, together with SDRs and gold.

The Target Zone Proposal

The Edison, Miller, and Williamson proposal calls for target zones for exchange rates among major industrialized countries. These zones would be wider than the range proposed for McKinnon's fixed rates system, perhaps 20 percent rather than 10 percent. Also the zones would be adjustable at specified intervals.

Williamson argues that "target zones offer escape from the major costs of floating while retaining the important advantages that flexible rates offer." We have seen, for example, that flexible exchange rates free monetary policy to pursue domestic goals. By allowing a fairly wide target zone and allowing for periodic changes, the target zone proposal seeks to retain that advantage. By committing participating countries to keep the exchange rate within the zone, the target zone approach aims at decreasing the volatility of exchange rates that has characterized the post-1973 period.

Policy Coordination

Both McKinnon's proposal for fixed exchange rates and the target zone proposal call for increased coordination of monetary and fiscal policy among industrialized countries. In McKinnon's proposal the United States, Japan, and Germany would also agree to use monetary and fiscal policy, each to stabilize its domestic producer price index—to set a zero-inflation target for this price index.

---

[14] For discussion of these proposals, see Ronald I. McKinnon, "Monetary and Exchange Rate Policies for International Financial Stability: A Proposal"; Rudiger Dornbusch, "Doubts about the McKinnon Standard"; and John Williamson, "Comment on McKinnon's Monetary Rule," *Journal of Economic Perspectives,* 2 (Winter 1988), pp. 83–119.

The Edison, Miller, and Williamson proposal also involves "a comprehensive set of rules for policy coordination among the main industrialized countries."[15] According to these rules, average world interest rate levels, interest rate differentials across nations, and fiscal policies would all be coordinated to meet agreed upon targets for inflation rates and nominal income growth in each country. Through policy coordination, proponents of target zones believe large swings in currency values such as the rise and fall in the value of the dollar between 1981 and 1988 will be avoided; policy coordination will make large movements in target zones each period unnecessary.[16]

20.7 • CONCLUSION

The question of whether the world economy functions better with fixed or with flexible exchange rates is a longstanding one. The large swings in exchange rates in the 1980s led to disenchantment with freely fluctuating exchange rates. But recurrent balance of payment crises had fostered criticism of a fixed exchange rate system in the 1960s and early 1970s. Advocates of a return to fixed exchange rates or to the target zone approach see international policy coordination as a means of preventing such crises.

The Plaza Accord in 1985 and the Louvre Agreement in 1987 were initial attempts at coordinating policy toward exchange rates. As implemented, however, these agreements have resulted in coordinated foreign exchange market intervention, but not coordinated setting of domestic monetary and fiscal policy. There are many obstacles to effective international policy coordination, not the least of which are different preferences of policymakers and different industrial structures in major world economies. The merits and possible mechanics of macroeconomic policy coordination is a subject of much current interest among both economists and policymakers.

Review Questions

1. Why do the balance of payments accounts always balance?

2. Explain how the exchange rate for a country is determined under:

    a. A fixed exchange rate system.

    b. A flexible exchange rate.

    c. A managed or dirty float.

---

[15] Williamson, "Comment on McKinnon's Monetary Rule," p. 114.

[16] A case *against* formal international macroeconomic policy coordination is made in Martin S. Feldstein, "Thinking About International Economic Coordination," *Journal of Economic Perspective*, 2 (Spring 1988), pp. 3–13.

3. Analyze the effects of an autonomous fall in the demand for a country's exports under fixed and flexible exchange rate systems. In each case indicate the effects on the country's balance of payments and on the exchange rate.

4. If central banks never intervened in foreign exchange markets, could there be deficits or surpluses in a country's balance of payments?

5. Describe the Bretton Woods system of exchange rate determination that was set up at the end of World War II and lasted until 1973.

6. Explain the relationship between the trade balance and the level of economic activity in a fixed exchange rate system. Why does this relationship create a potential conflict between the goals of internal and external balance?

7. Taking account of both the effect on the trade balance and the capital account, explain the relationships between balance of payments equilibrium and both expansionary monetary and fiscal policies within a fixed exchange rate system.

8. "Adoption of a system of flexible exchange rates would free monetary and fiscal policy for use in attaining domestic goals of full employment and price stability." Do you agree or disagree with this statement? Explain.

9. What are some of the relative advantages or disadvantages of fixed versus flexible exchange rates?

10. Illustrate graphically the effects in the foreign exchange market of an expansionary monetary policy carried out by the *foreign* country in our two-country framework. Consider the cases of both a fixed and a flexible exchange rate.

11. Explain the central elements of the *target zone* proposal for exchange rates. Why do some economists favor this approach over explicit fixed exchange rates?

Selected Readings

Artus, Jacques R., and Young, John H., "Fixed Versus Flexible Exchange Rates: A Renewal of the Debate," *IMF Staff Papers*, 26 (December 1979), pp. 654–98.

Black, Stanley W., *Floating Exchange Rates and National Economic Policy*. New Haven, Conn.: Yale University Press, 1977.

Bryant, Ralph C., *Money and Monetary Policy in Interdependent Nations*. Washington, D.C.: The Brookings Institution, 1980.

Dornbusch, Rudiger, "Exchange Rate Economics, 1986," *Economic Journal*, 95 (March 1987), pp. 1–18.

Dornbusch, Rudiger, *Dollars, Debts and Deficits*. Cambridge, Mass.: MIT Press, 1986.

Edison, Hali, Miller, Marcus, and Williamson, John, "On Evaluating and Extending the Target Zone Proposal," *Journal of Policy Modeling,* 9 (Spring 1987), pp. 199–224.

Friedman, Milton, "The Case for Flexible Exchange Rates," in Milton Friedman, *Essays in Positive Economics.* Chicago: University of Chicago Press, 1953.

Johnson, Harry G., "The Case for Flexible Exchange Rates, 1969," Federal Reserve Bank of St. Louis *Review,* 51 (June 1969), pp. 12–24.

Kindleberger, Charles P., "The Case for Fixed Exchange Rates, 1969," in *The International Adjustment Mechanism.* Boston: Federal Reserve Bank of Boston, 1969.

Krugman, Paul, *Exchange Rate Instability.* Cambridge, Mass.: MIT Press, 1989.

McKinnon, Ronald I., *Money in International Exchange: The Convertible Currency System.* New York: Oxford University Press, 1979.

McKinnon, Ronald I., "Monetary and Exchange Rate Policies for International Financial Stability: A Proposal," *Journal of Economic Perspectives,* 2 (Winter 1988), pp. 83–103.

Meade, James E., *The Balance of Payments,* Vol. 1: *The Theory of Economic Policy.* London: Oxford University Press, 1951.

Stern, Robert M., *The Balance of Payments: Theory and Economic Policy.* Chicago: Aldine, 1973.

Williamson, John, *The Exchange Rate System.* Washington, D.C.: Institute for International Economics, 1985.

Williamson, John, "Exchange Rate Management: The Role of Target Zones," *American Economic Review* 77 (May 1987), pp. 200–04.

An Open Economy Macroeconomic Model

In this appendix we construct an open economy version of the *IS–LM* curve model from Chapters 6 and 7. The model is then used to analyze the effects of monetary and fiscal policy in the open economy. We consider the conflicts which may arise for policymakers between considerations of internal and external balance in a system of fixed exchange rates. We illustrate why those conflicts do not arise in a flexible exchange rate system. The exchange rate effects of monetary and fiscal policy actions within a flexible exchange rate system are examined. The way in which a flexible rate system provides a degree of insulation from certain foreign shocks is also clarified.

A.1 • AN OPEN ECONOMY *IS–LM* MODEL

The closed economy *IS–LM* model consists of the following two equations:

$$M = L(Y, r) \tag{V.A.1}$$

$$S(Y) + T = I(r) + G \tag{V.A.2}$$

Equation (V.A.1) is the money market equilibrium or *LM* schedule and equation (V.A.2) is the goods market equilibrium or *IS* schedule. The model simultaneously determines the nominal interest rate (r) and the level of *real* income (Y), with the aggregate price level held constant. What changes will be required to analyze an open economy?

When we consider an open economy, the *LM* schedule will not need to be changed. Equation (V.A.1) states that the *real* money stock, which we assume to be controlled by the domestic policymaker, must in equilibrium

623

equal the real demand for money. It is the nominal stock of money that the policymaker controls, but with the assumption of a fixed price level, changes in the nominal money stock are changes in the real money stock as well.

The equation for the *IS* schedule (V.A.2) is derived from the goods market equilibrium condition for a closed economy:

$$C + S + T \equiv Y = C + I + G \qquad\qquad \text{(V.A.3)}$$

which when *C* is subtracted from both sides reduces to

$$S + T = I + G \qquad\qquad \text{(V.A.4)}$$

If we add imports (*Z*) and exports (*X*) to the model, (V.A.3) is replaced by[1]

$$C + S + T \equiv Y = C + I + G + X - Z \qquad\qquad \text{(V.A.5)}$$

and the *IS* equation becomes

$$S + T = I + G + X - Z \qquad\qquad \text{(V.A.6)}$$

If we bring imports over to the left-hand side and indicate the dependence of variables on income and the interest rate, the *IS* equation for an open economy can be written as

$$S(Y) + T + Z(Y) = I(r) + G + X \qquad\qquad \text{(V.A.7)}$$

Notice that, as discussed in Chapter 20, imports depend (positively) on the level of income. There may also be autonomous shifts in import demand, for example, due to changes in preferences for imported relative to domestic goods.

By a derivation analogous to that in Chapter 6, the open economy *IS* schedule can be shown to be downward-sloping, as drawn in Figure V.A.1. High values of the interest rate will result in low levels of investment. To satisfy equation (V.A.7), at such high levels of the interest rate, income must be low so that the levels of imports and saving will be low. Alternatively, at low levels of the interest rate, which result in high levels of investment demand, for goods market equilibrium saving and imports must be high; therefore, *Y* must be high.

Notice that the levels of taxes, government spending, and exports are taken as given; these are the factors that shift the *IS* schedule. Expansionary shocks such as an increase in government spending, a cut in taxes, or an increase in export demand will shift the *IS* schedule to the right. An autonomous increase in investment [a shift in the *I(r)* function] also would shift the *IS* schedule to the right, as would an autonomous *decline* in import

---

[1] Private transfer payments to foreigners should also appear on the left-hand side of equation (V.A.5), but we will ignore this relatively minor item in our model.

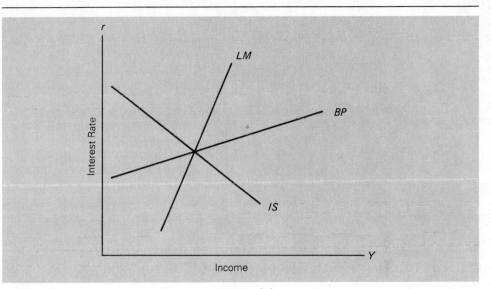

FIGURE V.A.1   Open Economy *IS–LM* Model
The *LM* schedule shows the combinations of *r* and *Y* which are points of equilibrium for the money market and the *IS* schedule shows combinations of *r* and *Y* that clear the goods market. The *BP* schedule shows the combinations of *r* and *Y* that will equate supply and demand in the foreign exchange market at a given exchange rate.

demand. An autonomous decline in import demand is expansionary because it is a shift in demand away from foreign goods to domestic output.

In addition to the *IS* and *LM* schedules, our open economy model will contain a balance of payments equilibrium schedule, the *BP* schedule in Figure V.A.1. This schedule plots all the interest rate–income combinations that result in balance of payments equilibrium at a given exchange rate. Balance of payments equilibrium means that the official reserve transaction balance is zero (no official reserve transactions). The equation for the *BP* schedule can be written as

$$X(\pi) - Z(Y, \pi) + F(r) = 0 \qquad \text{(V.A.8)}$$

where here we have made explicit the dependence on the exchange rate (π) of both imports and exports.[2] Equation (V.A.8) states that the sum of the

---

[2] Recall that π is the price of foreign currency measured in dollars. A rise in π will make imports more expensive and cause import demand to decline. A rise in π will make our exports less expensive to foreign buyers and export demand will rise.

trade balance $(X - Z)$ plus the capital inflow (F), which depends positively on the interest rate, must be zero for balance of payments equilibrium.

The BP schedule will be positively sloped, as shown in Figure V.A.1. As the level of income rises, import demand increases whereas export demand does not. To maintain balance of payments equilibrium the capital inflow must increase, which will happen if the interest rate is higher. Now consider factors that will shift the BP schedule. An increase in π will shift the schedule horizontally to the right. For a given level of the interest rate, which fixes the capital flow, at a higher exchange rate a higher level of income will be required for balance of payments equilibrium. This is because the higher exchange rate encourages exports and discourages imports; thus a higher level of income which will stimulate import demand is needed for balance of payments equilibrium. Similarly, an exogenous rise in export demand or fall in import demand will shift the BP schedule to the right. If exports rise, for example, at a given interest rate which again fixes the capital flow, a higher level of income and therefore of imports is required to restore balance of payments equilibrium. The BP schedule shifts to the right.

Having constructed the open economy $IS–LM$ model, we can now analyze the effects of various policy actions. To begin with, we will assume that the exchange rate is fixed.

A.2 • MONETARY AND FISCAL POLICY IN AN OPEN ECONOMY: FIXED EXCHANGE RATES

Monetary Policy: Fixed Exchange Rates

Consider the effects of an expansionary monetary policy action, an increase in the money stock from M_0 to M_1, as illustrated in Figure V.A.2. The increase in the money stock shifts the LM schedule to the right, from $LM(M_0)$ to $LM(M_1)$. The equilibrium point shifts from E_0 to E_1 with a fall in the interest rate from r_0 to r_1 and an increase in income from Y_0 to Y_1. What has happened to the balance of payments? First, note that all points below the BP schedule are points of balance of payments deficit, while all points above the schedule are points of surplus. As we move from an equilibrium point on the BP schedule to points below the schedule, for example, we are increasing income and/or reducing the interest rate and therefore causing a deficit in the balance of payments. Consequently, as we move from point E_0 to point E_1 following the increase in the money stock, the balance of payments moves into deficit. As discussed in Section 20.4, the expansionary monetary policy increases income, which stimulates imports and lowers the interest rate, which causes a capital outflow (F declines).

It is the fact that, beginning from a point of equilibrium, an expansionary monetary policy leads to a balance of payments deficit that raises potential

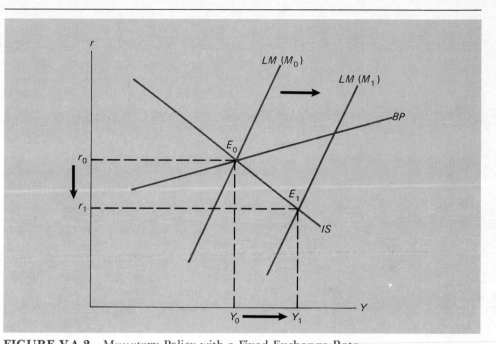

FIGURE V.A.2 Monetary Policy with a Fixed Exchange Rate
An increase in the quantity of money will shift the *LM* schedule from *LM(M0)* to
LM(M1). The equilibrium point shifts from E_0 to E_1. The rate of interest falls and
the level of income rises. The new equilibrium point is below the *BP* schedule,
indicating that the expansionary monetary policy has caused a deficit in the balance
of payments.

conflicts between domestic policy goals and external balance. If at point E_0
in Figure V.A.2 the level of income, Y_0, is low relative to full employment,
then the move to point E_1 and income level Y_1 may well be preferable on
domestic grounds. But at point E_1 there will be a deficit in the balance
of payments, and with limited foreign exchange reserves, such a situation
cannot be maintained indefinitely.

Fiscal Policy: Fixed Exchange Rates

The effects of an increase in government spending from G_0 to G_1 for the
fixed exchange rates case are illustrated in Figure V.A.3. The increase in
government spending shifts the *IS* schedule to the right from $IS(G_0)$ to
$IS(G_1)$, moving the equilibrium point from E_0 to E_1 in the graph. Income
rises from Y_0 to Y_1 and the interest rate rises from r_0 to r_1. As shown in
Figure V.A.3, at the new equilibrium point we are above the *BP* schedule;

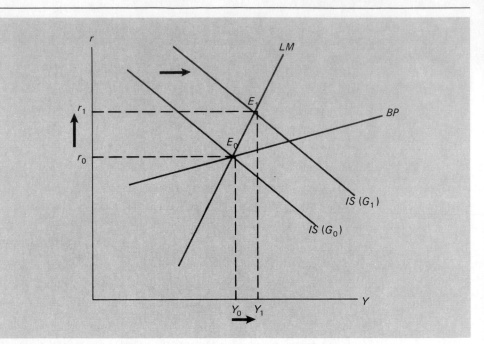

FIGURE V.A.3   Fiscal Policy with a Fixed Exchange Rate
An increase in the level of government spending shifts the *IS* schedule from *IS(G₀)* to *IS(G₁)*. The equilibrium point shifts from E_0 to E_1. The level of income and the interest rate rise. The new equilibrium point is above the *BP* schedule which indicates that, with a fixed exchange rate for the case where the *BP* schedule is flatter than the *LM* schedule, the expansionary fiscal policy results in surplus in the balance of payments.

there is a balance of payments surplus. We get this result because in Figure V.A.3 the *BP* schedule is flatter than the *LM* schedule. If, alternatively, the *BP* schedule were steeper than the *LM* schedule, as drawn in Figure V.A.4, it can be seen that an expansionary fiscal policy action would lead to a balance of payments deficit.

The *BP* schedule will be steeper the less responsive capital flows are to the rate of interest. The smaller the increase in the capital inflow for a given increase in the interest rate, the larger will be the rise in the interest rate required to maintain balance of payments equilibrium as we go to a higher income (and hence import) level; that is, the steeper will be the *BP* schedule. The *BP* schedule will also be steeper the larger the marginal propensity to import. With a higher marginal propensity to import, a given increase in income will produce a larger increase in imports. For equilibrium in the

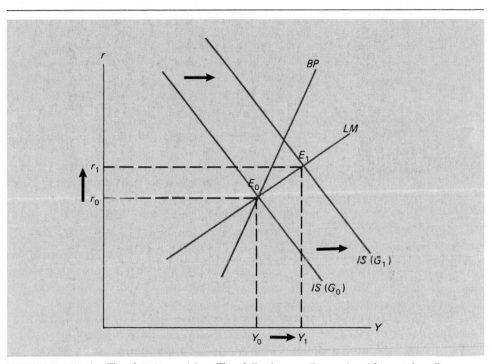

FIGURE V.A.4 Fiscal Policy with a Fixed Exchange Rate: An Alternative Outcome
As in Figure V.A.3, an increase in the level of government spending shifts the *IS*
schedule to the right, increasing both income and the rate of interest. In this case
where the *BP* schedule is steeper than the *LM* schedule, the new equilibrium point
(E_1) is below the *BP* schedule. The expansionary fiscal policy results in a balance of
payments deficit.

balance of payments, a larger compensatory increase in the capital inflow
and consequently a larger rise in the interest rate will be required.

The expansionary fiscal policy action depicted in Figures V.A.3 and V.A.4
causes income to increase, which leads to a deterioration in the trade balance and causes the interest rate to rise, resulting in an improvement in
the capital account. The foregoing discussion indicates that the steeper the
BP schedule, the larger the unfavorable effect (the effect on imports and
the trade balance) and the smaller the favorable effect (on capital flows).
Therefore, the steeper the *BP* schedule, the more likely it becomes that an
expansionary fiscal policy action will lead to a balance of payments deficit.

Finally, notice that it is the slope of the *BP* schedule relative to the slope
of the *LM* schedule that determines whether an expansionary fiscal policy
action will result in a balance of payments surplus or deficit. Given the slope

of the *BP* schedule, the steeper the *LM* schedule, clearly the more likely it is that the *LM* schedule will be steeper than the *BP* schedule—the condition for a surplus to result from an expansionary fiscal policy action. This follows since, *ceteris paribus*, the steeper the *LM* schedule, the larger the increase in the interest rate (which produces the favorable capital inflow) and the smaller the increase in income (which produces the unfavorable effect on the trade balance) as a result of the expansionary fiscal policy action.

A.3 • MONETARY AND FISCAL POLICY IN AN OPEN ECONOMY: FLEXIBLE EXCHANGE RATES

Monetary Policy: Flexible Exchange Rates

We turn now to the case in which the exchange rate is completely flexible; there is no central bank intervention. The exchange rate adjusts to equate supply and demand in the foreign exchange market. Consider, first, the same monetary policy action analyzed previously, an increase in the quantity of money from M_0 to M_1. The effects of this expansionary monetary policy action in the flexible exchange rate case are as illustrated in Figure V.A.5.

The initial effect of the increase in the money stock—the effect prior to an adjustment in the exchange rate—is to move the economy from point E_0 to point E_1. The interest rate falls from r_0 to r_1. Income rises from Y_0 to Y_1 and we move to a point below the *BP* schedule where there is an *incipient* balance of payments deficit. In a flexible exchange rate system, the exchange rate will rise (from π_0 to π_1) to clear the foreign exchange market. (This is the adjustment shown earlier in Figure 20.8.) The rise in the exchange rate will, as explained above, shift the *BP* schedule to the right; in Figure V.A.5 the schedule shifts from $BP(\pi_0)$ to $BP(\pi_1)$. The rise in the exchange rate also causes the *IS* schedule to shift to the right, from $IS(\pi_0)$ to $IS(\pi_1)$ in Figure V.A.5 because exports rise and imports fall with an increase in the exchange rate. The new equilibrium is shown at point E_2, with the interest rate r_2 and income at Y_2. The exchange rate adjustment reequilibrates the balance of payments following the expansionary monetary policy and eliminates the potential conflict between internal and external balance.

Notice also that the rise in income as a result of the expansionary monetary policy action is greater in the flexible rate case than in the fixed rate case. In the fixed exchange rate case income would rise only to Y_1 in Figure V.A.5 or Figure V.A.2. With a flexible exchange rate, the rise in the exchange rate will further stimulate income by increasing exports and reducing import demand (for a given income level). Monetary policy is therefore a more potent stabilization tool in a flexible exchange rate regime.

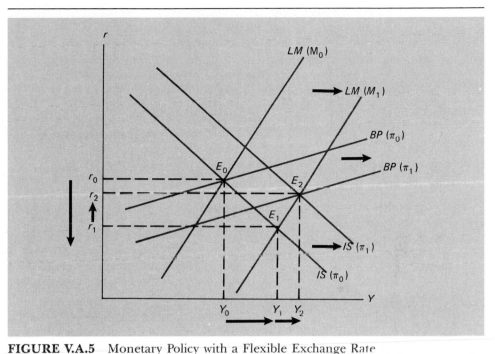

FIGURE V.A.5   Monetary Policy with a Flexible Exchange Rate
An increase in the money stock shifts the *LM* schedule to the right, moving the equilibrium point from E_0 to E_1. The point E_1 is below the *BP* schedule where there is an incipient balance of payments deficit. In the flexible exchange rate case, the exchange rate will rise, causing the *BP* schedule to shift to the right from $BP(\pi_0)$ to $BP(\pi_1)$ and the *IS* curve to shift right from $IS(\pi_0)$ to $IS(\pi_1)$. The final equilibrium point will be at E_2 *with an income level* Y_2, above Y_1 the new equilibrium for a fixed exchange rate

Fiscal Policy: Flexible Exchange Rates

Figure V.A.6 illustrates the effects of an increase in government spending from G_0 to G_1 for the flexible exchange rate case. The initial effect—meaning again the effect prior to the adjustment in the exchange rate—is to shift the *IS* schedule from $IS(G_0, \pi_0)$ to $IS(G_1, \pi_0)$ and move the economy from E_0 to E_1. The interest rate rises (from r_0 to r_1) and income increases (from Y_0 to Y_1). With the slopes of the *BP* and *LM* schedules as drawn in Figure V.A.6 (with the *BP* schedule flatter than the *LM* schedule), an incipient balance of surplus results from this expansionary policy action. If this is the case, the exchange rate must *fall* (from π_0 to π_1) to clear the foreign exchange market. A fall in the exchange rate will shift the *BP* schedule to the left in Figure V.A.6, from $BP(\pi_0)$ to $BP(\pi_1)$. The *IS* schedule will also shift

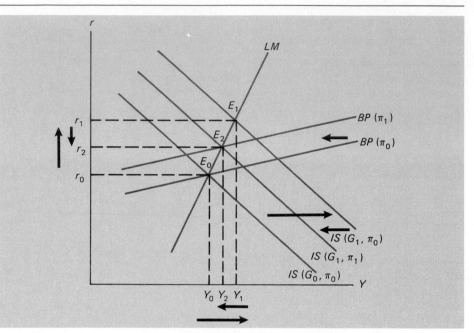

FIGURE V.A.6   Fiscal Policy with a Flexible Exchange Rate

An increase in government spending shifts the *IS* schedule to the right from $IS(G_0, \pi_0)$ to $IS(G_1, \pi_0)$ moving the equilibrium point from E_0 to E_1. With the *BP* schedule flatter than the *LM* schedule, E_1 is above the initial *BP* schedule, $BP(\pi_0)$. There is an incipient balance of payments surplus and the exchange rate will fall, shifting the *BP* schedule to the left to $BP(\pi_1)$ and shifting the *IS* schedule to the left from $IS(G_1, \pi_0)$ to $IS(G_1, \pi_1)$. The final equilibrium will be at E_2 with income level Y_2, below Y_1 the new equilibrium for a fixed exchange rate.

left, from $IS(G_1, \pi_0)$ to $IS(G_1, \pi_1)$ since the fall in the exchange rate will lower the level of exports and stimulate import demand. The exchange rate adjustment will work *in this case* as a partial offset to the expansionary effect of the fiscal policy action. The new equilibrium point will be at Y_2, which is above Y_0 but below Y_1, the level that would have resulted in the fixed exchange rate case.

There is not, however, a general relationship between the potency of fiscal policy and the type of exchange rate regime, as there was with monetary policy. If the *BP* schedule is steeper than the *LM* schedule, as we saw in Figure V.A.4, an expansionary fiscal policy will, for a given exchange rate, cause a balance of payments deficit. With an incipient balance of payments deficit in the flexible exchange rate regime, the exchange rate must rise to restore equilibrium in the foreign exchange market. The *BP* schedule and the *IS* schedule will shift to the right and reinforce the initial expansionary effect of the increase in government spending. In this case, as illustrated in Figure V.A.7, the expansionary fiscal policy action has a *larger* effect on income than it would have in the fixed exchange rate case (income rises to $Y_2 > Y_1$).

While the outcome in Figure V.A.7 is possible in theory, most economists believe that the outcome in Figure V.A.6 is more likely. They believe an expansionary fiscal policy will lower the exchange rate (raise the value of the domestic currency). This belief follows from the view that there is a relatively high degree of international capital mobility, which means that the BP schedule is relatively flat and therefore likely to be flatter than the LM schedule—the case in Figure V.A.6. Notice that this view is consistent with the experience of the United States where an expansionary fiscal policy in the early 1980s was accompanied by a large rise in the value of the dollar.

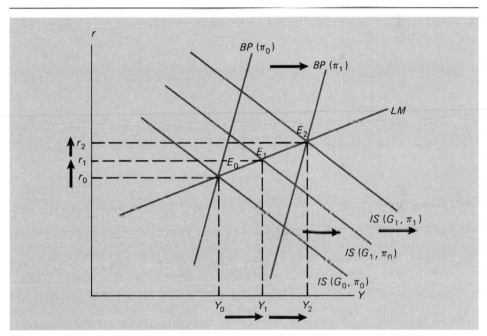

FIGURE V.A.7 Fiscal Policy with a Flexible Exchange Rate: An Alternative Outcome

As in Figure V.A.6 the increase in government spending shifts the IS schedule to the right, moving the equilibrium point from E_0 to E_1. With the BP schedule steeper than the LM schedule there is an incipient balance of payments deficit at E_1 and the exchange rate rises. The IS and BP schedules shift to the right to the new equilibrium point E_2 where the level of income Y_2 is above Y_1, the new equilibrium for a fixed exchange rate.

A.4 • INSULATION OF THE ECONOMY FROM FOREIGN SHOCKS UNDER FLEXIBLE EXCHANGE RATES

As a last application of our open economy IS–LM model, we examine how a flexible exchange rate system can insulate the domestic economy from certain foreign shocks. We consider the same shock discussed in Section 20.4, a fall in export demand resulting from a recession abroad. The effects on the domestic economy from such a shock are illustrated in Figure V.A.8.

The initial effect of the fall in export demand from X_0 to X_1 will be to shift the IS schedule to the left, from $IS(X_0, \pi_0)$ to $IS(X_1, \pi_0)$. The BP schedule will shift upward to the left since with a lower exogenous export demand a higher interest rate (with a higher capital inflow) and/or a lower level of income (with a lower level of imports) will be required for balance of payments equilibrium *at the initial exchange rate*. The economy moves from point E_0 to point E_1. The level of income initially falls to Y_1. Also, since E_1

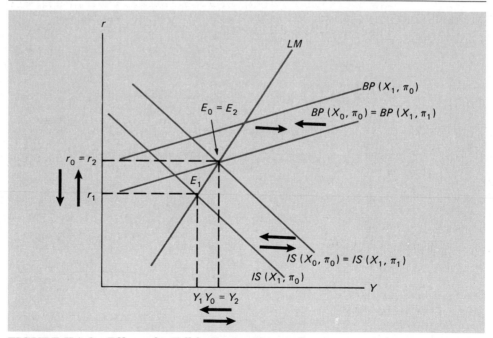

FIGURE V.A.8   Effect of a Fall in Export Demand
A fall in exports shifts the IS schedule to the left, which would move the equilibrium point from E_0 to E_1. At E_1 there is an incipient balance of payments deficit so the exchange rate rises. The IS and BP schedules shift to the right and the final point of equilibrium is at E_2 which coincides with the initial equilibrium point E_0.

is below the new *BP* schedule, the economy is at a point where there is an incipient balance of payments deficit. This would be the final result if the exchange rate were fixed. The foreign recession would depress income at home and create a balance of payments deficit.

With a flexible exchange rate, the incipient balance of payments deficit will cause a rise in the exchange rate. A rise in the exchange rate (from π_0 to π_1) will, as we have seen in earlier examples, cause the *IS* and *BP* schedules to shift to the right. In this simple *IS–LM* model, the rise in the exchange rate will cause these schedules to shift all the way back to their initial levels [i.e., $IS(X_1, \pi_1) = IS(X_0, \pi_0)$ and $BP(X_1, \pi_1) = BP(X_0, \pi_0)$]. The domestic economy will be completely insulated from foreign shocks to export demand. In more complicated models this complete insulation does not occur.[3] As a general point, however, it does hold that exchange rate adjustments that occur in a flexible exchange rate system provide a degree of insulation to the economy against certain foreign shocks: shocks that affect aggregate demand.

Review Questions

1. Explain why the *BP* schedule in Figure V.A.1 is upward sloping. What factors will cause a shift in the *BP* schedule? Explain.

2. Within the open economy *IS–LM* model, analyze the effects of the following policy actions for both the fixed and flexible exchange rate cases.
    a. A decline in the money stock from M_0 to M_1.
    b. A decrease in government spending from G_0 to G_1.
Include in your answer the effects of the policy action on both income and the interest rate, as well as the effects on the balance of payments and exchange rate.

3. Suppose that, rather than a foreign recession, the external shock to hit the economy was an expansionary boom abroad. Explain the effects that this shock would have on the domestic economy in both a fixed and, alternatively, a flexible exchange rate regime.

---

[3]The intuition behind the complete insulation result here is as follows. The rise in the exchange rate, which is just sufficient to shift the *BP* schedule back to the initial position $BP(\pi_0, Y_0)$, will just restore the trade balance to its initial level for each point along the *BP* schedule. This means that this rise in the exchange rate has caused a rise in exports and a fall in imports, which just counterbalances the initial drop in exports. From this it follows that the rise in the exchange rate is just sufficient to return the *IS* schedule to its initial level—the rise in exports and fall in imports caused by the rise in the exchange rate just counterbalance the effect *on aggregate demand* from the initial drop in exports. The new equilibrium is the same as the initial equilibrium, with both the capital flow and the trade balance back at their initial levels.

Selected Readings

Appleyard, Dennis R., and Field, Alfred J., *International Economics*. Homewood, Ill.: Irwin, 1992, Chaps. 24–27.

Dornbusch, Rudiger, *Open Economy Macroeconomics*. New York: Basic Books, 1980.

Kenen, Peter B., "Macroeconomic Theory and Policy: How the Closed Economy Was Opened," in Jones, Ronald W. and Kenen, Peter B., eds., *Handbook on International Economics*, Vol. 2. Amsterdam: North Holland, 1985.

Krueger, Anne O., *Exchange-Rate Determination*. Cambridge: Cambridge University Press, 1983.

Stern, Robert M., *The Balance of Payments: Theory and Economic Policy*. Chicago: Aldine, 1973.

Glossary

A

The **accelerator model** is a model of business investment which in its simplest form relates the level of investment to the rate of change in output. More complex forms take account of costs of adjustment and borrowing costs.

Aggregate demand is the sum of the demands for current output by each of the buying sectors of the economy: households, businesses, the government, and foreign purchasers of exports.

The **aggregate demand curve** measures the demand for total output at each value of the aggregate price level.

The **aggregate supply curve** is the macroeconomic analog to the individual market supply curve, which shows the output forthcoming at each level of product price. The aggregate supply curve shows the total output firms will supply at each value of the aggregate price level.

Automatic stabilizers are changes in taxes and government transfer payments that occur when the level of income changes. They help stabilize the economy.

The **autonomous expenditure multiplier** gives the change in equilibrium output per unit change in autonomous expenditures (e.g., government spending).

Autonomous expenditures are expenditures which are largely determined by factors other than current income.

B

The **balanced-budget multiplier** gives the change in equilibrium output that results from a one-unit increase or decrease in *both* taxes and government spending.

637

The **Board of Governors of the Federal Reserve** is composed of seven members (governors) appointed by the president of the United States with the advice and consent of the Senate for a term of 14 years. One member of the board is appointed chairman.

The **Bretton Woods system** was a pegged exchange rate system set up at the end of World War II.

C

The **Cambridge approach** is a version of the quantity theory of money that focuses on the demand for money ($M^d = kPy$).

The **capital account** in the balance of payments is a record of purchases of U.S. assets by foreign residents (capital inflows) and purchases of foreign assets by U.S. residents (capital outflows).

capital formation is growth in the stock of plant and equipment.

A **capital gain** is the increase in the market value of any asset above the price originally paid. The capital gain is realized when the asset is actually sold.

Capital goods are capital resources like factories, machinery, and railroads used to produce other goods.

A **capital loss** is the decrease in the market value of any asset below the price originally paid.

Constant returns to scale mean that increasing all inputs by a certain proportion (e.g., 100 percent) will cause output to rise by the same proportion (e.g., 100 percent).

Consumption is the household sector's demand for output for current use. *Consumption expenditures* consist of purchases of durable goods (e.g., autos and televisions), nondurable goods (e.g., food and newspapers), and services (e.g., haircuts and taxi rides).

The **consumption function** is the Keynesian relationship between income and consumption.

Corporate bonds are formal IOUs that require the corporation to pay a fixed sum of money (interest payment) annually until maturity and then, at maturity, a fixed sum of money to repay the initial amount borrowed (principal).

The **CPI** measures the retail prices of a fixed "market basket" of several thousand goods and services purchased by households.

The **current account** in the U.S. balance of payments is a record of U.S. merchandise exports and imports as well as trade in services and foreign transfer payments.

The **cyclical deficit** is the portion of the federal deficit that results from the economy being at a low level of economic activity.

Cyclical unemployment   results from fluctuations in the level of economic activity and consequent fluctuations in industry demand for workers.

D

The **deposit multiplier**   gives the increase in bank deposits per unit increase in bank reserves.

Depository institutions   are financial intermediaries whose main liabilities are deposits. These depository institutions include commercial banks, savings and loan associations, mutual savings banks, and credit unions.

Depreciation   is the portion of the capital stock that wears out each year.

E

Economies of scale   are present when a doubling of all inputs result in output *more* than doubling.

The **effective tax rate**   is the taxpayer's tax bill divided by her or his total income.

In **efficiency wage models**   the productivity of labor depends on the real wage workers are paid. In such models, the real wage is set to maximize the efficiency units of labor per dollar of expenditure, not to clear the labor market.

Elasticity   measures the percentage change in one variable per 1 percent change in another variable, for example, the elasticity of money demand with respect to the interest rate.

An **exchange rate**   is the value of one country's currency in terms of foreign currencies.

An **exchange rate system**   is a set of rules organizing the determination of exchange rates among currencies.

F

The **factors of production**   are labor, land, capital, and entrepreneurship.

The **Federal Reserve System**   (Federal Reserve for short) is composed of 12 regional Federal Reserve banks and the Board of Governors located in Washington.

Financial intermediaries   are institutions that accept funds from savers and make loans to ultimate borrowers (e.g., firms).

Fiscal stabilization policy   is the use of government spending and tax policies to affect the level of economic activity.

A **fixed input**   is one whose quantity cannot be changed during the period of time under consideration.

Frictional unemployment   is unemployment due to the time workers spend between jobs and to the time entrants or reentrants to the labor force need to find jobs.

G

Government purchases of goods and services are the part of current output that goes to the government sector—the federal government as well as state and local governments.

Government spending refers to government outlays for purchases, transfer payments, and subsidies.

The **Gramm–Rudman Act** mandated a move to a balanced budget in steps over five years, by *automatic* spending cuts if Congress failed to balance the budget by legislation.

Gross Domestic Product (GDP) is a measure of all currently produced final goods and services.

Gross National Product (GNP) is, like gross domestic product, a measure of aggregate national production. There are two differences between the two measures, both of which concern foreign transactions. GNP includes foreign earnings of U.S. corporations and earnings of U.S. residents working overseas; GDP does not include these items. Conversely, GDP includes earnings from current production in the United States that accrue to foreign residents and foreign-owned firms, while GNP excludes these items.

H

A **hyperinflation** is a period when the price level simply explodes. In the worst hyperinflation, inflation rates reach several thousand percent *per month*.

Hysteresis is a term indicating that the history of a variable affects its present value. Persistently high unemployment rates in many European countries have led economists to argue that unemployment exhibits hysteresis.

Human capital is the accumulation of investments in schooling, training, and health that raises the productive capacity of people.

I

The **implicit GNP deflator** is an index of the prices of goods and services include in GNP.

Indirect business taxes are general sales and excise taxes.

Induced expenditures are expenditures that are determined primarily by current income.

Insider–Outsider models provide one explanation of hysteresis in unemployment. Insiders (e.g., union members) are the only group that affects the real wage bargain. Outsiders (e.g., those who want jobs) do not. Recessions cause insiders to become outsiders. After the recession, with fewer insiders, the real wage rises and unemployment persists.

Intermediate targeting on a monetary aggregate   is a monetary policy strategy which aims at hitting money growth targets, with the ultimate goal of controlling the level of economic activity.

Investment   is the part of GNP purchased by the business sector plus residential construction.

L

Labor   comprises the physical energy, manual skill, and mental ability that humans apply to the production of goods and services.

Legal reserve requirements   specify that banks must hold a certain percentage (fraction) of deposits either in the form of vault cash (currency) or as deposits at regional Federal Reserve banks. They are what are called *fractional reserve requirements.*

The **life cycle hypothesis**   about consumption asserts that saving and consumption decisions of households reflect a plan for an optimal consumption pattern over their lifetime, subject to the constraint of their resources.

M

M1   is the narrowest of the money supply measures in the United States. It consists of currency plus *checkable* deposits. Two other measures, M2 and M3 are broader. They include all the components of M1 plus some additional bank deposits that have no or only limited provisions for checks.

Macroeconomics   is the study of economics in the large. It covers aggregate economic performance.

A **managed float**   for a country's exchange rate is a system in which, at some times, the exchange rate is allowed to respond to market forces while at other times the central bank *intervenes* to influence the exchange rate.

Marginal cost   is the extra, or additional, cost of producing one more unit of output.

The **marginal product**   of an input is the addition to total output due to the addition of an extra unit of that input (the quantity of other inputs being held constant.

The **marginal propensity to consume (MPC)**   is the increase in consumption per unit increase in disposable income.

The **marginal propensity to save (MPS)**   is the increase in saving per unit increase in disposable income.

Marginal revenue   is the added revenue associated with the sale of one more unit of output.

The **marginal revenue product (MRP)**   of any resource input is the extra revenue the firm gains by using one more unit of the input holding other inputs constant).

The **marginal tax rate** is the rate paid on each additional dollar earned from an activity.

The **marginal utility** of a good is the additional satisfaction a consumer derives from consuming one additional unit of that good.

Menu Costs refer to any type of cost that a firm incurs if it changes its product price.

The **merchandise trade balance** measures exports minus imports in the U.S. balance of payments.

The **monetary base** is equal to currency held by the public plus bank reserves.

Monetary policy is the central bank's use of control of the money supply and interest rates to influence the level of economic activity.

Money is whatever is commonly accepted as payment in exchange for goods and services (and payment of debts and taxes).

The **money multiplier** gives the increase in the the money supply per unit increase in the monetary base.

N

National income is the sum of the earnings of all factors of production that come from current production.

Natural rates of output, employment, and therefore unemployment, in the monetarist model are determined by *real* supply-side factors: the capital stock, the size of the labor force, and the level of technology. In our simple model, the natural rates of output, employment, and unemployment are the classical equilibrium levels of these variables (unemployment being confined to frictional and structural forms).

The **new classical policy ineffectiveness proposition** asserts that systematic monetary and fiscal policy actions that change aggregate demand will *not* affect output and employment even in the short run.

Nominal (or money) GNP is gross national product measured in current dollars.

The **nominal interest rate** is that stated on loan contracts, such as the annual percentage rate (APR), specified on consumer loans and credit card agreements.

O

Oligopoly is closer to monopoly than to perfect competition because it is typified by few firms (as few as two or three) and by moderately difficult entry. In product type, oligopoly markets may have either standardized or differentiated products.

The **open market** is the market of dealers in government securities in New York City.

The **Open Market Committee** is composed of 12 voting members: the 7 members of the Board of Governors and 5 of the presidents of regional Federal Reserve banks. Presidents of the regional banks serve on a rotating basis, with the exception of the president of the Federal Reserve Bank of New York, who is vice chairman and a permanent voting member of the committee.

Open-market operations are purchases and sales of government securities in the open market by the Federal Reserve. Open-market operations are the primary tool for control of the monetary base.

The **opportunity cost** of an action is the value of the best foregone alternative.

P

The **partisan (or partisan party) theory** views macroeconomic policy outcomes as the result of ideologically motivated decisions by leaders of different political parties. The parties represent constituencies with different preferences concerning macroeconomic variables.

Personal income is the national income accounts measure of the income received by persons from all sources.

The **Phillips curve** is the schedule showing the relationship between the unemployment and inflation rates.

Potential GNP (output) is the level that would be reached if productive resources (labor and capital) were being used at benchmark high levels.

A **price index** measures the aggregate price level relative to a chosen base year.

The **producer price index** measures the wholesale prices of approximately 3000 items.

A **production function** summarizes the relationship between total inputs and total outputs assuming a given technology.

Public choice is the application to macroeconomic policymaking of the microeconomic theory of how decisions are made.

Q

The **quantity theory of money** is the classical theory stating that the price level is proportional to the quantity of money. In the monetarist version the quantity theory is a theory of nominal GNP.

R

Rational expectations are expectations formed on the basis of all available relevant information concerning the variable being predicted. Moreover, economic agents are assumed to use available information intelligently; that is, they understand the relationships between the variables they observe and the variables they are trying to predict.

Real GNP   measures aggregate output in constant-valued dollars from a base year.

The **real interest rate**   is the nominal interest rate minus the anticipated rate of price inflation.

A **recession**   is a period when economic activity declines significantly relative to potential output, but less severely than in a depression such as that of the 1930s.

The **required reserve ratio**   is the percentage of deposits banks must hold as reserves.

S

Sticky price models   (or menu cost models) are those in which costs of changing prices present price adjustments when demand changes. Consequently, output falls when, for example, there is a decline in demand.

The **structural deficit**   is the part of the federal deficit that would exist even if the economy were at its potential level of output.

Structural unemployment,   like frictional unemployment, originates in the dynamic nature of the product and job mix in the economy, but structural unemployment lasts longer.

T

Target zones   for exchange rates are ranges within which policymakers try to maintain their currency's value. The target zones are jointly set by major industrialized nations.

Technological change   includes changes in technological knowledge (e.g., ways to employ robots in the production process), as well as new knowledge about how to organize businesses (managerial strategies).

The **trade deficit**   is the excess of imports over exports.

U

The **unemployment rate**   expresses the number of unemployed persons as a percentage of the labor force.

V

The **velocity of money**   is the rate at which money *turns over* in GNP transactions during a given period, that is, the average number of times each dollar is used in GNP transactions.

Index